THE WORLD'S CLASSICS

BEN JONSON

Five Plays

Edited with an Introduction by
G. A. WILKES

Oxford   New York

OXFORD UNIVERSITY PRESS

Oxford University Press, Walton Street, Oxford OX2 6DP

Oxford New York Toronto
Delhi Bombay Calcutta Madras Karachi
Petaling Jaya Singapore Hong Kong Tokyo
Nairobi Dar es Salaam Cape Town
Melbourne Auckland

and associated companies in
Berlin Ibadan

Oxford is a trade mark of Oxford University Press

British Library Cataloguing in Publication Data

Jonson, Ben
Five plays.—(The World's classics)
I. Title   II. Wilkes, G. A.
822'.3   PR2602
ISBN 0-19-281782-5

Library of Congress Cataloging in Publication Data

Jonson, Ben, 1573?-1637.
[Plays, Selections]
Ben Jonson: five plays/edited with an introduction
by G. A. Wilkes.
p. cm.—(The World's classics) Bibliography: p.
Contents: Every man in his humour—Sejanus—Volpone, or, The
fox—The alchemist—Bartholomew Fair.
1. Sejanus, Lucius Aelius, d. 31—Drama.   I. Wilkes, G. A.
(Gerald Alfred), 1927–.   II. Title.
PR2603.W54 1988   822'.3—dc19 87-27218
ISBN 0-19-281782-5 (pbk.)

Printed in Great Britain by
Hazell Watson & Viney Limited
Aylesbury, Bucks

BENJAMIN JONSON was born *c.*1572, and he died in 1637. narrowly escaped the gallows for killing an actor in a duel in 1598, and worked as a bricklayer and served as a soldier before he began to write. Jonson's varied career as a playwright extended through the reigns of Elizabeth, James I, and Charles I, and his reputation vied with Shakespeare's. He was the sole author of sixteen plays, and either wrote or collaborated in at least eight others, which have not all survived. He wrote over thirty court masques and entertainments, several in partnership with Inigo Jones. Jonson was also a poet of distinction, and it was as both poet and dramatist that he influenced the younger writers who declared themselves of 'the tribe of Ben'. The more engaging of his prose works are the commonplace book *Timber: or, Discoveries* and the *Conversations* with Drummond of Hawthornden.

G. A. WILKES is Challis Professor of English Literature at the University of Sydney. His publications include *The Thesis of Paradise Lost* (1961), and editions of *The Remains* of Fulke Greville, Lord Brooke (1965) and of Jonson's *Complete Plays* (1981–2).

CONTENTS

INTRODUCTION

IT is not easy to fix on a single image of Ben Jonson. We may think of him first as the boy put unwillingly to the craft of bricklaying, who then went soldiering in the Low Countries, began a turbulent career in the theatre by being imprisoned for his part in *The Isle of Dogs* and by killing Gabriel Spencer in a duel, and survived further friction with authority to become a legend at the Mermaid tavern for his conviviality and his corpulence. In another tradition, Jonson is the austere classicist of Elizabethan drama, writing with a high moral purpose and fastidiously editing his work for posterity. He figures in a third tradition as the comic playwright revelling in the bustle and clamour of London life, celebrating the rogue and the trickster, and presenting an ambivalent moral world.

Each of these versions is well founded, and much of the fascination of Jonson's work comes from the tensions set up amongst them. The combative, idiosyncratic Jonson rebukes his audience for failing to appreciate what is set before it, and disdains such current fashions as the sonnet, the essay, and the romance. His sense of mission is declared from one prologue to another, and is felt especially in his pride in dedicating *Volpone* to 'the two famous Universities', and in his repeated citing of the maxim of Florus, that while mayors and sheriffs are created every year, poets and kings are much rarer births. The plays themselves take such delight in the follies they expose that morality may seem to be subverted, with Jonson presiding as a lord of misrule.

The motto on the title-page of *Every Man in his Humour*, *Haut tamen invideas vati, quem pulpita pascunt* (You need not begrudge the poets who gain their living from the stage—Juvenal, vii. 93) may suggest a dramatist who is embattled, yet conscious of his own dignity. The quarto text had an additional line from Juvenal, *Quod non dant proceres, dabit Histrio* (What no great men give you, the stage-player shall—ix. 90). The prologue to *Every Man in his Humour*, dismissing other theatrical entertainments which are in vogue, asserts a serious role for the play which follows, although without explaining the 'humour' mentioned in its title.

The four humours of medieval physiology—blood, phlegm, choler, and melancholy—derived from the combination of the four elements, and the predominance of one or other of them was held to affect the personality. In a discussion of the concept in Jonson's next play, *Every Man out of his Humour*, Asper extended the basic sense of the word 'by metaphor' to apply to 'the general disposition' of any individual:

> As when some one peculiar quality
> Doth so possess a man that it doth draw
> All his affects, his spirits, and his power,
> In their confluctions, all to run one way;
> This may be truly said to be a humour.
>
> (Induction, 105-9)

Such a 'humour', as the mainspring of a person's conduct, is set apart from mere affectations and passing caprices, such as the wearing of a cable hatband or a three-piled ruff. This distinction is quickly blurred, however, when Cordatus comments:

> He speaks pure truth now; if an idiot
> Have but an apish or fantastic strain,
> It is his humour.
>
> (Induction, 115-17)

The concept is a flexible one. It will allow Jonson to explore such deep-seated traits as envy and avarice, and at the same time to exhibit any 'apish or fantastic strain', along with the casual extravagances of dress or behaviour which the strict theory would seem to proscribe. The influence of the theory of humours in *Every Man in his Humour*—even if Jonson had so formulated it at this time—is in any case joined to the medley of influences attributed to the *vetus comoedia* (the 'old comedy' loosely derived from Plautus and Terence and Aristophanes) with some admixture of the Tudor interlude and the *commedia dell'arte*. Thus Knowell is the *senex*, the 'old gentleman' of the cast list, out of sympathy with modern ideas and ready to deplore them. Brainworm is the clever slave, as able to outwit his master as he is to serve his interests; Bobadil is a version of the *miles gloriosus*, the braggart soldier. Kitely occupies the role of the husband suspicious of his wife's fidelity, a 'humour' he casts off at the end by quoting verse from 'a jealous man's part in a play' (v. v. 74). Master Stephen and Master Matthew are designated 'a country gull' and 'the town gull' respectively, familiar figures in the verse satires of the 1590s.

The contrast between these stock roles and the vitality of the play itself demonstrates how little Jonson is to be constricted by any framework. When it was first performed in 1598, *Every Man in his Humour* had Italianate characters and setting, although Jonson's Florence included the Mermaid tavern and the Cockney characters Cob and Tib. In the play as we now have it, revised for the Folio of 1616, the scene has been entirely transposed to England, and the play takes on extra life from the change. It is transacted in a single day, beginning with Knowell up so early that he intercepts the letter to his son from the city, where Cob the water-carrier is reproaching himself that 'It's six o'clock: I should ha' carried two turns by this', and concluding with Justice Clement's reconciling the warring parties with an invitation to a night of 'friendship, love, and laughter'.

The company invited to this supper with the 'old merry magistrate' (as he is described in the cast list) would have included Shakespeare, although we do not know which role he played. When he acted again in a work of Jonson's in 1603, it was in a much graver vein. The motto on the title-page of *Sejanus* is from Martial's *Epigrams*:

> *Non hic Centauros, non Gorgonas, Harpyiasque*
> *Invenies: Hominem pagina nostra sapit.*

(Not here will you find Centaurs, not Gorgons and
Harpies: our page smacks of man—x. iv. 9–10)

As part of advice on how 'to recognize your manners, know yourself', the epigraph signals a weighty intention, and the import of the play is made clearer in its full title: *Sejanus his Fall*. It is a study of the overreacher, a tragedy in a relatively simple form. Sejanus lacks the flamboyance that has been found attractive in a Tamburlaine or a Bussy D'Ambois, resorting much more to intrigue, and working through the agency of others. Although his fall may be attributed to errors of judgement springing from his ambition, it comes about essentially because in Tiberius he is dealing with a manipulator of superior skills and foresight, but of no higher morality. This makes *Sejanus* a somewhat clinical analysis of political power, with such men of principle as Arruntius in a muted choric role, Cordus and Gallus the blameless casualties in the contest, and the unreasoning savagery of it all shown in the poisonings and murders, and the dismemberment of Sejanus by the crowd at the end, and the strangling of his children. The Gemonies, the steps by the Tiber where the corpses of criminals were dragged by the hook, remain the characteristic image of the play.

The quotation on the title-page of *Volpone*, from Horace's *Art of Poetry* (l. 334), sets it in a less austere tradition:

> [*Aut prodesse volunt aut delectare poetae*]
> *Aut simul et iucunda et idonea dicere vitae.*

> (Poets would either profit, or delight,
> Or mixing sweet, and fit, teach life the right.)

Volpone is, however, another overreacher, who aspires beyond the material gains won by his roguery to exult in the discomfiture of his clients after his presumed death, so that his ambition is his undoing. Even then he survives, in a fashion, to speak the epilogue—which is in one way a concession to theatrical custom, but in another an index to the moral uncertainties of mature Jonsonian comedy.

The intention to 'place' the legacy-hunters is clear from the names they are given: Vulture, Raven, Crow. If the Fox and the Fly are not so easily stigmatized, it is because they operate with such resourcefulness and panache, and take such glee in their schemes as they prosper. Yet as *Volpone* is a play in which nearly all the relationships are based on self-interest, it is difficult for the sympathies to be engaged. We are drawn rather into a process in which stratagem begets stratagem, exposure is narrowly averted, the tables are turned and turned again. Such frail representatives of good as Celia and Bonario are borne along in this stream, and even the system of justice at the end seems an uncertain bulwark against the forces opposing it.

Jonson did not designate *Volpone* a 'comical satire', the term applied in the 1616 Folio to the plays preceding it, *Every Man out of his Humour*, *Cynthia's Revels*, and *Poetaster*. While it may not offer such a parade of follies as these do, *Volpone* is still a 'satire' in that we are alienated from the world it presents, and yet paradoxically drawn into it by sympathizing more with the witty rogue than with his dupe, so that we seem to endorse a milieu in which the trickster is king.

The epigraph to *The Alchemist*, from Lucretius' *De Rerum Natura*, is one of Jonson's most ambitious claims for his art (if he is not mocking a similar aspiration in alchemy itself):

> *petere inde coronam,*
> *Unde prius nulli velarint tempora Musae.*

(To seek a garland from where hitherto the Muses have crowned the brows of no one—i. 929–30; iv. 4–5)

The Alchemist is certainly a consummate display of Jonson's theatrical skill, as the whole action takes place in a house and a lane, and the different elements in the plot are set in motion with each knock at the door. The setting is London again, and a London so competitive and acquisitive that the philosophers' stone is a fitting emblem of its cupidity, and the greed and deceit of all those approaching the house is expressed equally in the treacheries in the partnership of those inside it. At the end of *Every Man in his Humour*, Justice Clement had acquitted Brainworm with the comment 'Thou hast done, or assisted to nothing, in my judgement, but deserves to be pardoned for the wit o' the offence' (v. iii. 96–8). The principle is carried further in *The Alchemist*, as Lovewit not only excuses Face with the comment 'I love a teeming wit, as I love my nourishment' (v. i. 16), but also helps himself to the goods in the house and to a new wife as well.

The Alchemist demonstrates how such 'classical' restraints as Jonson chooses to submit to—here, for example, the unity of place—seem to intensify his comic exuberance. The more the restrictions he places on himself, the greater his comic ingenuity. In *Volpone*, likewise, the house had been a microcosm in which Volpone cherished his riches, kept a company of grotesques for his delectation, and enticed Celia to his bed. His ventures out of this fortress, as Scoto of Mantua and as the disguised Captain, exposed him to a beating, and to his being outmanœuvred by Mosca. This way of focusing the action is extended in *Bartholomew Fair*, when the Fair and its booths are the only fixtures, and those plying their trade there mix with the citizens who come to see and to buy.

The idea of a pageant or exhibition is conveyed in the epigraph from Horace's *Epistles*:

> *Si foret in terris, rideret Democritus: nam*
> *Spectaret populum ludis attentius ipsis,*
> *Ut sibi praebentem, nimio spectacula plura.*

Scriptores autem narrare putaret asello
Fabellam surdo.

(If Democritus were still on earth, he would laugh: for he would
look more intently at the people than at the play itself, as
offering more shows by far: but as for the authors, he would
think that they were telling a tale to a deaf ass—II. i. 194,
197–200.)

While this is another of Jonson's reprimands to his audience, it also
dissolves the distinction between spectators and participants—carried
through in the induction to the play, the play itself, and the puppet-show
at the Fair. The hucksters and the citizens are labelled alike—Proctor
Littlewit and Jordan Knockem, Filcher and Sharkwell, Winwife and
Cokes—so that by these means there is no telling which is which. The
only consistent pattern is that any figure of authority is apt to be
subverted or ridiculed. This is the lot of Cokes's mentor, Wasp, of
Littlewit the Proctor, of the Puritan Zeal-of-the-Land Busy, and
especially of Justice Overdo, who frequents the Fair in disguise to detect
its iniquities, only to be deluded by a pickpocket and to be placed in the
stocks himself.

Although its satire may be more pervasive, *Bartholomew Fair* is more
indulgent of human frailty than any of the comedies before it. It seems to
be saying that human nature is like this, that ballad-singers and
gingerbread-women make a living by mild fraud like anyone else, and if
Ursula's bower is a place for recruiting ladies of fashion as whores, she
will offer them the relief of a chamberpot as she does so. Cokes and
Littlewit have a delight in simple things which is denied to such astute
personalities as Quarlous and Wasp. This play does not end with
Volpone or Face reviewing the action in an epilogue, but with Adam
Overdo inviting everyone to supper. This casts back to the first of
Jonson's 'humour' plays, but the 'humours' now do not recall Martial or
Juvenal, but more probably Chaucer.

G.A.W.

NOTE ON THE TEXT

Every Man in his Humour was first acted in 1598, and published in quarto in 1601, with a Florentine setting. *Sejanus*, when it was first performed in 1603, was the work of Jonson and 'a second pen'. He rewrote the part of his collaborator (probably George Chapman) when the play was published in quarto in 1605. *Volpone* was performed early in 1606 (the statement on the title-page, 'Acted in the yeere 1605', is probably an example of old style dating) and published in quarto in 1607; *The Alchemist* was first performed in 1610 and published in quarto in 1612. The quarto texts of all these plays were superseded for the most part by the text of *The Works* of Benjamin Jonson (1616), usually referred to as the 1616 Folio. *Bartholomew Fair*, acted in 1614, was not printed until the folio of 1631.

The texts of *Every Man in his Humour*, *Sejanus*, *Volpone*, and *The Alchemist* in the Herford and Simpson edition of Ben Jonson (Oxford, 1925–52) were based principally on the 1616 Folio, and the text of *Bartholomew Fair* on the folio of 1631. A modernized version of the Herford and Simpson text was given in *The Complete Plays*, ed. G. A. Wilkes (Oxford, 1981–2), with a new styling and annotation. The text of *The Complete Plays*, with some minor corrections, is reproduced in the present edition.

SELECT BIBLIOGRAPHY

EDITIONS: The standard edition of Ben Jonson is that of C. H. Herford and Percy and Evelyn Simpson, 11 vols. (Oxford, 1925–52). The text of volumes III–VI was presented in a modernized version by G. A. Wilkes in *The Complete Plays*, 4 vols. (Oxford, 1981–2). Individual plays have been edited in the New Mermaid series and the Yale Ben Jonson. The editions of *The Alchemist* by F. H. Mares (The Revels Plays, 1967), of *Bartholomew Fair* by E. A. Horsman (The Revels Plays, 1960), and of *Volpone* by John W. Creaser (The London Medieval and Renaissance Series, 1978) are especially informative. J. W. Lever has edited the quarto and folio texts of *Every Man in his Humour* in a parallel edition (Regents Renaissance Drama Series, 1971).

CRITICISM: While A. C. Swinburne's *A Study of Ben Jonson* (1889) is generous and enthusiastic, modern criticism would take its beginning from T. S. Eliot's essay of 1919 (in *Selected Essays*, 1932), or L. C. Knights, *Drama and Society in the Age of Jonson* (1937). Both are represented in *Ben Jonson: A Collection of Critical Essays* (Twentieth Century Views, 1963). This collection has been supplemented by two 'quadricentennial' tributes, *A Celebration of Ben Jonson*, ed. William Blissett, R. W. Van Fossen, and Julian Patrick (Toronto, 1973) and *Ben Jonson: Quadricentennial Essays*, ed. Mary Olive Thomas, as vol. VI, no. 1 of *Studies in the Literary Imagination* (Georgia, 1973).

The most succinct introduction to Jonson is J. B. Bamborough, *Ben Jonson* (Hutchinson University Library, 1970). Other monographs include George Parfitt, *Ben Jonson: Public Poet and Private Man* (1976), Alexander Leggatt, *Ben Jonson: His Vision and His Art* (1981), and Richard Dutton, *Ben Jonson* (1983).

The comedies have received most critical attention. Representative studies are John J. Enck, *Jonson and the comic truth* (1957), Edward B. Partridge, *The Broken Compass* (1958), James A. Barish, *Ben Jonson and the Language of Prose Comedy* (1960), J. A. Bryant, *The Compassionate Satirist* (1972), and L. A. Beaurline, *Jonson and Elizabethan Comedy* (1978). There have been two Macmillan Casebooks devoted to Jonson, one on *Volpone*, ed. Jonas A. Barish (1972) and one on *Every Man in his Humour* and *The Alchemist*, ed. R. V. Holdsworth (1978).

The staging of the plays is discussed by Franz Fricker, *Ben Jonson's Plays in Performance and the Jacobean Theatre* (Bern, 1972), Stephen Orgel, *The Illusion of Power: Political Theater in the English Renaissance* (1975) and by Ian Donaldson in 'Jonson's Magic Houses' (*Essays & Studies*, 1986). A particular aspect is explored by Mary Chan in *Music in the Theatre of Ben Jonson* (1980).

Jonson's work is illuminated by more general studies such as Oscar James Campbell, *Comicall Satyre and Shakespeare's Troilus and Cressida* (1938), Robert Ornstein, *The Moral Vision of Jacobean Tragedy* (1960), and Ian Donaldson, *The World Upside-Down: Comedy from Jonson to Fielding* (1974).

The most stimulating recent critical work is Anne Barton's *Ben Jonson, dramatist* (1984).

CHRONOLOGY

1572–3   Ben Jonson born (? 11 June 1572), posthumous son of a
         minister. His mother married for a second time a master-
         bricklayer of Westminster.
         Attended Westminster School under William Camden, to whom
         he owed 'All that I am in arts, all that I know' (*Ep.* xiv).

*c.*1588   Taken from school and put to the craft of bricklaying.
         Military service (date unknown) in the Low Countries, whence
         he returned and 'betook himself to his wonted studies'.

1594   'Benjamine Johnson and Anne Lewis maryed' (parish register
         of St. Magnus Martyr, 14 November).

*c.*1596   Conjectural experience as a strolling player.
         Presumed early version of *A Tale of a Tub*.

1597   Playwright in the employ of Henslowe (July).
         Imprisoned (*c.* August–October) for part in *The Isle of Dogs*.

1598   ? *The Case is Altered* performed by the Children of the Chapel.
         Every Man in his Humour acted by the Lord Chamberlain's Men
         at the Curtain (September).
         Named among the 'best for Tragedie' by Francis Meres in
         Palladis Tamia.
         Killed Gabriel Spencer in a duel (22 September) escaping the
         gallows by claiming right of clergy.
         While in prison, adopted the Catholic faith.

1599   Prosecuted for a debt, and imprisoned in the Marshalsea
         (January).
         Collaborated with Dekker and others in the lost tragedies, *Page
         of Plymouth* and *Robert II King of Scots*, for the Admiral's Men.
         Every Man out of his Humour acted by the Chamberlain's Men
         at the Globe in the winter, and at court at about Christmas.

1600   *Cynthia's Revels* acted by the Children of the Chapel at the
         Blackfriars (? December).

1601   *Cynthia's Revels* performed at court (6 January).

      Poetaster acted by the Children of the Chapel (? in spring).

      Paid £2 by Henslowe for additions to *The Spanish Tragedy* (25 September).

1602   Paid £10 for further additions to *The Spanish Tragedy*, and in earnest of *Richard Crookback* (22 June).

1603   Eldest son Benjamin died of the plague.

      Entertainment at Althorp for the new queen and prince on their journey from Edinburgh (25 June).

      Sejanus performed by the King's Men. Jonson called before the Privy Council to answer charges of Popery and treason.

1604   *Part of the King's Entertainment in Passing to his Coronation* (15 March).

      A Panegyre on the King's opening of Parliament (19 March).

      The Entertainment at Highgate (1 May).

1605   *The Masque of Blackness* (6 January), first of the series of court masques extending to *Chloridia* (1631).

      Every Man out of his Humour revived at court by the King's Men (8 January).

      Every Man in his Humour (? the revised version of the play) revived at court by the King's Men (2 February).

      Eastward Ho, written in collaboration with Chapman and Marston, acted at the Blackfriars by the Children of the Queen's Revels.

      All three playwrights imprisoned for the satire on the Scots.

      Present at a Catholic supper party given by Robert Catesby (October).

      Employed by the Privy Council in inquiries following the Gunpowder Plot (November).

1606   *Hymenaei* presented for the marriage of the Countess of Essex (5 January).

      Indicted as a recusant at the London Sessions (9 January), and cited as a recusant before the Consistory Court (January and April).

      Volpone, or The Fox acted by the King's Men at the Globe (? March) and later at the two universities.

      The Entertainment of the Two Kings at Theobalds (24 July).

Excursion to Scotland, reaching Edinburgh *c.* August, returning at the end of January 1619. Conversations with Drummond of Hawthornden.

1619   Formally inducted to the degree of Master of Arts at Oxford (17 July).

1620   *News from the New World* (17 January and 29 February).
An Entertainment at the Blackfriars (for the christening of Charles Cavendish, b. 20 May).
Pan's Anniversary (? 19 June).

1621   *The Gypsies Metamorphosed* presented at Burley-on-the-Hill (3 August), Belvoir (5 August), Windsor (September).

1622   *The Masque of Augurs* (6 January), with additions (5 or 6 May).

1623   *The Alchemist* revived for a court performance (1 January).
Time Vindicated presented in the Banqueting House at Whitehall (19 January).
Mentioned in a lawsuit (20 October) as 'Benjamin Johnson of Gresham Colledge' (hence conjectures that *Discoveries* and *The English Grammar* may be lecture notes).
Jonson's library destroyed in a fire.

1624   *Neptune's Triumph* (prepared for 6 January, not performed).
The Masque of Owls presented before Prince Charles at Kenilworth (19 August).
Volpone revived by the King's Men for a court performance (27 December).

1625   *The Fortunate Isles* (9 January).

1626   *The Staple of News* acted by the King's Men (soon after the coronation of Charles on 2 February), first at the Blackfriars and then at court.

1628   Jonson afflicted with palsy.
Appointed City Chronologer (September).
Interrogated about verses on the death of Buckingham (26 October).

1629   *The New Inn* acted at the Blackfriars by the King's Men (? 19 January).

Gift of £100 from King Charles, and pension increased from 100 marks to £100 yearly.

1630   *Volpone* revived by the King's Men (19 November).

1631   *Love's Triumph through Callipolis* (9 January).
        Chloridia (22 February).
        Every Man in his Humour revived by the King's Men at Blackfriars (18 February).
        Salary as City Chronologer withdrawn (November).
        The Alchemist revived by the King's Men (1 December).

1632   *The Magnetic Lady* acted by the King's Men at Blackfriars (? October), and possibly at court.

1633   *A Tale of a Tub* licensed to the Queen's Men (7 May), with passages ridiculing Inigo Jones as Vitruvius Hoop to be struck out; acted at the Cockpit.
        The King's Entertainment at Welbeck (21 May).

1634   *A Tale of a Tub* performed at Whitehall (14 January).
        Love's Welcome at Bolsover (30 July).
        Salary as City Chronologer resumed, as a pension, at the King's request (18 September).

1637   Death of Jonson (6 August).

ABBREVIATIONS

The following cue-titles have been adopted:

Alch.	*The Alchemist*
BF	*Bartholomew Fair*
CA	*The Case is Altered*
Chappell	W. Chappell, *Old English Popular Music* (ed. H. E. Wool-dridge, 2 vols., 1893–4)
CR	*Cynthia's Revels, or The Fountain of Self-Love*
DA	*The Devil is an Ass*
Disc.	*Timber, or Discoveries*
EH	*Eastward Ho*
EMI	*Every Man in his Humour*
EMO	*Every Man out of his Humour*
Ep.	*The Epigrams*
Florio	John Florio, *A World of Words* (1598)
H&S	*Ben Jonson*, edited by C. H. Herford and Percy and Evelyn Simpson (11 vols., 1925–52)
ML	*The Magnetic Lady, or Humours Reconciled*
Poet.	*Poetaster, or His Arraignment*
Sej.	*Sejanus his Fall*
SN	*The Staple of News*
SW	*Epicoene, or The Silent Woman*
TT	*A Tale of a Tub*
Volp.	*Volpone, or The Fox*

EVERY MAN IN HIS HUMOUR

Euery
MAN IN
HIS
HVMOVR.

A Comœdie.

Acted in the yeere 1598. By the then
Lord Chamberlaine his
Seruants.

The Author B. I.

IUVEN.

Haud tamen inuide.ts vati, quem pulpita paſcunt.

LONDON,

Printed by VVILLIAM STANSBY.

M. DC. XVI.

TO THE MOST
LEARNED, AND
MY HONOURED
FRIEND,

Mr Camden, CLARENTIAUX

SIR,

THERE are, no doubt, a supercilious race in the world, who will esteem all office done you in this kind an injury; so solemn a vice it is with them to use the authority of their ignorance to the crying-down of poetry or the professors. But my gratitude must not leave 5 to correct their error; since I am none of those that can suffer the benefits conferred upon my youth to perish with my age. It is a frail memory that remembers but present things. And had the favour of the times so conspired with my disposition, as it could have brought forth other, or better, you had had the same propor- 10 tion and number of the fruits, the first. Now, I pray you to accept this, such wherein neither the confession of my manners shall make you blush; nor of my studies, repent you to have been the instructor; and, for the profession of my thankfulness, I am sure it will, with good men, find either praise, or excuse. 15

Your true lover,
BEN. JONSON

Camden: William Camden the antiquary, Jonson's old schoolmaster (*Ep.* xiv) *Clarentiaux*: second King-at-arms in England 5 *the professors*: those following it as a serious pursuit

The Persons of the Play

Knowell, *an old gentleman*

Edward Knowell, *his son*

Brainworm, *the father's man*

Master Stephen, *a country gull*

Downright, *a plain squire*

Wellbred, *his half-brother*

Justice Clement, *an old merry magistrate*

Roger Formal, *his clerk*

Kitely, *a merchant*

Dame Kitely, *his wife*

Mistress Bridget, *his sister*

Master Matthew, *the town gull*

Cash, Kitely's *man*

Cob, *a waterbearer*

Tib, *his wife*

Captain Bobadil, *a Paul's-man*

The Scene

London

a Paul's-man: a lounger in the middle aisle of St. Paul's, then a fashionable resort and place of business

EVERY MAN IN
HIS HUMOUR

PROLOGUE

THOUGH need make many Poets, and some such
As art and nature have not bettered much;
Yet ours, for want, hath not so loved the stage,
As he dare serve the ill customs of the age:
Or purchase your delight at such a rate,   5
As, for it, he himself must justly hate.
To make a child, now swaddled, to proceed
Man, and then shoot up, in one beard and weed,
Past threescore years: or, with three rusty swords,
And help of some few foot-and-half-foot words,   10
Fight over York and Lancaster's long jars:
And in the tiring-house bring wounds to scars.
He rather prays you will be pleased to see
One such, today, as other plays should be.
Where neither Chorus wafts you o'er the seas;   15
Nor creaking throne comes down, the boys to please;
Nor nimble squib is seen, to make afeared
The gentlewomen; nor rolled bullet heard
To say it thunders; nor tempestuous drum
Rumbles, to tell you when the storm doth come;   20
But deeds, and language, such as men do use:
And persons, such as Comedy would choose,

10 *foot-and-half-foot words*: Horace's *sesquipedalia verba* (*Ars Poetica*, 79)
12 *tiring-house*: dressing rooms   15 *Chorus wafts you*: as in *Henry V* (cf. *EMO*,
Ind. 269-71)   18 *rolled bullet*: the cannonball rolled along the floor

When she would show an image of the times,
And sport with human follies, not with crimes.
25 Except, we make 'em such by loving still
Our popular errors, when we know they're ill.
I mean such errors, as you'll all confess
By laughing at them, they deserve no less:
Which when you heartily do, there's hope left, then,
30 You, that have so graced monsters, may like men.

ACT I, Scene i

[Before Knowell's house]

Enter Knowell, Brainworm

Kno. A GOODLY day toward! And a fresh morning! Brainworm,
Call up your young master: bid him rise, sir.
Tell him I have some business to employ him.
Bra. I will, sir, presently.
Kno.   But hear you, sirrah,
If he be at his book, disturb him not.
5   *Bra.*   Well, sir.   [*Exit*]
Kno. How happy yet should I esteem myself
Could I, by any practice, wean the boy
From one vain course of study he affects.
He is a scholar, if a man may trust
10 The liberal voice of fame, in her report
Of good account, in both our universities,
Either of which hath favoured him with graces:
But their indulgence must not spring in me
A fond opinion that he cannot err.
15 Myself was once a student; and, indeed,
Fed with the selfsame humour he is now,
Dreaming on naught but idle poetry,

30 *monsters*: ? like Caliban in *The Tempest* (cf. l. 19)   (*I. i*) 1 *toward*: in
prospect   4 *presently*: immediately   7 *practice*: device, scheme   10 *fame*:
Sej. II. 195 n.   12 *graces*: degrees   14 *fond*: foolish

That fruitless and unprofitable art,
Good unto none, but least to the professors,
Which then, I thought the mistress of all knowledge: 20
But since, time, and the truth have waked my judgement,
And reason taught me better to distinguish
The vain from the useful learnings.

[*Enter* Stephen]

Cousin Stephen!
What news with you, that you are here so early?

Ste. Nothing, but e'en come to see how you do, uncle.   25

Kno. That's kindly done, you are welcome, coz.

Ste. Aye, I know that, sir, I would not ha' come else.
How do my cousin Edward, uncle?

Kno. Oh, well, coz, go in and see: I doubt he be scarce stirring yet.

Ste. Uncle, afore I go in, can you tell me, an' he have e'er a book   30
of the sciences of hawking and hunting? I would fain borrow it.

Kno. Why, I hope you will not a-hawking now, will you?

Ste. No wusse; but I'll practise against next year, uncle: I have
bought me a hawk, and a hood and bells, and all; I lack nothing
but a book to keep it by.   35

Kno. Oh, most ridiculous.

Ste. Nay, look you now, you are angry, uncle: why you know, an'
a man have not skill in the hawking and hunting languages nowa-
days, I'll not give a rush for him. They are more studied than the
Greek or the Latin. He is for no gallant's company without 'em.   40
And by gad's lid, I scorn it, aye, so I do, to be a consort for every
humdrum, hang 'em scroyles, there's nothing in 'em, in the world.
What do you talk on it? Because I dwell at Hoxton, I shall keep
company with none but the archers of Finsbury? Or the citizens,
that come a-ducking to Islington ponds? A fine jest i' faith! 'Slid,   45
a gentleman mun show himself like a gentleman. Uncle, I pray
you be not angry, I know what I have to do, I trow, I am no novice.

Kno. You are a prodigal absurd cockscomb. Go to.

19 *professors*: cf. Ded. 5   30 *an'*: if   33 *wusse*: certainly   42 *scroyles*:
scoundrels   44 *archers of Finsbury*: a fraternity noted for their use of pseudo-
aristocratic titles (cf. *TT* III. vi. 3–6)   45 *ducking*: catching ducks   47 *I trow*:
I feel sure

Nay, never look at me, it's I that speak.
50 Take it as you will, sir, I'll not flatter you.
Ha' you not yet found means enow, to waste
That which your friends have left you, but you must
Go cast away your money on a kite,
And know not how to keep it when you ha' done?
55 Oh, it's comely! This will make you a gentleman!
Well, cousin, well! I see you are e'en past hope
Of all reclaim. Aye, so, now you are told on it,
You look another way.
    Ste.   What would you ha' me do?
    Kno. What would I have you do? I'll tell you, kinsman,
60 Learn to be wise, and practise how to thrive,
That would I have you do: and not to spend
Your coin on every bauble that you fancy,
Or every foolish brain that humours you.
I would not have you to invade each place,
65 Nor thrust yourself on all societies,
Till men's affections, or your own desert,
Should worthily invite you to your rank.
He that is so respectless in his courses
Oft sells his reputation at cheap market.
70 Nor would I you should melt away yourself
In flashing bravery, lest while you affect
To make a blaze of gentry to the world,
A little puff of scorn extinguish it,
And you be left, like an unsavoury snuff,
75 Whose property is only to offend.
I'd ha' you sober, and contain yourself;
Not that your sail be bigger than your boat:
But moderate your expenses now, at first,
As you may keep the same proportion still.
80 Nor stand so much on your gentility,
Which is an airy and mere borrowed thing,
From dead men's dust and bones: and none of yours
Except you make or hold it. Who comes here?

---

53 *kite*: a meaner type of hawk   71 *bravery*: finery, ostentation

ACT I, Scene ii

Enter Servant

Ser. Save you, gentlemen.

Ste. Nay, we do not stand much on our gentility, friend; yet you are welcome, and I assure you, mine uncle here is a man of a thousand a year, Middlesex land: he has but one son in all the world, I am his next heir (at the common law) Master Stephen, as 5 simple as I stand here, if my cousin die (as there's hope he will) I have a pretty living o' mine own too, beside, hard-by here.

Ser. In good time, sir.

Ste. In good time, sir? Why! And in very good time, sir. You do not flout, friend, do you? 10

Ser. Not I, sir.

Ste. Not you, sir? You were not best, sir; an' you should, here be them can perceive it, and that quickly too: go to. And they can give it again soundly too, and need be.

Ser. Why, sir, let this satisfy you: good faith, I had no such 15 intent.

Ste. Sir, an' I thought you had, I would talk with you, and that presently.

Ser. Good Master Stephen, so you may, sir, at your pleasure.

Ste. And so I would, sir, good my saucy companion! An' you 20 were out o' mine uncle's ground, I can tell you; though I do not stand upon my gentility neither in't.

Kno. Cousin! Cousin! Will this ne'er be left?

Ste. Whoreson base fellow! A mechanical serving-man! By this cudgel, and 'twere not for shame, I would—— 25

Kno. What would you do, you peremptory gull?
If you cannot be quiet, get you hence.
You see, the honest man demeans himself
Modestly towards you, giving no reply
To your unseasoned, quarrelling, rude fashion: 30
And still you huff it, with a kind of carriage

---

8 *In good time*: formula of polite acquiescence   26 *peremptory*: absolute
28 *demeans*: conducts

As void of wit as of humanity.

Go, get you in; 'fore heaven, I am ashamed

Thou hast a kinsman's interest in me.   [*Exit* Stephen]

35   *Ser.* I pray you, sir. Is this Master Knowell's house?

Kno. Yes, marry, is it, sir.

Ser. I should enquire for a gentleman here, one Master Edward
Knowell: do you know any such, sir, I pray you?

Kno. I should forget myself else, sir.

40   *Ser.* Are you the gentleman? Cry you mercy, sir: I was required
by a gentleman i' the city, as I rode out at this end o' the town, to
deliver you this letter, sir.

Kno. To me, sir! What do you mean? Pray you remember your
courtesy. 'To his most selected friend, Master Edward Knowell.'

45   What might the gentleman's name be, sir, that sent it? Nay, pray
you be covered.

Ser. One Master Wellbred, sir.

Kno. Master Wellbred! A young gentleman, is he not?

Ser. The same, sir, Master Kitely married his sister: the rich

50   merchant i' the Old Jewry.

Kno. You say very true. Brainworm.

[*Enter* Brainworm]

Bra. Sir.

Kno. Make this honest friend drink here: pray you go in.

[*Exeunt* Brainworm, servant]

This letter is directed to my son:

55   Yet I am Edward Knowell too, and may

With the safe conscience of good manners use

The fellow's error to my satisfaction.

Well, I will break it ope (old men are curious)

Be it but for the style's sake, and the phrase,

60   To see if both do answer my son's praises,

Who is almost grown the idolator

Of this young Wellbred: what have we here? What's this?

(*The letter*)

'Why, Ned, I beseech thee; has thou forsworn all thy friends i'
the Old Jewry? Or dost thou think us all Jews that inhabit there yet?

43–4 *remember your courtesy*: i.e. remove your hat (cf. l. 45–6)

If thou dost, come over, and but see our frippery: change an old 65
shirt for a whole smock with us. Do not conceive that antipathy
between us and Hoxton, as was between Jews and hogs-flesh. Leave
thy vigilant father alone, to number over his green apricots, evening
and morning, o' the north-west wall. An' I had been his son, I had
saved him the labour, long since; if, taking in all the young wenches 70
that pass by at the back door, and coddling every kernel of the fruit
for 'em, would ha' served. But, prithee, come over to me quickly,
this morning: I have such a present for thee (our Turkey company
never sent the like to the Grand-Signior). One is a rhymer, sir, o'
your own batch, your own leaven; but doth think himself Poet- 75
major, o' the town: willing to be shown, and worthy to be seen. The
other——I will not venture his description with you till you come,
because I would ha' you make hither with an appetite. If the worst
of 'em be not worth your journey, draw your bill of charges, as
unconscionable as any Guildhall verdict will give it you, and you 80
shall be allowed your *viaticum*.'   *From the* Windmill.'
From the bordello, it might come as well;
The Spittle: or Pict-hatch. Is this the man
My son hath sung so, for the happiest wit,
The choicest brain the times hath sent us forth?   85
I know not what he may be in the arts;
Nor what in schools: but surely, for his manners,
I judge him a profane and dissolute wretch:
Worse, by possession of such great good gifts,
Being the master of so loose a spirit.   90
Why, what unhallowed ruffian would have writ
In such a scurrilous manner to a friend!
Why should he think I tell my apricots?
Or play the Hesperian Dragon with my fruit,
To watch it? Well, my son, I'd thought   95

---

65 *frippery*: old-clothes shop   65-6 *an old shirt for a whole smock*: an old man
(i.e. Knowell) for a wench free of disease   71 *coddling*: stewing (? with quibble
on cods or cuddling)   73-4 gifts from the Levant Company to the Sultan were
noted for their munificence   80 *Guildhall verdict*: 'London jury' and 'Middlesex
jury' were bywords for injustice   81 *viaticum*: travelling-money   *the Windmill*:
tavern in the Old Jewry   82 *bordello*: brothel   83 *Spittle*: hospital, especially
for foul diseases   *Pict-hatch*: haunt of prostitutes   93 *tell*: count   94 *Hesperian
Dragon*: guarding the golden apples

You'd had more judgement, to have made election
Of your companions, than to have ta'en on trust
Such petulant, jeering gamesters, that can spare
No argument or subject from their jest.
100 But I perceive, affection makes a fool
Of any man, too much the father. Brainworm.

[*Enter* Brainworm]

    Bra. Sir.
    Kno. Is the fellow gone that brought this letter?
    Bra. Yes, sir, a pretty while since.
105   *Kno.* And where's your young master?
    Bra. In his chamber, sir.
    Kno. He spake not with the fellow! Did he?
    Bra. No, sir, he saw him not.
    Kno. Take you this letter, and deliver it my son,
110 But with no notice that I have opened it, on your life.
    Bra. Oh lord, sir, that were a jest, indeed!   [*Exit*]
    Kno. I am resolved, I will not stop his journey;
Nor practise any violent mean, to stay
The unbridled course of youth in him: for that,
115 Restrained, grows more impatient; and, in kind,
Like to the eager but the generous greyhound,
Who ne'er so little from his game withheld,
Turns head, and leaps up at his holder's throat.
There is a way of winning, more by love,
120 And urging of the modesty, than fear:
Force works on servile natures, not the free.
He that's compelled to goodness may be good;
But 'tis but for that fit: where others drawn
By softness and example, get a habit.
125 Then, if they stray, but warn 'em: and the same
They should for virtue have done, they'll do for shame.   [*Exit*]

---

98 *gamesters*: those who make game of everything

ACT I, Scene iii

[Knowell's house]

Enter Edward Knowell [*with a letter*], Brainworm

E. Kn. Did he open it, sayest thou?

Bra. Yes, o' my word, sir, and read the contents.

E. Kn. That scarce contents me. What countenance, prithee, made he i' the reading of it? Was he angry, or pleased?   5

Bra. Nay, sir, I saw him not read it, nor open it, I assure your worship.

E. Kn. No? How knowst thou, then, that he did either?

Bra. Marry, sir, because he charged me, on my life, to tell nobody that he opened it: which unless he had done, he would never fear to have it revealed.   10

E. Kn. That's true: well, I thank thee, Brainworm

[*He walks aside, reading*]

[*Enter* Stephen]

Ste. Oh, Brainworm, didst thou not see a fellow here in a what-sha'-call-him doublet! He brought mine uncle a letter e'en now.

Bra. Yes, Master Stephen, what of him?

Ste. Oh, I ha' such a mind to beat him—— Where is he? Canst   15
thou tell?

Bra. Faith, he is not of that mind: he is gone, Master Stephen.

Ste. Gone? Which way? When went he? How long since?

Bra. He is rid hence. He took horse at the street door.

Ste. And I stayed i' the fields! Whoreson scander-bag rogue!   20
Oh that I had but a horse to fetch him back again.

Bra. Why, you may ha' my master's gelding, to save your longing, sir.

Ste. But, I ha' no boots, that's the spite on't.

Bra. Why, a fine wisp of hay, rolled hard, Master Stephen.   25

---

20 *scander-bag*: Iskanderbeg, the Turkish name of George Castriot, who won the freedom of Albania (? hence 'adventurer')   25 *hay*: used as a substitute for boots

Ste. No faith, it's no boot to follow him now: let him e'en go, and hang. 'Pray thee, help to truss me a little. He does so vex me——

Bra. You'll be worse vexed when you are trussed, Master Stephen. Best keep unbraced; and walk yourself till you be cold: your choler
30 may founder you else.

Ste. By my faith, and so I will, now thou tellst me on't. How dost thou like my leg, Brainworm?

Bra. A very good leg, Master Stephen! But the woollen stocking does not commend it so well.

35 *Ste.* Foh, the stockings be good enough, now summer is coming on, for the dust. I'll have a pair of silk again' winter, that I go to dwell i' the town. I think my leg would show in a silk-hose.

Bra. Believe me, Master Stephen, rarely well.

Ste. In sadness, I think it would: I have a reasonable good leg.

40 *Bra.* You have an excellent good leg, Master Stephen, but I cannot stay to praise it longer now, and I am very sorry for it.

Ste. Another time will serve, Brainworm. Gramercy for this.

[*Exit* Brainworm]

E. Kn. (*laughs having read the letter*) Ha, ha, ha!

Ste. 'Slid, I hope, he laughs not at me, and he do——

45 *E. Kn.* Here was a letter, indeed, to be intercepted by a man's father, and do him good with him! He cannot but think most virtuously, both of me and the sender, sure; that make the careful costermonger of him in our familiar Epistles. Well, if he read this with patience, I'll be gelt, and troll ballads for Master John Trundle,
50 yonder, the rest of my mortality. It is true, and likely, my father may have as much patience as another man; for he takes much physic: and oft taking physic makes a man very patient. But would your packet, Master Wellbred, had arrived at him in such a minute of his patience; then we had known the end of it, which now is
55 doubtful, and threatens—— What! My wise cousin! Nay, then, I'll furnish our feast with one gull more toward the mess. He writes to me of a brace, and here's one, that's three: oh, for a fourth; Fortune, if ever thou'lt use thine eyes, I entreat thee——

26 *no boot*: no use   27 *truss*: tie the 'points' or laces fastening the breeches to the doublet ('trussed' in l. 28 is a quibble on 'beaten')   39 *sadness*: seriousness
48 *costermonger*: seller of apples (costards) and pears   *familiar Epistles*: i.e. as though their letters were like the *Epistles* of Cicero or Pliny (cf. III. i. 29)   49 *John Trundle*: bookseller and publisher of ballads and light literature, c. 1603-26   56 *mess*: set of four

Ste. Oh, now I see who he laughed at. He laughed at somebody
in that letter. By this good light, and he had laughed at me—— 60
E. Kn. How now, cousin Stephen, melancholy?
Ste. Yes, a little. I thought, you had laughed at me, cousin.
E. Kn. Why, what an' I had, coz, what would you ha' done?
Ste. By this light, I would ha' told mine uncle.
E. Kn. Nay, if you would ha' told your uncle, I did laugh at you, 65
coz.
Ste. Did you, indeed?
E. Kn. Yes, indeed.
Ste. Why, then——
E. Kn. What then? 70
Ste. I am satisfied, it is sufficient.
E. Kn. Why, be so gentle, coz. And I pray you let me entreat a
courtesy of you. I am sent for, this morning, by a friend in the Old
Jewry to come to him; it's but crossing over the fields to Moorgate:
will you bear me company? I protest, it is not to draw you into 75
bond, or any plot against the state, coz.
Ste. Sir, that's all one, and 'twere: you shall command me twice
so far as Moorgate to do you good in such a matter. Do you think
I would leave you? I protest——
E. Kn. No, no, you shall not protest, coz. 80
Ste. By my fackins, but I will, by your leave; I'll protest more to
my friend than I'll speak of, at this time.
E. Kn. You speak very well, coz.
Ste. Nay, not so neither, you shall pardon me: but I speak to
serve my turn. 85
E. Kn. Your turn, coz? Do you know what you say? A gentleman
of your sort, parts, carriage, and estimation, to talk o' your turn i'
this company, and to me, alone, like a tankard-bearer, at a conduit!
Fie. A wight, that, hitherto, his every step hath left the stamp of a
great foot behind him, as every word the savour of a strong spirit! 90
And he! This man! So graced, gilded, or (to use a more fit metaphor)
so tin-foiled by nature, as not ten housewives' pewter (again' a good

79 *protest*: an affected usage   81 *By my fackins*: 'By my faith'   86 *turn*:
an unfashionable word   87 *sort*: rank   88 *tankard-bearer*: a water-carrier
(tankard = hooped wooden vessel of about three gallons for fetching water from the
conduits)

time) shows more bright to the world than he! And he (as I said
last, so I say again, and still shall say it) this man! To conceal such
95 real ornaments as these, and shadow their glory, as a milliner's wife
does her wrought stomacher, with a smoky lawn, or a black cypress?
Oh, coz! It cannot be answered, go not about it. Drake's old ship,
at Deptford, may sooner circle the world again. Come, wrong not
the quality of your desert, with looking downward, coz; but hold
100 up your head, so: and let the Idea of what you are be portrayed i'
your face, that men may read i' your physiognomy, 'Here, within
this place, is to be seen the true, rare, and accomplished monster, or
miracle of nature', which is all one. What think you of this, coz?

Ste. Why, I do think of it; and I will be more proud, and melan-
105 choly, and gentleman-like, than I have been: I'll ensure you.

E. Kn. Why, that's resolute, Master Stephen! [*Aside*] Now, if I
can but hold him up to his height, as it is happily begun, it will do
well for a suburb-humour: we may hap have a match with the city,
and play him for forty pound. Come, coz.

110 *Ste.* I'll follow you.

E. Kn. Follow me? You must go before.

Ste. Nay, an' I must, I will. Pray you, show me, good cousin.

[*Exeunt*]

ACT I, Scene iv

[Before Cob's house]

Enter Master Matthew

Mat. I think this be the house: what, ho?

[*Enter* Cob]

Cob. Who's there? Oh, Master Matthew! Gi' your worship good-
morrow.

Mat. What! Cob! How dost thou, good Cob? Dost thou inhabit
5 here, Cob?

96 *wrought*: embroidered   *black cypress*: light transparent material resembling crepe
97 *answered*: justified   *old ship*: the *Golden Hind*, laid up at Deptford   100 *Idea*:
perfect pattern   105 *ensure*: guarantee   111 *go before*: i.e. like a servant

Cob. Aye, sir, I and my lineage ha' kept a poor house here, in our days.

Mat. Thy lineage, Monsieur Cob, what lineage? What lineage?

Cob. Why, sir, an ancient lineage, and a princely. Mine ancestry came from a king's belly, no worse man: and yet no man neither 10 (by your worship's leave, I did lie in that) but Herring the king of fish (from his belly, I proceed) one o' the monarchs o' the world, I assure you. The first red herring that was broiled in Adam and Eve's kitchen do I fetch my pedigree from, by the harrot's books. His cob was my great-great-mighty-great grandfather. 15

Mat. Why mighty? Why mighty? I pray thee.

Cob. Oh, it was a mighty while ago, sir, and a mighty great cob.

Mat. How knowst thou that?

Cob. How know I? Why, I smell his ghost, ever and anon.

Mat. Smell a ghost? Oh, unsavoury jest! And the ghost of a 20 herring, Cob!

Cob. Aye, sir, with favour of your worship's nose, Master Matthew, why not the ghost of a herring-cob, as well as the ghost of rasher-bacon?

Mat. Roger Bacon, thou wouldst say? 25

Cob. I say rasher-bacon. They were both broiled o' the coals? And a man may smell broiled meat, I hope? You are a scholar, upsolve me that now.

Mat. Oh, raw ignorance! Cob, canst thou show me of a gentle-man, one Captain Bobadil, where his lodging is? 30

Cob. Oh, my guest, sir! You mean.

Mat. Thy guest! Alas! Ha, ha.

Cob. Why do you laugh, sir? Do you not mean Captain Bobadil?

Mat. Cob, 'pray thee, advise thyself well: do not wrong the gentleman, and thyself too. I dare be sworn, he scorns thy house: 35 he! He lodge in such a base, obscure place, as thy house! Tut, I know his disposition so well, he would not lie in thy bed if thou'dst gi'it him.

Cob. I will not give it him, though, sir. Mass, I thought somewhat was in't, we could not get him to bed all night! Well, sir, though he 40

11–12 *Herring the king of fish*: cob = head of a herring   14 *harrot's*: herald's
25 *Roger Bacon*: the necromancer of the legend of the brazen head (ll. 54–5)
28 *upsolve*: clear up

lie not o' my bed, he lies o' my bench: an't please you to go up, sir,
you shall find him with two cushions under his head, and his cloak
wrapped about him, as though he had neither won nor lost, and yet
(I warrant) he ne'er cast better in his life than he has done tonight.

45 *Mat.* Why? Was he drunk?

Cob. Drunk, sir? You hear not me say so. Perhaps, he swallowed
a tavern-token, or some such device, sir: I have nothing to do
withal. I deal with water, and not with wine. Gi'me my tankard
there, ho. God b'w'you, sir. It's six o'clock: I should ha' carried
50 two turns by this. What ho? My stopple? Come.

Mat. Lie in a waterbearer's house! A gentleman of his havings!
Well, I'll tell him my mind.

[*Enter* Tib]

Cob. What Tib, show this gentleman up to the Captain. [*Exeunt*
Tib, Matthew] Oh, an' my house were the Brazen Head now!
55 Faith, it would e'en speak, 'Mo fools yet'. You should ha' some
now would take this Master Matthew to be a gentleman, at the least.
His father's an honest man, a worshipful fishmonger, and so forth;
and now does he creep and wriggle into acquaintance with all the
brave gallants about the town, such as my guest is: (oh, my guest
60 is a fine man) and they flout him invincibly. He useth every day to
a merchant's house (where I serve water), one Master Kitely's, i'
the Old Jewry; and here's the jest, he is in love with my master's
sister, Mistress Bridget, and calls her mistress: and there he will sit
you a whole afternoon sometimes, reading o' these same abominable,
65 vile (a pox on 'em, I cannot abide them) rascally verses, poyetry,
poyetry, and speaking of interludes, 'twill make a man burst
to hear him. And the wenches, they do so jeer, and tee-hee at him—
well, should they do so much to me, I'd forswear them all, by the
foot of Pharaoh. There's an oath! How many waterbearers shall you
70 hear swear such an oath? Oh, I have a guest (he teaches me), he
does swear the legiblest of any man christened: by St. George, the
foot of Pharaoh, the body of me, as I am a gentleman, and a soldier:

---

44 *cast*: (1) cast dice, (2) vomited   46–7 *swallowed a tavern-token*: euphemism
for getting drunk (tokens worth a halfpenny or a farthing were issued by tradesmen for
small change)   51 *havings*: qualities, deportment   57 *a worshipful fish-
monger*: i.e. a member of the city company   65 *poyetry*: indicating Cob's broad
pronunciation

such dainty oaths! And withal, he does take this same filthy roguish
tobacco, the finest, and cleanliest! It would do a man good to see
the fume come forth at his tunnels! Well, he owes me forty shillings   75
(my wife lent him out of her purse, by sixpence a time) besides his
lodging: I would I had it. I shall ha'it, he says, the next action.
Helter-skelter, hang sorrow, care'll kill a cat, up-tails all, and a
louse for the hangman.   [*Exit*]

ACT I, Scene v

[Cob's house]

Bobadil *is discovered lying on his bench*

Bob. Hostess, hostess.

[*Enter* Tib]

Tib. What say you, sir?

Bob. A cup o' thy small beer, sweet hostess.

Tib. Sir, there's a gentleman below would speak with you.

Bob. A gentleman! 'Ods so, I am not within.

Tib. My husband told him you were, sir.   5

Bob. What a plague—what meant he?

Mat. [*Within*] Captain Bobadil?

Bob. Who's there? Take away the basin, good hostess. Come
up, sir.   10

Tib. He would desire you to come up, sir. You come into a cleanly
house, here.

[*Enter* Matthew]

Mat. 'Save you, sir. 'Save you, captain.

Bob. Gentle Master Matthew! Is it you, sir? Please you sit down.

Mat. Thank you, good captain; you may see, I am somewhat   15
audacious.

Bob. Not so, sir. I was requested to supper last night by a sort of
gallants, where you were wished for, and drunk to, I assure you.

---

75 *tunnels*: nostrils   77 *action*: campaign   *care'll kill a cat*: proverbial
78 *up-tails all*: an old song (Chappell, i. 149)   (*I. v*) 17 *sort*: company

    Mat. Vouchsafe me, by whom, good captain.

20   *Bob.* Marry, by young Wellbred, and others. Why, hostess, a
stool here, for this gentleman.

    Mat. No haste, sir, 'tis very well.

    Bob. Body of me! It was so late ere we parted last night, I can
scarce open my eyes yet; I was but new risen as you came: how
25 passes the day abroad, sir? You can tell.

    Mat. Faith, some half-hour to seven: now trust me, you have an
exceeding fine lodging here, very neat, and private!

    Bob. Aye, sir: sit down, I pray you. Master Matthew, in any case,
possess no gentlemen of our acquaintance with notice of my lodging.

30   *Mat.* Who? I sir? No.

    Bob. Not that I need to care who know it, for the cabin is con-
venient, but in regard I would not be too popular, and generally
visited, as some are.

    Mat. True, captain, I conceive you.

35   *Bob.* For, do you see, sir, by the heart of valour in me (except it
be to some peculiar and choice spirits, to whom I am extraordinarily
engaged, as yourself, or so) I could not extend thus far.

    Mat. Oh Lord, sir, I resolve so.

    Bob. I confess I love a cleanly and quiet privacy, above all the
40 tumult and roar of fortune. What new book ha' you there? What!
'Go by, Hieronymo'!

    Mat. Aye, did you ever see it acted? Is't not well penned?

    Bob. Well penned? I would fain see all the poets of these times
pen such another play as that was! They'll prate and swagger, and
45 keep a stir of art and devices, when (as I am a gentleman) read 'em,
they are the most shallow, pitiful, barren fellows, that live upon the
face of the earth, again!

    Mat. Indeed, here are a number of fine speeches in this book!
'O eyes, no eyes, but fountains fraught with tears!' There's a
50 conceit! 'Fountains fraught with tears!' 'O life, no life, but lively
form of death!' Another! 'O world, no world, but mass of
public wrongs!' A third! 'Confused and filled with murder, and
misdeeds!' A fourth! Oh, the Muses! Is't not excellent? Is't not

---

34 *conceive*: understand   38 *I resolve so*: I am convinced (affected usage)
41 *'Go by, Hieronymo'*: stock quotation identifying Kyd's *The Spanish Tragedy* (ed.
Edwards, III. xii. 31)   49–53 *The Spanish Tragedy*: III. ii. 1–4

simply the best that ever you heard, captain? Ha? How do you
like it?

Bob. 'Tis good.   55

Mat. 'To thee, the purest object to my sense,
The most refined essence heaven covers,
Send I these lines, wherein I do commence
The happy state of turtle-billing lovers.   60
If they prove rough, unpolished, harsh, and rude,
Haste made the waste. Thus, mildly, I conclude.'

           (Bobadil *is making him ready all this while*)

Bob. Nay, proceed, proceed. Where's this?

Mat. This, sir? A toy o' mine own, in my nonage: the infancy of
my Muses! But when will you come and see my study? Good faith, 65
I can show you some very good things I have done of late——That
boot becomes your leg passing well, captain, methinks!

Bob. So, so, it's the fashion gentlemen now use.

Mat. Troth, captain, an' now you speak o' the fashion, Master
Wellbred's elder brother and I are fallen out exceedingly: this other 70
day, I happened to enter into some discourse of a hanger, which I
assure you, both for fashion and workmanship, was most peremp-
tory-beautiful and gentlemanlike! Yet he condemned and cried it
down for the most pied and ridiculous that ever he saw.

Bob. Squire Downright? The half-brother? Was't not?   75

Mat. Aye, sir, he.

Bob. Hang him, rook, he! Why, he has no more judgement than
a malt-horse. By St. George, I wonder you'd lose a thought upon
such an animal: the most peremptory absurd clown of Christendom
this day he is holden. I protest to you, as I am a gentleman and a 80
soldier, I ne'er changed words with his like. By his discourse, he
should eat nothing but hay. He was born for the manger, pannier,
or pack-saddle! He has not so much as a good phrase in his belly,
but all old iron, and rusty proverbs! A good commodity for some
smith to make hobnails of.   85

Mat. Aye, and he thinks to carry it away with his manhood still,
where he comes. He brags he will gi' me the *bastinado*, as I hear.

57–62 untraced   s.d. *making . . . ready*: getting dressed   64 *toy*: trifle
71 *hanger*: loop in sword belt   71–2 *peremptory*: absolutely   76 *rook*: gull,
simpleton   78 *malt-horse*: proverbially stupid (it draws liquor but drinks none)
87 *bastinado*: beating (strictly with a cane on the soles of the feet)

Bob. How! He the *bastinado*! How came he by that word, trow?

Mat. Nay, indeed, he said cudgel me; I termed it so, for my more

90 grace.

Bob. That may be: for I was sure, it was none of his word. But, when? When said he so?

Mat. Faith, yesterday, they say: a young gallant, a friend of mine told me so.

95 *Bob.* By the foot of Pharaoh, and 'twere my case now, I should send him a chartel, presently. The *bastinado*! A most proper, and sufficient dependance, warranted by the great Caranza. Come hither. You shall chartel him. I'll show you a trick or two you shall kill him with, at pleasure: the first *stoccata*, if you will, by this air.

100 *Mat.* Indeed, you have absolute knowledge i' the mystery, I have heard, sir.

Bob. Of whom? Of whom ha' you heard it, I beseech you?

Mat. Troth, I have heard it spoken of divers, that you have very rare, and un-in-one-breath-utter-able skill, sir.

105 *Bob.* By heaven, no, not I; no skill i' the earth: some small rudiments i' the science, as to know my time, distance, or so. I have professed it more for noblemen and gentlemen's use than mine own practice, I assure you. Hostess, accommodate us with another bed-staff here, quickly: lend us another bed-staff. [*Exit* Tib] The

110 woman does not understand the words of action. Look you, sir. Exalt not your point above this state, at any hand, and let your poniard maintain your defence, thus:

[*Enter* Tib]

(give it the gentleman, and leave us) [*Exit* Tib] so, sir. Come on: oh, twine your body more about, that you may fall to a more sweet

115 comely gentleman-like guard. So, indifferent. Hollow your body more, sir, thus. Now, stand fast o' your left leg, note your distance, keep your due proportion of time——oh, you disorder your point most irregularly!

88 *trow*: do you suppose?   96 *chartel*: cartel (written challenge)   97 *dependance*: a duellist's ground of quarrel   *Caranza*: Jeronimo de Carranza, author of a treatise on fencing and the rules of the duel   99 *stoccata*: thrust   108 *accommodate*: a vogue word   109 *bed-staff*: used for beating up the bed in making it   111 *state*: position

Mat. How is the bearing of it now, sir?

Bob. Oh, out of measure ill! A well-experienced hand would 120
pass upon you at pleasure.

Mat. How mean you, sir, pass upon me?

Bob. Why, thus, sir (make a thrust at me), come in, upon the
answer, control your point, and make a full career, at the body. The
best-practised gallants of the time, name it the *passada*: a most 125
desperate thrust, believe it!

Mat. Well, come, sir.

Bob. Why, you do not manage your weapon with any facility, or
grace to invite me: I have no spirit to play with you. Your dearth
of judgement renders you tedious.   130

Mat. But one *venue*, sir.

Bob. Venue! Fie. Most gross denomination, as ever I heard. Oh,
the *stoccata*, while you live, sir. Note that. Come, put on your cloak,
and we'll go to some private place, where you are acquainted, some
tavern, or so——and have a bit——I'll send for one of these fencers, 135
and he shall breath you, by my direction; and then I will teach you
your trick. You shall kill him with it, at the first, if you please. Why,
I will learn you, by the true judgement of the eye, hand, and foot,
to control any enemy's point i' the world. Should your adversary
confront you with a pistol, 'twere nothing, by this hand, you should, 140
by the same rule, control his bullet, in a line: except it were hail-
shot and spread. What money ha' you about you, Master Matthew?

Mat. Faith, I ha' not past a two shillings or so.

Bob. 'Tis somewhat with the least: but come. We will have a
bunch of radish, and salt, to taste our wine; and a pipe of tobacco, 145
to close the orifice of the stomach: and then we'll call upon young
Wellbred. Perhaps we shall meet the Corydon, his brother, there:
and put him to the question.   [*Exeunt*]

124 *career*: lunge   125 *passada*: forward thrust while the fencer advances one
foot   131 *venue*: pass (an unfashionable term)   147 *Corydon*: rustic

ACT II, Scene i

[Before Kitely's house]

Enter Kitely, Cash, Downright

Kit. THOMAS, come hither.
There lies a note, within upon my desk,
Here, take my key: it is no matter, neither.
Where is the boy?
    Cas.   Within, sir, i' the warehouse.
5   *Kit*. Let him tell over, straight, that Spanish gold,
And weigh it, with the pieces of eight. Do you
See the delivery of those silver stuffs,
To Master Lucar. Tell him, if he will,
He shall ha' the grograms, at the rate I told him,
10 And I will meet him on the Exchange anon.
    Cas. Good, sir.   [*Exit*]
    Kit. Do you see that fellow, brother Downright?
    Dow. Aye, what of him?
    Kit. He is a jewel, brother.
15 I took him of a child, up, at my door,
And christened him, gave him mine own name, Thomas,
Since bred him at the Hospital; where proving
A toward imp, I called him home, and taught him
So much as I have made him my cashier,
20 And given him, who had none, a surname, Cash:
And find him in his place so full of faith
That I durst trust my life into his hands.
    Dow. So would not I in any bastard's, brother,
As it is like he is, although I knew
25 Myself his father. But you said you had somewhat
To tell me, gentle brother, what is't? What is't?
    Kit. Faith, I am very loth to utter it,
As fearing it may hurt your patience:

---

6 *pieces of eight*: the Spanish *peso* worth eight reales   9 *grograms*: coarse fabric
17 *Hospital*: Christ's Hospital, which educated foundlings

But that I know your judgement is of strength,
Against the nearness of affection——
    Dow. What need this circumstance? Pray you be direct.
    Kit. I will not say how much I do ascribe
Unto your friendship; nor in what regard
I hold your love: but let my past behaviour,
And usage of your sister but confirm
How well I've been affected to your——
    Dow. You are too tedious, come to the matter, the matter.
    Kit. Then, without further ceremony, thus.
My brother Wellbred, sir, I know not how,
Of late is much declined in what he was,
And greatly altered in his disposition.
When he came first to lodge here in my house,
Ne'er trust me, if I were not proud of him:
Methought he bare himself in such a fashion,
So full of man, and sweetness in his carriage,
And (what was chief) it showed not borrowed in him,
But all he did, became him as his own,
And seemed as perfect, proper, and possessed
As breath, with life, or colour, with the blood.
But, now, his course is so irregular,
So loose, affected, and deprived of grace,
And he himself withal so far fallen off
From that first place, as scarce no note remains,
To tell men's judgements where he lately stood.
He's grown a stranger to all due respect,
Forgetful of his friends, and not content
To stale himself in all societies,
He makes my house here common as a mart,
A theatre, a public receptacle
For giddy humour, and diseased riot;
And here (as in a tavern, or a stews)
He and his wild associates spend their hours,
In repetition of lascivious jests,
Swear, leap, drink, dance, and revel night by night,
Control my servants: and indeed what not?

30

35

40

45

50

55

60

65

    53 *note*: sign, characteristic   57 *stale*: cheapen

Dow. 'Sdeynes, I know not what I should say to him, i' the whole
world! He values me at a cracked three-farthings, for aught I see:
it will never out o' the flesh that's bred i' the bone! I have told him
enough, one would think, if that would serve. But counsel to him
70 is as good, as a shoulder of mutton to a sick horse. Well! He knows
what to trust to, 'fore George. Let him spend, and spend, and
domineer till his heart ache; an' he think to be relieved by me, when
he is got into one o' your city pounds, the Counters, he has the
wrong sow by the ear, i' faith: and claps his dish at the wrong man's
75 door. I'll lay my hand o' my halfpenny, ere I part with't, to fetch
him out, I'll assure him.

Kit. Nay, good brother, let it not trouble you thus.

Dow. 'Sdeath, he mads me, I could eat my very spur-leathers for
anger! But why are you so tame? Why do you not speak to him, and
80 tell him how he disquiets your house?

Kit. Oh, there are divers reasons to dissuade, brother.
But would yourself vouchsafe to travail in it,
(Though but with plain and easy circumstance)
It would both come much better to his sense,
85 And savour less of stomach, or of passion.
You are his elder brother, and that title
Both gives and warrants you authority;
Which (by your presence seconded) must breed
A kind of duty in him, and regard:
90 Whereas if I should intimate the least,
It would but add contempt to his neglect,
Heap worse on ill, make up a pile of hatred
That, in the rearing, would come tottering down,
And in the ruin, bury all our love.
95 Nay, more than this, brother, if I should speak
He would be ready from his heat of humour,
And overflowing of the vapour in him,
To blow the ears of his familiars
With the false breath of telling what disgraces
100 And low disparagements I had put upon him.

---

66 *'Sdeynes*: 'by God's deynes' (? dignity)   67 *three-farthings*: a thin silver piece
coined by Elizabeth   73 *Counters*: the two city prisons   74–5 *wrong sow ... half-
penny*: proverbial   74 *dish*: the wooden dish which beggars clapped to attract alms

Whilst they, sir, to relieve him, in the fable,
Make their loose comments upon every word,
Gesture, or look I use; mock me all over,
From my flat cap unto my shining shoes:
And out of their impetuous rioting fancies,   105
Beget some slander, that shall dwell with me.
And what would that be, think you? Marry, this.
They would give out, because my wife is fair,
Myself but lately married, and my sister
Here sojourning a virgin in my house,   110
That I were jealous! Nay, as sure as death,
That they would say. And how that I had quarrelled
My brother purposely, thereby to find
An apt pretext to banish them my house.
    Dow. Mass, perhaps so; they're like enough to do it.   115
    Kit. Brother, they would, believe it: so should I
(Like one of these penurious quack-salvers)
But set the bills up, to mine own disgrace,
And try experiments upon myself:
Lend scorn and envy, opportunity   120
To stab my reputation, and good name——

ACT II, Scene ii

Enter Matthew, Bobadil

    Mat. I will speak to him——
    Bob. Speak to him? Away, by the foot of Pharaoh, you shall not,
you shall not do him that grace. The time of day to you, gentleman
o' the house. Is Master Wellbred stirring?
    Dow. How then? What should he do?
    Bob. Gentleman of the house, it is to you: is he within, sir?   5
    Kit. He came not to his lodging tonight, sir, I assure you.
    Dow. Why, do you hear? You.
    Bob. The gentleman-citizen hath satisfied me, I'll talk to no
scavenger.   *[Exit with* Matthew]   10

104 *flat cap*: the mark of the citizen   *shining*: i.e. blackened (unfashionably)
118 *bills*: advertisements   (*II. ii*) 7 *tonight*: last night

Dow. How, scavenger? Stay, sir, stay?

Kit. Nay, brother Downright.

Dow. 'Heart! Stand you away, and you love me.

Kit. You shall not follow him now, I pray you, brother, good
15 faith you shall not: I will over-rule you.

Dow. Ha? Scavenger? Well, go to, I say little: but, by this good
day (God forgive me I should swear) if I put it up so, say I am the
rankest cow that ever pissed. 'Sdeynes, and I swallow this, I'll ne'er
draw my sword in the sight of Fleet Street again, while I live; I'll
20 sit in a barn, with Madge-howlet and catch mice first. Scavenger?
'Heart, and I'll go near to fill that huge tumbrel-slop of yours, with
somewhat, and I have good luck: your Garagantua breech cannot
carry it away so.

Kit. Oh, do not fret yourself thus, never think on't.

25 *Dow.* These are my brother's consorts, these! These are his
Cam'rades, his walking mates! He's a gallant, a *Cavaliero* too, right
hangman cut! Let me not live, and I could not find in my heart to
swinge the whole ging of 'em, one after another, and begin with him
first. I am grieved it should be said he is my brother, and take these
30 courses. Well, as he brews, so he shall drink, 'fore George, again.
Yet, he shall hear on't, and that tightly too, and I live, i' faith.

Kit. But, brother, let your reprehension, then,
Run in an easy current, not o'er-high
Carried with rashness, or devouring choler;
35 But rather use the soft persuading way,
Whose powers will work more gently, and compose
The imperfect thoughts you labour to reclaim:
More winning, than enforcing the consent.

Dow. Aye, aye, let me alone for that, I warrant you.   *(Bell rings)*
40 *Kit.* How now? Oh, the bell rings to breakfast.
Brother, I pray you go in, and bear my wife
Company till I come; I'll but give order
For some dispatch of business, to my servants——

                                                    [*Exit* Downright]

11 *scavenger*: lit. street-cleaner, here a term of abuse   19 *Fleet Street*: noted
for affrays   20 *Madge*: popular name for the owl   21 *tumbrel-slop*: wide
puffed breeches   22 *Garagantua*: A reference to the folk-tales of the giant
Gargantua, rather than to Rabelais's work (*H&S* ix. 316–17)   26–7 *right hang-
man cut*: dressed ready for the hangman   28 *swinge*: thrash   *ging*: company

ACT II, Scene iii

Enter Cob

Kit. What, Cob? Our maids will have you by the back,
I' faith, for coming so late this morning.

Cob. Perhaps so, sir, take heed somebody have not them by the
belly, for walking so late in the evening.

(*He passes by with his tankard*)

Kit. Well, yet my troubled spirit's somewhat eased,   5
Though not reposed in that security
As I could wish. But I must be content.
Howe'er I set a face on't to the world,
Would I had lost this finger, at a venture,
So Wellbred had ne'er lodged within my house.   10
Why't cannot be, where there is such resort
Of wanton gallants and young revellers,
That any woman should be honest long.
Is't like, that factious beauty will preserve
The public weal of chastity, unshaken,   15
When such strong motives muster, and make head
Against her single peace? No, no. Beware,
When mutual appetite doth meet to treat,
And spirits of one kind, and quality,
Come once to parley, in the pride of blood: 20
It is no slow conspiracy that follows.
Well (to be plain) if I but thought the time
Had answered their affections: all the world
Should not persuade me, but I were a cuckold.
Marry, I hope, they ha'not got that start: 25
For opportunity hath balked 'em yet,
And shall do still, while I have eyes and ears
To attend the impositions of my heart.
My presence shall be as an iron bar
'Twixt the conspiring motions of desire: 30
Yea, every look, or glance, mine eye ejects,

1–4: cf. proverb 'The back of a herring, the belly of a wench are best'

Shall check occasion, as one doth his slave,
When he forgets the limits of prescription.

[*Enter* Dame Kiteley, Bridget]

Dam. Sister Bridget, pray you fetch down the rosewater above in
35 the closet. [*Exit* Bridget] Sweetheart, will you come in to breakfast?
    Kit. [*Aside*] An' she have overheard me now?
    Dam. I pray thee, good Mouse, we stay for you.
    Kit. [*Aside*] By heaven I would not for a thousand angels.
    Dam. What ail you, sweetheart, are you not well, speak, good
40 Mouse.
    Kit. Troth my head aches extremely, on a sudden.
    Dam. [*Putting her hand to his forehead*] Oh, the lord!
    Kit. How now? What?
    Dam. Alas, how it burns? Mouse, keep you warm, good truth it
45 is this new disease! There's a number are troubled withal! For
love's sake, sweetheart, come in, out of the air.
    Kit. [*Aside*] How simple, and how subtle are her answers?
A new disease, and many troubled with it!
Why, true: she heard me, all the world to nothing.
50   *Dam.* I pray thee, good sweetheart, come in; the air will do you
harm, in troth.
    Kit. [*Aside*] The air! She has me i' the wind! Sweetheart!
I'll come to you presently: 'twill away, I hope.
    Dam. Pray heaven it do.   [*Exit*]
55   *Kit.* A new disease? I know not, new, or old,
But it may well be called poor mortals' plague:
For, like a pestilence, it doth infect
The houses of the brain. First it begins
Solely to work upon the fantasy,
60 Filling her seat with such pestiferous air,
As soon corrupts the judgement; and from thence
Sends like contagion to the memory:
Still each to other giving the infection.

34 *rose-water*: taken when eating fruit   45 *new disease*: term given to forms of
fever which were imperfectly diagnosed   46 *air*: thought harmful to invalids
52 *i' the wind*: of the hart (so 'sweetheart') scenting the hunter   58 *houses of the
brain*: according to the old anatomists, imagination (at the front), reason (in the middle),
and memory (at the back)

Which, as a subtle vapour, spreads itself
Confusedly through every sensive part,   65
Till not a thought, or motion, in the mind,
Be free from the black poison of suspect.
Ah, but what misery is it, to know this?
Or, knowing it, to want the mind's erection,
In such extremes? Well, I will once more strive,   70
(In spite of this black cloud) myself to be,
And shake the fever off, that thus shakes me.   [*Exit*]

ACT II, Scene iv

[Moorfields]

Enter Brainworm [*disguised*]

Bra. 'Slid, I cannot choose but laugh, to see myself translated
thus, from a poor creature to a creator; for now must I create an
intolerable sort of lies, or my present profession loses the grace: and
yet the lie to a man of my coat is as ominous a fruit as the *Fico*. Oh
sir, it holds for good polity ever, to have that outwardly in vilest   5
estimation, that inwardly is most dear to us. So much for my
borrowed shape. Well, the truth is, my old master intends to follow
my young, dry foot over Moorfields to London this morning: now
I, knowing of this hunting-match, or rather conspiracy, and to
insinuate with my young master (for so must we that are blue   10
waiters, and men of hope and service do, or perhaps we may wear
motley at the year's end, and who wears motley, you know) have got
me afore, in this disguise, determining here to lie in *ambuscado*, and
intercept him in the midway. If I can but get his cloak, his purse,
his hat, nay, anything, to cut him off, that is, to stay his journey,   15
Veni, vidi, vici, I may say with Captain Caesar, I am made for ever,
i' faith. Well, now must I practise to get the true garb of one of

4 *the Fico*: the gesture of thrusting the thumb between the forefingers, or of swell-
ing the cheek by putting the thumb in the mouth   8 *dry foot*: by the mere
scent   10 *blue*: the colour of servingmen's dress   11-12 *wear motley*: be
made fools of   17 *garb*: style

these lance-knights, my arm here, and my—young master! And his
cousin, Master Stephen, as I am true counterfeit man of war, and
20 no soldier!

[*Enter* Edward Knowell, Stephen]

E. Kn. So, sir, and how then, coz?

Ste. 'Sfoot, I have lost my purse, I think.

E. Kn. How? Lost your purse? Where? When had you it?

Ste. I cannot tell, stay.

25 *Bra.* 'Slid, I am afeared, they will know me, would I could get by
them.   [*Goes aside*]

E. Kn. What? Ha' you it?

Ste. No, I think I was bewitched, I——

E. Kn. Nay, do not weep the loss, hang it, let it go.

30 *Ste.* Oh, it's here: no, and it had been lost, I had not cared, but
for a jet ring Mistress Mary sent me.

E. Kn. A jet ring? Oh, the posy, the posy?

Ste. Fine, i' faith! 'Though fancy sleep, my love is deep.' Meaning
that though I did not fancy her, yet she loved me dearly.

35 *E. Kn.* Most excellent!

Ste. And then, I sent her another, and my posy was: 'The deeper,
the sweeter, I'll be judged by St. Peter.'

E. Kn. How, by St. Peter? I do not conceive that!

Ste. Marry, St. Peter, to make up the metre.

40 *E. Kn.* Well, there the Saint was your good patron, he helped you
at your need: thank him, thank him.

Bra. (*He is come back*) I cannot take leave on 'em, so: I will
venture, come what will. Gentlemen, please you change a few
crowns, for a very excellent good blade, here? I am a poor gentle-
45 man, a soldier, one that (in the better state of my fortunes) scorned
so mean a refuge, but now it is the humour of necessity, to have it so.
You seem to be gentlemen, well affected to martial men, else I
should rather die with silence than live with shame: however,
vouchsafe to remember, it is my want speaks, not myself. This condi-
50 tion agrees not with my spirit——

E. Kn. Where hast thou served?

18 *lance-knights*: mercenary footsoldiers, especially armed with lance or pike
31 *jet*: a favourite material for cheap rings because of its electrical attraction
32 *posy*: inscription   36–7 a drinking proverb

Bra. May it please you, sir, in all the late wars of Bohemia, Hungaria, Dalmatia, Poland, where not, sir? I have been a poor servitor, by sea and land, any time this fourteen years, and followed the fortunes of the best commanders in Christendom. I was twice 55 shot at the taking of Aleppo, once at the relief of Vienna; I have been at Marseilles, Naples, and the Adriatic gulf, a gentleman-slave in the galleys, thrice, where I was most dangerously shot in the head, through both the thighs, and yet, being thus maimed, I am void of maintenance, nothing left me but my scars, the noted marks 60 of my resolution.

Ste. How will you sell this rapier, friend?

Bra. Generous sir, I refer it to your own judgement; you are a gentleman, give me what you please.

Ste. True, I am a gentleman, I know that, friend: but what 65 though? I pray you say, what would you ask?

Bra. I assure you, the blade may become the side or thigh of the best prince in Europe.

E. Kn. Aye, with a velvet scabbard, I think.

Ste. Nay, and't be mine, it shall have a velvet scabbard, coz, that's 70 flat: I'd not wear it as 'tis, and you would give me an angel.

Bra. At your worship's pleasure, sir; nay, 'tis a most pure Toledo.

Ste. I had rather it were a Spaniard! But tell me, what shall I give you for it? An' it had a silver hilt——

E. Kn. Come, come, you shall not buy it; hold, there's a shilling, 75 fellow, take thy rapier.

Ste. Why, but I will buy it now, because you say so, and there's another shilling, fellow. I scorn to be outbidden. What, shall I walk with a cudgel, like Higgin-Bottom? And may have a rapier, for money? 80

E. Kn. You may buy one in the city.

Ste. Tut, I'll buy this i' the field, so I will, I have a mind to't, because 'tis a field rapier. Tell me your lowest price.

E. Kn. You shall not buy it, I say.

Ste. By this money, but I will, though I give more than 'tis worth. 85

52 *the late wars*: of Ferdinand of Hungary against the Turks   56 *Aleppo*: taken by Selim I in 1516   *Vienna*: relieved in 1529   69 *velvet scabbard*: a fashionable affectation   71 *angel*: gold coin with the image of the archangel Michael   73 *Spaniard*: Stephen is unaware that Toledo is in Spain   79 *Higgin-Bottom*: ? a type of belligerence (*H&S* ix. 366)

E. Kn. Come away, you are a fool.

Ste. Friend, I am a fool, that's granted: but I'll have it, for that word's sake. Follow me, for your money.

Bra. At your service, sir.   [*Exeunt*]

ACT II, Scene v

Enter Knowell

Kno. I cannot lose the thought, yet, of this letter,
Sent to my son: nor leave to admire the change
Of manners and the breeding of our youth,
Within the kingdom, since myself was one.
5 When I was young, he lived not in the stews,
Durst have conceived a scorn and uttered it
On a grey head; age was authority
Against a buffoon: and a man had then
A certain reverence paid unto his years,
10 That had none due unto his life. So much
The sanctity of some prevailed, for others.
But now we all are fallen; youth, from their fear:
And age, from that which bred it, good example.
Nay, would ourselves were not the first, even parents,
15 That did destroy the hopes in our own children:
Or they not learned our vices in their cradles,
And sucked in our ill customs with their milk.
Ere all their teeth be born, or they can speak,
We make their palates cunning! The first words
20 We form their tongues with are licentious jests!
Can it call, whore? Cry, bastard? Oh, then, kiss it,
A witty child! Can't swear? The father's darling!
Give it two plums. Nay, rather than 't shall learn
No bawdy song, the mother herself will teach it!
25 But this is in the infancy; the days
Of the long coat: when it puts on the breeches,

2 *admire*: wonder at   14–34 Quintilian, I. ii. 6–8   19 *cunning*: knowing
26 *long coat*: worn by the child (*BF* I. iv. 103)

It will put off all this. Aye, it is like:
When it is gone into the bone already.
No, no: this dye goes deeper than the coat,
Or shirt, or skin. It stains, unto the liver,
And heart, in some. And rather than it should not,   30
Note, what we fathers do! Look, how we live!
What mistresses we keep! At what expense,
In our sons' eyes! Where they may handle our gifts,
Hear our lascivious courtships, see our dalliance,   35
Taste of the same provoking meats with us,
To ruin of our states! Nay, when our own
Portion is fled, to prey on their remainder,
We call them into fellowship of vice!
Bait 'em with the young chambermaid, to seal!   40
And teach 'em all bad ways, to buy affliction!
This is one path! But there are millions more,
In which we spoil our own, with leading them.
Well, I thank heaven, I never yet was he,
That travelled with my son, before sixteen,   45
To show him the Venetian courtesans.
Nor read the grammar of cheating I had made
To my sharp boy, at twelve: repeating still
The rule, 'Get money'; still, 'Get money, boy';
'No matter by what means; money will do   50
More, boy, than my Lord's letter.' Neither have I
Dressed snails, or mushrooms curiously before him,
Perfumed my sauces, and taught him to make 'em;
Preceding still, with my grey gluttony,
At all the ordinaries: and only feared   55
His palate should degenerate, not his manners.
These are the trade of fathers, now! However
My son, I hope, hath met within my threshold
None of these household precedents, which are strong
And swift to rape youth to their precipice.   60
But let the house at home be ne'er so clean-
Swept, or kept sweet from filth, nay, dust, and cobwebs:

30 *liver*: seat of the passions   40 *seal*: e.g. some document conveying property
52 *curiously*: exotically   55 *ordinaries*: public eating-houses

If he will live abroad with his companions,
In dung and leystalls, it is worth a fear.
65 Nor is the danger of conversing less
Than all that I have mentioned of example.

[*Enter* Brainworm *disguised*]

Bra. [*Aside*] My master? Nay, faith, have at you: I am fleshed
now, I have sped so well. Worshipful sir, I beseech you, respect the
estate of a poor soldier; I am ashamed of this base course of life
70 (God's my comfort) but extremity provokes me to't, what remedy?
Kno. I have not for you, now.
Bra. By the faith I bear unto truth, gentleman, it is no ordinary
custom in me, but only to preserve manhood. I protest to you, a
man I have been, a man I may be, by your sweet bounty.
75 *Kno.* 'Pray thee, good friend, be satisfied.
Bra. Good sir, by that hand, you may do the part of a kind
gentleman; in lending a poor soldier the price of two cans of beer
(a matter of small value) the king of heaven shall pay you, and I
shall rest thankful: sweet worship——
80 *Kno.* Nay, and you be so importunate——
Bra. Oh, tender sir, need will have his course: I was not made to
this vile use! Well, the edge of the enemy could not have abated me
so much. It's hard when a man hath served in his Prince's cause,
and be thus (*He weeps*)—Honourable worship, let me derive a small
85 piece of silver from you, it shall not be given in the course of time,
by this good ground, I was fain to pawn my rapier last night for a
poor supper, I had sucked the hilts long before, I am a pagan else:
sweet honour.
Kno. Believe me, I am taken with some wonder,
90 To think a fellow of thy outward presence
Should, in the frame, and fashion of his mind,
Be so degenerate and sordid-base!
Art thou a man? And sham'st thou not to beg?
To practise such a servile kind of life?
95 Why, were thy education ne'er so mean,
Having thy limbs, a thousand fairer courses

---

64 *leystalls*: dungheaps   77 *price* . . . *beer*: twopence   85 *not* . . . *time*:
i.e. you will one day be repaid

Offer themselves to thy election.
Either the wars might still supply thy wants,
Or service of some virtuous gentleman,
Or honest labour: nay, what can I name,
But would become thee better than to beg?   100
But men of thy condition feed on sloth,
As doth the beetle on the dung she breeds in,
Not caring how the metal of your minds
Is eaten with the rust of idleness.
Now, afore me, whate'er he be that should   105
Relieve a person of thy quality,
While thou insists in this loose desperate course,
I would esteem the sin not thine, but his.

    Bra. Faith, sir, I would gladly find some other course, if so—— 110
    Kno. Aye, you'd gladly find it, but you will not seek it.

    Bra. Alas, sir, where should a man seek? In the wars, there's no
ascent by desert in these days, but——and for service, would it
were as soon purchased, as wished for (the air's my comfort) I
know, what I would say——   115

    Kno. What's thy name?

    Bra. Please you, Fitzsword, sir.

    Kno. Fitzsword?
Say, that a man should entertain thee now,
Wouldst thou be honest, humble, just, and true?   120

    Bra. Sir, by the place, and honour of a soldier——

    Kno. Nay, nay, I like not those affected oaths;
Speak plainly, man: what thinkst thou of my words?

    Bra. Nothing, sir, but wish my fortunes were as happy, as my
service should be honest.   125

    Kno. Well, follow me, I'll prove thee, if thy deeds
Will carry a proportion to thy words.   [*Exit*]

    Bra. Yes, sir, straight, I'll but garter my hose. Oh, that my belly
were hooped now, for I am ready to burst with laughing! Never was
bottle or bagpipe fuller. 'Slid, was there ever seen a fox in years to   130
betray himself thus? Now shall I be possessed of all his counsels:
and, by that conduit, my young master. Well, he is resolved to
prove my honesty; faith, and I am resolved to prove his patience: oh,

114 *purchased*: acquired   119 *entertain*: engage   126 *prove*: test

I shall abuse him intolerably. This small piece of service will bring
135 him clean out of love with the soldier for ever. He will never come
within the sign of it, the sight of a cassock, or a musket-rest again.
He will hate the musters at Mile End for it, to his dying day. It's
no matter, let the world think me a bad counterfeit, if I cannot give
him the slip at an instant: why, this is better than to have stayed
140 his journey! Well, I'll follow him: oh, how I long to be employed.
                                                                [*Exit*]

ACT III, Scene i

[A street near the Windmill Tavern]

Enter Matthew, Wellbred, Bobadil

Mat. YES faith, sir, we were at your lodging to seek you, too.

Wel. Oh, I came not there tonight.

Bob. Your brother delivered us as much.

Wel. Who? My brother Downright?

5   *Bob.* He. Master Wellbred, I know not in what kind you hold me,
but let me say to you this: as sure as honour, I esteem it so much
out of the sunshine of reputation, to throw the least beam of regard,
upon such a——

Wel. Sir, I must hear no ill words of my brother.

10   *Bob.* I protest to you, as I have a thing to be saved about me, I
never saw any gentleman-like part——

Wel. Good captain, 'faces about', to some other discourse.

Bob. With your leave, sir, and there were no more men living
upon the face of the earth, I should not fancy him, by St. George.

15   *Mat.* Troth, nor I, he is of a rustical cut, I know not how: he
doth not carry himself like a gentleman of fashion——

Wel. Oh, Master Matthew, that's a grace peculiar but to a few;
quos aequus amavit Jupiter.

---

136 *cassock*: soldier's cloak   *musket-rest*: pole with semicircular top, carried sus-
pended from the shoulder   137 *Mile End*: commonly used as a military training-
ground   139 *slip*: quibble on 'slip' as a counterfeit coin   (*III. i*) 17–18 Virgil,
Aeneid, vi. 129 ('those whom gracious Jove has loved')

Mat. I understand you, sir.

Wel. No question, you do, or you do not, sir.   20

(Young Knowell *enters* [*with* Stephen])

Ned Knowell! By my soul, welcome; how dost thou, sweet spirit,
my genius? 'Slid, I shall love Apollo and the mad Thespian girls
the better, while I live, for this; my dear fury: now, I see there's
some love in thee! Sirrah, these be the two I writ to thee of (nay,
what a drowsy humour is this now? Why dost thou not speak?).   25

E. Kn. Oh, you are a fine gallant, you sent me a rare letter!

Wel. Why, was't not rare?

E. Kn. Yes, I'll be sworn, I was ne'er guilty of reading the like;
match it in all Pliny, or Symmachus epistles, and I'll have my
judgement burned in the ear for a rogue: make much of thy vein,   30
for it is inimitable. But I mar'l what camel it was, that had the
carriage of it? For doubtless, he was no ordinary beast that
brought it!

Wel. Why?

E. Kn. Why, sayest thou? Why dost thou think that any reason-   35
able creature, especially in the morning (the sober time of the day
too) could have mista'en my father for me?

Wel. 'Slid, you jest, I hope?

E. Kn. Indeed, the best use we can turn it to, is to make a jest
on't now: but I'll assure you, my father had the full view o' your   40
flourishing style, some hour before I saw it.

Wel. What a dull slave was this? But, sirrah, what said he to it,
i' faith?

E. Kn. Nay, I know not what he said: but I have a shrewd guess
what he thought.   45

Wel. What? What?

E. Kn. Marry, that thou art some strange dissolute young fellow,
and I a grain or two better, for keeping thee company.

Wel. Tut, that thought is like the moon in her last quarter, 'twill
change shortly: but, sirrah, I pray thee be acquainted with my two   50
hang-bys, here; thou wilt take exceeding pleasure in 'em if thou

22 *genius*: tutelary spirit   *Apollo*: as god of poetry (Thespian girls = the Muses)
29 *Symmachus*: scholar and statesman (consul in AD 391) whose letters, like Pliny's,
were collected in several volumes   31 *mar'l*: wonder

hear'st 'em once go: my wind-instruments. I'll wind 'em up——
but what strange piece of silence is this? [*Indicating* Stephen] The
sign of the dumb man?

55   *E. Kn.* Oh, sir, a kinsman of mine, one that may make your music
the fuller, and he please, he has his humour, sir.

Wel. Oh, what is't? What is't?

E. Kn. Nay, I'll neither do your judgement, nor his folly that
wrong, as to prepare your apprehension: I'll leave him to the mercy
60 o' your search, if you can take him, so.

Wel. Well, Captain Bobadil, Master Matthew, pray you know
this gentleman here, he is a friend of mine, and one that will deserve
your affection. (*To* Master Stephen) I know not your name, sir, but
I shall be glad of any occasion, to render me more familiar to you.

65   *Ste.* My name is Master Stephen, sir, I am this gentleman's own
cousin, sir, his father is mine uncle, sir, I am somewhat melancholy,
but you shall command me, sir, in whatsoever is incident to a
gentleman.

Bob. (*To* Knowell) Sir, I must tell you this, I am no general man,
70 but for Master Wellbred's sake (you may embrace it, at what height
of favour you please) I do communicate with you: and conceive
you to be a gentleman of some parts, I love few words.

E. Kn. And I fewer, sir. I have scarce enow, to thank you.

Mat. (*To* Master Stephen) But are you indeed, sir? So given to it?
75   *Ste.* Aye, truly, sir, I am mightily given to melancholy.

Mat. Oh, it's your only fine humour, sir, your true melancholy
breeds your perfect fine wit, sir: I am melancholy myself divers
times, sir, and then do I no more but take pen and paper presently,
and overflow you half a score, or a dozen of sonnets, at a sitting.
80   (*E. Kn.* Sure, he utters them then, by the gross.)

Ste. Truly, sir, and I love such things, out of measure.

E. Kn. [*Aside*] I' faith, better than in measure, I'll undertake.

Mat. Why, I pray you, sir, make use of my study, it's at your
service.

85   *Ste.* I thank you, sir, I shall be bold, I warrant you; have you a
stool there, to be melancholy upon?

Mat. That I have, sir, and some papers there of mine own doing,

54 *sign*: i.e. a painted tavern sign   80 *utters*: quibble on the commercial sense
'put into circulation'

at idle hours, that you'll say there's some sparks of wit in 'em, when
you see them.

Wel. [*Aside*] Would the sparks would kindle once, and become a   90
fire amongst 'em, I might see self-love burnt for her heresy.

Ste. Cousin, is it well? Am I melancholy enough?

E. Kn. Oh aye, excellent!

Wel. Captain Bobadil: why muse you so?

E. Kn. He is melancholy, too.   95

Bob. Aye, faith, sir, I was thinking of a most honourable piece
of service, was performed tomorrow, being St. Mark's day: shall be
some ten years, now?

E. Kn. In what place, captain?

Bob. Why, at the beleaguering of Strigonium, where, in less than   100
two hours, seven hundred resolute gentlemen, as any were in
Europe, lost their lives upon the breach. I'll tell you, gentlemen, it
was the first, but the best leaguer, that ever I beheld, with these
eyes, except the taking in of——what do you call it, last year, by
the Genoese, but that (of all other) was the most fatal and dangerous   105
exploit that ever I was ranged in, since I first bore arms before the
face of the enemy, as I am a gentleman, and soldier.

Ste. So, I had as lief, as an angel, I could swear as well as that
gentleman!

E. Kn. Then you were a servitor, at both it seems! At Strigonium?   110
And what do you call't?

Bob. Oh lord, sir? By St. George, I was the first man that entered
the breach: and had I not effected it with resolution, I had been
slain, if I had had a million of lives.

E. Kn. [*Aside*] 'Twas pity you had not ten; a cat's, and your own,   115
i' faith. But, was it possible?

(*Mat.* Pray you, mark this discourse, sir.

Ste. So, I do.)

Bob. I assure you (upon my reputation) 'tis true, and yourself
shall confess.   120

E. Kn. [*Aside*] You must bring me to the rack first.

Bob. Observe me judicially, sweet sir, they had planted me three
demi-culverins, just in the mouth of the breach; now, sir (as we

100 *Strigonium*: Graan in Hungary, retaken from the Turks in 1595   103 *leaguer*:
siege   123 *demi-culverins*: cannon of about 4½-inch bore

were to give on) their master gunner (a man of no mean skill and
125 mark, you must think) confronts me with his linstock, ready to give
fire; I spying his intendment, discharged my petronel in his
bosom, and with these single arms, my poor rapier, ran violently,
upon the Moors, that guarded the ordnance, and put 'em pell-mell
to the sword.

130   *Wel.* To the sword? To the rapier, captain?

       E. Kn. Oh, it was a good figure observed, sir! But did you all
this, captain, without hurting your blade?

       Bob. Without any impeach o' the earth: you shall perceive, sir.
It is the most fortunate weapon that ever rid on poor gentleman's
135 thigh: shall I tell you, sir? You talk of Morglay, Excalibur,
Durindana, or so? Tut, I lend no credit to that is fabled of 'em,
I know the virtue of mine own, and therefore I dare, the boldlier,
maintain it.

       Ste. I mar'l whether it be a Toledo, or no?

140   *Bob.* A most perfect Toledo, I assure you, sir.

       Ste. I have a countryman of his here.

       Mat. Pray you, let's see, sir: yes faith, it is!

       Bob. This a Toledo? Pish.

       Ste. Why do you pish, captain?

145   *Bob.* A Fleming, by heaven, I'll buy them for a guilder, a piece,
an' I would have a thousand of them.

       E. Kn. How say you, cousin? I told you thus much?

       Wel. Where bought you it, Master Stephen?

       Ste. Of a scurvy rogue soldier, a hundred of lice go with him; he
150 swore it was a Toledo.

       Bob. A poor provant rapier, no better.

       Mat. Mass, I think it be, indeed! Now I look on't, better.

       E. Kn. Nay, the longer you look on't, the worse. Put it up, put
it up.

155   *Ste.* Well, I will put it up, but by——(I ha' forgot the captain's
oath, I thought to ha' sworn by it) an' e'er I meet him——

       Wel. Oh, it is past help now, sir, you must have patience.

---

124 *give on*: make the assault   125 *linstock*: staff with a forked head for hold-
ing a lighted match   126 *petronel*: large pistol or carbine   135–6 *Morglay,
Excalibur, Durindana*: the swords of Bevis of Hampton, Arthur, and Orlando
145 *guilder*: Dutch coin worth 1s. 8d.   151 *provant*: supplied by the govern-
ment stores

Ste. Whoreson cony-catching rascal! I could eat the very hilts for anger!

E. Kn. A sign of good digestion! You have an ostrich stomach, 160 cousin.

Ste. A stomach? Would I had him here, you should see, an' I had a stomach.

Wel. It's better as 'tis: come, gentlemen, shall we go?

ACT III, Scene ii

Enter Brainworm

E. Kn. A miracle, cousin, look here! Look here!

Ste. Oh, God's lid, by your leave, do you know me, sir?

Bra. Aye, sir, I know you, by sight.

Ste. You sold me a rapier, did you not?

Bra. Yes, marry, did I, sir.   5

Ste. You said it was a Toledo, ha?

Bra. True, I did so.

Ste. But, it is none?

Bra. No, sir, I confess it, it is none.

Ste. Do you confess it? Gentlemen, bear witness, he has confessed 10 it. By God's will, and you had not confessed it——

E. Kn. Oh cousin, forbear, forbear.

Ste. Nay, I have done, cousin.

Wel. Why you have done like a gentleman, he has confessed it, what would you more?   15

Ste. Yet, by his leave, he is a rascal, under his favour, do you see?

E. Kn. Aye, by his leave, he is, and under favour: a pretty piece of civility! Sirrah, how dost thou like him?

Wel. Oh, it's a most precious fool, make much on him: I can compare him to nothing more happily than a drum; for everyone 20 may play upon him.

---

158 *cony-catching*: swindling   163 *stomach*: vexation, and martial readiness
(*III. ii*) 16 *by his leave . . . under his favour*: qualifying phrases in the etiquette of the quarrel, to allow for backing down

E. Kn. No, no, a child's whistle were far the fitter.

Bra. Sir, shall I entreat a word with you?

E. Kn. With me, sir? You have not another Toledo to sell,
25 ha' you?   [*They go aside*]

Bra. You are conceited, sir, your name is Master Knowell, as I
take it?

E. Kn. You are i' the right; you mean not to proceed in the
catechism, do you?

30   *Bra.* No, sir, I am none of that coat.

E. Kn. Of as bare a coat, though; well, say, sir.

Bra. Faith, sir, I am but servant to the drum extraordinary, and
indeed (this smoky varnish being washed off, and three or four
patches removed) I appear your worship's in reversion, after the
35 decease of your good father, Brainworm.

E. Kn. Brainworm! 'Slight, what breath of a conjurer hath blown
thee hither in this shape?

Bra. The breath o' your letter, sir, this morning: the same that
blew you to the Windmill, and your father after you.

40   *E. Kn.* My father?

Bra. Nay, never start, 'tis true, he has followed you over the
fields, by the foot, as you would do a hare i' the snow.

E. Kn. Sirrah, Wellbred, what shall we do, sirrah? My father is
come over, after me.

45   *Wel.* Thy father? Where is he?

Bra. At Justice Clement's house here, in Colman Street, where
he but stays my return; and then——

Wel. Who's this? Brainworm?

Bra. The same, sir.

50   *Wel.* Why how, i' the name of wit, com'st thou transmuted, thus?

Bra. Faith, a device, a device: nay, for the love of reason, gentle-
men, and avoiding the danger, stand not here, withdraw, and I'll
tell you all.

Wel. But, art thou sure, he will stay thy return?

55   *Bra.* Do I live, sir? What a question is that?

Wel. We'll prorogue his expectation then, a little: Brainworm, thou

---

26 *conceited*: pleasant, witty   30 *that coat*: i.e. the clergy   32 *extraordinary*:
i.e. not a regular soldier   36 *conjurer*: wizard   46 *Colman Street*: the Bond
Street of the period   51 *device*: stratagem

shalt go with us. Come on, gentlemen, nay, I pray thee, sweet Ned,
droop not: 'heart, and our wits be so wretchedly dull, that one old
plodding brain can outstrip us all, would we were e'en pressed, to
make porters of; and serve out the remnant of our days in Thames 60
Street, or at Custom House Quay, in a civil war, against the
car-men.

Bra. Amen, Amen, Amen, say I.   [*Exeunt*]

ACT III, Scene iii

[Kitely's warehouse]

Enter Kitely, Cash

Kit. What says he, Thomas? Did you speak with him?

Cas. He will expect you, sir, within this half-hour.

Kit. Has he the money ready, can you tell?

Cas. Yes, sir, the money was brought in, last night.

Kit. Oh, that's well: fetch me my cloak, my cloak.   [*Exit* Cash] 5
Stay, let me see, an hour, to go and come;
Aye, that will be the least: and then 'twill be
An hour, before I can dispatch with him;
Or very near: well, I will say two hours.
Two hours? Ha? Things never dreamt of yet   10
May be contrived, aye, and effected too,
In two hours' absence: well, I will not go.
Two hours; no, fleering opportunity,
I will not give your subtlety that scope,
Who will not judge him worthy to be robbed,   15
That sets his doors wide open to a thief,
And shows the felon where his treasure lies?
Again, what earthy spirit but will attempt
To taste the fruit of beauty's golden tree,
When leaden sleep seals up the dragon's eyes?   20
I will not go. Business, go by, for once.

---

59 *pressed*: conscripted   62 *car-men*: carters, given to jostling for space
(*III. iii*) 13 *fleering*: mocking

No beauty, no; you are of too good caract,
To be left so, without a guard, or open!
Your lustre too'll enflame, at any distance,
25 Draw courtship to you, as a jet doth straws,
Put motion in a stone, strike fire from ice,
Nay, make a porter leap you, with his burden!
You must be then kept up, close, and well-watched,
For, give you opportunity, no quicksand
30 Devours, or swallows swifter! He that lends
His wife (if she be fair) or time, or place,
Compels her to be false. I will not go.
The dangers are too many. And, then, the dressing
Is a most main attractive! Our great heads,
35 Within the city, never were in safety,
Since our wives wore these little caps: I'll change 'em,
I'll change 'em, straight, in mine. Mine shall no more
Wear three-piled acorns, to make my horns ache.
Nor will I go. I am resolved for that.

[*Enter* Cash *with cloak*]

40 Carry in my cloak again. Yet, stay. Yet, do too.
I will defer going, on all occasions.
    Cas. Sir. Snare, your scrivener, will be there with the bonds.
    Kit. That's true! Fool on me! I had clean forgot it,
I must go. What's a-clock?
    Cas.   Exchange time, sir.
45 *Kit.* [*Aside*] 'Heart, then will Wellbred presently be here too,
With one or other of his loose consorts.
I am a knave, if I know what to say,
What course to take, or which way to resolve.
My brain, methinks, is like an hour-glass,
50 Wherein my imaginations run like sands,
Filling up time; but then are turned, and turned,
So that I know not what to stay upon,
And less to put in act. It shall be so.

22 *caract*: carat (confused with 'charact', a sign or mark)   36 *little caps*: velvet
caps fashionable in the city   38 *three-piled*: the richest quality (with quibble on
the 'russet pile' on a hart's horns)   44 *Exchange time*: after ten

Nay, I dare build upon his secrecy,
He knows not to deceive me. Thomas?
   Cas.   Sir.   55
   Kit. [*Aside*] Yet now, I have bethought me, too, I will not.
Thomas, is Cob within?
   Cas.   I think he be, sir.
   Kit. [*Aside*] But he'll prate too, there's no speech of him.
No, there were no man o' the earth to Thomas,
If I durst trust him; there is all the doubt.
But should he have a chink in him, I were gone,   60
Lost i' my fame for ever: talk for the Exchange.
The manner he hath stood with, till this present,
Doth promise no such change! What should I fear then?
Well, come what will, I'll tempt my fortune, once.   65
Thomas——you may deceive me, but, I hope——
Your love, to me, is more——
   Cas.   Sir, if a servant's
Duty, with faith, may be called love, you are
More than in hope; you are possessed of it.
   Kit. I thank you, heartily, Thomas; gi' me your hand: 70
With all my heart, good Thomas. I have, Thomas,
A secret to impart unto you——but
When once you have it, I must seal your lips up:
(So far, I tell you, Thomas).
   Cas.   Sir, for that——
   Kit. Nay, hear me out. Think, I esteem you, Thomas,   75
When, I will let you in, thus, to my private.
It is a thing sits, nearer, to my crest,
Then thou art 'ware of, Thomas. If thou shouldst
Reveal it, but——
   Cas.   How? I reveal it?
   Kit.   Nay,
I do not think thou wouldst; but if thou shouldst: 80
'Twere a great weakness.
   Cas.   A great treachery.
Give it no other name.
   Kit.   Thou wilt not do't, then?

59 *to*: to be compared with   77 *crest*: honour, self-esteem

 Cas. Sir, if I do, mankind disclaim me, ever.

 Kit. [*Aside*] He will not swear, he has some reservation,

85 Some concealed purpose, and close meaning, sure:

Else (being urged so much) how should he choose,

But lend an oath to all this protestation?

He's no precisian, that I am certain of.

Nor rigid Roman Catholic. He'll play,

90 At fayles, and tick-tack, I have heard him swear.

What should I think of it? Urge him again,

And by some other way? I will do so.

Well, Thomas, thou hast sworn not to disclose;

Yes, you did swear?

 Cas.   Not yet, sir, but I will,

Please you——

95 *Kit.*   No, Thomas, I dare take thy word.

But; if thou wilt swear, do, as thou thinkst good;

I am resolved without it; at thy pleasure.

 Cas. By my soul's safety then, sir, I protest.

My tongue shall ne'er take knowledge of a word,

100 Delivered me in nature of your trust.

 Kit. It's too much, these ceremonies need not,

I know thy faith to be as firm as rock.

Thomas, come hither, near: we cannot be

Too private in this business. So it is,

105 (Now, he has sworn, I dare the safelier venture)

I have of late, by divers observations——

(But, whether his oath can bind him, yea, or no;

Being not taken lawfully? Ha? Say you?

I will ask counsel, ere I do proceed:)

110 Thomas, it will be now too long to stay,

I'll spy some fitter time soon, or tomorrow.

 Cas. Sir, at your pleasure?

 Kit.   I will think. And, Thomas,

I pray you search the books 'gainst my return,

For the receipts 'twixt me, and Traps.

 Cas.   I will, sir.

83 *disclaim*: disown   88 *precisian*: Puritan   90 *fayles, and tick-tack*:
varieties of backgammon   103 *near*: (neere) old comparative of 'nigh'   108 *law-
fully*: i.e. before a magistrate

Kit. And, hear you, if your mistress' brother, Wellbred,   115
Chance to bring hither any gentlemen,
Ere I come back, let one straight bring me word.
  Cas. Very well, sir.
  Kit.   To the Exchange; do you hear?
Or here in Colman Street, to Justice Clement's.
Forget it not, nor be not out of the way.   120
  Cas. I will not, sir.
  Kit.   I pray you have a care on't.
Or whether he come, or no, if any other,
Stranger, or else, fail not to send me word.
  Cas. I shall not, sir.
  Kit.   Be't your special business
Now, to remember it.
  Cas.   Sir. I warrant you.   125
  Kit. But, Thomas, this is not the secret, Thomas,
I told you of.
  Cas.   No, sir. I do suppose it.
  Kit. Believe me, it is not.
  Cas.   Sir. I do believe you.
  Kit. By heaven, it is not, that's enough. But, Thomas,
I would not, you should utter it, do you see?   130
To any creature living, yet, I care not.
Well, I must hence. Thomas, conceive thus much.
It was a trial of you, when I meant
So deep a secret to you, I mean not this,
But that I have to tell you, this is nothing, this.   135
But, Thomas, keep this from my wife, I charge you,
Locked up in silence, midnight, buried here.
No greater hell, than to be slave to fear.   [*Exit*]
  Cas. Locked up in silence, midnight, buried here.
Whence should this flood of passion (trow) take head? Ha?   140
Best dream no longer of this running humour,
For fear I sink! The violence of the stream
Already hath transported me so far,
That I can feel no ground at all! But soft,
Oh, 'tis our waterbearer: somewhat has crossed him, now.   145

  140 *trow*: do you suppose?

ACT III, Scene iv

Enter Cob

Cob. Fasting days? What tell you me of fasting days? 'Slid, would they were all on a light fire for me. They say the whole world shall be consumed with fire one day, but would I had these ember weeks, and villainous Fridays burnt, in the meantime, and then——

5   *Cas.* Why, how now, Cob, what moves thee to this choler? Ha?

Cob. Collar, Master Thomas? I scorn your collar, I, sir, I am none o' your carthorse, though I carry and draw water. An' you offer to ride me, with your collar, or halter either, I may hap show you a jade's trick, sir.

10   *Cas.* Oh, you'll slip your head out of the collar? Why, goodman Cob, you mistake me.

Cob. Nay, I have my rheum, and I can be angry as well as another, sir.

Cas. Thy rheum, Cob? Thy humour, thy humour? Thou 15 mistakst.

Cob. Humour? Mack, I think it be so, indeed: what is that humour? Some rare thing, I warrant.

Cas. Marry, I'll tell thee, Cob: it is a gentleman-like monster, bred in the special gallantry of our time by affectation; and fed by 20 folly.

Cob. How? Must it be fed?

Cas. Oh, aye, humour is nothing, if it be not fed. Didst thou never hear that? It's a common phrase, 'Feed my humour'.

Cob. I'll none on it: humour, avaunt, I know you not, be gone. 25 Let who will make hungry meals for your monstership, it shall not be I. Feed you, quoth he? 'Slid, I ha' much ado to feed myself; especially, on these lean rascally days, too; and 't had been any other day but a fasting day (a plague on them all for me) by this light, one might have done the commonwealth good service, and have 30 drowned them all i' the flood, two or three hundred thousand years

---

1 *Fasting days*: Fridays, Saturdays, Ember days, vigils and Lent (appointed for the benefit of the fishing trade)   2 *on a light fire*: ablaze   12 *rheum*: mucous discharge (here an affectation for 'humour')   16 *Mack*: distortion of 'mass'

ago. Oh, I do stomach them hugely! I have a maw now, and 'twere for Sir Bevis his horse, against 'em.

Cas. I pray thee, good Cob, what makes thee so out of love with fasting days?

Cob. Marry, that which will make any man out of love with 'em, 35 I think: their bad conditions, and you will needs know. First, they are of a Flemish breed, I'm sure on't, for they raven up more butter than all the days of the week beside; next, they stink of fish, and leek-porridge miserably: thirdly, they'll keep a man devoutly hungry all day, and at night send him supperless to bed. 40

Cas. Indeed, these are faults, Cob.

Cob. Nay, and this were all, 'twere something, but they are the only known enemies to my generation. A fasting day no sooner comes, but my lineage goes to rack, poor cobs they smoke for it, they are made martyrs o' the gridiron, they melt in passion: and 45 your maids too know this, and yet would have me turn Hannibal, and eat my own fish and blood: (*He pulls out a red herring*) my princely coz, fear nothing; I have not the heart to devour you, and I might be made as rich as King Cophetua. Oh that I had room for my tears, I could weep salt-water enough now to preserve the lives 50 of ten thousand of my kin. But I may curse none but these filthy Almanacks, for an't were not for them, these days of persecution would ne'er be known. I'll be hanged, an' some fishmonger's son do not make of 'em; and puts in more fasting days than he should do, because he would utter his father's dried stock-fish and stinking 55 conger.

Cas. 'Slight, peace, thou'lt be beaten like a stock-fish, else: here is Master Matthew. Now must I look out for a messenger to my master. [*Exeunt*]

32 *Bevis*: Bevis of Southampton, whose horse was Arundell   37 *Flemish*: noted consumers of butter   46 *Hannibal*: blunder for 'cannibal'   49 *Cophetua*: wealthy African king of the ballad 'King Cophetua and the Beggar-maid'   55 *utter*: put on the market (III. i. 80)   *stock-fish*: dried cod (beaten before boiling)   56 *conger*: large species of eel

ACT III, Scene v

Enter Wellbred, Edward Knowell, Brainworm, Bobadil,
Matthew, Stephen

Wel. Beshrew me, but it was an absolute good jest, and exceedingly well carried!

E. Kn. Aye, and our ignorance maintained it as well, did it not?

Wel. Yes faith, but was't possible thou shouldst not know him?
5 I forgive Master Stephen, for he is stupidity itself!

E. Kn. 'Fore God, not I, and I might have been joined patent with one of the seven wise masters, for knowing him. He had so writhen himself, into the habit of one of your poor Infantry, your decayed, ruinous, worm-eaten gentlemen of the round: such as
10 have vowed to sit on the skirts of the city, let your Provost, and his half-dozen of halberdiers do what they can; and have translated begging out of the old hackney pace, to a fine easy amble, and made it run as smooth, of the tongue, as a shove-groat shilling. Into the likeness of one of these Reformados had he moulded himself so
15 perfectly, observing every trick of their action, as varying the accent, swearing with an emphasis, indeed all, with so special and exquisite a grace, that (hadst thou seen him) thou wouldst have sworn he might have been Sergeant-Major, if not Lieutenant-Colonel to the regiment.

20 *Wel.* Why, Brainworm, who would have thought thou hadst been such an artificer?

E. Kn. An artificer! An architect! Except a man had studied begging all his lifetime, and been a weaver of language, from his infancy, for the clothing of it! I never saw his rival.

25 *Wel.* Where got'st thou this coat, I mar'l?

Bra. Of a Houndsditch man, sir. One of the devil's near kinsmen, a broker.

---

6 *joined patent*: lit. sharing by letters patent in a privilege or office   7 *seven wise masters*: Bias, Pittacus, Cleobulus, Periander, Solon, Chilon, Thales   9 *round*: military patrol (usually for inspecting the sentries)   10 *sit on the skirts of*: harry 13 *shove-groat shilling*: worn smooth in playing shovel-board   14 *Reformados*: officers of a 're-formed' or disbanded company   18 *Sergeant-Major*: field officer next in rank to the lieutenant-colonel   22 *artificer*: artist   23 *weaver of language*: spinner of yarns   26 *Houndsditch*: the brokers' quarter

Wel. That cannot be, if the proverb hold; for, a crafty knave needs no broker.

Bra. True, sir, but I did need a broker, *ergo*.

Wel. [*Aside*] Well put off!—No crafty knave, you'll say.   30

E. Kn. Tut, he has more of these shifts.

Bra. And yet where I have one, the broker has ten, sir.

[*Enter* Cash]

Cas. Francis, Martin, ne'er a one to be found, now? What a spite's this?   35

Wel. How now, Thomas? Is my brother Kitely within?

Cas. No, sir, my master went forth e'en now: but Master Downright is within. Cob, what Cob? Is he gone too?

Wel. Whither went your master? Thomas, canst thou tell?

Cas. I know not, to Justice Clement's, I think, sir. Cob!   40

E. Kn. Justice Clement, what's he?

Wel. Why, dost thou not know him? He is a city-magistrate, a Justice here, an excellent good lawyer, and a great scholar: but the only mad, merry, old fellow in Europe! I showed him you, the other day.   45

E. Kn. Oh, is that he? I remember him now. Good faith, and he has a very strange presence, methinks; it shows as if he stood out of the rank from other men: I have heard many of his jests i' the university. They say, he will commit a man for taking the wall of his horse.   50

Wel. Aye, or wearing his cloak off one shoulder, or serving of God: anything indeed, if it come in the way of his humour.

Cas. Gaspar, Martin, Cob! 'Heart, where should they be, trow?

(Cash *goes in and out, calling*)

Bob. Master Kitely's man, 'pray thee vouchsafe us the lighting of this match.   55

Cas. Fire on your match, no time but now to vouchsafe? Francis! Cob!

Bob. Body of me! Here's the remainder of seven pound, since yesterday was seven-night. 'Tis your right Trinidado! Did you never take any, Master Stephen?   60

30 *ergo*: therefore   49 *the wall*: i.e. the cleaner and safer part of the street
51–2 *serving of God*: cf. Dogberry in *Much Ado*, IV. ii. 15–20   59 *Trinidado*:
tobacco from Trinidad, reputed the best

Ste. No, truly, sir; but I'll learn to take it now, since you commend it so.

Bob. Sir, believe me, upon my relation, for what I tell you, the world shall not reprove. I have been in the Indies (where this herb
65 grows) where neither myself, nor a dozen gentlemen more (of my knowledge) have received the taste of any other nutriment, in the world, for the space of one and twenty weeks, but the fume of this simple only. Therefore, it cannot be, but 'tis most divine! Further, take it in the nature, in the true kind so, it makes an antidote, that
70 (had you taken the most deadly poisonous plant in all Italy) it should expel it, and clarify you, with as much ease, as I speak. And for your green wound, your Balsamum, and your St. John's wort are all mere gulleries, and trash to it, especially your Trinidado: your Nicotian is good too. I could say what I know of the virtue of
75 it, for the expulsion of rheums, raw humours, crudities, obstructions, with a thousand of this kind; but I profess myself no quacksalver. Only, thus much, by Hercules, I do hold it, and will affirm it (before any prince in Europe) to be the most sovereign and precious weed that ever the earth tendered to the use of man.

80   *E. Kn.* [*Aside*] This speech would ha' done decently in a tobacco trader's mouth!

[*Enter* Cash, Cob]

Cas. At Justice Clement's, he is: in the middle of Colman Street.
Cob. Oh, oh?
Bob. Where's the match I gave thee? Master Kitely's man?
85   *Cas.* [*Aside*] Would his match, and he, and pipe, and all were at Sancto Domingo! I had forgot it.   [*Exit*]
Cob. By God's me, I mar'l, what pleasure or felicity they have in taking this roguish tobacco! It's good for nothing but to choke a man, and fill him full of smoke and embers: there were four died
90 out of one house, last week, with taking of it, and two more the bell went for, yesternight; one of them (they say) will ne'er scape it: he voided a bushel of soot yesterday, upward, and downward. By the stocks, an' there were no wiser men than I, I'd have it present

68 *simple*: medicament made from a single ingredient; a herb so applied   72 *St. John's wort*: herb used as an ointment and as a draught   74 *Nicotian*: after Jaques Nicot, who introduced tobacco to France (also generic name of tobacco plant)

whipping, man, or woman, that should but deal with a tobacco
pipe; why, it will stifle them all in the end, as many as use it; it's 95
little better than ratsbane, or rosaker.

                              (Bobadil *beats him with a cudgel*)
    All. Oh, good captain, hold, hold.
    Bob. You base cullion, you.

                    [*Enter* Cash]

    Cas. Sir, here's your match: come, thou must needs be talking,
too, thou art well enough served.   100
    Cob. Nay, he will not meddle with his match, I warrant you:
well it shall be a dear beating, and I live.
    Bob. Do you prate? Do you murmur?
    E. Kn. Nay, good captain, will you regard the humour of a fool?
Away, knave.   105
    Wel. Thomas, get him away.   [*Exit* Cash *with* Cob]
    Bob. A whoreson filthy slave, a dungworm, an excrement! Body o'
Caesar, but that I scorn to let forth so mean a spirit, I'd ha' stabbed
him to the earth.
    Wel. Marry, the law forbid, sir.   110
    Bob. By Pharaoh's foot, I would have done it.
    Ste. Oh, he swears admirably! 'By Pharaoh's foot', 'body of
Caesar', I shall never do it, sure, upon mine honour, and by St.
George, no, I ha' not the right grace.
    Mat. Master Stephen, will you any? By this air, the most divine 115
tobacco that ever I drunk!
    Ste. None, I thank you, sir. Oh, this gentleman does it, rarely
too! But nothing like the other. 'By this air', as I am a gentleman:
'by——'   [*Exeunt* Matthew, Bobadil]
    Bra. Master, glance, glance! Master Wellbred!   120
                    (Master Stephen *is practising, to the post*)
    Ste. As I have somewhat to be saved, I protest——
    Wel. You are a fool: it needs no affidavit.
    E. Kn. Cousin, will you any tobacco?
    Ste. I, sir! Upon my reputation——
    E. Kn. How now, cousin!   125

    96 *ratsbane, or rosaker*: preparations of arsenic   98 *cullion*: rascal (lit. 'testicle')
101 *meddle with his match*: BF I. iv. 92

 Ste. I protest, as I am a gentleman, but no soldier, indeed——

 Wel. No, Master Stephen? As I remember your name is entered in the artillery garden?

 Ste. Aye, sir, that's true: cousin, may I swear, as I am a soldier,
130 by that?

 E. Kn. Oh yes, that you may. It's all you have for your money.

 Ste. Then, as I am a gentleman, and a soldier, it is divine tobacco!

 Wel. But soft, where's Master Matthew? Gone?

 Bra. No, sir, they went in here.

135 *Wel*. Oh, let's follow them: Master Matthew is gone to salute his mistress, in verse. We shall ha' the happiness to hear some of his poetry now. He never comes unfurnished. Brainworm?

 Ste. Brainworm? Where? Is this Brainworm?

 E. Kn. Aye, cousin, no words of it, upon your gentility.

140 *Ste*. Not I, body of me, by this air, St. George, and the foot of Pharaoh.

 Wel. Rare! Your cousin's discourse is simply drawn out with oaths.

 E. Kn. 'Tis larded with 'em. A kind of French dressing, if you
145 love it.

[Exeunt]

ACT III, Scene vi

[Justice Clement's house]
Enter Kitely, Cob

 Kit. Ha? How many are there, sayest thou?

 Cob. Marry, sir, your brother, Master Wellbred——

 Kit. Tut, beside him: what strangers are there, man?

 Cob. Strangers? Let me see, one, two; mass, I know not well,
5 there are so many.

 Kit. How? So many?

 Cob. Aye, there's some five, or six of them, at the most.

 Kit. [*Aside*] A swarm, a swarm,

---

128 *artillery garden*: training ground of the Honourable Artillery Company
144 *French dressing*: alluding to the reputation of the French for swearing

Spite of the devil, how they sting my head
With forked stings, thus wide, and large! But, Cob,　　10
How long hast thou been coming hither, Cob?

Cob. A little while, sir.

Kit. Didst thou come running?

Cob. No, sir.

Kit. [*Aside*] Nay, then I am familiar with thy haste!　　15
Bane to my fortunes: what meant I to marry?
I, that before was ranked in such content,
My mind at rest too, in so soft a peace,
Being free master of mine own free thoughts,
And now become a slave? What? Never sigh,　　20
Be of good cheer, man: for thou art a cuckold,
'Tis done, 'tis done! Nay, when such flowing store,
Plenty itself, falls in my wife's lap,
The cornucopiae will be mine, I know. But, Cob,
What entertainment had they? I am sure　　25
My sister and my wife would bid them welcome! Ha?

Cob. Like enough, sir, yet, I heard not a word of it.

Kit. [*Aside*] No: their lips were sealed with kisses, and the voice
Drowned in a flood of joy, at their arrival,
Had lost her motion, state, and faculty.　　30
Cob, which of them was it, that first kissed my wife?
(My sister, I should say) my wife, alas,
I fear not her: ha? Who was it, sayst thou?

Cob. By my troth, sir, will you have the truth of it?

Kit. Oh, aye, good Cob: I pray thee, heartily.　　35

Cob. Then, I am a vagabond, and fitter for Bridewell, than your
worship's company, if I saw anybody to be kissed, unless they
would have kissed the post in the middle of the warehouse; for
there I left them all, at their tobacco, with a pox.

Kit. How? Were they not gone in, then, ere thou camst?　　40

Cob. Oh, no, sir.

Kit. Spite of the devil! What do I stay here, then? Cob, follow
me.　　　　　　　　　　　　　　　　　　　　　　　　[*Exit*]

---

23 *in my wife's lap*: as in the wooing of Danae by Zeus　　24 *cornucopiae*: the
horn of plenty (with pun on the cuckold's horns)　　36 *Bridewell*: workhouse and
place of correction

Cob. Nay, soft and fair, I have eggs on the spit; I cannot go yet,
45 sir. Now am I for some five and fifty reasons hammering, ham-
mering revenge: oh, for three or four gallons of vinegar to sharpen
my wits. Revenge: vinegar revenge: vinegar and mustard revenge:
nay, and he had not lain in my house, 'twould never have grieved
me, but being my guest, one, that I'll be sworn, my wife has lent
50 him her smock off her back, while his one shirt has been at washing;
pawned her neckerchers for clean bands for him; sold almost all
my platters to buy him tobacco; and he to turn monster of ingrati-
tude, and strike his lawful host! Well, I hope to raise up an host of
fury for it: here comes Justice Clement.

ACT III, Scene vii

Enter Clement, Knowell, Formal

Cle. What's Master Kitely gone? Roger?

For. Aye, sir.

Cle. 'Heart of me! What made him leave us so abruptly! How
now, sirrah? What make you here? What would you have, ha?

5   *Cob.* And't please your worship, I am a poor neighbour of your
worship's——

Cle. A poor neighbour of mine? Why, speak, poor neighbour.

Cob. I dwell, sir, at the sign of the water-tankard, hard by the
green lattice: I have paid scot and lot there, any time this eighteen
10 years.

Cle. To the green lattice?

Cob. No, sir, to the parish: marry, I have seldom scaped scot-free,
at the lattice.

Cle. Oh, well! What business has my poor neighbour with me?

15 *Cob.* And't like your worship, I am come, to crave the peace of
your worship.

Cle. Of me, knave? Peace of me, knave? Did I e'er hurt thee?
Or threaten thee? Or wrong thee? Ha?

Cob. No, sir, but your worship's warrant, for one that has

---

44 *I have eggs on the spit*: i.e. I am very busy (proverbial)   51 *bands*: collars
(*III. vii*) 9 *scot and lot*: parish taxes   11 *green lattice*: denoting an inn

wronged me, sir: his arms are at too much liberty, I would fain have them bound to a treaty of peace, an' my credit could compass it, with your worship.

Cle. Thou goest far enough about for't, I'm sure.

Kno. Why, dost thou go in danger of thy life for him? Friend?

Cob. No, sir; but I go in danger of my death, every hour, by his means: an' I die within a twelve-month and a day, I may swear, by the law of the land, that he killed me.

Cle. How? How, knave? Swear he killed thee? And by the law? What pretence? What colour hast thou for that?

Cob. Marry, and't please your worship, both black, and blue; colour enough, I warrant you. I have it here, to show your worship.

Cle. What is he, that gave you this, sirrah?

Cob. A gentleman, and a soldier, he says he is, o' the city here.

Cle. A soldier o' the city? What call you him?

Cob. Captain Bobadil.

Cle. Bobadil? And why did he bob and beat you, sirrah? How began the quarrel betwixt you: ha? Speak truly, knave, I advise you.

Cob. Marry, indeed, and please your worship, only because I spake against their vagrant tobacco, as I came by 'em, when they were taking on't, for nothing else.

Cle. Ha? You speak against tobacco? Formal, his name.

For. What's your name, sirrah?

Cob. Oliver, sir, Oliver Cob, sir.

Cle. Tell Oliver Cob, he shall go to the jail, Formal.

For. Oliver Cob, my master, Justice Clement, says, you shall go to the jail.

Cob. Oh, I beseech your worship, for God's sake, dear Master Justice.

Cle. Nay, God's precious: and such drunkards, and tankards, as you are, come to dispute of tobacco once; I have done! Away with him.

Cob. Oh, good Master Justice, sweet old gentleman.

Kno. Sweet Oliver, would I could do thee any good: Justice Clement, let me entreat you, sir.

---

26 *twelve-month and a day*: legal period for determining cause of death from injury   31 *colour*: specious ground   36 *bob*: deceive, cheat   53 *Sweet Oliver*: stock epithet for Orlando's rival in *Orlando Furioso*

55   *Cle.* What? A threadbare rascal! A beggar! A slave that never drunk out of better than pisspot metal in his life! And he to deprave and abuse the virtue of an herb, so generally received in the courts of princes, the chambers of nobles, the bowers of sweet ladies, the cabins of soldiers! Roger, away with him, by God's precious——
60 I say, go to.

  Cob. Dear Master Justice; let me be beaten again, I have deserved it: but not the prison, I beseech you.

  Kno. Alas, poor Oliver!

  Cle. Roger, make him a warrant (he shall not go) I but fear the
65 knave.

  For. Do not stink, sweet Oliver, you shall not go, my master will give you a warrant.

  Cob. Oh, the Lord maintain his worship, his worthy worship.

  Cle. Away, dispatch him. [*Exeunt* Formal, Cob] How now,
70 Master Knowell! In dumps? In dumps? Come, this becomes not.

  Kno. Sir, would I could not feel my cares——

  Cle. Your cares are nothing! They are like my cap, soon put on, and as soon put off. What? Your son is old enough to govern himself: let him run his course, it's the only way to make him a staid
75 man. If he were an unthrift, a ruffian, a drunkard, or a licentious liver, then you had reason; you had reason to take care: but, being none of these, mirth's my witness, an' I had twice so many cares as you have, I'd drown them all in a cup of sack. Come, come, let's try it: I muse, your parcel of a soldier returns not all this while.

                               [*Exeunt*]

ACT IV, Scene i

[Kitely's house]
Enter Downright, Dame Kitely

  Dow. WELL, sister, I tell you true: and you'll find it so, in the end.

  Dam. Alas, brother, what would you have me to do? I cannot help it: you see, my brother brings 'em in here, they are his friends.

56 *pisspot metal*: pewter   59 *cabins*: tents   64 *fear*: frighten   79 *parcel*: fragment (contemptuous)

Dow. His friends? His fiends. 'Slud, they do nothing but haunt 5
him, up and down, like a sort of unlucky sprites, and tempt him to
all manner of villainy that can be thought of. Well, by this light, a
little thing would make me play the devil with some of 'em; and
'twere not more for your husband's sake than anything else, I'd
make the house too hot for the best on 'em: they should say, and 10
swear, hell were broken loose, ere they went hence. But, by God's
will, 'tis nobody's fault but yours: for an' you had done, as you
might have done, they should have been parboiled, and baked too,
every mother's son, ere they should ha' come in, e'er a one of 'em.

Dam. God's my life! Did you ever hear the like? What a strange 15
man is this! Could I keep out all them, think you? I should put
myself against half a dozen men? Should I? Good faith, you'd mad
the patientest body in the world, to hear you talk so, without any
sense, or reason!

ACT IV, Scene ii

Enter Bridget, Matthew, Bobadil [*followed by*]
Wellbred, Stephen, Edward Knowell, Brainworm

Bri. Servant (in troth), you are too prodigal
Of your wit's treasure, thus to pour it forth
Upon so mean a subject as my worth?

Mat. You say well, mistress; and I mean, as well.

Dow. Hoy-day, here is stuff!

Wel. Oh, now stand close: pray heaven, she can get him to read: 5
he should do it, of his own natural impudency.

Bri. Servant, what is this same, I pray you?

Mat. Marry, an elegy, an elegy, an odd toy——

Dow. To mock an ape withal. Oh, I could sew up his mouth now. 10

Dam. Sister, I pray you, let's hear it.

Dow. Are you rhyme-given, too?

Mat. Mistress, I'll read it, if you please.

Bri. Pray you do, servant.

---

13 *parboiled*: boiled thoroughly   (*IV. ii*) 1 *Servant*: lover   10 *mock an ape*:
dupe a simpleton (proverbial)

15   *Dow.* Oh, here's no foppery! Death, I can endure the stocks
better.   [*Exit*]

E. Kn. What ails thy brother? Can he not hold his water, at
reading of a ballad?

Wel. Oh, no: a rhyme to him is worse than cheese or a bagpipe.
20 But mark, you lose the protestation.

Mat. Faith, I did it in an humour; I know not how it is: but,
please you come near, sir. This gentleman has judgement, he knows
how to censure of a——pray you, sir, you can judge.

Ste. Not I, sir: upon my reputation, and by the foot of Pharaoh.

25   *Wel.* Oh, chide your cousin for swearing.

E. Kn. Not I, so long as he does not forswear himself.

Bob. Master Matthew, you abuse the expectation of your dear
mistress and her fair sister: fie, while you live, avoid this prolixity.

Mat. I shall, sir: well, *Incipere dulce*.

30   *E. Kn.* How! *Insipere dulce?* A sweet thing to be a fool, indeed.

Wel. What, do you take *Incipere* in that sense?

E. Kn. You do not, you? This was your villainy, to gull him with
a *mot*.

Wel. Oh, the bencher's phrase: *pauca verba, pauca verba*.

35   *Mat.* 'Rare creature, let me speak without offence,
Would God my rude words had the influence,
To rule thy thoughts, as thy fair looks do mine,
Then shouldst thou be his prisoner, who is thine.'

E. Kn. This is in *Hero and Leander*?

40   *Wel.* Oh, aye! Peace, we shall have more of this.

Mat. 'Be not unkind, and fair, misshapen stuff
Is of behaviour boisterous, and rough:'

Wel. How like you that, sir?

(Master Stephen *answers with shaking his head*)

E. Kn. 'Slight, he shakes his head like a bottle, to feel and there
45 be any brain in it!

Mat. But observe the catastrophe now,
'And I in duty will exceed all other,

23 *censure*: judge   29 *Incipere dulce*: 'It is sweet to begin'   31 *Insipere*:
referring to Horace's *dulce est desipere in loco* (*Odes*, iv. 12): 'It is sweet to play the fool
on the appropriate occasion'   33 *mot*: tag, adage   34 *bencher*: ale-house
lounger   *pauca verba*: catch-phrase ('Talk less', i.e. and drink more)   35–8, 41–2,
47–8 loosely quoted from Marlowe's *Hero and Leander* (ed. Brooke, ll. 199 ff.)

As you in beauty do excel love's mother.'

E. Kn. Well, I'll have him free of the wit-brokers, for he utters nothing but stolen remnants.   50

Wel. Oh, forgive it him.

E. Kn. A filching rogue? Hang him. And, from the dead? It's worse than sacrilege.

Wel. Sister, what ha' you here? Verses? Pray you, let's see. Who made these verses? They are excellent good!   55

Mat. Oh, Master Wellbred, 'tis your disposition to say so, sir. They were good i' the morning, I made 'em, *extempore*, this morning.

Wel. How? *Extempore?*

Mat. Aye, would I might be hanged else; ask Captain Bobadil.   60
He saw me write them, at the——(pox on it) the Star, yonder.

Bra. Can he find, in his heart, to curse the stars, so?

E. Kn. Faith, his are even with him: they ha' cursed him enough already.

Ste. Cousin, how do you like this gentleman's verses?   65

E. Kn. Oh, admirable! The best that ever I heard, coz.

Ste. Body o' Caesar! They are admirable!
The best, that ever I heard, as I am a soldier.

[*Enter* Downright]

Dow. I am vexed, I can hold ne'er a bone of me still! Heart, I think they mean to build and breed here!   70

Wel. Sister, you have a simple servant here, that crowns your beauty, with such encomions, and devices: you may see what it is to be the mistress of a wit! That can make your perfections so transparent, that every bleary eye may look through them, and see him drowned over head, and ears, in the deep well of desire. Sister   75
Kitely, I marvel you get you not a servant, that can rhyme, and do tricks, too.

Dow. Oh, monster! Impudence itself! Tricks?

Dam. Tricks, brother? What tricks?

Bri. Nay, speak, I pray you, what tricks?   80

Dam. Aye, I never spare anybody here: but say, what tricks?

---

49 *free*: admitted to the company of   77 *do tricks*: taken by the others in a
sexual sense

Bri. Passion of my heart! Do tricks?

Wel. 'Slight, here's a trick vied, and revied! Why, you monkeys, you? What a caterwauling do you keep? Has he not given you
85 rhymes, and verses, and tricks?

Dow. Oh, the fiend!

Wel. Nay, you, lamp of virginity, that take it in snuff so! Come and cherish this tame poetical fury in your servant, you'll be begged else, shortly, for a concealment: go to, reward his muse. You cannot
90 give him less than a shilling, in conscience, for the book he had it out of cost him a teston, at least. How now, gallants? Master Matthew? Captain? What? All sons of silence? No spirit?

Dow. Come, you might practise your ruffian-tricks somewhere else, and not here, I wusse; this is no tavern nor drinking-school to
95 vent your exploits in.

Wel. How now! Whose cow has calved?

Dow. Marry, that has mine, sir. Nay, boy, never look askance at me, for the matter; I'll tell you of it, aye, sir, you, and your companions, mend yourselves, when I ha' done?

100 *Wel.* My companions?

Dow. Yes, sir, your companions, so I say, I am not afraid of you, nor them neither: your hang-bys here. You must have your poets and your potlings, your *soldados* and *foolados*, to follow you up and down the city, and here they must come to domineer and swagger.
105 Sirrah, you, ballad-singer, and slops, your fellow there, get you out; get you home: or, by this steel, I'll cut off your ears, and that presently.

Wel. 'Slight, stay, let's see what he dare do: cut off his ears? Cut a whetstone. You are an ass, do you see? Touch any man here, and
110 by this hand, I'll run my rapier to the hilts in you.

Dow. Yea, that would I fain see, boy.

(They all draw, and they of the house make out to part them)

Dam. Oh Jesu! Murder. Thomas, Gaspar!

Bri. Help, help, Thomas.

83 *vied, and revied*: offered in challenge, and challenged in return (gambling)
87 *take it in snuff*: take offence at it   88-9 *begged . . . for a concealment*: an allusion to the claiming on forfeit of monastery lands which had not passed to the crown
91 *teston*: sixpence   94 *wusse*: cf. I. i. 33   103 *soldados*: soldiers (*foolado* is a nonce-word)   105 *slops*: II. ii. 21   108-9 *cut a whetstone*: the miraculous feat of Accius Naevius (Livy, i. 36)

[*Enter* Cash]

E. Kn. Gentlemen, forbear, I pray you.

Bob. Well, sirrah, you, Holofernes: by my hand, I will pink your 115
flesh full of holes with my rapier for this; I will, by this good
heaven: nay, let him come, let him come, gentlemen, by the body
of St. George, I'll not kill him.

(*They offer to fight again, and are parted*)

Cas. Hold, hold, good gentlemen.

Dow. You whoreson, bragging coistrel!   120

ACT IV, Scene iii

Enter Kitely

Kit. Why, how now? What's the matter? What's the stir here?
Whence springs the quarrel? Thomas! Where is he?
Put up your weapons, and put off this rage.
My wife and sister, they are cause of this,
What, Thomas? Where is this knave?   5

Cas. Here, sir.

Wel. Come, let's go: this is one of my brother's ancient humours,
this.

Ste. I am glad nobody was hurt by his ancient humour.

[*Exeunt* Wellbred, Stephen, Bobadil, Matthew,
Edward Knowell, Brainworm]

Kit. Why, how now, brother, who enforced this brawl?   10

Dow. A sort of lewd rake-hells, that care neither for God, nor the
devil! And they must come here to read ballads, and roguery, and
trash! I'll mar the knot of 'em ere I sleep, perhaps: especially Bob,
there: he that's all manner of shapes! And *Songs and Sonnets*, his
fellow.   15

Bri. Brother, indeed, you are too violent,
Too sudden, in your humour: and, you know
My brother Wellbred's temper will not bear

---

115 *Holofernes*: tyrant, bully   120 *coistrel*: knave   (*IV. iii*) 8 *ancient*:
oldfashioned   14 *shapes*: referring again to Bobadil's breeches   *Songs and
Sonnets*: original title (1557) of *Tottel's Miscellany*

Any reproof, chiefly in such a presence,
20 Where every slight disgrace he should receive
Might wound him in opinion and respect.

Dow. Respect? What talk you of respect 'mong such,
As ha' nor spark of manhood, nor good manners?
'Sdeynes, I am ashamed to hear you! Respect?   [*Exit*]
25   *Bri.* Yes, there was one a civil gentleman,
And very worthily demeaned himself!

Kit. Oh, that was some love of yours, sister!

Bri. A love of mine? I would it were no worse, brother!
You'd pay my portion sooner than you think for.

30 *Dam.* Indeed, he seemed to be a gentleman of an exceeding fair
disposition, and of very excellent good parts!   [*Exit with* Bridget]

Kit. Her love, by heaven! My wife's minion!
Fair disposition? Excellent good parts?
Death, these phrases are intolerable!
35 Good parts? How should she know his parts?
His parts? Well, well, well, well, well, well!
It is too plain, too clear: Thomas, come hither.
What, are they gone?

Cas.   Aye, sir, they went in.
My mistress and your sister——
40   *Kit.* Are any of the gallants within?

Cas. No, sir, they are all gone.

Kit. Art thou sure of it?

Cas. I can assure you, sir.

Kit. What gentleman was that they praised so, Thomas?
45   *Cas.* One, they call him Master Knowell, a handsome young
gentleman, sir.

Kit. Aye, I thought so: my mind gave me as much.
I'll die, but they have hid him i' the house,
Somewhere; I'll go and search: go with me, Thomas.
50 Be true to me, and thou shalt find me a master.   [*Exeunt*]

---

26 *demeaned*: comported   29 *portion*: dowry   31 *parts*: qualities

ACT IV, Scene iv

[Before Cob's house]

Enter Cob

Cob. [*Knocks*] What, Tib, Tib, I say.

Tib. [*Within*] How now, what cuckold is that knocks so hard?

[*Enter* Tib]

Oh, husband, is't you? What's the news?

Cob. Nay, you have stunned me, i' faith! You ha' given me a
knock o' the forehead, will stick by me! Cuckold? 'Slid, cuckold? 5

Tib. Away, you fool, did I know it was you that knocked? Come,
you may call me as bad, when you list.

Cob. May I? Tib, you are a whore.

Tib. You lie in your throat, husband.

Cob. How, the lie? And in my throat, too? Do you long to be 10
stabbed, ha?

Tib. Why, you are no soldier, I hope?

Cob. Oh, must you be stabbed by a soldier? Mass, that's true!
When was Bobadil here? Your captain? That rogue, that foist,
that fencing Burgullian? I'll tickle him, i' faith. 15

Tib. Why, what's the matter? Trow!

Cob. Oh, he has basted me, rarely, sumptuously! But I have it
here in black and white; for his black and blue: shall pay him. Oh,
the Justice! The honestest old brave Trojan in London! I do
honour the very flea of his dog. A plague on him though, he put 20
me once in a villainous filthy fear; marry, it vanished away, like
the smoke of tobacco; but I was smoked soundly first. I thank the
devil, and his good angel, my guest. Well, wife, or Tib (which you
will) get you in, and lock the door, I charge you, let nobody in to
you; wife, nobody in, to you: those are my words. Not Captain 25
Bob himself, nor the fiend, in his likeness; you are a woman; you

---

13 *stabbed*: with sexual innuendo
15 *Burgullian*: Burgonians were noted swordsmen
warrant   19 *Trojan*: term of commendation
the Folio continues the innuendo

14 *foist*: rogue (lit. pickpocket)
18 *black and white*: i.e. the
24, 25 *nobody*: 'no body' in

have flesh and blood enough in you, to be tempted: therefore, keep the door shut, upon all comers.

 Tib. I warrant you, there shall nobody enter here, without my
30 consent.

 Cob. Nor with your consent, sweet Tib, and so I leave you.

 Tib. It's more, than you know, whether you leave me so.

 Cob. How?

 Tib. Why, sweet.

35 *Cob.* Tut, sweet, or sour, thou art a flower,
Keep close thy door, I ask no more.   [*Exeunt*]

ACT IV, Scene v

[The Windmill Tavern]

Enter Edward Knowell, Brainworm [*disguised*], Wellbred,
Stephen

 Ed. K. Well, Brainworm, perform this business happily, and thou makest a purchase of my love forever.

 Wel. I'faith, now let thy spirits use their best faculties. But, at any hand, remember the message to my brother: for there's no
5 other means to start him.

 Bra. I warrant you, sir, fear nothing: I have a nimble soul has waked all forces of my fancy by this time, and put 'em in true motion. What you have possessed me withal, I'll discharge it amply, sir. Make it no question.

10 *Wel.* Forth, and prosper, Brainworm. [*Exit* Brainworm] Faith, Ned, how dost thou approve of my abilities in this device?

 E. Kn. Troth, well, howsoever: but it will come excellent, if it take.

 Wel. Take, man? Why, it cannot choose but take, if the circum-
15 stances miscarry not: but, tell me, ingenuously, dost thou affect my sister Bridget, as thou pretend'st?

 E. Kn. Friend, am I worth belief?

 Wel. Come, do not protest. In faith, she is a maid of good orna-ment, and much modesty: and except I conceived very worthily of
20 her, thou shouldest not have her.

  5 *start*: bring an animal from its lair (hunting)   16 *pretend'st*: profess

E. Kn. Nay, that I am afraid will be a question yet, whether I shall have her, or no?

Wel. 'Slid, thou shalt have her; by this light, thou shalt.

E. Kn. Nay, do not swear.

Wel. By this hand, thou shalt have her: I'll go fetch her, presently. 25 'Point but where to meet, and as I am an honest man, I'll bring her.

E. Kn. Hold, hold, be temperate.

Wel. Why, by——what shall I swear by? Thou shalt have her, as I am——

E. Kn. 'Pray thee, be at peace, I am satisfied: and do believe 30 thou wilt omit no offered occasion, to make my desires complete.

Wel. Thou shalt see, and know, I will not.   [*Exeunt*]

ACT IV, Scene vi

[A street in the Old Jewry]

Enter Formal, Knowell

For. Was your man a soldier, sir?

Kno. Aye, a knave, I took him begging o' the way,
This morning, as I came over Moorfields!

[*Enter* Brainworm *disguised*]

Oh, here he is! You have made fair speed, believe me:
Where, i' the name of sloth, could you be thus——   5

Bra. Marry, peace be my comfort, where I thought I should have had little comfort of your worship's service.

Kno. How so?

Bra. Oh, sir! Your coming to the city, your entertainment of me, and your sending me to watch——indeed, all the circumstances 10 either of your charge, or my employment, are as open to your son, as to yourself!

Kno. How should that be! Unless that villain, Brainworm,
Have told him of the letter, and discovered
All that I strictly charged him to conceal? 'Tis so!   15

Bra. I am, partly, o' the faith, 'tis so indeed.

Kno. But how should he know thee to be my man?

Bra. Nay, sir, I cannot tell; unless it be by the black art! Is not
your son a scholar, sir?

20 *Kno.* Yes, but I hope his soul is not allied
Unto such hellish practice: if it were,
I had just cause to weep my part in him,
And curse the time of his creation.
But where didst thou find them, Fitzsword?

25 *Bra.* You should rather ask, where they found me, sir, for, I'll
be sworn I was going along in the street, thinking nothing, when (of a
sudden) a voice calls, Master Knowell's man; another cries, soldier:
and thus, half a dozen of 'em, till they had called me within a house
where I no sooner came, but they seemed men, and out flew all
30 their rapiers at my bosom, with some three or four score oaths to
accompany 'em, and all to tell me, I was but a dead man, if I did
not confess where you were, and how I was employed, and about
what; which, when they could not get out of me (as I protest, they
must ha' dissected and made an anatomy o' me first, and so I told
35 'em) they locked me up into a room i' the top of a high house,
whence, by great miracle (having a light heart) I slid down, by a
bottom of pack-thread, into the street, and so 'scaped. But, sir,
thus much I can assure you, for I heard it, while I was locked up,
there were a great many rich merchants, and brave citizens' wives
40 with 'em at a feast, and your son, Master Edward, withdrew with
one of 'em, and has 'pointed to meet her anon, at one Cob's house, a
waterbearer, that dwells by the wall. Now, there, your worship shall
be sure to take him, for there he preys, and fail he will not.

Kno. Nor will I fail to break his match, I doubt not.
45 Go thou along with Justice Clement's man,
And stay there for me. At one Cob's house, sayst thou?

Bra. Aye, sir, there you shall have him. [*Exit* Knowell] [*Aside*]
Yes? Invisible? Much wench, or much son! 'Slight, when he has
stayed there, three or four hours, travelling with the expectation of
50 wonders, and at length be delivered of air: oh, the sport, that I
should then take, to look on him, if I durst! But, now, I mean to
appear no more afore him in this shape. I have another trick to act

29 *seemed*: were seen to be   37 *bottom*: ball, skein   39 *brave*: finely
dressed   49 *travelling*: with play on 'travailing'

yet. Oh that I were so happy, as to light on a nupson, now, of this Justice's novice. Sir, I make you stay somewhat long.

For. Not a whit, sir. 'Pray you, what do you mean, sir?   55

Bra. I was putting up some papers——

For. You ha' been lately in the wars, sir, it seems.

Bra. Marry have I, sir; to my loss: and expense of all, almost——

For. Troth, sir, I would be glad to bestow a pottle of wine o' you, if it please you to accept it——   60

Bra. Oh, sir——

For. But, to hear the manner of your services, and your devices in the wars, they say they be very strange, and not like those a man reads in the Roman histories, or sees at Mile End.

Bra. No, I assure you, sir, why, at any time when it please you, 65 I shall be ready to discourse to you, all I know: [*Aside*] and more too, somewhat.

For. No better time than now, sir; we'll go to the Windmill: there we shall have a cup of neat grist, we call it. I pray you, sir, let me request you, to the Windmill.   70

Bra. I'll follow you, sir, [*Aside*] and make grist o' you, if I have good luck.   [*Exeunt*]

ACT IV, Scene vii

Enter Matthew, Edward Knowell, Bobadil, Stephen

Mat. Sir, did your eyes ever taste the like clown of him, where we were today, Master Wellbred's half-brother? I think the whole earth cannot show his parallel, by this daylight.

E. Kn. We were now speaking of him: Captain Bobadil tells me he is fallen foul o' you, too.   5

Mat. Oh, aye, sir, he threatened me, with the bastinado.

Bob. Aye, but I think I taught you prevention, this morning, for that—— You shall kill him, beyond question: if you be so generously minded.

Mat. Indeed, it is a most excellent trick!   10

---

53 *nupson*: simpleton   69 *grist*: the product of a windmill, i.e. the tavern's liquor   71 *grist*: profit, advantage

Bob. Oh, you do not give spirit enough to your motion, you are too tardy, too heavy! Oh, it must be done like lightning, hay?

(*He practises at a post*)

Mat. Rare captain!

Bob. Tut, 'tis nothing, and 't be not done in a——*punto*!

15 *E. Kn.* Captain, did you ever prove yourself upon any of our masters of defence, here?

Mat. Oh, good sir! Yes, I hope, he has.

Bob. I will tell you, sir. Upon my first coming to the city, after my long travail, for knowledge (in that mystery only) there came
20 three, or four of 'em to me, at a gentleman's house, where it was my chance to be resident at that time, to entreat my presence at their schools, and withal so much importuned me, that (I protest to you as I am a gentleman) I was ashamed of their rude demeanour, out of all measure: well, I told 'em, that to come to a public school,
25 they should pardon me, it was opposite (in diameter) to my humour, but, if so they would give their attendance at my lodging, I protested to do them what right or favour I could, as I was a gentleman, and so forth.

E. Kn. So, sir, then you tried their skill?

30 *Bob.* Alas, soon tried! You shall hear, sir. Within two or three days after, they came; and, by honesty, fair sir, believe me, I graced them exceedingly, showed them some two or three tricks of prevention, have purchased 'em since a credit, to admiration! They cannot deny this: and yet now, they hate me, and why? Because I am
35 excellent, and for no other vile reason on the earth.

E. Kn. This is strange and barbarous! As ever I heard!

Bob. Nay, for a more instance of their preposterous natures, but note, sir. They have assaulted me some three, four, five, six of them together, as I have walked alone, in divers skirts i' the town, as
40 Turnbull, Whitechapel, Shoreditch, which were then my quarters, and since upon the Exchange, at my lodging, and at my ordinary: where I have driven them afore me, the whole length of a street, in the open view of all our gallants, pitying to hurt them, believe me. Yet, all this lenity will not o'ercome their spleen: they will be doing

---

12 *hay?*: the Italian *hai* ('you have it') on a thrust reaching the antagonist   14 *punto*: instant (cf. l. 67)   19 *travail*: IV. vi. 49   40 *Turnbull, Whitechapel, Shoreditch*: disreputable areas

with a pismire, raising a hill, a man may spurn abroad, with his foot, 45
at pleasure. By myself, I could have slain them all, but I delight not
in murder. I am loth to bear any other than this bastinado for 'em:
yet, I hold it good policy, not to go disarmed, for though I be
skilful, I may be oppressed with multitudes.

E. Kn. Aye, believe me, may you, sir: and (in my conceit) our 50
whole nation should sustain the loss by it, if it were so.

Bob. Alas, no: what's a peculiar man, to a nation? Not seen.

E. Kn. Oh, but your skill, sir!

Bob. Indeed, that might be some loss; but, who respects it? I will
tell you, sir, by the way of private, and under seal; I am a gentleman, 55
and live here obscure, and to myself: but were I known to Her
Majesty, and the Lords (observe me) I would undertake (upon this
poor head, and life) for the public benefit of the state, not only to
spare the entire lives of her subjects in general, but to save the one
half, nay, three parts of her yearly charge, in holding war, and 60
against what enemy soever. And how would I do it, think you?

E. Kn. Nay, I know not, nor can I conceive.

Bob. Why thus, sir. I would select nineteen, more, to myself,
throughout the land; gentlemen they should be of good spirit,
strong, and able constitution, I would choose them by an instinct, 65
a character, that I have: and I would teach these nineteen the
special rules, as your *Punto*, your *Reverso*, your *Stoccata*, your
Imbroccata, your *Passada*, your *Montanto*: till they could all play
very near, or altogether as well as myself. This done, say the enemy
were forty thousand strong, we twenty would come into the field, 70
the tenth of March, or thereabouts; and we would challenge twenty
of the enemy; they could not, in their honour, refuse us, well, we
would kill them: challenge twenty more, kill them; twenty more,
kill them; twenty more, kill them too; and thus, would we kill,
every man, his twenty a day, that's twenty score; twenty score, 75
that's two hundred; two hundred a day, five days a thousand;
forty thousand; forty times five, five times forty, two hundred days
kills them all up, by computation. And this, will I venture my poor

45 *pismire*: ant (i.e. 'busy as ants')   50 *conceit*: opinion   52 *peculiar*:
individual   67 *Punto*: a thrust with the point   *Reverso*: a back-stroke   *Stoccata*:
I. v. 115   68 *Imbroccata*: 'a thrust at fence, or a venie given over the dagger'
(Florio)   *Passada*: I. v. 125   *Montanto*: an upright thrust

gentleman-like carcass, to perform (provided, there be no treason
80 practised upon us) by fair, and discreet manhood, that is, civilly by
the sword.

E. Kn. Why, are you so sure of your hand, captain, at all times?

Bob. Tut, never miss thrust, upon my reputation with you.

E. Kn. I would not stand in Downright's state, then, an' you
85 meet him, for the wealth of any one street in London.

Bob. Why, sir, you mistake me! If he were here now, by this
welkin, I would not draw my weapon on him! Let this gentleman
do his mind: but I will bastinado him (by the bright sun) wherever
I meet him.

90   *Mat.* Faith, and I'll have a fling at him, at my distance.

                          (Downright *walks over the stage*)

E. Kn. Gods so', look, where he is: yonder he goes.

Dow. What peevish luck have I, I cannot meet with these bragging
rascals?

Bob. It's not he? Is it?

95   *E. Kn.* Yes faith, it is he.

Mat. I'll be hanged, then, if that were he.

E. Kn. Sir, keep your hanging good, for some greater matter, for
I assure you, that was he.

Ste. Upon my reputation, it was he.

100   *Bob.* Had I thought it had been he, he must not have gone so:
but I can hardly be induced to believe it was he, yet.

E. Kn. That I think, sir. But see, he is come again!

Dow. Oh, Pharaoh's foot, have I found you? Come, draw, to your
tools: draw, gipsy, or I'll thrash you.

105   *Bob.* Gentleman of valour, I do believe in thee, hear me——

Dow. Draw your weapon, then.

Bob. Tall man, I never thought on it, till now (body of me) I had
a warrant of the peace, served on me, even now, as I came along,
by a waterbearer; this gentleman saw it, Master Matthew.

110   *Dow.* 'Sdeath, you will not draw, then?

                          (*He beats him, and disarms him:* Matthew *runs away*)

Bob. Hold, hold, under thy favour, forbear.

Dow. Prate again, as you like this, you whoreson foist, you.

104 *gipsy*: rogue   107 *Tall*: bold

You'll control the point, you? Your consort is gone? Had he stayed,
he had shared with you, sir.   [*Exit*]

Bob. Well, gentlemen, bear witness, I was bound to the peace, by 115
this good day.

E. Kn. No faith, it's an ill day, captain, never reckon it other: but
say you were bound to the peace, the law allows you to defend
yourself: that'll prove but a poor excuse.

Bob. I cannot tell, sir. I desire good construction, in fair sort. I 120
never sustained the like disgrace (by heaven) sure I was struck with
a planet thence, for I had no power to touch my weapon.

E. Kn. Aye, like enough, I have heard of many that have been
beaten under a planet: go, get you to a surgeon. [*Exit* Bobadil]
'Slid, an' these be your tricks, your *passadas*, and your *mountantos*, 125
I'll none of them. Oh, manners! That this age should bring forth
such creatures! That Nature should be at leisure to make 'em.
Come, coz.

Ste. Mass, I'll ha' this cloak.

E. Kn. God's will, 'tis Downright's.   130

Ste. Nay, it's mine now, another might have ta'en up, as well as
I: I'll wear it, so I will.

E. Kn. How, an' he see it? He'll challenge it, assure yourself.

Ste. Aye, but he shall not ha' it; I'll say, I bought it.

E. Kn. Take heed, you buy it not too dear, coz.   [*Exeunt*] 135

ACT IV, Scene viii

[Kitely's house]

Enter Kitely, Wellbred, Dame Kitely, Bridget

Kit. Now, trust me, brother, you were much to blame,
To incense his anger, and disturb the peace
Of my poor house, where there are sentinels
That every minute watch to give alarms
Of civil war, without adjection   5
Of your assistance, or occasion.

121–2 *struck with a planet*: a way of accounting for an inexplicable malady
(*IV. viii*) 5 *adjection*: addition

Wel. No harm done, brother, I warrant you: since there is no
harm done. Anger costs a man nothing: and a tall man is never his
own man, till he be angry. To keep his valour in obscurity is to keep
himself, as it were, in a cloak-bag. What's a musician, unless he
play? What's a tall man, unless he fight? For, indeed, all this, my
wise brother stands upon, absolutely: and that made me fall in with
him so resolutely.

Dam. Aye, but what harm might have come of it, brother?

Wel. Might, sister? So might the good warm clothes your husband
wears be poisoned, for anything he knows: or the wholesome wine
he drunk, even now, at the table——

Kit. Now, God forbid: oh me. Now, I remember,
My wife drunk to me, last; and changed the cup:
And bade me wear this cursed suit today.
See, if heaven suffer murder undiscovered!
I feel me ill; give me some mithridate,
Some mithridate and oil, good sister, fetch me;
Oh, I am sick at heart! I burn, I burn.
If you will save my life, go, fetch it me.

Wel. Oh, strange humour! My very breath has poisoned him.

Bri. Good brother, be content, what do you mean? The strength
of these extreme conceits will kill you.

Dam. Beshrew your heart-blood, brother Wellbred, now;
For putting such a toy into his head.

Wel. Is a fit simile, a toy? Will he be poisoned with a simile?
Brother Kitely, what a strange and idle imagination is this? For
shame, be wiser. O' my soul, there's no such matter.

Kit. Am I not sick? How am I, then, not poisoned? Am I not
poisoned? How am I, then, so sick?

Dam. If you be sick, your own thoughts make you sick.

Wel. His jealousy is the poison, he has taken.

[*Enter* Brainworm] (*He comes disguised like* Justice Clement's *man*)

Bra. Master Kitely, my master, Justice Clement, salutes you; and
desires to speak with you, with all possible speed.

Kit. No time, but now? When, I think, I am sick? Very sick!
Well, I will wait upon his worship. Thomas! Cob! I must seek

---

22 *mithridate*: antidote against poison or infection

them out, and set 'em sentinels, till I return. Thomas, Cob, Thomas!

                                           [*Exit*]

Wel. This is perfectly rare, Brainworm! But how got'st thou this apparel of the Justice's man?

Bra. Marry, sir, my proper fine penman would needs bestow the 45 grist o' me, at the Windmill, to hear some martial discourse; where so I marshalled him, that I made him drunk, with admiration! And, because too much heat was the cause of his distemper, I stripped him stark naked, as he lay along asleep, and borrowed his suit, to deliver this counterfeit message in, leaving a rusty armour 50 and an old brown bill to watch him, till my return: which shall be, when I ha' pawned his apparel, and spent the better part o' the money, perhaps.

Wel. Well, thou art a successful merry knave, Brainworm, his absence will be a good subject for more mirth. I pray thee, return 55 to thy young master, and will him to meet me, and my sister Bridget, at the Tower instantly: for, here, tell him, the house is so stored with jealousy, there is no room for love to stand upright in. We must get our fortunes committed to some larger prison, say; and, than the Tower, I know no better air: nor where the liberty 60 of the house may do us more present service. Away.

                                      [*Exit* Brainworm]

[*Enter* Kitely, Cash]

Kit. Come hither, Thomas. Now, my secret's ripe,
And thou shalt have it: lay to both thine ears.
Hark, what I say to thee. I must go forth, Thomas.
Be careful of thy promise, keep good watch,   65
Note every gallant, and observe him well,
That enters in my absence, to thy mistress:
If she would show him rooms, the jest is stale,
Follow 'em, Thomas, or else hang on him,
And let him not go after; mark their looks;
Note, if she offer but to see his band,   70
Or any other amorous toy, about him;
But praise his leg; or foot; or if she say,

---

45 *penman*: clerk (i.e. Formal)   57 *Tower*: where they could be married at once, as the precincts of the Tower were extra-parochial

The day is hot, and bid him feel her hand,
75 How hot it is; oh, that's a monstrous thing!
Note me all this, good Thomas, mark their sighs,
And if they do but whisper, break 'em off:
I'll bear thee out in it. Wilt thou do this?
Wilt thou be true, my Thomas?

    Cas.   As truth's self, sir.

80   *Kit.* Why, I believe thee: where is Cob, now? Cob?   [*Exit*]
    Dam. He's ever calling for Cob! I wonder, how he employs
Cob so!

    Wel. Indeed, sister, to ask how he employs Cob, is a necessary
question for you, that are his wife, and a thing not very easy for
85 you to be satisfied in: but this I'll assure you, Cob's wife is an
excellent bawd, sister, and, oftentimes, your husband haunts her
house, marry, to what end, I cannot altogether accuse him, imagine
you what you think convenient. But, I have known, fair hides have
foul hearts, ere now, sister.

90   *Dam.* Never said you truer than that, brother, so much I can tell
you for your learning. Thomas, fetch your cloak, and go with me,
I'll after him presently: I would to fortune, I could take him there,
i'faith. I'd return him his own, I warrant him.   [*Exit with* Cash]

    Wel. So, let 'em go: this may make sport anon. Now, my fair
95 sister-in-law, that you knew, but how happy a thing it were to be
fair, and beautiful?

    Bri. That touches not me, brother.

    Wel. That's true; that's even the fault of it: for, indeed, beauty
stands a woman in no stead, unless it procure her touching. But,
100 sister, whether it touch you, or no, it touches your beauties; and
I am sure, they will abide the touch; an' they do not, a plague of
all ceruse, say I: and it touches me too in part, though not in the——
Well, there's a dear and respected friend of mine, sister, stands very
strongly, and worthily affected toward you, and hath vowed to
105 inflame whole bonfires of zeal, at his heart, in honour of your per-
fections. I have already engaged my promise to bring you, where
you shall hear him confirm much more. Ned Knowell is the man,
sister. There's no exception against the party. You are ripe for a

---

93 *return him his own*: pay him back in kind   99 *touching*: i.e. sexual contact
102 *ceruse*: a cosmetic of white lead

husband; and a minute's loss to such an occasion is a great trespass
in a wise beauty. What say you, sister? On my soul, he loves you. 110
Will you give him the meeting?

   Bri. Faith, I had very little confidence in mine own constancy,
brother, if I durst not meet a man: but this motion of yours savours
of an old knight-adventurer's servant, a little too much, methinks.

   Wel. What's that, sister?   115

   Bri. Marry, of the squire.

   Wel. No matter if it did, I would be such an one for my friend,
but see! Who is returned to hinder us?

[*Enter* Kitely]

   Kit. What villainy is this? Called out on a false message?
This was some plot! I was not sent for. Bridget,   120
Where's your sister?

   Bri.   I think she be gone forth, sir.

   Kit. How! Is my wife gone forth? Whither, for God's sake?

   Bri. She's gone abroad with Thomas.

   Kit. Abroad with Thomas? Oh, that villain dors me.
He hath discovered all unto my wife!   125
Beast that I was, to trust him: whither, I pray you,
Went she?

   Bri.   I know not, sir.

   Wel.   I'll tell you, brother,
Whither I suspect she's gone.

   Kit.   Whither, good brother?

   Wel. To Cob's house, I believe: but, keep my counsel.

   Kit. I will, I will: to Cob's house? Doth she haunt Cob's?   130
She's gone a' purpose, now, to cuckold me,
With that lewd rascal, who, to win her favour,
Hath told her all.   [*Exit*]

   Wel.   Come, he's once more gone.
Sister, let's lose no time; the affair is worth it.   [*Exeunt*]

---

116 *squire*: i.e. the 'apple-squire' or pandar   124 *dors*: hoaxes, mocks

ACT IV, Scene ix

[A street]
Enter Matthew, Bobadil

Mat. I wonder, captain, what they will say of my going away? Ha?

Bob. Why, what should they say? But as of a discreet gentleman?
Quick, wary, respectful of nature's fair lineaments: and that's all?

Mat. Why, so! But what can they say of your beating?

5 *Bob.* A rude part, a touch with soft wood, a kind of gross battery
used, laid on strongly, borne most patiently: and that's all.

Mat. Aye, but, would any man have offered it in Venice? As
you say?

Bob. Tut, I assure you, no: you shall have there your *Nobilis*,
10 your *Gentelezza*, come in bravely upon your *reverse*, stand you
close, stand you firm, stand you fair, save your *retricato* with his
left leg, come to the *assalto* with the right, thrust with brave steel,
defy your base wood! But, wherefore do I awake this remembrance?
I was fascinated, by Jupiter: fascinated: but I will be unwitched,
15 and revenged, by law.

Mat. Do you hear? Is't not best to get a warrant, and have him
arrested, and brought before Justice Clement?

Bob. It were not amiss, would we had it.

Mat. Why, here comes his man, let's speak to him.

20 *Bob.* Agreed, do you speak.

[*Enter* Brainworm *disguised as* Formal]

Mat. Save you, sir.

Bra. With all my heart, sir.

Mat. Sir, there is one Downright, hath abused this gentleman,
and myself, and we determine to make our amends by law; now,
25 if you would do us the favour, to procure a warrant, to bring him
afore your master, you shall be well considered, I assure you, sir.

Bra. Sir, you know my service is my living, such favours as these,
gotten of my master, is his only preferment, and therefore, you must
consider me, as I may make benefit of my place.

9–10 *Nobilis* . . . *Gentelezza*: nobility . . . gentility (blunderingly expressed)
11 *retricato*: unexplained   12 *assalto*: aggressive lunge

Mat. How is that, sir?   30

Bra. Faith, sir, the thing is extraordinary, and the gentleman may be of great accompt: yet be what he will, if you will lay me down a brace of angels, in my hand, you shall have it, otherwise not.

Mat. How shall we do, captain? He asks a brace of angels, you have no money?   35

Bob. Not a cross, by fortune.

Mat. Nor I, as I am a gentleman, but twopence, left of my two shillings in the morning for wine, and radish: let's find him some pawn.

Bob. Pawn? We have none to the value of his demand.   40

Mat. Oh, yes. I'll pawn this jewel in my ear, and you may pawn your silk stockings, and pull up your boots, they will ne'er be missed: it must be done, now.

Bob. Well, an' there be no remedy: I'll step aside, and pull 'em off.

Mat. Do you hear, sir? We have no store of money at this time,   45
but you shall have good pawns: look you, sir, this jewel, and that gentleman's silk stockings, because we would have it dispatched, ere we went to our chambers.

Bra. I am content, sir; I will get you the warrant presently, what's his name, say you? Downright?   50

Mat. Aye, aye, George Downright.

Bra. What manner of man is he?

Mat. A tall big man, sir; he goes in a cloak, most commonly, of silk russet, laid about with russet lace.

Bra. 'Tis very good, sir.   55

Mat. Here, sir, here's my jewel.

Bob. And here, are stockings.

Bra. Well, gentlemen, I'll procure you this warrant presently, but, who will you have to serve it?

Mat. That's true, captain: that must be considered.   60

Bob. Body o'me, I know not! 'Tis service of danger!

Bra. Why, you were best get one o' the varlets o' the city, a serjeant. I'll appoint you one, if you please.

Mat. Will you, sir? Why, we can wish no better.

---

34 *brace of angels*: the lawful fee was 10 groats   36 *cross*: silver penny or half-penny so marked   62 *varlet*: synonymous with 'serjeant', a city officer serving warrants etc.

65   *Bob.* We'll leave it to you, sir.   *[Exit with* Matthew]

   Bra. This is rare! Now, will I go pawn this cloak of the Justice's man's, at the brokers, for a varlet's suit, and be the varlet myself; and get either more pawns, or more money of Downright, for the arrest.   *[Exit]*

ACT IV, Scene x

[Before Cob's house]

Enter Knowell

   Kno. Oh, here it is, I am glad: I have found it now.
Ho? Who is within, here?

   Tib. [*Within*] I am within, sir, what's your pleasure?

   Kno. To know, who is within, besides yourself.

5   *Tib.* Why, sir, you are no constable, I hope?

   Kno. Oh! Fear you the constable? Then, I doubt not,
You have some guests within, deserve that fear,
I'll fetch him straight.

   Tib.   O' God's name, sir.

   Kno. Go to. Come, tell me, is not young Knowell here?

10   *Tib.* Young Knowell? I know none such, sir, o' mine honesty.

   Kno. Your honesty? Dame, it flies too lightly from you:
There is no way, but, fetch the constable.

   Tib. The constable? The man is mad, I think.

[*Enter* Cash, Dame Kitely]

   Cas. Ho, who keeps house here?

15   *Kno.* Oh, this is the female copes-mate of my son?
Now shall I meet him straight.

   Dam.   Knock, Thomas, hard.

   Cas. Ho, good wife?

   Tib.   Why, what's the matter with you?

   Dam. Why, woman, grieves it you to ope' your door?
Belike, you get something, to keep it shut.

[*Enter* Tib]

20   *Tib.* What mean these questions, 'pray ye?

    (*IV. x*) 15 *copes-mate*: associate, paramour

Dam. So strange you make it? Is not my husband here?
Kno. Her husband!
Dam.   My tried husband, Master Kitely.
Tib. I hope he needs not to be tried, here.
Dam. No, dame: he does it not for need, but pleasure.
Tib. Neither for need, nor pleasure, is he here.   25
Kno. This is but a device, to balk me withal.

[*Enter* Kitely *in his cloak*]

Soft, who is this? 'Tis not my son, disguised?
   Dam. (*She spies her husband come: and runs to him*) Oh, sir, have
       I forestalled your honest market?
Found your close walks? You stand amazed, now, do you?
I'faith (I am glad) I have smoked you yet at last!   30
What is your jewel trow? In: come, let's see her;
(Fetch forth your huswife, dame) if she be fairer,
In any honest judgement, than myself,
I'll be content with it: but, she is change,
She feeds you fat, she soothes your appetite,   35
And you are well? Your wife, an honest woman,
Is meat twice sod to you, sir? Oh, you treacher!
   Kno. She cannot counterfeit thus palpably.
   Kit. Out on thy more than strumpet's impudence!
Steal'st thou thus to thy haunts? And have I taken   40
Thy bawd, and thee, and thy companion,
(*Pointing to old Knowell*) This hoary-headed lecher, this old goat,
Close at your villainy, and wouldst thou 'scuse it,
With this stale harlot's jest, accusing me?
(*To him*) Oh, old incontinent, dost not thou shame,   45
When all thy powers in chastity is spent,
To have a mind so hot? And to entice,
And feed the enticements of a lustful woman?
   Dam. Out, I defy thee, I, dissembling wretch.
   Kit. Defy me, strumpet? Ask thy pandar, here,   (*By* Thomas) 50
Can he deny it? Or that wicked elder?
   Kno. Why, hear you, sir.
   Kit.   Tut, tut, tut: never speak.

---

37 *twice sod*: unpalatable (sod = boiled)   *treacher*: deceiver   50 s.d. *By*: referring to

Thy guilty conscience will discover thee.

    Kno. What lunacy is this, that haunts this man?

55   *Kit.* Well, goodwife BA'D, Cob's wife; and you,
That make your husband such a hoddie-doddie;
And you, young apple-squire; and old cuckold-maker;
I'll ha' you every one before a Justice:
Nay, you shall answer it, I charge you go.

60   *Kno.* Marry, with all my heart, sir: I go willingly.
Though I do taste this as a trick, put on me,
To punish my impertinent search; and justly:
And half forgive my son, for the device.

    Kit. Come, will you go?

    Dam.   Go? To thy shame, believe it.

                 [*Enter* Cob]

65   *Cob.* Why, what's the matter, here? What's here to do?

    Kit. Oh, Cob, art thou come? I have been abused,
And i' thy house. Never was man so wronged!

    Cob. 'Slid, in my house? My master Kitely? Who wrongs you
in my house?

70   *Kit.* Marry, young lust in old; and old in young, here:
Thy wife's their bawd, here have I taken 'em.

    Cob. How? Bawd? Is my house come to that? Am I preferred
thither? Did I charge you to keep your doors shut, Isobel? And do
you let 'em lie open for all comers?

                  (*He falls upon his wife and beats her*)

75   *Kno.* Friend, know some cause, before thou beat'st thy wife,
This's madness in thee.

    Cob.   Why? Is there no cause?

    Kit. Yes, I'll show cause before the Justice, Cob.
Come, let her go with me.

    Cob.   Nay, she shall go.

    Tib. Nay, I will go. I'll see, an' you may be allowed to make
80 a bundle o' hemp, o' your right and lawful wife thus, at every
cuckoldly knave's pleasure. Why do you not go?

    Kit. A bitter quean. Come, we'll ha' you tamed.   [*Exeunt*]

---

55 *BA'D*: pun on 'bawd'; Kitely spells out the word   56 *hoddie-doddie*:
cuckold, noodle   73 *Isobel*: ? for Jezebel   82 *quean*: jade, strumpet

ACT IV, Scene xi

[A street]

Enter Brainworm

Bra. Well, of all my disguises yet, now am I most like myself: being in this serjeant's gown. A man of my present profession, never counterfeits, till he lays hold upon a debtor, and says, he rests him, for then he brings him to all manner of unrest. A kind of little kings we are, bearing the diminutive of a mace, made like a young arti- 5 choke, that always carries pepper and salt in itself. Well, I know not what danger I undergo by this exploit; pray heaven, I come well off.

[*Enter* Matthew, Bobadil]

Mat. See, I think, yonder is the varlet, by his gown.
Bob. Let's go in quest of him.   10
Mat. 'Save you, friend, are not you here, by appointment of Justice Clement's man?
Bra. Yes, an't please you, sir: he told me two gentlemen had willed him to procure a warrant from his master (which I have about me) to be served on one Downright.   15
Mat. It is honestly done of you both; and see, where the party comes, you must arrest: serve it upon him, quickly, afore he be aware——

[*Enter* Stephen *in* Downright's *cloak*]

Bob. Bear back, Master Matthew.
Bra. Master Downright, I arrest you, i' the Queen's name, and 20 must carry you afore a Justice, by virtue of this warrant.
Ste. Me, friend? I am no Downright, I. I am Master Stephen, you do not well to arrest me, I tell you, truly: I am in nobody's bonds, nor books, I, I would you should know it. A plague on you heartily, for making me thus afraid afore my time.   25
Bra. Why, now are you deceived, gentlemen?

---

3 *rests*: arrests   5 *mace*: badge of the City serjeant (with quibble on 'mace' as 'spice')

Bob. He wears such a cloak, and that deceived us: but see, here a comes, indeed! This is he, officer.

[*Enter* Downright]

Dow. Why, how now, signior gull! Are you turned filcher of late?
30 Come, deliver my cloak.

Ste. Your cloak, sir? I bought it, even now, in open market.

Bra. Master Downright, I have a warrant I must serve upon you, procured by these two gentlemen.

Dow. These gentlemen? These rascals?

35 *Bra.* Keep the peace, I charge you, in Her Majesty's name.

Dow. I obey thee. What must I do, officer?

Bra. Go before Master Justice Clement, to answer what they can object against you, sir. I will use you kindly, sir.

Mat. Come, let's before, and make the Justice, captain——

40 *Bob.* The varlet's a tall man! Afore heaven!

[*Exit with* Matthew]

Dow. Gull, you'll gi'me my cloak?

Ste. Sir, I bought it, and I'll keep it.

Dow. You will.

Ste. Aye, that I will.

45 *Dow.* Officer, there's thy fee, arrest him.

Bra. Master Stephen, I must arrest you.

Ste. Arrest me, I scorn it. There, take your cloak, I'll none on't.

Dow. Nay, that shall not serve your turn now, sir. Officer, I'll go with thee, to the Justice's: bring him along.

50 *Ste.* Why, is not here your cloak? What would you have?

Dow. I'll ha' you answer it, sir.

Bra. Sir, I'll take your word; and this gentleman's, too: for his appearance.

Dow. I'll ha' no words taken. Bring him along.

55 *Bra.* Sir, I may choose to do that: I may take bail.

Dow. 'Tis true, you may take bail, and choose; at another time: but you shall not, now, varlet. Bring him along, or I'll swinge you.

Bra. Sir, I pity the gentleman's case. Here's your money again.

Dow. 'Sdeynes, tell not me of my money, bring him away, I say.

60 *Bra.* I warrant you he will go with you of himself, sir.

39 *make*: prepare   51 *answer*: be accountable for   57 *swinge*: thrash

Dow. Yet more ado?

Bra. [*Aside*] I have made a fair mash on't.

Ste. Must I go?

Bra. I know no remedy, Master Stephen.

Dow. Come along, afore me, here. I do not love your hanging 65
look behind.

Ste. Why, sir. I hope you cannot hang me for it. Can he, fellow?

Bra. I think not, sir. It is but a whipping matter, sure!

Ste. Why, then, let him do his worst, I am resolute.   [*Exeunt*]

ACT V, Scene i

[Justice Clement's house]

Enter Clement, Knowell, Kitely, Dame Kitely, Cash, Tib, Cob

Cle. NAY, but stay, stay, give me leave: my chair, sirrah. You,
Master Knowell, say you went thither to meet your son.

Kno. Aye, sir.

Cle. But who directed you thither?   5

Kno. That did mine own man, sir.

Cle. Where is he?

Kno. Nay, I know not, now; I left him with your clerk: and
appointed him to stay here for me.

Cle. My clerk? About what time was this?   10

Kno. Marry, between one and two, as I take it.

Cle. And what time came my man with the false message to you,
Master Kitely?

Kit. After two, sir.

Cle. Very good: but, Mistress Kitely, how that you were at 15
Cob's? Ha?

Dam. An' please you, sir, I'll tell you: my brother, Wellbred,
told me that Cob's house was a suspected place——

Cle. So it appears, methinks: but, on.

Dam. And that my husband used thither, daily.   20

Cle. No matter, so he used himself well, mistress.

20 *used thither*: constantly resorted there

Dam. True, sir, but you know, what grows, by such haunts, oftentimes.

Cle. I see, rank fruits of a jealous brain, Mistress Kitely: but did
25 you find your husband there, in that case, as you suspected?

Kit. I found her there, sir.

Cle. Did you so? That alters the case. Who gave you knowledge of your wife's being there?

Kit. Marry, that did my brother Wellbred.

30 *Cle.* How? Wellbred first tell her? Then tell you, after? Where is Wellbred?

Kit. Gone with my sister, sir, I know not whither.

Cle. Why, this is a mere trick, a device; you are gulled in this most grossly, all! Alas, poor wench, wert thou beaten for this?

35 *Tib.* Yes, most pitifully, and't please you.

Cob. And worthily, I hope: if it shall prove so.

Cle. Aye, that's like, and a piece of a sentence.

[*Enter* Servant]

How now, sir? What's the matter?

Ser. Sir, there's a gentleman, i'the court without, desires to
40 speak with your worship.

Cle. A gentleman? What's he?

Ser. A soldier, sir, he says.

Cle. A soldier? Take down my armour, my sword, quickly: a soldier speak with me! Why, when knaves? Come on, come on,
45 hold my cap there, so; give me my gorget, my sword: stand by, I will end your matters, anon——— (*He arms himself*) Let the soldier enter, now, sir, what ha' you to say to me?

ACT V, Scene ii

Enter Bobadil, Matthew

Bob. By your worship's favour——

Cle. Nay, keep out, sir, I know not your pretence, you send me word, sir, you are a soldier: why, sir, you shall be answered, here, here be them have been amongst soldiers. Sir, your pleasure.

37 *piece of a sentence*: instance of a wise saying (Cob's 'if it shall prove so')
45 *gorget*: armour protecting the throat　　　(*V. ii*) 2 *pretence*: claim

Bob. Faith, sir, so it is, this gentleman, and myself, have been 5
most uncivilly wronged, and beaten, by one Downright, a coarse
fellow, about the town, here, and for mine own part, I protest,
being a man in no sort given to this filthy humour of quarrelling, he
hath assaulted me in the way of my peace; despoiled me of mine
honour; disarmed me of my weapons; and rudely, laid me along, 10
in the open streets: when I not so much as once offered to resist him.

Cle. Oh, God's precious! Is this the soldier? Here, take my
armour off quickly, 'twill make him swoon, I fear; he is not fit to
look on't, that will put up a blow.

Mat. An't please your worship, he was bound to the peace. 15

Cle. Why, and he were, sir, his hands were not bound, were they?

[*Enter* Servant]

Ser. There's one of the varlets of the city, sir, has brought two
gentlemen, here, one upon your worship's warrant.

Cle. My warrant?

Ser. Yes, sir. The officer says, procured by these two. 20

Cle. Bid him, come in. Set by this picture.

[*Enter* Downright, Brainworm, Stephen]

What, Master Downright! Are you brought at Master Freshwater's
suit, here!

ACT V, Scene iii

Dow. I'faith, sir. And here's another brought at my suit.

Cle. What are you, sir?

Ste. A gentleman, sir. Oh, uncle!

Cle. Uncle? Who? Master Knowell?

Kno. Aye, sir! This is a wise kinsman of mine. 5

Ste. God's my witness, uncle, I am wronged here monstrously,
he charges me with stealing of his cloak, and would I might never
stir, if I did not find it in the street, by chance.

Dow. Oh, did you find it, now? You said you bought it erewhile.

Ste. And you said I stole it; nay, now my uncle is here, I'll do 10
well enough, with you.

---

21 *this picture*: i.e. Bobadil   22 *Freshwater*: soldier without experience

Cle. Well, let this breathe awhile; you, that have cause to complain, there, stand forth: had you my warrant for this gentleman's apprehension?

15   *Bob.* Aye, an't please your worship.

Cle. Nay, do not speak in passion so: where had you it?

Bob. Of your clerk, sir.

Cle. That's well! An' my clerk can make warrants, and my hand not at 'em! Where is the warrant? Officer, have you it?

20   *Bra.* No, sir, your worship's man, Master Formal, bid me do it, for these gentlemen, and he would be my discharge.

Cle. Why, Master Downright, are you such a novice, to be served, and never see the warrant?

Dow. Sir. He did not serve it on me.

25   *Cle.* No? How then?

Dow. Marry, sir, he came to me, and said, he must serve it, and he would use me kindly, and so——

Cle. Oh, God's pity, was it so, sir? He must serve it? Give me my longsword there, and help me off; so. Come on, sir varlet, I

30 must cut off your legs, sirrah: nay, stand up, I'll use you kindly; I must cut off your legs, I say.

                     (*He flourishes over him with his longsword*)

Bra. Oh, good sir, I beseech you; nay, good Master Justice.

Cle. I must do it; there is no remedy. I must cut off your legs, sirrah, I must cut off your ears, you rascal, I must do it; I must cut

35 off your nose, I must cut off your head.

Bra. Oh, good your worship.

Cle. Well, rise, how dost thou do, now? Dost thou feel thyself well? Hast thou no harm?

Bra. No, I thank your good worship, sir.

40   *Cle.* Why, so! I said, I must cut off thy legs, and I must cut off thy arms, and I must cut off thy head; but, I did not do it: so, you said, you must serve this gentleman, with my warrant, but you did not serve him. You knave, you slave, you rogue, do you say you must? Sirrah, away with him, to the jail, I'll teach you a trick, for

45 your *must*, sir.

Bra. Good sir, I beseech you, be good to me.

Cle. Tell him he shall to the jail, away with him, I say.

16 *passion*: i.e. strong feeling, here 'sorrow'

Bra. Nay, sir, if you will commit me, it shall be for committing more than this: I will not lose, by my travail, any grain of my fame certain.   [*He throws off his disguise*] 50

Cle. How is this!

Kno. My man, Brainworm!

Ste. Oh yes, uncle. Brainworm has been with my cousin Edward, and I, all this day.

Cle. I told you all, there was some device!   55

Bra. Nay, excellent Justice, since I have laid myself thus open to you; now, stand strong for me: both with your sword, and your balance.

Cle. Body o' me, a merry knave! Give me a bowl of sack: if he belong to you, Master Knowell, I bespeak your patience.   60

Bra. That is it, I have most need of. Sir, if you'll pardon me, only; I'll glory in all the rest of my exploits.

Kno. Sir, you know, I love not to have my favours come hard from me. You have your pardon: though I suspect you shrewdly for being of counsel with my son, against me.   65

Bra. Yes, faith, I have, sir; though you retained me doubly this morning, for yourself: first, as Brainworm; after, as Fitzsword. I was your reformed soldier, sir. 'Twas I sent you to Cob's, upon the errand, without end.

Kno. Is it possible! Or that thou shouldst disguise thy language 70 so, as I should not know thee?

Bra. Oh, sir, this has been the day of my metamorphosis! It is not that shape alone that I have run through today. I brought this gentleman, Master Kitely, a message too, in the form of Master Justice's man, here, to draw him out o' the way, as well as your 75 worship: while Master Wellbred might make a conveyance of Mistress Bridget, to my young master.

Kit. How! My sister stolen away?

Kno. My son is not married, I hope!

Bra. Faith, sir, they are both as sure as love, a priest, and three 80 thousand pound (which is her portion) can make 'em: and by this time are ready to bespeak their wedding supper at the Windmill, except some friend, here, prevent 'em, and invite 'em home.

---

58 *balance*: i.e. the scales of justice   69 *end*: purpose   80 *sure*:
betrothed   83 *prevent*: anticipate

Cle. Marry, that will I (I thank thee, for putting me in mind on't).
85 Sirrah, go you, and fetch 'em hither, upon my warrant. Neither's
friends have cause to be sorry, if I know the young couple aright.
Here, I drink to thee, for thy good news. But, I pray thee, what hast
thou done with my man Formal?

Bra. Faith, sir, after some ceremony past, as making him drunk,
90 first with story, and then with wine (but all in kindness) and strip-
ping him to his shirt: I left him in that cool vein, departed, sold
your worship's warrant to these two, pawned his livery for that
varlet's gown, to serve it in; and thus have brought myself, by my
activity, to your worship's consideration.

95 *Cle.* And I will consider thee, in another cup of sack. Here's to
thee, which having drunk of, this is my sentence. Pledge me. Thou
hast done, or assisted to nothing, in my judgement, but deserves to
be pardoned for the wit o' the offence. If thy master, or any man
here, be angry with thee, I shall suspect his engine, while I know
100 him for't. How now? What noise is that!

[*Enter* Servant]

Ser. Sir, it is Roger is come home.
Cle. Bring him in, bring him in.

[*Enter* Formal]

What! Drunk in arms, against me? Your reason, your reason for
this.

ACT V, Scene iv

For. I beseech your worship to pardon me; I happened into ill
company by chance, that cast me into a sleep, and stripped me of
all my clothes——

Cle. Well, tell him, I am Justice Clement, and do pardon him:
5 but, what is this to your armour! What may that signify?

For. And't please you, sir, it hung up i' the room, where I was
stripped; and I borrowed it of one o' the drawers, to come home in,
because I was loth to do penance through the street i' my shirt.

Cle. Well, stand by a while.

99 *engine*: wit

[*Enter* Edward Knowell, Wellbred, Bridget]

Who be these? Oh, the young company, welcome, welcome. Gi' 10
you joy. Nay, Mistress Bridget, blush not; you are not so fresh a
bride, but the news of it is come hither afore you. Master Bride-
groom, I ha' made your peace, give me your hand: so will I for all
the rest, ere you forsake my roof.

ACT V, Scene v

E. Kn. We are the more bound to your humanity, sir.

Cle. Only these two have so little of man in 'em, they are no part
of my care.

Wel. Yes, sir, let me pray you for this gentleman, he belongs to
my sister, the bride.   5

Cle. In what place, sir?

Wel. Of her delight, sir, below the stairs, and in public: her
poet, sir.

Cle. A poet? I will challenge him myself, presently, at extempore.
  'Mount up thy Phlegon muse, and testify,   10
    How Saturn, sitting in an ebon cloud,
  Disrobed his podex white as ivory,
    And, through the welkin, thundered all aloud.'

Wel. He is not for extempore, sir. He is all for the pocket-muse,
please you command a sight of it.   15

Cle. Yes, yes, search him for a taste of his vein.

Wel. You must not deny the Queen's Justice, sir, under a writ o'
rebellion.

Cle. What! All this verse? Body o' me, he carries a whole realm,
a commonwealth of paper, in's hose! Let's see some of his subjects! 20
  'Unto the boundless Ocean of thy face,
    Runs this poor river charged with streams of eyes.'
How? This is stolen!

E. Kn. A parody! A parody! With a kind of miraculous gift, to
make it absurder than it was.   25

(*V. v*) 10 *Phlegon*: one of the horses of the sun   19 *realm*: pronounced 'ream'
21–2 burlesqued from the opening sonnet of Daniel's *Delia*

Cle. Is all the rest, of this batch? Bring me a torch; lay it together, and give fire. Cleanse the air. Here was enough to have infected the whole city, if it had not been taken in time! See, see, how our poet's glory shines! Brighter, and brighter! Still it increases! Oh, now,
30 it's at the highest: and, now, it declines as fast! You may see. *Sic transit gloria mundi.*

Kno. There's an emblem for you, son, and your studies!

Cle. Nay, no speech, or act of mine be drawn against such, as profess it worthily. They are not born every year, as an alderman.
35 There goes more to the making of a good poet, than a sheriff, Master Kitely. You look upon me! Though, I live i' the city here, amongst you, I will do more reverence to him when I meet him, than I will to the mayor, out of his year. But, these paper-pedlars! These ink-dabblers! They cannot expect reprehension, or reproach.
40 They have it with the fact.

E. Kn. Sir, you have saved me the labour of a defence.

Cle. It shall be discourse for supper; between your father and me, if he dare undertake me. But, to dispatch away these, you sign o' the soldier, and picture o' the poet (but, both so false, I will not ha'
45 you hanged out at my door till midnight) while we are at supper, you two shall penitently fast it out in my court, without; and, if you will, you may pray there, that we may be so merry within, as to forgive, or forget you, when we come out. Here's a third, because, we tender your safety, shall watch you, he is provided for the
50 purpose. Look to your charge, sir.

Ste. And what shall I do?

Cle. Oh! I had lost a sheep, an' he had not bleated! Why, sir, you shall give Master Downright his cloak: and I will entreat him to take it. A trencher, and a napkin, you shall have, i' the buttery, and
55 keep Cob and his wife company, here; whom I will entreat first to be reconciled: and you to endeavour with your wit, to keep 'em so.

Ste. I'll do my best.

Cob. Why, now I see thou art honest, Tib, I receive thee as my dear, and mortal wife, again.

30 *Sic . . .*: 'So passes away the glory of this world'   32 *emblem*: picture with a motto   34-5 *alderman . . . poet*: a favourite maxim of Jonson's (adapted from Florus) that while new aldermen and sheriffs might be created annually, a poet or a king is born once in an age (*Disc.* 2433)   40 *fact*: deed, crime   43 *sign*: i.e. like a tavern sign   48 *a third*: Formal

Tib. And, I you, as my loving, and obedient husband.   60

Cle. Good complement! It will be their bridal night too. They are
married anew. Come, I conjure the rest, to put off all discontent.
You, Master Downright, your anger; you, Master Knowell, your
cares; Master Kitely, and his wife, their jealousy.

For, I must tell you both, while that is fed,   65
Horns i' the mind are worse than o' the head.

Kit. Sir, thus they go from me, kiss me, sweetheart.
  'See, what a drove of horns fly, in the air,
  Winged with my cleansed, and my credulous breath!
  Watch 'em, suspicious eyes, watch, where they fall.   70
  See, see! On heads, that think th'have none at all!
  Oh, what a plenteous world of this, will come!
  When air rains horns, all may be sure of some.'
I ha' learned so much verse out of a jealous man's part in a play.

Cle. 'Tis well, 'tis well! This night we'll dedicate to friendship,   75
love, and laughter. Master bridegroom, take your bride, and lead;
everyone, a fellow. Here is my mistress, Brainworm! To whom all
my addresses of courtship shall have their reference. Whose
adventures, this day, when our grandchildren shall hear to be made
a fable, I doubt not, but it shall find both spectators, and applause.   80
                                                            [*Exeunt*]

THE END

THE END.

SEJANUS
his Fall

SEIANVS

his

FALL.

A Tragœdie.

Acted, in the yeere 1 6 0 3.
By the K. MAIESTIES
SERVANTS.

The Author B. I.

MART.

*Non hic Centauros, non Gorgonas, Harpyiasq̃
Inuenies: Hominem paginanostra sapit.*

LONDON,
Printed by WILLIAM STANSBY,

M. DC. XVI.

The title-page of the 1616 Folio.

TO THE NO LESS
NOBLE, BY VERTUE,
THAN BLOOD:
Esmé

L. AUBIGNY

MY LORD,

IF ever any ruin were so great, as to survive; I think this be one I
send you: the *Fall of Sejanus*. It is a poem that (if I well remember)
in your Lordship's sight, suffered no less violence from our people
here, than the subject of it did from the rage of the people of Rome;
but, with a different fate, as (I hope) merit: for this hath out-lived
their malice, and begot itself a greater favour than he lost, the love
of good men. Amongst whom, if I make your Lordship the first it
thanks, it is not without a just confession of the bond your benefits
have, and ever shall hold upon me.

Your Lordship's most faithful honourer,

BEN. JONSON.

To the Readers

THE following, and voluntary labours of my friends, prefixed to
my book, have relieved me in much, whereat (without them) I
should necessarily have touched: now, I will only use three or four
short, and needful notes, and so rest.

First, if it be objected, that what I publish is no true poem, in the
strict laws of time, I confess it: as also in the want of a proper
chorus, whose habit, and moods are such, and so difficult, as not

---

5 *L. Aubigny*: Esmé Stuart, Seigneur d'Aubigné (1574-1624), who gave Jonson
hospitality for five years (*Ep.* cxxvii)   9 *violence*: the accusations which led
to Jonson's appearance before the Privy Council   (*To the Readers*) 1 *prefixed*:
the commendatory poems in the quarto text

any, whom I have seen since the Ancients (no, not they who have
most presently affected laws) have yet come in the way of. Nor is it
10 needful, or almost possible, in these our times, and to such auditors,
as commonly things are presented, to observe the old state and
splendour of dramatic poems, with preservation of any popular
delight. But of this I shall take more seasonable cause to speak, in
my observations upon Horace his *Art of Poetry*, which (with the text
15 translated) I intend shortly to publish. In the meantime, if in truth
of argument, dignity of persons, gravity and height of elocution,
fullness and frequency of sentence, I have discharged the other
offices of a tragic writer, let not the absence of these forms be im-
puted to me, wherein I shall give you occasion hereafter (and
20 without my boast) to think I could better prescribe, than omit the
due use, for want of a convenient knowledge.

The next is, lest in some nice nostril, the quotations might
savour affected, I do let you know that I abhor nothing more; and
have only done it to show my integrity in the story, and save myself
25 in those common torturers, that bring all wit to the rack: whose
noses are ever like swine spoiling and rooting up the Muses'
gardens, and their whole bodies, like moles, as blindly working
under earth to cast any, the least, hills upon virtue.

Whereas, they are in Latin and the work in English, it was pre-
30 supposed, none but the learned would take the pains to confer them,
the authors themselves being all in the learned tongues, save one,
with whose English side I have had little to do: to which it may be
required, since I have quoted the page, to name what edition I
followed. *Tacit. Lips.* in 4°. *Antwerp. edit.* 600. *Dio. Folio Hen. Step.*
35 92. For the rest, as *Sueton, Seneca.* etc. the chapter doth sufficiently
direct, or the edition is not varied.

Lastly I would inform you, that this book, in all numbers, is not
the same with that which was acted on the public stage, wherein
a second pen had good share: in place of which I have rather chosen,

---

14 *observations upon Horace*: lost in Jonson's fire   16 *elocution*: 'an applying
of apt wordes and sentences to the matter' (Thomas Wilson)   17 *sentence*: the
sententia of the rhetoricians: aphorisms   22 *nice*: fastidious   31 *save one*: Richard
Greneway's translation of *The Annales of Corn. Tacitus* (1598)   33 *what edition*:
Tacitus, *Opera* (*Justus Lipsius recensuit*, Antwerp, 1600); Dion Cassius, *Romanorum
Historiarium libri XXV* [Lat. couplets by Henri Estienne] (1592). This refers to the
marginal notes in the quarto.   39 *a second pen*: probably Chapman's

to put weaker (and no doubt less pleasing) of mine own, than to 40
defraud so happy a genius of his right, by my loathed usurpation.

Fare you well. And if you read farther of me, and like, I shall not
be afraid of it though you praise me out.

Neque enim mihi cornea fibra est.

But that I should plant my felicity, in your general saying *Good*, 45
or *Well*, etc. were a weakness which the better sort of you might
worthily contemn, if not absolutely hate me for.

BEN. JONSON and no such,

Quem Palma negata macrum, donata reducit opimum.

The Argument

AELIUS Sejanus, son to Sejus Strabo, a gentleman of Rome, and
born at Vulsinium, after his long service in court, first under
Augustus, afterward Tiberius, grew into that favour with the latter,
and won him by those arts, as there wanted nothing but the name
to make him a co-partner of the Empire. Which greatness of his, 5
Drusus, the Emperor's son, not brooking, after many smothered
dislikes (it one day breaking out) the Prince struck him publicly on
the face. To revenge which disgrace, Livia, the wife of Drusus
(being before corrupted by him to her dishonour, and the discovery
of her husband's counsels) Sejanus practiseth with, together with 10
her physician, called Eudemus, and one Lygdus, an eunuch, to
poison Drusus. This their inhuman act having successful and un-
suspected passage, it emboldeneth Sejanus to further and more
insolent projects, even the ambition of the Empire: where finding
the lets he must encounter to be many and hard, in respect of the 15
issue of Germanicus (who were next in hope for the succession) he
deviseth to make Tiberius' self his means, and instils into his ears
many doubts and suspicions, both against the Princes and their
mother Agrippina: which Caesar jealously hearkening to, as

44 Persius, *Sat.* I. 47 ('certainly my innards are not made of horn')   49 Horace,
Epist. II. i. 181 ('whom the denial of the palm sends home lean, its bestowal plump')
(*The Argument*) 10 *practiseth*: plots   15 *lets*: hindrances

20 covetously consenteth to their ruin, and their friends'. In this time,
the better to mature and strengthen his design, Sejanus labours to
marry Livia, and worketh (with all his engine) to remove Tiberius
from the knowledge of public business, with allurements of a quiet
and retired life: the latter of which, Tiberius (out of a proneness to
25 lust, and a desire to hide those unnatural pleasures, which he could
not so publicly practise) embraceth: the former enkindleth his fears,
and there, gives him first cause of doubt, or suspect toward Sejanus.
Against whom he raiseth (in private) a new instrument, one Ser-
torius Macro, and by him underworketh, discovers the other's
30 counsels, his means, his ends, sounds the affections of the Senators,
divides, distracts them: at last, when Sejanus least looketh, and is
most secure (with pretext of doing him an unwonted honour in the
Senate) he trains him from his guards, and with a long doubtful
letter, in one day, hath him suspected, accused, condemned, and
35 torn in pieces, by the rage of the people.

22 *engine*: craft   33 *trains*: entices

The Persons of the Play

Tiberius, *Emperor of Rome*
Drusus senior, *his son*
Agrippina, *widow of Germanicus*
Nero
Drusus junior } *her sons*
Caligula

Supporters of Agrippina
Titius Sabinus
Caius Silius
Sosia, *his wife*
Cremutius Cordus
Lucius Arruntius
Marcus Lepidus
Asinius Gallus
Memmius Regulus

Sertorius Macro
Gracinus Laco

Sejanus
Livia, *wife of Drusus senior*

Supporters of Sejanus
Latiaris
Satrius
Pinnarius Natta
Quintus Haterius
Terentius
Eudemus
Julius Posthumus
Afer
Varro
Fulcinius Trio
Cotta
Rufus
Opsius
Pomponius
Minutius
Sanquinius

Flamen [*priest*]
Tubicines [*trumpeters*]
Tribuni [*tribunes*]
Nuntius [*messenger*]
Servus [*slave*]

Praecones [*heralds*]
Tibicines [*flute-players*]
Lictores [*lictors*]
Ministri [*assistants to
the priest*]

The Scene

Rome

SEJANUS

ACT I

[A state-room in the palace]

Enter Sabinus *and* Silius, [*followed by*] Latiaris

Sab. HAIL, Caius Silius.
Sil.   Titius Sabinus, hail.
You're rarely met in court!
Sab.   Therefore, well met.
Sil. 'Tis true. Indeed, this place is not our sphere.
Sab. No, Silius, we are no good enginers;
We want the fine arts and their thriving use,   5
Should make us graced, or favoured of the times.
We have no shift of faces, no cleft tongues,
No soft and glutinous bodies, that can stick,
Like snails, on painted walls, or, on our breasts,
Creep up, to fall, from that proud height, to which   10
We did by slavery, not by service, climb.
We are no guilty men, and then no great;
We have nor place in court, office in state,
That we can say we owe unto our crimes.
We burn with no black secrets, which can make   15
Us dear to the pale authors; or live feared
Of their still waking jealousies, to raise
Ourselves a fortune by subverting theirs.
We stand not in the lines, that do advance
To that so courted point.

---

4 *enginers*: schemers   7 *shift*: change   17 *jealousies*: suspicions

[*Enter* Satrius *and* Natta *at a distance*]

20 *Sil.*   But yonder lean
 A pair that do.
  (*Sab.*   Good cousin Latiaris.)
  Sil. Satrius Secundus and Pinnarius Natta,
 The great Sejanus' clients: there be two
 Know more than honest counsels, whose close breasts
25 Were they ripped up to light, it would be found
 A poor and idle sin, to which their trunks
 Had not been made fit organs. These can lie,
 Flatter, and swear, forswear, deprave, inform,
 Smile, and betray; make guilty men; then beg
30 The forfeit lives, to get the livings; cut
 Men's throats with whisperings; sell to gaping suitors
 The empty smoke, that flies about the palace;
 Laugh, when their patron laughs; sweat, when he sweats;
 Be hot, and cold with him; change every mood,
35 Habit and garb, as often as he varies;
 Observe him, as his watch observes his clock;
 And true, as turquoise in the dear lord's ring,
 Look well, or ill with him, ready to praise
 His lordship, if he spit, or but piss fair,
40 Have an indifferent stool, or break wind well,
 Nothing can scape their catch.
  Sab.   Alas! These things
 Deserve no note, conferred with other vile
 And filthier flatteries, that corrupt the times,
 When, not alone our gentries chief are fain
45 To make their safety from such sordid acts,
 But all our consuls, and no little part
 Of such as have been praetors, yea, the most
 Of senators* (that else not use their voices)

---

* *Pedarii* [the section of the Senate with a silent vote]

---

  20 *lean*: have a tendency 29 *beg*: i.e. as a reward for informing 35 *garb*:
demeanor 36 *watch*: the clumsy Elizabethan pocket-watch had to be regulated
by a public clock 37 *turquoise*: thought to change colour when the wearer was
not well

Start up in public Senate, and there strive
Who shall propound most abject things, and base,   50
So much, as oft Tiberius hath been heard,
Leaving the court, to cry, O race of men,
Prepared for servitude! Which showed that he
Who least the public liberty could like,
As loathly brooked their flat servility.   55
  Sil. Well, all is worthy of us, were it more,
Who with our riots, pride, and civil hate,
Have so provoked the justice of the gods.
We, that (within these fourscore years) were born
Free, equal lords of the triumphed world,   60
And knew no masters, but affections,
To which betraying first our liberties,
We since became the slaves to one man's lusts;
And now to many: every ministering spy
That will accuse and swear, is lord of you,   65
Of me, of all, our fortunes and our lives.
Our looks are called to question, and our words,
How innocent soever, are made crimes;
We shall not shortly dare to tell our dreams,
Or think, but 'twill be treason.
  Sab.   Tyrant's arts   70
Are to give flatterers, grace; accusers, power;
That those may seem to kill whom they devour.

[*Enter* Cordus, Arruntius]

Now, good Cremutius Cordus.
  Cor.   Hail to your lordship.
  Nat. Who's that salutes your cousin?   (*They whisper*)
  Lat.   'Tis one Cordus,
A gentleman of Rome: one, that has writ   75
Annals of late, they say, and very well.
  Nat. Annals? Of what times?
  Lat.   I think of Pompey's,
And Caius Caesar's; and so down to these.
  Nat. How stands he affected to the present state?

60 *triumphed*: conquered

80 Is he or Drusian? Or Germanican?
Or ours? Or neutral?
    Lat.   I know him not so far.
    Nat. Those times are somewhat queasy to be touched.
Have you or seen, or heard part of his work?
    Lat. Not I, he means they shall be public shortly.
    Nat. Oh, Cordus do you call him?
    Lat.   Aye.
85   *Sab.*   But these our times
Are not the same, Arruntius.
    Arr.   Times? The men,
The men are not the same: 'tis we are base,
Poor and degenerate from the exalted strain
Of our great fathers. Where is now the soul
90 Of godlike Cato? He, that durst be good,
When Caesar durst be evil; and had power,
As not to live his slave, to die his master.
Or where the constant Brutus, that (being proof
Against all charm of benefits) did strike
95 So brave a blow into the monster's heart
That sought unkindly to captive his country?
Oh, they are fled the light. Those mighty spirits
Lie raked up with their ashes in their urns,
And not a spark of their eternal fire
100 Glows in a present bosom. All's but blaze,
Flashes, and smoke, wherewith we labour so,
There's nothing Roman in us; nothing good,
Gallant or great: 'tis true, that Cordus says,
'Brave Cassius was the last of all that race'.
               (Drusus *passeth by* [*attended by* Haterius])
    Sab. Stand by, lord Drusus.
105   *Hat.*   The Emperor's son, give place.
    Sil. I like the prince well.
    Arr.   A riotous youth,
There's little hope of him.
    Sab.   That fault his age
Will, as it grows, correct. Methinks he bears

    96 *unkindly*: unnaturally   *captive*: make captive

Himself each day more nobly than other,
And wins no less on men's affections   110
Than doth his father lose. Believe me, I love him,
And chiefly for opposing to Sejanus.

  Sil. And I, for gracing his young kinsmen so,
The sons of Prince Germanicus. It shows
A gallant clearness in him, a straight mind,   115
That envies not, in them, their father's name.

  Arr. His name was, while he lived, above all envy;
And being dead, without it. O, that man!
If there were seeds of the old virtue left,
They lived in him.

  Sil.   He had the fruits, Arruntius,   120
More than the seeds. Sabinus and myself
Had means to know him, within; and can report him.
We were his followers (he would call us friends).
He was a man most like to virtue; in all,
And every action, nearer to the gods   125
Than men, in nature; of a body as fair
As was his mind; and no less reverend
In face, than fame. He could so use his state,
Tempering his greatness with his gravity,
As it avoided all self-love in him,   130
And spite in others. What his funerals lacked
In images and pomp, they had supplied
With honourable sorrow, soldiers' sadness,
A kind of silent mourning, such as men
(Who know no tears, but from their captives) use   135
To show in so great losses.

  Cor.   I thought once,
Considering their forms, age, manner of deaths,
The nearness of the places where they fell,
To have paralleled him with great Alexander:
For both were of best feature, of high race,   140
Yeared but to thirty, and, in foreign lands,
By their own people, alike made away.

---

  132 *images*: painted masks of the deceased and his ancestors   140 *feature*:
appearance (not the face alone)   *race*: family

Sab. I know not, for his death, how you might wrest it:
But, for his life, it did as much disdain
145 Comparison with that voluptuous, rash,
Giddy, and drunken Macedon's, as mine
Doth with my bondman's. All the good in him,
(His valour and his fortune) he made his;
But he had other touches of late Romans,
150 That more did speak him: Pompey's dignity,
The innocence of Cato, Caesar's spirit,
Wise Brutus' temperance, and every virtue,
Which, parted unto others, gave them name,
Flowed mixed in him. He was the soul of goodness:
155 And all our praises of him are like streams
Drawn from a spring, that still rise full, and leave
The part remaining greatest.
  Arr.   I am sure
He was too great for us, and that they knew
Who did remove him hence.
  Sab.   When men grow fast
160 Honoured and loved, there is a trick in state
(Which jealous princes never fail to use)
How to decline that growth with fair pretext,
And honourable colours of employment,
Either by embassy, the war, or such,
165 To shift them forth into another air,
Where they may purge and lessen; so was he:
And had his seconds there, sent by Tiberius,
And his more subtle dam, to discontent him;
To breed and cherish mutinies; detract
170 His greatest actions; give audacious check
To his commands; and work to put him out
In open act of treason. All which snares
When his wise cares prevented, a fine poison
Was thought on, to mature their practices.
  Cor. Here comes Sejanus.

143 *wrest*: interpret (with implication of distortion) 153 *parted*: distributed
163 *colours*: outward appearances 167 *seconds*: subordinates 168 *dam*: Livia
173 *prevented*: anticipated

Sil.   Now observe the stoops,   175
The bendings and the falls.
    Arr.   Most creeping base!
        (Sejanus, Satrius, Terentius, etc., *pass over the stage*)
    Sej. I note 'em well: no more. Say you.
    Sat.   My lord,
There is a gentleman of Rome would buy——
    Sej. How call you him you talked with?
    Sat.   Please your lordship,
It is Eudemus, the physician   180
To Livia, Drusus's wife.
    Sej.   On with your suit.
Would buy, you said——
    Sat.   A tribune's place, my lord.
    Sej. What will he give?
    Sat.   Fifty *sestertia*.
    Sej. Livia's physician, say you, is that fellow?
    Sat. It is, my lord; your lordship's answer?
    Sej.   To what?   185
    Sat. The place, my lord. 'Tis for a gentleman,
Your lordship will well like of, when you see him;
And one you may make yours, by the grant.
    Sej. Well, let him bring his money, and his name.
    Sat. Thank your lordship. He shall, my lord.
    Sej.   Come hither.   190
Know you this same Eudemus? Is he learned?
    Sat. Reputed so, my lord: and of deep practice.
    Sej. Bring him in, to me, in the gallery;
And take you cause, to leave us there, together:
I would confer with him, about a grief.——On.   190
        [*Exeunt* Sejanus, Satrius, Terentius, etc.]
    Arr. So, yet! Another? Yet? O desperate state
Of grovelling honour! Seest thou this, O sun,
And do we see thee after? Methinks, day
Should lose his light, when men do lose their shames,
And, for the empty circumstance of life,   200
Betray their cause of living.

  175 *stoops*: bows   192 *of deep practice*: expert in intrigue   195 *grief*: illness

    Sil.   Nothing so
Sejanus can repair, if Jove should ruin.
He is the now court-god; and well applied
With sacrifice of knees, of crooks and cringe,
205 He will do more than all the house of heaven
Can for a thousand hecatombs. 'Tis he
Makes us our day or night; Hell and Elysium
Are in his look: we talk of Rhadamanth,
Furies and fire-brands; but 'tis his frown
210 That is all these, where, on the adverse part,
His smile is more, than e'er yet poets feigned
Of bliss, and shades, nectar——
    Arr.   A serving boy?
I knew him, at Caius' trencher, when for hire,
He prostituted his abused body
215 To that great gourmand, fat Apicius;
And was the noted pathic of the time.
    Sab. And, now, the second face of the whole world.
The partner of the empire, hath his image
Reared equal with Tiberius, borne in ensigns,
220 Commands, disposes every dignity,
Centurions, tribunes, heads of provinces,
Praetors and consuls, all that heretofore
Rome's general suffrage gave, is now his sale.
The gain, or rather spoil, of all the earth,
One, and his house, receives.
225   *Sil.*   He hath of late
Made him a strength too, strangely, by reducing
All the praetorian bands into one camp,
Which he commands: pretending that the soldier
By living loose and scattered, fell to riot;
230 And that if any sudden enterprise
Should be attempted, their united strength
Would be far more, than severed; and their life
More strict, if from the city more removed.
    Sab. Where now he builds what kind of forts he please,

208 *Rhadamanth*: one of the judges of the underworld   215 *Apicius*: the most
celebrated epicure of his age   216 *pathic*: catamite

Is hard to court the soldier, by his name,   235
Woos, feasts the chiefest men of action,
Whose wants, not loves, compel them to be his.
And, though he ne'er were liberal by kind,
Yet to his own dark ends he's most profuse,
Lavish, and letting fly, he cares not what   240
To his ambition.
    Arr.   Yet, hath he ambition?
Is there that step in state can make him higher?
Or more? Or anything he is, but less?
    Sil. Nothing, but Emperor.
    Arr.   The name Tiberius
I hope, will keep; how e'er he hath foregone   245
The dignity and power.
    Sil.   Sure, while he lives.
    Arr. And dead, it comes to Drusus. Should he fail,
To the brave issue of Germanicus;
And they are three: too many (ha?) for him
To have a plot upon?
    Sab.   I do not know   250
The heart of his designs; but, sure, their face
Looks farther than the present.
    Arr.   By the gods,
If I could guess he had but such a thought,
My sword should cleave him down from head to heart,
But I would find it out: and with my hand   255
I'd hurl his panting brain about the air,
In mites, as small as *atomi*, to undo
The knotted bed——
    Sab.   You are observed, Arruntius.
    Arr. Death! I dare tell him so; and all his spies:
                        (*He turns to* Sejanus' *clients*)
You, sir, I would, do you look? And you.
    Sab.   Forbear.   [*They retire*] 260

Enter Satrius, Eudemus

238 *kind*: nature

Sat. Here, he will instant be; let's walk a turn.
You're in a muse, Eudemus?

　　Eud.　　　　　　　　　Not I, sir.
I wonder he should mark me out so! Well,
Jove and Apollo form it for the best.

265　*Sat.* Your fortune's made unto you now, Eudemus,
If you can but lay hold upon the means;
Do but observe his humour, and——believe it——
He's the noblest Roman, where he takes——
Here comes his lordship.

　　Sej.　　　　　　　　　Now, good Satrius.

　　Sat. This is the gentleman, my lord.

270　*Sej.*　　　　　　　　　　Is this?
Give me your hand, we must be more acquainted.
Report, sir, hath spoke out your art and learning:
And I am glad I have so needful cause,
(However in itself painful and hard)

275 To make me known to so great virtue. Look,
Who's that, Satrius?　　　　　　　　[*Exit* Satrius]

　　　　　　　　　I have a grief, sir,
That will desire your help. Your name's Eudemus?

　　Eud. Yes.

　　Sej.　　Sir?

　　Eud.　　　　　It is, my lord.

　　Sej.　　　　　　　　　I hear you are
Physician to Livia, the princess?

280　*Eud.* I minister unto her, my good lord.

　　Sej. You minister to a royal lady, then.

　　Eud. She is, my lord, and fair.

　　Sej.　　　　　　　　　That's understood
Of all their sex, who are, or would be so;
And those that would be, physic soon can make 'em:

285 For those that are, their beauties fear no colours.

　　Eud. Your lordship is conceited.

　　Sej.　　　　　　　　　Sir, you know it.
And can (if need be) read a learned lecture,
On this and other secrets. Pray you tell me,

285 *colours*: II. 60–4 (with quibble on 'fear no foe')　　　286 *conceited*: witty

What more of ladies, besides Livia,
Have you your patients?
 Eud.   Many, my good lord.   290
The great Augusta, Urgulania,
Mutilia Prisca and Plancina, divers——
 Sej. And, all these tell you the particulars
Of every several grief? How first it grew,
And then increased, what action caused that;   295
What passion that: and answer to each point
That you will put 'em.
 Eud.   Else, my lord, we know not
How to prescribe the remedies.
 Sej.   Go to,
You're a subtle nation, you physicians!
And grown the only cabinets, in court,   300
To ladies' privacies. Faith, which of these
Is the most pleasant lady, in her physic?
Come, you are modest now.
 Eud.   'Tis fit, my lord.
 Sej. Why, sir, I do not ask you of their urines,
Whose smell's most violet? Or whose siege is best? 305
Or who makes hardest faces on her stool?
Which lady sleeps with her own face a nights?
Which puts her teeth off, with her clothes, in court?
Or which her hair? Which her complexion?
And in which box she puts it? These were questions 310
That might, perhaps, have put your gravity
To some defence of blush. But, I enquired,
Which was the wittiest? Merriest? Wantonest?
Harmless interrogatories, but conceits.
Methinks Augusta should be most perverse,   315
And froward in her fit?
 Eud.   She's so, my lord.
 Sej. I knew it. And Mutilia the most jocund?
 Eud. 'Tis very true, my lord.
 Sej.   And why would you
Conceal this from me, now? Come, what's Livia?

---

305 *siege*: evacuation   314 *conceits*: fancies, whims   316 *froward*: refractory

320 I know, she's quick, and quaintly spirited,
And will have strange thoughts, when she's at leisure;
She tells 'em all to you?
  Eud.   My noblest lord,
He breathes not in the empire, or on earth,
Whom I would be ambitious to serve
325 (In any act, that may preserve mine honour)
Before your lordship.
  Sej.   Sir, you can lose no honour,
By trusting aught to me. The coarsest act
Done to my service, I can so requite,
As all the world shall style it honourable:
330 Your idle, virtuous definitions
Keep honour poor, and are as scorned as vain:
Those deeds breathe honour, that do suck in gain.
  Eud. But, good my lord, if I should thus betray
The counsels of my patient, and a lady's
335 Of her high place and worth, what might your lordship,
(Who presently are to trust me with your own)
Judge of my faith?
  Sej.   Only the best, I swear.
Say now, that I should utter you my grief,
And with it, the true cause; that it were love;
340 And love to Livia: you should tell her this?
Should she suspect your faith? I would you could
Tell me as much, from her; see if my brain
Could be turned jealous.
  Eud.   Happily, my lord,
I could, in time, tell you as much, and more;
345 So I might safely promise but the first,
To her, from you.
  Sej.   As safely, my Eudemus,
(I now dare call thee so) as I have put
The secret into thee.
  Eud.   My lord——
  Sej.   Protest not.
Thy looks are vows to me, use only speed,

343 *jealous*: suspicious   *Happily*: perchance

And but affect her with Sejanus' love,   350
Thou art a man, made to make consuls. Go.
   Eud. My lord, I'll promise you a private meeting
This day, together.
     Sej.   Canst thou?
     Eud.   Yes.
     Sej.   The place?
   Eud. My gardens, whither I shall fetch your lordship.
   Sej. Let me adore my Aesculapius.   355
Why, this indeed is physic! And outspeaks
The knowledge of cheap drugs or any use
Can be made out of it! More comforting
Than all your opiates, juleps, apozemes,
Magistral syrups, or—begone, my friend,   360
Not barely styled, but created so;
Expect things, greater than thy largest hopes,
To overtake thee: Fortune shall be taught
To know how ill she hath deserved thus long,
To come behind thy wishes. Go, and speed.   [*Exit* Eudemus] 365
Ambition makes more trusty slaves than need.
These fellows, by the favour of their art,
Have, still, the means to tempt, oft-times, the power.
If Livia will be now corrupted, then
Thou hast the way, Sejanus, to work out   370
His secrets, who (thou knowest) endures thee not,
Her husband Drusus: and to work against them.
Prosper it, Pallas, thou, that betterest wit;
For Venus hath the smallest share in it.

Enter Tiberius, Drusus, Haterius

   Tib. (*One kneels to him*) We not endure these flatteries, let him
     stand;   375
Our empire, ensigns, axes, rods, and state
Take not away our human nature from us:
Look up, on us, and fall before the gods.

---

355 *Aesculapius*: god of medicine   359 *apozemes*: decoctions or infusions
376 *axes, rods*: the *fasces*, bundle of rods with axes in the middle, carried before the
chief magistrate by the lictors (III. 470)

 Sej. How like a god speaks Caesar!

 Arr.   There, observe!
380 He can endure that second, that's no flattery.
Oh, what is it, proud slime will not believe
Of his own worth, to hear it equal praised
Thus with the gods?

 Cor.   He did not hear it, sir.

 Arr. He did not? Tut, he must not, we think meanly.
385 'Tis your most courtly, known confederacy,
To have your private parasite redeem
What he, in public subtlety, will lose
To making him a name.

 Hat. [*Giving him letters*] Right mighty lord——

 Tib. We must make up our ears, 'gainst these assaults
390 Of charming tongues; we pray you use no more
These contumelies to us: style not us
Or lord, or mighty, who profess our self
The servant of the Senate, and are proud
To enjoy them our good, just and favouring lords.

 Cor. Rarely dissembled.

395 *Arr.*   Prince-like, to the life.

 Sab. When power, that may command, so much descends,
Their bondage, whom it stoops to, it intends.

 Tib. Whence are these letters?

 Hat.   From the Senate.

 Tib.   So.

          [*Latiarus gives him letters*]
Whence these?

 Lat. From thence too.

 Tib.   Are they sitting, now?

 Lat. They stay thy answer, Caesar.

400 *Sil.*   If this man
Had but a mind allied unto his words,
How blessed a fate were it to us, and Rome?
We could not think that state for which to change,
Although the aim were our old liberty:
405 The ghosts of those that fell for that, would grieve

 397 *intends*: aims at

Their bodies lived not, now, again to serve.
Men are deceived, who think there can be thrall
Beneath a virtuous prince. Wished liberty
Ne'er lovelier looks, than under such a crown.
But when his grace is merely but lip-good,   410
And that no longer than he airs himself
Abroad in public, there, to seem to shun
The strokes and stripes of flatterers, which within
Are lechery unto him, and so feed
His brutish sense with their afflicting sound,   415
As (dead to virtue) he permits himself
Be carried like a pitcher, by the ears,
To every act of vice: this is a case
Deserves our fear, and doth presage the nigh
And close approach of blood and tyranny.   420
Flattery is midwife unto princes' rage:
And nothing sooner, doth help forth a tyrant,
Than that, and whisperers' grace, who have the time,
The place, the power, to make all men offenders.
   Arr. He should be told this: and be bid dissemble   425
With fools and blind men: we that know the evil,
Should hunt the palace rats, or give them bane;
Fright hence these worse than ravens, that devour
The quick, where they but prey upon the dead:
He shall be told it.
   Sab.   Stay, Arruntius,   430
We must abide our opportunity:
And practise what is fit, as what is needful.
It is not safe to enforce a sovereign's ear:
Princes hear well, if they at all will hear.
   Arr. Ha? Say you so? Well. In the meantime, Jove,   435
(Say not, but I do call upon thee now.)
Of all wild beasts, preserve me from a tyrant;
And of all tame, a flatterer.
   Sil.   'Tis well prayed.
   Tib. Return the lords this voice, we are their creature:
And it is fit, a good and honest prince,   440

423 *whisperers' grace*: tolerance of informers   427 *bane*: ratsbane (arsenic)

Whom they, out of their bounty, have instructed
With so dilate and absolute a power,
Should owe the office of it to their service,
And good of all and every citizen.
445 Nor shall it e'er repent us, to have wished
The Senate just, and favouring lords unto us,
Since their free loves do yield no less defence
To a prince's state, than his own innocence.
Say then, there can be nothing in their thought
450 Shall want to please us, that hath pleased them;
Our suffrage rather shall prevent, than stay
Behind their wills: 'tis empire, to obey
Where such, so great, so grave, so good determine.
Yet, for the suit of Spain, to erect a temple
455 In honour of our mother and ourself,
We must (with pardon of the Senate) not
Assent thereto. Their lordships may object
Our not denying the same late request
Unto the Asian cities: we desire
460 That our defence, for suffering that, be known
In these brief reasons, with our after purpose.
Since deified Augustus hindered not
A temple to be built, at Pergamum,
In honour of himself, and sacred Rome,
465 We, that have all his deeds and words observed
Ever, in place of laws, the rather followed
That pleasing precedent, because, with ours,
The Senate's reverence also, there, was joined.
But as to have once received it may deserve
470 The gain of pardon, so, to be adored
With the continued style, and note of gods,
Through all the provinces, were wild ambition,
And no less pride. Yea, even Augustus' name
Would early vanish, should it be profaned
475 With such promiscuous flatteries. For our part,
We here protest it, and are covetous

441 *instructed*: provided   442 *dilate*: extended   451 *prevent*: anticipate
471 *note*: repute

Posterity should know it, we are mortal;
And can but deeds of men: 'twere glory enough,
Could we be truly a prince. And, they shall add
Abounding grace unto our memory,   480
That shall report us worthy our forefathers,
Careful of your affairs, constant in dangers,
And not afraid of any private frown
For public good. These things shall be to us
Temples and statues, reared in your minds,   485
The fairest and most during imagery:
For those of stone, or brass, if they become
Odious in judgement of posterity,
Are more contemned, as dying sepulchres,
Than ta'en for living monuments. We then   490
Make here our suit, alike to gods, and men,
The one, until the period of our race,
To inspire us with a free, and quiet mind,
Discerning both divine and human laws;
The other, to vouchsafe us after death,   495
An honourable mention and fair praise,
To accompany our actions and our name:
The rest of greatness princes may command,
And (therefore) may neglect, only, a long,
A lasting, high, and happy memory   500
They should, without being satisfied, pursue.
Contempt of fame begets contempt of virtue.
  Nat. Rare!
  Sat.   Most divine!
  Sej.   The oracles are ceased,
That only Caesar, with their tongue, might speak.
  Arr. Let me be gone, most felt, and open this!   505
  Cor. Stay.
  Arr.   What? To hear more cunning, and fine words,
With their sound flattered, ere their sense be meant?
  Tib. Their choice of Antium, there to place the gift*

---

* *Fortuna equestris* [an equestrian statue to the Goddess Fortuna]

478 *can*: are capable of   492 *period of our race*: end of our life

Vowed to the goddess, for our mother's health,
510 We will the Senate know, we fairly like;
As also, of their grant to Lepidus,
For his repairing the Aemilian place,
And restoration of those monuments.
Their grace too in confining of Silanus
515 To the other isle Cythera, at the suit
Of his religious sister, much commends
Their policy, so tempered with their mercy.
But, for the honours, which they have decreed
To our Sejanus, to advance his statue
520 In Pompey's theatre (whose ruining fire
His vigilance and labour kept restrained
In that one loss) they have, therein, outgone
Their own great wisdoms, by their skilful choice,
And placing of their bounties, on a man
525 Whose merit more adorns the dignity
Than that can him: and gives a benefit,
In taking, greater, than it can receive.
Blush not, Sejanus, thou great aid of Rome,
Associate of our labours, our chief helper,
530 Let us not force thy simple modesty
With offering at thy praise, for more we cannot,
Since there's no voice can take it. No man, here,
Receive our speeches, as hyperboles;
For we are far from flattering our friend,
535 (Let envy know) as from the need to flatter.
Nor let them ask the causes of our praise;
Princes have still their grounds reared with themselves,
Above the poor low flats of common men,
And, who will search the reasons of their acts,
540 Must stand on equal bases. Lead, away.
Our loves unto the Senate.   [*Exeunt* Tiberius, Sejanus, etc.]
   Arr.   Caesar.
   Sab.   Peace.
   Cor. Great Pompey's theatre was never ruined
Till now, that proud Sejanus hath a statue

519 *advance*: erect

Reared on his ashes.

   Arr.   Place the shame of soldiers,
Above the best of generals? Crack the world!   545
And bruise the name of Romans into dust,
Ere we behold it!

   Sil.   Check your passion;
Lord Drusus tarries.

   Dru.   Is my father mad?
Weary of life and rule, lords? Thus to heave
An idol up with praise! Make him his mate!   550
His rival in the empire!

   Arr.   O, good prince!

   Dru. Allow him statues? Titles? Honours? Such,
As he himself refuseth?

   Arr.   Brave, brave Drusus!

   Dru. The first ascents to sovereignty are hard,
But, entered once, there never wants or means,   555
Or ministers, to help the aspirer on.

   Arr. True, gallant Drusus.

   Dru.   We must shortly pray
To modesty, that he will rest contented——

   Arr. Aye, where he is, and not write emperor.

          Sejanus *enters, followed with clients*

   Sej. There is your bill, and yours; bring you your man: 560
I have moved for you, too, Latiaris.

   Dru.   What?
Is your vast greatness grown so blindly bold,
That you will over us?

   Sej.   Why, then give way.

   Dru. Give way, Colossus? Do you lift? Advance you?
Take that.   (Drusus *strikes him*)

   Arr.   Good! Brave! Excellent brave prince!   565

   Dru. Nay, come, approach. What? Stand you off? At gaze?
It looks too full of death for thy cold spirits.
Avoid mine eye, dull camel, or my sword
Shall make thy bravery fitter for a grave,
Than for a triumph. I'll advance a statue,   570

   551 *rival*: partner   559 *write*: designate himself   564 *lift*: rise up

O'your own bulk; but it shall be on the cross:
Where I will nail your pride, at breadth, and length,
And crack those sinews, which are yet but stretched
With your swollen fortune's rage.
  Arr.   A noble prince!
575 *All.* A Castor, a Castor, a Castor, a Castor!
            [Exeunt all but Sejanus]
  Sej. He that, with such wrong moved, can bear it through
With patience, and an even mind, knows how
To turn it back. Wrath, covered, carries fate:
Revenge is lost, if I profess my hate.
580 What was my practice late, I'll now pursue
As my fell justice. This hath styled it new.   *[Exit]*

Chorus——*of musicians*

ACT II

[The garden of Eudemus]

Enter Sejanus, Livia, Eudemus

  Sej. Physician, thou art worthy of a province,
For the great favours done unto our loves;
And, but that greatest Livia bears a part
In the requital of thy services,
5 I should alone despair of aught like means,
To give them worthy satisfaction.
  Liv. Eudemus (I will see it) shall receive
A fit and full reward for his large merit.
But for this potion, we intend to Drusus,
10 (No more our husband, now) whom shall we choose
As the most apt and abled instrument,
To minister it to him?
  Eud.   I say, Lygdus.

575 *Castor*: a celebrated gladiator of the day who had once struck a knight; also a
cognomen of Drusus because of his violence 580 *practice*: treachery

Sej. Lygdus? What's he?
Liv.   An eunuch Drusus loves.
Eud. Aye, and his cup-bearer.
Sej.   Name not a second.
If Drusus love him, and he have that place,   15
We cannot think a fitter.
Eud.   True, my lord,
For free access and trust are two main aids.
  Sej. Skilful physician!
Liv.   But he must be wrought
To the undertaking, with some laboured art.
  Sej. Is he ambitious?
Liv.   No.
Sej.   Or covetous?   20
Liv. Neither.
Eud.   Yet, gold is a good general charm.
  Sej. What is he then?
Liv.   Faith, only wanton, light.
  Sej. How! Is he young? And fair?
Eud.   A delicate youth.
  Sej. Send him to me, I'll work him. Royal lady,
Though I have loved you long, and with that height   25
Of zeal and duty (like the fire, which more
It mounts, it trembles) thinking naught could add
Unto the fervour, which your eye had kindled;
Yet, now I see your wisdom, judgement, strength,
Quickness, and will, to apprehend the means   30
To your own good and greatness, I protest
Myself through rarefied, and turned all flame
In your affection: such a spirit as yours,
Was not created for the idle second
To a poor flash, as Drusus; but to shine   35
Bright, as the moon, among the lesser lights,
And share the sovereignty of all the world.
Then Livia triumphs in her proper sphere,
When she and her Sejanus shall divide
The name of Caesar; and Augusta's star   40
Be dimmed with glory of a brighter beam:

When Agrippina's fires are quite extinct,
And the scarce-seen Tiberius borrows all
His little light from us, whose folded arms
45 Shall make one perfect orb. [*Knocking within*] Who's that? Eudemus,
Look, 'tis not Drusus? [*Exit* Eudemus] Lady, do not fear.
   Liv. Not I, my lord. My fear and love of him
Left me at once.
   Sej.   Illustrious lady! Stay——
   Eud. [*Within*] I'll tell his lordship.

[*Enter* Eudemus]

   Sej.   Who is it, Eudemus?
50   *Eud.* One of your lordship's servants, brings you word
The Emperor hath sent for you.
   Sej.   Oh! Where is he?
With your fair leave, dear Princess. I'll but ask
A question, and return.   (*He goes out*)
   Eud.   Fortunate Princess!
How are you blessed in the fruition
55 Of this unequalled man, this soul of Rome,
The empire's life, and voice of Caesar's world!
   Liv. So blessed, my Eudemus, as to know
The bliss I have, with what I ought to owe
The means that wrought it. How do I look today?
60   *Eud.* Excellent clear, believe it. This same fucus
Was well laid on.
   Liv.   Methinks, 'tis here not white.
   Eud. Lend me your scarlet, lady. 'Tis the sun
Hath given some little taint unto the ceruse,
You should have used of the white oil I gave you.
                         [*He paints her cheeks*]
65 Sejanus, for your love! His very name
Commandeth above Cupid, or his shafts——
   (*Liv.* Nay, now you have made it worse.
   Eud.   I'll help it straight.)
And, but pronounced, is a sufficient charm

60 *fucus*: cosmetic paint   63 *ceruse*: cosmetic of white lead

Against all rumour; and of absolute power
To satisfy for any lady's honour.   70
    (*Liv.* What do you now, Eudemus?
    Eud.   Make a light fucus,
To touch you o'er withal.) Honoured Sejanus!
What act (though ne'er so strange and insolent)
But that addition will at least bear out,
If't do not expiate?
    Liv.   Here, good physician.   75
    Eud. I like this study to preserve the love
Of such a man, that comes not every hour
To greet the world. 'Tis now well, lady, you should
Use of the dentifrice I prescribed you too,
To clear your teeth, and the prepared pomatum,   80
To smooth the skin: a lady cannot be
Too curious of her form, that still would hold
The heart of such a person, made her captive,
As you have his: who, to endear him more
In your clear eye, hath put away his wife,   85
The trouble of his bed, and your delights,
Fair Apicata, and made spacious room
To your new pleasures.
    Liv.   Have not we returned
That, with our hate of Drusus, and discovery
Of all his counsels?
    Eud.   Yes, and wisely, lady,   90
The ages that succeed, and stand far off
To gaze at your high prudence, shall admire
And reckon it an act, without your sex:
It hath that rare appearance. Some will think
Your fortune could not yield a deeper sound,   95
Than mixed with Drusus; but, when they shall hear
That, and the thunder of Sejanus meet,
Sejanus, whose high name doth strike the stars,
And rings about the concave, great Sejanus,
Whose glories, style, and titles are himself,   100

----

74 *addition*: title   80 *pomatum*: scented ointment   82 *curious*: studious
93 *without*: beyond

The often iterating of Sejanus:
They then will lose their thoughts, and be ashamed
To take acquaintance of them.

[*Enter* Sejanus]

 Sej.   I must make
A rude departure, lady. Caesar sends
105 With all his haste both of command, and prayer.
Be resolute in our plot; you have my soul,
As certain yours, as it is my body's.
And, wise physician, so prepare the poison
As you may lay the subtle operation
110 Upon some natural disease of his.
Your eunuch send to me. I kiss your hands,
Glory of ladies, and commend my love
To your best faith and memory.
 Liv.   My lord,
I shall but change your words. Farewell. Yet, this
115 Remember for your heed, he loves you not;
You know what I have told you: his designs
Are full of grudge, and danger. We must use
More than a common speed.
 Sej.   Excellent lady,
How you do fire my blood!
 Liv.   Well, you must go?
120 The thoughts be best, are least set forth to show. [*Exit* Sejanus]
 Eud. When will you take some physic, lady?
 Liv.   When
I shall, Eudemus: but let Drusus' drug
Be first prepared.
 Eud. Were Lygdus made, that's done;
I have it ready. And tomorrow morning,
125 I'll send you a perfume, first to resolve,
And procure sweat, and then prepare a bath
To cleanse and clear the cutis; against when,

---

 114 *change*: exchange, give back 123 *made*: prepared, primed 127 *cutis*: skin

I'll have an excellent new fucus made,
Resistive 'gainst the sun, the rain, or wind,
Which you shall lay on with a breath, or oil,   130
As you best like, and last some fourteen hours.
This change came timely, lady, for your health;
And the restoring your complexion,
Which Drusus' choler had almost burnt up:
Wherein your fortune hath prescribed you better   135
Than art could do.

    Liv.   Thanks, good physician,
I'll use my fortune (you shall see) with reverence.
Is my coach ready?

    Eud.   It attends your highness.   [*Exeunt*]

[A room in the palace]

Enter Sejanus

  Sej. If this be not revenge, when I have done
And made it perfect, let Egyptian slaves,   140
Parthians, and barefoot Hebrews brand my face,
And print my body full of injuries.
Thou lost thyself, child Drusus, when thou thoughtst
Thou couldst outskip my vengeance: or outstand
The power I had to crush thee into air.   145
Thy follies now shall taste what kind of man
They have provoked, and this thy father's house
Crack in the flame of my incensed rage,
Whose fury shall admit no shame, or mean.
Adultery? It is the lightest ill,   150
I will commit. A race of wicked acts
Shall flow out of my anger, and o'erspread
The world's wide face, which no posterity
Shall e'er approve, nor yet keep silent: things,
That for their cunning, close, and cruel mark,   155
Thy father would wish his; and shall (perhaps)
Carry the empty name, but we the prize.
On then, my soul, and start not in thy course;

140–1 *Egyptian . . . Parthians . . . Hebrews*: symbols of oriental subjection

Though heaven drop sulphur, and hell belch out fire,
160 Laugh at the idle terrors. Tell proud Jove,
Between his power and thine, there is no odds.
'Twas only fear first in the world made gods.

Enter Tiberius [*attended*]

   Tib. Is yet Sejanus come?
   Sej.   He's here, dread Caesar.
   Tib. Let all depart that chamber, and the next:
                         [*Exeunt* attendants]
165 Sit down, my comfort. When the master-prince
Of all the world, Sejanus, saith, he fears;
Is it not fatal?
   Sej.   Yes, to those are feared.
   Tib. And not to him?
   Sej.   Not if he wisely turn
That part of fate he holdeth, first on them.
170   *Tib.* That nature, blood, and laws of kind forbid.
   Sej. Do policy and state forbid it?
   Tib.   No.
   Sej. The rest of poor respects, then, let go by:
State is enough to make the act just, them guilty.
   Tib. Long hate pursues such acts.
   Sej.   Whom hatred frights,
Let him not dream on sovereignty.
175   *Tib.*   Are rites
Of faith, love, piety, to be trod down?
Forgotten? And made vain?
   Sej.   All for a crown.
The prince, who shames a tyrant's name to bear,
Shall never dare do anything, but fear;
180 All the command of sceptres quite doth perish
If it begin religious thoughts to cherish:
Whole empires fall, swayed by those nice respects.
It is the licence of dark deeds protects
Even states most hated: when no laws resist
185 The sword, but that it acteth what it list.

   170 *kind*: kinship   171 *state*: reasons of state

Tib. Yet so, we may do all things cruelly,
Not safely:
    Sej.   Yes, and do them thoroughly.
    Tib. Knows yet, Sejanus, whom we point at?
    Sej.   Aye,
Or else my thought, my sense, or both do err:
'Tis Agrippina?
    Tib.   She; and her proud race.   190
    Sej. Proud? Dangerous, Caesar. For in them apace
The father's spirit shoots up. Germanicus
Lives in their looks, their gait, their form, to upbraid us
With his close death, if not revenge the same.
    Tib. The act's not known.
    Sej.   Not proved. But whispering fame 195
Knowledge, and proof doth to the jealous give,
Who, than to fail, would their own thought believe.
It is not safe, the children draw long breath,
That are provoked by a parent's death.
    Tib. It is as dangerous, to make them hence,   200
If nothing but their birth be their offence.
    Sej. Stay, till they strike at Caesar: then their crime
Will be enough, but late, and out of time
For him to punish.
    Tib.   Do they purpose it?
    Sej. You know, sir, thunder speaks not till it hit. 205
Be not secure: none swiftlier are oppressed
Than they whom confidence betrays to rest.
Let not your daring make your danger such:
All power's to be feared, where 'tis too much.
The youths are (of themselves) hot, violent,   210
Full of great thought; and that male-spirited dame,
Their mother, slacks no means to put them on,
By large allowance, popular presentings,
Increase of train, and state, suing for titles,
Hath them commended with like prayers, like vows, 215
To the same gods, with Caesar: days and nights

---

194 *close*: veiled in secrecy   195 *fame*: Lat. *fama*, good or ill report   196 *jealous*:
suspicious   197 *than to fail*: i.e. rather than fail of proof   206 *secure*: careless

She spends in banquets and ambitious feasts
For the nobility: where Caius Silius,
Titius Sabinus, old Arruntius,
220 Asinius Gallus, Furnius, Regulus,
And others of that discontented list,
Are the prime guests. There, and to these, she tells
Whose niece she was, whose daughter, and whose wife,
And then must they compare her with Augusta,
225 Aye, and prefer her too, commend her form,
Extol her fruitfulness; at which a shower
Falls for the memory of Germanicus,
Which they blow over straight, with windy praise,
And puffing hopes of her aspiring sons:
230 Who, with these hourly ticklings, grow so pleased,
And wantonly conceited of themselves,
As now, they stick not to believe they're such
As these do give 'em out; and would be thought
(More than competitors) immediate heirs.
235 Whilst to their thirst of rule they win the rout
(That's still the friend of novelty) with hope
Of future freedom, which on every change,
That greedily, though emptily, expects.
Caesar, 'tis age in all things breeds neglects,
240 And princes that will keep old dignity,
Must not admit too youthful heirs stand by;
Not their own issue: but so darkly set
As shadows are in picture, to give height,
And lustre to themselves.
    Tib.   We will command
245 Their rank thoughts down, and with a stricter hand
Than we have yet put forth, their trains must bate,
Their titles, feasts and factions.
    Sej.   Or your state.
But how, sir, will you work?
    Tib.   Confine 'em.
    Sej.   No.
They are too great, and that too faint a blow

    223 *niece*: granddaughter

To give them now: it would have served at first,   250
When, with the weakest touch, their knot had burst.
But, now, your care must be, not to detect
The smallest cord or line of your suspect,
For such, who know the weight of princes' fear,
Will, when they find themselves discovered, rear   255
Their forces, like seen snakes, that else would lie
Rolled in their circles, close: naught is more high,
Daring, or desperate, than offenders found;
Where guilt is, rage and courage both abound.
The course must be, to let 'em still swell up,   260
Riot, and surfeit on blind fortune's cup;
Give 'em more place, more dignities, more style,
Call 'em to court, to senate: in the while,
Take from their strength some one or twain or more
Of the main fautors; (it will fright the store)   265
And by some by-occasion. Thus, with slight
You shall disarm them first, and they (in night
Of their ambition) not perceive the train,
Till, in the engine, they are caught, and slain.
    Tib. We would not kill, if we knew how to save;   270
Yet, than a throne, 'tis cheaper give a grave.
Is there no way to bind them by deserts?
    Sej. Sir, wolves do change their hair, but not their hearts.
While thus your thought unto a mean is tied,
You neither dare enough, nor do provide.   275
All modesty is fond; and chiefly where
The subject is no less compelled to bear,
Than praise his sovereign's acts.
    Tib.   We can no longer
Keep on our mask to thee, our dear Sejanus;
Thy thoughts are ours, in all, and we but proved   280
Their voice, in our designs, which by assenting
Hath more confirmed us, than if heartening Jove
Had from his hundred statues bid us strike,

---

  252 *detect*: reveal   265 *fautors*: supporters   268 *train*: snare   269 *engine*:
trap   275 *provide*: prepare beforehand   276 *fond*: foolish   280 *proved*: made
trial of

And at the stroke clicked all his marble thumbs.
But, who shall first be struck?
285   *Sej.*   First, Caius Silius;
He is the most of mark, and most of danger:
In power, and reputation equal strong,
Having commanded an imperial army
Seven years together, vanquished Sacrovir
290 In Germany, and thence obtained to wear
The ornaments triumphal. His steep fall,
By how much it doth give the weightier crack,
Will send more wounding terror to the rest,
Command them stand aloof, and give more way
295 To our surprising of the principal.
      Tib. But what, Sabinus?
      Sej.   Let him grow awhile,
His fate is not yet ripe: we must not pluck
At all together, lest we catch ourselves.
And there's Arruntius too, he only talks.
300 But Sosia, Silius' wife, would be wound in
Now, for she hath a fury in her breast
More than hell ever knew; and would be sent
Thither in time. Then, is there one Cremutius
Cordus, a writing fellow, they have got
305 To gather notes of the precedent times,
And make them into annals; a most tart
And bitter spirit (I hear) who, under colour
Of praising those, doth tax the present state,
Censures the men, the actions, leaves no trick,
310 No practice unexamined, parallels
The times, the governments, a professed champion,
For the old liberty——
      Tib.   A perishing wretch.
As if there were that chaos bred in things,
That laws and liberty would not rather choose
315 To be quite broken, and ta'en hence by us,
Than have the stain to be preserved by such.

284 like the spectators at a gladiatorial contest, indicating a death verdict
289 *Sacrovir*: leader of a rebellion in Gaul in A.D. 21   309 *Censures*: judges

Have we the means to make these guilty, first?
   Sej. Trust that to me: let Caesar, by his power,
But cause a formal meeting of the Senate,
I will have matter and accusers ready.   320
   Tib. But how? Let us consult.
   Sej.   We shall misspend
The time of action. Counsels are unfit
In business, where all rest is more pernicious
Than rashness can be. Acts of this close kind
Thrive more by execution than advice.   325
There is no lingering in that work begun,
Which cannot praised be, until through done.
   Tib. Our edict shall, forthwith, command a court.
While I can live, I will prevent earth's fury:
Ἐμοῦ δανόντος γαῖα μιχδήτω τυρί.   [*Exit*] 330

Enter Posthumus

   Pos. My lord Sejanus——
   Sej.   Julius Posthumus,
Come with my wish! What news from Agrippina's?
   Pos. Faith, none. They all lock up themselves a'late;
Or talk in character: I have not seen
A company so changed. Except they had   335
Intelligence by augury of our practice.
   Sej. When were you there?
   Pos.   Last night.
   Sej.   And what guests found
   Pos. Sabinus, Silius (the old list) Arruntius,   [you?
Furnius and Gallus.
   Sej.   Would not these talk?
   Pos.   Little.
And yet we offered choice of argument.   340
Satrius was with me.
   Sej.   Well: 'tis guilt enough
Their often meeting. You forgot to extol
The hospitable lady?

---

330 'When I die, let fire overwhelm the earth'   334 *character*: cipher

   Pos.   No, that trick
Was well put home, and had succeeded too,
345 But that Sabinus coughed a caution out;
For she began to swell.
   Sej.   And may she burst.
Julius, I would have you go instantly,
Unto the palace of the great Augusta,
And (by your kindest friend*) get swift access;
350 Acquaint her with these meetings: tell the words
You brought me (the other day) of Silius,
Add somewhat to 'em. Make her understand
The danger of Sabinus, and the times,
Out of his closeness. Give Arruntius' words
355 Of malice against Caesar; so, to Gallus:
But (above all) to Agrippina. Say,
(As you may truly) that her infinite pride,
Propped with the hopes of her too fruitful womb,
With popular studies gapes for sovereignty;
360 And threatens Caesar. Pray Augusta then,
That for her own, great Caesar's, and the pub-
lic safety, she be pleased to urge these dangers.
Caesar is too secure (he must be told,
And best he'll take it from a mother's tongue).
365 Alas! What is it for us to sound, to explore,
To watch, oppose, plot, practise, or prevent,
If he, for whom it is so strongly laboured,
Shall, out of greatness, and free spirit, be
Supinely negligent? Our city's now
370 Divided as in time o' the civil war,
And men forbear not to declare themselves
Of Agrippina's party. Every day
The faction multiplies; and will do more
If not resisted: you can best enlarge it
375 As you find audience. Noble Posthumus,
Commend me to your Prisca: and pray her,

---

* Mutilia Prisca

359 *popular studies*: the devotion of the people

She will solicit this great business
To earnest and most present execution,
With all her utmost credit with Augusta.
   Pos. I shall not fail in my instructions.   [*Exit*] 380
   Sej. This second (from his mother) will well urge
Our late design, and spur on Caesar's rage,
Which else might grow remiss. The way to put
A prince in blood is to present the shapes
Of dangers greater than they are (like late,   385
Or early shadows) and, sometimes, to feign
Where there are none, only to make him fear;
His fear will make him cruel: and once entered,
He doth not easily learn to stop, or spare
Where he may doubt. This have I made my rule,   390
To thrust Tiberius into tyranny,
And make him toil, to turn aside those blocks,
Which I alone, could not remove with safety.
Drusus once gone, Germanicus' three sons
Would clog my way; whose guards have too much faith   395
To be corrupted: and their mother known
Of too-too unreproved a chastity
To be attempted, as light Livia was.
Work then, my art, on Caesar's fears, as they
On those they fear, till all my lets be cleared: 400
And he in ruins of his house, and hate
Of all his subjects, bury his own state:
When, with my peace and safety, I will rise,
By making him the public sacrifice.   [*Exit*]

[Agrippina's house]

Enter Satrius, Natta

   Sat. They are grown exceeding circumspect and wary.   405
   Nat. They have us in the wind: and yet, Arruntius
Cannot contain himself.

---

378 *present*: immediate   381 *second*: support   400 *lets*: obstacles   406 *in
the wind*: *EMI* II. iii. 52 n.

 Sat.   Tut, he's not yet
Looked after, there are others more desired,
That are more silent.
 Nat.   Here he comes. Away.   [*Exeunt*]

    Enter Sabinus, Arruntius, Cordus

410 *Sab.* How is it that these beagles haunt the house
Of Agrippina?
 Arr.   Oh, they hunt, they hunt.
There is some game here lodged, which they must rouse,
To make the great ones sport.
 Cor.   Did you observe
How they inveighed 'gainst Caesar?
 Arr.   Aye, baits, baits,
415 For us to bite at: would I have my flesh
Torn by the public hook, these qualified hangmen
Should be my company.
 Cor.   Here comes another.

           (Afer *passeth by*)

 Arr. Aye, there's a man, Afer the orator!
One that hath phrases, figures and fine flowers,
420 To strew his rhetoric with, and doth make haste
To get him note, or name, by any offer
Where blood or gain be objects; steeps his words,
When he would kill, in artificial tears:
The crocodile of Tiber! Him I love,
425 That man is mine. He hath my heart, and voice,
When I would curse, he, he.
 Sab.   Contemn the slaves,
Their present lives will be their future graves.   [*Exeunt*]

    Enter Silius, Agrippina, Nero, Sosia

 Sil. May it please your highness not forget yourself,
I dare not, with my manners, to attempt
Your trouble farther.
430 *Agr.*   Farewell, noble Silius.

  416 *the public hook*: by which the body of the executed criminal was dragged to the
Gemonian steps, and then to the Tiber

Sil. Most royal princess.

Agr.   Sosia stays with us?

Sil. She is your servant, and doth owe your grace
An honest, but unprofitable love.

   Agr. How can that be, when there's no gain, but virtue's?

   Sil. You take the moral, not the politic sense.   435
I meant, as she is bold and free of speech,
Earnest to utter what her zealous thought
Travails withal, in honour of your house;
Which act, as it is simply borne in her,
Partakes of love and honesty, but may,   440
By the over-often and unseasoned use,
Turn to your loss, and danger: for your state
Is waited on by envies, as by eyes;
And every second guest your tables take,
Is a fee'd spy, to observe who goes, who comes,   445
What conference you have, with whom, where, when,
What the discourse is, what the looks, the thoughts
Of every person there, they do extract,
And make into a substance.

   Agr.   Hear me, Silius,
Were all Tiberius' body stuck with eyes,   450
And every wall and hanging in my house
Transparent, as this lawn I wear, or air;
Yea, had Sejanus both his ears as long
As to my inmost closet: I would hate
To whisper any thought, or change an act,   455
To be made Juno's rival. Virtue's forces
Show ever noblest in conspicuous courses.

   Sil. 'Tis great, and bravely spoken, like the spirit
Of Agrippina: yet, your highness knows,
There is nor loss nor shame in providence: 460
Few can, what all should do, beware enough.
You may perceive with what officious face,
Satrius and Natta, Afer, and the rest
Visit your house of late, to enquire the secrets;
And with what bold and privileged art they rail   465

460 *providence*: taking steps beforehand

Against Augusta: yea, and at Tiberius,
Tell tricks of Livia and Sejanus, all
To excite and call your indignation on,
That they might hear it at more liberty.

   Agr. You are too suspicious, Silius.

470   *Sil.*   Pray the gods,
I be so Agrippina: but I fear
Some subtle practice. They that durst to strike
At so examp'less, and unblam'd a life
As that of the renowned Germanicus,

475 Will not sit down, with that exploit alone:
He threatens many, that hath injured one.

   Ner. 'Twere best rip forth their tongues, sear out their eyes,
When next they come.

   Sos.   A fit reward for spies.

Enter Drusus *junior*

   Dru. Hear you the rumour?
   Agr.   What?
   Dru.   Drusus is dying.
   Agr. Dying?
   Ner.   That's strange!

480   *Agr.*   You were with him, yesternight.
   Dru. One met Eudemus, the physician,
Sent for but now: who thinks he cannot live.

   Sil. Thinks? If't be arrived at that, he knows,
Or none.

   Agr.   This is quick! What should be his disease?
   Sil. Poison. Poison——
   Agr.   How, Silius!

485   *Ner.*   What's that?
   Sil. Nay, nothing. There was (late) a certain blow
Given o' the face.

   Ner.   Aye, to Sejanus?
   Sil.   True.
   Dru. And, what of that?
   Sil.   I'm glad I gave it not.

---

473 *examp'less*: unexampled   484 *should be*: is said to be

Ner. But, there is somewhat else?
Sil.   Yes, private meetings,
With a great lady, at a physician's,   490
And a wife turned away——
Ner.   Ha!
Sil.   Toys, mere toys:
What wisdom's now i'the streets? I'the common mouth?
Dru. Fears, whisperings, tumults, noise, I know not what:
They say, the Senate sit.
Sil.   I'll thither, straight;
And see what's in the forge.
Agr.   Good Silius do.   495
Sosia and I will in.
Sil.   Haste you, my lords,
To visit the sick prince: tender your loves
And sorrows to the people. This Sejanus
(Trust my divining soul) hath plots on all:
No tree that stops his prospect but must fall.   [*Exeunt*] 500

Chorus——*of musicians*

ACT III

[The Senate]

Enter Sejanus, Varro, Latiaris, Cotta, Afer, Praecones,
Lictores

Sej. 'TIS only you must urge against him, Varro,
Nor I, nor Caesar may appear therein,
Except in your defence, who are the Consul:
And, under colour of late enmity
Between your father and his, may better do it,   5
As free from all suspicion of a practice.
Here be your notes, what points to touch at; read:
Be cunning in them. Afer has them too.
Var. But is he summoned?

---

491 *Toys*: trifles   (*III*) 6 *practice*: plot   8 *cunning*: well versed

  Sej.   No. It was debated
10 By Caesar, and concluded as most fit
To take him unprepared.
  Afe.   And prosecute
All under name of treason.
  Var.   I conceive.

    [*Enter* Sabinus, Gallus, Lepidus, Arruntius]

  Sab. Drusus being dead, Caesar will not be here.
  Gal. What should the business of this Senate be?
15 *Arr.* That can my subtle whisperers tell you: we,
That are the good-dull-noble lookers-on,
Are only called to keep the marble warm.
What should we do with those deep mysteries,
Proper to these fine heads? Let them alone.
20 Our ignorance may, perchance, help us be saved
From whips and furies.
  Gal.   See, see, see, their action!
  Arr. Aye, now their heads do travail, now they work;
Their faces run like shuttles, they are weaving
Some curious cobweb to catch flies.
  Sab.   Observe,
They take their places.
  Arr.   What so low?
25 *Gal.*   Oh yes,
They must be seen to flatter Caesar's grief
Though but in sitting.
  Var.   Bid us silence.
  Pra.   Silence.
  Var. 'Fathers Conscript, may this our present meeting
Turn fair, and fortunate to the Commonwealth.'

     [*Enter* Silius]

  Sej. See, Silius enters.
  Sil.   Hail, grave Fathers.

---

12 *conceive:* understand 24 *curious*: intricate 28 *Fathers Conscript*:
patres et conscripti, the members of the Senate

Lic.   Stand.   30
Silius, forbear thy place.
   Sen.   How!
   Pra.   Silius, stand forth,
The Consul hath to charge thee.
   Lic.   Room for Caesar.
   Arr. Is he come too? Nay then expect a trick.
   Sab. Silius accused? Sure he will answer nobly.

Enter Tiberius

   Tib. We stand amazed, Fathers, to behold   35
This general dejection. Wherefore sit
Rome's Consuls thus dissolved, as they had lost
All the remembrance both of style and place?
It not becomes. No woes are of fit weight
To make the honour of the empire stoop: 40
Though I, in my peculiar self, may meet
Just reprehension, that so suddenly,
And in so fresh a grief, would greet the Senate,
When private tongues, of kinsmen, and allies,
(Inspired with comforts) lothly are endured,   45
The face of men not seen, and scarce the day,
To thousands, that communicate our loss.
Nor can I argue these of weakness; since
They take but natural ways: yet I must seek
For stronger aids, and those fair helps draw out   50
From warm embraces of the commonwealth.
Our mother, great Augusta, is struck with time,
Ourself impressed with aged characters,
Drusus is gone, his children young, and babes,
Our aims must now reflect on those, that may   55
Give timely succour to these present ills,
And are our only glad-surviving hopes,
The noble issue of Germanicus,
Nero and Drusus: might it please the Consul
Honour them in (they both attend without).   60

---

37 *dissolved*: discomposed   47 *communicate*: share
8126018   K

I would present them to the Senate's care,
And raise those suns of joy, that should drink up
These floods of sorrow, in your drowned eyes.
   Arr. By Jove, I am not Oedipus enough,
65 To understand this Sphinx.
   Sab.   The princes come.

Enter Nero, Drusus *junior*

   Tib. Approach, you noble Nero, noble Drusus,
These princes, Fathers, when their parent died,
I gave unto their uncle, with this prayer,
That, though he had proper issue of his own,
70 He would no less bring up and foster these
Than that self-blood; and by that act confirm
Their worths to him and to posterity:
Drusus ta'en hence, I turn my prayers to you,
And, 'fore our country and our gods, beseech
75 You take and rule Augustus' nephew's sons,
Sprung of the noblest ancestors; and so
Accomplish both my duty, and your own.
Nero and Drusus, these shall be to you
In place of parents, these your fathers, these,
80 And not unfitly: for you are so born,
As all your good, or ill's the commonwealth's.
Receive them, you strong guardians; and blessed gods,
Make all their actions answer to their bloods:
Let their great titles find increase by them,
85 Not they by titles. Set them, as in place,
So in example, above all the Romans:
And may they know no rivals, but themselves.
Let fortune give them nothing; but attend
Upon their virtue: and that still come forth
90 Greater than hope, and better than their fame.
Relieve me, Fathers, with your general voice.
   Sen. 'May all the gods consent to Caesar's wish,
And add to any honours, that may crown
The hopeful issue of Germanicus.'*

   * A form of speaking they had.

 Tib. We thank you, reverend Fathers, in their right.   95
 Arr. If this were true now! But the space, the space
Between the breast and lips——Tiberius' heart
Lies a thought farther, than another man's.
 Tib. My comforts are so flowing in my joys,
As, in them, all my streams of grief are lost,   100
No less than are land-waters in the sea,
Or showers in rivers; though their cause was such,
As might have sprinkled even the gods with tears:
Yet since the greater doth embrace the less,
We covetously obey.
  (*Arr*.   Well acted, Caesar.)   105
 Tib. And now I am the happy witness made
Of your so much desired affections,
To this great issue, I could wish, the fates
Would here set peaceful period to my days;
However, to my labours, I entreat   110
And beg it of this Senate some fit ease.
  (*Arr*. Laugh, Fathers, laugh: ha' you no spleens about you?)
 Tib. The burden is too heavy, I sustain
On my unwilling shoulders; and I pray
It may be taken off, and reconferred   115
Upon the Consuls, or some other Romans,
More able, and more worthy.
  (*Arr*.   Laugh on, still.)
 Sab. Why, this doth render all the rest suspected!
 Gal. It poisons all.
 Arr.   Oh, do you taste it then?
 Sab. It takes away my faith to anything   120
He shall hereafter speak.
 Arr.   Aye, to pray that,
Which would be to his head as hot as thunder,
('Gainst which he wears that charm*) should but the court
Receive him at his word.
 Gal.   Hear.

---

* A wreath of laurel.

112 *spleens*: the seat of laughter

 Tib.   For myself,
125 I know my weakness, and so little covet
(Like some gone past) the weight that will oppress me,
As my ambition is the counter-point.
 (*Arr.* Finely maintained; good still.)
 Sej.   But Rome, whose blood,
Whose nerves, whose life, whose very frame relies
130 On Caesar's strength, no less than heaven on Atlas,
Cannot admit it but with general ruin.
 (*Arr.* Ah! Are you there, to bring him off?)
 Sej.   Let Caesar
No more than urge a point so contrary
To Caesar's greatness, the grieved Senate's vows,
Or Rome's necessity.
135 (*Gal.*   He comes about.
 Arr. More nimbly than Vertumnus.)
 Tib.   For the public,
I may be drawn, to show, I can neglect
All private aims; though I affect my rest:
But, if the Senate still command me serve,
140 I must be glad to practise my obedience.
 (*Arr.* You must, and will, sir. We do know it.)
 Sen.   'Caesar,
Live long, and happy, great, and royal Caesar,
The gods preserve thee, and thy modesty,
Thy wisdom, and thy innocence.'*
 (*Arr.*   Where is't?
The prayer's made before the subject.)
145 *Sen.*   'Guard
His meekness, Jove, his piety, his care,
His bounty——'
 Arr. And his subtlety, I'll put in:
Yet he'll keep that himself, without the gods.
All prayers are vain for him.

* Another form of speaking.

---

 127 *counter-point*: exact opposite 136 *Vertumnus*: the god who presided over
changing year 138 *affect*: cherish

 Tib.   We will not hold
Your patience, Fathers, with long answer; but   150
Shall still contend to be what you desire,
And work to satisfy so great a hope:
Proceed to your affairs.
 Arr.   Now, Silius, guard thee;
The curtain's drawing. Afer advanceth.
 Pra.   Silence.
 Afe. Cite Caius Silius.
 Pra.   Caius Silius.
 Sil.   Here.   155
 Afe. The triumph that thou hadst in Germany
For thy late victory on Sacrovir,
Thou hast enjoyed so freely, Caius Silius,
As no man it envied thee; nor would Caesar,
Or Rome admit, that thou wert then defrauded 160
Of any honours, thy deserts could claim,
In the fair service of the commonwealth:
But now, if, after all their loves and graces,
(Thy actions, and their courses being discovered)
It shall appear to Caesar, and this Senate,   165
Thou hast defiled those glories, with thy crimes——
 Sil. Crimes?
 Afe. Patience, Silius.
 Sil.   Tell thy mule of patience,
I am a Roman. What are my crimes? Proclaim them.
Am I too rich? Too honest for the times?
Have I or treasure, jewels, land, or houses   170
That some informer gapes for? Is my strength
Too much to be admitted? Or my knowledge?
These now are crimes.
 Afe.   Nay, Silius, if the name
Of crime so touch thee, with what impotence
Wilt thou endure the matter to be searched? 175
 Sil. I tell thee, Afer, with more scorn, than fear:
Employ your mercenary tongue, and art.
Where's my accuser?

 174 *impotence*: lack of self-restraint

Var.   Here.

Arr.   Varro? The Consul?
Is he thrust in?

  Var.   'Tis I accuse thee, Silius.
180 Against the majesty of Rome and Caesar,
I do pronounce thee here a guilty cause,
First, of beginning, and occasioning,
Next, drawing out the war in Gallia,
For which thou late triumph'st; dissembling long
185 That Sacrovir to be an enemy,
Only to make thy entertainment more,
Whilst thou and thy wife Sosia polled the province;
Wherein, with sordid-base desire of gain,
Thou hast discredited thy action's worth
And been a traitor to the state.

190 *Sil.*   Thou liest.

  Arr. I thank thee, Silius, speak so still, and often.

  Var. If I not prove it, Caesar, but unjustly
Have called him into trial, here I bind
Myself to suffer what I claim 'gainst him;
195 And yield, to have what I have spoke, confirmed
By judgement of the court, and all good men.

  Sil. Caesar, I crave to have my cause deferred,
Till this man's Consulship be out.

  Tib.   We cannot,
Nor may we grant it.

  Sil.   Why? Shall he design
200 My day of trial? Is he my accuser?
And must he be my judge?

  Tib.   It hath been usual,
And is a right, that custom hath allowed
The magistrate to call forth private men;
And to appoint their day: which privilege
205 We may not in the Consul see infringed,
By whose deep watches and industrious care
It is so laboured, as the commonwealth
Receive no loss, by any oblique course.

  186 *entertainment*: employment 187 *polled*: pillaged

Sil. Caesar, thy fraud is worse than violence.

Tib. Silius, mistake us not, we dare not use   210
The credit of the Consul to thy wrong,
But only do preserve his place and power
So far as it concerns the dignity,
And honour of the state.

  Arr.   Believe him, Silius.

  Cot. Why, so he may, Arruntius.

  Arr.   I say so.   215
And he may choose too.

  Tib.   By the Capitol,
And all our gods, but that the dear republic,
Our sacred laws, and just authority
Are interested therein, I should be silent.

  Afe. Please Caesar to give way unto his trial.   220
He shall have justice.

  Sil.   Nay, I shall have law;
Shall I not, Afer? Speak.

  Afe.   Would you have more?

  Sil. No, my well-spoken man, I would no more;
Nor less: might I enjoy it natural,
Not taught to speak unto your present ends,   225
Free from thine, his, and all your unkind handling.
Furious enforcing, most unjust presuming,
Malicious, and manifold applying,
Foul wresting, and impossible construction.

  Afe. He raves, he raves.

  Sil.   Thou durst not tell me so,   230
Hadst thou not Caesar's warrant. I can see
Whose power condemns me.

  Var.   This betrays his spirit.
This doth enough declare him what he is.

  Sil. What am I? Speak.

  Var.   An enemy to the state.

  Sil. Because I am an enemy to thee,   235
And such corrupted ministers of the state,
That here art made a present instrument

219 *interested*: concerned and involved (in reputation)

To gratify it with thine own disgrace.
   Sej. This, to the Consul, is most insolent!
And impious!
240   *Sil.*   Aye, take part. Reveal yourselves.
Alas, I scent not your confederacies?
Your plots, and combinations? I not know
Minion Sejanus hates me; and that all
This boast of law, and law, is but a form,
245 A net of Vulcan's filing, a mere engine,
To take that life by a pretext of justice,
Which you pursue in malice? I want brain
Or nostril to persuade me, that your ends,
And purposes are made to what they are,
250 Before my answer? O, you equal gods,
Whose justice not a world of wolf-turned men
Shall make me to accuse (how e'er provoked)
Have I for this so oft engaged myself?
Stood in the heat and fervour of a fight,
255 When Phoebus sooner hath forsook the day
Than I the field? Against the blue-eyed Gauls?
And crisped Germans? When our Roman eagles
Have fanned the fire, with their labouring wings,
And no blow dealt, that left not death behind it?
260 When I have charged, alone, into the troops
Of curled Sicambrians, routed them, and came
Not off with backward ensigns of a slave,
But forward marks, wounds on my breast and face,
Were meant to thee, O Caesar, and thy Rome?
265 And have I this return? Did I, for this,
Perform so noble, and so brave defeat,
On Sacrovir? (O Jove, let it become me
To boast my deeds, when he, whom they concern,
Shall thus forget them.)
   Afe.   Silius, Silius,
270 These are the common customs of thy blood,

---

242 *combinations*: factions, conspiracies   245 *net of Vulcan's*: Vulcan
entrapped Mars and Venus in a net of finely woven wires and exposed their adultery
248 *nostril*: perception   250 *equal*: just   257 *crisped:* curly-haired

When it is high with wine, as now with rage:
This well agrees, with that intemperate vaunt,
Thou lately madst at Agrippina's table,
That when all other of the troops were prone
To fall into rebellion, only yours   275
Remained in their obedience. You were he,
That saved the empire; which had then been lost,
Had but your legions, there, rebelled, or mutinied.
Your virtue met, and fronted every peril.
You gave to Caesar, and to Rome their surety.   280
Their name, their strength, their spirit, and their state,
Their being was a donative from you.

   Arr. Well worded, and most like an orator.

   Tib. Is this true, Silius?

   Sil.   Save thy question, Caesar.
Thy spy, of famous credit, hath affirmed it.   285

   Arr. Excellent Roman!

   Sab.   He doth answer stoutly.

   Sej. If this be so, there needs no farther cause
Of crime against him.

   Var.   What can more impeach
The royal dignity, and state of Caesar,
Than to be urged with a benefit   290
He cannot pay?

   Cot.   In this, all Caesar's fortune
Is made unequal to the courtesy.

   Lat. His means are clean destroyed, that should requite.

   Gal. Nothing is great enough for Silius' merit.

   Arr. Gallus on that side too?

   Sil.   Come, do not hunt,   295
And labour so about for circumstance,
To make him guilty, whom you have foredoomed:
Take shorter ways, I'll meet your purposes.
The words were mine, and more I now will say:
Since I have done thee that great service, Caesar,   300
Thou still hast feared me; and, in place of grace,
Returned me hatred: so soon, all best turns,

   285 *famous*: infamous   288 *crime*: accusation

With doubtful princes, turn deep injuries
In estimation, when they greater rise,
305 Than can be answered. Benefits, with you,
Are of no longer pleasure, than you can
With ease restore them; that transcended once,
Your studies are not how to thank, but kill.
It is your nature, to have all men slaves
310 To you, but you acknowledging to none.
The means that makes your greatness, must not come
In mention of it; if it do, it takes
So much away, you think: and that, which helped,
Shall soonest perish, if it stand in eye,
315 Where it may front, or but upbraid the high.

    Cot. Suffer him speak no more.
    Var.   Note but his spirit.
    Afe. This shows him in the rest.
    Lat.   Let him be censured.
    Sej. He hath spoke enough to prove him Caesar's foe.
    Cot. His thoughts look through his words.
    Sej.   A censure.
    Sil.   Stay.
320 Stay, most officious Senate, I shall straight
Delude thy fury. Silius hath not placed
His guards within him against fortune's spite
So weakly, but he can escape your gripe
That are but hands of fortune: she herself
325 When virtue doth oppose, must lose her threats.
All that can happen in humanity,
The frown of Caesar, proud Sejanus' hatred,
Base Varro's spleen, and Afer's bloodying tongue,
The Senate's servile flattery, and these
330 Mustered to kill, I am fortified against;
And can look down upon: they are beneath me.
It is not life whereof I stand enamoured:
Nor shall my end make me accuse my fate.
The coward, and the valiant man must fall,
335 Only the cause, and manner how, discerns them:

    317 *censured*: judged   335 *discerns*: distinguishes

Which then are gladdest, when they cost us dearest.
Romans, if any here be in this Senate,
Would know to mock Tiberius' tyranny,
Look upon Silius, and so learn to die.   [*Stabs himself*]

   Var. Oh, desperate act!
   Arr.   An honourable hand!   340
   Tib. Look, is he dead?
   Sab.   'Twas nobly struck, and home.
   Arr. My thought did prompt him to it. Farewell, Silius.
Be famous ever for thy great example.
   Tib. We are not pleased in this sad accident
That thus hath stalled and abused our mercy,   345
Intended to preserve thee, noble Roman:
And to prevent thy hopes.
   Arr.   Excellent wolf!
Now he is full, he howls.
   Sej.   Caesar doth wrong
His dignity, and safety, thus to mourn
The deserved end of so professed a traitor,   350
And doth, by this his lenity, instruct
Others as factious, to the like offence.
   Tib. The confiscation merely of his state
Had been enough.
   Arr.   Oh, that was gaped for then?
   Var. Remove the body.
   Sej.   Let citation   355
Go out for Sosia.
   Gal.   Let her be proscribed.
And for the goods, I think it fit that half
Go to the treasure, half unto the children.
   Lep. With leave of Caesar, I would think that fourth
Part, which the law doth cast on the informers,   360
Should be enough; the rest go to the children:
Wherein the Prince shall show humanity,
And bounty, not to force them by their want
(Which in their parents' trespass they deserved)
To take ill courses.

   345 *stalled*: brought to a standstill

    Tib.   It shall please us.
365   *Arr.*   Aye,
Out of necessity. This Lepidus
Is grave and honest, and I have observed
A moderation still in all his censures.
    Sab. And bending to the better——Stay, who's this?
370 Cremutius Cordus? What? Is he brought in?
    Arr. More blood unto the banquet? Noble Cordus,
I wish thee good: be as thy writings, free,
And honest.
    Tib.   What is he?
    Sej.   For the annals, Caesar.

Enter Cordus, Satrius, Natta

    Pra. Cremutius Cordus.
    Cor.   Here.
    Pra.   Satrius Secundus,
375 Pinnarius Natta, you are his accusers.
    Arr. Two of Sejanus' bloodhounds, whom he breeds
With human flesh, to bay at citizens.
    Afe. Stand forth before the Senate, and confront him.
    Sat. I do accuse thee here, Cremutius Cordus,
380 To be a man factious and dangerous,
A sower of sedition in the state,
A turbulent and discontented spirit,
Which I will prove from thine own writings, here,
The annals thou hast published; where thou bit'st
385 The present age, and with a viper's tooth,
Being a member of it, dar'st that ill
Which never yet degenerous bastard did
Upon his parent.
    Nat.   To this, I subscribe;
And, forth a world of more particulars,
390 Instance in only one: comparing men,
And times, thou praisest Brutus, and affirm'st
That Cassius was the last of all the Romans.

---

    385 *viper's tooth*: believed to eat through the parent's body at birth

Cot. How! What are we then?

Var.   What is Caesar? Nothing?

Afe. My lords, this strikes at every Roman's private,
In whom reigns gentry, and estate of spirit,   395
To have a Brutus brought in parallel,
A parricide, an enemy of his country,
Ranked, and preferred to any real worth
That Rome now holds. This is most strangely invective.
Most full of spite, and insolent upbraiding.   400
Nor is't the time alone is here disprized,
But the whole man of time, year, Caesar's self
Brought in disvalue; and he aimed at most
By oblique glance of his licentious pen.
Caesar, if Cassius were the last of Romans,   405
Thou hast no name.

Tib.   Let's hear him answer. Silence.

Cor. So innocent I am of fact, my lords,
As but my words are argued; yet those words
Not reaching either prince, or prince's parent:
The which your law of treason comprehends.   410
Brutus and Cassius I am charged to have praised:
Whose deeds, when many more, besides myself,
Have writ, not one hath mentioned without honour.
Great Titus Livius, great for eloquence,
And faith, amongst us, in his history,   415
With so great praises Pompey did extol,
As oft Augustus called him a Pompeian:
Yet this not hurt their friendship. In his book
He often names Scipio, Afranius,
Yea, the same Cassius, and this Brutus too,   420
As worthiest men; not thieves, and parricides,
Which notes, upon their fames, are now imposed.
Asinius Pollio's writings quite throughout
Give them a noble memory; so Messalla
Renowned his general Cassius: yet both these   425
Lived with Augustus, full of wealth, and honours.

---

394 *private*: personal concern or honour   397 *parricide*: traitor   401 *dis-*
prized: belittled   407 *fact*: crime   422 *notes*: brands

To Cicero's book, where Cato was heaved up
Equal with heaven, what else did Caesar answer,
Being then Dictator, but with a penned oration,
430 As if before the judges? Do but see
Antonius' letters; read but Brutus' pleadings:
What vile reproach they hold against Augustus,
False I confess, but with much bitterness.
The epigrams of Bibaculus and Catullus,
435 Are read, full stuffed with spite of both the Caesars;
Yet deified Julius, and no less Augustus!
Both bore them, and contemned them: (I not know
Promptly to speak it, whether done with more
Temper, or wisdom) for such obloquies
440 If they despised be, they die suppressed,
But, if with rage acknowledged, they are confessed.
The Greeks I slip, whose licence not alone,
But also lust did scape unpunished:
Or where some one (by chance) exception took,
445 He words with words revenged. But, in my work,
What could be aimed more free, or farther off
From the time's scandal, than to write of those,
Whom death from grace, or hatred had exempted?
Did I, with Brutus and with Cassius,
450 Armed, and possessed of the Philippi fields,
Incense the people in the civil cause,
With dangerous speeches? Or do they, being slain
Seventy years since, as by their images
(Which not the conqueror hath defaced) appears,
455 Retain that guilty memory with writers?
Posterity pays every man his honour.
Nor shall there want, though I condemned am,
That will not only Cassius well approve,
And of great Brutus' honour mindful be,
460 But that will, also, mention make of me.
    Arr. Freely, and nobly spoken.
    Sab.   With good temper,
I like him, that he is not moved with passion.

    442 *slip*: pass over   453 *images*: statues

Arr. He puts 'em to their whisper.

Tib.   Take him hence,
We shall determine of him at next sitting.

Cot. Meantime, give order that his books be burnt,   465
To the Aediles.

Sej.   You have well advised.

Afe. It fits not such licentious things should live
To upbraid the age.

Arr.   If the age were good, they might.

Lat. Let 'em be burnt.

Gal.   All sought, and burnt, today.

Pra. The court is up, lictors, resume the fasces.   470

                    [*Exeunt all but* Arruntius, Sabinus, Lepidus]

Arr. Let 'em be burnt! Oh, how ridiculous
Appears the Senate's brainless diligence,
Who think they can, with present power, extinguish
The memory of all succeeding times!

Sab. 'Tis true, when (contrary) the punishment   475
Of wit, doth make the authority increase.
Nor do they aught, that use this cruelty
Of interdiction, and this rage of burning;
But purchase to themselves rebuke and shame,
And to the writers an eternal name.   480

Lep. It is an argument the times are sore,
When virtue cannot safely be advanced;
Nor vice reproved.

Arr.   Aye, noble Lepidus,
Augustus well foresaw what we should suffer,
Under Tiberius, when he did pronounce   485
The Roman race most wretched, that should live
Between so slow jaws, and so long a bruising.   [*Exeunt*]

                        [A room in the palace]

                      Enter Tiberius, Sejanus

Tib. This business hath succeeded well, Sejanus:
And quite removed all jealousy of practice

    489 *jealousy of practice*: suspicion of plotting

490 'Gainst Agrippina, and our nephews. Now,
We must bethink us how to plant our engines
For the other pair, Sabinus and Arruntius,
And Gallus too (how e'er he flatter us)
His heart we know.
  Sej.   Give it some respite, Caesar.
495 Time shall mature, and bring to perfect crown,
What we, with so good vultures, have begun:
Sabinus shall be next.
  Tib.   Rather Arruntius.
  Sej. By any means, preserve him. His frank tongue
Being lent the reins, will take away all thought
500 Of malice, in your course against the rest.
We must keep him to stalk with.
  Tib.   Dearest head,
To thy most fortunate design I yield it.
  Sej. Sir——I have been so long trained up in grace,
First, with your father, great Augustus, since,
505 With your most happy bounties so familiar,
As I not sooner would commit my hopes
Or wishes to the gods than to your ears.
Nor have I ever, yet, been covetous
Of over-bright and dazzling honours: rather
510 To watch and travail in great Caesar's safety,
With the most common soldier.
  Tib.   'Tis confessed.
  Sej. The only gain, and which I count most fair
Of all my fortunes, is that mighty Caesar
Hath thought me worthy his alliance.* Hence
Begin my hopes.
  Tib. H'mh?
515 *Sej.*   I have heard, Augustus
In the bestowing of his daughter, thought
But even of gentlemen of Rome: if so,
(I know not how to hope so great a favour)

---

* His daughter was betrothed to Claudius, his son.

  496 *good vultures*: used in augury

But if a husband should be sought for Livia,
And I be had in mind, as Caesar's friend,   520
I would but use the glory of the kindred.
It should not make me slothful, or less caring
For Caesar's state; it were enough to me
It did confirm, and strengthen my weak house,
Against the now unequal opposition   525
Of Agrippina; and for dear regard
Unto my children, this I wish: myself
Have no ambition farther, than to end
My days in service of so dear a master.

  Tib. We cannot but commend thy piety,   530
Most-loved Sejanus, in acknowledging
Those bounties; which we, faintly, such remember.
But to thy suit. The rest of mortal men,
In all their drifts and counsels, pursue profit:
Princes, alone, are of a different sort,   535
Directing their main actions still to fame.
We therefore will take time to think, and answer.
For Livia, she can best, herself, resolve
If she will marry after Drusus, or
Continue in the family; besides   540
She hath a mother and a grandam yet,
Whose nearer counsels she may guide her by:
But I will simply deal. That enmity
Thou fear'st in Agrippina would burn more,
If Livia's marriage should (as 'twere in parts)   545
Divide the imperial house; an emulation
Between the women might break forth: and discord
Ruin the sons and nephews on both hands.
What if it cause some present difference?
Thou art not safe, Sejanus, if thou prove it.   550
Canst thou believe, that Livia, first the wife
To Caius Caesar, then my Drusus, now
Will be contented to grow old with thee,
Born but a private gentleman of Rome?

  530 *piety*: dutiful affection   534 *drifts*: schemes   550 *prove it*: put it to
the proof

555 And raise thee with her loss, if not her shame?
Or say that I should wish it, canst thou think
The Senate, or the people (who have seen
Her brother, father, and our ancestors,
In highest place of empire) will endure it?
560 The state thou hold'st already is in talk;
Men murmur at thy greatness; and the nobles
Stick not, in public, to upbraid thy climbing
Above our father's favours, or thy scale:
And dare accuse me, from their hate to thee.
565 Be wise, dear friend. We would not hide these things
For friendship's dear respect. Nor will we stand
Adverse to thine, or Livia's designments.
What we had purposed to thee, in our thought,
And with what near degrees of love to bind thee,
570 And make thee equal to us: for the present,
We will forbear to speak. Only, thus much
Believe, our loved Sejanus, we not know
That height in blood, or honour, which thy virtue,
And mind to us, may not aspire with merit.
575 And this we'll publish, on all watched occasion
The Senate, or the people shall present.
    Sej. I am restored, and to my sense again,
Which I had lost in this so blinding suit.
Caesar hath taught me better to refuse,
580 Than I knew how to ask. How pleaseth Caesar
To embrace my late advice, for leaving Rome?
    Tib. We are resolved.
    Sej. [*Giving paper*]   Here are some motives more,
Which I have thought on since, may more confirm.
    Tib. Careful Sejanus! We will straight peruse them:
585 Go forward in our main design, and prosper.   [*Exit*]
    Sej. If those but take, I shall: dull, heavy Caesar!
Wouldst thou tell me, thy favours were made crimes?
And that my fortunes were esteemed thy faults?
That thou, for me, wert hated? And not think
590 I would with winged haste prevent that change,

      574 *aspire*: mount up to

When thou mightst win all to thyself again,
By forfeiture of me? Did those fond words
Fly swifter from thy lips, than this my brain,
This sparkling forge, created me an armour
To encounter chance, and thee? Well, read my charms,   595
And may they lay that hold upon thy senses,
As thou hadst snuffed up hemlock, or ta'en down
The juice of poppy and of mandrakes. Sleep,
Voluptuous Caesar, and security
Seize on thy stupid powers, and leave them dead   600
To public cares, awake but to thy lusts,
The strength of which makes thy libidinous soul
Itch to leave Rome; and I have thrust it on:
With blaming of the city business,
The multitude of suits, the confluence   605
Of suitors, then their importunacies,
The manifold distractions he must suffer,
Besides ill rumours, envies, and reproaches,
All which, a quiet and retired life,
(Larded with ease and pleasure) did avoid;   610
And yet, for any weighty and great affair,
The fittest place to give the soundest counsels.
By this, shall I remove him both from thought
And knowledge of his own most dear affairs;
Draw all dispatches through my private hands;   615
Know his designments, and pursue mine own;
Make mine own strengths, by giving suits and places;
Conferring dignities and offices:
And these, that hate me now, wanting access
To him, will make their envy none, or less.   620
For when they see me arbiter of all,
They must observe: or else, with Caesar fall.   [*Exit*]

Enter Tiberius

Tib. To marry Livia? Will no less, Sejanus,
Content thy aims? No lower object? Well!

---

597 *hemlock*: an opiate (like poppy and mandragora), reputed also to cause hallucinations   599 *security*: carelessness

625 Thou know'st how thou art wrought into our trust;
    Woven in our design; and think'st we must
    Now use thee, whatsoe'er thy projects are:
    'Tis true. But yet with caution, and fit care.
    And, now we better think—who's there, within?
        Ser. [*Within*] Caesar?
630   *Tib.*   To leave our journey off, were sin
    'Gainst our decreed delights; and would appear
    Doubt: or (what less becomes a prince) low fear.
    Yet, doubt hath law, and fears have their excuse,
    Where princes' states plead necessary use;
635 As ours doth now: more in Sejanus' pride,
    Than all fell Agrippina's hates beside.
    Those are the dreadful enemies we raise
    With favours, and make dangerous with praise;
    The injured by us may have will alike,
640 But 'tis the favourite hath the power to strike:
    And fury ever boils more high and strong,
    Heat' with ambition, than revenge of wrong.
    'Tis then a part of supreme skill, to grace
    No man too much; but hold a certain space
645 Between the ascender's rise, and thine own flat,
    Lest, when all rounds be reached, his aim be that.
    'Tis thought—

                    [*Enter* Servus]

                    Is Macro in the palace? See:
    If not, go, seek him, to come to us [*Exit* Servus]—He
    Must be the organ, we must work by now;
650 Though none less apt for trust: need doth allow
    What choice would not. I've heard that aconite
    Being timely taken hath a healing might
    Against the scorpion's stroke; the proof we'll give:
    That, while two poisons wrestle, we may live.
655 He hath a spirit too working, to be used
    But to the encounter of his like; excused
    Are wiser sovereigns then, that raise one ill

    646 *rounds*: rungs   651 *aconite*: herbal poison said to cure serpents' stings

Against another, and both safely kill:
The prince, that feeds great natures, they will sway him;
Who nourisheth a lion, must obey him.   660

[*Enter* Macro, Servus]

   Tib. Macro, we sent for you.
   Mac.   I heard so, Caesar.
   Tib. (Leave us awhile) [*Exit* Servus] When you shall know, good
     Macro,
The causes of our sending, and the ends;
You then will hearken nearer: and be pleased
You stand so high, both in our choice, and trust.   665
   Mac. The humblest place in Caesar's choice, or trust,
May make glad Macro proud; without ambition:
Save to do Caesar service.
   Tib.   Leave our courtings.
We are in purpose, Macro, to depart
The city for a time, and see Campania;   670
Not for our pleasures, but to dedicate
A pair of temples, one to Jupiter
At Capua, the other at Nola, to Augustus:
In which great work, perhaps, our stay will be
Beyond our will produced. Now, since we are   675
Not ignorant what danger may be born
Out of our shortest absence, in a state
So subject unto envy, and embroiled
With hate and faction; we have thought on thee,
(Amongst a field of Romans) worthiest Macro,   680
To be our eye and ear, to keep strict watch
On Agrippina, Nero, Drusus, aye,
And on Sejanus: not that we distrust
His loyalty, or do repent one grace
Of all that heap we have conferred on him: 685
(For that were to disparage our election,
And call that judgement now in doubt, which then
Seemed as unquestioned as an oracle),

---

  668 *our courtings*: courting us   675 *produced*: prolonged   686 *election*:
choice

But, greatness hath his cankers. Worms and moths
690 Breed out of too fit matter, in the things
Which after they consume, transferring quite
The substance of their makers, into themselves.
Macro is sharp, and apprehends. Besides,
I know him subtle, close, wise, and well-read
695 In man and his large nature. He hath studied
Affections, passions, knows their springs, their ends,
Which way, and whether they will work: 'tis proof
Enough, of his great merit, that we trust him.
Then, to a point—because our conference
700 Cannot be long without suspicion—
Here, Macro, we assign thee, both to spy,
Inform, and chastise; think, and use thy means,
Thy ministers, what, where, on whom thou wilt;
Explore, plot, practise: all thou dost in this,
705 Shall be, as if the Senate, or the Laws
Had given it privilege, and thou thence styled
The saver both of Caesar, and of Rome.
We will not take thy answer, but in act:
Whereto, as thou proceed'st, we hope to hear
710 By trusted messengers. If't be enquired
Wherefore we called you, say, you have in charge
To see our chariots ready, and our horse.
Be still our loved, and (shortly) honoured Macro.   [*Exit*]
    Mac. I will not ask why Caesar bids do this:
715 But joy that he bids me. It is the bliss
Of courts to be employed; no matter how:
A prince's power makes all his actions virtue.
We whom he works by are dumb instruments,
To do, but not enquire: his great intents
720 Are to be served, not searched. Yet, as that bow
Is most in hand, whose owner best doth know
To affect his aims, so let that statesman hope
Most use, most price, can hit his prince's scope.
Nor must he look at what, or whom to strike,
725 But loose at all; each mark must be alike.

    722 *affect*: achieve   723 *scope*: intent

Were it to plot against the fame, the life
Of one with whom I twinned; remove a wife
From my warm side, as loved as is the air;
Practise away each parent; drawn mine heir
In compass, though but one; work all my kin   730
To swift perdition; leave no untrained engine,
For friendship, or for innocence; nay, make
The gods all guilty: I would undertake
This, being imposed me, both with gain and ease.
The way to rise, is to obey, and please.   735
He that will thrive in state, he must neglect
The trodden paths, that truth and right respect;
And prove new, wilder ways: for virtue, there,
Is not that narrow thing she is elsewhere.
Men's fortune there is virtue; reason, their will;   740
Their licence, law; and their observance, skill.
Occasion is their foil; conscience, their stain;
Profit, their lustre: and what else is, vain.
If then it be the lust of Caesar's power
To have raised Sejanus up, and in an hour   745
O'erturn him, tumbling, down, from height of all,
We are his ready engine: and his fall
May be our rise. It is no uncouth thing
To see fresh buildings from old ruins spring.   [*Exit*]

Chorus——of musicians

ACT IV

[Agrippina's house]

Enter Gallus, Agrippina

Gal. You must have patience, royal Agrippina.
Agr. I must have vengeance, first: and that were nectar
Unto my famished spirits. O, my fortune,

729–30 *draw . . . In compass*: involve in a trap   730 *but one*: i.e. a single heir
731 *no untrained engine*: no snare unset   744 *lust*: wish   747 *engine*:
instrument   748 *uncouth*: strange, unknown

Let it be sudden thou prepar'st against me;
5 Strike all my powers of understanding blind,
And ignorant of destiny to come:
Let me not fear, that cannot hope.
      Gal.   Dear Princess,
These tyrannies on yourself are worse than Caesar's.
      Agr. Is this the happiness of being born great?
10 Still to be aimed at? Still to be suspected?
To live the subject of all jealousies?
At the least colour made, if not the ground
To every painted danger? Who would not
Choose once to fall, than thus to hang for ever?
      Gal. You might be safe, if you would—
15   *Agr.*   What, my Gallus?
Be lewd Sejanus's strumpet? Or the bawd
To Caesar's lusts, he now is gone to practise?
Not these are safe, where nothing is. Yourself,
While thus you stand but by me, are not safe.
20 Was Silius safe? Or the good Sosia safe?
Or was my niece, dear Claudia Pulchra, safe?
Or innocent Furnius? They, that latest have
(By being made guilty) added reputation
To Afer's eloquence? Oh, foolish friends,
25 Could not so fresh example warn your loves,
But you must buy my favours with that loss
Unto yourselves: and when you might perceive
That Caesar's cause of raging must forsake him,
Before his will? Away, good Gallus, leave me.
30 Here to be seen is danger; to speak, treason:
To do me least observance is called faction.
You are unhappy in me, and I in all.
Where are my sons? Nero? And Drusus? We
Are they, be shot at; let us fall apart:
35 Not, in our ruins, sepulchre our friends.
Or shall we do some action, like offence,
To mock their studies, that would make us faulty?

----

  12 *colour*: pretext   13 *painted*: feigned   31 *observance*: courtesy
37 *studies*: schemes

And frustrate practice, by preventing it?
The danger's like: for, what they can contrive,
They will make good. No innocence is safe,   40
When power contests. Nor can they trespass more,
Whose only being was all crime, before.

[*Enter* Nero, Drusus, Caligula]

  Ner. You hear, Sejanus is come back from Caesar?
  Gal. No. How? Disgraced?
  Dru.   More graced now, than ever.
  Gal. By what mischance?
  Cal.   A fortune, like enough   45
Once to be bad.
  Dru.   But turned too good, to both.
  Gal. What was't?
  Ner.   Tiberius sitting at his meat,
In a farmhouse they call Spelunca, sited
By the seaside, among the Fundane hills,
Within a natural cave, part of the grot   50
About the entry fell, and overwhelmed
Some of the waiters; others ran away.
Only Sejanus, with his knees, hands, face,
O'erhanging Caesar, did oppose himself
To the remaining ruins, and was found   55
In that so labouring posture by the soldiers
That came to succour him. With which adventure,
He hath so fixed himself in Caesar's trust,
As thunder cannot move him, and is come
With all the height of Caesar's praise, to Rome.   60
  Agr. And power to turn those ruins all on us,
And bury whole posterities beneath them.
Nero and Drusus and Caligula,
Your places are the next, and therefore most
In their offence. Think on your birth and blood,   65
Awake your spirits, meet their violence,
'Tis princely, when a tyrant doth oppose;
And is a fortune sent to exercise

  39 *like*: the same

Your virtue, as the wind doth try strong trees,
70 Who by vexation grow more sound and firm.
After your father's fall, and uncle's fate,
What can you hope, but all the change of stroke
That force or sleight can give? Then stand upright;
And though you do not act, yet suffer nobly.
75 Be worthy of my womb, and take strong cheer;
What we do know will come, we should not fear.   [*Exeunt*]

[The street]

Enter Macro

 Mac. Returned so soon? Renewed in trust and grace?
Is Caesar then so weak? Or hath the place
But wrought this alteration, with the air;
80 And he, on next remove, will all repair?
Macro, thou art engaged: and what before
Was public, now must be thy private, more.
The weal of Caesar, fitness did imply;
But thine own fate confers necessity
85 On thy employment: and the thoughts borne nearest
Unto ourselves, move swiftest still, and dearest.
If he recover, thou art lost: yea, all
The weight of preparation to his fall
Will turn on thee, and crush thee. Therefore, strike
90 Before he settle, to prevent the like
Upon thyself. He doth his vantage know,
That makes it home, and gives the foremost blow.   [*Exit*]

[Agrippina's house]

Enter Latiaris, Rufus, Opsius

 Lat. It is a service great Sejanus will
See well requited, and accept of nobly.
95 Here place yourselves, between the roof and ceiling,
And when I bring him to his words of danger,
Reveal yourselves, and take him.

   80 *remove*: stage of his journey

Ruf.   Is he come?

Lat. I'll now go fetch him.   [*Exit*]

Ops.   With good speed. I long

To merit from the state in such an action.

Ruf. I hope it will obtain the Consulship   100

For one of us.

Ops.   We cannot think of less,

To bring in one so dangerous as Sabinus.

Ruf. He was a follower of Germanicus,

And still is an observer of his wife

And children, though they be declined in grace;   105

A daily visitant, keeps them company

In private and in public, and is noted

To be the only client of the house.

Pray Jove he will be free to Latiaris.

Ops. He is allied to him, and doth trust him well.   110

Ruf. And he'll requite his trust?

Ops.   To do an office

So grateful to the state, I know no man

But would strain nearer bonds than kindred——

Ruf.   List,

I hear them come.

Ops.   Shift to our holes, with silence.   [*They retire*]

Enter Latiaris, Sabinus

Lat. It is a noble constancy you show   115

To this afflicted house: that not like others,

The friends of season, you do follow fortune,

And in the winter of their fate, forsake

The place whose glories warmed you. You are just,

And worthy such a princely patron's love,   120

As was the world's-renowned Germanicus:

Whose ample merit when I call to thought,

And see his wife and issue, objects made

To so much envy, jealousy, and hate,

It makes me ready to accuse the gods   125

Of negligence, as men of tyranny.

104 *is an observer of*: is attentive to

    Sab. They must be patient, so must we.
    Lat.   O Jove.
What will become of us, or of the times,
When, to be high, or noble, are made crimes?
130 When land and treasure are most dangerous faults?
    Sab. Nay, when our table, yea our bed assaults
Our peace and safety? When our writings are,
By any envious instruments that dare
Apply them to the guilty, made to speak
135 What they will have, to fit their tyrannous wreak?
When ignorance is scarcely innocence;
And knowledge made a capital offence?
When not so much, but the bare empty shade
Of liberty is reft us? And we made
140 The prey to greedy vultures and vile spies,
That first transfix us with their murdering eyes?
    Lat. Methinks, the genius of the Roman race
Should not be so extinct, but that bright flame
Of liberty might be revived again,
145 Which no good man but with his life, should lose,
And we not sit like spent and patient fools,
Still puffing in the dark at one poor coal,
Held on by hope, till the last spark is out.
The cause is public, and the honour, name,
150 The immortality of every soul
That is not bastard, or a slave in Rome,
Therein concerned: whereto, if men would change
The wearied arm, and for the weighty shield
So long sustained, employ the ready sword,
155 We might have some assurance of our vows.
This ass's fortitude doth tire us all.
It must be active valour must redeem
Our loss, or none. The rock, and our hard steel
Should meet, to enforce those glorious fires again,
160 Whose splendour cheered the world, and heat gave life
No less than doth the sun's.
    Sab.   'Twere better stay

   135 *wreak*: vengeance

In lasting darkness, and despair of day.
No ill should force the subject undertake
Against the sovereign, more than hell should make
The gods do wrong. A good man should, and must   165
Sit rather down with loss, than rise unjust.
Though, when the Romans first did yield themselves
To one man's power, they did not mean their lives,
Their fortunes, and their liberties should be
His absolute spoil, as purchased by the sword.   170

Lat. Why, we are worse, if to be slaves, and bond
To Caesar's slave, be such, the proud Sejanus!
He that is all, does all, gives Caesar leave
To hide his ulcerous and anointed face
With his bald crown at Rhodes, while he here stalks   175
Upon the heads of Romans, and their princes,
Familiarly to empire.

Sab.   Now you touch
A point indeed, wherein he shows his art,
As well as power.

Lat.   And villainy in both.
Do you observe where Livia lodges? How   180
Drusus came dead? What men have been cut off?

Sab. Yes, those are things removed: I nearer looked,
Into his later practice, where he stands
Declared a master in his mystery.
First, ere Tiberius went, he wrought his fear   185
To think that Agrippina sought his death.
Then put those doubts in her; sent her oft word,
Under the show of friendship, to beware
Of Caesar, for he laid to poison her;
Drove them to frowns, to mutual jealousies,   190
Which, now, in visible hatred are burst out.
Since, he hath had his hired instruments
To work on Nero, and to heave him up;
To tell him Caesar's old; that all the people,
Yea, all the army have their eyes on him;   195

170 *purchased*: won   182 *removed*: remote   184 *mystery*: trade   189 *laid*:
plotted

That both do long to have him undertake
Something of worth, to give the world a hope;
Bids him to court their grace. The easy youth,
Perhaps, gives ear, which straight he writes to Caesar;
200 And with this comment: See yond dangerous boy;
Note but the practice of the mother, there;
She's tying him, for purposes at hand,
With men of sword. Here's Caesar put in fright
'Gainst son and mother. Yet, he leaves not thus.
205 The second brother Drusus (a fierce nature,
And fitter for his snares, because ambitious,
And full of envy) him he clasps and hugs,
Poisons with praise, tells him what hearts he wears,
How bright he stands in popular expectance;
210 That Rome doth suffer with him in the wrong
His mother does him by preferring Nero:
Thus sets he them asunder, each 'gainst other,
Projects the course that serves him to condemn,
Keeps in opinion of a friend to all,
And all drives on to ruin.
215 *Lat.*   Caesar sleeps,
And nods at this?
     Sab.   Would he might ever sleep,
Bogged in his filthy lusts.

                    [*Enter* Opsius, Rufus]

     Ops.   Treason to Caesar!
     Ruf. Lay hands upon the traitor, Latiaris,
Or take the name thyself.
     Lat.   I am for Caesar.
     Sab. Am I then catched?
220 *Ruf.*   How think you, sir? You are.
     Sab. Spies of this head! So white! So full of years!
Well, my most reverend monsters, you may live
To see yourselves thus snared.
     Ops.   Away with him.

     222 *reverend*: awe-inspiring

Lat. Hale him away.

Ruf.   To be a spy for traitors
Is honourable vigilance.

Sab.   You do well,   225
My most officious instruments of state;
Men of all uses: drag me hence, away.
The year is well begun, and I fall fit,
To be an offering to Sejanus. Go.

Ops. Cover him with his garments, hide his face.   230

Sab. It shall not need. Forbear your rude assault;
The fault's not shameful, villainy makes a fault.   [*Exeunt*]

[The street]

Enter Macro, Caligula

Mac. Sir, but observe how thick your dangers meet
In his clear drifts! Your mother, and your brothers,
Now cited to the Senate! Their friend, Gallus,   235
Feasted today by Caesar, since committed!
Sabinus, here we met, hurried to fetters!
The senators all struck with fear and silence,
Save those whose hopes depend not on good means,
But force their private prey from public spoil!   240
And you must know, if here you stay, your state
Is sure to be the subject of his hate,
As now the object.

Cal.   What would you advise me?

Mac. To go for Capreae presently: and there
Give up yourself, entirely, to your uncle.   245
Tell Caesar, since your mother is accused
To fly for succours to Augustus' statue,
And to the army, with your brethren, you
Have rather chose to place your aids in him,
Than live suspected; or in hourly fear   250
To be thrust out by bold Sejanus' plots:

228 *The year*: Sabinus is a New Year's sacrifice to the god Sejanus   230 *the procedure when a criminal was condemned to death*   234 *clear drifts*: patent
intrigues   239–40 cf. III. 357–61

Which, you shall confidently urge, to be
Most full of peril to the state, and Caesar,
As being laid to his peculiar ends,
255 And not to be let run, with common safety.
All which, upon the second, I'll make plain,
So both shall love and trust with Caesar gain.
    Cal. Away then, let's prepare us for our journey.   [*Exeunt*]

Enter Arruntius

    Arr. Still, dost thou suffer, heaven? Will no flame,
260 No heat of sin make thy just wrath to boil
In thy distempered bosom, and o'erflow
The pitchy blazes of impiety,
Kindled beneath thy throne? Still canst thou sleep,
Patient, while vice doth make an antic face
265 At thy dread power, and blow dust, and smoke
Into thy nostrils? Jove, will nothing wake thee?
Must vile Sejanus pull thee by the beard,
Ere thou wilt open thy black-lidded eye,
And look him dead? Well! Snore on, dreaming gods:
270 And let this last of that proud giant race
Heave mountain upon mountain, 'gainst your state——
Be good unto me, Fortune, and you powers,
Whom I, expostulating, have profaned;
I see (what's equal with a prodigy)
275 A great, a noble Roman, and an honest,
Live an old man!

[*Enter* Lepidus]

                O, Marcus Lepidus,
When is our turn to bleed? Thyself, and I
(Without our boast) are almost all the few
Left to be honest, in these impious times.
280   *Lep.* What we are left to be, we will be, Lucius,
Though tyranny did stare as wide as death
To fright us from it.

---

256 *upon the second*: giving support   264 *antic*: grotesque   270 *giant race*:
destroyed by Jupiter for its presumption

Arr.   'T hath so, on Sabinus.

Lep. I saw him now drawn from the Gemonies,
And, what increased the direness of the fact,
His faithful dog, upbraiding all us Romans,   285
Never forsook the corpse, but seeing it thrown
Into the stream leapt in, and drowned with it.

Arr. O act! To be envied him of us men!
We are the next, the hook lays hold on, Marcus:
What are thy arts, good patriot, teach them me,   290
That have preserved thy hairs to this white dye,
And kept so reverend and so dear a head
Safe on his comely shoulders?

Lep.   Arts, Arruntius?
None, but the plain and passive fortitude,
To suffer, and be silent; never stretch   295
These arms against the torrent; live at home,
With my own thoughts, and innocence about me,
Not tempting the wolves' jaws: these are my arts.

Arr. I would begin to study 'em, if I thought
They would secure me. May I pray to Jove,   300
In secret, and be safe? Aye, or aloud?
With open wishes? So I do not mention
Tiberius, or Sejanus? Yes, I must,
If I speak out. 'Tis hard, that. May I think,
And not be racked? What danger is't to dream?   305
Talk in one's sleep? Or cough? Who knows the law?
May I shake my head, without a comment? Say
It rains, or it holds up, and not be thrown
Upon the Gemonies? These now are things,
Whereon men's fortune, yea their fate depends.   310
Nothing hath privilege 'gainst the violent ear.
No place, no day, no hour, we see, is free——
Not our religious, and most sacred times——
From some one kind of cruelty: all matter,
Nay all occasion pleaseth. Madmen's rage,   315
The idleness of drunkards, women's nothing,
Jesters' simplicity, all, all is good

---

283 *Gemonies*: cf. II. 416 n.   305 *racked*: tortured

That can be catched at. Nor is now the event
Of any person, or for any crime,
320 To be expected; for, 'tis always one:
Death, with some little difference of place,
Or time——what's this? Prince Nero? Guarded?

Enter Laco, Nero, Lictors

   Lac. On, lictors, keep your way. My lords, forbear.
On pain of Caesar's wrath, no man attempt
Speech with the prisoner.
325   *Ner.*   Noble friends, be safe:
To lose yourselves for words were as vain hazard,
As unto me small comfort. Fare you well.
Would all Rome's sufferings in my fate did dwell.
   Lac. Lictors, away.   [*Exit* Nero, *guarded*]
   Lep.   Where goes he, Laco?
   Lac.   Sir,
330 He's banished into Pontia, by the Senate.
   Arr. Do I see? And hear? And feel? May I trust sense?
Or doth my phantasy form it?
   Lep.   Where's his brother?
   Lac. Drusus is prisoner in the palace.
   Arr.   Ha?
I smell it now: 'tis rank. Where's Agrippina?
335   *Lac.* The princess is confined, to Pandataria.
   Arr. Bolts, Vulcan; bolts, for Jove! Phoebus thy bow;
Stern Mars, thy sword; and blue-eyed maid, thy spear;
Thy club, Alcides: all the armoury
Of heaven is too little!——Ha? To guard
340 The gods, I meant. Fine, rare dispatch! This same
Was swiftly borne! Confined? Imprisoned? Banished?
Most tripartite! The cause, sir?
   Lac.   Treason.
   Arr.   Oh?
The complement of all accusings? That
Will hit, when all else fails.

---

318 *event*: outcome   337 *blue-eyed maid*: Pallas Athene   343 *complement*:
that which makes complete, fulfils

  Lep.   This turn is strange!
But yesterday, the people would not hear,   345
Far less objected, but cried, Caesar's letters
Were false and forged; that all these plots were malice;
And that the ruin of the prince's house
Was practised 'gainst his knowledge. Where are now
Their voices? Now, that they behold his heirs   350
Locked up, disgraced, led into exile?
  Arr.   Hushed.
Drowned in their bellies. Wild Sejanus' breath
Hath, like a whirlwind, scattered that poor dust
With this rude blast.   (*He turns to* Laco *and the rest*)
                    We'll talk no treason, sir,
If that be it you stand for? Fare you well.   355
We have no need of horse-leeches. Good spy,
Now you are spied, begone.   [*Exeunt* Laco, Lictors]
  Lep.   I fear, you wrong him.
He has the voice to be an honest Roman.
  Arr. And trusted to this office? Lepidus,
I'd sooner trust Greek Sinon than a man   360
Our state employs. He's gone: and being gone,
I dare tell you (whom I dare better trust)
That our night-eyed Tiberius doth not see
His minion's drifts; or, if he do, he is not
So arrant subtle as we fools do take him: 365
To breed a mongrel up, in his own house,
With his own blood, and, if the good gods please,
At his own throat, flesh him to take a leap.
I do not beg it, heaven: but, if the fates
Grant it these eyes, they must not wink.
  Lep.   They must   370
Not see it, Lucius.
  Arr.   Who should let 'em?
  Lep.   Zeal,
And duty; with the thought, he is our prince.

---

360 *Sinon*: who duped the Trojans into receiving the wooden horse   363 *night-eyed*: because when awakened at night, he could for a time see as clearly as if it were day

Arr. He is our monster: forfeited to vice
So far, as no racked virtue can redeem him.
375 His loathed person fouler than all crimes:
An emperor only in his lusts. Retired,
From all regard of his own fame, or Rome's,
Into an obscure island, where he lives,
Acting his tragedies with a comic face,
380 Amidst his rout of Chaldees: spending hours,
Days, weeks, and months, in the unkind abuse
Of grave astrology, to the bane of men,
Casting the scope of men's nativities,
And having found aught worthy in their fortune,
385 Kill, or precipitate them in the sea,
And boast, he can mock fate. Nay, muse not: these
Are far from ends of evil, scarce degrees.
He hath his slaughterhouse, at Capreae,
Where he doth study murder, as an art:
390 And they are dearest in his grace, that can
Devise the deepest tortures. Thither, too,
He hath his boys, and beauteous girls ta'en up,
Out of our noblest houses, the best formed,
Best nurtured, and most modest: what's their good
395 Serves to provoke his bad. Some are allured,
Some threatened; others, by their friends detained,
Are ravished hence, like captives, and, in sight
Of their most grieved parents, dealt away
Unto his spintries, sellaries, and slaves,
400 Masters of strange, and new-commented lusts,
For which wise nature hath not left a name.
To this (what most strikes us, and bleeding Rome)
He is, with all his craft, become the ward
To his own vassal, a stale catamite:
405 Whom he, upon our low and suffering necks,
Hath raised from excrement to side the gods,
And have his proper sacrifice in Rome:

379 *comic face*: comic mask   380 *Chaldees*: the astrologers   381 *unkind*:
unnatural   399 *spintries, sellaries*: male prostitutes   400 *new-commented*: newly
invented   406 *side*: rival

Which Jove beholds, and yet will sooner rive
A senseless oak with thunder, than his trunk.

Enter Laco, Pomponius, Minutius

   Lac. These letters make men doubtful what to expect,   410
Whether his coming, or his death.
   Pom.   Troth, both:
And which comes soonest, thank the gods for.
   (*Arr.*   List,
Their talk is Caesar, I would hear all voices.)
   Min. One day, he's well, and will return to Rome;
The next day, sick; and knows not when to hope it.   415
   Lac. True, and today, one of Sejanus' friends
Honoured by special writ; and on the morrow
Another punished——
   Pom.   By more special writ.
   Min. This man receives his praises of Sejanus;
A second, but slight mention; a third, none;   420
A fourth, rebukes. And thus he leaves the Senate
Divided and suspended, all uncertain.
   Lac. These forked tricks, I understand 'em not,
Would he would tell us whom he loves or hates,
That we might follow, without fear or doubt.   425
   (*Arr.* Good Heliotrope! Is this your honest man?
Let him be yours so still. He is my knave.)
   Pom. I cannot tell, Sejanus still goes on,
And mounts, we see: new statues are advanced,
Fresh leaves of titles, large inscriptions read,   430
His fortune sworn by, himself new gone out
Caesar's colleague in the fifth Consulship,
More altars smoke to him than all the gods:
What would we more?
   (*Arr.*   That the dear smoke would choke him,
That would I more.
   Lep.   Peace, good Arruntius.)   435
   Lac. But there are letters come, they say, ev'n now,
Which do forbid that last.

   426 *Heliotrope*: the flower which turned to follow the sun

 Min.   Do you hear so?

 Lac.   Yes.

 Pom. By Pollux, that's the worst.

 (*Arr.*   By Hercules, best.)

 Min. I did not like the sign, when Regulus,

440 Whom all we know no friend unto Sejanus,

Did, by Tiberius' so precise command,

Succeed a fellow in the Consulship:

It boded somewhat.

 Pom.   Not a mote. His partner,

Fulcinius Trio, is his own, and sure.

       [*Enter* Terentius]

445 Here comes Terentius. He can give us more.

       (*They whisper with* Terentius)

 Lep. I'll ne'er believe but Caesar hath some scent

Of bold Sejanus' footing. These cross points

Of varying letters, and opposing Consuls,

Mingling his honours, and his punishments,

450 Feigning now ill, now well, raising Sejanus,

And then depressing him, as now of late

In all reports we have it, cannot be

Empty of practice: 'tis Tiberius' art.

For, having found his favourite grown too great,

455 And, with his greatness, strong; that all the soldiers

Are, with their leaders, made at his devotion;

That almost all the Senate are his creatures,

Or hold on him their main dependances,

Either for benefit, or hope, or fear;

460 And that himself hath lost much of his own,

By parting unto him; and by the increase

Of his rank lusts and rages, quite disarmed

Himself of love, or other public means,

To dare an open contestation,

465 His subtlety hath chose this doubling line,

To hold him even in: not so to fear him,

As wholly put him out, and yet give check

  461 *parting unto*: sharing with   466 *fear*: frighten

Unto his farther boldness. In meantime,
By his employments, makes him odious
Unto the staggering rout, whose aid (in fine)   470
He hopes to use, as sure, who (when they sway)
Bear down, o'erturn all objects in their way.
   Arr. You may be a Lynceus, Lepidus: yet, I
See no such cause, but that a politic tyrant,
Who can so well disguise it, should have ta'en   475
A nearer way: feigned honest, and come home
To cut his throat, by law.
   Lep.   Aye, but his fear
Would ne'er be masked, all-be his vices were.
   Pom. His lordship then is still in grace?
   Ter.   Assure you,
Never in more, either of grace, or power.   480
   Pom. The gods are wise, and just.
   (*Arr.*   The fiends they are.
To suffer thee belie 'em?)
   Ter.   I have here
His last and present letters, where he writes him
The 'Partner of his cares', and 'his Sejanus'——
   Lac. But is that true, it is prohibited,   485
To sacrifice unto him?
   Ter.   Some such thing
Caesar makes scruple of, but forbids it not;
No more than to himself: says, he could wish
It were forborne to all.
   Lac.   Is it no other?
   Ter. No other, on my trust. For your more surety,   490
Here is that letter too.
   (*Arr.*   How easily
Do wretched men believe what they would have!
Looks this like plot?
   Lep.   Noble Arruntius, stay.)
   Lac. He names him here without his titles.
   (*Lep.*   Note.
   Arr. Yes, and come off your notable fool. I will.)   495

473 *Lynceus*: one of the lynx-eyed Argonauts   478 *all-be*: although

Lac. No other than Sejanus.

Pom.   That's but haste
In him that writes. Here he gives large amends.

   Min. And with his own hand written?

Pom.   Yes.

Lac.   Indeed?

500   *Ter.* Believe it, gentlemen, Sejanus' breast
Never received more full contentments in
Than at this present.

Pom.   Takes he well the escape
Of young Caligula, with Macro?

Ter.   Faith,
At the first air it somewhat troubled him.

   (*Lep.* Observe you?

Arr.   Nothing. Riddles. Till I see
505 Sejanus struck, no sound thereof strikes me.)

                         [*Exit with* Lepidus]

   Pom. I like it not. I muse he would not attempt
Somewhat against him in the Consulship,
Seeing the people 'gin to favour him.

   Ter. He doth repent it now; but he has employed
510 Pagonianus after him: and he holds
That correspondence, there, with all that are
Near about Caesar, as no thought can pass
Without his knowledge, thence, in act to front him.

   Pom. I gratulate the news.

Lac.   But how comes Macro
515 So in trust, and favour with Caligula?

   Pom. Oh sir, he has a wife; and the young prince
An appetite: he can look up, and spy
Flies in the roof, when there are fleas in bed;
And hath a learned nose to assure his sleeps.
520 Who, to be favoured of the rising sun,
Would not lend little of his waning moon?
'Tis the safest ambition. Noble Terentius.

   Ter. The night grows fast upon us. At your service.   [*Exeunt*]

                  Chorus——*of musicians*

517-19 the marks of the pandar husband, as in Juvenal, *Sat*. i. 56-7

Act V

[Sejanus's house]

Enter Sejanus

Sej. SWELL, swell, my joys: and faint not to declare
Yourselves as ample as your causes are.
I did not live, till now; this my first hour,
Wherein I see my thoughts reached by my power.
But this, and gripe my wishes. Great, and high,   5
The world knows only two, that's Rome, and I.
My roof receives me not; 'tis air I tread:
And at each step I feel my advanced head
Knock out a star in heaven! Reared to this height,
All my desires seem modest, poor and slight,   10
That did before sound impudent. 'Tis place,
Not blood, discerns the noble and the base.
Is there not something more, than to be Caesar?
Must we rest there? It irks, to have come so far,
To be so near a stay. Caligula,   15
Would thou stood'st stiff, and many, in our way.
Winds lose their strength when they do empty fly,
Unmet of woods or buildings; great fires die,
That want their matter to withstand them; so,
It is our grief, and will be our loss, to know   20
Our power shall want opposites; unless
The gods, by mixing in the cause, would bless
Our fortune with their conquest. That were worth
Sejanus's strife: durst fates but bring it forth.

Enter Terentius, [Servus]

Ter. Safety to great Sejanus.
Sej.   Now, Terentius?   25
Ter. Hears not my lord the wonder?
Sej.   Speak it, no.
Ter. I meet it violent in the people's mouths,
Who run in routs to Pompey's theatre,

23 *their conquest*: our conquest of them

To view your statue: which, they say, sends forth
30 A smoke, as from a furnace, black and dreadful.
    Sej. Some traitor hath put fire in: (you, go see).   [*Exit* Servus]
And let the head be taken off, to look
What 'tis——some slave hath practised an imposture,
To stir the people.

[*Enter* Servus, Satrius, Natta]

                    How now? Why return you?
35   *Sat.* The head, my lord, already is ta'en off,
I saw it: and, at opening, there leapt out
A great and monstrous serpent!
    Sej.   Monstrous! Why?
Had it a beard? And horns? No heart? A tongue
Forked as flattery? Looked it of the hue,
To such as live in great men's bosoms? Was
40 The spirit of it Macro's?
    Nat.   May it please
The most divine Sejanus, in my days,
And by his sacred fortune, I affirm it,
I have not seen a more extended, grown,
Foul, spotted, venomous, ugly——
45   *Sej.*   O, the fates!
What a wild muster's here of attributes,
To express a worm, a snake?
    Ter.   But how that should
Come there, my lord!
    Sej.   What! And you too, Terentius?
I think you mean to make it a prodigy
In your reporting?
50   *Ter.*   Can the wise Sejanus
Think heaven hath meant it less?
    Sej.   O, superstition!
Why, then the falling of our bed, that brake
This morning, burdened with the populous weight
Of our expecting clients, to salute us;

  33 *imposture*: deception   54 *expecting*: awaiting

Or running of the cat, betwixt our legs,   55
As we set forth unto the Capitol,
Were prodigies.
    Ter.   I think them ominous!
And would they had not happened. As, today,
The fate of some your servants! Who, declining
Their way, not able, for the throng, to follow,   60
Slipped down the Gemonies, and brake their necks!
Besides, in taking your last augury,
No prosperous bird appeared, but croaking ravens
Flagged up and down: and from the sacrifice
Flew to the prison, where they sat all night,   65
Beating the air with their obstreperous beaks!
I dare not counsel, but I could entreat
That great Sejanus would attempt the gods
Once more with sacrifice.
    Sej.   What excellent fools
Religion makes of men? Believes Terentius,   70
(If these were dangers, as I shame to think them)
The gods could change the certain course of fate?
Or, if they could, they would (now, in a moment)
For a beef's fat, or less, be bribed to invert
Those long decrees? Then think the gods, like flies,   75
Are to be taken with the steam of flesh
Or blood, diffused about their altars: think
Their power as cheap, as I esteem it small.
Of all the throng, that fill the Olympian hall,
And (without pity) lade poor Atlas's back,   80
I know not that one deity, but Fortune,
To whom, I would throw up, in begging smoke,
One grain of incense: or whose ear I'd buy
With thus much oil. Her, I, indeed, adore;
And keep her grateful image in my house,   85
Sometimes belonging to a Roman king,
But, now called mine, as by the better style:
To her, I care not, if, for satisfying

---

59 *declining*: turning aside from   64 *Flagged*: flew unsteadily   69 *excellent*:
exceptional   85 *grateful*: pleasing

Your scrupulous fancies, I go offer. Bid
90 Our priest prepare us honey, milk, and poppy,
His masculine odours, and night-vestments: say,
Our rites are instant, which performed, you'll see
How vain and worthy laughter your fears be.   [*Exeunt*]

Enter Cotta, Pomponius

  Cot. Pomponius! Whither in such speed?
  Pom.   I go
To give my lord Sejanus notice——
95   *Cot.*   What?
  Pom. Of Macro.
  Cot.   Is he come?
  Pom.   Entered but now
The house of Regulus.
  Cot.   The opposite Consul?
  Pom. Some half-hour since.
  Cot.   And by night too! Stay, sir;
I'll bear you company.
  Pom.   Along, then——   [*Exeunt*]

[Regulus' house]

Enter Macro, Regulus [*and* attendant]

100   *Mac.* 'Tis Caesar's will, to have a frequent Senate.
And therefore must your edict lay deep mulct
On such as shall be absent.
  Reg.   So it doth.
Bear it my fellow Consul to adscribe.
  Mac. And tell him it must early be proclaimed;
The place, Apollo's temple.   [*Exit* attendant]
105   *Reg.*   That's remembered.
  Mac. And at what hour.
  Reg.   Yes.
  Mac.   You do forget

91 *masculine odours*: 'mascula tura' was the name given to the best kind of frankin-
cense   100 *a frequent Senate*: a full muster (Lat. *senatus frequens*)   101 *mulct*:
fine   103 *adscribe*: subscribe

To send one for the Provost of the watch?

    Reg. I have not: here he comes.

                          [Enter Laco]

  Mac.   Gracinus Laco,
You are a friend most welcome: by and by,
I'll speak with you. (You must procure this list   110
Of the Praetorian cohorts, with the names
Of the Centurions, and their Tribunes.
    Reg.   Aye.)
    Mac. I bring you letters, and a health from Caesar——
    Lac. Sir, both come well.
    Mac.   (And hear you, with your note,
Which are the eminent men, and most of action.   115
    Reg. That shall be done you too.)   *(The Consul goes out)*
    Mac.   Most worthy Laco,
Caesar salutes you. (Consul! Death, and furies!
Gone now?) the argument will please you, sir.
(Hough! Regulus? The anger of the gods
Follow his diligent legs, and overtake 'em,   120
In likeness of the gout.) *(Returns)* Oh, good my lord,
We lacked you present; I would pray you send
Another to Fulcinius Trio straight,
To tell him you will come and speak with him:
(The matter we'll devise) to stay him there,   125
While I, with Laco, do survey the watch.   *(Goes out again)*
What are your strengths, Gracinus?
    Lac.   Seven cohorts.
    Mac. You see, what Caesar writes: and (——Gone again?
He has sure a vein of mercury in his feet)
Knew you what store of the praetorian soldiers   130
Sejanus holds about him for his guard?
    Lac. I cannot the just number: but, I think,
Three centuries.
    Mac.   Three? Good.
    Lac.   At most, not four.

---

129 *mercury*: messenger of the gods   132 *cannot*: do not know   *just*: exact

 Mac. And who be those Centurions?

 Lac.   That the Consul
Can best deliver you.

135 *Mac.*   (When he's away:
Spite, on his nimble industry.) Gracinus,
You find what place you hold, there, in the trust
Of royal Caesar?

 Lac.   Aye, and I am——

 Mac.   Sir,
The honours, there proposed, are but beginnings
Of his great favours.

 Lac.   They are more——

140 *Mac.*   I heard him
When he did study, what to add——

 Lac.   My life,
And all I hold——

 Mac.   You were his own first choice;
Which doth confirm as much as you can speak:
And will (if we succeed) make more——Your guards
Are seven cohorts, you say?

 Lac.   Yes.

145 *Mac.*   Those we must
Hold still in readiness, and undischarged.

 Lac. I understand so much. But how it can——

 Mac. Be done without suspicion, you'll object?

 Reg. (*Returns*) What's that?

 Lac.   The keeping of the watch in arms,
When morning comes.

150 *Mac.*   The Senate shall be met and set
So early in the temple, as all mark
Of that will be avoided.

 Reg.   If we need,
We have commission to possess the palace;
Enlarge Prince Drusus, and make him our chief.

155 *Mac.* (That secret would have burnt his reverend mouth,
Had he not spit it out, now:) by the gods,
You carry things too——let me borrow a man,
Or two, to bear these——That of freeing Drusus,

Caesar projected as the last, and utmost;
Not else to be remembered.

[*Enter* servants]

  Reg.   Here are servants.   160
  Mac. [*Giving letters*] These to Arruntius, these to Lepidus,
This bear to Cotta, this to Latiaris.
If they demand you of me: say, I have ta'en
Fresh horse, and am departed. [*Exeunt* servants] You, my lord,
To your colleague, and be you sure, to hold him   165
With long narration of the new fresh favours
Meant to Sejanus, his great patron; I,
With trusted Laco, here, are for the guards:
Then, to divide. For night hath many eyes,
Whereof, though most do sleep, yet some are spies.   [*Exeunt*] 170

[Sejanus' house]

Enter Praecones, Flamen, Ministri, Sejanus, Terentius,
Satrius, etc.

  Pra. Be all profane far hence; fly, fly far off:
Be absent far. Far hence be all profane.
  Fla. We have been faulty, but repent us now,
And bring pure hands, pure vestments, and pure minds.
         (Tubicines, Tibicines *sound, while the* Flamen *washes*)
  Min. Pure vessels.
  Min.   And pure offerings.
  Min.   Garlands pure.   175
  Fla. Bestow your garlands: and, with reverence, place
The vervin on the altar.
  Pra.   Favour your tongues.

(*While they sound again, the* Flamen *takes of the honey, with his
finger, and tastes, then ministers to all the rest: so of the milk, in
an earthen vessel, he deals about: which done, he sprinkleth, upon
the altar, milk; then imposeth the honey, and kindleth his gums, and*

177 *vervin: verbenae*, the boughs and leafage used in sacrificing *Favour your tongues*:
Favete linguis: be silent, in order not to utter any word of ill omen

after censing about the altar placeth his censer thereon, into which
they put several branches of poppy, and the music ceasing, proceed)

Fla. Great mother Fortune, Queen of human state,
Rectress of action, arbitress of fate,
180 To whom all sway, all power, all empire bows,
Be present, and propitious to our vows.

    Pra. Favour it with your tongues.

    Min. Be present, and propitious to our vows.
Accept our offering, and be pleased, great goddess.

    Ter. See, see, the image stirs!

185   *Sat.*   And turns away!

    Nat. Fortune averts her face!

    Fla.   Avert, you gods,
The prodigy. Still! Still! Some pious rite
We have neglected. Yet! Heaven, be appeased.
And be all tokens false, or void, that speak
Thy present wrath.

190   *Sej.*   Be thou dumb, scrupulous priest:
And gather up thyself, with these thy wares,
Which I, in spite of thy blind mistress, or
Thy juggling mystery, religion, throw
Thus, scorned on the earth. [*Overturns the altar*] Nay, hold thy look
195 Averted, till I woo thee, turn again;
And thou shalt stand, to all posterity,
The eternal game, and laughter, with thy neck
Writhed to thy tail, like a ridiculous cat.
Avoid these fumes, these superstitious lights,
200 And all these cozening ceremonies: you,
Your pure, and spiced conscience.

                    [*Exeunt all but* Sejanus, Terentius, Satrius, Natta]
                        I, the slave,
And mock of fools, scorn on my worthy head,
That have been titled, and adored a god,
Yea, sacrificed unto, myself, in Rome,
205 No less than Jove: and I be brought to do
A peevish giglet rites? Perhaps the thought,

---

200 *cozening*: deceiving   201 *spiced*: dainty, over-particular   206 *giglet*:
a wanton woman

And shame of that made Fortune turn her face,
Knowing herself the lesser deity,
And but my servant. Bashful queen, if so,
Sejanus thanks thy modesty. Who's that?   210

Enter Pomponius, Minutius

Pom. His fortune suffers, till he hears my news:
I have waited here too long. Macro, my lord——
    Sej. Speak lower, and withdraw.   [*Takes him aside*]
    Ter.   Are these things true?
    Min. Thousands are gazing at it, in the streets.
    Sej. What's that?
    Ter.   Minutius tells us here, my lord,   215
That a new head being set upon your statue
A rope is since found wreathed about it! and,
But now, a fiery meteor, in the form
Of a great ball, was seen to roll along
The troubled air, where yet it hangs, unperfect,   220
The amazing wonder of the multitude!
    Sej. No more. That Macro's come is more than all!
    Ter. Is Macro come?
    Pom.   I saw him.
    Ter.   Where? With whom?
    Pom. With Regulus.
    Sej.   Terentius——
    Ter.   My lord?
    Sej. Send for the Tribunes, we will straight have up   225
More of the soldiers, for our guard. [*Exit* Terentius] Minutius,
We pray you, go for Cotta, Latiaris,
Trio the Consul, or what Senators
You know are sure, and ours. [*Exit* Minutius] You, my good Natta,
For Laco, Provost of the watch. [*Exit* Natta] Now, Satrius,   230
The time of proof comes on. Arm all our servants,
And without tumult. [*Exit* Satrius] You, Pomponius,
Hold some good correspondence with the Consul;
Attempt him, noble friend. [*Exit* Pomponius] These things begin
To look like dangers now, worthy my fates.   235

220 *unperfect*: its flight uncompleted

Fortune, I see thy worst: let doubtful states
And things uncertain hang upon thy will:
Me surest death shall render certain still.
Yet, why is, now, my thought turned toward death,
240 Whom fates have let go on so far, in breath,
Unchecked, or unreproved? I, that did help
To fell the lofty cedar of the world,
Germanicus; that at one stroke, cut down
Drusus, that upright elm; withered his vine;
245 Laid Silius and Sabinus, two strong oaks,
Flat on the earth; besides those other shrubs,
Cordus, and Sosia, Claudia Pulchra,
Furnius, and Gallus, which I have grubbed up;
And since, have set my axe so strong and deep
250 Into the root of spreading Agrippine;
Lopped off, and scattered her proud branches, Nero,
Drusus, and Caius too, although replanted;
If you will, Destinies, that after all,
I faint, now, ere I touch my period,
255 You are but cruel: and I already have done
Things great enough. All Rome hath been my slave;
The Senate sat an idle looker-on
And witness of my power; when I have blushed
More to command, than it to suffer; all
260 The Fathers have sat ready and prepared
To give me empire, temples, or their throats,
When I would ask 'em; and, what crowns the top,
Rome, Senate, people, all the world have seen
Jove, but my equal; Caesar, but my second.
265 'Tis then your malice, fates, who, but your own,
Envy, and fear, to have any power long known.   [*Exit*]

Enter Terentius, Tribunes

Ter. Stay here: I'll give his lordship you are come.

Enter Minutius, Cotta, Latiaris

244 *his vine*: his wife, Livia (elm and vine used as a marriage metaphor)
267 *give*: tell

Min. Marcus Terentius, pray you tell my lord,
Here's Cotta and Latiaris.
    Ter.   Sir, I shall.   [*Exit*]
    Cot. My letter is the very same with yours;   270
Only requires me to be present there,
And give my voice, to strengthen his design.
    Lat. Names he not what it is?   (*They confer their letters*)
    Cot.   No, nor to you.
    Lat. 'Tis strange, and singular doubtful!
    Cot.   So it is?
It may be all is left to lord Sejanus.   275

Enter Natta, Laco

    Nat. Gentlemen, where's my lord?
    Tri.   We wait him here.
    Cot. The Provost Laco? What's the news?
    Lat.   My lord——

Enter Sejanus

    Sej. Now, my right dear, noble, and trusted friends;
How much I am a captive to your kindness!
Most worthy Cotta, Latiaris; Laco,   280
Your valiant hand; and gentlemen, your loves.
I wish I could divide myself unto you;
Or that it lay, within our narrow powers,
To satisfy for so enlarged bounty.
Gracinus, we must pray you, hold your guards   285
Unquit, when morning comes. Saw you the Consul?
    Min. Trio will presently be here, my lord.
    Cot. They are but giving order for the edict,
To warn the Senate.
    Sej.   How! The Senate?
    Lat.   Yes.
This morning, in Apollo's temple.
    Cot.   We   290
Are charged, by letter, to be there, my lord.

---

286 *Unquit*: not dismissed

Sej. By letter? Pray you let's see!

Lat.   Knows not his lordship?

Cot. It seems so!

Sej.   A Senate warned? Without my knowledge?
And on this sudden? Senators by letters
Required to be there! Who brought these?

295 *Cot.*   Macro.

Sej. Mine enemy! And when?

Cot.   This midnight.

Sej.   Time,
With every other circumstance, doth give
It hath some strain of engine in't!

[Enter Satrius]

                                    How now?

Sat. My lord, Sertorius Macro is without,
300 Alone, and prays to have private conference
In business of high nature with your lordship,
(He says to me) and which regards you much.

Sej. Let him come here.

Sat.   Better, my lord, withdraw,
You will betray what store and strength of friends
305 Are now about you, which he comes to spy.

Sej. Is he not armed?

Sat.   We'll search him.

Sej.   No, but take
And lead him to some room, where you, concealed,
May keep a guard upon us. [*Exit* Satrius] Noble Laco,
You are our trust: and, till our own cohorts
310 Can be brought up, your strengths must be our guard.
Now, good Minutius, honoured Latiaris, (*He salutes them humbly*)
Most worthy, and my most unwearied friends:
I return instantly.   [*Exit*]

Lat.   Most worthy lord!

Cot. His lordship is turned instant kind, methinks,
315 I have not observed it in him, heretofore.

---

298 *engine*: trickery   304 *store*: quantity

   1st Tri. 'Tis true, and it becomes him nobly.
   Min.   I
Am rapt withal.
   2nd Tri.   By Mars, he has my lives,
Were they a million, for this only grace.
   Lac. Aye, and to name a man!
   Lat.   As he did me!
   Min. And me!
   Lat.   Who would not spend his life and fortunes,   320
To purchase but the look of such a lord?
   Lac. [*Aside*] He, that would nor be lord's fool, nor the world's.
                            [*They retire*]

Enter Sejanus, Macro, Satrius [*above*]

   Sej. Macro! Most welcome, as most coveted friend!
Let me enjoy my longings. When arrived you?
   Mac. About the noon of night.
   Sej.   Satrius, give leave. [*Exit* Satrius] 325
   Mac. I have been, since I came, with both the Consuls,
On a particular design from Caesar.
   Sej. How fares it with our great and royal master?
   Mac. Right plentifully well; as with a prince,
That still holds out the great proportion   330
Of his large favours, where his judgement hath
Made once divine election: like the god,
That wants not, nor is wearied to bestow
Where merit meets his bounty, as it doth
In you, already the most happy, and ere   335
The sun shall climb the south, most high Sejanus.
Let not my lord be amused. For, to this end
Was I by Caesar sent for, to the isle,
With special caution to conceal my journey;
And thence had my dispatch as privately   340
Again to Rome; charged to come here by night;
And only to the Consuls make narration
Of his great purpose: that the benefit

   337 *amused*: puzzled

Might come more full and striking, by how much
345 It was less looked for, or aspired by you,
Or least informed to the common thought.
    Sej. What may this be? Part of myself, dear Macro!
If good, speak out: and share with your Sejanus.
    Mac. If bad, I should for ever loathe myself,
350 To be the messenger to so good a lord.
I do exceed my instructions, to acquaint
Your lordship with thus much; but 'tis my venture
On your retentive wisdom: and because
I would no jealous scruple should molest
355 Or rack your peace of thought. For, I assure
My noble lord, no Senator yet knows
The business meant: though all, by several letters,
Are warned to be there, and give their voices,
Only to add unto the state and grace
Of what is purposed.
360   *Sej.*   You take pleasure, Macro,
Like a coy wench, in torturing your lover.
What can be worth this suffering?
    Mac.   That which follows,
The tribunitial dignity, and power:
Both which Sejanus is to have this day
365 Conferred upon him, and by public Senate.
    Sej. Fortune, be mine again; thou hast satisfied
For thy suspected loyalty.
    Mac.   My lord,
I have no longer time, the day approacheth,
And I must back to Caesar.
370   *Sej.*   Where's Caligula?
    Mac. That I forgot to tell your lordship. Why,
He lingers yonder, about Capreae,
Disgraced; Tiberius hath not seen him yet:
He needs would thrust himself to go with me,
Against my wish, or will, but I have quitted
375 His forward trouble, with as tardy note

---

    363 *tribunitial dignity*: an office that gave the holder the right of veto in state business,
and made his person sacrosanct   374 *quitted*: repaid

As my neglect, or silence could afford him.
Your lordship cannot now command me aught,
Because I take no knowledge that I saw you,
But I shall boast to live to serve your lordship:
And so take leave.
  Sej.   Honest, and worthy Macro,   380
Your love and friendship. Who's there? Satrius,
Attend my honourable friend forth. [*Exit* Macro] O!
How vain and vile a passion is this fear?
What base, uncomely things it makes men do?
Suspect their noblest friends, as I did this,   385
Flatter poor enemies, entreat their servants,
Stoop, court, and catch at the benevolence
Of creatures, unto whom, within this hour,
I would not have vouchsafed a quarter-look,
Or piece of face? By you, that fools call gods,   390
Hang all the sky with your prodigious signs,
Fill earth with monsters, drop the scorpion down
Out of the zodiac, or the fiercer lion,
Shake off the loosened globe from her long hinge,
Roll all the world in darkness, and let loose   395
The enraged winds to turn up groves and towns;
When I do fear again, let me be struck
With forked fire, and unpitied die:
Who fears, is worthy of calamity.   [*Exit*]

Enter Pomponius, Regulus, Trio

  Pom. Is not my lord here?
  Ter.   Sir, he will be straight.   400
  Cot. What news, Fulcinius Trio?
  Tri.   Good, good tidings.
(But, keep it to yourself.) My lord Sejanus
Is to receive this day, in open Senate,
The tribunitial dignity.
  Cot.   Is't true?
  Tri. No words; not to your thought: but, sir, believe it. 405

389 *a quarter-look*: a face almost averted   394 *hinge*: axis

Lat. What says the Consul?
Cot.   (Speak it not again,)
He tells me, that today my lord Sejanus——
       (*Tri.* I must entreat you Cotta, on your honour
Not to reveal it.
       Cot.   On my life, sir.)
Lat.   Say.

410   *Cot.* Is to receive the tribunitial power.
But, as you are an honourable man,
Let me conjure you, not to utter it:
For it is trusted to me, with that bond.
       Lat. I am Harpocrates.
       Ter.   Can you assure it?

415   *Pom.* The Consul told it me, but keep it close.
       Min. Lord Latiaris, what's the news?
       Lat.   I'll tell you,
But you must swear to keep it secret——

Enter Sejanus

Sej. I knew the fates had on their distaff left
More of our thread, than so.
       Reg.   Hail, great Sejanus.
       Tri. Hail, the most honoured.
       Cot.   Happy.

420   *Lat.*   High Sejanus.
       Sej. Do you bring prodigies too?
       Tri.   May all presage
Turn to those fair effects, whereof we bring
Your lordship news.
       Reg.   May't please my lord withdraw.
       Sej. Yes. (*To some that stand by*) (I will speak with you, anon.)
       Ter.   My lord,
What is your pleasure for the Tribunes?

425   *Sei.*   Why,
Let 'em be thanked, and sent away.
       Min.   My lord——

414 *Harpocrates*: god of silence and secrecy

Lac. Will't please your lordship to command me——
Sej.   No.
You are troublesome.
   Min.   The mood is changed.
   1st Tri.   Not speak?
   2nd Tri. Nor look?
   Lac.   Aye. He is wise, will make him friends
Of such, who never love, but for their ends.   [*Exeunt*]

[Before the Temple of Apollo]

Enter Arruntius, Lepidus, *divers other* Senators *passing by them*   430

   Arr. Aye, go, make haste; take heed you be not last
To tender your 'All hail', in the wide hall
Of huge Sejanus: run, a lictor's pace;
Stay not to put your robes on; but away
With the pale troubled ensigns of great friendship   435
Stamped i' your face! Now, Marcus Lepidus,
You still believe your former augury?
Sejanus must go downward? You perceive
His wane approaching fast?
   Lep.   Believe me, Lucius,
I wonder at this rising!
   Arr.   Aye, and that we   440
Must give our suffrage to it? You will say,
It is to make his fall more steep, and grievous?
It may be so. But think it, they that can
With idle wishes 'ssay to bring back time:
In cases desperate, all hope is crime.   445
See, see! What troops of his officious friends
Flock to salute my lord! And start before
My great, proud lord! To get a lord-like nod!
Attend my lord, unto the senate-house!
Bring back my lord! Like servile ushers, make   450
Way for my lord! Proclaim his idol lordship,
More than ten criers, or six noise of trumpets!
Make legs, kiss hands, and take a scattered hair
From my lord's eminent shoulder! See, Sanquinius!

   452 *noise*: bands

455 With his slow belly, and his dropsy! Look,
What toiling haste he makes! Yet, here's another,
Retarded with the gout, will be afore him!
Get thee Liburnian porters, thou gross fool,
To bear thy obsequious fatness, like thy peers.
460 They are met! The gout returns, and his great carriage.

        Lictors, Consuls, Sejanus, etc. pass over the stage

  Lic. Give way, make place; room for the Consul.
  San.   Hail,
Hail, great Sejanus.
    Hat.   Hail, my honoured lord.
    Arr. We shall be marked anon, for our not-hail.
    Lep. That is already done.
    Arr.   It is a note
465 Of upstart greatness, to observe and watch
For these poor trifles, which the noble mind
Neglects and scorns.
    Lep.   Aye, and they think themselves
Deeply dishonoured, where they are omitted,
As if they were necessities, that helped
470 To the perfection of their dignities:
And hate the men, that but refrain 'em.
    Arr.   Oh!
There is a farther cause of hate. Their breasts
Are guilty, that we know their obscure springs,
And base beginnings: thence the anger grows. On. Follow.

                                   [Exeunt]

              Enter Macro, Laco

475   *Mac.* When all are entered, shut the temple doors;
And bring your guards up to the gate.
    Lac.   I will.
    Mac. If you shall hear commotion in the Senate,
Present yourself: and charge on any man
Shall offer to come forth.
    Lac.   I am instructed.   *[Exeunt]*

458 *Liburnian*: Illyrian slaves after whom the *liburna* (a sedan-chair) was named
464 *note*: sign, characteristic

[The Temple of Apollo]

The Senate

Enter Haterius, Trio, Sanquinius, Cotta, Regulus,
Sejanus, Pomponius, Latiaris, Lepidus, Arruntius,
Praecones, Lictores

Hat. How well his lordship looks today!
Tri.   As if   480
He had been born, or made for this hour's state.
   Cot. Your fellow Consul's come about, methinks?
Tri. Aye, he is wise.
San.   Sejanus trusts him well.
Tri. Sejanus is a noble, bounteous lord.
Hat. He is so, and most valiant.
Lat.   And most wise.   485
Sen. He's everything.
Lat.   Worthy of all, and more
Than bounty can bestow.
   Tri.   This dignity
Will make him worthy.
Pom.   Above Caesar.
San.   Tut,
Caesar is but the rector of an isle,
He of the empire.
   Tri.   Now he will have power   490
More to reward than ever.
Cot.   Let us look
We be not slack in giving him our voices.
   Lat. Not I.
San.   Nor I.
Cot.   The readier we seem
To propagate his honours, will more bind
His thought to ours.
   Hat.   I think right with your lordship.   495
It is the way to have us hold our places.
   San. Aye, and get more.
Lat.   More office, and more titles.

Pom. I will not lose the part I hope to share
In these his fortunes, for my patrimony.

500   *Lat.* See, how Arruntius sits, and Lepidus.

   Tri. Let 'em alone, they will be marked anon.

   1st Sen. I'll do with others.

   2nd Sen.   So will I.

   3rd Sen.   And I.

Men grow not in the state, but as they are planted
Warm in his favours.

   Cot.   Noble Sejanus!

   Hat. Honoured Sejanus!

505   *Lat.*   Worthy, and great Sejanus!

   Arr. Gods! How the sponges open, and take in!
And shut again! Look, look! Is not he blessed
That gets a seat in eye-reach of him? More,
That comes in ear, or tongue-reach? Oh, but most,
510 Can claw his subtle elbow, or with a buzz
Fly-blow his ears.

   Pra.   Proclaim the Senate's peace;
And give last summons by the edict.

   Pra.   Silence:
In name of Caesar and the Senate. Silence.

'Memmius Regulus, and Fulcinius Trio, Consuls, these present
515 kalends of June, with the first light, shall hold a senate, in the temple
of Apollo Palatine, all that are Fathers, and are registered Fathers,
that have right of entering the Senate, we warn, or command, you
be frequently present, take knowledge the business is the common-
wealth's, whosoever is absent, his fine, or mulct, will be taken, his
520 excuse will not be taken.'

   Tri. Note who are absent, and record their names.

   Reg. Fathers Conscript. May what I am to utter,
Turn good and happy for the commonwealth.
And thou Apollo, in whose holy house
525 We here are met, inspire us all, with truth,
And liberty of censure, to our thought.
The majesty of great Tiberius Caesar

---

515 *kalends*: first day of the month   516 *registered*: Lat. *conscripti*, as at
III. 28 n.   518 *frequently*: in full muster (l. 100)

Propounds to this grave Senate the bestowing
Upon the man he loves, honoured Sejanus,
The tribunitial dignity, and power;   530
Here are his letters, signed with his signet:
What pleaseth now the Fathers to be done?
 Sen. Read, read 'em, open, publicly, read 'em.
 Cot. Caesar hath honoured his own greatness much,
In thinking of this act.
 Tri.   It was a thought   535
Happy, and worthy Caesar.
 Lat.   And the lord,
As worthy it, on whom it is directed!
 Hat. Most worthy!
 San.   Rome did never boast the virtue
That could give envy bounds, but his: Sejanus——
 1st Sen. Honoured and noble!
 2nd Sen.   Good, and great Sejanus!   540
 Arr. O, most tame slavery and fierce flattery!
 Pra.   Silence.

(*The Epistle is read*)

'Tiberius Caesar

To the Senate

Greeting

If you, Conscript Fathers, with your children, be in health, it is
abundantly well: we with our friends here, are so. The care of the
commonwealth, howsoever we are removed in person, cannot be
absent to our thought; although, oftentimes, even to princes most   545
present, the truth of their own affairs is hid: than which, nothing
falls out more miserable to a state, or makes the art of governing
more difficult. But since it hath been our easeful happiness to enjoy
both the aids, and industry of so vigilant a Senate, we profess to have
been the more indulgent to our pleasures, not as being careless of our   550
office, but rather secure of the necessity. Neither do these common
rumours of many and infamous libels published against our retire-
ment, at all afflict us; being born more out of men's ignorance than

their malice: and will, neglected, find their own grave quickly;
555 whereas too sensibly acknowledged, it would make their obloquy
ours. Nor do we desire their authors (though found) be censured,
since in a free state (as ours) all men ought to enjoy their minds, and
tongues free.'

    (*Arr.* The lapwing, the lapwing.)

560 'Yet, in things, which shall worthily, and more near concern the
majesty of a prince, we shall fear to be so unnaturally cruel to our
own fame, as to neglect them. True it is, Conscript Fathers, that we
have raised Sejanus, from obscure, and almost unknown gentry,

    (*Sen.* How! How!)

565 'to the highest, and most conspicuous point of greatness, and (we
hope) deservingly; yet, not without danger: it being a most bold
hazard in that sovereign, who, by his particular love to one, dares
adventure the hatred of all his other subjects.'

    (*Arr.* This touches, the blood turns.)

570 'But we affie in your loves, and understandings, and do no way
suspect the merit of our Sejanus to make our favours offensive
to any.'

    (*Sen.* Oh! Good, good.)

'Though we could have wished his zeal had run a calmer course
,575 against Agrippina, and our nephews, howsoever the openness of
their actions declared them delinquents; and, that he would have
remembered, no innocence is so safe, but it rejoiceth to stand in the
sight of mercy: the use of which in us, he hath so quite taken away,
toward them, by his loyal fury, as now our clemency would be
580 thought but wearied cruelty, if we should offer to exercise it.'

    (*Arr.* I thank him, there I looked for it. A good fox!)

'Some there be, that would interpret this his public severity to be
particular ambition; and that, under a pretext of service to us, he
doth but remove his own lets: alleging the strengths he hath made
585 to himself, by the Praetorian soldiers, by his faction in Court, and
Senate, by the offices he holds himself, and confers on others, his
popularity, and dependents, his urging (and almost driving) us to
this our unwilling retirement, and lastly his aspiring to be our son-
in-law.'

    559 *lapwing*: supposed to cry at a distance from its nest, to deceive searchers
    570 *affie in*: trust in

  (*Sen.* This is strange!   590

  Arr. I shall anon believe your vultures, Marcus.)

'Your wisdoms, Conscript Fathers, are able to examine, and censure these suggestions. But, were they left to our absolving voice, we durst pronounce them, as we think them, most malicious.'

  (*Sen.* Oh, he has restored all, list.)   595

'Yet, are they offered to be averred, and on the lives of the informers. What we should say, or rather what we should not say, lords of the Senate, if this be true, our gods, and goddesses confound us if we know! Only, we must think, we have placed our benefits ill: and conclude, that, in our choice, either we were wanting to the gods, or   600 the gods to us.'   (*The* Senators *shift their places*)

  (*Arr.* The place grows hot, they shift.)

'We have not been covetous, honourable Fathers, to change; neither is it now any new lust that alters our affection, or old loathing: but those needful jealousies of state, that warn wiser princes hourly, to   605 provide their safety; and do teach them how learned a thing it is to beware of the humblest enemy; much more of those great ones, whom their own employed favours have made fit for their fears.'

  (*1st Sen.* Away.

  2nd Sen.   Sit farther.

  Cot.   Let's remove——

  Arr. Gods! How the leaves drop off, this little wind!)   610

'We therefore desire, that the offices he holds, be first seized by the Senate; and himself suspended from all exercise of place, or power——'

  (*Sen.* How!

  San.   By your leave.

  Arr.   Come, porpoise—where's Haterius? His gout keeps him most miserably constant—   615 Your dancing shows a tempest.)

  Sej.   Read no more.

  Reg. Lords of the Senate, hold your seats: read on.

  Sej. These letters, they are forged.

  Reg.   A guard, sit still.

Laco enters with the guards

605 *jealousies*: anxieties   606 *provide*: II. 460   615 *porpoise*: cf. l. 455—the 'dancing' was taken as a storm warning

Arr. There's change.

Reg.   Bid silence, and read forward.

620   *Pra*. Silence——'and himself suspended from all exercise of place,
or power, but till due and mature trial be made of his innocency,
which yet we can faintly apprehend the necessity, to doubt. If,
Conscript Fathers, to your more searching wisdoms, there shall
appear farther cause (or of farther proceeding, either to seizure of
625 lands, goods, or more——) it is not our power that shall limit your
authority, or our favour, that must corrupt your justice: either were
dishonourable in you, and both uncharitable to ourself. We would
willingly be present with your counsels in this business, but the
danger of so potent a faction (if it should prove so) forbids our
630 attempting it: except one of the Consuls would be entreated for our
safety, to undertake the guard of us home, then we should most
readily adventure. In the meantime, it shall not be fit for us to
importune so judicious a Senate, who know how much they hurt
the innocent, that spare the guilty: and how grateful a sacrifice, to
635 the gods, is the life of an ingrateful person. We reflect not, in this,
on Sejanus (notwithstanding, if you keep an eye upon him——and
there is Latiaris a Senator, and Pinnarius Natta, two of his most
trusted ministers, and so professed, whom we desire not to have
apprended) but as the necessity of the cause exacts it.'

Reg. A guard on Latiaris.

640   *Arr*.   Oh, the spy!
The reverend spy is caught, who pities him?
Reward, sir, for your service: now, you ha' done
Your property, you see what use is made?
Hang up the instrument.

Sej.   Give leave.

Lac.   Stand, stand,
645 He comes upon his death, that doth advance
An inch toward my point.

Sej.   Have we no friends here?

Arr. Hushed. Where now are all the hails, and acclamations?

Enter Macro

Mac. Hail, to the Consuls, and this noble Senate.

Sej. [*Aside*] Is Macro here? Oh, thou art lost Sejanus.

Mac. Sit still, and unaffrighted, reverend Fathers.   650
Macro, by Caesar's grace, the new-made Provost,
And now possessed of the praetorian bands,
An honour late belonged to that proud man,
Bids you, be safe: and to your constant doom
Of his deservings, offers you the surety   655
Of all the soldiers, tribunes, and centurions,
Received in our command.

Reg.   Sejanus, Sejanus,
Stand forth, Sejanus.

Sej.   Am I called?

Mac.   Aye, thou,
Thou insolent monster, art bid stand.

Sej.   Why, Macro,
It hath been otherwise, between you and I?   660
This court that knows us both, hath seen a difference,
And can (if it be pleased to speak) confirm,
Whose insolence is most.

Mac.   Come down, Typhoeus,
If mine be most, lo, thus I make it more;
Kick up thy heels in air, tear off thy robe,   665
Play with thy beard and nostrils. Thus 'tis fit,
And no man take compassion of thy state,
To use the ingrateful viper, tread his brains
Into the earth.

Reg.   Forbear.

Mac.   If I could lose
All my humanity now, 'twere well to torture   670
So meriting a traitor. Wherefore, Fathers,
Sit you amazed, and silent? And not censure
This wretch, who in the hour he first rebelled
'Gainst Caesar's bounty, did condemn himself?
Phlegra, the field, where all the sons of earth   675
Mustered against the gods, did ne'er acknowledge
So proud and huge a monster.

---

654 *doom*: judgement   663 *Typhoeus*: one of the giants who did battle with
the gods   675 *Phlegra*: the battlefield where Zeus struck down the giants

   Reg.   Take him hence.
And all the gods guard Caesar.
   Tri.   Take him hence.
   Hat. Hence.
   Cot.   To the dungeon with him.
   San.   He deserves it.
   Sen. Crown all our doors with bays.
680   *San.*   And let an ox
With gilded horns, and garlands, straight be led
Unto the Capitol.
   Hat.   And sacrificed
To Jove, for Caesar's safety.
   Tri.   All our gods
Be present still to Caesar.
   Cot.   Phoebus.
   San.   Mars.
   Hat. Diana.
   San.   Pallas.
685   *Sen.*   Juno, Mercury,
All guard him.
   Mac.   Forth, thou prodigy of men. [*Exit* Sejanus, *guarded*]
   Cot. Let all the traitor's titles be defaced.
   Tri. His images and statues be pulled down.
   Hat. His chariot-wheels be broken.
   Arr.   And the legs
690 Of the poor horses, that deserved naught,
Let them be broken too.
   Lep.   O, violent change,
And whirl of men's affections!
   Arr.   Like, as both
Their bulks and souls were bound on Fortune's wheel,
And must act only with her motion!
                      [*Exeunt all but* Lepidus, Arruntius]
695   *Lep.* Who would depend upon the popular air,
Or voice of men, that have today beheld,
That which if all the gods had foredeclared,
Would not have been believed, Sejanus' fall?
He, that this morn rose proudly, as the sun?

And, breaking through a mist of clients' breath,   700
Came on as gazed at, and admired, as he
When superstitious Moors salute his light!
That had our servile nobles waiting him
As common grooms; and hanging on his look,
No less than human life on destiny!   705
That had men's knees as frequent, as the gods;
And sacrifices, more, than Rome had altars:
And this man fall! Fall? Aye, without a look,
That durst appear his friend; or lend so much
Of vain relief, to his changed state, as pity!   710
  Arr. They, that before like gnats played in his beams,
And thronged to circumscribe him, now not seen!
Nor deign to hold a common seat with him!
Others, that waited him unto the Senate,
Now inhumanely ravish him to prison,   715
Whom, but this morn, they followed as their lord!
Guard through the streets, bound like a fugitive!
Instead of wreaths, give fetters; strokes, for stoops:
Blind shame, for honours; and black taunts, for titles!
Who would trust slippery chance?
  Lep.   They, that would make   720
Themselves her spoil: and foolishly forget,
When she doth flatter, that she comes to prey.
Fortune, thou hadst no deity, if men
Had wisdom: we have placed thee so high,
By fond belief in thy felicity.   725
  Sen. The gods guard Caesar. All the gods guard Caesar.
                         (*Shout within*)

Enter Macro, Regulus, Senators

  Mac. Now great Sejanus, you that awed the state,
And sought to bring the nobles to your whip,
That would be Caesar's tutor, and dispose
Of dignities and offices! That had   730
The public head still bare to your designs,

---

702 *Moors*: believed by the Romans to worship the sun   717 *fugitive*: runaway
slave

And made the general voice to echo yours!
That looked for salutations, twelve score off,
And would have pyramids, yea, temples reared
735 To your huge greatness! Now you lie as flat,
As was your pride advanced.
    Reg.   Thanks, to the gods.
    Sen. And praise to Macro, that hath saved Rome.
Liberty, liberty, liberty. Lead on,
And praise to Macro, that hath saved Rome.
                   [Exeunt all but Arruntius, Lepidus]
740   *Arr.* I prophesy, out of this Senate's flattery,
That this new fellow, Macro, will become
A greater prodigy in Rome, than he
That now is fallen.

[*Enter* Terentius]

    Ter.   O you, whose minds are good,
And have not forced all mankind, from your breasts;
745 That yet have so much stock of virtue left,
To pity guilty states, when they are wretched:
Lend your soft ears to hear, and eyes to weep
Deeds done by men, beyond the acts of furies.
The eager multitude, who never yet
750 Knew why to love, or hate, but only pleased
To express their rage of power, no sooner heard
The murmur of Sejanus in decline,
But with that speed, and heat of appetite,
With which they greedily devour the way
755 To some great sports, or a new theatre,
They filled the Capitol, and Pompey's cirque;
Where, like so many mastiffs, biting stones,
As if his statues now were sensive grown
Of their wild fury, first, they tear them down:
760 Then fastening ropes, drag them along the streets,
Crying in scorn, this, this was that rich head
Was crowned with garlands, and with odours, this

---

733 *twelve score off*: i.e. yards, a common length for a shot in archery   744 *mankind*: human feeling

That was in Rome so reverenced! Now
The furnace, and the bellows shall to work,
The great Sejanus crack, and piece, by piece, 765
Drop in the founder's pit.
   Lep.   O, popular rage!
   Ter. The whilst, the Senate, at the temple of Concord,
Make haste to meet again, and thronging cry,
Let us condemn him, tread him down in water,
While he doth lie upon the bank; away: 770
Where some, more tardy, cry unto their bearers,
He will be censured ere we come, run knaves;
And use that furious diligence, for fear
Their bondmen should inform against their slackness,
And bring their quaking flesh unto the hook: 775
The rout, they follow with confused voice,
Crying, they are glad, say they could ne'er abide him;
Enquire, what man he was? What kind of face?
What beard he had? What nose? What lips? Protest,
They ever did presage he would come to this: 780
They never thought him wise, nor valiant: ask
After his garments, when he dies? What death?
And not a beast of all the herd demands,
What was his crime? Or, who were his accusers?
Under what proof, or testimony, he fell? 785
There came (says one) a huge, long, worded letter
From Capreae against him. Did there so?
Oh, they are satisfied, no more.
   Lep.   Alas!
They follow fortune, and hate men condemned,
Guilty, or not.
   Arr.   But had Sejanus thrived 790
In his design, and prosperously oppressed
The old Tiberius, then, in that same minute,
These very rascals, that now rage like furies,
Would have proclaim'd Sejanus emperor.
   Lep. But what hath followed?
   Ter.   Sentence, by the Senate; 795
To lose his head: which was no sooner off,

But that, and the unfortunate trunk were seized
By the rude multitude; who not content
With what the forward justice of the state
800 Officiously had done, with violent rage
Have rent it limb from limb. A thousand heads,
A thousand hands, ten thousand tongues, and voices,
Employed at once in several acts of malice!
Old men not staid with age, virgins with shame,
805 Late wives with loss of husbands, mothers of children,
Losing all grief in joy of his sad fall,
Run quite transported with their cruelty!
These mounting at his head, these at his face,
These digging out his eyes, those with his brain,
810 Sprinkling themselves, their houses, and their friends;
Others are met, have ravished thence an arm,
And deal small pieces of the flesh for favours;
These with a thigh; this hath cut off his hands;
And this his feet; these fingers, and these toes;
815 That hath his liver; he his heart: there wants
Nothing but room for wrath, and place for hatred!
What cannot oft be done, is now o'erdone.
The whole, and all of what was great Sejanus,
And next to Caesar did possess the world,
820 Now torn and scattered, as he needs no grave,
Each little dust covers a little part:
So lies he nowhere, and yet often buried!

[*Enter* Nuntius]

   Arr. More of Sejanus?
   Nun.   Yes.
   Lep.   What can be added?
We know him dead.
   Nun.   Then, there begin your pity.
825 There is enough behind, to melt even Rome
And Caesar into tears: since never slave
Could yet so highly offend, but tyranny,
In torturing him, would make him worth lamenting.
A son and daughter, to the dead Sejanus,

Of whom there is not now so much remaining　　　　830
As would give fastening to the hangman's hook,
Have they drawn forth for farther sacrifice;
Whose tenderness of knowledge, unripe years,
And childish silly innocence was such,
As scarce would lend them feeling of their danger:　　835
The girl so simple, as she often asked,
Where they would lead her? For what cause they dragged her?
Cried, she would do no more. That she could take
Warning with beating. And because our laws
Admit no virgin immature to die,　　　　　840
The wittily and strangely-cruel Macro,
Delivered her to be deflowered and spoiled
By the rude lust of the licentious hangman,
Then, to be strangled with her harmless brother.

   Lep. O, act, most worthy hell, and lasting night,　　845
To hide it from the world!

   Nun.　　　　　　　Their bodies thrown
Into the Gemonies, I know not how,
Or by what accident returned, the mother,
The expulsed Apicata, finds them there;
Whom when she saw lie spread on the degrees,　　850
After a world of fury on herself,
Tearing her hair, defacing of her face,
Beating her breasts and womb, kneeling amazed,
Crying to heaven, then to them; at last,
Her drowned voice gat up above her woes:　　855
And with such black and bitter execrations,
(As might affright the gods, and force the sun
Run backward to the east, nay, make the old
Deformed Chaos rise again, to o'erwhelm
Them, us, and all the world) she fills the air;　　860
Upbraids the heavens with their partial dooms,
Defies their tyrannous powers, and demands,
What she, and those poor innocents have transgressed,
That they must suffer such a share in vengeance,

---

834 *silly*: simple　　841 *wittily*: ingeniously　　850 *degrees*: steps　　861 *partial dooms*: unjust decrees

865 Whilst Livia, Lygdus, and Eudemus live,
    Who, as she says, and firmly vows, to prove it
    To Caesar and the Senate, poisoned Drusus?
       Lep. Confederates with her husband?
       Nun.   Aye.
       Lep.   Strange act!
       Arr. And strangely opened: what says now my monster,
870 The multitude? They reel now? Do they not?
       Nun. Their gall is gone, and now they 'gin to weep
    The mischief they have done.
       Arr.   I thank 'em, rogues!
       Nun. Part are so stupid, or so flexible,
    As they believe him innocent; all grieve:
875 And some, whose hands yet reek with his warm blood,
    And grip the part which they did tear of him,
    Wish him collected, and created new.
       Lep. How Fortune plies her sports, when she begins
    To practise 'em! Pursues, continues, adds!
880 Confounds, with varying her impassioned moods!
       Arr. Dost thou hope, Fortune, to redeem thy crimes?
    To make amends, for thy ill-placed favours,
    With these strange punishments? Forbear, you things,
    That stand upon the pinnacles of state,
885 To boast your slippery height; when you do fall,
    You pash yourselves in pieces, ne'er to rise:
    And he that lends you pity, is not wise.
       Ter. Let this example move the insolent man,
    Not to grow proud, and careless of the gods:
890 It is an odious wisdom, to blaspheme,
    Much more to slighten, or deny their powers.
    For, whom the morning saw so great, and high,
    Thus low, and little, 'fore the even doth lie.   [*Exeunt*]

THE END

886 *pash*: break violently

VOLPONE *or* THE FOX

VOLPONE,

OR
THE FOXE.

A Comœdie.

Acted in the yeere 1605. By
the K. MAIESTIES
SERVANTS.

The Author B. I.

HORAT.
Simul & iucunda, & idonea dicere vitæ.

LONDON,

Printed by WILLIAM STANSBY.

M. DC. XVI.

The title-page of the 1616 Folio.

TO

THE MOST

NOBLE AND

MOST EQVALL

SISTERS

THE TWO FAMOVS

VNIVERSITIES

FOR THEIR LOVE

AND

ACCEPTANCE

SHEWN TO HIS POEME IN THE

PRESENTATION

BEN. IONSON

THE GRATEFVLL ACKNOWLEDGER

DEDICATES

BOTH IT AND HIMSELFE.

NEVER (most equal Sisters) had any man a wit so presently excellent, as that it could raise itself; but there must come both matter, occasion, commenders, and favourers to it. If this be true, and that the fortune of all writers doth daily prove it, it behoves the careful to provide well toward these accidents: and having acquired them, 5 to preserve that part of reputation most tenderly, wherein the benefit of a friend is also defended. Hence is it that I now render myself grateful, and am studious to justify the bounty of your act: to which, though your mere authority were satisfying, yet, it being an age wherein Poetry, and the professors of it hear so ill on all 10 sides, there will a reason be looked for in the subject. It is certain, nor can it with any forehead be opposed, that the too much licence of Poetasters, in this time, hath much deformed their mistress; that every day, their manifold and manifest ignorance doth stick unnatural reproaches upon her. But for their petulancy, 15 it were an act of the greatest injustice, either to let the learned suffer; or so divine a skill (which indeed should not be attempted with unclean hands) to fall under the least contempt. For if men will impartially, and not a-squint, look toward the offices and function of a Poet, they will easily conclude to themselves the impossibility 20 of any man's being the good Poet, without first being a good man. He that is said to be able to inform young men to all good disciplines, inflame grown men to all great virtues, keep old men in their best and supreme state, or as they decline to childhood, recover them to their first strength; that comes forth the interpreter and arbiter of 25 nature, a teacher of things divine, no less than human, a master in manners; and can alone (or with a few) effect the business of mankind: this, I take him, is no subject for pride and ignorance to exercise their railing rhetoric upon. But, it will here be hastily answered, that the writers of these days are other things; that not 30 only their manners, but their natures are inverted; and nothing remaining with them of the dignity of Poet, but the abused name,

---

1 *presently*: instantly   10 *professors*: those practising it   *hear so ill*: have such an evil reputation   12 *forehead*: assurance   20–1 *impossibility* . . . *good man*: Strabo, *Geographica*, I. ii. 5   22–8 Minturno, *De Poeta* (1559), p. 8   22 *inform*: shape, mould

which every scribe usurps: that now, especially in dramatic, or (as
they term it) stage-poetry, nothing but ribaldry, profanation, blas-
35 phemy, all licence of offence to God and man is practised. I dare
not deny a great part of this (and am sorry, I dare not) because in
some men's abortive features (and would they had never boasted
the light) it is over-true. But, that all are embarked in this bold
adventure for hell, is a most uncharitable thought, and, uttered, a
40 more malicious slander. For my particular, I can (and from a most
clear conscience) affirm, that I have ever trembled to think toward
the least profaneness; have loathed the use of such foul and un-
washed bawdry as is now made the food of the scene. And howso-
ever I cannot escape, from some, the imputation of sharpness, but
45 that they will say I have taken a pride, or lust, to be bitter, and not
my youngest infant but hath come into the world with all his teeth;
I would ask of these supercilious politiques, what nation, society,
or general order, or state I have provoked? What public person?
Whether I have not (in all these) preserved their dignity, as mine
50 own person, safe? My works are read, allowed (I speak of those
that are entirely mine); look into them: what broad reproofs have
I used? Where have I been particular? Where personal? Except
to a mimic, cheater, bawd, or buffoon, creatures (for their in-
solencies) worthy to be taxed? Yet, to which of these so pointingly
55 as he might not, either ingenuously have confessed, or wisely
dissembled his disease? But it is not rumour can make men guilty,
much less entitle me to other men's crimes. I know that nothing
can be so innocently writ, or carried, but may be made obnoxious
to construction; marry, whilst I bear mine innocence about me,
60 I fear it not. Application is now grown a trade with many; and there
are that profess to have a key for the deciphering of everything:
but let wise and noble persons take heed how they be too credulous,
or give leave to these invading interpreters, to be over-familiar with
their fames, who cunningly, and often, utter their own virulent
65 malice under other men's simplest meanings. As for those, that will
(by faults which charity hath raked up, or common honesty con-

---

37 *features*: creations   45 *lust*: delight   46 *youngest*: *Sejanus*, which brought
Jonson before the Privy Council   51 *entirely mine*: referring to collaboration in
Sej. and *EH*   53 *mimic*: actor   58 *obnoxious*: liable   60 *Application*: i.e.
identifying the characters with particular people   64 *fames*: reputations   *utter*:
give currency to   66 *raked up*: covered

cealed) make themselves a name with the multitude, or (to draw
their rude and beastly claps) care not whose living faces they
entrench with their petulant styles; may they do it, without a rival,
for me: I choose rather to live graved in obscurity, than share with 70
them in so preposterous a fame. Nor can I blame the wishes of
those severe and wiser patriots, who providing the hurts these
licentious spirits may do in a state, desire rather to see fools and
devils, and those antique relics of barbarism retrieved, with all other
ridiculous and exploded follies, than behold the wounds of private 75
men, of princes, and nations. For, as Horace makes Trebatius
speak, among these

> ——Sibi quisqe timet, quamquam est intactus, et odit.

And men may justly impute such rages, if continued, to the writer,
as his sports. The increase of which lust in liberty, together with 80
the present trade of the stage, in all their misc'line interludes, what
learned or liberal soul doth not already abhor? Where nothing but
the filth of the time is uttered, and that with such impropriety of
phrase, such plenty of solecisms, such dearth of sense, so bold
prolepses, so racked metaphors, with brothelry, able to violate the 85
ear of a pagan, and blasphemy, to turn the blood of a Christian to
water. I cannot but be serious in a cause of this nature, wherein my
fame, and the reputations of divers honest and learned are the ques-
tion; when a name, so full of authority, antiquity, and all great
mark, is (through their insolence) become the lowest scorn of the 90
age: and those men subject to the petulancy of every vernaculous
orator, that were wont to be the care of kings, and happiest mon-
archs. This is it, that hath not only rapt me to present indignation,
but made me studious heretofore; and, by all my actions, to stand
off from them: which may most appear in this my latest work 95
(which you, most learned Arbitresses, have seen, judged, and to
my crown, approved) wherein I have laboured, for their instruction
and amendment, to reduce not only the ancient forms, but manners
of the scene, the easiness, the propriety, the innocence, and last the

---

71 *preposterous*: upsetting the natural order   72 *patriots*: fellow-countrymen
providing: foreseeing   74 *antique*: (1) antiquated (2) grotesque   77 Horace,
Sat. II. i. 23 (*Poet.* III. v. 41–2)   81 *misc'line interludes*: *ludi miscelli*, variety
entertainments   85 *prolepses*: anachronisms   89 *name*: i.e. of poet   98 *reduce*:
bring back

100 doctrine, which is the principal end of poesy, to inform men in the
best reason of living. And though my catastrophe may, in the strict
rigour of comic law, meet with censure, as turning back to my
promise, I desire the learned and charitable critic to have so much
faith in me, to think it was done of industry: for with what ease I
105 could have varied it nearer his scale (but that I fear to boast my
own faculty) I could here insert. But my special aim being to put the
snaffle in their mouths, that cry out, we never punish vice in our
interludes, etc. I took the more liberty; though not without some
lines of example, drawn even in the ancients themselves, the goings-
110 out of whose comedies are not always joyful, but oft times, the
bawds, the servants, the rivals, yea, and the masters are mulcted:
and fitly, it being the office of a comic Poet, to imitate justice, and
instruct to life, as well as purity of language, or stir up gentle
affections. To which, I shall take the occasion elsewhere to speak.
115 For the present (most reverenced Sisters) as I have cared to be
thankful for your affections past, and here made the understanding
acquainted with some ground of your favours, let me not despair
their continuance, to the maturing of some worthier fruits: wherein,
if my Muses be true to me, I shall raise the despised head of Poetry
120 again, and stripping her out of those rotten and base rags, where-
with the times have adulterated her form, restore her to her primi-
tive habit, feature, and majesty, and render her worthy to be em-
braced and kissed of all the great and master-spirits of our world.
As for the vile and slothful, who never affected an act worthy of
125 celebration, or are so inward with their own vicious natures, as they
worthily fear her; and think it a high point of policy to keep her in
contempt with their declamatory and windy invectives: she shall
out of just rage incite her servants (who are *genus irritabile*) to spout
ink in their faces, that shall eat, farther than their marrow, into their
130 fames; and not Cinnamus the barber, with his art, shall be able to
take out the brands, but they shall live, and be read, till the wretches
die, as things worst deserving of themselves in chief, and then of all
mankind.

104 *of industry*: intentionally   111 *mulcted:* punished   114 *elsewhere*: in
the lost commentary on Horace's *Art of Poetry*   128 *genus irritabile:* 'a peevish
tribe' (Horace, *Epist*. II. i. 102)   130 *Cinnamus*: celebrated in Martial (VI. lxiv.
24–6) for his skill in removing brands

The Persons of the Play

Volpone, *a Magnifico*
Mosca, *his Parasite*
Voltore, *an Advocate*
Corbaccio, *an old gentleman*
Corvino, *a merchant*
Avocatori, *four Magistrates*
Notario, *the Register*
Nano, *a dwarf*
Castrone, *an eunuch*
Grege [*the crowd*]
Sir Politic Would-be, *a knight*

Peregrine, *a gentleman-traveller*
Bonario, *a young gentleman*
Fine Madam Would-be, *the knight's wife*
Celia, *the merchant's wife*
Commandadori, *Officers*
Mercatori, *three merchants*
Androgyno, *a hermaphrodite*
Servitore, *a servant*
Women

The Scene

Venice

VOLPONE,

OR

THE FOX

THE ARGUMENT

V olpone, childless, rich, feigns sick, despairs,
O ffers his state to hopes of several heirs,
L ies languishing; his parasite receives
P resents of all, assures, deludes: then weaves
O ther cross-plots, which open themselves, are told.   5
N ew tricks for safety are sought; they thrive: when, bold,
E ach tempts the other again, and all are sold.

PROLOGUE

Now, luck yet send us, and a little wit
    Will serve, to make our play hit;
According to the palates of the season,
    Here is rhyme, not empty of reason:
This we were bid to credit, from our poet,   5
    Whose true scope, if you would know it,
In all his poems, still, hath been this measure,
    To mix profit with your pleasure;
And not as some (whose throats their envy failing)
    Cry hoarsely, all he writes is railing: 10

---

3 *parasite*: one kept at another's expense, repaying him with flattery; but see
Mosca's speech at III. i (mosca = fly)   (*Prologue*) 8 Horace, *Ars Poetica*, 343-4
9 *as some*: Marston, in the prologue to *The Dutch Curtezan* (1605)

And when his plays come forth, think they can flout them,
   With saying, he was a year about them.
To these there needs no lie, but this his creature,
   Which was, two months since, no feature;
15 And though he dares give them five lives to mend it,
   'Tis known, five weeks fully penned it:
From his own hand, without a co-adjutor,
   Novice, journeyman, or tutor.
Yet, thus much I can give you, as a token
20   Of his play's worth, no eggs are broken;
Nor quaking custards with fierce teeth affrighted,
   Wherewith your rout are so delighted;
Nor hales he in a gull, old ends reciting,
   To stop gaps in his loose writing;
25 With such a deal of monstrous and forced action
   As might make Bedlam a faction:
Nor made he his play, for jests, stolen from each table,
   But makes jests, to fit his fable.
And so presents quick comedy, refined,
30   As best critics have designed,
The laws of time, place, persons he observeth,
   From no needful rule he swerveth.
All gall and copperas from his ink he draineth,
   Only, a little salt remaineth;
Wherewith he'll rub your cheeks, till red with laughter,
35   They shall look fresh, a week after.

14 *feature*: creation   17 *co-adjutor*: collaborator (of equal standing)   18 *Novice*:
a second hand learning his business   *journeyman*: underwriter engaged for a section
of the play   *tutor*: who superintended and corrected   21 *custards*: referring to
the huge custard set on the Lord Mayor's table at city feasts for the fool to jump into,
a practice burlesqued on the stage   23 *ends*: tags, quotations (perhaps glancing
at Gonzago in Marston's *Parasitaster*)   26 i.e. recruit supporters from Bedlam
33 *gall . . . copperas*: both bitter; salt, not used in ink-making, allows a pun on the
sense 'wit'

ACT I, Scene i

[Volpone's house]

Enter Volpone, Mosca

Volp. Good morning to the day; and next, my gold:
Open the shrine, that I may see my saint.

[Mosca *reveals the treasure*]

Hail the world's soul, and mine. More glad than is
The teeming earth to see the longed-for sun
Peep through the horns of the celestial ram,   5
Am I, to view thy splendour, darkening his:
That lying here, amongst my other hoards,
Show'st like a flame by night; or like the day
Struck out of chaos, when all darkness fled
Unto the centre. Oh, thou son of Sol,   10
(But brighter than thy father) let me kiss,
With adoration, thee, and every relic
Of sacred treasure in this blessed room.
Well did wise poets, by thy glorious name,
Title that age, which they would have the best;   15
Thou being the best of things: and far transcending
All style of joy, in children, parents, friends,
Or any other waking dream on earth.
Thy looks, when they to Venus did ascribe,
They should have given her twenty thousand Cupids;   20
Such are thy beauties, and our loves! Dear saint,
Riches, the dumb god, that giv'st all men tongues:
That canst do naught, and yet mak'st men do all things;
The price of souls; even hell, with thee to boot,
Is made worth heaven! Thou art virtue, fame,   25
Honour, and all things else! Who can get thee,
He shall be noble, valiant, honest, wise——

    Mos. And what he will, sir. Riches are in fortune
A greater good than wisdom is in nature.

---

5 *celestial ram*: Aries, which the sun enters on 21 March   19 *Venus*: 'aurea
Venus' in Virgil and Ovid   22 *dumb god*: silence is golden

30   *Volp.* True, my beloved Mosca. Yet, I glory
     More in the cunning purchase of my wealth
     Than in the glad possession; since I gain
     No common way: I use no trade, no venture;
     I wound no earth with ploughshares; fat no beasts
35   To feed the shambles; have no mills for iron,
     Oil, corn, or men, to grind 'em into powder;
     I blow no subtle glass; expose no ships
     To threatenings of the furrow-faced sea;
     I turn no moneys in the public bank;
     Nor usure private——
40   *Mos.*   No, sir, nor devour
     Soft prodigals. You shall ha' some will swallow
     A melting heir as glibly as your Dutch
     Will pills of butter, and ne'er purge for't;
     Tear forth the fathers of poor families
45   Out of their beds, and coffin them, alive,
     In some kind, clasping prison, where their bones
     May be forthcoming, when the flesh is rotten:
     But your sweet nature doth abhor these courses;
     You loathe the widow's, or the orphan's tears
50   Should wash your pavements; or their piteous cries
     Ring in your roofs; and beat the air, for vengeance.——
     Volp. Right, Mosca, I do loathe it.
     Mos.   And besides, sir,
     You are not like the thresher that doth stand
     With a huge flail, watching a heap of corn,
55   And, hungry, dares not taste the smallest grain,
     But feeds on mallows and such bitter herbs;
     Nor like the merchant, who hath filled his vaults
     With Romagnía, and rich Candian wines,
     Yet drinks the lees of Lombard's vinegar:
60   You will not lie in straw, whilst moths and worms
     Feed on your sumptuous hangings and soft beds.

---

31 *purchase*: acquisition   35 *shambles*: slaughter house   *mills for iron*: the
smelting consumed timber   37 *glass*: for which Venice was famed   42 *Dutch*:
noted for their consumption of butter   58 *Romagnía*: a sweet wine of Greek origin
Candian: e.g. Malmsey, from Greece and Crete (Candy)

You know the use of riches, and dare give, now,
From that bright heap, to me, your poor observer,
Or to your dwarf, or your hermaphrodite,
Your eunuch, or what other household-trifle   65
Your pleasure allows maintenance.——

   Volp.   Hold thee, Mosca,
                                    [*Gives him money*]

Take, of my hand; thou strik'st on truth, in all:
And they are envious, term thee parasite.
Call forth my dwarf, my eunuch, and my fool,
And let 'em make me sport. [*Exit* Mosca] What should I do,   70
But cocker up my genius, and live free
To all delights my fortune calls me to?
I have no wife, no parent, child, ally,
To give my substance to; but whom I make,
Must be my heir: and this makes men observe me.   75
This draws new clients, daily, to my house,
Women, and men, of every sex and age,
That bring me presents, send me plate, coin, jewels
With hope, that when I die (which they expect
Each greedy minute) it shall then return,   80
Tenfold, upon them; whilst some, covetous
Above the rest, seek to engross me, whole,
And counterwork the one unto the other,
Contend in gifts, as they would seem, in love:
All which I suffer, playing with their hopes,   85
And am content to coin 'em into profit,
And look upon their kindness, and take more,
And look on that; still bearing them in hand,
Letting the cherry knock against their lips,
And draw it, by their mouths, and back again. How now!   90

---

  66 *Hold thee*: Hold for yourself   71 *cocker up*: indulge   75 *observe*: court,
defer to (l. 63)   88 *bearing them in hand*: deluding them with false hopes   89 *cherry
knock*: as in the game of bob-cherry

ACT I, Scene ii

Enter Nano, Androgyno, Castrone, Mosca

Nan. Now, room for fresh gamesters, who do will you to know,
  They do bring you neither play, nor university show;
And therefore do entreat you, that whatsoever they rehearse,
  May not fare a whit the worse, for the false pace of the verse.
5 If you wonder at this, you will wonder more, ere we pass,
  For know, here [*Pointing to* Androgyno] is enclosed the soul of
      Pythagoras,
That juggler divine, as hereafter shall follow;
  Which soul (fast and loose, sir) came first from Apollo,
And was breathed into Aethalides, Mercurius his son,
10 Where it had the gift to remember all that ever was done.
From thence it fled forth, and made quick transmigration
  To goldy-locked Euphorbus, who was killed, in good fashion,
At the siege of old Troy, by the cuckold of Sparta.
  Hermotimus was next (I find it, in my charta)
15 To whom it did pass, where no sooner it was missing,
  But with one Pyrrhus of Delos it learned to go a-fishing:
And thence did it enter the Sophist of Greece.
  From Pythagore, she went into a beautiful piece,
Hight Aspasia, the meretrix; and the next toss of her
20 Was, again, of a whore, she became a philosopher,
Crates the Cynic: (as itself doth relate it)
  Since, kings, knights, and beggars, knaves, lords, and fools gat it,
Besides, ox and ass, camel, mule, goat, and brock,
  In all which it hath spoke, as in the cobbler's cock.

---

4 *false pace*: the four-stressed line of the moralities (*DA* I. i. 44 ff.)
6 *Pythagoras*: the transmigration of his soul is traced in Lucian's *Gallus* (the dialogue
of the cobbler and the cock), and in the *De Philosophorum Vitis* of Diogenes Laertius
7 *juggler*: magician, trickster   8 *fast and loose*: a game of deception described in
H&S ix. 691   9 *Aethalides*: herald of the Argonauts, with the gift from Mercury
of remembering everything   12 *Euphorbus*: the Trojan who first wounded Patroclus
13 *cuckold*: Menelaus   14 *Hermotimus*: famous prophet of Clazomenae   17 *Sophist*:
Pythagoras   19 *Aspasia*: mistress of Pericles ('meretrix' puns on 'merry tricks')
21 *Crates*: disciple of Diogenes the Cynic who scorned riches and was negligent in
dress   23 *brock*: badger

But I come not here, to discourse of that matter,   25
  Or his one, two, or three, or his greath oath, by quater,
His musics, his trigon, his golden thigh,
  Or his telling how elements shift: but I
Would ask how of late thou hast suffered translation,
  And shifted thy coat, in these days of reformation?   30
And. Like one of the reformed, a fool, as you see,
  Counting all old doctrine heresy.
Nan. But not on thine own forbid meats hast thou ventured?
  And. On fish, when first a Carthusian I entered.
Nan. Why, then thy dogmatical silence hath left thee?   35
  And. Of that an obstreperous lawyer bereft me.
Nan. Oh wonderful change! When sir lawyer forsook thee,
  For Pythagore's sake, what body then took thee?
And. A good dull mule.
Nan.   And how! By that means,
  Thou wert brought to allow of the eating of beans?   40
And. Yes.
Nan.   But, from the mule, into whom didst thou pass?
  And. Into a very strange beast, by some writers called an ass;
By others, a precise, pure, illuminate brother,
  Of those devour flesh, and sometimes one another:
And will drop you forth a libel, or a sanctified lie,   45
  Betwixt every spoonful of a nativity-pie.
Nan. Now quit thee, for heaven, of that profane nation;
  And gently, report thy next transmigration.
And. To the same that I am.
Nan.   A creature of delight?
  And (what is more than a fool) an hermaphrodite?   50
Now 'pray thee, sweet soul, in all thy variation,
  Which body wouldst thou choose to take up thy station?
And. Troth, this I am in, even here would I tarry.

---

26 *one, two, or three*: Pythagorean theory of number as principle of harmony (cf. musics, l. 27)   26-7 *quater ... trigon*: triangle of ten dots with a base of four (by which oaths were sworn)   30 *shifted*: changed   32 *old doctrine*: pre-Reformation teaching   33 *forbid meats*: including fish and beans   34 *fish*: taken jocularly as the staple diet of Carthusians   35 *silence*: enjoined on the Pythagoreans for five years   39 *mule*: the lawyer's mount   43 *precise ... brother*: Puritan 46 *nativity*: Puritan term for Christmas (avoiding the Popish 'mas')

Nan. 'Cause here, the delight of each sex thou canst vary?

55 *And.* Alas, those pleasures be stale and forsaken;

No, 'tis your fool wherewith I am so taken,

The only one creature, that I can call blessed:

For all other forms I have proved most distressed.

Nan. Spoke true, as thou wert in Pythagoras still.

60   This learned opinion we celebrate will,

Fellow eunuch (as behoves us) with all our wit, and art,

  To dignify that, whereof ourselves are so great, and special a part.

Vol. Now very, very pretty: Mosca, this

  Was thy invention?

Mos.   If it please my patron,

Not else.

Vol.   It doth, good Mosca.

65 *Mos.*   Then it was, sir.

SONG

Fools, they are the only nation

Worth men's envy, or admiration;

Free from care, or sorrow-taking,

Selves and others merry making:

70   All they speak or do is sterling.

Your fool, he is your great man's darling,

And your ladies' sport and pleasure;

Tongue and bauble are his treasure.

E'en his face begetteth laughter,

75   And he speaks truth, free from slaughter;

He's the grace of every feast,

And sometimes the chiefest guest:

Hath his trencher and his stool,

When wit waits upon the fool.

80   Oh, who would not be

He, he, he?   (*One knocks without*)

Volp. Who's that? Away.   [*Exeunt* Nano, Castrone]

            Look Mosca.

Mos.   Fool, be gone,

                         [*Exit* Androgyno]

73 *bauble*: the fool's mace (also phallus)   75 *free from slaughter*: i.e. with impunity

'Tis Signior Voltore, the advocate,
I know him by his knock.
   Volp.   Fetch me my gown,
My furs, and night-caps; say my couch is changing: 85
And let him entertain himself awhile,
Without i' the gallery. [*Exit* Mosca] Now, now, my clients
Begin their visitation! Vulture, kite,
Raven, and gor-crow, all my birds of prey,
That think me turning carcass, now they come: 90
I am not for 'em yet.

               [*Enter* Mosca]

              How now? The news?
   Mos. A piece of plate, sir.
   Volp.   Of what bigness?
   Mos.   Huge,
Massy, and antique, with your name inscribed,
And arms ingraven.
   Volp.   Good! And not a fox
Stretched on the earth, with fine delusive sleights,   95
Mocking a gaping crow? Ha, Mosca?
   Mos.   Sharp, sir.
   Volp. Give me my furs. Why dost thou laugh so, man?
   Mos. I cannot choose, sir, when I apprehend
What thoughts he has (without) now, as he walks:
That this might be the last gift he should give;   100
That this would fetch you; if you died today,
And gave him all, what he should be tomorrow;
What large return would come of all his ventures;
How he should worshipped be, and reverenced;
Ride, with his furs, and foot-cloths; waited on   105
By herds of fools and clients; have clear way
Made for his mule, as lettered as himself;

---

88 *vulture*: Voltore   *kite*: Lady Would-be   89 *Raven*: Corvino   *gor-crow*: carrion crow (Corbaccio)   94–5 *fox Stretched on the earth*: i.e. feigning death to entice predators   96 *gaping crow*: in Aesop's fable of the fox who praises the raven's singing and catches the cheese from its beak (V. viii. 11–14)   105 *foot-cloths*: i.e. on a caparisoned steed

Be called the great and learned advocate:
And then concludes, there's naught impossible.
   Volp. Yes, to be learned, Mosca.
110 *Mos.*   Oh no: rich
Implies it. Hood an ass with reverend purple,
So you can hide his two ambitious ears,
And he shall pass for a cathedral doctor.
   Volp. My caps, my caps, good Mosca, fetch him in.
   Mos. Stay, sir, your ointment for your eyes.
115 *Volp.*   That's true;
Dispatch, dispatch: I long to have possession
Of my new present.
   Mos.   That, and thousands more,
I hope to see you lord of.
   Volp.   Thanks, kind Mosca.
   Mos. And that, when I am lost in blended dust,
120 And hundred such, as I am, in succession——
   Volp. Nay, that were too much, Mosca.
   Mos.   You shall live,
Still, to delude these harpies.
   Volp.   Loving Mosca,
'Tis well, my pillow now, and let him enter.   [*Exit* Mosca]
Now, my feigned cough, my physic, and my gout,
125 My apoplexy, palsy, and catarrhs,
Help, with your forced functions, this my posture,
Wherein, this three year, I have milked their hopes.
He comes, I hear him: uh, uh, uh, uh, oh!

ACT I, Scene iii

Enter Mosca, Voltore

   Mos. You still are, what you were, sir. Only you,
Of all the rest, are he commands his love:
And you do wisely to preserve it thus,
With early visitation, and kind notes

---

112 *ambitious*: towering   126 *posture*: imposture   (*I. iii*) 4 *notes*: tokens

Of your good meaning to him, which, I know,   5
Cannot but come most grateful. Patron, sir.
Here's Signior Voltore is come——
   Volp.   What say you?
   Mos. Sir, Signior Voltore is come this morning,
To visit you.
   Volp.   I thank him.
   Mos.   And hath brought
A piece of antique plate, bought of St Mark,   10
With which he here presents you.
   Volp.   He is welcome.
Pray him, to come more often.
   Mos.   Yes.
   Volt.   What says he?
   Mos. He thanks you, and desires you see him often.
   Volp. Mosca.
   Mos.   My patron?
   Volp.   Bring him near, where is he?
I long to feel his hand.
   Mos.   The plate is here, sir.   15
   Volt. How fare you, sir?
   Volp.   I thank you, Signior Voltore.
Where is the plate? Mine eyes are bad.
   Volt.   I'm sorry,
To see you still thus weak.
   Mos. [*Aside*]   That he is not weaker.
   Volp. You are too munificent.
   Volt.   No, sir, would to heaven,
I could as well give health to you, as that plate.   20
   Volp. You give, sir, what you can. I thank you. Your love
Hath taste in this, and shall not be unanswered.
I pray you see me often.
   Volt.   Yes, I shall, sir.
   Volp. Be not far from me.
   Mos.   Do you observe that, sir?
   Volp. Hearken unto me still: it will concern you.   25
   Mos. You are a happy man, sir, know your good.

10 *of St Mark*: i.e. of a goldsmith's shop in the market-place

Volp. I cannot now last long——

Mos.   You are his heir, sir.

Volt. Am I?

Volp.   I feel me going, uh, uh, uh, uh.

I am sailing to my port, uh, uh, uh, uh?

30 And I am glad, I am so near my haven.

    Mos. Alas, kind gentleman, well, we must all go——

    Volt. But, Mosca——

    Mos.   Age will conquer.

    Volt.   'Pray thee hear me.

Am I inscribed his heir, for certain?

    Mos.   Are you?

I do beseech you, sir, you will vouchsafe

35 To write me, i' your family. All my hopes

Depend upon your worship. I am lost,

Except the rising sun do shine on me.

    Volt. It shall both shine and warm thee, Mosca.

    Mos.   Sir.

I am a man, that have not done your love

40 All the worst offices: here I wear your keys,

See all your coffers and your caskets locked,

Keep the poor inventory of your jewels,

Your plate and moneys, am your steward, sir,

Husband your goods here.

    Volt.   But am I sole heir?

45   *Mos.* Without a partner, sir, confirmed this morning;

The wax is warm yet, and the ink scarce dry

Upon the parchment.

    Volt.   Happy, happy, me!

By what good chance, sweet Mosca?

    Mos.   Your desert, sir;

I know no second cause.

    Volt.   Thy modesty

50 Is loth to know it; well, we shall requite it.

    Mos. He ever liked your course, sir, that first took him.

I oft have heard him say, how he admired

Men of your large profession, that could speak

35 *write me*: in the 'household book' in which the names of servants were entered

To every cause, and things mere contraries,
Till they were hoarse again, yet all be law;   55
That, with most quick agility, could turn,
And return; make knots, and undo them;
Give forked counsel; take provoking gold
On either hand, and put it up: these men,
He knew, would thrive, with their humility.   60
And (for his part) he thought, he should be blessed
To have his heir of such a suffering spirit,
So wise, so grave, of so perplexed a tongue,
And loud withal, that would not wag, nor scarce
Lie still, without a fee; when every word   65
Your worship but lets fall, is a *cecchine!*   (*Another knocks*)
Who's that? One knocks, I would not have you seen, sir.
And yet——pretend you came and went in haste;
I'll fashion an excuse. And, gentle sir,
When you do come to swim, in golden lard,   70
Up to the arms, in honey, that your chin
Is born up stiff with fatness of the flood,
Think on your vassal; but remember me:
I ha' not been your worst of clients.
    Volt.   Mosca——
    Mos. When will you have your inventory brought, sir?   75
Or see a copy of the will? (Anon!)
I'll bring 'em to you, sir. Away, be gone,
Put business i' your face.   [*Exit* Voltore]
    Volp.   Excellent, Mosca!
Come hither, let me kiss thee.
    Mos.   Keep you still, sir.
Here is Corbaccio.
    Volp.   Set the plate away,   80
The vulture's gone, and the old raven's come.

58 *provoking*: 'provoke' in the sense of having one's case taken up   63 *perplexed*:
involved in doubt   66 *cecchine*: sequin, gold coin worth 9*s.*

ACT I, Scene iv

Mos. Betake you to your silence and your sleep:
Stand there, and multiply. [*Puts plate aside*] Now, shall we see
A wretch, who is indeed more impotent,
Than this can feign to be; yet hopes to hop
Over his grave.

[*Enter* Corbaccio]

Signior Corbaccio!
5 You're very welcome, sir.
  Corb.   How does your patron?
  Mos. Troth, as he did, sir, no amends.
  Corb.   What? Mends he?
  Mos. No, sir: he is rather worse.
  Corb.   That's well. Where is he?
  Mos. Upon his couch, sir, newly fallen asleep.
  Corb. Does he sleep well?
  Mos.   No wink, sir, all this night,
10 Nor yesterday, but slumbers.
  Corb.   Good! He should take
Some counsel of physicians: I have brought him
An opiate here, from mine own doctor——
  Mos. He will not hear of drugs.
  Corb.   Why? I myself
Stood by, while 'twas made; saw all the ingredients:
15 And know it cannot but most gently work.
My life for his, 'tis but to make him sleep.
  Volp. [*Aside*] Aye, his last sleep, if he would take it.
  Mos.   Sir,
He has no faith in physic.
  Corb.   Say you? Say you?
20   *Mos.* He has no faith in physic: he does think,
Most of your doctors are the greater danger,
And worse disease to escape. I often have
Heard him protest that your physician
Should never be his heir.
  Corb.   Not I his heir?

11 *slumbers*: dozes

Mos. Not your physician, sir.

Corb.   Oh, no, no, no,   25
I do not mean it.

Mos.   No sir, nor their fees
He cannot brook: he says, they flay a man,
Before they kill him.

Corb.   Right, I do conceive you.

Mos. And then, they do it by experiment;
For which the law not only doth absolve 'em,   30
But gives them great reward: and he is loth
To hire his death, so.

Corb.   It is true, they kill,
With as much licence as a judge.

Mos.   Nay, more;
For he but kills, sir, where the law condemns,
And these can kill him too.

Corb.   Aye, or me: 35
Or any man. How does his apoplexy?
Is that strong on him still?

Mos.   Most violent.
His speech is broken, and his eyes are set,
His face drawn longer than 'twas wont——

Corb.   How? how?
Stronger than he was wont?

Mos.   No, sir: his face   40
Drawn longer than 'twas wont.

Corb.   Oh, good.

Mos.   His mouth
Is ever gaping, and his eyelids hang.

Corb.   Good.

Mos. A freezing numbness stiffens all his joints,
And makes the colour of his flesh like lead.

Corb.   'Tis good.

Mós. His pulse beats slow and dull.

Corb.   Good symptoms still.   45

Mos. And from his brain——

Corb.   Ha? How? Not from his brain?

28 *conceive*: understand

    Mos. Yes, sir, and from his brain——
    Corb.   I conceive you, good.
    Mos. Flows a cold sweat, with a continual rheum,
Forth the resolved corners of his eyes.
50   *Corb.* Is't possible? Yet I am better, ha!
How does he, with the swimming of his head?
    Mos. Oh, sir, 'tis past the scotomy; he now
Hath lost his feeling, and hath left to snort:
You hardly can perceive him, that he breathes.
55   *Corb.* Excellent, excellent, sure I shall outlast him:
This makes me young again, a score of years.
    Mos. I was a-coming for you, sir.
    Corb.   Has he made his will?
What has he given me?
    Mos.   No, sir.
    Corb.   Nothing? ha?
    Mos. He has not made his will, sir.
    Corb.   Oh, oh, oh.
60 What then did Voltore, the lawyer, here?
    Mos. He smelt a carcass, sir, when he but heard
My master was about his testament;
(As I did urge him to it, for your good——)
    Corb. He came unto him, did he? I thought so.
65   *Mos.* Yes, and presented him this piece of plate.
    Corb. To be his heir?
    Mos.   I do not know, sir.
    Corb.   True,
I know it too.
    Mos. [*Aside*] By your own scale, sir.
    Corb.   Well,
I shall prevent him yet. See, Mosca, look
Here, I have brought a bag of bright *cecchines*,
Will quite weigh down his plate.
70   *Mos.*   Yea, marry, sir!
This is true physic, this your sacred medicine,
No talk of opiates, to this great elixir.

---

    48 *rheum*: mucous discharge   49 *resolved*: relaxed   52 *scotomy*: dizziness
68 *prevent*: forestall

Corb. 'Tis *aurum palpabile*, if not *potabile*.

Mos. It shall be ministered to him, in his bowl?

Corb. Aye, do, do, do.

Mos.   Most blessed cordial!   75
This will recover him.

Corb.   Yes, do, do, do.

Mos. I think, it were not best, sir.

Corb.   What?

Mos.   To recover him.

Corb. Oh, no, no, no; by no means.

Mos.   Why, sir, this
Will work some strange effect, if he but feel it.

Corb. 'Tis true, therefore forbear, I'll take my venture: 80
Give me it again.

Mos.   At no hand, pardon me;
You shall not do yourself that wrong, sir. I
Will so advise you, you shall have it all.

Corb. How?

Mos.   All, sir, 'tis your right, your own; no man
Can claim a part: 'tis yours, without a rival,   85
Decreed by destiny.

Corb.   How? How, good Mosca?

Mos. I'll tell you, sir. This fit he shall recover——

Corb. I do conceive you.

Mos.   And on first advantage
Of his 'gained sense, will I reimportune him
Unto the making of his testament: 90
And show him this.

Corb.   Good, good.

Mos.   'Tis better yet,
If you will hear, sir.

Corb.   Yes, with all my heart.

Mos. Now, would I counsel you, make home with speed;
There, frame a will: whereto you shall inscribe
My master your sole heir.

Corb.   And disinherit   95

73 *palpabile* . . .: palpable, if not drinkable (*aurum* . . . *potabile* = cordial prepared
from gold)

My son?

   Mos. Oh, sir, the better: for that colour

Shall make it much more taking.

   Corb.   Oh, but colour?

   Mos. This will, sir, you shall send it unto me.

Now, when I come to enforce (as I will do)

100 Your cares, your watchings, and your many prayers,

Your more than many gifts, your this day's present,

And, last, produce your will; where (without thought,

Or least regard, unto your proper issue,

A son so brave, and highly meriting)

105 The stream of your diverted love hath thrown you

Upon my master, and made him your heir:

He cannot be so stupid, or stone dead,

But, out of conscience, and mere gratitude——

   Corb. He must pronounce me, his?

   Mos.   'Tis true.

   Corb.   This plot

Did I think on before.

110   *Mos.*   I do believe it.

   Corb. Do you not believe it?

   Mos.   Yes, sir.

   Corb.   Mine own project.

   Mos. Which when he hath done, sir——

   Corb.   Published me his heir?

   Mos. And you so certain to survive him——

   Corb.   Aye.

   Mos. Being so lusty a man——

   Corb.   'Tis true.

   Mos.   Yes, sir——

115   *Corb.* I thought on that too. See, how he should be

The very organ, to express my thoughts!

   Mos. You have not only done yourself a good——

   Corb. But multiplied it on my son?

   Mos.   'Tis right, sir.

   Corb. Still, my invention.

   Mos.   'Las sir, heaven knows,

---

96 *colour*: outward appearance   100 *watchings*: i.e. at night

It hath been all my study, all my care,   120
(I e'en grow grey withal) how to work things——
   Corb. I do conceive, sweet Mosca.
   Mos.   You are he,
For whom I labour here.
   Corb.   Aye, do, do, do:
I'll straight about it.
   Mos. [*Aside*]   Rook go with you, raven.
   Corb. I know thee honest.
   Mos. [*Aside*]   You do lie, sir——
   Corb.   And——   125
   Mos. [*Aside*] Your knowledge is no better than your ears, sir.
   Corb. I do not doubt, to be a father to thee.
   Mos. [*Aside*] Nor I, to gull my brother of his blessing.
   Corb. I may ha' my youth restored to me, why not?
   Mos. [*Aside*] Your worship is a precious ass——
   Corb.   What sayst thou?   130
   Mos. I do desire your worship to make haste, sir.
   Corb. 'Tis done, 'tis done, I go.   [*Exit*]
   Volp. [*Leaping from his couch*]   Oh, I shall burst;
Let out my sides, let out my sides——
   Mos.   Contain
Your flux of laughter, sir: you know, this hope
Is such a bait, it covers any hook.   135
   Volp. Oh, but thy working, and thy placing it!
I cannot hold; good rascal, let me kiss thee:
I never knew thee in so rare a humour.
   Mos. Alas, sir, I but do as I am taught;
Follow your grave instructions; give 'em words;   140
Pour oil into their ears: and send them hence.
   Volp. 'Tis true, 'tis true. What a rare punishment
Is avarice to itself?
   Mos.   Aye, with our help, sir.
   Volp. So many cares, so many maladies,
So many fears attending on old age,   145
Yea, death so often called on, as no wish

---

124 *Rook go with you*: Be fooled (rook = simpleton)   128 *gull my brother*: as
Jacob did Esau   140 *give 'em words*: deceive them   141 *oil*: i.e. flattery

Can be more frequent with 'em, their limbs faint,
Their senses dull, their seeing, hearing, going,
All dead before them; yea, their very teeth,
150 Their instruments of eating, failing them:
Yet this is reckoned life! Nay, here was one,
Is now gone home, that wishes to live longer!
Feels not his gout, nor palsy, feigns himself
Younger, by scores of years, flatters his age,
155 With confident belying it, hopes he may
With charms, like Aeson, have his youth restored:
And with these thoughts so battens, as if fate
Would be as easily cheated on, as he,
And all turns air! (*Another knocks*) Who's that there now? A third?
160   *Mos.* Close, to your couch again: I hear his voice.
It is Corvino, our spruce merchant.
    Volp. [*Lying down again*]   Dead.
    Mos. Another bout, sir, with your eyes. [*Anointing them*] Who's
    there?

ACT I, Scene v

Enter Corvino

    Mos. Signior Corvino! Come most wished for! Oh,
How happy were you, if you knew it, now!
    Corv. Why? What? Wherein?
    Mos.   The tardy hour is come, sir.
    Corv. He is not dead?
    Mos.   Not dead, sir, but as good;
He knows no man.
    Corv.   How shall I do then?
5   *Mos.*   Why, sir?
    Corv. I have brought him, here, a pearl.
    Mos.   Perhaps he has
So much remembrance left as to know you, sir;
He still calls on you, nothing but your name

---

156 *Aeson . . . restored*: by Medea's magic   157 *battens*: thrives

Is in his mouth. Is your pearl orient, sir?

Corv. Venice was never owner of the like.   10

Volp. Signior Corvino.

Mos.   Hark.

Volp.   Signior Corvino.

Mos. He calls you, step and give it him. He's here, sir,
And he has brought you a rich pearl.

Corv.   How do you, sir?
Tell him, it doubles the twelfth carat.

Mos.   Sir,
He cannot understand, his hearing's gone;   15
And yet it comforts him, to see you——

Corv.   Say,
I have a diamond for him, too.

Mos.   Best show it, sir,
Put it into his hand; 'tis only there
He apprehends: he has his feeling yet.
See, how he grasps it!

Corv.   'Las, good gentleman!   20
How pitiful the sight is!

Mos.   Tut, forget, sir.
The weeping of an heir should still be laughter,
Under a visor.

Corv.   Why? Am I his heir?

Mos. Sir, I am sworn, I may not show the will,
Till he be dead. But, here has been Corbaccio,   25
Here has been Voltore, here were others too,
I cannot number 'em, they were so many,
All gaping here for legacies; but I,
Taking the vantage of his naming you,
(Signior Corvino, Signior Corvino) took   30
Paper, and pen, and ink, and there I asked him,
Whom he would have his heir? 'Corvino.' Who
Should be executor? 'Corvino.' And,
To any question he was silent to,
I still interpreted the nods he made   35
(Through weakness) for consent: and sent home the others,

9 *orient*: of pure lustre   23 *visor*: mask

Nothing bequeathed them, but to cry and curse.

 Corv. Oh, my dear Mosca. (*They embrace*) Does he not
  perceive us?

 Mos. No more than a blind harper. He knows no man,
40 No face of friend, nor name of any servant,
Who 'twas that fed him last, or gave him drink:
Not those he hath begotten, or brought up
Can he remember.

 Corv.   Has he children?

 Mos.   Bastards,
Some dozen, or more, that he begot on beggars,
45 Gipsies, and Jews, and black-moors, when he was drunk.
Knew you not that, sir? 'Tis the common fable,
The dwarf, the fool, the eunuch are all his;
He's the true father of his family,
In all, save me: but he has given 'em nothing.

50 *Corv.* That's well, that's well. Art sure he does not hear us?

 Mos. Sure, sir? Why, look you, credit your own sense.

         [*He shouts in* Volpone's *ear*]

The pox approach, and add to your diseases,
If it would send you hence the sooner, sir.
For your incontinence, it hath deserved it
55 Throughly, and throughly, and the plague to boot.
(You may come near, sir) would you would once close
Those filthy eyes of yours, that flow with slime,
Like two frog-pits; and those same hanging cheeks,
Covered with hide instead of skin: (nay, help, sir)
60 That look like frozen dish-clouts, set on end.

 Corv. Or like an old smoked wall, on which the rain
Ran down in streaks.

 Mos.   Excellent, sir, speak out;
You may be louder yet: a culverin
Discharged in his ear, would hardly bore it.

65 *Corv.* His nose is like a common sewer, still running.

 Mos. 'Tis good! And what his mouth?

 Corv.   A very draught.

---

39 *blind harper*: proverbial for a nondescript in a crowd 39–43, 57–9, 63–4 Juvenal,
Sat. x. 232–6, 191–4, 214–15 63 *culverin*: hand-gun 66 *draught*: sink, privy

Mos. Oh, stop it up——
Corv.   By no means.
Mos.   'Pray you let me.
'Faith, I could stifle him, rarely, with a pillow,
As well as any woman that should keep him.
   Corv. Do as you will, but I'll be gone.
   Mos.   Be so;   70
It is your presence makes him last so long.
   Corv. I pray you, use no violence.
   Mos.   No, sir? Why?
Why should you be thus scrupulous? 'Pray you, sir.
   Corv. Nay, at your discretion.
   Mos.   Well, good sir, be gone.
   Corv. I will not trouble him now, to take my pearl?   75
   Mos. Puh, nor your diamond. What a needless care
Is this afflicts you? Is not all, here, yours?
Am not I here? Whom you have made? Your creature?
That owe my being to you?
   Corv.   Grateful Mosca!
Thou art my friend, my fellow, my companion,   80
My partner, and shalt share in all my fortunes.
   Mos. Excepting one.
   Corv.   What's that?
   Mos.   Your gallant wife, sir.
                              [*Exit* Corvino]
Now, is he gone: we had no other means,
To shoot him hence, but this.
   Volp.   My divine Mosca!
Thou hast today outgone thyself. (*Another knocks*) Who's there?   85
I will be troubled with no more. Prepare
Me music, dances, banquets, all delights;
The Turk is not more sensual, in his pleasures,
Than will Volpone. [*Exit* Mosca] Let me see, a pearl?
A diamond? Plate? *Cecchines?* Good morning's purchase;   90
Why, this is better than rob churches yet:
Or fat, by eating, once a month, a man.
                [*Enter* Mosca]
Who is't?

 Mos. The beauteous Lady Would-be, sir,
Wife, to the English knight, Sir Politic Would-be,
95 (This is the style, sir, is directed me)
Hath sent to know, how you have slept tonight,
And if you would be visited.

 Volp.   Not now.
Some three hours hence——

  Mos.   I told the squire so much.

 Volp. When I am high with mirth and wine: then, then.
100 'Fore heaven, I wonder at the desperate valour
Of the bold English, that they dare let loose
Their wives to all encounters!

  Mos.   Sir, this knight
Had not his name for nothing, he is politic,
And knows, how e'er his wife affect strange airs,
105 She hath not yet the face to be dishonest.
But had she Signior Corvino's wife's face——

  Volp. Has she so rare a face?

  Mos.   Oh, sir, the wonder,
The blazing star of Italy! A wench
O' the first year! A beauty, ripe, as harvest!
110 Whose skin is whiter than a swan, all over!
Than silver, snow, or lilies! A soft lip,
Would tempt you to eternity of kissing!
And flesh that melteth in the touch to blood!
Bright as your gold! And lovely as your gold!

  Volp. Why had not I known this before?

115 *Mos.*   Alas, sir.
Myself but yesterday discovered it.

  Volp. How might I see her?

  Mos.   Oh, not possible;
She's kept as warily as is your gold:
Never does come abroad, never takes air,
120 But at a window. All her looks are sweet,
As the first grapes or cherries: and are watched
As near as they are.

  96 *tonight*: last night 105 *face*: beauty 109 *O' the first year*: a term of
commendation (*CR* V. iv. 477)

Volp.   I must see her——
Mos.   Sir.
There is a guard of ten spies thick upon her;
All his whole household: each of which is set
Upon his fellow, and have all their charge,   125
When he goes out, when he comes in, examined.
    Volp. I will go see her, though but at her window.
    Mos. In some disguise, then.
    Volp.   That is true. I must
Maintain mine own shape, still, the same: we'll think.

                                                    [*Exeunt*]

ACT II, Scene i

[The Square, before Corvino's house]

Enter Sir Politic Would-be, Peregrine

    Pol. SIR, to a wise man, all the world's his soil.
It is not Italy, nor France, nor Europe,
That must bound me, if my fates call me forth.
Yet, I protest, it is no salt desire
Of seeing countries, shifting a religion,   5
Nor any disaffection to the state
Where I was bred, and, unto which I owe
My dearest plots, hath brought me out; much less
That idle, antique, stale, grey-headed project
Of knowing men's minds and manners, with Ulysses: 10
But a peculiar humour of my wife's,
Laid for this height of Venice, to observe,
To quote, to learn the language, and so forth——
I hope you travel, sir, with licence?
    Per.   Yes.
    Pol. I dare the safelier converse—— How long, sir,   15
Since you left England?
    Per.   Seven weeks.

---

4 *salt*: wanton   12 *height*: latitude   13 *quote*: take mental note of
14 *licence*: from the Lords of the Council

 Pol.   So lately!
You ha' not been with my lord ambassador?
 Per. Not yet, sir.
 Pol.   'Pray you, what news, sir, vents our climate?
I heard, last night, a most strange thing reported
20 By some of my lord's followers, and I long
To hear how 'twill be seconded!
 Per.   What was't, sir?
 Pol. Marry, sir, of a raven, that should build
In a ship royal of the King's.
 Per. [*Aside*]   This fellow
Does he gull me, trow? Or is gulled? Your name, sir?
 Pol. My name is Politic Would-be.
25 *Per.* [*Aside*]   Oh, that speaks him.
A knight, sir?
 Pol.   A poor knight, sir.
 Per.   Your lady
Lies here in Venice for intelligence
Of tires, and fashions, and behaviour,
Among the courtesans? The fine Lady Would-be?
30 *Pol.* Yes, sir, the spider and the bee oft-times
Suck from one flower.
 Per.   Good Sir Politic!
I cry you mercy; I have heard much of you:
'Tis true, sir, of your raven.
 Pol.   On your knowledge?
 Per. Yes, and your lions whelping, in the Tower.
 Pol. Another whelp!
 Per.   Another, sir.
35 *Pol.*   Now, heaven!
What prodigies be these? The fires at Berwick!
And the new star! These things concurring, strange!
And full of omen! Saw you those meteors?
 Per. I did, sir.

17 *ambassador*: Sir Henry Wotton, from 1604 to 1612 18 *vents*: publishes
22 *raven ... build*: an evil portent (should = it is said) 28 *tires*: dresses 34 *lions whelping*: as they had in August 1604 and February 1605 36 *fires at Berwick*: reported in January 1605 37 *the new star*: discovered by Kepler in October 1604

Pol.   Fearful! Pray you sir, confirm me,
Were there three porpoises seen, above the bridge,   40
As they give out?
   Per.   Six, and a sturgeon, sir.
   Pol. I am astonished!
   Per.   Nay, sir, be not so;
I'll tell you a greater prodigy than these——
   Pol. What should these things portend!
   Per.   The very day
(Let me be sure) that I put forth from London,   45
There was a whale discovered in the river,
As high as Woolwich, that had waited there
(Few know how many months) for the subversion
Of the Stode-Fleet.
   Pol.   Is't possible? Believe it,
'Twas either sent from Spain, or the Arch Dukes!   50
Spinola's whale, upon my life, my credit!
Will they not leave these projects? Worthy sir,
Some other news.
   Per.   Faith, Stone, the fool, is dead;
And they do lack a tavern fool, extremely.
   Pol. Is Mas' Stone dead!
   Per.   He's dead, sir, why? I hope   55
You thought him not immortal? [*Aside*] Oh, this knight
(Were he well-known) would be a precious thing
To fit our English stage: he that should write
But such a fellow, should be thought to feign
Extremely, if not maliciously.
   Pol.   Stone dead!   60
   Per. Dead. Lord! How deeply, sir, you apprehend it?
He was no kinsman to you?
   Pol.   That I know of.

---

40 *porpoises* and 46 *a whale*: observed in January 1606   49 *Stode-Fleet*: the fleet
of the English Merchant Adventurers at Stade, on the mouth of the Elbe   50 *the
Arch Dukes*: i.e. the Infanta Isabella and her husband Albert, rulers of the Netherlands
51 *Spinola*: general in chief of the Spanish army in the Netherlands from 1604; he was
supposed to have a whale that would drown London 'by snuffing up the Thames and
spouting it upon the City'   53 *Stone, the fool*: anecdotes of him are given in *H&S*
ix. 701

Well! That same fellow was an unknown fool.
   Per. And yet you knew him, it seems?
   Pol.   I did so. Sir,
65 I knew him one of the most dangerous heads
Living within the state, and so I held him.
   Per. Indeed, sir?
   Pol.   While he lived, in action.
He has received weekly intelligence,
Upon my knowledge, out of the Low Countries,
70 (For all parts of the world) in cabbages;
And those dispensed again, to ambassadors,
In oranges, musk-melons, apricots,
Lemons, pome-citrons, and such like: sometimes,
In Colchester oysters, and your Selsey cockles.
   Per. You make me wonder!
75   *Pol.*   Sir, upon my knowledge.
Nay, I have observed him, at your public ordinary,
Take his advertisement from a traveller
(A concealed statesman) in a trencher of meat:
And instantly, before the meal was done,
Convey an answer in a toothpick.
80   *Per.*   Strange!
How could this be, sir?
   Pol.   Why, the meat was cut
So like his character, and so laid, as he
Must easily read the cipher.
   Per.   I have heard
He could not read, sir.
   Pol.   So 'twas given out,
85 In policy by those that did employ him:
But he could read, and had your languages,
And to it, as sound a noddle——
   Per.   I have heard, sir,
That your baboons were spies; and that they were
A kind of subtle nation, near to China.

---

   70 *cabbages*: an import from Holland   73 *pome-citrons*: large citrons   76 *ordinary*:
public eating-house   82 *character*: cipher (the carving of meat in fantastic shapes was a
fashion of the time)

Pol. Aye, aye, your Mamuluchi. Faith, they had   90
Their hand in a French plot or two; but they
Were so extremely given to women, as
They made discovery of all: yet I
Had my advices here (on Wednesday last)
From one of their own coat, they were returned,   95
Made their relations (as the fashion is)
And now stand fair for fresh employment.
 Per. [*Aside*]   'Heart!
This, Sir Pol. will be ignorant of nothing.
It seems, sir, you know all?
 Pol.   Not all, sir. But,
I have some general notions; I do love   100
To note, and to observe: though I live out,
Free from the active torrent, yet I'd mark
The currents and the passages of things,
For mine own private use; and know the ebbs
And flows of state.
 Per.   Believe it, sir, I hold   105
Myself, in no small tie unto my fortunes
For casting me thus luckily upon you;
Whose knowledge (if your bounty equal it)
May do me great assistance, in instruction
For my behaviour and my bearing, which   110
Is yet so rude and raw——
 Pol.   Why? Came you forth
Empty of rules for travel?
 Per.   Faith, I had
Some common ones, from out that vulgar grammar,
Which he that cried Italian to me taught me.
 Pol. Why, this it is, that spoils all our brave bloods;   115
Trusting our hopeful gentry unto pedants:
Fellows of outside, and mere bark. You seem
To be a gentleman, of ingenuous race——
I not profess it, but my fate hath been

90 *Mamuluchi*: Mamelukes (of Egypt, unrelated to baboons or China) 94 *advices*:
dispatches 96 *relations:* reports 113 *grammar*: containing phrases and precepts
118 *ingenuous race*: noble stock

120 To be, where I have been consulted with,
    In this high kind, touching some great men's sons,
    Persons of blood and honour——
          Per.   Who be these, sir?

ACT II, Scene ii

Enter Mosca, Nano [*disguised*]

   Mos. Under that window, there it must be. The same.
   Pol. Fellows, to mount a bank! Did your instructor
In the dear tongues never discourse to you
Of the Italian mountebanks?
      Per.   Yes, sir.
      Pol.   Why,
Here shall you see one.
 5   *Per.*   They are quack-salvers,
Fellows that live by vending oils and drugs?
   Pol. Was that the character he gave you of them?
   Per. As I remember.
   Pol.   Pity his ignorance.
They are the only knowing men of Europe!
10 Great general scholars, excellent physicians,
Most admired statesmen, professed favourites,
And cabinet counsellors to the greatest princes!
The only languaged men, of all the world!
      Per. And I have heard, they are most lewd impostors;
15 Made all of terms and shreds; no less beliers
Of great men's favours than their own vile medicines;
Which they will utter upon monstrous oaths:
Selling that drug for twopence, ere they part,
Which they have valued at twelve crowns before.
20   *Pol.* Sir, calumnies are answered best with silence:
Yourself shall judge. Who is it mounts, my friends?
      Mos. Scoto of Mantua, sir.

---

2 *bank*: platform   3 *dear*: esteemed   14 *lewd*: ignorant   15 *terms*:
i.e. cant   17 *utter*: put forth to the public   22 *Scoto of Mantua*: professional
actor famed in England as a juggler

Pol.   Is't he? Nay, then
I'll proudly promise, sir, you shall behold
Another man than has been phant'sied to you.
I wonder, yet, that he should mount his bank   25
Here in this nook, that has been wont to appear
In face of the Piazza! Here, he comes.

                    Enter Volpone, Grege

Volp. [*To* Nano] Mount, Zany.
Gre.   Follow, follow, follow, follow, follow.
Pol. See how the people follow him! He's a man
May write ten thousand crowns, in bank, here. Note,   30
Mark but his gesture: I do use to observe
The state he keeps, in getting up!
Per.   'Tis worth it, sir.

Volp. 'Most noble gentlemen, and my worthy patrons, it may
seem strange, that I, your Scoto Mantuano, who was ever wont to
fix my bank in face of the public Piazza, near the shelter of the 35
portico, to the Procuratìa, should, now (after eight months' absence
from this illustrious city of Venice) humbly retire myself into an
obscure nook of the Piazza.'

Pol. Did not I, now, object the same?
Per.   Peace, sir.

Volp. 'Let me tell you: I am not, as your Lombard proverb saith, 40
cold on my feet; or content to part with my commodities at a
cheaper rate than I accustomed: look not for it. Nor that the
calumnious reports of that impudent detractor, and shame to our
profession, Alessandro Buttone, I mean, who gave out, in public,
I was condemned a '*sforzato* to the galleys, for poisoning the   45
Cardinal Bembo's—cook, hath at all attached, much less dejected
me. No, no, worthy gentlemen, to tell you true, I cannot endure to
see the rabble of these ground *ciarlitani*, that spread their cloaks
on the pavement, as if they meant to do feats of activity, and then
come in, lamely, with their mouldy tales out of Boccaccio, like stale 50

---

28 *Zany*: mountebank's attendant   36 *Procuratìa*: the Procuratie Vecchie with
an arcade of fifty arches running along the north side of the Piazza di San Marco
41 *cold on my feet*: i.e. forced by circumstances to sell my wares cheap   44 *Buttone*:
untraced   45 *'sforzato*: prisoner   46 *Bembo*: Pietro Bembo (1470–1547), the
humanist   48 *ciarlitani*: the poorer mountebanks, who stood on the ground

Tabarine, the fabulist: some of them discoursing their travels, and
of their tedious captivity in the Turks' galleys, when indeed (were
the truth known) they were the Christians' galleys, where very
temperately, they ate bread, and drunk water, as a wholesome
55 penance (enjoined them by their confessors) for base pilferies.'

Pol. Note but his bearing, and contempt of these.

Volp. 'These turdy-facy-nasty-paty-lousy-fartical rogues, with
one poor groats-worth of unprepared antimony, finely wrapped up
in several '*scartoccios*, are able, very well, to kill their twenty a week,
60 and play; yet these meagre starved spirits, who have half-stopped
the organs of their minds with earthy oppilations, want not their
favourers among your shrivelled, salad-eating artisans: who are
overjoyed that they may have their half-pe'rth of physic, though it
purge 'em into another world, it makes no matter.'

65 *Pol.* Excellent! Ha' you heard better language, sir?

Volp. 'Well, let 'em go. And gentlemen, honourable gentlemen,
know, that for this time, our bank, being thus removed from the
clamours of the *canaglia*, shall be the scene of pleasure and delight:
for, I have nothing to sell, little, or nothing to sell.'

Pol. I told you, sir, his end.

70 *Per.*   You did so, sir.

Volp. 'I protest, I and my six servants are not able to make of
this precious liquor so fast as it is fetched away from my lodging
by gentlemen of your city; strangers of the terra-firma; worshipful
merchants; aye, and senators too, who, ever since my arrival, have
75 detained me to their uses, by their splendidous liberalities. And
worthily. For what avails your rich man to have his magazines
stuffed with *moscadelli*, or of the purest grape, when his physicians
prescribe him (on pain of death) to drink nothing but water, cocted
with aniseeds? Oh, health! Health! The blessing of the rich! The
80 riches of the poor! Who can buy thee at too dear a rate, since there
is no enjoying this world without thee? Be not then so sparing of
your purses, honourable gentlemen, as to abridge the natural course
of life——'

---

51 *Tabarine*: zany in a troop of Italian comedians who visited France in 1572
59 '*scartoccios*: term applied to apothecaries' packages   61 *oppilations*: obstructions
62 *salad-eating*: contemptuous reference to Italian diet   68 *canaglia*: canaille
73 *terra-firma*: the Continental possessions of the old Venetian state   76 *magazines*:
storehouses   77 *moscadelli*: muscatel   78 *cocted*: boiled

Per. You see his end?

Pol.   Aye, is it not good?

Volp. 'For, when a humid flux, or catarrh, by the mutability of   85
air, falls from your head, into an arm, or shoulder, or any other
part; take you a ducat, or your *cecchine* of gold, and apply to the
place affected: see, what good effect it can work. No, no, 'tis this
blessed *unguento*, this rare extraction, that hath only power to
disperse all malignant humours, that proceed, either of hot, cold,   90
moist, or windy causes——'

Per. I would he had put in dry to.

Pol.   'Pray you, observe.

Volp. 'To fortify the most indigest, and crude stomach, aye, were
it of one, that (through extreme weakness) vomited blood, applying
only a warm napkin to the place, after the unction, and fricace;   95
for the *vertigine*, in the head, putting but a drop into your nostrils,
likewise, behind the ears; a most sovereign and approved remedy:
the *mal-caduco*, cramps, convulsions, paralyses, epilepsies, *tremor-
cordia*, retired-nerves, ill vapours of the spleen, stoppings of the
liver, the stone, the strangury, *hernia ventosa, iliaca passio*; stops a   100
disenteria immediately; easeth the torsion of the small guts; and
cures *melancolia hypocondriaca*, being taken and applied according
to my printed receipt. (*Pointing to his bill and his glass*) For this is
the physician, this the medicine; this counsels, this cures; this gives
the direction, this works the effect: and (in sum) both together may   105
be termed an abstract of the theoric and practice in the Aesculapian
art. 'Twill cost you eight crowns. And, Zan Fritada, 'pray thee sing
a verse, extempore, in honour of it.'

Pol. How do you like him, sir?

Per.   Most strangely, I!

Pol. Is not his language rare?

Per.   But alchemy,   110
I never heard the like: or Broughton's books.

---

95 *fricace*: rubbing   98 *mal-caduco*: falling sickness   98–99 *tremor-cordia*:
palpitation of the heart   99 *retired-nerves*: shrunken sinews   100 *strangury*:
slow and painful urination   *hernia ventosa*: ? flatulent hernia   *iliaca passio*: similar
to colic   101 *torsion of the small guts*: gripes   106 *Aesculapian*: of Aescula-
pius, god of medicine   107 *Zan Fritada*: (Ital. *fritata*, 'pancake') a versatile
zany   111 *Broughton*: Hugh Broughton (1549–1612), Puritan divine and rabbinical
scholar

Song

Had old Hippocrates, or Galen,
(That to their books put medicines all in)
But known this secret, they had never
115 (Of which they will be guilty ever)
Been murderers of so much paper,
Or wasted many a hurtless taper:
No Indian drug had e'er been famed,
Tobacco, sassafras not named;
120 Ne yet, of guacum one small stick, sir,
Nor Raymond Lully's great elixir.
Ne had been known the Danish Gonswart,
Or Paracelsus, with his long-sword.

Per. All this, yet, will not do, eight crowns is high.

125 *Volp.* 'No more. Gentlemen, if I had but time to discourse to you the miraculous effects of this my oil, surnamed *oglio del Scoto*; with the countless catalogue of those I have cured of the aforesaid, and many more diseases; the patents and privileges of all the princes and commonwealths of Christendom; or but the depositions 130 of those that appeared on my part, before the signiory of the Sanitâ, and most learned college of physicians; where I was authorized, upon notice taken of the admirable virtues of my medicaments, and mine own excellency, in matter of rare and unknown secrets, not only to disperse them publicly in this famous city, but in all the 135 territories that happily joy under the government of the most pious and magnificent states of Italy. But may some other gallant fellow say, Oh, there be divers that make profession to have as good, and as experimented receipts, as yours. Indeed, very many have essayed, like apes in imitation of that, which is really and essentially in me,

---

112 *Hippocrates . . . Galen*: the traditional authorities in medicine, one the originator and the other the expositor of the theory of humours   119 *sassafras*: medicinal extract from bark of the sassafras tree   120 *guacum*: drug from the resin of the guaiacum (*lignum vitae*)   121 *Raymond Lully's*: Raymond Lull or Lully (1235–1315), reputed to have the secret of the elixir, as Paracelsus (1493–1541) had of the stone   122 *Danish Gonswart*: not satisfactorily identified   123 *long-sword*: in the pommel of which Paracelsus reputedly kept his 'chief quintessences'   130 *the signiory of the Sanitâ*: the 'health-masters' who had the authority to license physicians and mountebanks to practise

to make of this oil; bestowed great cost in furnaces, stills, alembics, 140
continual fires, and preparation of the ingredients (as indeed there
goes to it six hundred several simples, besides some quantity of
human fat, for the conglutination, which we buy of the anatomists)
but, when these practitioners come to the last decoction, blow,
blow, puff, puff, and all flies in *fumo*: ha, ha, ha. Poor wretches! 145
I rather pity their folly and indiscretion than their loss of time and
money; for those may be recovered by industry: but to be a fool
born is a disease incurable. For myself, I always from my youth
have endeavoured to get the rarest secrets, and book them; either in
exchange, or for money: I spared nor cost, nor labour, where any- 150
thing was worthy to be learned. And, gentlemen, honourable gentle-
men, I will undertake (by virtue of chemical art) out of the honour-
able hat that covers your head, to extract the four elements; that is
to say, the fire, air, water, and earth, and return you your felt with-
out burn or stain. For whilst others have been at the *balloo*, I have 155
been at my book: and am now past the craggy paths of study, and
come to the flowery plains of honour and reputation.'

Pol. I do assure you, sir, that is his aim.

Volp. 'But, to our price.'

Per.   And that withal, Sir Pol.

Volp. 'You all know (honourable gentlemen) I never valued this 160
ampulla, or vial, at less than eight crowns, but for this time, I am
content, to be deprived of it for six; six crowns is the price; and less
in courtesy, I know you cannot offer me: take it, or leave it, howso-
ever, both it, and I, am at your service. I ask you not, as the value
of the thing, for then I should demand of you a thousand crowns, 165
so the Cardinals Montalto, Fernese, the great duke of Tuscany, my
gossip, with divers other princes have given me; but I despise
money: only to show my affection to you, honourable gentlemen,
and your illustrious state here, I have neglected the messages of
these princes, mine own offices, framed my journey hither, only to 170
present you with the fruits of my travels. Tune your voices once

---

140 *alembics*: crucibles   142 *simples*: *EMI* III. v. 68 n.   145 *fumo*: smoke,
vapour   155 *balloo*: game in which an inflated leather ball was driven to and fro
by a flat piece of wood fixed to the arm   166 *Montalto*: Felice Peretti, Cardinal
di Montalto in 1570, later Pope Sixtus V   *Fernese*: Alessandro Ferneze, Pope Paul
III in 1534   *duke of Tuscany*: office created by Pius V in 1569, and conferred on
Cosimo de' Medici   167 *gossip*: godsib; godfather

more to the touch of your instruments, and give the honourable
assembly some delightful recreation.'

 Per. What monstrous and most painful circumstance
175 Is here, to get some three or four *gazets*!
Some threepence, i'the whole, for that 'twill come to.

SONG

You that would last long, list to my song,
Make no more coil, but buy of this oil.
Would you be ever fair? And young?
180 Stout of teeth? And strong of tongue?
Tart of palate? Quick of ear?
Sharp of sight? Of nostril clear?
Moist of hand? And light of foot?
(Or I will come nearer to't)
185 Would you live free from all diseases?
Do the act your mistress pleases;
Yet fright all aches from your bones?
Here's a medicine for the nones.

 Volp. 'Well, I am in a humour (at this time) to make a present of
190 the small quantity my coffer contains: to the rich, in courtesy, and
to the poor, for God's sake. Wherefore, now mark; I asked you six
crowns; and six crowns, at other times, you have paid me; you shall
not give me six crowns, nor five, nor four, nor three, nor two, nor
one; nor half a ducat; no, nor a *muccinigo*: six—pence it will cost
195 you, or six hundred pound—expect no lower price, for by the
banner of my front, I will not bate a *bagatine*, that I will have only
a pledge of your loves, to carry something from amongst you, to
show I am not contemned by you. Therefore, now, toss your hand-
kerchiefs, cheerfully, cheerfully; and be advertised, that the first
200 heroic spirit, that deigns to grace me, with a handkerchief, I will
give it a little remembrance of something, beside, shall please it
better than if I had presented it with a double pistolet.'

 175 *gazet*: coin valued at about three farthings 178 *coil*: fuss 187 *aches*
. . . *bones*: symptoms of venereal disease ('aches' is a disyllable) 188 *for the nones*:
for the nonce, for the occasion 194 *ducat*: worth about 4s. 8d. *muccinigo*: worth
about 9d. 196 *banner*: advertising his wares *bagatine*: worth about a third of
a farthing 198–9 *handkerchiefs*: with the money knotted in the corner
202 *pistolet*: Spanish gold coin worth from 16s. 8d. to 18s.

Per. Will you be that heroic spark, Sir Pol?
                (Celia *at the window throws down her handkerchief*)
Oh, see! The window has prevented you.

Volp. 'Lady, I kiss your bounty: and for this timely grace you   205
have done your poor Scoto of Mantua, I will return you, over and
above my oil, a secret, of that high and inestimable nature, shall
make you for ever enamoured on that minute, wherein your eye
first descended on so mean (yet not altogether to be despised) an
object. Here is a powder, concealed in this paper, of which, if I   210
should speak to the worth, nine thousand volumes were but as one
page, that page as a line, that line as a word: so short is this pilgrim-
age of man (which some call life) to the expressing of it. Would I
reflect on the price? Why, the whole world were but as an empire,
that empire as a province, that province as a bank, that bank as a   215
private purse, to the purchase of it. I will, only, tell you; it is the
powder that made Venus a goddess (given her by Apollo) that kept
her perpetually young, cleared her wrinkles, firmed her gums, filled
her skin, coloured her hair; from her, derived to Helen, and at the
sack of Troy (unfortunately) lost: till now, in this our age, it was as   220
happily recovered, by a studious antiquary, out of some ruins of Asia,
who sent a moiety of it to the court of France (but much sophisti-
cated) wherewith the ladies there now colour their hair. The rest
(at this present) remains with me; extracted, to a quintessence: so
that, wherever it but touches, in youth it perpetually preserves, in   225
age restores the complexion; seats your teeth, did they dance
like virginal jacks, firm as a wall; makes them white as ivory, that
were black as——'

ACT II, Scene iii

Enter Corvino

Corv. Spite o' the devil, and my shame! Come down here;
                (*He beats away the mountebank, etc.*)
Come down: no house but mine to make your scene?

---

204 *prevented*: forestalled   222–3 *sophisticated*: adulterated   227 *virginal
jacks*: upright staves fitted with quills, which plucked the strings of the virginals when
the keys were struck

Signior Flaminio, will you down, sir? Down?
What, is my wife your Franciscina? Sir?
5 No windows on the whole Piazza here
To make your properties, but mine? But mine?
Heart! Ere tomorrow I shall be new-christened,
And called the *Pantalone di besogniosi*
About the town.   [*Exit*]

    Per.   What should this mean, Sir Pol?
10 *Pol.* Some trick of state, believe it. I will home.
    Per. It may be some design on you.
    Pol.   I know not.
I'll stand upon my guard.
    Per.   It is your best, sir.
    Pol. This three weeks, all my advices, all my letters,
They have been intercepted.
    Per.   Indeed, sir?
Best have a care.
    Pol.   Nay, so I will.
15 *Per.* [*Aside*]   This knight,
I may not lose him, for my mirth, till night.   [*Exeunt*]

ACT II, Scene iv

[Volpone's house]
Enter Volpone, Mosca

    Volp. Oh, I am wounded.
    Mos.   Where, sir?
    Volp.   Not without;
Those blows were nothing: I could bear them ever.
But angry Cupid, bolting from her eyes,
Hath shot himself into me, like a flame;

---

   3 *Flaminio*: Flaminio Scala, noted actor and author of a collection of scenari, *Il Teatro delle Favole* (1611): also stock name for the lover in the Comedy of Arts
   4 *Franciscina*: the servant-maid of the Comedy of Arts   8 *Pantalone di besogniosi*: Pantaloon (of the paupers) stock character in the Comedy of Arts, often depicted as a jealous dotard or cuckold   (*II. iv*) 3 *bolting*: springing

Where now he flings about his burning heat,   5
As in a furnace, an ambitious fire,
Whose vent is stopped. The fight is all within me.
I cannot live, except thou help me, Mosca;
My liver melts, and I, without the hope
Of some soft air from her refreshing breath,   10
Am but a heap of cinders.
    Mos.   'Las, good sir!
Would you had never seen her.
    Volp.   Nay, would thou
Hadst never told me of her.
    Mos.   Sir, 'tis true;
I do confess, I was unfortunate,
And you unhappy: but I'm bound in conscience,   15
No less than duty, to effect my best
To your release of torment, and I will, sir.
    Volp. Dear Mosca, shall I hope?
    Mos.   Sir, more than dear,
I will not bid you to despair of aught,
Within a human compass.
    Volp.   Oh, there spoke   20
My better angel. Mosca, take my keys,
Gold, plate, and jewels, all's at thy devotion;
Employ them how thou wilt; nay, coin me, too:
So thou in this but crown my longings. Mosca?
    Mos. Use but your patience.
    Volp.   So I have.
    Mos.   I doubt not   25
To bring success to your desires.
    Volp.   Nay, then,
I not repent me of my late disguise.
    Mos. If you can horn him, sir, you need not.
    Volp.   True:
Besides, I never meant him for my heir.
Is not the colour o' my beard and eyebrows   30
To make me known?
    Mos.   No jot.

---

9 *liver*: classically, the seat of the violent passions   28 *horn him*: cuckold him

    Volp.   I did it well.

    Mos. So well, would I could follow you in mine,
With half the happiness; and yet I would
Escape your epilogue.

    Volp.   But, were they gulled
With a belief, that I was Scoto?

35   *Mos.*   Sir,
Scoto himself could hardly have distinguished!
I have not time to flatter you now, we'll part:
And, as I prosper, so applaud my art.   *[Exeunt]*

ACT II, Scene v

[Corvino's house]

Enter Corvino, Celia

    Corv. Death of mine honour, with the city's fool?
A juggling, tooth-drawing, prating mountebank?
And at a public window? Where whilst he,
With his strained action, and his dole of faces,
5   To his drug-lecture draws your itching ears,
A crew of old, unmarried, noted lechers,
Stood leering up, like satyrs: and you smile,
Most graciously! And fan your favours forth,
To give your hot spectators satisfaction!
10 What, was your mountebank their call? Their whistle?
Or were you enamoured on his copper rings?
His saffron jewel, with the toad-stone in it?
Or his embroidered suit, with the cope-stitch,
Made of a hearse-cloth? Or his old tilt-feather?
15 Or his starched beard? Well! You shall have him, yes.
He shall come home, and minister unto you
The fricace, for the mother. Or, let me see,

---

34 *epilogue*: i.e. the beating   *(II. v)* 4 *dole*: deceit, trickery   12 *toad-stone*:
jewel resembling that supposedly found in the head of a toad   13 *cope-stitch*:
used in embroidering the edge of a cope   17 *fricace*: massage   *mother*: hysteria
(with equivoque)

I think, you had rather mount? Would you not mount?
Why, if you'll mount, you may; yes truly, you may:
And so, you may be seen, down to the foot.   20
Get you a cithern, lady vanity,
And be a dealer with the virtuous man;
Make one: I'll but protest myself a cuckold,
And save your dowry. I am a Dutchman, I!
For, if you thought me an Italian,   25
You would be damned, ere you did this, you whore:
Thouldst tremble, to imagine that the murder
Of father, mother, brother, all thy race,
Should follow, as the subject of my justice!
    Cel. Good sir, have patience!
    Corv.   What couldst thou propose   30
Less to thyself, than, in this heat of wrath,
And stung with my dishonour, I should strike [*Taking his sword*]
This steel into thee, with as many stabs,
As thou wert gazed upon with goatish eyes?
    Cel. Alas, sir, be appeased! I could not think   35
My being at the window should more now
Move your impatience than at other times.
    Corv. No? Not to seek and entertain a parley
With a known knave? Before a multitude?
You were an actor, with your handkerchief!   40
Which he, most sweetly, kissed in the receipt,
And might (no doubt) return it, with a letter,
And point the place where you might meet: your sisters,
Your mothers, or your aunts might serve the turn.
    Cel. Why, dear sir, when do I make these excuses?   45
Or ever stir abroad, but to the church?
And that so seldom——
    Corv.   Well, it shall be less;
And thy restraint, before, was liberty,
To what I now decree: and therefore, mark me.
First, I will have this bawdy light dammed up;   50

21 *cithern*: musical instrument like a guitar   *lady vanity*: a character in the morality
plays   22 *dealer*: bawd or prostitute   24 *dowry*: forfeited by a widow proved
to have been unfaithful   *Dutchman*: i.e. phlegmatic

And, till it be done, some two or three yards off
I'll chalk a line: o'er which, if thou but chance
To set thy desperate foot, more hell, more horror,
More wild, remorseless rage shall seize on thee
55 Than on a conjurer, that had heedless left
His circle's safety, ere his devil was laid.
Then, here's a lock, which I will hang upon thee;
And, now I think on't, I will keep thee backwards;
Thy lodging shall be backwards; thy walks backwards;
60 Thy prospect—all be backwards; and no pleasure,
That thou shalt know, but backwards: nay, since you force
My honest nature, know it is your own
Being too open makes me use you thus.
Since you will not contain your subtle nostrils
65 In a sweet room, but they must snuff the air
Of rank and sweaty passengers—— (*Knock within*) One knocks.
Away, and be not seen, pain of thy life;
Not look toward the window: if thou dost——
(Nay stay, hear this) let me not prosper, whore,
70 But I will make thee an anatomy,
Dissect thee mine own self, and read a lecture
Upon thee to the city and in public.
Away. [*Exit* Celia] Who's there?

[*Enter* Servitore]

Ser. 'Tis Signior Mosca, sir.

ACT II, Scene vi

Corv. Let him come in, his master's dead: there's yet
Some good, to help the bad.

[*Enter* Mosca]
                                                    My Mosca, welcome,
I guess your news.

56 *circle's safety*: within which he was secure from the power of the devils he had
conjured; he could not leave it until they had returned to the spirit world (*Poet.* IV.
viii. 10–13)   57 *lock*: girdle of chastity   58 *backwards*: at the rear of the house

Mos.   I fear you cannot, sir.
Corv. Is't not his death?
Mos.   Rather the contrary.
Corv. Not his recovery?
Mos.   Yes, sir.
Corv.   I am cursed,   5
I am bewitched, my crosses meet to vex me.
How? How? How? How?
Mos.   Why, sir, with Scoto's oil!
Corbaccio and Voltore brought of it,
Whilst I was busy in an inner room——
   Corv. Death! That damned mountebank! But for the law,   10
Now I could kill the rascal: it cannot be
His oil should have that virtue. Ha' not I
Known him a common rogue, come fiddling in
To the *ostería*, with a tumbling whore,
And, when he has done all his forced tricks, been glad   15
Of a poor spoonful of dead wine, with flies in it?
It cannot be. All his ingredients
Are a sheep's gall, a roasted bitch's marrow,
Some few sod earwigs, pounded caterpillars,
A little capon's grease, and fasting spittle: 20
I know 'em, to a dram.
Mos.   I know not, sir,
But some on't, there, they poured into his ears,
Some in his nostrils, and recovered him;
Applying but the fricace.
Corv.   Pox o' that fricace.
Mos. And since, to seem the more officious,   25
And flattering of his health, there they have had
(At extreme fees) the college of physicians
Consulting on him, how they might restore him;
Where one would have a cataplasm of spices,
Another, a flayed ape clapped to his breast,   30
A third would ha' it a dog, a fourth an oil
With wild cat's skins: at last, they all resolved

---

14 *ostería*: inn   *tumbling*: acrobat (with equivoque)   16 *dead*: stale
19 *sod*: boiled   25 *officious*: dutiful   29 *cataplasm*: poultice

That to preserve him was no other means
But some young woman must be straight sought out,
35 Lusty, and full of juice, to sleep by him;
And to this service (most unhappily,
And most unwillingly) am I now employed,
Which here I thought to pre-acquaint you with,
For your advice, since it concerns you most,
40 Because, I would not do that thing might cross
Your ends, on whom I have my whole dependance, sir:
Yet, if I do it not, they may delate
My slackness to my patron, work me out
Of his opinion; and there all your hopes,
45 Ventures, or whatsoever, are all frustrate.
I do but tell you, sir. Besides, they are all
Now striving, who shall first present him. Therefore——
I could entreat you, briefly, conclude somewhat:
Prevent 'em if you can.
    Corv.   Death to my hopes!
50 This is my villainous fortune! Best to hire
Some common courtesan?
    Mos.   Aye, I thought on that, sir.
But they are all so subtle, full of art,
And age again doting, and flexible,
So as——I cannot tell——we may perchance
Light on a quean, may cheat us all.
55   *Corv.*   'Tis true.
    Mos. No, no: it must be one, that has no tricks, sir,
Some simple thing, a creature, made unto it;
Some wench you may command. Ha' you no kinswoman?
God's so—— Think, think, think, think, think, think, think, sir.
60 One o' the doctors offered there his daughter.
    Corv. How!
    Mos.   Yes, Signior Lupo, the physician,
    Corv. His daughter?
    Mos.   And a virgin, sir. Why? Alas
He knows the state of 's body, what it is;
That naught can warm his blood, sir, but a fever;

    42 *delate*: report

Nor any incantation raise his spirit: 65
A long forgetfulness hath seized that part.
Besides, sir, who shall know it? Some one, or two——
    Corv. I pray thee give me leave. [*He walks aside*] If any man
But I had had this luck—— The thing, in itself,
I know, is nothing—— Wherefore should not I   70
As well command my blood and my affections
As this dull doctor? In the point of honour,
The cases are all one, of wife, and daughter.
    Mos. [*Aside*] I hear him coming.
    Corv.   She shall do't: 'Tis done.
Slight, if this doctor, who is not engaged,   75
Unless it be for his counsel (which is nothing)
Offer his daughter, what should I, that am
So deeply in? I will prevent him: wretch!
Covetous wretch! Mosca, I have determined.
    Mos. How, sir?
    Corv.   We'll make all sure. The party, you wot of,   80
Shall be mine own wife, Mosca.
    Mos.   Sir. The thing,
(But that I would not seem to counsel you)
I should have motioned to you, at the first:
And, make your count, you have cut all their throats.
Why! 'Tis directly taking a possession!   85
And, in his next fit, we may let him go.
'Tis but to pull the pillow from his head,
And he is throttled: it had been done before,
But for your scrupulous doubts.
    Corv.   Aye, a plague on't,
My conscience fools my wit. Well, I'll be brief,   90
And so be thou, lest they should be before us;
Go home, prepare him, tell him with what zeal
And willingness I do it: swear it was
On the first hearing (as thou mayest do, truly)
Mine own free motion.
    Mos.   Sir, I warrant you,   95
I'll so possess him with it, that the rest

74 *coming*: yielding   78 *prevent*: forestall

Of his starved clients shall be banished, all;
And only you received. But come not, sir,
Until I send, for I have something else
100 To ripen, for your good (you must not know it).
     Corv. But do not you forget to send, now.
     Mos.   Fear not.   [*Exit*]

ACT II, Scene vii

     Corv. Where are you, wife? My Celia? Wife?

               [*Enter* Celia]
                                        What, blubbering?
Come, dry those tears. I think thou thoughtst me in earnest?
Ha? By this light, I talked so but to try thee.
Methinks the lightness of the occasion
5 Should ha' confirmed thee. Come, I am not jealous.
     Cel. No?
     Corv.   Faith, I am not, I, nor never was:
It is a poor, unprofitable humour.
Do not I know, if women have a will,
They'll do 'gainst all the watches o' the world?
10 And that the fiercest spies are tamed with gold?
Tut, I am confident in thee, thou shalt see it:
And see, I'll give thee cause too, to believe it.
Come, kiss me. Go, and make thee ready straight,
In all thy best attire, thy choicest jewels,
15 Put 'em all on, and with 'em thy best looks:
We are invited to a solemn feast
At old Volpone's, where it shall appear
How far I am free from jealousy, or fear.   [*Exeunt*]

    11 *confident*: trusting

ACT III, Scene i

[A street]

Enter Mosca

Mos. I FEAR I shall begin to grow in love
With my dear self, and my most prosperous parts,
They do so spring and burgeon; I can feel
A whimsy i' my blood: I know not how,
Success hath made me wanton. I could skip   5
Out of my skin now, like a subtle snake,
I am so limber. Oh! Your parasite
Is a most precious thing, dropped from above,
Not bred 'mongst clods and clot-poles, here on earth.
I muse, the mystery was not made a science,   10
It is so liberally professed! Almost
All the wise world is little else, in nature,
But parasites, or sub-parasites. And yet,
I mean not those that have your bare town-art,
To know who's fit to feed 'em; have no house,   15
No family, no care, and therefore mould
Tales for men's ears, to bait that sense; or get
Kitchen-invention, and some stale receipts
To please the belly and the groin; nor those,
With their court-dog-tricks, that can fawn and fleer,   20
Make their revenue out of legs and faces,
Echo my-Lord, and lick away a moth:
But your fine, elegant rascal, that can rise
And stoop (almost together) like an arrow;
Shoot through the air, as nimbly as a star;   25
Turn short, as doth a swallow; and be here,
And there, and here, and yonder, all at once;
Present to any humour, all occasion;
And change a visor swifter than a thought!
This is the creature had the art born with him;   30
Toils not to learn it, but doth practise it
Out of most excellent nature: and such sparks
Are the true parasites, others but their zanies.

9 *clot-poles*: thick heads   20 *fleer*: laugh obsequiously   29 *visor*: mask

ACT III, Scene ii

Enter Bonario

  Mos. Who's this? Bonario? Old Corbaccio's son?
The person I was bound to seek. Fair sir,
You are happ'ly met.
    Bon.   That cannot be, by thee.
  Mos. Why, sir?
    Bon.   Nay, 'pray thee know thy way, and leave me:
5 I would be loth to interchange discourse
With such a mate as thou art.
    Mos.   Courteous sir,
Scorn not my poverty.
    Bon.   Not I, by heaven:
But thou shalt give me leave to hate thy baseness.
  Mos. Baseness?
    Bon.   Aye, answer me, is not thy sloth
10 Sufficient argument? Thy flattery?
Thy means of feeding?
    Mos.   Heaven, be good to me.
These imputations are too common, sir,
And easily stuck on virtue, when she's poor;
You are unequal to me, and howe'er
15 Your sentence may be righteous, yet you are not,
That ere you know me, thus proceed in censure:
St Mark bear witness 'gainst you, 'tis inhuman.
  Bon. [*Aside*] What? Does he weep? The sign is soft and good!
I do repent me that I was so harsh.
20   *Mos.* 'Tis true, that, swayed by strong necessity,
I am enforced to eat my careful bread
With too much obsequy; 'tis true, beside,
That I am fain to spin mine own poor raiment,
Out of my mere observance, being not born
25 To a free fortune: but that I have done
Base offices, in rending friends asunder,

---

  2 *bound*: on my way   6 *mate*: fellow (contemptuous)   14 *unequal*:
unjust   24 *observance*: I. i. 75

Dividing families, betraying counsels,
Whispering false lies, or mining men with praises,
Trained their credulity with perjuries,
Corrupted chastity, or am in love   30
With mine own tender ease, but would not rather
Prove the most rugged and laborious course,
That might redeem my present estimation;
Let me here perish, in all hope of goodness.

    Bon. [*Aside*] This cannot be a personated passion!   35
I was to blame, so to mistake thy nature;
'Pray thee forgive me: and speak out thy business.

    Mos. Sir, it concerns you; and though I may seem
At first to make a main offence, in manners,
And in my gratitude, unto my master,   40
Yet, for the pure love, which I bear all right,
And hatred of the wrong, I must reveal it.
This very hour, your father is in purpose
To disinherit you——

    Bon.   How!

    Mos.   And thrust you forth,
As a mere stranger to his blood; 'tis true, sir: 45
The work no way engageth me, but as
I claim an interest in the general state
Of goodness and true virtue, which I hear
To abound in you: and, for which mere respect,
Without a second aim, sir, I have done it.   50

    Bon. This tale hath lost thee much of the late trust,
Thou hadst with me; it is impossible:
I know not how to lend it any thought,
My father should be so unnatural.

    Mos. It is a confidence, that well becomes   55
Your piety; and formed (no doubt) it is,
From your own simple innocence: which makes
Your wrong more monstrous and abhorred. But, sir,
I now will tell you more. This very minute,
It is, or will be doing: and, if you   60

28 *mining*: undermining   29 *trained*: deceived   45 *mere*: absolute
56 *piety*: filial affection

Shall be but pleased to go with me, I'll bring you,
(I dare not say where you shall see, but) where
Your ear shall be a witness of the deed;
Hear yourself written bastard: and professed
The common issue of the earth.

65   *Bon.*   I'm 'mazed!
      Mos. Sir, if I do it not, draw your just sword,
And score your vengeance on my front and face;
Mark me your villain. You have too much wrong,
And I do suffer for you, sir. My heart
Weeps blood, in anguish——

70   *Bon.*   Lead. I follow thee.   [*Exeunt*]

ACT III, Scene iii

[Volpone's house]

Enter Volpone, Nano, Androgyno, Castrone

Volp. Mosca stays long, methinks. Bring forth your sports
And help to make the wretched time more sweet.
      Nan. Dwarf, fool, and eunuch, well met here we be.
A question it were now, whether of us three,
5 Being, all, the known delicates of a rich man,
      In pleasing him, claim the precedency can?
      Cas. I claim for myself.
      And.   And so doth the fool.
      Nan. 'Tis foolish indeed: let me set you both to school.
First, for your dwarf, he's little, and witty,
10   And everything, as it is little, is pretty;
Else, why do men say to a creature of my shape,
      So soon as they see him, it's a pretty little ape?
And why a pretty ape? But for pleasing imitation
      Of greater men's action, in a ridiculous fashion.
15 Beside, this feat body of mine doth not crave
      Half the meat, drink, and cloth, one of your bulks will have.

---

65 *issue of the earth*: of unknown parentage (*Alch.* IV. ii. 13)   (*III. iii*) 5 *delicates*:
favourites   15 *feat*: adroit, elegant

Admit, your fool's face be the mother of laughter,
   Yet, for his brain, it must always come after:
And though that do feed him, it's a pitiful case,
   His body is beholding to such a bad face.   (*One knocks*) 20
   Volp. Who's there? My couch, away, look, Nano, see:
Give me my caps, first—— go, enquire. [*Exeunt* Nano, *etc.*] Now,
   Cupid
Send it be Mosca, and with fair return.

               [*Enter* Nano]

   Nan. It is the beauteous madam——
   Volp.   Would-be—is it?
   Nan. The same.
   Volp.   Now, torment on me; squire her in: 25
For she will enter, or dwell here for ever.
Nay, quickly, that my fit were past. [*Exit* Nano] I fear
A second hell too, that my loathing this
Will quite expel my appetite to the other:
Would she were taking, now, her tedious leave.   30
Lord, how it threats me, what I am to suffer!

ACT III, Scene iv

Enter Nano, Lady Politic Would-be

   Lad. I thank you, good sir. 'Pray you signify
Unto your patron I am here. This band
Shows not my neck enough (I trouble you, sir,
Let me request you, bid one of my women
Come hither to me) in good faith, I am dressed   5
Most favourably today, it is no matter,
'Tis well enough.

             [*Enter* 1st Woman]

           Look, see, these petulant things!
How they have done this!
   Volp. [*Aside*]   I do feel the fever

---

1 Lady Politic Would-be's speeches are indebted to the *De Muliere Loquaci* of
Libanius of Antioch   2 *band*: collar

Entering in at mine ears; oh for a charm
To fright it hence.
10   *Lad.*   Come nearer: is this curl
In his right place? Or this? Why is this higher
Than all the rest? You ha' not washed your eyes yet?
Or do they not stand even i' your head?
Where's your fellow? Call her.   [*Exit* 1st Woman]
      Nan. [*Aside*]   Now, St Mark
15 Deliver us: anon, she'll beat her women,
Because her nose is red.

                    [*Enter* 1st *and* 2nd Women]

      Lad.   I pray you, view
This tire, forsooth: are all things apt, or no?
      Wom. One hair a little, here, sticks out, forsooth.
      Lad. Does 't so forsooth? And where was your dear sight
20 When it did so, forsooth? What now? Bird-eyed?
And you, too? 'Pray you both approach, and mend it.
Now (by that light) I muse, you are not ashamed!
I, that have preached these things so oft unto you,
Read you the principles, argued all the grounds,
25 Disputed every fitness, every grace,
Called you to counsel of so frequent dressings——
      Nan. [*Aside*] More carefully than of your fame or honour.
      Lad. Made you acquainted what an ample dowry
The knowledge of these things would be unto you,
30 Able, alone, to get you noble husbands
At your return: and you, thus, to neglect it?
Besides, you seeing what a curious nation
The Italians are, what will they say of me?
The English lady cannot dress herself;
35 Here's a fine imputation to our country!
Well, go your ways, and stay i' the next room.
This fucus was too coarse too, it's no matter.
Good sir, you'll give 'em entertainment?   [*Exeunt* Nano, Women]
      Volp. [*Aside*] The storm comes toward me.

17 *tire*: head-dress   20 *bird-eyed*: i.e. with the look of a fearful bird   32 *curious*:
particular   37 *fucus*: cosmetic paint

Lad.   How does my Volp?

Volp. Troubled with noise, I cannot sleep; I dreamt   40
That a strange fury entered now my house,
And with the dreadful tempest of her breath,
Did cleave my roof asunder.

Lad.   Believe me, and I
Had the most fearful dream, could I remember it——

Volp. [*Aside*] Out on my fate; I ha' given her the occasion   45
How to torment me: she will tell me hers.

Lad. Methought, the golden mediocrity
Polite, and delicate——

Volp.   Oh, if you do love me,
No more; I sweat and suffer at the mention
Of any dream: feel, how I tremble yet.   50

Lad. Alas, good soul! The passion of the heart.
Seed-pearl were good now, boiled with syrup of apples,
Tincture of gold, and coral, citron-pills,
Your elicampane root, myrobalanes——

Volp. [*Aside*] Ay me, I have ta'en a grasshopper by the wing. 55

Lad. Burnt silk, and amber, you have muscadel
Good i' the house——

Volp.   You will not drink, and part?

Lad. No, fear not that. I doubt, we shall not get
Some English saffron (half a dram would serve)
Your sixteen cloves, a little musk, dried mints,   60
Bugloss, and barley-meal——

Volp. [*Aside*]   She's in again,
Before, I feigned diseases, now I have one.

Lad. And these applied, with a right scarlet-cloth——

Volp. [*Aside*] Another flood of words! A very torrent!

Lad. Shall I, sir, make you a poultice?

Volp.   No, no, no;   65
I'm very well: you need prescribe no more.

---

47 *golden mediocrity*: ? the golden mean   51 *the passion of the heart*: heartburn
53 *Tincture of gold*: *aurum potabile* (I. iv. 73)   54 *elicampane*: *Inula Helenium*,
the yellow-flowered plant used to make a tonic   *myrobalanes*: plum-like fruit
55 *grasshopper by the wing*: proverbial (*Poet.* Ap. Dial., 113–14)   61 *Bugloss*: herb
recommended as cure for melancholy   63 *scarlet-cloth*: used in the treatment of
smallpox

Lad. I have, a little, studied physic; but, now,
I'm all for music: save, i' the forenoons,
An hour or two for painting. I would have
70 A lady, indeed, to have all, letters, and arts,
Be able to discourse, to write, to paint,
But principal (as Plato holds) your music
(And so does wise Pythagoras, I take it)
Is your true rapture; when there is concent
75 In face, in voice, and clothes: and is, indeed,
Our sex's chiefest ornament.
　　Volp.　　　　　　　　The poet,
As old in time, as Plato, and as knowing,
Says that your highest female grace is silence.
　　Lad. Which o' your poets? Petrarch? Or Tasso? Or Dante?
80 Guerrini? Ariosto? Aretine?
Cieco di Hadria? I have read them all.
　　Volp. [*Aside*] Is everything a cause, to my destruction?
　　Lad. I think I ha' two or three of 'em about me.
　　Volp. [*Aside*] The sun, the sea will sooner both stand still,
85 Than her eternal tongue! Nothing can 'scape it.
　　Lad. Here's *Pastor Fido*——
　　Volp. [*Aside*]　　　　　Profess obstinate silence,
That's now my safest.
　　Lad.　　　　　　All our English writers,
I mean such as are happy in the Italian,
Will deign to steal out of this author mainly;
90 Almost as much as from Montagnie:
He has so modern and facile a vein,
Fitting the time, and catching the court-ear.
Your Petrarch is more passionate, yet he,
In days of sonneting, trusted 'em with much:
95 Dante is hard, and few can understand him.

---

74 *concent*: harmony　　　76 *The poet*: Sophocles, *Ajax*, 293　　　80 *Guerrini*:
Guarini (1537–1612), author of the *Pastor Fido Aretine*: Pietro Aretino (1492–1556),
comedian and satirist, who wrote sixteen *Sonnetti lussuriosi* to illustrate the obscene
designs of Giulio Romano (l. 97)　　　81 *Cieco di Hadria*: Luigi Groto (1541–85),
'the blind man of Adria', who translated the first book of the *Iliad* and celebrated the
battle of Lepanto　　　94 *trusted 'em with much*: left much for later poets 'to steal
out of'

But, for a desperate wit, there's Aretine!
Only, his pictures are a little obscene——
You mark me not?
  Volp.   Alas, my mind's perturbed.
  Lad. Why, in such cases, we must cure ourselves,
Make use of our philosophy——
  Volp.   O'y me.   100
  Lad. And as we find our passions do rebel,
Encounter 'em with reason; or divert 'em,
By giving scope unto some other humour
Of lesser danger: as in politic bodies,
There's nothing more doth overwhelm the judgement,   105
And clouds the understanding, than too much
Settling and fixing, and (as 'twere) subsiding
Upon one object. For the incorporating
Of these same outward things, into that part,
Which we call mental, leaves some certain faeces,   110
That stop the organs, and, as Plato says,
Assassinates our knowledge.
  Volp. [*Aside*]   Now, the spirit
Of patience help me.
  Lad.   Come, in faith, I must
Visit you more, a-days; and make you well:
Laugh, and be lusty.
  Volp. [*Aside*]   My good angel save me.   115
  Lad. There was but one sole man, in all the world,
With whom I ere could sympathise; and he
Would lie you often, three, four hours together,
To hear me speak: and be, sometime, so rapt,
As he would answer me quite from the purpose,   120
Like you, and you are like him, just. I'll discourse
And't be but only, sir, to bring you asleep,
How we did spend our time and loves together,
For some six years.
  Volp.   Oh, oh, oh, oh, oh, oh.
  Lad. For we were *coaetanei*, and brought up——   125
  Volp. [*Aside*] Some power, some fate, some fortune rescue me.

111 *as Plato says*: a false attribution   125 *coaetanei*: contemporaries (an affectation)

ACT III, Scene v

Enter Mosca

  Mos. God save you, madam.
  Lad.   Good sir.
  Volp.   Mosca? Welcome,
Welcome to my redemption.
  Mos.   Why, sir?
  Volp.   Oh,
Rid me of this my torture, quickly, there;
My Madam, with the everlasting voice:
5 The bells, in time of pestilence, ne'er made
Like noise, or were in that perpetual motion;
The cockpit comes not near it. All my house,
But now, steamed like a bath, with her thick breath.
A lawyer could not have been heard; nor scarce
10 Another woman, such a hail of words
She has let fall. For hell's sake, rid her hence.
  Mos. Has she presented?
  Volp.   Oh, I do not care,
I'll take her absence, upon any price,
With any loss.
  Mos.   Madam——
  Lad.   I ha' brought your patron
A toy, a cap here, of mine own work——
15   *Mos.*   'Tis well,
I had forgot to tell you, I saw your knight,
Where you'd little think it——
  Lad.   Where?
  Mos.   Marry,
Where yet, if you make haste, you may apprehend him,
20 Rowing upon the water in a gondola,
With the most cunning courtesan of Venice.
  Lad. Is't true?
  Mos.   Pursue 'em, and believe your eyes:

---

7 *cockpit*: noisy from the cries of those wagering on the outcome   15 *toy*: trifle

Leave me to make your gift. [*Exit* Lady] I knew, 'twould take.
For lightly, they that use themselves most licence,
Are still most jealous.
   Volp.   Mosca, hearty thanks,
For thy quick fiction, and delivery of me.   25
Now, to my hopes, what sayest thou?

[Enter Lady]

   Lad.   But, do you hear, sir?——
   Volp. [*Aside*] Again; I fear a paroxysm.
   Lad.   Which way
Rowed they together?
   Mos.   Toward the Rialto.
   Lad. I pray you lend me your dwarf.
   Mos.   I pray you, take him.

[Exit Lady]

Your hopes, sir, are like happy blossoms, fair,   30
And promise timely fruit, if you will stay
But the maturing; keep you at your couch,
Corbaccio will arrive straight, with the will:
When he is gone, I'll tell you more.   [*Exit*]
   Volp.   My blood,
My spirits are returned; I am alive: 35
And like your wanton gamester, at primero,
Whose thought had whispered to him, not go less,
Methinks I lie, and draw—for an encounter.

[He retires to his couch]

ACT III, Scene vi

Enter Mosca, Bonario

   Mos. Sir, here concealed, you may hear all. But 'pray you
Have patience, sir; (*One knocks*) the same's your father, knocks:
I am compelled to leave you.
   Bon.   Do so.   [*Exit* Mosca]
                  Yet
Cannot my thought imagine this a truth.   [*He retires*]

---

   23 *lightly*: commonly   36 *primero*: card-game, in which 'go less', 'draw', and
'encounter' are technical terms

ACT III, Scene vii

Enter Mosca, Corvino, Celia

Mos. Death on me! You are come too soon, what meant you?
Did not I say, I would send?

    Corv.   Yes, but I feared
You might forget it, and then they prevent us.

    Mos. [*Aside*] Prevent? Did e'er man haste so for his horns?
5 A courtier would not ply it so, for a place.
Well, now there's no helping it, stay here;
I'll presently return.

    Corv.   Where are you, Celia?
You know not wherefore I have brought you hither?

    Cel. Not well, except you told me.

    Corv.   Now I will:
Hark hither.   [*They converse apart*]

10   *Mos.* (*To* Bonario) Sir, your father hath sent word,
It will be half an hour ere he come;
And therefore, if you please to walk the while
Into that gallery——at the upper end,
There are some books to entertain the time:
15 And I'll take care no man shall come unto you, sir.

    Bon. [*Aside*] Yes, I will stay there, I do doubt this fellow.

                              [*He retires*]

    Mos. There, he is far enough; he can hear nothing:
And, for his father, I can keep him off.

    Corv. Nay, now, there is no starting back; and therefore,
20 Resolve upon it: I have so decreed.
It must be done. Nor would I move it afore,
Because I would avoid all shifts and tricks,
That might deny me.

    Cel.   Sir, let me beseech you,
Affect not these strange trials; if you doubt
25 My chastity, why lock me up, for ever:
Make me the heir of darkness. Let me live,
Where I may please your fears, if not your trust.

    Corv. Believe it, I have no such humour, I.

All that I speak, I mean; yet I am not mad:
Not horn-mad, see you? Go to, show yourself   30
Obedient, and a wife.
   Cel.   Oh heaven!
   Corv.   I say it,
Do so.
   Cel. Was this the train?
   Corv.   I've told you reasons;
What the physicians have set down; how much
It may concern me; what my engagements are;
My means; and the necessity of those means,   35
For my recovery: wherefore, if you be
Loyal, and mine, be won, respect my venture.
   Cel. Before your honour?
   Corv.   Honour? Tut, a breath;
There's no such thing in nature: a mere term
Invented to awe fools. What, is my gold   40
The worse for touching? Clothes, for being looked on?
Why, this is no more. An old, decrepit wretch,
That has no sense, no sinew; takes his meat
With other's fingers; only knows to gape,
When you do scald his gums; a voice; a shadow;   45
And what can this man hurt you?
   Cel. [*Aside*]   Lord! What spirit
Is this hath entered him?
   Corv.   And for your fame,
That's such a jig; as if I would go tell it,
Cry it on the Piazza! Who shall know it?
But he that cannot speak it; and this fellow,   50
Whose lips are i' my pocket: save yourself,
If you'll proclaim it, you may. I know no other
Should come to know it.
   Cel.   Are heaven and saints then nothing?
Will they be blind, or stupid?
   Corv.   How?
   Cel.   Good sir,
Be jealous still, emulate them; and think   55

   32 *train*: scheme   47 *fame*: reputation   48 *jig*: farce

What hate they burn with, toward every sin.

    Corv. I grant you: if I thought it were a sin,
I would not urge you. Should I offer this
To some young Frenchman, or hot Tuscan blood,
60 That had read Aretine, conned all his prints,
Knew every quirk within lust's labyrinth,
And were professed critic in lechery;
And I would look upon him, and applaud him,
This were a sin: but here, 'tis contrary,
65 A pious work, mere charity, for physic,
And honest policy, to assure mine own.

    Cel. Oh heaven! Canst thou suffer such a change?

    Volp. Thou art mine honour, Mosca, and my pride,
My joy, my tickling, my delight! Go, bring 'em.

    Mos. Please you draw near, sir.

70   *Corv.*   Come on, what——
You will not be rebellious? By that light——

    Mos. Sir, Signior Corvino, here, is come to see you.

    Volp. Oh.

    Mos.   And hearing of the consultation had,
So lately, for your health, is come to offer,
Or rather, sir, to prostitute——

75   *Corv.*   Thanks, sweet Mosca.

    Mos. Freely, unasked, or unentreated——

    Corv.   Well.

    Mos. As the true, fervent instance of his love,
His own most fair and proper wife; the beauty,
Only of price, in Venice——

    Corv.   'Tis well urged.

80   *Mos.* To be your comfortress, and to preserve you.

    Volp. Alas, I'm past already! 'Pray you, thank him
For his good care and promptness, but for that,
'Tis a vain labour, e'en to fight 'gainst heaven;
Applying fire to a stone: (uh, uh, uh, uh)
85 Making a dead leaf grow again. I take
His wishes gently, though; and you may tell him,
What I've done for him: marry, my state is hopeless!

    61 *quirk*: sudden twist

Will him to pray for me; and to use his fortune
With reverence, when he comes to it.
    Mos.   Do you hear, sir?
Go to him, with your wife.
    Corv.   Heart of my father!   90
Wilt thou persist thus? Come, I pray thee, come.
Thou seest 'tis nothing, Celia. By this hand,
I shall grow violent. Come, do it, I say.
    Cel. Sir, kill me, rather: I will take down poison,
Eat burning coals, do anything——
    Corv.   Be damned.   95
Heart, I will drag thee hence, home, by the hair;
Cry thee a strumpet through the streets; rip up
Thy mouth unto thine ears; and slit thy nose,
Like a raw rochet—— Do not tempt me, come.
Yield, I am loth—— Death! I will buy some slave,   100
Whom I will kill, and bind thee to him, alive;
And at my window hang you forth: devising
Some monstrous crime, which I, in capital letters,
Will eat into thy flesh, with aqua-fortis,
And burning corsives, on this stubborn breast.   105
Now, by the blood thou hast incensed, I'll do it.
    Cel. Sir, what you please, you may, I am your martyr.
    Corv. Be not thus obstinate, I ha' not deserved it:
Think who it is entreats you. 'Pray thee, sweet;
Good faith, thou shalt have jewels, gowns, attires,   110
What thou wilt think, and ask. Do but go kiss him.
Or touch him, but. For my sake. At my suit.
This once. No? Not? I shall remember this.
Will you disgrace me, thus? Do you thirst my undoing?
    Mos. Nay, gentle lady, be advised.
    Corv.   No, no.   115
She has watched her time. God's precious, this is scurvy;
'Tis very scurvy: and you are——
    Mos.   Nay, good sir.
    Corv. An errant locust, by heaven, a locust. Whore,

---

  99 *Like a . . . rochet*: like a fish (the red gurnet)   104 *aqua-fortis*: nitric acid
118 *errant*: (1) wandering, (2) arrant   *locust*: consuming plague

Crocodile, that hast thy tears prepared,
Expecting how thou'lt bid 'em flow.

120   *Mos.*   Nay, 'pray you, sir,
She will consider.
       Cel.   Would my life would serve
To satisfy.
       Corv.   'Sdeath if she would but speak to him,
And save my reputation, 'twere somewhat;
But, spitefully to effect my utter ruin.

125   *Mos.* Aye, now you have put your fortune in her hands.
Why i' faith, it is her modesty, I must quit her;
If you were absent, she would be more coming;
I know it: and dare undertake for her.
What woman can, before her husband? 'Pray you,
Let us depart, and leave her here.

130   *Corv.*   Sweet Celia,
Thou mayst redeem all yet; I'll say no more:
If not, esteem yourself as lost. Nay, stay there. [*Exit with* Mosca]
       Cel. Oh God, and his good angels! Whither, whither
Is shame fled human breasts? That with such ease,

135 Men dare put off your honours and their own?
Is that, which ever was a cause of life,
Now placed beneath the basest circumstance?
And modesty an exile made, for money?
       Volp. (*He leaps off from his couch*) Aye, in Corvino, and such
earth-fed minds,

140 That never tasted the true heaven of love.
Assure thee, Celia, he that would sell thee,
Only for hope of gain, and that uncertain,
He would have sold his part of paradise
For ready money, had he met a cope-man.

145 Why art thou 'mazed, to see me thus revived?
Rather applaud thy beauty's miracle;
'Tis thy great work: that hath, not now alone,
But sundry times, raised me, in several shapes,
And but this morning, like a mountebank,

150 To see thee at thy window. Aye, before

126 *quit*: acquit   127 *coming*: yielding   144 *cope-man*: dealer

I would have left my practice, for thy love,
In varying figures, I would have contended
With the blue Proteus, or the horned flood.
Now, art thou welcome.

  Cel.   Sir!

  Volp.   Nay, fly me not.

Nor let thy false imagination   155
That I was bedrid make thee think I am so:
Thou shalt not find it. I am now as fresh,
As hot, as high, and in as jovial plight,
As when, in that so celebrated scene,
At recitation of our comedy,   160
For entertainment of the great Valois,
I acted young Antinous; and attracted
The eyes and ears of all the ladies present,
To admire each graceful gesture, note, and footing.

SONG

    Come, my Celia, let us prove,   165
    While we can, the sports of love;
    Time will not be ours forever,
    He, at length, our good will sever;
    Spend not then his gifts in vain.
    Suns that set may rise again: 170
    But if once we lose this light,
    'Tis with us perpetual night.
    Why should we defer our joys?
    Fame and rumour are but toys.
    Cannot we delude the eyes   175
    Of a few poor household-spies?
    Or his easier ears beguile,
    Thus removed by our wile?
    'Tis no sin love's fruits to steal;

---

151 *practice*: scheming   153 *blue Proteus*: *caeruleus Proteus*, who changed his shape at will *horned flood*: the river-god Achelous who fought Hercules in the shapes of a serpent and a bull   161 *Valois*: Duke of Anjou and King of Poland, entertained by the Doge and senators of Venice in 1574   162 *Antinous*: favourite of the Emperor Hadrian, famed for his beauty   165–72: from Catullus' *Vivamus, mea Lesbia, atque amemus*

180   But the sweet thefts to reveal:
             To be taken, to be seen,
             These have crimes accounted been.

   Cel. Some serene blast me, or dire lightning strike
This my offending face.
       Volp.   Why droops my Celia?
185 Thou hast in place of a base husband, found
A worthy lover: use thy fortune well,
With secrecy, and pleasure. See, behold,
What thou art queen of; not in expectation,
As I feed others: but possessed, and crowned.
190 See, here, a rope of pearl; and each, more orient
Than that the brave Egyptian queen caroused:
Dissolve, and drink 'em. See, a carbuncle,
May put out both the eyes of our St Mark;
A diamond would have bought Lollia Paulina,
195 When she came in, like star-light, hid with jewels
That were the spoils of provinces; take these,
And wear, and lose 'em: yet remains an ear-ring
To purchase them again, and this whole state.
A gem, but worth a private patrimony,
200 Is nothing: we will eat such at a meal.
The heads of parrots, tongues of nightingales,
The brains of peacocks, and of ostriches
Shall be our food: and could we get the phoenix,
(Though nature lost her kind) she were our dish.
205   *Cel.* Good sir, these things might move a mind affected
With such delights; but I, whose innocence
Is all I can think wealthy, or worth the enjoying,
And which once lost, I have naught to lose beyond it,
Cannot be taken with these sensual baits:
If you have conscience——
210   *Volp.*   'Tis the beggar's virtue,
If thou hast wisdom, hear me, Celia.

---

183 *serene*: noxious dew   191 *Egyptian queen*: Cleopatra, who drank a price-
less pearl dissolved in vinegar   193 *eyes of our St Mark*: perhaps the famous
carbuncle in the Treasury of St. Mark at Venice   194 *Lollia Paulina*: wife of
Caligula who appeared at a banquet covered in jewels

Thy baths shall be the juice of July-flowers,
Spirit of roses, and of violets,
The milk of unicorns, and panther's breath
Gathered in bags, and mixed with Cretan wines.   215
Our drink shall be prepared gold and amber;
Which we will take, until my roof whirl round
With the vertigo: and my dwarf shall dance,
My eunuch sing, my fool make up the antic.
Whilst, we, in changed shapes, act Ovid's tales,   220
Thou, like Europa now, and I like Jove,
Then I like Mars, and thou like Erycine,
So, of the rest, till we have quite run through
And wearied all the fables of the gods.
Then will I have thee in more modern forms,   225
Attired like some sprightly dame of France,
Brave Tuscan lady, or proud Spanish beauty;
Sometimes, unto the Persian Sophy's wife;
Or the Grand Signior's mistress; and, for change,
To one of our most artful courtesans,   230
Or some quick Negro, or cold Russian;
And I will meet thee in as many shapes:
Where we may, so, transfuse our wandering souls,
Out at our lips, and score up sums of pleasures,

> That the curious shall not know,   235
> How to tell them, as they flow;
> And the envious, when they find
> What their number is, be pined.

Cel. If you have ears that will be pierced; or eyes
That can be opened; a heart, may be touched;   240
Or any part, that yet sounds man, about you:
If you have touch of holy saints, or heaven,

212 *July-flowers*: gillyflowers   214 *milk of unicorns*: imaginary   *panther's breath*: thought to entice other creatures to it   219 *antic*: caper   220 *Ovid's tales*: the *Metamorphoses*   221 *Europa*: carried off by Zeus while he was in the form of a bull   222 *Erycine*: Venus   228 *Sophy's*: Shah's   229 *Grand Signior*: Sultan of Turkey   235-8 Catullus, vii. 9-12

Do me the grace to let me 'scape. If not,
Be bountiful, and kill me. You do know
245 I am a creature hither ill-betrayed,
By one whose shame I would forget it were.
If you will deign me neither of these graces,
Yet feed your wrath, sir, rather than your lust;
It is a vice, comes nearer manliness,
250 And punish that unhappy crime of nature,
Which you miscall my beauty: flay my face,
Or poison it with ointments for seducing
Your blood to this rebellion. Rub these hands
With what may cause an eating leprosy,
255 E'en to my bones and marrow: anything,
That may disfavour me, save in my honour.
And I will kneel to you, pray for you, pay down
A thousand hourly vows, sir, for your health,
Report, and think you virtuous——

Volp.   Think me cold,
260 Frozen, and impotent, and so report me?
That I had Nestor's hernia, thou wouldst think.
I do degenerate and abuse my nation,
To play with opportunity thus long:
I should have done the act, and then have parleyed.
Yield, or I'll force thee.

Cel.   Oh! Just God.
265 *Volp.*   In vain——
  Bon. (He leaps out from where Mosca *had placed him)* Forbear,
    foul ravisher, libidinous swine,
Free the forced lady, or thou diest, impostor.
But that I am loth to snatch thy punishment
Out of the hand of justice, thou shouldst yet
270 Be made the timely sacrifice of vengeance,
Before this altar, and this dross, thy idol.
Lady, let's quit the place, it is the den
Of villainy; fear naught, you have a guard:
And he, ere long, shall meet his just reward.   [*Exit with* Celia]

261 *Nestor's hernia*: Juvenal, *Sat.* vi. 326   262 *nation*: i.e. the reputation of
Italians

Volp. Fall on me, roof, and bury me in ruin,   275
Become my grave, that wert my shelter. Oh!
I am unmasked, unspirited, undone,
Betrayed to beggary, to infamy——

ACT III, Scene viii

Enter Mosca [*bleeding*]

Mos. Where shall I run, most wretched shame of men,
To beat out my unlucky brains?
    Volp.   Here, here.
What! Dost thou bleed?
    Mos.   Oh, that his well-driven sword
Had been so courteous to have cleft me down,
Unto the navel; ere I lived to see   5
My life, my hopes, my spirits, my patron, all
Thus desperately engaged, by my error.
    Volp. Woe, on thy fortune.
    Mos.   And my follies, sir.
    Volp. Thou'st made me miserable.
    Mos.   And myself, sir.
Who would have thought he would have harkened so?   10
    Volp. What shall we do?
    Mos.   I know not, if my heart
Could expiate the mischance, I'd pluck it out.
Will you be pleased to hang me? Or cut my throat?
And I'll requite you, sir. Let's die like Romans,
Since we have lived like Grecians.   (*They knock without*)
    Volp.   Hark, who's there?   15
I hear some footing, officers, the Saffi,
Come to apprehend us! I do feel the brand
Hissing already at my forehead: now,
Mine ears are boring.
    Mos.   To your couch, sir, you

---

14 *like Romans*: i.e. by suicide   15 *like Grecians*: dissolutely   16 *Saffi*: sergeants

20 Make that place good, however. Guilty men
Suspect what they deserve still.

                [*Enter* Corbaccio]
                  Signior Corbaccio!

ACT III, Scene ix

  Corb. Why! How now? Mosca!

           [*Enter* Voltore, *behind*]

  Mos.   Oh, undone, amazed, sir.
Your son, I know not, by what accident,
Acquainted with your purpose to my patron,
Touching your will, and making him your heir;
5 Entered our house with violence, his sword drawn,
Sought for you, called you wretch, unnatural,
Vowed he would kill you.
    Corb.   Me?
    Mos.   Yes, and my patron.
    Corb. This act shall disinherit him indeed:
Here is the will.
    Mos.   'Tis well, sir.
    Corb.   Right and well.
Be you as careful now, for me.
10   *Mos.*   My life, sir,
Is not more tendered, I am only yours.
    Corb. How does he? Will he die shortly, thinkst thou?
    Mos.   I fear
He'll outlast May.
    Corb.   Today?
    Mos.   No, last out May, sir.
    Corb. Couldst thou not gi' him a dram?
    Mos.   Oh, by no means, sir.
    Corb. Nay, I'll not bid you.   [*He retires*]
15 *Volt.* [*Comes forward*]   This is a knave, I see.
    Mos. How, Signior Voltore! [*Aside*] Did he hear me?
    Volt.   Parasite.

Mos. Who's that? Oh, sir, most timely welcome——
Volt.   Scarce,
To the discovery of your tricks, I fear.
You are his, only? And mine, also? Are you not?
   Mos. Who? I, sir!
   Volt.   You, sir. What device is this   20
About a will?
   Mos.   A plot for you, sir.
   Volt.   Come,
Put not your foists upon me, I shall scent 'em.
   Mos. Did you not hear it?
   Volt.   Yes, I hear, Corbaccio
Hath made your patron, there, his heir.
   Mos.   'Tis true,
By my device, drawn to it by my plot,   25
With hope——
   Volt.   Your patron should reciprocate?
And you have promised?
   Mos.   For your good, I did, sir.
Nay more, I told his son, brought, hid him here,
Where he might hear his father pass the deed;
Being persuaded to it, by this thought, sir,   30
That the unnaturalness, first, of the act,
And then his father's oft disclaiming in him,
(Which I did mean to help on) would sure enrage him
To do some violence upon his parent.
On which the law should take sufficient hold,   35
And you be stated in a double hope:
Truth be my comfort and my conscience,
My only aim was to dig you a fortune
Out of these two, old rotten sepulchres——
   (*Volt.* I cry thee mercy, Mosca.)
   Mos.   Worth your patience,   40
And your great merit, sir. And, see the change!
   Volt. Why? What success?

---

22 *foists*: quibble on foist = trick, and foist = stench   32 *disclaiming in*:
disowning   36 *stated*: settled   38–9 reference to the treasure found in
old monuments   42 *success*: result

    Mos.   Most hapless! You must help, sir.
Whilst we expected the old raven, in comes
Corvino's wife, sent hither, by her husband——
    Volt. What, with a present?
45   *Mos.*   No, sir, on visitation:
(I'll tell you how, anon) and, staying long,
The youth, he grows impatient, rushes forth,
Seizeth the lady, wounds me, makes her swear,
Or he would murder her, that was his vow,
50 To affirm my patron to have done her rape:
Which how unlike it is, you see! And hence,
With that pretext, he's gone, to accuse his father;
Defame my patron; defeat you——
    Volt.   Where's her husband?
Let him be sent for straight.
    Mos.   Sir, I'll go fetch him.
    Volt. Bring him to the Scrutineo.
55   *Mos.*   Sir, I will.
    Volt. This must be stopped.
    Mos.   Oh, you do nobly, sir.
Alas, 'twas laboured all, sir, for your good;
Nor was there want of counsel in the plot:
But fortune can, at any time, o'erthrow
60 The projects of a hundred learned clerks, sir.
    Corb. [*Coming forward*] What's that?
    Volt.   Wilt please you, sir, to go along?
                           [*Exit with* Corbaccio]
    Mos. Patron, go in, and pray for our success.
    Volp. Need makes devotion: heaven your labour bless. [*Exeunt*]

ACT IV, Scene i

[A street]
Enter Politic, Peregrine

    Pol. I TOLD you, sir, it was a plot: you see
What observation is. You mentioned me

  55 *Scrutineo*: Senate-house

For some instructions: I will tell you, sir,
Since we are met here, in this height of Venice,
Some few particulars I have set down,   5
Only for this meridian; fit to be known
Of your crude traveller, and they are these.
I will not touch, sir, at your phrase, or clothes,
For they are old.
    Per.   Sir, I have better.
    Pol.   Pardon,
I meant, as they are themes.
    Per.   Oh, sir, proceed: 10
I'll slander you no more of wit, good sir.
    Pol. First, for your garb, it must be grave and serious;
Very reserved and locked; not tell a secret,
On any terms, not to your father; scarce
A fable, but with caution; make sure choice   15
Both of your company and discourse; beware
You never speak a truth——
    Per.   How!
    Pol.   Not to strangers,
For those be they you must converse with most;
Others I would not know, sir, but at distance,
So as I still might be a saver in 'em: 20
You shall have tricks else, passed upon you hourly.
And then, for your religion, profess none;
But wonder at the diversity of all;
And for your part protest, were there no other
But simply the laws o' the land, you could content you: 25
Nic. Machiavel and Monsieur Bodin, both,
Were of this mind. Then must you learn the use
And handling of your silver fork at meals;
The metal of your glass: these are main matters,
With your Italian, and to know the hour   30

---

11 *slander*: ? accuse   12 *garb*: outward bearing   15 *fable*: fiction
20 *be a saver*: insure against loss (gambling)   26–7 *Machiavel . . . of this mind*:
a false attribution   26 *Bodin*: Jean Bodin (1530–96), author of *Six Livres de la
République* (1576), and advocate of religious toleration (for reasons of state)   28 *fork*:
not yet widely used in England   29 *metal*: material for making glass, in its molten
state

When you must eat your melons and your figs.
    Per. Is that a point of state too?
    Pol.   Here it is.
For your Venetian, if he see a man
Preposterous, in the least, he has him straight;
35 He has: he strips him. I'll acquaint you, sir,
I now have lived here, 'tis some fourteen months;
Within the first week, of my landing here,
All took me for a citizen of Venice:
I knew the forms, so well——
    Per. [*Aside*]   And nothing else.
40   *Pol.* I had read Contarene, took me a house,
Dealt with my Jews, to furnish it with movables——
Well, if I could but find one man, one man,
To mine own heart, whom I durst trust, I would——
    Per. What? What, sir?
    Pol.   Make him rich; make him a fortune:
45 He should not think again. I would command it.
    Per. As how?
    Pol.   With certain projects that I have:
Which, I may not discover.
    Per. [*Aside*]   If I had
But one to wager with, I would lay odds, now,
He tells me instantly.
    Pol.   One is (and that
50 I care not greatly who knows) to serve the state
Of Venice with red herrings, for three years,
And at a certain rate, from Rotterdam,
Where I have correspondence. There's a letter,
Sent me from one o' the States, and to that purpose;
55 He cannot write his name, but that's his mark.
    Per. He is a chandler?
    Pol.   No, a cheesemonger.
There are some other too, with whom I treat,
About the same negotiation;

---

34 *Preposterous*: Ded. 71   40 *Contarene*: the *De Magistratibus et Republica Venetorum* (1589) of Gasparo Contarini   54 *States*: member of the States-General of Holland

And I will undertake it: for, 'tis thus,
I'll do't with ease, I've cast it all. Your hoy 60
Carries but three men in her, and a boy;
And she shall make me three returns a year:
So, if there come but one of three I save,
If two, I can defalk. But, this is now,
If my main project fail.

  Per.   Then you have others? 65

  Pol. I should be loth to draw the subtle air
Of such a place, without my thousand aims.
I'll not dissemble, sir, where e'er I come,
I love to be considerative; and, 'tis true,
I have at my free hours thought upon 70
Some certain goods, unto the state of Venice,
Which I do call my cautions: and, sir, which
I mean (in hope of pension) to propound
To the Great Council, then unto the forty,
So to the ten. My means are made already—— 75

  Per. By whom?

  Pol.   Sir, one, that though his place be obscure,
Yet he can sway, and they will hear him. He's
A commandadore.

  Per.   What, a common sergeant?

  Pol. Sir, such, as they are, put it in their mouths,
What they should say, sometimes: as well as greater. 80
I think I have my notes to show you——

  Per.   Good, sir,

  Pol. But you shall swear unto me, on your gentry,
Not to anticipate——

  Per.   I, sir?

  Pol.   Nor reveal
A circumstance—— My paper is not with me.

  Per. Oh, but, you can remember, sir.

  Pol.   My first is 85
Concerning tinder-boxes. You must know,

---

60 *cast*: calculated *hoy*: small vessel used for short trips in the carrying trade (rigged as a sloop) 64 *defalk*: reduce the amount 72 *cautions*: precautions 74 *Great Council . . . the forty . . . the ten*: the ruling bodies of Venice

No family is, here, without its box.
Now, sir, it being so portable a thing,
Put case, that you or I were ill affected
90 Unto the state; sir, with it in our pockets,
Might not I go into the Arsenal?
Or you? Come out again? And none the wiser?
    Per. Except yourself, sir.
    Pol.   Go to, then. I, therefore,
Advertise to the state, how fit it were,
95 That none but such as were known patriots,
Sound lovers of their country, should be suffered
To enjoy them in their houses: and even those,
Sealed, at some office, and at such a bigness,
As might not lurk in pockets.
    Per.   Admirable!
100   *Pol.* My next is, how to enquire and be resolved
By present demonstration, whether a ship,
Newly arrived from Soría, or from
Any suspected part of all the Levant,
Be guilty of the plague: and where they use,
105 To lie out forty, fifty days, sometimes,
About the Lazaretto, for their trial;
I'll save that charge and loss unto the merchant,
And in an hour clear the doubt.
    Per.   Indeed, sir?
    Pol. Or—— I will lose my labour.
    Per.   'My faith, that's much.
110   *Pol.* Nay, sir, conceive me. 'Twill cost me, in onions,
Some thirty livres——
    Per.   Which is one pound sterling.
    Pol. Beside my waterworks: for this I do, sir.
First, I bring in your ship, 'twixt two brick walls;
(But those the state shall venture): on the one
115 I strain me a fair tarpaulin; and in that
I stick my onions, cut in halves: the other
Is full of loopholes, out at which, I thrust

    89 *Put case*: suppose   102 *Soría*: Syria (Ital. form)   110 *onions*: a specific
against the plague

The noses of my bellows; and those bellows
I keep, with waterworks, in perpetual motion,
Which is the easiest matter of a hundred.   120
Now, sir, your onion, which doth naturally
Attract the infection, and your bellows, blowing
The air upon him, will show instantly
By his changed colour, if there be contagion,
Or else remain as fair as at the first.   125
Now 'tis known, 'tis nothing.

    Per.   You are right, sir.
    Pol. I would I had my note.
    Per.   'Faith, so would I:
But you ha' done well, for once, sir.
    Pol.   Were I false,
Or would be made so, I could show you reasons,
How I could sell this state, now, to the Turk;   130
Spite of their galleys, or their——
    Per.   Pray you, Sir Pol.
    Pol. I have 'em not about me.
    Per.   That I feared.
They're there, sir?
    Pol.   No, this is my diary,
Wherein I note my actions of the day.
    Per. 'Pray you, let's see, sir. What is here? *Notandum*,   135
A rat had gnawn my spur-leathers; notwithstanding,
I put on new, and did go forth: but first
I threw three beans over the threshold. *Item*,
I went and bought two toothpicks, whereof one
I burst, immediately, in a discourse   140
With a Dutch merchant, 'bout *ragion del stato*.
From him I went and paid a *moccinigo*,
For piecing my silk stockings; by the way,
I cheapened sprats; and at St Mark's I urined.
'Faith, these are politic notes!
    Pol.   Sir, I do slip   145
No action of my life, thus, but I quote it.

---

140 *burst*: broke   141 *ragion del stato*: reasons of state   143 *piecing*: mending
144 *cheapened*: asked the price of

Per. Believe me it is wise!
Pol.   Nay, sir, read forth.

ACT IV, Scene ii

Enter Lady Politic Would-be, Nano, Women

Lad. Where should this loose knight be, trow? Sure, he's housed.
Nan. Why, then he's fast.
Lad.   Aye, he plays both, with me:
I pray you, stay. This heat will do more harm
To my complexion than his heart is worth.
5 I do not care to hinder, but to take him.
How it comes off!   [*Rubbing her cheeks*]
Wom.   My master's yonder.
Lad.   Where?
Wom. With a young gentleman.
Lad.   That same's the party!
In man's apparel. 'Pray you, sir, jog my knight:
I will be tender to his reputation,
How ever he demerit.
Pol.   My lady!
10 *Per.*   Where?
Pol. 'Tis she indeed, sir, you shall know her. She is,
Were she not mine, a lady of that merit,
For fashion, and behaviour; and for beauty
I durst compare——
Per.   It seems you are not jealous,
That dare commend her.
15 *Pol.*   Nay, and for discourse——
Per. Being your wife, she cannot miss that.
Pol.   Madam,
Here is a gentleman, 'pray you, use him fairly,
He seems a youth, but he is——
Lad.   None?
Pol.   Yes, one
Has put his face, as soon, into the world——

2 *fast*: secure   *both*: i.e. fast and loose (I. ii. 8)   5 *take*: catch

Lad. You mean, as early? But today?

Pol.   How's this!   20

Lad. Why in this habit, sir, you apprehend me.
Well, Master Would-be, this doth not become you;
I had thought the odour, sir, of your good name
Had been more precious to you; that you would not
Have done this dire massacre on your honour;   25
One of your gravity and rank, besides!
But, knights, I see, care little for the oath
They make to ladies: chiefly their own ladies.

Pol. Now, by my spurs (the symbol of my knighthood)

(Per. Lord! How his brain is humbled, for an oath.)   30

Pol. I reach you not.

Lad.   Right, sir, your policy
May bear it through thus. Sir, a word with you.
I would be loth to contest publicly
With any gentlewoman; or to seem
Froward, or violent (as the courtier says)   35
It comes too near rusticity in a lady,
Which I would shun, by all means: and however
I may deserve from Master Would-be, yet,
To have one fair gentlewoman, thus, be made
The unkind instrument to wrong another,   40
And one she knows not, aye, and to persever;
In my poor judgement, is not warranted
From being a solecism in our sex,
If not in manners.

Per.   How is this!

Pol.   Sweet madam,
Come nearer to your aim.

Lad.   Marry, and will, sir.   45
Since you provoke me with your impudence,
And laughter of your light land-siren here,
Your Sporus, your hermaphrodite——

Per. [*Aside*]   What's here?

29–30 a reference to the indiscriminate creation of knights by James I (*Alch.* II. ii.
86–7)   35 *Froward*: refractory   *the courtier*: Castiglione's *Il Cortegiano* (1528)
48 *Sporus*: Nero's favourite, a eunuch dressed as a woman

Poetic fury and historic storms!

50   *Pol.* The gentleman, believe it, is of worth,
And of our nation.

    Lad.   Aye, your Whitefriars' nation?
Come, I blush for you, Master Would-be, I;
And am ashamed you should ha' no more forehead,
Than thus to be the patron or St George

55   To a lewd harlot, a base fricatrice,
A female devil, in a male outside.

    Pol.   Nay,
And you be such a one! I must bid adieu
To your delights. The case appears too liquid.   [*Exit*]

    Lad. Aye, you may carry it clear, with your state-face!

60   But for your carnival concupiscence,
Who here is fled for liberty of conscience,
From furious persecution of the marshal,
Her will I disciple.

    Per.   This is fine, i'faith!
And do you use this often? Is this part

65   Of your wit's exercise, 'gainst you have occasion?
Madam——

    Lad.   Go to, sir.

    Per.   Do you hear me, lady?
Why, if your knight have set you to beg shirts,
Or to invite me home, you might have done it
A nearer way by far.

    Lad.   This cannot work you,
Out of my snare.

70   *Per.*   Why? Am I in it then?
Indeed, your husband told me you were fair,
And so you are; only your nose inclines,
That side, that's next the sun, to the queen-apple.

    Lad. This cannot be endured, by any patience.

51 *Whitefriars*: sanctuary (and also resort) for those liable to arrest   53 *fore-head*: shame   55 *fricatrice*: prostitute   60 *carnival*: a wench as licentious as the carnival   61 *liberty of conscience*: freedom in religion (cf. 'persecution', 'disciple')   62 *marshal*: prison officer   63 *disciple*: discipline i.e. whip   73 *next the sun*: i.e. it is red   *queen-apple*: an early variety

ACT IV, Scene iii

Enter Mosca

Mos. What's the matter, madam?

Lad.   If the Senate
Right not my quest in this, I will protest 'em
To all the world no aristocracy.

Mos. What is the injury, lady?

Lad.   Why, the callet
You told me of, here I have ta'en disguised.   5

Mos. Who? This? What means your ladyship? The creature
I mentioned to you is apprehended now,
Before the Senate, you shall see her——

Lad.   Where?

Mos. I'll bring you to her. This young gentleman
I saw him land this morning, at the port.   10

Lad. Is't possible! How has my judgement wandered!
Sir, I must, blushing, say to you, I have erred:
And plead your pardon.

Per.   What! More changes yet?

Lad. I hope, you ha' not the malice to remember
A gentlewoman's passion. If you stay,   15
In Venice, here, please you to use me, sir——

Mos. Will you go, madam?

Lad.   'Pray you, sir, use me. In faith,
The more you see me, the more I shall conceive
You have forgot our quarrel.   [*Exeunt* Lady, Mosca, *etc.*]

Per.   This is rare!
Sir Politic Would-be? No, Sir Politic bawd!   20
To bring me, thus, acquainted with his wife!
Well, wise Sir Pol: since you have practised thus
Upon my freshmanship, I'll try your salt-head,
What proof it is against a counter-plot.   [*Exit*]

---

4 *callet*: lewd woman   16–19 *use . . . conceive*: taken by Peregrine as an
overture   23 *salt-head*: quibble on 'salt' as opposed to 'fresh', and 'salt' meaning
'wanton'

ACT IV, Scene iv

[The Scrutineo]

Enter Voltore, Corbaccio, Corvino, Mosca

Volt. Well, now you know the carriage of the business,
Your constancy is all that is required
Unto the safety of it.
Mos.   Is the lie
Safely conveyed amongst us? Is that sure?
Knows every man his burden?
Corv.   Yes.
5   *Mos.*   Then, shrink not.
Corv. But knows the advocate the truth?
Mos.   Oh, sir,
By no means. I devised a formal tale,
That salved your reputation. But be valiant, sir.
Corv. I fear no one but him; that this his pleading
Should make him stand for a co-heir——
10   *Mos.*   Co-halter.
Hang him: we will but use his tongue, his noise,
As we do croaker's, here.   [*Pointing to* Corbaccio]
Corv.   Aye, what shall he do?
Mos. When we ha' done, you mean?
Corv.   Yes.
Mos.   Why, we'll think,
Sell him for *mummia*, he's half dust already.   (*To* Voltore)
15   Do not you smile to see this buffalo,   [*Pointing to* Corvino]
How he doth sport it with his head?—— [*Aside*] I should
If all were well and past. (*To* Corbaccio) Sir, only you
Are he, that shall enjoy the crop of all,
And these not know for whom they toil.
Corb.   Aye, peace.
Mos. (*To* Corvino) But you shall eat it. [*Aside*] Much! (*Then to*
20   Voltore *again*) Worshipful sir,

---

12 *croaker's*: Corbaccio's   14 *mummia*: used as a medicine   15-16 *buffalo*
... *head*: referring to the cuckold's horns

Mercury sit upon your thundering tongue,
Or the French Hercules, and make your language
As conquering as his club, to beat along,
(As with a tempest) flat, our adversaries:
But, much more, yours, sir.
    Volt.   Here they come, ha' done.   25
    Mos. I have another witness, if you need, sir,
I can produce.
    Volt.   Who is it?
    Mos.   Sir, I have her.

ACT IV, Scene v

Enter 4 Avocatori, Bonario, Celia, Notario, Commandadori

    1st Avo. The like of this the Senate never heard of.
    2nd Avo. 'Twill come most strange to them when we report it.
    4th Avo. The gentlewoman has been ever held
Of unreproved name.
    3rd Avo.   So, the young man.
    4th Avo. The more unnatural part that of his father.   5
    2nd Avo. More of the husband.
    1st Avo.   I not know to give
His act a name, it is so monstrous!
    4th Avo. But the impostor, he is a thing created
To exceed example!
    1st Avo.   And all after times!
    2nd Avo. I never heard a true voluptuary   10
Described, but him.
    3rd Avo.   Appear yet those were cited?
    Not. All but the old magnifico, Volpone.
    1st Avo. Why is not he here?
    Mos.   Please your fatherhoods,
Here is his advocate. Himself's so weak,
So feeble——

---

21 *Mercury*: as god of eloquence   22 *French Hercules*: symbol of eloquence
(*IV. v*) s.d. *Commandadori*: officers of justice

4th Avo.   What are you?

15   *Bon.*   His parasite,
His knave, his pandar: I beseech the court,
He may be forced to come, that your grave eyes
May bear strong witness of his strange impostures.

Volt. Upon my faith and credit, with your virtues,
20 He is not able to endure the air.

2nd Avo. Bring him, however.

3rd Avo.   We will see him.

4th Avo.
                                                    Fetch him.
                                            [*Exeunt* Officers]

Volt. Your fatherhoods' fit pleasures be obeyed,
But sure, the sight will rather move your pities,
Than indignation; may it please the court,
25 In the meantime, he may be heard in me:
I know this place most void of prejudice,
And therefore crave it, since we have no reason
To fear our truth should hurt our cause.

3rd Avo.   Speak free.

Volt. Then know, most honoured fathers, I must now
30 Discover, to your strangely abused ears,
The most prodigious, and most frontless piece
Of solid impudence and treachery,
That ever vicious nature yet brought forth
To shame the state of Venice. This lewd woman,
35 That wants no artificial looks or tears
To help the visor she has now put on,
Hath long been known a close adulteress
To that lascivious youth there; not suspected,
I say, but known; and taken in the act,
40 With him; and by this man, the easy husband,
Pardoned: whose timeless bounty makes him, now,
Stand here, the most unhappy, innocent person
That ever man's own goodness made accused.
For these, not knowing how to owe a gift
45 Of that dear grace, but with their shame, being placed
So above all powers of their gratitude,

31 *frontless*: shameless   37 *close*: secret   41 *timeless*: untimely, premature

Began to hate the benefit: and in place
Of thanks, devise to extirp the memory
Of such an act. Wherein, I pray your fatherhoods,
To observe the malice, yea, the rage of creatures   50
Discovered in their evils; and what heart
Such take, even from their crimes. But that, anon,
Will more appear. This gentleman, the father,
Hearing of this foul fact, with many others,
Which daily struck at his too-tender ears,   55
And grieved in nothing more, than that he could not
Preserve himself a parent (his son's ills
Growing to that strange flood) at last decreed
To disinherit him.
    1st Avo.   These be strange turns!
    2nd Avo. The young man's fame was ever fair and honest.   60
    Volt. So much more full of danger is his vice,
That can beguile so, under shade of virtue.
But as I said, my honoured sires, his father
Having this settled purpose (by what means
To him betrayed, we know not) and this day   65
Appointed for the deed; that parricide,
(I cannot style him better) by confederacy
Preparing this his paramour to be there,
Entered Volpone's house (who was the man
Your fatherhoods must understand, designed   70
For the inheritance) there, sought his father:
But with what purpose sought he him, my lords?
I tremble to pronounce it, that a son
Unto a father, and to such a father
Should have so foul, felonious intent.   75
It was, to murder him. When, being prevented
By his more happy absence, what then did he?
Not check his wicked thoughts; no, now new deeds:
(Mischief doth ever end, where it begins)
An act of horror, fathers! He dragged forth   80
The aged gentleman, that had there lain, bed-rid,
Three years and more, out off his innocent couch,

     48 *extirp*: root out   54 *fact*: crime

Naked, upon the floor, there left him; wounded
His servant in the face; and with this strumpet,
85 The stale to his forged practice, who was glad
To be so active (I shall here desire
Your fatherhoods to note but my collections,
As most remarkable) thought, at once, to stop
His father's ends; discredit his free choice,
90 In the old gentleman; redeem themselves,
By laying infamy upon this man,
To whom, with blushing, they should owe their lives.
   1st Avo. What proofs have you of this?
   Bon.   Most honoured fathers,
I humbly crave, there be no credit given
To this man's mercenary tongue.
95   *2nd Avo.*   Forbear.
   Bon. His soul moves in his fee.
   3rd Avo.   Oh, sir.
   Bon.   This fellow,
For six *sols* more, would plead against his maker.
   4st Avo. You do forget yourself.
   Volt.   Nay, nay, grave fathers,
Let him have scope: can any man imagine
100 That he will spare his accuser, that would not
Have spared his parent?
   1st Avo.   Well, produce your proofs.
   Cel. I would I could forget I were a creature.
   Volt. Signior Corbaccio.
   4th Avo.   What is he?
   Volt.   The father.
   2nd Avo. Has he had an oath?
   Not.   Yes.
   Corb.   What must I do now?
   Not. Your testimony's craved.
105   *Corb.*   Speak to the knave?
I'll ha' my mouth, first, stopped with earth; my heart
Abhors his knowledge: I disclaim in him.
   1st Avo. But, for what cause?

85 *stale*: decoy   97 *sols*: worth a halfpenny   102 *creature*: ? human being

Corb.   The mere portent of nature.
He is an utter stranger to my loins.

Bon. Have they made you to this!

Corb.   I will not hear thee,   110
Monster of men, swine, goat, wolf, parricide,
Speak not, thou viper.

Bon.   Sir, I will sit down,
And rather wish my innocence should suffer
Than I resist the authority of a father.

Volt. Signior Corvino.

2nd Avo.   This is strange!

1st Avo.   Who's this?   115

Not. The husband.

4th Avo.   Is he sworn?

Not.   He is.

3rd Avo.   Speak then.

Corv. This woman (please your fatherhoods) is a whore,
Of most hot exercise, more than a partridge,
Upon record——

1st Avo.   No more.

Corv.   Neighs like a jennet.

Not. Preserve the honour of the court.

Corv.   I shall,   120
And modesty of your most reverend ears.
And yet I hope that I may say, these eyes
Have seen her glued unto that piece of cedar,
That fine well-timbered gallant: and that, here,
The letters may be read, thorough the horn,   125
That make the story perfect.

Mos.   Excellent! Sir.

Corv. There is no shame in this, now, is there?

Mos.   None.

Corv. Or if I said, I hoped that she were onward
To her damnation, if there be a hell
Greater than whore and woman; a good catholic   130

---

110 *made*: wrought   118 *partridge*: ? byword for lechery   119 *jennet*:
small Spanish horse   124 *here*: i.e. on his forehead   125 *horn*: quibble on
cuckold's horns and the hornbook (*Poet.* IV. v. 67 n.)   126 *perfect*: complete

May make the doubt.

3rd Avo.   His grief hath made him frantic.

1st Avo. Remove him hence.

2nd Avo.   Look to the woman.   (*She swoons*)

Corv.   Rare!

Prettily feigned! Again!

4th Avo.   Stand from about her.

1st Avo. Give her the air.

3rd Avo.   What can you say?

Mos.   My wound,

135 May it please your wisdoms, speaks for me, received
In aid of my good patron, when he missed
His sought-for father, when that well-taught dame
Had her cue given her, to cry out a rape.

   Bon. Oh, most laid impudence! Fathers——

3rd Avo.   Sir, be silent,

140 You had your hearing free, so must they theirs.

   2nd Avo. I do begin to doubt the imposture here.

   4th Avo. This woman has too many moods.

Volt.   Grave fathers,

She is a creature of a most professed
And prostituted lewdness.

   Corv.   Most impetuous!

Unsatisfied, grave fathers!

145 *Volt.*   May her feignings
Not take your wisdoms: but this day she baited
A stranger, a grave knight, with her loose eyes,
And more lascivious kisses. This man saw 'em
Together, on the water, in a gondola.

150   *Mos.* Here is the lady herself, that saw 'em too,
Without; who then had in the open streets
Pursued them, but for saving her knight's honour.

   1st Avo. Produce that lady.

   2nd Avo.   Let her come.   [*Exit* Mosca]

   4th Avo.   These things,

They strike with wonder!

   3rd Avo.   I am turned a stone!

139 *laid*: designed, plotted

ACT IV, Scene vi

Enter Mosca, Lady Politic Would-be

Mos. Be resolute, madam.

Lad. [*Pointing to* Celia]   Aye, this same is she.
Out, thou chameleon harlot; now thine eyes
Vie tears with the hyena: dar'st thou look
Upon my wronged face? I cry your pardons.
I fear I have, forgettingly, transgressed   5
Against the dignity of the court——

2nd Avo.   No, madam.

Lad. And been exorbitant——

4th Avo.   You have not, lady.
These proofs are strong.

Lad.   Surely I had no purpose
To scandalize your honours, or my sex's.

3rd Avo. We do believe it.

Lad.   Surely, you may believe it.   10

2nd Avo. Madam, we do.

Lad.   Indeed, you may; my breeding
Is not so coarse——

4th Avo.   We know it.

Lad.   To offend
With pertinacy——

3rd Avo.   Lady.

Lad.   Such a presence:
No, surely.

1st Avo. We well think it.

Lad.   You may think it.

1st Avo. Let her o'ercome. What witnesses have you,   15
To make good your report?

Bon.   Our consciences.

Cel. And heaven, that never fails the innocent.

4th Avo. These are no testimonies.

Bon.   Not in your courts,
Where multitude, and clamour overcomes.

3 *hyena*: type of treachery (*CA* V. v. 19 n.)

    1st Avo. Nay, then you do wax insolent.
20   *Volt.*   Here, here,
The testimony comes, that will convince,
And put to utter dumbness their bold tongues.
                       (Volpone *is brought in, as impotent*)
See here, grave fathers, here's the ravisher,
The rider on men's wives, the great impostor,
25 The grand voluptuary! Do you not think,
These limbs should affect venery? Or these eyes
Covet a concubine? 'Pray you, mark these hands.
Are they not fit to stroke a lady's breasts?
Perhaps he doth dissemble?
    Bon.   So he does.
    Volt. Would you ha' him tortured?
30   *Bon.*   I would have him proved.
    Volt. Best try him, then, with goads, or burning irons;
Put him to the strappado: I have heard,
The rack hath cured the gout, faith, give it him,
And help him of a malady, be courteous.
35 I'll undertake, before these honoured fathers,
He shall have yet as many left diseases,
As she has known adulterers, or thou strumpets.
Oh, my most equal hearers, if these deeds,
Acts, of this bold and most exorbitant strain,
40 May pass with sufferance, what one citizen,
But owes the forfeit of his life, yea fame,
To him that dares traduce him? Which of you
Are safe, my honoured fathers? I would ask
(With leave of your grave fatherhoods) if their plot
45 Have any face, or colour like to truth?
Or if, unto the dullest nostril, here,
It smell not rank, and most abhorred slander?
I crave your care of this good gentleman,
Whose life is much endangered by their fable;
50 And, as for them, I will conclude with this,

    21 *convince*: overpower   30 *proved*: tested   32 *strappado*: torture by being
hoisted in the air by the hands, which were first tied behind the back   38 *equal*:
fair, just   45 *colour*: appearance   46 *nostril*: i.e. perception

That vicious persons when they are hot, and fleshed
In impious acts, their constancy abounds:
Damned deeds are done with greatest confidence.
   1st Avo. Take 'em to custody, and sever them.
   2nd Avo. 'Tis pity two such prodigies should live.   55
                 [*Celia and* Bonario *are taken out*]
   1st Avo. Let the old gentleman be returned, with care:
I'm sorry, our credulity wronged him.   [*Volpone is taken out*]
   4th Avo. These are two creatures!
   3rd Avo.   I have an earthquake in me!
   2nd Avo. Their shame (even in their cradles) fled their faces.
   4th Avo. You've done a worthy service to the state, sir,   60
In their discovery.
   1st Avo.   You shall hear, ere night,
What punishment the court decrees upon 'em.
   Volt. We thank your fatherhoods.   [*Exeunt* Avocatori, etc]
                     How like you it?
   Mos.   Rare.
I'd ha' your tongue, sir, tipped with gold for this;
I'd ha' you be the heir to the whole city;   65
The earth I'd have want men, ere you want living:
They're bound to erect your statue in St Mark's.
Signior Corvino, I would have you go,
And show yourself, that you have conquered.
   Corv.   Yes.
   Mos. It was much better, that you should profess   70
Yourself a cuckold thus, than that the other
Should have been proved.
   Corv.   Nay, I considered that:
Now, it is her fault.
   Mos.   Then, it had been yours.
   Corv. True, I do doubt this advocate still.
   Mos.   I'faith,
You need not, I dare ease you of that care.   75
   Corv. I trust thee, Mosca.
   Mos.   As your own soul, sir.
                     [*Exit* Corvino]

52 Juvenal, *Sat.* xiii. 237

Corb.   Mosca.

Mos. Now for your business, sir.

Corb.   How? Ha' you business?

Mos. Yes, yours, sir.

Corb.   Oh, none else?

Mos.   None else, not I.

Corb. Be careful then.

Mos.   Rest you, with both your eyes, sir.

Corb. Despatch it.

Mos.   Instantly.

80   *Corb.*   And look that all,
Whatever, be put in, jewels, plate, moneys,
Household-stuff, bedding, curtains.

Mos.   Curtain-rings, sir,
Only, the advocate's fee must be deducted.

Corb. I'll pay him now: you'll be too prodigal.

Mos. Sir, I must tender it.

85   *Corb.*   Two *cecchines* is well?

Mos. No, six, sir.

Corb.   'Tis too much.

Mos.   He talked a great while,
You must consider that, sir.

Corb.   Well, there's three——

Mos. I'll give it him.

Corb.   Do so, and there's for thee.   [*Exit*]

Mos. Bountiful bones! What horrid strange offence

90   Did he commit 'gainst nature, in his youth,
Worthy this age? You see, sir, how I work
Unto your ends; take you no notice.

Volt.   No,
I'll leave you.   [*Exit*]

Mos.   All, is yours; the devil, and all:
Good advocate. Madam, I'll bring you home.

Lad. No, I'll go see your patron.

95   *Mos.*   That you shall not:
I'll tell you why. My purpose is to urge
My patron to reform his will; and for

89–91 Juvenal, *Sat.* x. 254–5

The zeal you've shown today, whereas before
You were but third, or fourth, you shall be now
Put in the first: which would appear as begged,   100
If you were present. Therefore——

    Lad.   You shall sway me.   [*Exeunt*]

ACT V, Scene i

[*Volpone's house*]
Enter Volpone

   Volp. WELL, I am here; and all this brunt is past:
I ne'er was in dislike with my disguise
Till this fled moment; here 'twas good, in private,
But in your public, *cave*, whilst I breathe.
'Fore God, my left leg 'gan to have the cramp;   5
And I apprehended, straight, some power had struck me
With a dead palsy: well, I must be merry,
And shake it off. A many of these fears
Would put me into some villainous disease,
Should they come thick upon me: I'll prevent 'em.   10
Give me a bowl of lusty wine, to fright
This humour from my heart; (hum, hum, hum)   (*He drinks*)
'Tis almost gone, already: I shall conquer.
Any device now, of rare, ingenious knavery,
That would possess me with a violent laughter,   15
Would make me up again! So, so, so, so.   (*Drinks again*)
This heat is life; 'tis blood, by this time: Mosca!

ACT V, Scene ii

Enter Mosca

   Mos. How now, sir? Does the day look clear again?
Are we recovered? And wrought out of error,
Into our way? To see our path before us?

    4 *cave*: beware, look out

Is our trade free, once more?

    Volp.   Exquisite Mosca!

    Mos. Was it not carried learnedly?

5   *Volp*.   And stoutly.

Good wits are greatest in extremities.

    Mos. It were a folly beyond thought to trust

Any grand act unto a cowardly spirit:

You are not taken with it enough, methinks?

10   *Volp*. Oh, more than if I had enjoyed the wench:

The pleasure of all womankind's not like it.

    Mos. Why, now you speak, sir. We must here be fixed;

Here we must rest; this is our masterpiece:

We cannot think to go beyond this.

    Volp.   True,

Thou'st played thy prize, my precious Mosca.

15   *Mos*.   Nay, sir,

To gull the court——

    Volp.   And quite divert the torrent,

Upon the innocent.

    Mos.   Yes, and to make

So rare a music out of discords——

    Volp.   Right.

That, yet, to me's the strangest! How thou'st borne it!

20 That these (being so divided 'mongst themselves)

Should not scent somewhat, or in me, or thee,

Or doubt their own side.

    Mos.   True, they will not see't.

Too much light blinds 'em, I think. Each of 'em

Is so possessed, and stuffed with his own hopes,

25 That anything unto the contrary,

Never so true, or never so apparent,

Never so palpable, they will resist it——

    Volp. Like a temptation of the devil.

    Mos.   Right, sir.

Merchants may talk of trade, and your great signiors

30 Of land that yields well; but if Italy

7–8 Plautus, *Pseudolus*, 576   15 *played thy prize*: played your part in the
contest (*SW* I. i. 157)   30–2 Plautus, *Epidicus*, 306–7

Have any glebe more fruitful than these fellows,
I am deceived. Did not your advocate rare?
    Volp. Oh 'My most honoured fathers, my grave fathers,
Under correction of your fatherhoods,
What face of truth, is here? If these strange deeds   35
May pass, most honoured fathers——' I had much ado
To forbear laughing.
    Mos.   It seemed to me, you sweat sir.
    Volp. In troth, I did a little.
    Mos.   But confess, sir,
Were you not daunted?
    Volp.   In good faith, I was
A little in a mist; but not dejected: 40
Never, but still myself.
    Mos.   I think it, sir.
Now (so truth help me) I must needs say this, sir,
And, out of conscience, for your advocate:
He's taken pains, in faith, sir, and deserved,
(In my poor judgement, I speak it, under favour,   45
Not to contrary you, sir) very richly——
Well——to be cozened.
    Volp.   'Troth, and I think so too,
By that I heard him, in the latter end.
    Mos. Oh, but before, sir; had you heard him first,
Draw it to certain heads, then aggravate,   50
Then use his vehement figures—— I looked still,
When he would shift a shirt; and doing this
Out of pure love, no hope of gain——
    Volp.   'Tis right.
I cannot answer him, Mosca, as I would,
Not yet; but for thy sake; at thy entreaty,   55
I will begin, e'en now, to vex 'em all:
This very instant.
    Mos.   Good, sir.
    Volp.   Call the dwarf
And eunuch forth.
    Mos.   Castrone, Nano.   [*Enter* Nano, Castrone]

    52 *shift a shirt*: i.e. from his violent gestures

Nan.   Here.

Volp. Shall we have a jig now?

Mos.   What you please, sir.

Volp.   Go,

60 Straight, give out about the streets, you two,
That I am dead; do it with constancy,
Sadly, do you hear? Impute it to the grief
Of this late slander.   [*Exeunt* Nano, Castrone]

Mos.   What do you mean, sir?

Volp.   Oh,

I shall have, instantly, my vulture, crow,

65 Raven, come flying hither, on the news
To peck for carrion, my she-wolf, and all,
Greedy, and full of expectation——

Mos. And then to have it ravished from their mouths?

Volp. 'Tis true, I will ha' thee put on a gown,

70 And take upon thee, as thou wert mine heir;
Show 'em a will: open that chest, and reach
Forth one of those, that has the blanks. I'll straight
Put in thy name.

Mos.   It will be rare, sir.

Volp.   Aye,

When they e'en gape, and find themselves deluded——

Mos. Yes.

75   *Volp.*   And thou use them scurvily. Despatch,
Get on thy gown.

Mos.   But, what, sir, if they ask
After the body?

Volp.   Say, it was corrupted.

Mos. I'll say it stunk, sir; and was fain to have it
Coffined up instantly, and sent away.

80   *Volp.* Anything, what thou wilt. Hold, here's my will.
Get thee a cap, a count-book, pen and ink,
Papers afore thee; sit, as thou wert taking
An inventory of parcels: I'll get up,
Behind the curtain, on a stool, and hearken;

85 Sometime peep over; see how they do look;

62 *Sadly*: seriously

With what degrees their blood doth leave their faces!
Oh, 'twill afford me a rare meal of laughter.
  Mos. Your advocate will turn stark dull upon it.
  Volp. It will take off his oratory's edge.
  Mos. But your *clarissimo*, old round-back, he   90
Will crump you, like a hog-louse, with the touch.
  Volp. And what Corvino?
  Mos.   Oh, sir, look for him,
Tomorrow morning, with a rope and a dagger,
To visit all the streets; he must run mad.
My Lady too, that came into the court,   95
To bear false witness for your worship——
  Volp.   Yes,
And kissed me 'fore the fathers; when my face
Flowed all with oils.
  Mos.   And sweat, sir. Why, your gold
Is such another medicine, it dries up
All those offensive savours! It transforms   100
The most deformed, and restores 'em lovely,
As 'twere the strange poetical girdle.* Jove
Could not invent to himself a shroud more subtle,
To pass Acrisius' guards. It is the thing
Makes all the world her grace, her youth, her beauty.   105
  Volp. I think she loves me.
  Mos.   Who? The lady, sir?
She's jealous of you.
  Volp.   Dost thou say so?
  Mos.   Hark,
There's some already.
  Volp.   Look.
  Mos.   It is the vulture:
He has the quickest scent.

* Cestus

---

90 *clarissimo*: a grandee of Venice   91 *crump*: curl up   98–105 Lucian,
Gallus, 722   102 *girdle*: 'wherein all the joyes and delights of love, were woven'
(*Challenge at Tilt*, 51–2)   104 *Acrisius*: father of Danae, who locked her in the
tower   107 *jealous of*: watchful of her interests in

Volp.   I'll to my place,
Thou, to thy posture.
     Mos.   I am set.
110   *Volp.*   But Mosca,
Play the artificer now, torture 'em, rarely.   [*He retires*]

ACT V, Scene iii

Enter Voltore

Volt. How now, my Mosca?
Mos.   Turkey carpets, nine——
Volt. Taking an inventory? That is well.
Mos. Two suits of bedding, tissue——
Volt.   Where's the will?
Let me read that the while.   [*Corbaccio is carried in*]
Corb.   So, set me down:
And get you home.   [*Exeunt* porters]
5   *Volt.*   Is he come now to trouble us?
Mos. Of cloth of gold, two more——
Corb.   Is it done, Mosca?
Mos. Of several velvets, eight——
Volt.   I like his care.
Corb. Dost thou not hear?

[*Enter* Corvino]

Corv.   Ha? Is the hour come, Mosca?
Volp. (Volpone *peeps from behind a traverse*) Aye, now they
    muster.
Corv.   What does the advocate here?
Or this Corbaccio?

[*Enter* Lady Would-be]

Corb.   What do these here?
10   *Lad.*   Mosca?
Is his thread spun?

---

3 *tissue*: rich cloth, often woven with gold or silver   9 s.d. *traverse*: low screen
11 *thread*: i.e. of life

 Mos.   Eight chests of linen——

 Volp.   Oh,

My fine Dame Would-be too!

 Corv.   Mosca, the will,

That I may show it these, and rid 'em hence.

 Mos. Six chests of diaper, four of damask—— There.

 Corb. Is that the will?

 Mos.   Down-beds, and bolsters——

 Volp.   Rare! 15

Be busy still. Now they begin to flutter:

They never think of me. Look, see, see, see!

How their swift eyes run over the long deed,

Unto the name, and to the legacies,

What is bequeathed them there——

 Mos.   Ten suits of hangings—— 20

 Volp. Aye, i'their garters, Mosca. Now their hopes

Are at the gasp.

 Volt.   Mosca the heir!

 Corb.   What's that?

 Volp. My advocate is dumb, look to my merchant,

He has heard of some strange storm, a ship is lost,

He faints: my lady will swoon. Old glazen-eyes, 25

He hath not reached his despair yet.

 Corb.   All these

Are out of hope, I'm sure the man.

 Corv.   But, Mosca——

 Mos. Two cabinets——

 Corv.   Is this in earnest?

 Mos.   One

Of ebony.——

 Corv.   Or do you but delude me?

 Mos. The other, mother of pearl—I am very busy. 30

Good faith, it is a fortune thrown upon me——

Item, one salt of agate——not my seeking.

 Lad. Do you hear, sir?

 Mos.   A perfumed box——'pray you forbear,

---

14 *diaper*: patterned linen fabric   20-1 *hangings . . . garters*: i.e. suicide
25 *glazen-eyes*: Corbaccio wears spectacles (l. 63)   32 *salt*: salt-cellar

You see I am troubled——made of an onyx——
   Lad.   How!
35   *Mos.* Tomorrow, or next day, I shall be at leisure
To talk with you all.
   Corv.   Is this my large hope's issue?
   Lad. Sir, I must have a fairer answer.
   Mos.   Madam!
Marry, and shall: 'pray you, fairly quit my house.
Nay, raise no tempest with your looks; but hark you:
40 Remember what your ladyship offered me,
To put you in, an heir; go to, think on't.
And what you said, e'en your best madams did
For maintenance, and why not you? Enough.
Go home, and use the poor Sir Pol, your knight, well;
45 For fear I tell some riddles: go, be melancholic.   [*Exit* Lady]
   Volp. Oh, my fine devil!
   Corv.   Mosca, 'pray you a word.
   Mos. Lord! Will not you take your despatch hence yet?
Methinks, of all, you should have been the example.
Why should you stay here? With what thought? What promise?
50 Hear you, do not you know, I know you an ass?
And that you would most fain have been a wittol,
If fortune would have let you? That you are
A declared cuckold, on good terms? This pearl,
You'll say, was yours? Right: this diamond?
55 I'll not deny it, but thank you. Much here, else?
It may be so. Why, think that these good works
May help to hide your bad: I'll not betray you,
Although you be but extraordinary,
And have it only in title, it sufficeth.
60 Go home, be melancholic too, or mad.   [*Exit* Corvino]
   Volp. Rare, Mosca! How his villainy becomes him!
   Volt. Certain, he doth delude all these, for me.
   Corb. Mosca, the heir?
   Volp.   Oh, his four eyes have found it!
   Corb. I'm cozened, cheated, by a parasite-slave;
Harlot, thou'st gulled me.

---

51 *wittol*: conniver in his wife's dishonour   65 *Harlot*: rascal

Mos.   Yes, sir. Stop your mouth,   65
Or I shall draw the only tooth is left.
Are not you he, that filthy covetous wretch,
With the three legs, that here, in hope of prey,
Have, any time this three year, snuffed about,
With your most grovelling nose; and would have hired   70
Me to the poisoning of my patron? Sir?
Are not you he, that have today in court
Professed the disinheriting of your son?
Perjured yourself? Go home, and die, and stink;
If you but croak a syllable, all comes out: 75
Away and call your porters, go, go, stink.   [*Exit* Corbaccio]

Volp. Excellent varlet!

Volt.   Now, my faithful Mosca,
I find thy constancy.

Mos.   Sir?

Volt.   Sincere.

Mos.   A table
Of porphyry——I mar'l, you'll be thus troublesome.

Volt. Nay, leave off now, they are gone.

Mos.   Why? Who are you?   80
What? Who did send for you? Oh, cry you mercy,
Reverend sir! Good faith, I am grieved for you,
That any chance of mine should thus defeat
Your (I must needs say) most deserving travels:
But, I protest, sir, it was cast upon me,   85
And I could, almost, wish to be without it,
But that the will o' the dead must be observed.
Marry, my joy is that you need it not,
You have a gift, sir (thank your education),
Will never let you want, while there are men   90
And malice to breed causes. Would I had
But half the like, for all my fortune, sir.
If I have any suits (as I do hope,
Things being so easy, and direct, I shall not)
I will make bold with your obstreperous aid,   95
(Conceive me) for your fee, sir. In meantime,

68 *three legs*: i.e. his stick   84 *travels*: labours

You, that have so much law, I know ha' the conscience,
Not to be covetous of what is mine.
Good sir, I thank you for my plate: 'twill help
100 To set up a young man. Good faith, you look
As you were costive; best go home, and purge, sir. [*Exit* Voltore]
    Volp. Bid him eat lettuce well: my witty mischief,
Let me embrace thee. Oh, that I could now
Transform thee to a Venus—— Mosca, go,
105 Straight, take my habit of *clarissimo*;
And walk the streets; be seen, torment 'em more:
We must pursue, as well as plot. Who would
Have lost this feast?
    Mos.   I doubt it will lose them.
    Volp. Oh, my recovery shall recover all.
110 That I could now but think on some disguise,
To meet 'em in: and ask 'em questions.
How I would vex 'em still, at every turn?
    Mos. Sir, I can fit you.
    Volp.   Canst thou?
    Mos.   Yes, I know
One o' the *commandadori*, sir, so like you,
115 Him will I straight make drunk, and bring you his habit.
    Volp. A rare disguise, and answering thy brain!
Oh, I will be a sharp disease unto 'em.
    Mos. Sir, you must look for curses——
    Volp.   Till they burst;
The fox fares ever best when he is cursed.   [*Exeunt*]

ACT V, Scene iv

[Sir Politic Would-be's house]
Enter Peregrine, 3 Mercatori

Per. Am I enough disguised?
1st Mer.   I warrant you.
Per. All my ambition is to fright him only.

102 *lettuce*: for constipation   119 *cursed*: i.e. for escaping

2nd Mer. If you could ship him away, 'twere excellent.
3rd Mer. To Zant, or to Aleppo?
Per.   Yes, and ha' his
Adventures put i' the book of voyages,   5
And his gulled story registered, for truth?
Well, gentlemen, when I am in, a while,
And that you think us warm in our discourse,
Know your approaches.
    1st Mer.   Trust it to our care.   [*Exeunt* Mercatori]

                    [*Enter* Woman]

Per. Save you, fair lady. Is Sir Pol. within?   10
Wom. I do not know, sir.
Per.   'Pray you, say unto him,
Here is a merchant, upon earnest business,
Desires to speak with him.
    Wom.   I will see, sir.   [*Exit*]
Per.   'Pray you.
I see the family is all female here.

                    [*Enter* Woman]

Wom. He says, sir, he has weighty affairs of state,   15
That now require him whole; some other time
You may possess him.
    Per.   'Pray you, say again,
If those require him whole, these will exact him,
Whereof I bring him tidings.   [*Exit* Woman]
                    What might be
His grave affair of state now? How to make   20
Bolognian sausages here in Venice, sparing
One o' the ingredients.

                    [*Enter* Woman]

    Wom.   Sir, he says, he knows
By your word, tidings, that you are no statesman,
And therefore wills you stay.

---

4 *Zant*: an Ionian island under Venetian rule   5 *book of voyages*: such as
Hakluyt's, then in vogue   6 *gulled story*: the story of his gulling   14 *female*:
weak, simple   18 *exact him*: draw him forth   23 *tidings*: the 'statesman'
would have said 'intelligence'

Per.   Sweet, 'pray you return him,
25 I have not read so many proclamations,
And studied them for words, as he has done,
But—— Here he deigns to come.   [*Exit* Woman]

                    [*Enter* Sir Politic Would-be]

Pol.   Sir, I must crave
Your courteous pardon. There hath chanced today
Unkind disaster, 'twixt my lady and me:
30 And I was penning my apology
To give her satisfaction, as you came, now.

    Per. Sir, I am grieved, I bring you worse disaster;
The gentleman you met at the port, today,
That told you he was newly arrived——

Pol.   Aye, was
A fugitive punk?
35   *Per.*   No, sir, a spy set on you:
And he has made relation to the Senate,
That you professed to him to have a plot
To sell the state of Venice to the Turk.

    Pol. Oh me!

    Per.   For which, warrants are signed by this time,
40 To apprehend you, and to search your study,
For papers——

    Pol.   Alas, sir. I have none, but notes
Drawn out of play-books——

    Per.   All the better, sir.

    Pol. And some essays. What shall I do?

    Per.   Sir, best
Convey yourself into a sugar-chest,
45 Or, if you could lie round, a frail were rare:
And I could send you aboard.

    Pol.   Sir, I but talked so,
For discourse sake, merely.   (*They knock without*)

    Per.   Hark, they are there.

    Pol. I am a wretch, a wretch.

    Per.   What, will you do, sir?

----
43 *essays*: despised by Jonson (*Disc.* 719–29)   45 *frail*: rush basket

Ha' you ne'er a currant-butt to leap into?
They'll put you to the rack, you must be sudden.   50
    Pol. Sir, I have an engine——
    3rd Mer. [*Without*]   Sir Politic Would-be?
    2nd Mer. Where is he?
    Pol.   That I have thought upon, before time.
    Per. What is it?
    Pol.   (I shall ne'er endure the torture.)
Marry, it is, sir, of a tortoise-shell,
Fitted for these extremities: 'pray you sir, help me.   55
Here, I've a place, sir, to put back my legs,
Please you to lay it on, sir, with this cap,
And my black gloves, I'll lie, sir, like a tortoise,
Till they are gone.
    Per.   And call you this an engine?
    Pol. Mine own device—— good sir, bid my wife's women   60
To burn my papers.   (*They rush in*)
    1st Mer.   Where's he hid?
    3rd Mer.   We must,
And will, sure, find him.
    2nd Mer.   Which is his study?
    1st Mer.   What
Are you, sir?
    Per.   I'm a merchant, that came here
To look upon this tortoise.
    3rd Mer.   How?
    1st Mer.   St Mark!
What beast is this?
    Per.   It is a fish.
    2nd Mer.   Come out here.   65
    Per. Nay, you may strike him, sir, and tread upon him:
He'll bear a cart.
    1st Mer.   What, to run over him?
    Per.   Yes.
    3rd Mer. Let's jump upon him.

49 *currant-butt*: cask for holding currants or currant wine   51 *engine*: device,
stratagem   54 *tortoise*: associated emblematically with silence, policy, and the
motto 'home is best'

2nd Mer.   Can he not go?
Per.   He creeps, sir.
1st Mer. Let's see him creep.
Per.   No, good sir, you will hurt him.
70 *2nd Mer.* Heart, I'll see him creep; or prick his guts.
3rd Mer. Come out here.
Per.   'Pray you sir (creep a little).
1st Mer.   Forth.
2nd Mer. Yet further.
Per.   Good sir (creep).
2nd Mer.   We'll see his legs.
3rd Mer. God's so, he has garters!
1st Mer.   Aye, and gloves!
2nd Mer.   Is this
Your fearful tortoise?   (*They pull off the shell and discover him*)
Per.   Now, Sir Pol, we are even;
75 For your next project, I shall be prepared:
I am sorry, for the funeral of your notes, sir.
   1st Mer. 'Twere a rare motion, to be seen in Fleet Street!
   2nd Mer. Aye, i'the term.
   1st Mer.   Or Smithfield, in the fair.
   3rd Mer. Methinks, 'tis but a melancholic sight!
   Per. Farewell, most politic tortoise.   [*Exit with* Mercatori]
80 *Pol.*   Where's my lady?

[*Enter* Woman]

Knows she of this?
   Wom.   I know not, sir.
   Pol.   Enquire.   [*Exit* Woman]
Oh, I shall be the fable of all feasts;
The freight of the *gazetti*; ship-boys' tale;
And, which is worst, even talk for ordinaries.

[*Enter* Woman]

85 *Wom.* My lady's come most melancholic, home,
And says, sir, she will straight to sea, for physic.

---

77 *motion*: puppet show   78 *term*: the London season, corresponding to the
law terms   78 *the fair*: Bartholemew Fair   83 *freight of the gazetti*: theme
of the news-sheets

Pol. And I, to shun this place and clime for ever;
Creeping, with house, on back: and think it well,
To shrink my poor head in my politic shell.   [*Exeunt*]

ACT V, Scene v

[Volpone's house]

Enter Volpone, Mosca, *the first in the habit of a* Commandadore:
the other, of a Clarissimo

Volp. Am I then like him?
   Mos.   Oh, sir, you are he:
No man can sever you.
   Volp.   Good.
   Mos.   But, what am I?
   Volp. 'Fore heav'n, a brave *clarissimo*, thou becom'st it!
Pity thou wert not born one.
   Mos. [*Aside*]   If I hold
My made one, 'twill be well.
   Volp.   I'll go and see   5
What news, first, at the court.   [*Exit*]
   Mos.   Do so. My Fox
Is out on his hole, and ere he shall re-enter
I'll make him languish in his borrowed case,
Except he come to composition with me:
Androgyno, Castrone, Nano!

[*They enter*]

   All.   Here.   10
   Mos. Go recreate yourselves abroad; go, sport.   [*Exeunt*]
So, now I have the keys, and am possessed.
Since he will needs be dead afore his time,
I'll bury him, or gain by him. I'm his heir:
And so will keep me, till he share at least.   15

---

7 *out on his hole*: as in the children's game fox-in-the-hole   8 *case*: dress
9 *composition*: mutual arrangement

To cozen him of all were but a cheat
Well placed; no man would construe it a sin:
Let his sport pay for't, this is called the Fox-trap.   [*Exit*]

ACT V, Scene vi

[*A street*]

Enter Corbaccio, Corvino

Corb. They say, the court is set.
Corv.   We must maintain
Our first tale good, for both our reputations.
Corb. Why? Mine's no tale: my son would there have killed me.
Corv. That's true, I had forgot: mine is, I am sure.
But, for your will, sir.
5   *Corb*.   Aye, I'll come upon him
For that hereafter, now his patron's dead.

[*Enter* Volpone, *disguised*]

Volp. Signior Corvino! And Corbaccio! Sir,
Much joy unto you.
Corv.   Of what?
Volp.   The sudden good,
Dropped down upon you——
Corb.   Where?
Volp.   (And, none knows how)
From old Volpone, sir.
10 *Corb*.   Out, arrant knave.
Volp. Let not your too much wealth, sir, make you furious.
Corb. Away, thou varlet.
Volp.   Why sir?
Corb.   Dost thou mock me?
Volp. You mock the world, sir, did you not change wills?
Corb. Out, harlot.
Volp.   Oh! Belike you are the man,
15 Signior Corvino? 'Faith, you carry it well;
You grow not mad withal: I love your spirit.

You are not over-leavened with your fortune.
You should ha' some would swell now, like a wine-fat,
With such an autumn—— Did he gi' you all, sir?
   Corv. Avoid, you rascal.
   Volp.   Troth, your wife has shown   20
Herself a very woman: but you are well,
You need not care, you have a good estate,
To bear it out, sir, better by this chance.
Except Corbaccio have a share?
   Corb.   Hence, varlet.
   Volp. You will not be a'known, sir: why, 'tis wise.   25
Thus do all gamesters, at all games, dissemble.
No man will seem to win.   [*Exeunt* Corbaccio, Corvino]
                Here, comes my vulture,
Heaving his beak up i' the air, and snuffing.

ACT V, Scene vii

Enter Voltore

   Volt. Outstripped thus, by a parasite? A slave?
Would run on errands? And make legs, for crumbs?
Well, what I'll do——
   Volp.   The court stays for your worship.
I e'en rejoice, sir, at your worship's happiness,
And that it fell into so learned hands,   5
That understand the fingering——
   Volt.   What do you mean?
   Volp. I mean to be a suitor to your worship,
For the small tenement, out of reparations;
That, at the end of your long row of houses,
By the *piscaria*: it was, in Volpone's time,   10
Your predecessor, ere he grew diseased,
A handsome, pretty, customed, bawdy-house,

---

17 *over-leavened*: puffed-up   18 *wine-fat*: vat   20 *Avoid*: Be gone
25 *a'known*: acknowledged   (*V. vii*) 8 *reparations*: repair   10 *piscaria*:
fish-market

As any was in Venice (none dispraised)
But fell with him; his body and that house
Decayed together.
15 *Volt.*   Come, sir, leave your prating.
  Volp. Why, if your worship give me but your hand,
That I may ha' the refusal; I have done.
'Tis a mere toy to you, sir; candle rents:
As your learn'd worship knows——
    Volt.   What do I know?
20 *Volp.* Marry no end of your wealth, sir, God decrease it.
  Volt. Mistaking knave! What, mock'st thou my misfortune?
  Volp. His blessing on your heart, sir, would 'twere more.

                                    [*Exit* Voltore]
Now, to my first, again; at the next corner.

ACT V, Scene viii

Enter Corbaccio, Corvino (Mosca, *passant*)

  Corb. See, in our habit! See the impudent varlet!
  Corv. That I could shoot mine eyes at him, like gun-stones.
  Volp. But, is this true, sir, of the parasite?
  Corb. Again, to afflict us? Monster!
  Volp.   In good faith, sir,
5 I'm heartily grieved a beard of your grave length
Should be so over-reached. I never brooked
That parasite's hair, methought his nose should cozen:
There still was somewhat, in his look, did promise
The bane of a *clarissimo.*
    Corb.   Knave——
  Volp.   Methinks,
10 Yet you, that are so traded i' the world,
A witty merchant, the fine bird, Corvino,
That have such moral emblems on your name,

---

18 *toy:* trifle   *candle rents:* from property which is continually deteriorating
(*V. viii*) 2 *gun-stones:* stone cannonballs   10 *traded:* experienced   12 *emblems:*
fables expressed pictorially

Should not have sung your shame; and dropped your cheese:
To let the Fox laugh at your emptiness.

   Corv. Sirrah, you think the privilege of the place,   15
And your red saucy cap, that seems (to me)
Nailed to your jolt-head, with those two *cecchines*,
Can warrant your abuses; come you, hither:
You shall perceive, sir, I dare beat you. Approach.

   Volp. No haste, sir, I do know your valour well: 20
Since you durst publish what you are, sir.

   Corv.   Tarry,
I'd speak with you.

   Volp. [*Retreating*] Sir, sir, another time——

   Corv. Nay, now.

   Volp.   Oh God, sir! I were a wise man,
Would stand the fury of a distracted cuckold.

   Corb. What! Come again?   (Mosca *walks by 'em*)

   Volp.   Upon 'em, Mosca; save me.   25

   Corb. The air's infected, where he breathes.

   Corv.   Let's fly him.
                                 [*Exeunt*]

   Volp. Excellent basilisk! Turn upon the vulture.

ACT V, Scene ix

Enter Voltore

   Volt. Well, flesh-fly, it is summer with you now;
Your winter will come on.

   Mos.   Good advocate,
'Pray thee, not rail, nor threaten out of place thus;
Thou'lt make a solecism (as madam says).
Get you a biggin more: your brain breaks loose.   5

   Volt. Well, sir.

---

13 *dropped your cheese*: I. ii. 94–6   17 *jolt-head*: blockhead *cecchines*: gilt
buttons (in a commandadore's cap)   27 *basilisk*: fabled reptile hatched from a
cock's egg, and reputed to kill with its mere glance   (*V. ix*) 1 *flesh-fly*: blowfly
(with play on 'Mosca')   5 *biggin*: lawyer's skull-cap

   Volp.   Would you ha' me beat the insolent slave?
Throw dirt upon his first good clothes?
   Volt.   This same
Is, doubtless, some familiar!
   Volp.   Sir, the court
In troth stays for you. I am mad, a mule,
10 That never read Justinian, should get up
And ride an advocate. Had you no quirk,
To avoid gullage, sir, by such a creature?
I hope you do but jest; he has not done it:
This's but confederacy, to blind the rest.
You are the heir?
15   *Volt.*   A strange, officious,
Troublesome knave! Thou dost torment me.
   Volp.   I know——
It cannot be, sir, that you should be cozened;
'Tis not within the wit of man to do it:
You are so wise, so prudent, and 'tis fit,
20 That wealth and wisdom still should go together.   *[Exeunt]*

ACT V, Scene x

[The Scrutineo]

Enter 4 Avocatori, Notario, Commandadori, Bonario,
Celia, Corbaccio, Corvino

   1st Avo. Are all the parties here?
   Not.   All but the advocate.
   2nd Avo. And here he comes.

[*Enter* Voltore, Volpone]

   1st Avo.   Then bring 'em forth to sentence
   Volt. Oh, my most honoured fathers, let your mercy
Once win upon your justice, to forgive——
I am distracted——

---

   8 *familiar*: (1) member of same household, (2) attendant demon   9 *mule*: the
lawyer's mount (I. ii. 107)   10 *Justinian*: i.e. the *Corpus Juris Civilis* compiled
under Justinian   11 *quirk*: trick

(*Volp.*   What will he do now?)
Volt.   Oh,   5
I know not which to address myself to first,
Whether your fatherhoods, or these innocents——
(*Corv.* Will he betray himself?)
Volt.   Whom, equally,
I have abused, out of most covetous ends——
(*Corv.* The man is mad!
Corb.   What's that?
Corv.   He is possessed.)   10
Volt. For which; now struck in conscience, here I prostrate
Myself, at your offended feet, for pardon.   [*He kneels*]
1st and 2nd Avo. Arise.
Cel.   Oh heaven, how just thou art!
Volp. [*Aside*]   I'm caught
I' mine own noose——
Corv.   Be constant, sir, naught now
Can help, but impudence.
1st Avo.   Speak forward.
Com.   Silence.   15
Volt. It is not passion in me, reverend fathers,
But only conscience, conscience, my good sirs,
That makes me now tell truth. That parasite,
That knave hath been the instrument of all.
2nd Avo. Where is that knave? Fetch him.
Volp.   I go.   [*Exit*]
Corv.   Grave fathers,   20
This man's distracted; he confessed it now:
For, hoping to be old Volpone's heir,
Who now is dead——
3rd Avo.   How?
2nd Avo.   Is Volpone dead?
Corv. Dead since, grave fathers——
Bon.   Oh, sure vengeance!
1st Avo.   Stay,
Then he was no deceiver?
Volt.   Oh no, none: 25

10 *possessed*: i.e. of a devil

The parasite, grave fathers.

Corv.   He does speak,
Out of mere envy, 'cause the servant's made
The thing, he gaped for; please your fatherhoods,
This is the truth: though, I'll not justify
30 The other, but he may be some-deal faulty.

Volt. Aye, to your hopes, as well as mine, Corvino:
But I'll use modesty. Pleaseth your wisdoms
To view these certain notes, and but confer them;
As I hope favour, they shall speak clear truth.

Corv. The devil has entered him!
35 *Bon.*   Or bides in you.

4th Avo. We have done ill, by a public officer,
To send for him, if he be heir.

2nd Avo.   For whom?

4th Avo. Him, that they call the parasite.

3rd Avo.   'Tis true;
He is a man, of great estate, now left.

40 *4th Avo.* Go you, and learn his name; and say, the court
Entreats his presence here; but to the clearing
Of some few doubts.   [*Exit* Notario]

2nd Avo.   This same's a labyrinth!

1st Avo. Stand you unto your first report?

Corv.   My state,
My life, my fame——

(*Bon.*   Where is't?)

Corv.   Are at the stake.

1st Avo. Is yours so too?
45 *Corb.*   The advocate's a knave:
And has a forked tongue——

(*2nd Avo.*   Speak to the point.)

Corb. So is the parasite, too.

1st Avo.   This is confusion.

Volt. I do beseech your fatherhoods, read but those.

[*Giving them papers*]

Corv. And credit nothing, the false spirit hath writ:
50 It cannot be but he is possessed, grave fathers.   [*Exeunt*]

30 *some-deal*: in some part

ACT V, Scene xi

[A street]

Enter Volpone

Volp. To make a snare for mine own neck! And run
My head into it, wilfully! With laughter!
When I had newly 'scaped, was free and clear!
Out of mere wantonness! Oh, the dull devil
Was in this brain of mine when I devised it;   5
And Mosca gave it second: he must now
Help to sear up this vein, or we bleed dead.

[*Enter* Nano, Androgyno, Castrone]

How now! Who let you loose? Whither go you, now?
What? To buy gingerbread? Or to drown kitlings?

Nan. Sir, Master Mosca called us out of doors,   10
And bids us all go play, and took the keys.

And.   Yes.

Volp. Did Master Mosca take the keys? Why, so!
I am farther in. These are my fine conceits!
I must be merry, with a mischief to me!
What a vile wretch was I, that could not bear   15
My fortune soberly? I must ha' my crotchets!
And my conundrums! Well, go you, and seek him:
His meaning may be truer than my fear.
Bid him, he straight come to me, to the court;
Thither will I, and if 't be possible,   20
Unscrew my advocate upon new hopes:
When I provoked him, then I lost myself.   [*Exeunt*]

ACT V, Scene xii

[The Scrutineo]

Enter 4 Avocatori, *etc, as before*

1st Avo. These things can ne'er be reconciled. He, here,
Professeth that the gentleman was wronged;

And that the gentlewoman was brought thither,
Forced by her husband: and there left.

   Volt.   Most true.

   Cel. How ready is heaven to those that pray!

5   *1st Avo.*   But, that
Volpone would have ravished her, he holds
Utterly false; knowing his impotence.

   Corv. Grave fathers, he is possessed; again, I say,
Possessed: nay, if there be possession,
And obsession, he has both.

10   *3rd Avo.*   Here comes our officer.

                   [*Enter* Volpone]

   Volp. The parasite will straight be here, grave fathers.

   4th Avo. You might invent some other name, sir varlet.

   3rd Avo. Did not the notary meet him?

   Volp.   Not that I know.

   4th Avo. His coming will clear all.

   2nd Avo.   Yet it is misty.

   Volt. May it please your fatherhoods——

15   *Volp.* (*Whispers the* Advocate)   Sir, the parasite
Willed me to tell you, that his master lives;
That you are still the man; your hopes the same;
And this was only a jest——

   Volt.   How?

   Volp.   Sir, to try
If you were firm, and how you stood affected.

   Volt. Art sure he lives?

   Volp.   Do I live, sir?

20   *Volt.*   Oh me!
I was too violent.

   Volp.   Sir, you may redeem it,
They said you were possessed; fall down, and seem so:
I'll help to make it good. (Voltore *falls*) God bless the man!
(Stop your wind hard, and swell) see, see, see, see!

25 He vomits crooked pins! His eyes are set,

---

     9 *possession*: entrance of the evil spirit within the body   10 *obsession*: influence
from without   25 *vomits crooked pins*: as did some frauds of the time (cf. the
'blue toad' at l. 31, and *H&S* ix. 731–2)

Like a dead hare's, hung in a poulter's shop!
His mouth's running away! Do you see, signior?
Now, 'tis in his belly.
   (*Corv.*   Aye, the devil!)
   Volp. Now, in his throat.
   (*Corv.*   Aye, I perceive it plain.)
   Volp. 'Twill out, 'twill out; stand clear. See, where it flies!   30
In shape of a blue toad, with a bat's wings!
Do not you see it, sir?
   Corb.   What? I think I do.
   Corv. 'Tis too manifest.
   Volp.   Look! He comes to himself!
   Volt. Where am I?
   Volp.   Take good heart, the worst is past, sir.
You are dispossessed.
   1st Avo.   What accident is this?   35
   2nd Avo. Sudden, and full of wonder!
   3rd Avo.   If he were
Possessed, as it appears, all this is nothing.
   Corv. He has been often subject to these fits,
   1st Avo. Show him that writing, do you know it, sir?
   Volp. Deny it, sir, forswear it, know it not.   40
   Volt. Yes, I do know it well, it is my hand:
But all that it contains is false.
   Bon.   Oh practice!
   2nd Avo. What maze is this!
   1st Avo.   Is he not guilty, then,
Whom you, there, name the parasite?
   Volt.   Grave fathers,
No more than his good patron old Volpone.   45
   4th Avo. Why, he is dead?
   Volt.   Oh no, my honoured fathers.
He lives——
   1st Avo.   How! Lives?
   Volt.   Lives.
   2nd Avo.   This is subtler yet!
   3rd Avo. You said, he was dead?

   27 *running away*: i.e. awry

Volt.   Never.
3rd Avo.   You said so?
Corv.   I heard so.
4th Avo. Here comes the gentleman, make him way.

[*Enter* Mosca *as* Clarissimo]
   3rd Avo.   A stool.
50   *4th Avo.* A proper man! And were Volpone dead,
A fit match for my daughter.
      3rd Avo.   Give him way.
   Volp. Mosca, I was almost lost, the advocate
Had betrayed all; but now it is recovered:
All's o' the hinge again——say, I am living.
55   *Mos.* What busy knave is this! Most reverend fathers,
I sooner had attended your grave pleasures,
But that my order for the funeral
Of my dear patron did require me——
      (*Volp.*   Mosca!)
      Mos. Whom I intend to bury, like a gentleman.
      Volp. [*Aside*] Aye, quick, and cozen me of all.
60   *2nd Avo.*   Still stranger!
More intricate!
      1st Avo.   And come about again!
   4th Avo. It is a match, my daughter is bestowed.
      (*Mos.* Will you gi' me half?
      Volp.   First, I'll be hanged.
      Mos.   I know,
Your voice is good, cry not so loud.)
      1st Avo.   Demand
65 The advocate. Sir, did not you affirm
Volpone was alive?
   Volp.   Yes, and he is;
This gent'man told me so (thou shalt have half).
   Mos. Whose drunkard is this same? Speak some, that know him:
I never saw his face. (I cannot now
Afford it you so cheap.

50 *proper*: handsome   54 *o' the hinge*: opposite of 'off the hinge' (*SW* III.
ii. 34)   60 *quick*: alive

Volp.   No?)
1st Avo.   What say you?   70
Volt. The officer told me.
Volp.   I did, grave fathers,
And will maintain he lives, with mine own life.
And that this creature told me. (I was born,
With all good stars my enemies.)
    Mos.   Most grave fathers,
If such an insolence, as this, must pass   75
Upon me, I am silent: 'twas not this,
For which you sent, I hope.
    2nd Avo.   Take him away.
    (*Volp.* Mosca!)
    3rd Avo.   Let him be whipped.
    (*Volp.*   Wilt thou betray me?
Cozen me?)
    3rd Avo. And taught to bear himself
Toward a person of his rank.
    4th Avo.   Away.   80
    Mos. I humbly thank your fatherhoods.
    Volp. [*Aside*]   Soft, soft: whipped?
And lose all that I have? If I confess,
It cannot be much more.
    4th Avo.   Sir, are you married?
    Volp. [*Aside*] They'll be allied anon; I must be resolute:
The Fox shall, here, uncase. (*He puts off his disguise*)
    (*Mos.*   Patron.)
    Volp.   Nay, now,   85
My ruins shall not come alone; your match
I'll hinder sure: my substance shall not glue you,
Nor screw you, into a family.
    (*Mos.*   Why, patron!)
    Volp. I am Volpone, and this is my knave;
This, his own knave; this, avarice's fool;   90
This, a chimera of wittol, fool, and knave;
And, reverend fathers, since we all can hope

73–4 Plautus, *Mostellaria*, 562–3   85 *uncase*: strip off his disguise   91 *chimera*: mythical beast with head of a lion, body of a goat, and tail of a serpent.

Naught but a sentence, let's not now despair it.
You hear me brief.

    Corv.   May it please your fatherhoods——

    Com.   Silence.

95   *1st Avo.* The knot is now undone, by miracle!

    2nd Avo. Nothing can be more clear.

    3rd Avo.   Or can more prove
These innocent.

    1st Avo.   Give 'em their liberty.

    Bon. Heaven could not long let such gross crimes be hid.

    2nd Avo. If this be held the high way to get riches,
May I be poor.

100   *3rd Avo.*   This 's not the gain, but torment.

    1st Avo. These possess wealth, as sick men possess fevers,
Which, trulier, may be said to possess them.

    2nd Avo. Disrobe that parasite.

    Corv., Mos.   Most honoured fathers.

    1st Avo. Can you plead aught to stay the course of justice?
If you can, speak.

    Corv., Volt.   We beg favour,

105   *Cel.*   And mercy.

    1st Avo. You hurt your innocence, suing for the guilty.
Stand forth; and, first, the parasite. You appear
To have been the chiefest minister, if not plotter,
In all these lewd impostures; and now, lastly,
110 Have, with your impudence, abused the court,
And habit of a gentleman of Venice,
Being a fellow of no birth or blood:
For which, our sentence is, first thou be whipped;
Then live perpetual prisoner in our galleys.

    Volp. I thank you, for him.

115   *Mos.*   Bane to thy wolfish nature.

    1st Avo. Deliver him to the Saffi.   [Mosca *is taken out*]

                            Thou, Volpone,
By blood and rank a gentleman, canst not fall
Under like censure; but our judgement on thee
Is, that thy substance all be straight confiscate

101-2 Seneca, *Ep.* cxix, 12

To the hospital of the *Incurabili*:   120
And, since the most was gotten by imposture,
By feigning lame, gout, palsy, and such diseases,
Thou art to lie in prison, cramped with irons,
Till thou be'st sick and lame indeed. Remove him.

   Volp. This is called mortifying of a Fox.   [*He is taken out*] 125

   1st Avo. Thou, Voltore, to take away the scandal
Thou hast given all worthy men, of thy profession,
Art banished from their fellowship, and our state.
Corbaccio, bring him near. We here possess
Thy son of all thy state; and confine thee   130
To the monastery of San' Spirito:
Where, since thou knewst not how to live well here,
Thou shalt be learned to die well.

   Corb.   Ha! What said he?

   Com. You shall know anon, sir.

   1st Avo.   Thou, Corvino, shalt
Be straight embarked from thine own house, and rowed   135
Round about Venice, through the Grand Canal,
Wearing a cap, with fair, long ass's ears,
Instead of horns: and, so to mount (a paper
Pinned on thy breast) to the *berlino*——

   Corv.   Yes,
And have mine eyes beat out with stinking fish,   140
Bruised fruit, and rotten eggs—— 'Tis well. I'm glad,
I shall not see my shame, yet.

   1st Avo.   And to expiate
Thy wrongs done to thy wife, thou art to send her
Home, to her father, with her dowry trebled:
And these are all your judgements.

   All.   Honoured fathers.   145

   1st Avo. Which may not be revoked. Now you begin,
When crimes are done and past, and to be punished,
To think what your crimes are: away with them.
Let all that see these vices thus rewarded

125 *mortifying*: cookery term for hanging a carcase after it has been killed
136 *Grand Canal*: the 'main street' of Venice   139 *berlino*: pillory   146–8 Juvenal,
Sat. xiii. 237–9

150 Take heart, and love to study 'em. Mischiefs feed
Like beasts, till they be fat, and then they bleed.   [*Exeunt*]

Volpone

The seasoning of a play is the applause.
Now, though the Fox be punished by the laws,
He yet doth hope there is no suffering due
For any fact which he hath done 'gainst you;
5 If there be, censure him: here he, doubtful, stands.
If not, fare jovially, and clap your hands.

THE END

4 *fact*: crime   6 *jovially*: as though under the planetary influence of Jupiter (as the source of mirth and joy)

THE ALCHEMIST

THE
ALCHEMIST.

A Comœdie.

Acted in the yeere 1610. By the
Kings MAIESTIES
Seruants.

The Author B. I.

LVCRET.

————*petere inde coronam,*
Vnde priùs nulli velarint tempora Musæ.

LONDON,
Printed by VVILLIAM STANSBY

M. DC. XVI.

The title-page of the 1616 Folio.

TO THE LADY, MOST

DESERVING HER NAME,

AND BLOOD:

Mary,

LA[DY] WROTH

MADAM,
In the age of sacrifices, the truth of religion was not in the greatness
and fat of the offerings, but in the devotion and zeal of the sacrificers:
else, what could a handful of gums have done in the sight of a
hecatomb? Or how might I appear at this altar, except with those
affections that no less love the light and witness than they have the 5
conscience of your virtue? If what I offer bear an acceptable odour,
and hold the first strength, it is your value of it, which remembers,
where, when, and to whom it was kindled. Otherwise, as the times
are, there comes rarely forth that thing, so full of authority or example,
but by assiduity and custom grows less, and loses. This yet safe in 10
your judgement (which is a Sidney's) is forbidden to speak more; lest
it talk or look like one of the ambitious Faces of the time: who, the
more they paint, are the less themselves.

Your La[dyship's]
true honourer, 15
BEN. JONSON.

Mary, La[dy] Wroth: also spelled Worth ('most deserving her name'). Daughter
of Robert, Lord Sidney, and niece of Sir Philip Sidney, she was the author of
Urania and of a collection of sonnets   1–2 Seneca, *De Beneficiis*, I. vi. 2
6 *conscience*: consciousness

To the Reader

If thou beest more, thou art an Understander, and then I trust thee.
If thou art one that tak'st up, and but a Pretender, beware at what
hands thou receiv'st thy commodity; for thou wert never more fair
in the way to be cozened (than in this Age) in Poetry, especially in
5 Plays: wherein now the concupiscence of dances and antics so
reigneth, as to run away from Nature and be afraid of her, is the only
point of art that tickles the spectators. But how out of purpose and
place do I name Art? When the professors are grown so obstinate
contemners of it, and presumers on their own naturals, as they are
10 deriders of all diligence that way, and by simple mocking at the
terms, when they understand not the things, think to get off wittily
with their ignorance. Nay, they are esteemed the more learned and
sufficient for this, by the many, through their excellent vice of judge-
ment. For they commend writers as they do fencers or wrestlers;
15 who if they come in robustuously, and put for it with a great deal of
violence, are received for the braver fellows: when many times their
own rudeness is the cause of their disgrace, and a little touch of their
adversary gives all that boisterous force the foil. I deny not, but that
these men, who always seek to do more than enough, may sometime
20 happen on something that is good and great; but very seldom. And
when it comes it doth not recompense the rest of their ill. It sticks out
perhaps and is more eminent, because all is sordid and vile about it:
as lights are more discerned in a thick darkness than a faint shadow.
I speak not this out of a hope to do good on any man against his will;
25 for I know, if it were put to the question of theirs and mine, the worse
would find more suffrages: because the most favour common errors.
But I give thee this warning, that there is a great difference between
those that (to gain the opinion of copy) utter all they can, however
unfitly; and those that use election and a mean. For it is only the
30 disease of the unskilful to think rude things greater than polished:
or scattered more numerous than composed.

    (To the Reader) [*Folio omits*] **2** *one that tak'st up*: a speculator   **5** *dances*
and antics: ? aimed at Shakespeare; cf. *BF*, Ind. 112–6   **8** *the professors*: those
practising it   **8–14**, **18–23**, **27–31** cf. *Disc.* 745–75 (translated from Quintilian)
9 *naturals*: mental endowment   **13** *excellent*: pre-eminent   **14–18** cf. *Disc.*
634–42 (from Quintilian)   **28** *copy*: copiousness   *can*: know   **31** *numerous*:
harmonious

The Persons of the Play

Subtle, *the alchemist*
Face, *the housekeeper*
Dol Common, *their colleague*
Dapper, *a clerk*
Abel Drugger, *a tobacco-man*
Lovewit, *master of the house*
Epicure Mammon, *a knight*
Surly, *a gamester*

Tribulation Wholesome, *a pastor of Amsterdam*
Ananias, *a deacon there*
Kastril, *the angry boy*
Dame Pliant, *his sister, a widow*
Neighbours
Officers
Mutes

The Scene

London

THE ALCHEMIST

THE ARGUMENT

T he sickness hot, a master quit, for fear,
H is house in town: and left one servant there.
E ase him corrupted, and gave means to know
A cheater and his punk; who, now brought low,
L eaving their narrow practice, were become   5
C ozeners at large: and only wanting some
H ouse to set up, with him they here contract,
E ach for a share, and all begin to act.
M uch company they draw, and much abuse,
I n casting figures, telling fortunes, news,   10
S elling of flies, flat bawdry, with the stone:
T ill it, and they, and all in fume are gone.

PROLOGUE

FORTUNE, that favours fools, these two short hours
   We wish away; both for your sakes, and ours,
Judging spectators: and desire in place
   To the author justice, to ourselves but grace.
Our scene is London, 'cause we would make known   5
   No country's mirth is better than our own.
No clime breeds better matter, for your whore,
   Bawd, squire, impostor, many persons more,

---

1 *sickness*: the plague   4 *punk*: whore   10 *casting figures*: I. i. 96 n.
11 *flies*: familiar demons   *stone*: the philosophers' stone, for turning base metals to
gold   12 *fume*: smoke, vapour   (*Prologue*) 8 *squire*: pander

Whose manners, now called humours, feed the stage:
10   And which have still been subject for the rage
Or spleen of comic writers. Though this pen
      Did never aim to grieve, but better men;
Howe'er the age he lives in doth endure
      The vices that she breeds, above their cure.
15 But when the wholesome remedies are sweet,
      And in their working, gain and profit meet,
He hopes to find no spirit so much diseased,
      But will, with such fair correctives, be pleased.
For here, he doth not fear, who can apply.
20   If there be any, that will sit so nigh
Unto the stream, to look what it doth run,
      They shall find things they'd think, or wish, were done;
They are so natural follies, but so shown,
      As even the doers may see, and yet not own.

ACT I, Scene i

[Lovewit's house and the lane outside]

Enter Face [*with a sword*], Subtle [*with a phial*], Dol Common

Fac. BELIEVE'T, I will.
Sub.   Thy worst. I fart at thee.
Dol. Ha' you your wits? Why gentlemen! For love——
Fac. Sirrah, I'll strip you——
Sub.   What to do? Lick figs
Out at my——
      Fac.   Rogue, rogue, out of all your sleights.
5   *Dol.* Nay, look ye! Sovereign, General, are you madmen?
      Sub. Oh, let the wild sheep loose. I'll gum your silks
With good strong water, an' you come.
      Dol.   Will you have

---

9 *humours*: a use of the term resisted in *EMO*, Ind. 110–17   12 *better*: i.e.
improve   (I. i) 3 *figs*: piles, but see *H&S* x. 54   7 *strong water*: cf. the
'corsive waters' of I. iii. 102   *come*: approach

The neighbours hear you? Will you betray all?
Hark, I hear somebody.

   Fac.   Sirrah——
   Sub.   I shall mar
All that the tailor has made, if you approach.   10

   Fac. You most notorious whelp, you insolent slave,
Dare you do this?

   Sub.   Yes faith, yes faith.
   Fac.   Why! Who
Am I, my mongrel? Who am I?

   Sub.   I'll tell you,
Since you know not yourself——

   Fac.   Speak lower, rogue.
   Sub. Yes. You were once (time's not long past) the good,   15
Honest, plain, livery-three-pound-thrum; that kept
Your master's worship's house, here, in the Friars,
For the vacations——

   Fac.   Will you be so loud?
   Sub. Since, by my means, translated suburb-captain.
   Fac. By your means, Doctor dog?

   Sub.   Within man's memory,   20
All this, I speak of.

   Fac.   Why, I pray you, have I
Been countenanced by you? Or you, by me?
Do but collect, sir, where I met you first.

   Sub. I do not hear well.
   Fac.   Not of this, I think it.
But I shall put you in mind, sir, at Pie Corner,   25
Taking your meal of steam in, from cooks' stalls,
Where, like the father of hunger, you did walk
Piteously costive, with your pinched-horn-nose,
And your complexion, of the Roman wash,

---

  10 *the tailor*: 'The tailor makes the man' (proverb)   16 *livery-three-pound-thrum*:
shabbily dressed, poorly paid underling   17 *Friars*: Blackfriars   18 *vacations*:
i.e. the law vacations   19 *suburb-captain*: bogus captain (l. 127), preying on the
disreputable life of the suburbs (cf. Pistol in *2 Henry IV*, II. iv. 131–41)   24 *hear
well*: *Volp.* Ded. 10   25 *Pie Corner*: near Smithfield (named not from the cook-
shops, but from an inn with the sign of a magpie)   29 *Roman wash*: ? for a skin
disease

30 Stuck full of black and melancholic worms,
   Like powder-corns, shot, at the artillery yard.
       Sub. I wish you could advance your voice a little.
       Fac. When you went pinned up in the several rags
   You'd raked and picked from dunghills, before day,
35 Your feet in mouldy slippers, for your kibes,
   A felt of rug, and a thin threaden cloak,
   That scarce would cover your no-buttocks——
       Sub.   So, sir!
       Fac. When all your alchemy, and your algebra,
   Your minerals, vegetals, and animals,
40 Your conjuring, cozening, and your dozen of trades,
   Could not relieve your corpse, with so much linen
   Would make you tinder, but to see a fire;
   I ga' you countenance, credit for your coals,
   Your stills, your glasses, your materials,
45 Built you a furnace, drew you customers,
   Advanced all your black arts; lent you, beside,
   A house to practise in——
       Sub.   Your master's house?
       Fac. Where you have studied the more thriving skill
   Of bawdry, since.
       Sub.   Yes, in your master's house.
50 You, and the rats, here, kept possession.
   Make it not strange. I know, yo'were one could keep
   The buttery-hatch still locked, and save the chippings,
   Sell the dole-beer to *aqua-vitae*-men,
   The which, together with your Christmas vails,
55 At post and pair, your letting out of counters,
   Made you a pretty stock, some twenty marks,
   And gave you credit to converse with cobwebs,
   Here, since your mistress's death hath broke up house.
       Fac. You might talk softlier, rascal.

---

31 *powder-corns*: grains of gunpowder   *artillery yard*: EMI III. v. 128 n.
35 *kibes*: chilblains   36 *felt of rug*: hat made of coarse frieze   53 *dole-beer*:
distributed, with dole-bread, from well-to-do households   *aqua-vitae-men*: distillers
of spirits   54 *vails*: gratuities   55 *post and pair*: a card-game   *counters*:
used instead of coin in gambling, and 'let out' for a gratuity   56 *marks*: worth
13*s.* 4*d.* each

Sub.   No, you scarab,
I'll thunder you in pieces. I will teach you   60
How to beware to tempt a fury again
That carries tempest in his hand and voice.
  Fac. The place has made you valiant.
  Sub.   No, your clothes.
Thou vermin, have I ta'en thee, out of dung,
So poor, so wretched, when no living thing   65
Would keep thee company, but a spider, or worse?
Raised thee from brooms and dust and watering pots?
Sublimed thee, and exalted thee, and fixed thee
I' the third region, called our state of grace?
Wrought thee to spirit, to quintessence, with pains   70
Would twice have won me the philosophers' work?
Put thee in words and fashion? Made thee fit
For more than ordinary fellowships?
Given thee thy oaths, thy quarrelling dimensions?
Thy rules, to cheat at horse-race; cock-pit, cards,   75
Dice, or whatever gallant tincture else?
Made thee a second in mine own great art?
And have I this for thank? Do you rebel?
Do you fly out, i' the projection?
Would you be gone now?
  Dol.   Gentlemen, what mean you?   80
Will you mar all?
  Sub.   Slave, thou hadst had no name——
  Dol. Will you undo yourselves, with civil war?
  Sub. Never been known, past *equi clibanum*,
The heat of horse-dung, underground, in cellars,
Or an ale-house, darker than deaf John's: been lost   85
To all mankind, but laundresses and tapsters,
Had not I been.
  Dol.   D'you know who hears you, Sovereign?
  Fac. Sirrah——

---

  59 *scarab*: dung beetle   68 *sublimed . . . fixed*: cf. II. i. 100   69 *the third*:
purest of the three regions of air (upper, middle, lower)   71 *philosophers' work*:
philosophers' stone   73 *ordinary*: (1) commonplace, (2) public eating-house
74 *oaths*: part of the equipment of the gallant   *dimensions*: limits, rules   79 *projec-*
tion: climax of the alchemical transformation (II. ii. 5)   85 *deaf John's*: untraced

Dol.   Nay, General, I thought you were civil——

Fac. I shall turn desperate, if you grow thus loud.

Sub. And hang thyself, I care not.

90 *Fac.*   Hang thee, collier,

And all thy pots and pans, in picture I will,

Since thou hast moved me.——

   Dol.   (Oh, this'll o'erthrow all.)

Fac. Write thee up bawd, in Paul's; have all thy tricks

Of cozening with a hollow coal, dust, scrapings,

95 Searching for things lost, with a sieve and shears,

Erecting figures, in your rows of houses,

And taking in of shadows, with a glass,

Told in red letters: and a face, cut for thee,

Worse than Gamaliel Ratsey's.

   Dol.   Are you sound?

Ha' you your senses, masters?

100 *Fac.*   I will have

A book, but barely reckoning thy impostures,

Shall prove a true philosophers' stone, to printers.

   Sub. Away, you trencher-rascal.

   Fac.   Out you dog-leach,

The vomit of all prisons——

   Dol.   Will you be

Your own destructions, gentlemen?

105 *Fac.*   Still spewed out

For lying too heavy o' the basket.

   Sub.   Cheater.

Fac. Bawd.

   Sub.   Cowherd.

   Fac.   Conjurer.

---

90 *collier*: noted for giving false weight, hence 'rogue'   93 *Paul's*: EMI,
Persons, n.   94 *hollow coal*: filled with 'scrapings' that seem to turn into silver in
the fire   95 *sieve*: balanced on a pair of shears, supported by two persons, so that
it may turn about on the naming of the thief   96 *Erecting figures*: making a diagram
of the position of the planets to cast horoscopes   *houses*: the signs of the zodiac
97 *glass*: crystal or beryl, the reflections in which would answer questions, if read by
a virgin   98 *in red letters*: for emphasis, as in rubricated headings and titles
99 *Gamaliel Ratsey*: highwayman who wore a hideous mask   106 *too heavy o'*
the basket: i.e. eating more than his share of the scraps collected for prisoners (*EH* V.
iii. 46)

Sub.   Cutpurse.
Fac.   Witch.
Dol.   Oh me!
We are ruined! Lost! Ha' you no more regard
To your reputations? Where's your judgement? 'Slight,
Have yet some care of me, o' your republic——   110
    Fac. Away this brach. I'll bring thee, rogue, within
The statute of sorcery, *tricesimo tertio*,
Of Harry the Eight: aye, and (perhaps) thy neck
Within a noose, for laundering gold, and barbing it.
    Dol. You'll bring your head within a cockscomb, will you?   115
            (*She catcheth out* Face *his sword: and breaks* Subtle's *glass*)
And you, sir, with your *menstrue*, gather it up.
'Sdeath, you abominable pair of stinkards,
Leave off your barking, and grow one again,
Or, by the light that shines, I'll cut your throats.
I'll not be made a prey unto the marshal,   120
For ne'er a snarling dog-bolt o' you both.
Ha' you together cozened all this while,
And all the world, and shall it now be said
Yo've made most courteous shift to cozen yourselves?
[*To* Face] You will accuse him? You will bring him in   125 (
Within the statute? Who shall take your word?
A whoreson, upstart, apocryphal captain,
Whom not a puritan in Blackfriars will trust
So much as for a feather! [*To* Subtle] And you, too,
Will give the cause, forsooth? You will insult,   130
And claim a primacy in the divisions?
You must be chief? As if you, only, had
The powder to project with? And the work
Were not begun out of equality?
The venture tripartite? All things in common?   135

110 *republic*: common-weal, joint interests   111 *brach*: bitch   112 *statute*:
of 1541, forbidding sorcery   114 *laundering . . . barbing*: washing off the surface
and clipping   115 *cockscomb*: the fool's head-dress   116 *menstrue*: liquid for
dissolving metals   120 *marshal*: *Volp.* IV. ii. 62 n.   121 *dog-bolt*: (1) blunt-
headed arrow, (2) tool to be put to any use   122 *cozened*: (1) cheated, (2) acted
as cronies   128 *a puritan, in Blackfriars*: who traded in feathers   130 *insult*:
brag, vaunt

Without priority? 'Sdeath, you perpetual curs,
Fall to your couples again, and cozen kindly,
And heartily, and lovingly, as you should,
And lose not the beginning of a term,
140 Or, by this hand, I shall grow factious too,
And take my part, and quit you.
  Fac.   'Tis his fault,
He ever murmurs, and objects his pains,
And says the weight of all lies upon him.
  Sub. Why, so it does.
  Dol.   How does it? Do not we
Sustain our parts?
145 *Sub.*   Yes, but they are not equal.
  Dol. Why, if your part exceed today, I hope
Ours may, tomorrow, match it.
  Sub.   Aye, they may.
  Dol. May, murmuring mastiff? Aye, and do. Death on me!
Help me to throttle him. [*Seizes* Subtle *by the throat*]
  Sub.   Dorothy, mistress Dorothy,
150 'Ods precious, I'll do anything. What do you mean?
  Dol. Because o' your fermentation, and cibation?
  Sub. Not I, by heaven——
  Dol.   Your *Sol* and *Luna*—— help me.
  Sub. Would I were hanged then. I'll conform myself.
  Dol. Will you, sir, do so then, and quickly: swear.
  Sub. What should I swear?
155 *Dol.*   To leave your factions, sir.
And labour, kindly, in the common work.
  Sub. Let me not breathe, if I meant aught beside.
I only used those speeches as a spur
To him.
  Dol. I hope we need no spurs, sir. Do we?
  Fac. 'Slid, prove today, who shall shark best.
160 *Sub.*   Agreed.

---

137 *couples*: hunting dogs worked in pairs   139 *term*: of the Inns of Court,
corresponding to the London season   151 *fermentation*: the sixth process in the
conversion of metal to gold *cibation*: the seventh process, feeding in fresh substances
to compensate for evaporation 152 *Sol and Luna*: gold and silver

Dol. Yes, and work close, and friendly.

Sub.   'Slight, the knot
Shall grow the stronger, for this breach, with me.

Dol. Why so, my good baboons! Shall we go make
A sort of sober, scruffy, precise neighbours,
(That scarce have smiled twice, sin' the king came in)   165
A feast of laughter at our follies? Rascals,
Would run themselves from breath, to see me ride,
Or you to have but a hole to thrust your heads in,
For which you should pay ear-rent? No, agree.
And may Don Provost ride a-feasting, long,   170
In his old velvet jerkin, and stained scarfs,
(My noble Sovereign, and worthy General)
Ere we contribute a new crewel garter
To his most worsted worship.

Sub.   Royal Dol!
Spoken like Claridiana, and thyself!   175

Fac. For which, at supper, thou shalt sit in triumph,
And not be styled Dol Common, but Dol Proper,
Dol Singular: the longest cut, at night,
Shall draw thee for his Dol Particular.

Sub. Who's that? One rings. To the window, Dol. Pray heaven,   180
The master do not trouble us this quarter.

Fac. Oh, fear not him. While there dies one a week
O'the plague, he's safe from thinking toward London.
Beside, he's busy at his hopyards now:
I had a letter from him. If he do,   185
He'll send such word, for airing o' the house
As you shall have sufficient time to quit it:
Though we break up a fortnight, 'tis no matter.

Sub. Who is it, Dol?

Dol.   A fine young quodling.

Fac.   Oh,
My lawyer's clerk, I lighted on last night   190

164 *sort*: set   *precise*: Puritanical   167 *ride*: be carted as a whore (*SW* III. v. 75)
169 *pay ear-rent*: lose your ears in the pillory   173 *crewel garter*: pun on 'cruel'
and 'crewel' (worsted yarn)   175 *Claridiana*: heroine of *The Mirror of Knighthood*
(*CR* III. v. 28 n.)   177–9 punning on grammatical terms (with sexual innuendo)
178 *cut*: straw   189 *quodling*: raw youth (lit. half-grown apple)

In Holborn, at the Dagger. He would have
(I told you of him) a familiar,
To rifle with, at horses, and win cups.
 Dol. Oh, let him in.
 Sub.   Stay. Who shall do't?
 Fac.   Get you
195 Your robes on. I will meet him, as going out.
 Dol. And what shall I do?
 Fac.   Not be seen, away.   *[Exit* Dol]
Seem you very reserved.
 Sub.   Enough.   *[Exit]*
 Fac.   God b'w'you, sir.
I pray you, let him know that I was here.
His name is Dapper. I would gladly have stayed, but——

ACT I, Scene ii

 Dap. *[Without]* Captain, I am here.
 Fac.   Who's that? He's come, I think, Doctor.

[*Enter* Dapper]

Good faith, sir, I was going away.
 Dap.   In truth,
I'm very sorry, Captain.
 Fac.   But I thought
Sure, I should meet you.
 Dap.   Aye, I'm very glad.
5 I had a scurvy writ or two to make,
And I had lent my watch last night, to one
That dines today at the sheriff's: and so was robbed
Of my pass-time.

[*Enter* Subtle *in his robes*]

Is this the cunning man?
 Fac. This is his worship.

---

191 *the Dagger*: tavern famous for its pies   192 *familiar*: *Volp.* V. ix. 8
193 *rifle*: gamble   (*I. ii*) 6 *watch*: a sign of social distinction   8 *pass-time*:
timepiece   *cunning-man*: i.e. 'possessing magical knowledge or skill' (*OED*)

Dap.   Is he a Doctor?
Fac.   Yes.
Dap. And ha' you broke with him, Captain?
Fac.   Aye.
Dap.   And how?   10
Fac. Faith, he does make the matter, sir, so dainty,
I know not what to say——
Dap.   Not so, good Captain.
Fac. Would I were fairly rid on't, believe me.
Dap. Nay, now you grieve me, sir. Why should you wish so?
I dare assure you. I'll not be ungrateful.   15
Fac. I cannot think you will, sir. But the law
Is such a thing—— And then, he says, Read's matter
Falling so lately——
Dap.   Read? He was an ass,
And dealt, sir, with a fool.
Fac.   It was a clerk, sir.
Dap. A clerk?
Fac.   Nay, hear me, sir, you know the law   20
Better, I think——
Dap.   I should, sir, and the danger.
You know I showed the statute to you?
Fac.   You did so.
Dap. And will I tell, then? By this hand of flesh,
Would it might never write good court-hand more,
If I discover. What do you think of me,   25
That I am a Chiause?
Fac.   What's that?
Dap.   The Turk, was here——
As one would say, do you think I am a Turk?
Fac. I'll tell the Doctor so.
Dap.   Do, good sweet Captain.
Fac. Come, noble Doctor, 'pray thee, let's prevail,
This is the gentleman, and he is no Chiause.   30

10 *broke with*: confided in (or perhaps 'negotiated with')   17 *Read*: Simon
Read, who in 1607 invoked spirits to recover stolen money   24 *court-hand*: legal
script hard for a layman to decipher   26 *Chiause*: title (chaush = messenger) of
the Turk Mustapha, expensively entertained in England by the Levant merchants in
1607, and considered to have duped them (hence 'chouse' = to cheat)

Sub. Captain, I have returned you all my answer.
I would do much, sir, for your love—— But this
I neither may, nor can.

    Fac.   Tut, do not say so.
You deal now with a noble fellow, Doctor,
35 One that will thank you richly, and he's no Chiause:
Let that, sir, move you.

    Sub.   Pray you, forbear——

    Fac.   He has
Four angels, here——

    Sub.   You do me wrong, good sir.

    Fac. Doctor, wherein? To tempt you, with these spirits?

    Sub. To tempt my art, and love, sir, to my peril.
40 'Fore heaven, I scarce can think you are my friend,
That so would draw me to apparent danger.

    Fac. I draw you? A horse draw you, and a halter,
You, and your flies together——

    Dap.   Nay, good Captain.

    Fac. That know no difference of men.

    Sub.   Good words, sir.
45 *Fac.* Good deeds, Sir Doctor dogs-meat. 'Slight I bring you
No cheating Clim-o'the-Cloughs, or Claribels,
That look as big as five-and-fifty, and flush,
And spit out secrets, like hot custard——

    Dap.   Captain.

    Fac. Nor any melancholic underscribe,
50 Shall tell the Vicar: but a special gentle,
That is the heir to forty marks a year,
Consorts with the small poets of the time,
Is the sole hope of his old grandmother,
That knows the law, and writes you six fair hands,
55 Is a fine clerk, and has his ciphering perfect,

37-8 *angels*: *EMI* II. iv. 71 n.   42 *horse draw you*: i.e. to be hanged
43 *flies*: Argument, 11   46 *Clim-o'the-Clough*: the outlaw in the ballad
Claribel: the 'lewd' knight of *The Faerie Queene*, IV. ix. 20   47 *five-and-fifty,
and flush*: an invincible hand in cards   50 *Vicar*: the vicar-general, who
could act with the authority of the bishop   54 *six fair hands*: court-hand,
secretary (English and French), Italic, Roman, and chancellery   55 *ciphering*:
arithmetic

Will take his oath, o' the Greek Xenophon,
If need be, in his pocket: and can court
His mistress, out of Ovid.

   Dap.   Nay, dear Captain.

   Fac. Did you not tell me so?

   Dap.   Yes, but I'd ha'you
Use Master Doctor with some more respect.   60

   Fac. Hang him proud stag, with his broad velvet head.
But for your sake, I'd choke, ere I would change
An article of breath with such a puck-fist——
Come, let's be gone.

   Sub.   Pray you, let me speak with you.

   Dap. His worship calls you, Captain.

   Fac.   I am sorry   65
I e'er embarked myself in such a business.

   Dap. Nay, good sir. He did call you.

   Fac.   Will he take, then?

   Sub. First, hear me——

   Fac.   Not a syllable, 'less you take.

   Sub. Pray ye, sir——

   Fac.   Upon no terms, but an *assumpsit*.

   Sub. Your humour must be law. (*He takes the money*)

   Fac.   Why now, sir, talk.   70
Now, I dare hear you with mine honour. Speak.
So may this gentleman too.

   Sub.   Why, sir——

   Fac.   No whispering.

   Sub. 'Fore heaven, you do not apprehend the loss
You do yourself in this.

   Fac.   Wherein? For what?

   Sub. Marry, to be so importunate for one,   75
That, when he has it, will undo you all:
He'll win up all the money i' the town.

   Fac. How!

---

56 *Xenophon*: altered from *Testament* in the quarto, avoiding scriptural reference
61 *velvet head*: Subtle's doctor's cap (likened to the 'velvet' or down on a deer's horn)
63 *puck-fist*: the puff-ball fungus, hence 'empty boaster'   69 *assumpsit*: verbal
promise, made fast by a fee

Sub.   Yes. And blow up gamester after gamester,
As they do crackers, in a puppet play.
80 If I do give him a familiar,
Give you him all you play for; never set him:
For he will have it.

Fac.   You're mistaken, Doctor.
Why, he does ask one but for cups, and horses,
A rifling fly: none o' your great familiars.

85 *Dap.* Yes, Captain, I would have it, for all games.

Sub. I told you so.

Fac.   'Slight, that's a new business!
I understood you, a tame bird, to fly
Twice in a term, or so; on Friday nights,
When you had left the office: for a nag,
Of forty or fifty shillings.

90 *Dap.*   Aye, 'tis true, sir,
But I do think, now, I shall leave the law,
And therefore——

Fac.   Why, this changes quite the case!
D'you think that I dare move him?

Dap.   If you please, sir,
All's one to him, I see.

Fac.   What! For that money?
95 I cannot with my conscience. Nor should you
Make the request, methinks.

Dap.   No, sir, I mean
To add consideration.

Fac.   Why then, sir,
I'll try. Say, that it were for all games, Doctor?

Sub. I say, then, not a mouth shall eat for him
100 At any ordinary, but o' the score,
That is a gaming mouth, conceive me.

Fac.   Indeed!

Sub. He'll draw you all the treasure of the realm,
If it be set him.

Fac.   Speak you this from art?

81 *set him*: mark him down as prey   97 *consideration*: compensation   100 *o'the score*: on credit, i.e. no gambler will be left with ready money for a dinner

Sub. Aye, sir, and reason too: the ground of art.
He's o' the only best complexion,   105
The Queen of Faery loves.
    Fac.   What! Is he!
    Sub.   Peace.
He'll overhear you. Sir, should she but see him——
    Fac. What?
    Sub.   Do not you tell him.
    Fac.   Will he win at cards too?
    Sub. The spirits of dead Holland, living Isaac,
You'd swear were in him: such a vigorous luck   110
As cannot be resisted. 'Slight, he'll put
Six o' your gallants to a cloak, indeed.
    Fac. A strange success, that some man shall be born to!
    Sub. He hears you, man——
    Dap.   Sir, I'll not be ingrateful.
    Fac. Faith, I have a confidence in his good nature: 115
You hear, he says, he will not be ingrateful.
    Sub. Why, as you please, my venture follows yours.
   ·*Fac.* Troth, do it, Doctor. Think him trusty, and make him.
He may make us both happy in an hour:
Win some five thousand pound, and send us two on't.   120
    Dap. Believe it, and I will, sir.
    Fac.   And you shall, sir.
You have heard all?
    Dap.   No, what was't? Nothing, I sir.
    Fac. Nothing?
    Dap.   A little, sir. (Face *takes him aside*)
    Fac.   Well, a rare star
Reigned at your birth.
    Dap.   At mine, sir? No.
    Fac.   The Doctor
Swears that you are——
    Sub.   Nay, Captain, you'll tell all, now.   125
    Fac. Allied to the Queen of Faery.

---

109 *dead Holland, living Isaac*: the Dutch alchemists, John and John Isaac Holland
112 *cloak*: the last garment relinquished by a gallant, as it concealed the loss of the rest
119 *happy*: rich (cf. *beatus*)

Dap.   Who? That I am?
Believe it, no such matter——
    Fac.   Yes, and that
You were born with a caul o' your head.
    Dap.   Who says so?
    Fac.   Come.
You know it well enough, though you dissemble it.
    Dap. I-fac, I do not. You are mistaken.
130   *Fac.*   How!
Swear by your fac? And in a thing so known
Unto the Doctor? How shall we, sir, trust you
I'the other matter? Can we ever think,
When you have won five or six thousand pound,
You'll send us shares in't, by this rate?
135   *Dap.*   By Jove, sir,
I'll win ten thousand pound, and send you half.
I-fac's no oath.
    Sub.   No, no, he did but jest.
    Fac. Go to. Go, thank the Doctor. He's your friend
To take it so.
    Dap.   I thank his worship.
    Fac.   So?
Another angel.
    Dap.   Must I?
140   *Fac.*   Must you? 'Slight,
What else is thanks? Will you be trivial? [Dapper *gives money*]
                                        Doctor,
When must he come, for his familiar?
    Dap. Shall I not ha' it with me?
    Sub.   Oh, good sir!
There must a world of ceremonies pass,
145 You must be bathed and fumigated first;
Besides, the Queen of Faery does not rise
Till it be noon.
    Fac.   Not if she danced tonight.
    Sub. And she must bless it.

128 *caul*: considered a lucky omen (and a safeguard against drowning)   130 *I-fac*:
'in faith', too mild to be binding as an oath (l. 137)   147 *tonight*: last night

Fac.   Did you never see
Her royal Grace yet?
   Dap.   Whom?
   Fac.   Your aunt of Faery?
   Sub. Not since she kissed him in the cradle, Captain,   150
I can resolve you that.
   Fac.   Well, see her Grace,
What e'er it cost you, for a thing that I know!
It will be somewhat hard to compass: but,
However, see her. You are made, believe it,
If you can see her. Her Grace is a lone woman,   155
And very rich, and if she take a fancy,
She will do strange things. See her, at any hand.
'Slid, she may hap to leave you all she has!
It is the Doctor's fear.
   Dap.   How will't be done then?
   Fac. Let me alone, take you no thought. Do you   160
But say to me, Captain, I'll see her Grace.
   Dap. Captain, I'll see her Grace.   (*One knocks without*)
   Fac.   Enough.
   Sub.   Who's there?
Anon. (*Conduct him forth, by the back way.*)
Sir, against one o'clock, prepare yourself.
Till when you must be fasting; only, take   165
Three drops of vinegar in at your nose;
Two at your mouth; and one at either ear;
Then bathe your fingers' ends; and wash your eyes;
To sharpen your five senses; and cry 'hum',
Thrice; and then 'buzz', as often; and then, come.   [*Exit*] 170
   Fac. Can you remember this?
   Dap.   I warrant you.
   Fac. Well then, away. 'Tis but your bestowing
Some twenty nobles 'mong her Grace's servants;
And put on a clean shirt. You do not know
What grace her Grace may do you in clean linen.   [*Exeunt*] 175

151 *resolve you*: convince you of   173 *nobles*: worth 6s. 8d.   175 *clean
linen*: held in esteem by the fairies (III. iv. 137–9)

ACT I, Scene iii

Enter Subtle, Abel Drugger

Sub. Come in (good wives, I pray you forbear me now.
Troth I can do you no good, till afternoon):
What is your name, say you, Abel Drugger?
  Dru.   Yes, sir.
  Sub. A seller of tobacco?
  Dru.   Yes sir.
  Sub.   'Umh.
Free of the Grocers?
  Dru.   Aye, and't please you.
5 *Sub.*   Well——
Your business, Abel?
  Dru.   This, and't please your worship,
I am a young beginner, and am building
Of a new shop, and't like your worship; just,
At corner of a street: (here's the plot on't.)
10 And I would know by art, sir, of your worship,
Which way I should make my door, by necromancy.
And where my shelves. And which should be for boxes.
And which for pots. I would be glad to thrive, sir.
And I was wished to your worship by a gentleman,
15 One Captain Face, that says you know men's planets,
And their good angels, and their bad.
  Sub.   I do,
If I do see 'em——

[*Enter* Face]

  Fac.   What! My honest Abel?
Thou art well met, here!
  Dru.   Troth, sir, I was speaking,
Just, as your worship came here, of your worship.
20 I pray you, speak for me to Master Doctor.
  Fac. He shall do anything. Doctor, do you hear?
This is my friend, Abel, an honest fellow,

---

5 *Free*: admitted to the company 9 *plot*: groundplan

He lets me have good tobacco, and he does not
Sophisticate it with sack-lees, or oil,
Nor washes it in muscadel, and grains,   25
Nor buries it in gravel underground,
Wrapped up in greasy leather, or pissed clouts:
But keeps it in fine lily-pots, that opened,
Smell like conserve of roses, or French beans.
He has his maple block, his silver tongs,   30
Winchester pipes, and fire of juniper.
A neat, spruce-honest-fellow, and no goldsmith.
   Sub. He's a fortunate fellow, that I am sure on——
   Fac. Already, sir, ha' you found it? Lo' thee Abel!
   Sub. And in right way toward riches——
   Fac.   Sir.
   Sub.   This summer,   35
He will be of the clothing of his company:
And next spring, called to the scarlet. Spend what he can.
   Fac. What, and so little beard?
   Sub.   Sir, you must think,
He may have a receipt, to make hair come.
But he'll be wise, preserve his youth, and fine for't: 40
His fortune looks for him another way.
   Fac. 'Slid, Doctor, how canst thou know this so soon?
I am amused, at that!
   Sub.   By a rule, Captain,
In metoposcopy, which I do work by,
A certain star i'the forehead, which you see not.   45
Your chestnut, or your olive-coloured face
Does never fail: and your long ear doth promise.
I knew't, by certain spots too, in his teeth,
And on the nail of his mercurial finger.
   Fac. Which finger's that?   50

---

24 *Sophisticate*: adulterate   28 *lily-pots*: ornamental jars   29 *French beans*: broad beans, with fragrant flowers   30 *maple block*: for shredding the leaf   *silver tongs*: for holding the lighted coal   31 *Winchester*: famous for the manufacture of tobacco pipes   *juniper*: supposed to burn for a year   32 *goldsmith*: usurer   36 *clothing*: livery   37 *scarlet*: dress of the sheriff   40 *fine for't*: pay the fine for refusing office   43 *amused*: puzzled   44 *metoposcopy*: judging a man's character and fortune from his forehead and face

    Sub.   His little finger. Look.
You were born upon a Wednesday?
    Dru.   Yes, indeed, sir.
    Sub. The thumb, in chiromanty, we give Venus;
The forefinger to Jove; the midst, to Saturn;
The ring to Sol; the least, to Mercury:
55 Who was the lord, sir, of his horoscope,
His house of life being Libra, which foreshowed,
He should be a merchant, and should trade with balance.
    Fac. Why, this is strange! Is't not, honest Nab?
    Sub. There is a ship now, coming from Ormus,
60 That shall yield him such a commodity
Of drugs—— This is the west, and this the south?
    Dru. Yes, sir.
    Sub.   And those are your two sides?
    Dru.   Aye, sir.
    Sub. Make me your door, then, south; your broad side, west:
And on the east side of your shop, aloft,
65 Write *Mathlai, Tarmiel,* and *Baraborat*;
Upon the north part, *Rael, Velel, Thiel.*
They are the names of those Mercurial spirits,
That do fright flies from boxes.
    Dru.   Yes, sir.
    Sub.   And
Beneath your threshold, bury me a lodestone
70 To draw in gallants, that wear spurs. The rest,
They'll seem to follow.
    Fac.   That's a secret, Nab!
    Sub. And on your stall, a puppet, with a vice,
And a court-fucus to call city-dames.
You shall deal much, with minerals.
    Dru.   Sir, I have,

---

52 *chiromanty*: telling fortunes from the hand   56 *house of life being Libra*: so
that Venus would be the ruling planet, not Mercury (substituted to tempt Drugger with
the prospect of commercial success)   57 *balance*: quibble on the zodiacal sign for
Libra   64–7 based on the *Heptameron, seu Elementa magica Pietri de Abano
philosophi* appended to Cornelius Agrippa's *De Occulta Philosophia* (? Paris, 1567)
71 *seem*: be seen   72 *vice*: the mechanical contrivance (device) for working it
73 *court-fucus*: cosmetic paint used at court

At home, already——
   Sub.   Aye, I know, you have arsenic,   75
Vitriol, sal-tartar, argaile, alkali,
Cinoper: I know all. This fellow, Captain,
Will come, in time, to be a great distiller,
And give a say (I will not say directly,
But very fair) at the philosophers' stone.   80
   Fac. Why, how now, Abel! Is this true?
   Dru.   Good Captain,
What must I give?
   Fac.   Nay, I'll not counsel thee.
Thou hearst, what wealth (he says, spend what thou canst)
Th'art like to come to.
   Dru.   I would gi' him a crown.
   Fac. A crown! And toward such a fortune? Heart,   85
Thou shalt rather gi' him thy shop. No gold about thee?
   Dru. Yes, I have a portague, I ha' kept this half year.
   Fac. Out on thee, Nab; 'Slight, there was such an offer——
'Shalt keep 't no longer, I'll gi' it him for thee?
Doctor, Nab prays your worship, to drink this: and swears   90
He will appear more grateful, as your skill
Does raise him in the world.
   Dru.   I would entreat
Another favour of his worship.
   Fac.   What is't, Nab?
   Dru. But to look over, sir, my almanack,
And cross out my ill-days, that I may neither   95
Bargain, nor trust upon them.
   Fac.   That he shall, Nab.
Leave it, it shall be done, 'gainst afternoon.
   Sub. And a direction for his shelves.
   Fac.   Now, Nab?
Art thou well pleased, Nab?
   Dru.   Thank sir, both your worships.

---

76 *Vitriol*: sulphuric acid   *sal-tartar*: carbonate of potash   *argaile*: crude cream
of tartar   *alkali*: soda-ash   77 *Cinoper*: cinnabar, red mercuric sulphide
79 *give a say*: make an attempt   84 *crown*: worth 5s.   87 *portague*: Portuguese
gold coin worth from £3. 5s. 0d. to £4. 10s. 0d.   95 *ill-days*: unlucky days
96 *trust*: give credit

Fac. Away. [*Exit* Drugger]

100 Why, now, you smoky persecuter of nature!
Now, do you see, that something's to be done,
Beside your beech-coal, and your corsive waters,
Your cross-lets, crucibles, and cucurbits?
You must have stuff, brought home to you, to work on?
105 And yet you think I am at no expense,
In searching out these veins, then following 'em,
Then trying 'em out. 'Fore God, my intelligence
Costs me more money than my share oft comes to,
In these rare works.
    Sub.   You're pleasant, sir. How now?

ACT I, Scene iv

Enter Dol

Fac. What says my dainty Dolkin?
    Dol.   Yonder fishwife
Will not away. And there's your giantess,
The bawd of Lambeth.
    Sub.   Heart, I cannot speak with 'em.
    Dol. Not afore night, I have told 'em, in a voice,
5 Thorough the trunk, like one of your familiars.
But I have spied Sir Epicure Mammon——
    Sub.   Where?
    Dol. Coming along, at far end of the lane,
Slow of his feet, but earnest of his tongue,
To one that's with him.
    Sub.   Face, go you, and shift.   [*Exit* Face]
10 Dol, you must presently make ready too——
    Dol. Why, what's the matter?
    Sub.   Oh, I did look for him
With the sun's rising: 'marvel, he could sleep!

---

102 *beech*: preferred for charcoal (II. ii. 22-3)   103 *cross-lets*: melting pots
cucurbits: retorts, originally in shape of a gourd   107 *intelligence*: information
(*I. iv*) 5 *trunk*: speaking-tube   9 *shift*: change clothes   10 *presently make
ready*: dress at once

This is the day, I am to perfect for him
The magisterium, our great work, the stone;
And yield it, made, into his hands: of which,   15
He has this month talked, as he were possessed.
And now he's dealing pieces on't, away.
Methinks I see him, entering ordinaries,
Dispensing for the pox; and plaguey-houses,
Reaching his dose; walking Moorfields for lepers;   20
And offering citizens' wives pomander-bracelets,
As his preservative, made of the elixir;
Searching the spittle, to make old bawds young;
And the highways for beggars to make rich:
I see no end of his labours. He will make   25
Nature ashamed of her long sleep: when art,
Who's but a stepdame, shall do more than she,
In her best love to mankind, ever could.
If his dream last, he'll turn the age, to gold.   [*Exeunt*]

ACT II, Scene i

Enter Sir Epicure Mammon, Surly

Mam. COME on, sir. Now you set your foot on shore
In *novo orbe*; here's the rich Peru:
And there within, sir, are the golden mines,
Great Solomon's Ophir! He was sailing to't
Three years, but we have reached it in ten months.   5
This is the day wherein to all my friends,
I will pronounce the happy word, 'be rich'.
This day you shall be *spectatissimi*.
You shall no more deal with the hollow die,
Or the frail card. No more be at charge of keeping   10

14 *magisterium*: the master principle   20 *Moorfields*: resort of lepers forbidden the city   21 *pomander-bracelets*: made of scented paste, as a supposed safeguard against infection   23 *spittle*: hospital, especially for foul diseases   (*II i.*) 4 *Ophir*: where Solomon was reputed to have made gold with the philosophers' stone   5 *Three years*: the interval between shipments of gold from Tharshish (1 Kgs. 10: 22) 8 *spectatissimi*: specially looked up to

The livery-punk, for the young heir, that must
Seal, at all hours, in his shirt. No more,
If he deny, ha' him beaten to't, as he is
That brings him the commodity. No more
15 Shall thirst of satin, or the covetous hunger
Of velvet entrails, for a rude-spun cloak,
To be displayed at Madam Augusta's, make
The sons of sword and hazard fall before
The golden calf, and on their knees, whole nights,
20 Commit idolatry with wine and trumpets:
Or go a-feasting, after drum and ensign.
No more of this. You shall start up young Viceroys,
And have your punks and punkettees, my Surly.
And unto thee I speak it first, 'be rich'.
Where is my Subtle, there? Within hough?
25   *Fac.* (*Within*)   Sir.
He'll come to you, by and by.
   Mam.   That's his fire-drake,
His lungs, his Zephyrus, he that puffs his coals,
Till he firk nature up, in her own centre.
You are not faithful, sir. This night I'll change
30 All that is metal in my house to gold.
And early in the morning will I send
To all the plumbers and the pewterers,
And buy their tin and lead up: and to Lothbury,
For all the copper.
   Sur.   What, and turn that too?
35   *Mam.* Yes, and I'll purchase Devonshire and Cornwall,
And make them perfect Indies! You admire now?
   Sur. No faith.
   Mam.   But when you see the effects of the great medicine!

---

11 *livery-punk*: prostitute retained to induce men to seal agreements for the 'commodity' fraud, foisting goods upon them as part of the loan or repayment (III. iv. 90)
16 *entrails*: i.e. lining   17 *Madam Augusta's*: ? suggested by Juvenal's 'meretrix Augusta' (*Sat.* vi. 118)   18 *hazard*: card-game   26 *fire-drake*: (1) fiery dragon, (2) fiery meteor, (3) worker around the fire   27 *lungs*: the alchemist's drudge who blew the coals   28 *firk*: stir   29 *faithful*: ready to believe   33 *Lothbury*: the street of the copper founders   36 *make them . . . Indies*: i.e. by turning their copper and tin to gold   *admire*: marvel

Of which one part projected on a hundred
Of Mercury, or Venus, or the Moon,
Shall turn it to as many of the Sun;   40
Nay, to a thousand, so *ad infinitum*:
You will believe me.
   Sur.   Yes, when I see't, I will.
But if my eyes do cozen me so (and I
Giving 'em no occasion) sure, I'll have
A whore, shall piss 'em out, next day.
   Mam.   Ha! Why?   45
Do you think I fable with you? I assure you,
He that has once the flower of the sun,
The perfect ruby, which we call elixir,
Not only can do that, but by its virtue,
Can confer honour, love, respect, long life,   50
Give safety, valour: yea, and victory,
To whom he will. In eight and twenty days,
I'll make an old man of fourscore a child.
   Sur. No doubt, he's that already.
   Mam.   Nay, I mean,
Restore his years, renew him, like an eagle,   55
To the fifth age; make him get sons and daughters,
Young giants; as our philosophers have done
(The ancient patriarchs afore the flood)
But taking, once a week, on a knife's point,
The quantity of a grain of mustard, of it: 60
Become stout Marses, and beget young Cupids.
   Sur. The decayed vestals of Pict-hatch would thank you,
That keep the fire alive there.
   Mam.   'Tis the secret
Of nature, naturized 'gainst all infections,
Cures all diseases, coming of all causes,   65
A month's grief in a day; a year's in twelve:
And of what age soever, in a month.

39 *Venus*: copper   *Moon*: silver   40 *Sun*: gold   47 *flower of the sun*:
the philosophers' stone   48 *ruby*: the colour needed for perfect transmutation
55 *like an eagle*: Ps. 103: 5   56 *fifth age*: Dan. 2: 36–44   58 *patriarchs*: e.g.
Noah was said to have possessed the elixir and to have begotten Shem, Ham, and Japhet
62 *Pict-hatch*: noted for brothels   64 *naturized*: endowed with its special property

Past all the doses of your drugging doctors.
I'll undertake, withal, to fright the plague
Out o' the kingdom, in three months.
    Sur.   And I'll   70
Be bound, the players shall sing your praises then,
Without their poets.
    Mam.   Sir, I'll do't. Meantime,
I'll give away so much unto my man,
Shall serve the whole city, with preservative,
Weekly, each house his dose, and at the rate——   75
    Sur. As he that built the waterwork, does with water?
    Mam. You are incredulous.
    Sur.   Faith, I have a humour,
I would not willingly be gulled. Your stone
Cannot transmute me.
    Mam.   Pertinax, my Surly,
Will you believe antiquity? Records?   80
I'll show you a book, where Moses, and his sister,
And Solomon have written of the art;
Aye, and a treatise penned by Adam.
    Sur.   How!
    Mam. O' the philosophers' stone, and in high Dutch.
    Sur. Did Adam write, sir, in high Dutch?
    Mam.   He did: 85
Which proves it was the primitive tongue.
    Sur.   What paper?
    Mam. On cedar board.
    Sur.   Oh that, indeed (they say)
Will last 'gainst worms.
    Mam.   'Tis like your Irish wood
'Gainst cobwebs. I have a piece of Jason's fleece, too,
Which was no other than a book of alchemy,
Writ in large sheepskin, a good fat ram-vellum.   90

71 *the players*: who had to close the theatres during the plague   76 *waterwork*:
the much admired system for conveying Thames water to houses by lead pipes
81–3 alchemical writings (detailed in *H&S* x. 71) were commonly attributed to Adam,
Moses, Miriam, and Solomon   85 *Adam . . . in high Dutch*: the claim of Goropius
in his *Origines Antverpianae* (1569)   88 *Irish wood*: supposedly protected against
insects by the special power of St. Patrick

Such was Pythagoras' thigh, Pandora's tub;
And all that fable of Medea's charms,
The manner of our work: the bulls, our furnace,
Still breathing fire; our *argent-vive*, the dragon: 95
The dragon's teeth, mercury sublimate,
That keeps the whiteness, hardness, and the biting;
And they are gathered into Jason's helm,
(The alembic) and then sowed in Mars his field,
And thence sublimed so often, till they are fixed.   100
Both this, the Hesperian garden, Cadmus' story,
Jove's shower, the boon of Midas, Argus' eyes,
Boccace his Demogorgon, thousands more,
All abstract riddles of our stone. How now?

ACT II, Scene ii

Enter Face

  Mam. Do we succeed? Is our day come? And holds it?
  Fac. The evening will set red upon you, sir;
You have colour for it, crimson: the red ferment
Has done his office. Three hours hence, prepare you
To see projection.
  Mam.   Pertinax, my Surly,   5
Again, I say to thee, aloud: 'be rich'.
This day thou shalt have ingots: and tomorrow,

---

92 *Pythagoras' thigh*: made of gold   *tub*: Pandora's box (*poculum*) was equated with the stone in Delrio's *Disquisitiones Magicae*   93 *Medea's charms*: in restoring Aeson's youth (like an elixir) and in casting a spell on the dragon guarding the golden fleece   94 *bulls*: the fire-breathing bulls Jason nad to yoke and plough with 95 *argent-vive*: quicksilver   96 *dragon's teeth*: which sown in 'Mars his field' (l. 99) sprang up as men (Mars = iron)   98 *Jason's helm*: the cap on the cucurbit, conveying the vapour into another receiver to be condensed   100 *fixed*: transformed from a fluid or volatile to a permanent state (I. i. 68)   101 *Hesperian garden*: with golden apples guarded by a dragon   *Cadmus*: who also sowed dragon's teeth from which armed men sprang up   102 *Jove's shower*: the shower of gold in which he wooed Danae   *Argus' eyes*: transformed into the peacock's tail (II. ii. 27) 103 *Demogorgon* the 'parent of all things' (and so the source of subsequent mutations) (*II. ii*) 3 *crimson*: cf. 'ruby' (II. i. 48)

Give lords the affront. Is it, my Zephyrus, right?
Blushes the bolt's-head?

    Fac.   Like a wench with child, sir,
10 That were but now discovered to her master.

    Mam. Excellent witty Lungs! My only care is,
Where to get stuff enough now, to project on,
This town will not half serve me.

    Fac.   No, sir? Buy
The covering off o' churches.

    Mam.   That's true.

    Fac.   Yes.
15 Let 'em stand bare, as do their auditory.
Or cap 'em, new, with shingles.

    Mam.   No, good thatch:
Thatch will lie light upo' the rafters, Lungs.
Lungs, I will manumit thee, from the furnace;
I will restore thee thy complexion, Puff,
20 Lost in the embers; and repair this brain,
Hurt wi' the fume o'the metals.

    Fac.   I have blown, sir,
Hard, for your worship; thrown by many a coal,
When 'twas not beech; weighed those I put in, just,
To keep your heat still even; these bleared-eyes
25 Have waked, to read your several colours, sir,
Of the pale citron, the green lion, the crow,
The peacock's tail, the plumed swan.

    Mam.   And lastly,
Thou hast descried the flower, the *sanguis agni*?

    Fac. Yes, sir.

    Mam.   Where's master?

    Fac.   At's prayers, sir, he,
30 Good man, he's doing his devotions,
For the success.

    Mam.   Lungs, I will set a period,

---

    8 *Give lords the affront*: look them boldly in the face   9 *bolt's-head*: globular
flask with long cylindrical neck   23 *just*: exactly   25-8 *colours*: showing
stages in the alchemical process (*H&S* x. 73, 83) before the appearance of a constant
red (the flower, the *sanguis agni*)   30 *devotions*: cf. ll. 97–100

To all thy labours: thou shalt be the master
Of my seraglio.
   Fac.   Good, sir.
   Mam.   But do you hear?
I'll geld you, Lungs.
   Fac.   Yes, sir.
   Mam.   For I do mean
To have a list of wives and concubines,   35
Equal with Solomon; who had the stone
Alike with me: and I will make me a back
With the elixir that shall be as tough
As Hercules, to encounter fifty a night.
Th'art sure, thou saw'st it blood?
   Fac.   Both blood, and spirit, sir.   40
   Mam. I will have all my beds blown up; not stuffed:
Down is too hard. And then, mine oval room,
Filled with such pictures, as Tiberius took
From Elephantis, and dull Aretine
But coldly imitated. Then, my glasses,   45
Cut in more subtle angles, to disperse
And multiply the figures, as I walk
Naked between my *succubae*. My mists
I'll have of perfume, vapoured 'bout the room,
To loose ourselves in; and my baths, like pits   50
To fall into: from whence we will come forth,
And roll us dry in gossamer and roses.
(Is it arrived at ruby?)——— Where I spy
A wealthy citizen, or rich lawyer,
Have a sublimed pure wife, unto that fellow   55
I'll send a thousand pound, to be my cuckold.
   Fac. And I shall carry it?
   Mam.   No. I'll ha' no bawds,
But fathers and mothers. They will do it best.
Best of all others. And my flatterers

---

39 *fifty*: the daughters of King Thespius   44 *Elephantis*: known as an erotic
writer from references in Martial and in Suetonius (*Tiberius*, 43) *Aretine*: *Volp.* III.
iv. 80 n.   48 *succubae*: demons assuming female shape to have intercourse with
men

60 Shall be the pure and gravest of Divines,
   That I can get for money. My mere fools,
   Eloquent burgesses, and then my poets,
   The same that writ so subtly of the fart,
   Whom I will entertain, still, for that subject.
65 The few that would give out themselves to be
   Court and town-stallions, and, each where, belie
   Ladies, who are known most innocent, for them;
   Those will I beg to make me eunuchs of:
   And they shall fan me with ten ostrich tails
70 Apiece made in a plume to gather wind.
   We will be brave, Puff, now we ha' the medicine.
   My meat shall all come in in Indian shells,
   Dishes of agate, set in gold, and studded
   With emeralds, sapphires, hyacinths, and rubies.
75 The tongues of carps, dormice, and camels' heels,
   Boiled i' the spirit of Sol, and dissolved pearl,
   (Apicius' diet, 'gainst the epilepsy)
   And I will eat these broths with spoons of amber,
   Headed with diamond and carbuncle.
80 My footboy shall eat pheasants, calvered salmons,
   Knots, godwits, lampreys: I myself will have
   The beards of barbels, served instead of salads;
   Oiled mushrooms; and the swelling unctuous paps
   Of a fat pregnant sow, newly cut off,
85 Dressed with an exquisite and poignant sauce;
   For which, I'll say unto my cook, there's gold,
   Go forth, and be a knight.

  Fac.   Sir, I'll go look
A little, how it heightens.   *[Exit]*

  Mam.   Do. My shirts

---

63 *the fart*: poems on the subject found their way into print in *Musarum Deliciae*
(1656) 64 *entertain*: retain 68 *beg*: as was done with fools and lunatics (*EMO*
III. v. 12 n.) 74 *hyacinths*: the precious stone (jacinth) 77 *Apicius*: supposed
to have eaten camel's heels as a preservative against the plague 80 *calvered*: cut
up while still alive 81 *Knots*: birds larger than snipe *godwits*: marsh-birds
valued as a delicacy *lampreys*: eel-like fish 82 *barbels*: fish of the carp species
87 *knight*: a reference to the indiscriminate creation of knights under James (II. vi. 54)

I'll have of taffeta-sarsnet, soft, and light
As cobwebs; and for all my other raiment   90
It shall be such as might provoke the Persian;
Were he to teach the world riot anew.
My gloves of fishes' and birds'-skins, perfumed
With gums of paradise, and eastern air——
    Sur. And do you think to have the stone, with this?   95
    Mam. No, I do think, to have all this, with the stone.
    Sur. Why, I have heard, he must be *homo frugi*,
A pious, holy, and religious man,
One free from mortal sin, a very virgin.
    Mam. That makes it, sir, he is so. But I buy it.   100
My venture brings it me. He, honest wretch,
A notable, superstitious, good soul,
Has worn his knees bare, and his slippers bald,
With prayer and fasting for it: and, sir, let him
Do it alone, for me, still. Here he comes,   105
Not a profane word afore him: 'tis poison.

ACT II, Scene iii

Enter Subtle

    Mam. Good morrow, father.
    Sub.   Gentle son, good morrow,
And to your friend there. What is he, is with you?
    Mam. An heretic, that I did bring along,
In hope, sir, to convert him.
    Sub.   Son, I doubt
You're covetous, that thus you meet your time   5
I' the just point: prevent your day, at morning.
This argues something, worthy of a fear
Of importune and carnal appetite.
Take heed you do not cause the blessing leave you,
With your ungoverned haste. I should be sorry   10
To see my labours, now, e'en at perfection,

_____

89 *sarsnet*: soft, semi-transparent fabric of taffeta weave (made by the Saracens)
91 *the Persian*: Sardanapalus, a byword for luxury   94 *of paradise*: from the
East, supposed site of the garden of Eden   (*II. iii*) 6 *prevent*: anticipate

Got by long watching and large patience,
Not prosper, where my love and zeal hath placed 'em.
Which (heaven I call to witness, with yourself,
15 To whom I have poured my thoughts) in all my ends,
Have looked no way, but unto public good,
To pious uses, and dear charity,
Now grown a prodigy with men. Wherein
If you, my son, should now prevaricate,
20 And to your own particular lusts employ
So great and catholic a bliss: be sure,
A curse will follow, yea, and overtake
Your subtle and most secret ways.

  Mam.   I know, sir,
You shall not need to fear me. I but come,
To ha' you confute this gentleman.

25   *Sur.*   Who is,
Indeed, sir, somewhat costive of belief
Toward your stone: would not be gulled.

  Sub.   Well, son,
All that I can convince him in, is this,
The work is done: bright Sol is in his robe.
30 We have a medicine of the triple Soul,
The glorified spirit. Thanks be to heaven,
And make us worthy of it. Ulenspiegel!

  Fac. [*Within*] Anon, sir.

       [*Enter* Face]

  Sub.   Look well to the register,
And let your heat, still, lessen by degrees,
To the aludels.

  Fac. Yes, sir.

35   *Sub.*   Did you look
O'the bolt's-head yet?

  Fac.   Which, on D sir?

---

12 *watching*: i.e. at night   19 *prevaricate*: deviate from the right path
21 *catholic*: general (opposed to 'particular', l. 20)   30 *triple Soul*: the vital,
natural, and animal spirits (in the heart, liver, and brain respectively), all necessary to
the proper union of soul and body 32 *Ulenspiegel*: Owlglass (buffoon, knave)
hero of the German jestbooks (*Poet.* III. iv. 122) 33 *register*: sliding plate con-
trolling the draught 35 *aludels*: pear-shaped pots of earthenware

    Sub.   Aye.
What's the complexion?
    Fac.   Whitish.
    Sub.   Infuse vinegar,
To draw his volatile substance, and his tincture:
And let the water in glass E be filtered,
And put into the gripe's egg. Lute him well;   40
And leave him closed in *balneo.*
    Fac.   I will, sir.   [*Exit*]
    Sur. What a brave language here is? Next to canting?
    Sub. I have another work; you never saw, son,
That three days since passed the philosopher's wheel,
In the lent heat of Athanor; and's become   45
Sulphur o' nature.
    Mam.   But 'tis for me?
    Sub.   What need you?
You have enough, in that is, perfect.
    Mam.   Oh, but——
    Sub. Why, this is covetise!
    Mam.   No, I assure you,
I shall employ it all, in pious uses,
Founding of colleges and grammar schools,
Marrying young virgins, building hospitals,   50
And now and then a church.

                            [*Enter* Face]

    Sub.   How now?
    Fac.   Sir, please you,
Shall I not change the filter?
    Sub.   Marry, yes.
And bring me the complexion of glass B.   [*Exit* Face]
    Mam. Ha' you another?
    Sub.   Yes, son, were I assured   55
Your piety were firm, we would not want

    40 *gripe's egg*: vessel shaped like a vulture's egg   *Lute*: enclose in clay   41 *balneo*:
a sand- or water-bath   42 *canting*: thieves' slang   44 *philosopher's wheel*: the
cycle of alchemical processes   45 *lent*: slow   *Athanor*: digesting furnace
maintaining a steady heat   46 *Sulphur o' nature*: supposed, in combination with
mercury, to form gold   48 *covetise*: a disqualification (cf. II. ii. 96–9)

The means to glorify it. But I hope the best:
I mean to tinct C in sand-heat tomorrow,
And give him imbibition.
 Mam.   Of white oil?
60 *Sub.* No, sir, of red. F is come over the helm too,
I thank my Maker, in St Mary's bath,
And shows *lac virginis.* Blessed be heaven.
I sent you of his faeces there, calcined.
Out of that calx, I' ha' won the salt of Mercury.
65 *Mam.* By pouring on your rectified water?
 Sub. Yes, and reverberating in Athanor.

        [*Enter* Face]

How now? What colour says it?
 Fac.   The ground black, sir.
 Mam. That's your crow's-head?
 Sur.   Your cockscomb's, is it not?
 Sub. No, 'tis not perfect, would it were the crow.
That work wants something.
 (*Sur.*   Oh, I looked for this.
70 The hay is a-pitching.)
 Sub.   Are you sure, you loosed 'em
I' their own menstrue?
 Fac.   Yes, sir, and then married 'em,
And put 'em in a bolt's-head, nipped to digestion,
According as you bade me; when I set
75 The liquor of Mars to circulation,
In the same heat.
 Sub.   The process, then, was right.
 Fac. Yes, by the token, sir, the retort brake,
And what was saved, was put into the pelican,
And signed with Hermes' seal.

---

59 *imbibition*: steeping in liquid 60 *helm*: II. i. 98 61 *St Mary's bath*:
balneum Mariae, a water-bath 62 *lac virginis*: 'water of mercury' 63 *faeces*:
sediment *calcined*: burnt to a powder (calx) 64 *salt of Mercury*: oxide of
mercury 65 *rectified*: purified by repeated distillation 66 *reverberating*: heating
in a furnace where the flames beat back from the top on the substance in the bottom
68 *crow's-head*: II. ii. 26 71 *hay*: net placed ('pitched') as a snare before rabbit
holes 75 *liquor of Mars*: molten iron 78 *pelican*: vessel with long neck curved to re-
enter it 79 *Hermes' seal*: i.e. hermetically sealed by heating and twisting the neck

 Sub.   I think 'twas so.
We should have a new amalgama.
(*Sur.*   Oh, this ferret   80
Is rank as any polecat.)
 Sub.   But I care not.
Let him e'en die; we have enough beside,
In embrion. H has his white shirt on?
 Fac.   Yes, sir,
He's ripe for inceration: he stands warm,
In his ash-fire. I would not, you should let   85
Any die now, if I might counsel, sir,
For luck's sake to the rest. It is not good.
 Mam. He says right.
 (*Sur.*   Aye, are you bolted?)
 Fac.   Nay, I know't, sir,
I've seen the ill fortune. What is some three ounces
Of fresh materials?
 Mam.   Is't no more?
 Fac.   No more, sir,   90
Of gold, t' amalgam, with some six of mercury.
 Mam. Away, here's money. What will serve?
 Fac.   Ask him, sir.
 Mam. How much?
 Sub,   Give him nine pound: you may gi' him ten.
 Sur. Yes, twenty, and be cozened, do.
 Mam.   There 'tis.
 Sub. This needs not. But that you will have it, so,   95
To see conclusions of all. For two
Of our inferior works are at fixation.
A third is in ascension. Go your ways.
Ha' you set the oil of *Luna* in *kemia*?
 Fac. Yes, sir.

---

80 *amalgama*: mixture of metals with mercury   84 *inceration*: gradual admixture
of fluid to dry matter until it reaches the consistency of wax   88 *bolted*: driven
into the net (l. 71) by the ferret (l. 80)   97 *fixation*: II. i. 100   98 *ascension*:
distillation, evaporation   99 *oil of Luna*: white elixir   *kemia*: chymia (chemical
analysis)

  Sub.   And the philosopher's vinegar?

100 *Fac.*   Aye.   [*Exit*]

  Sur. We shall have a salad.

  Mam.   When do you make projection?

  Sub. Son, be not hasty, I exalt our medicine,

By hanging him in *balneo vaporoso*;

And giving him solution; then congeal him;

105 And then dissolve him; then again congeal him;

For look, how oft I iterate the work,

So many times, I add unto his virtue.

As, if at first, one ounce convert a hundred,

After his second loose, he'll turn a thousand;

110 His third solution, ten; his fourth, a hundred.

After his fifth, a thousand thousand ounces

Of any imperfect metal, into pure

Silver, or gold, in all examinations,

As good as any of the natural mine.

115 Get you your stuff here, against afternoon,

Your brass, your pewter, and your andirons.

  Mam. Not those of iron?

  Sub.   Yes. You may bring them, too.

We'll change all metals.

  Sur.   I believe you, in that.

  Mam. Then I may send my spits?

  Sub.   Yes, and your racks.

120 *Sur.* And dripping-pans, and pot-hangers, and hooks?

Shall he not?

  Sub.   If he please.

  Sur.   To be an ass.

  Sub. How, sir!

  Mam.   This gent'man, you must bear withal.

I told you, he had no faith.

  Sur.   And little hope, sir,

But much less charity, should I gull myself.

  100 *philosopher's vinegar*: mercury   101 *salad*: term seriously applied to the
combination of gold, salt, sulphur (= oil) and mercury (= vinegar)   103 *balneo
vaporoso*: vapour bath   109 *loose*: loosening, i.e. solution   116 *andirons*:
metal bars supporting the fire

   Sub. Why, what have you observed, sir, in our art,   125
Seems so impossible?
   Sur.   But your whole work, no more.
That you should hatch gold in a furnace, sir,
As they do eggs, in Egypt!
   Sub.   Sir, do you
Believe that eggs are hatched so?
   Sur.   If I should?
   Sub. Why, I think that the greater miracle.   130
No egg, but differs from a chicken more,
Than metals in themselves.
   Sur.   That cannot be.
The egg's ordained by nature to that end:
And is a chicken in *potentia*.
   Sub. The same we say of lead, and other metals,   135
Which would be gold, if they had time.
   Mam.   And that
Our art doth further.
   Sub.   Aye, for 'twere absurd
To think that nature, in the earth, bred gold
Perfect, i'the instant. Something went before.
There must be remote matter.
   Sur.   Aye, what is that?   140
   Sub. Marry, we say——
   Mam.   Aye, now it heats: stand, father.
Pound him to dust——
   Sub.   It is, of the one part,
A humid exhalation, which we call
Materia liquida, or the unctuous water;
On the other part, a certain crass and viscous   145
Portion of earth; both which, concorporate,
Do make the elementary matter of gold:
Which is not, yet, *propria materia*,
But common to all metals, and all stones.
For where it is forsaken of that moisture,   150

128 *eggs, in Egypt*: reportedly hatched in dunghills and ovens   131–76 Subtle's argument is taken from Delrio's *Disquisitiones Magicae*, i. 83, 73–5, 69–70 (*H&S* x. 81–2)   148 *propria materia*: a particular and distinct substance

And hath more dryness, it becomes a stone;
Where it retains more of the humid fatness,
It turns to sulphur, or to quick-silver:
Who are the parents of all other metals.
155 Nor can this remote matter suddenly
Progress so from extreme unto extreme,
As to grow gold, and leap o'er all the means.
Nature doth, first, beget the imperfect; then
Proceeds she to the perfect. Of that airy,
160 And oily water, mercury is engendered;
Sulphur o'the fat and earthy part: the one
(Which is the last) supplying the place of male,
The other of the female, in all metals.
Some do believe hermaphrodeity,
165 That both do act and suffer. But these two
Make the rest ductile, malleable, extensive.
And even in gold, they are; for we do find
Seeds of them, by our fire, and gold in them:
And can produce the species of each metal
170 More perfect thence than nature doth in earth.
Beside, who doth not see, in daily practice,
Art can beget bees, hornets, beetles, wasps,
Out of the carcasses and dung of creatures;
Yea, scorpions, of an herb, being ritely placed:
175 And these are living creatures, far more perfect
And excellent than metals.
    Mam.   Well said, father!
Nay, if he take you in hand, sir, with an argument,
He'll bray you in a mortar.
    Sur.   'Pray you, sir, stay.
Rather, then I'll be brayed, sir, I'll believe,
180 That Alchemy is a pretty kind of game,
Somewhat like tricks o'the cards, to cheat a man,
With charming.
    Sub.   Sir?

---

157 *means*: intermediate stages   166 *extensive*: capable of extension   174 *an herb*: basil   *ritely*: with all due rites   178 *bray*: pound into small pieces
182–207 from Delrio, i. 69, 70

 Sur.   What else are all your terms,
Whereon no one o' your writers grees with other?
Of your elixir, your *lac virginis*,
Your stone, your medicine, and your chrysosperm,   185
Your sal, your sulphur, and your mercury,
Your oil of height, your tree of life, your blood,
Your marcasite, your tutty, your magnesia,
Your toad, your crow, your dragon, and your panther,
Your sun, your moon, your firmament, your adrop,   190
Your lato, azoch, zernich, chibrit, heautarit,
And then, your red man, and your white woman,
With all your broths, your menstrues, and materials,
Of piss, and egg-shells, women's terms, man's blood,
Hair o' the head, burnt clouts, chalk, merds, and clay,   195
Powder of bones, scalings of iron, glass,
And worlds of other strange ingredients,
Would burst a man to name?
 Sub.   And all these, named
Intending but one thing: which art our writers
Used to obscure their art.
 Mam.   Sir, so I told him,   200
Because the simple idiot should not learn it,
And make it vulgar.
 Sub.   Was not all the knowledge
Of the Egyptians writ in mystic symbols?
Speak not the Scriptures oft in parables?
Are not the choicest fables of the Poets,   205
That were the fountains, and first springs of wisdom,
Wrapped in perplexed allegories?
 Mam.   I urged that,
And cleared to him, that Sisyphus was damned

---

 185 *chrysosperm*: seed of gold   187 *oil of height*: cf. l. 99   188 *marcasite*:
iron pyrites *tutty*: crude zinc oxide   189 *toad . . . crow*: black colours
appearing during the process (*panther* = spotted, *dragon* = mercury)   190 *firma-
ment*: the sphere beyond the planets, in alchemy = the stone (*H&S* x. 78)   *adrop*:
lead   191 *lato*: latten, a metal resembling brass *azoch*: quicksilver *zernich*:
orpiment, trisulphide of arsenic *chibrit*: sulphur *heautarit*: mercury   192 *red
man . . . white woman*: sulphur and mercury, the fixed and the volatile   194 *terms*:
menses   195 *merds*: ordure

To roll the ceaseless stone only because
210 He would have made ours common. (Dol *is seen*) Who is this?
    Sub. God's precious—— What do you mean? Go in, good lady,
Let me entreat you. [*She retires*] Where's this varlet?

[*Enter* Face]

    Fac.   Sir?
    Sub. You very knave! Do you use me, thus?
    Fac.   Wherein, sir?
    Sub. Go in, and see, you traitor. Go.   [*Exit* Face]
    Mam.   Who is it, sir?
    Sub. Nothing, sir. Nothing.
215   *Mam.*   What's the matter? Good sir!
I have not seen you thus distempered. Who is't?
    Sub. All arts have still had, sir, their adversaries,
But ours the most ignorant. (Face *returns*) What now?
    Fac. 'Twas not my fault, sir, she would speak with you.
    Sub. Would she, sir? Follow me.   [*Exit*]
    Mam.   Stay, Lungs.
220   *Fac.*   I dare not, sir.
    Mam. Stay man, what is she?
    Fac.   A lord's sister, sir.
    Mam. How! 'Pray thee stay?
    Fac.   She's mad, sir, and sent hither——
(He'll be mad too.
    Mam.   I warrant thee.) Why sent hither?
    Fac. Sir, to be cured.
    Sub. [*Within*]   Why, rascal!
    Fac.   Lo you. Here, sir.
                         (*He goes out*)

225   *Mam.* 'Fore God, a Bradamante, a brave piece.
    Sur. Heart, this is a bawdy house! I'll be burnt else.
    Mam. Oh, by this light, no. Do not wrong him. He's
Too scrupulous, that way. It is his vice.
No, he's a rare physician, do him right.

---

209 *ceaseless stone*: which would roll down the hill again when nearing the top: Sisyphus' punishment for betraying the secrets of the gods   225 *Bradamante*: martial heroine in Ariosto's *Orlando Furioso*

An excellent Paracelsian! And has done   230
Strange cures with mineral physic. He deals all
With spirits, he. He will not hear a word
Of Galen, or his tedious recipes.
How now, Lungs!   (Face *again*)
   Fac.   Softly, sir, speak softly. I meant
To ha' told your worship all. This must not hear.   235
   Mam. No, he will not be gulled; let him alone.
   Fac. You're very right, sir, she is a most rare scholar;
And is gone mad with studying Broughton's works.
If you but name a word, touching the Hebrew,
She falls into her fit, and will discourse   240
So learnedly of genealogies,
As you would run mad, too, to hear her, sir.
   Mam. How might one do to have conference with her, Lungs?
   Fac. Oh, divers have run mad upon the conference.
I do not know, sir: I am sent in haste,   245
To fetch a vial.
   Sur.   Be not gulled, Sir Mammon.
   Mam. Wherein? 'Pray ye, be patient.
   Sur.   Yes, as you are.
And trust confederate knaves, and bawds, and whores.
   Mam. You are too foul, believe it. Come, here, Ulen.
One word.
   Fac.   I dare not, in good faith. [*Going*]
   Mam.   Stay, knave.   250
   Fac. He's extreme angry, that you saw her, sir.
   Mam. Drink that. [*Giving money*] What is she, when she's out of
     her fit?
   Fac. Oh, the most affablest creature, sir! So merry!
So pleasant! She'll mount you up, like quick-silver,
Over the helm; and circulate, like oil,   255
A very vegetal: discourse of state,
Of mathematics, bawdry, anything——

---

230 *Paracelsian*: disciple of Paracelsus (believed to have had the secret of the stone)
who first applied a knowledge of chemistry to medicine   233 *Galen*: representing
traditional medicine   238 *Broughton*: Hugh Broughton (1549-1612), Puritan divine
and rabbinical scholar

Mam. Is she no way accessible? No means,
No trick, to give a man a taste of her—— wit——
Or so?——

    Sub. [Within]   Ulen!

260   *Fac.*   I'll come to you again, sir.   *[Exit]*

    Mam. Surly, I did not think one o' your breeding
Would traduce personages of worth.

    Sur.   Sir Epicure,
Your friend to use: yet still loth to be gulled.
I do not like your philosophical bawds.

265 Their stone is lechery enough to pay for,
Without this bait.

    Mam.   'Heart, you abuse yourself.
I know the lady, and her friends, and means,
The original of this disaster. Her brother
Has told me all.

    Sur.   And yet, you ne'er saw her
Till now?

270 *Mam.*   Oh, yes, but I forgot. I have (believe it)
One o'the treacherou'st memories, I do think,
Of all mankind. ·

    Sur.   What call you her, brother?

    Mam.   My lord——
He wi'not have his name known, now I think on't.

    Sur. A very treacherous memory!

    Mam.   O' my faith——

275 *Sur.* Tut, if you ha' it not about you, pass it,
Till we meet next.

    Mam.   Nay, by this hand, 'tis true.
He's one I honour, and my noble friend,
And I respect his house.

    Sur.   Heart! Can it be,
That a grave sir, a rich, that has no need,

280 A wise sir, too, at other times, should thus
With his own oaths and arguments make hard means
To gull himself? And this be your elixir,

    268 *original*: source, cause   282 *And*: if

Your *lapis mineralis*, and your lunary,
Give me your honest trick yet, at primero,
Or gleek; and take your *lutum sapientis*, 285
Your *menstruum simplex*: I'll have gold before you
And with less danger of the quick-silver;
Or the hot sulphur.

[*Enter* Face]

Fac. [*To* Surly]   Here's one from Captain Face, sir,
Desires you meet him i'the Temple church,
Some half hour hence, and upon earnest business. 290

(*He whispers* Mammon)

Sir, if you please to quit us now; and come
Again, within two hours; you shall have
My master busy examining o' the works;
And I will steal you in, unto the party,
That you may see her converse. Sir, shall I say,
You'll meet the Captain's worship? 295

Sur.   Sir, I will.   [*He walks aside*]
But, by attorney, and to a second purpose.
Now, I am sure, it is a bawdy-house;
I'll swear it, were the marshal here, to thank me:
The naming this Commander doth confirm it.
Don Face! Why, he's the most authentic dealer 300
I' these commodities! The superintendent
To all the queinter traffickers in town.
He is their Visitor, and does appoint
Who lies with whom; and at what hour; what price;
Which gown; and in what smock; what fall; what tire. 305
Him will I prove, by a third person, to find
The subtleties of this dark labyrinth:
Which, if I do discover, dear Sir Mammon,
You'll give your poor friend leave, though no philosopher,
To laugh: for you that are, 'tis thought, shall weep. 310

283 *lunary*: (1) the fern moonwort, (2) mercury   284 *primero . . . gleek*: card-
games   285 *lutum sapientis*: sealing paste   286 *menstruum simplex*: plain
solvent   287 *quick-silver*: for treating venereal disease   288 *sulphur*: for skin
diseases   289 *Temple church*: used for business appointments   303 *queinter*:
quibble on quaint = pudendum   304 *Visitor*: official inspector   306 *fall*:
collar lying flat (distinct from ruff)   307 *prove*: test

 Fac. Sir. He does pray, you'll not forget.

  Sur.   I will not, sir.

Sir Epicure, I shall leave you?

  Mam.   I follow you, straight. [*Exit* Surly]

 Fac. But do so, good sir, to avoid suspicion.

This gent'man has a parlous head.

315 *Mam.*   But wilt thou, Ulen,

Be constant to thy promise?

  Fac.   As my life, sir.

 Mam. And wilt thou insinuate what I am? And praise me?

And say I am a noble fellow?

  Fac.   Oh, what else, sir?

And that you'll make her royal, with the stone,

320 An empress; and yourself king of Bantam.

  Mam. Wilt thou do this?

  Fac.   Will I, sir?

  Mam.   Lungs, my Lungs!

I love thee.

  Fac. Send your stuff, sir, that my master

May busy himself, about projection.

  Mam. Th'hast witched me, rogue: take, go. [*Giving money*]

  Fac.   Your jack and all,

325 *Mam.* Thou art a villain—— I will send my jack; [sir.

And the weights too. Slave, I could bite thine ear.

Away, thou dost not care for me.

  Fac.   Not I, sir?

  Mam. Come, I was born to make thee, my good weasel;

Set thee on a bench: and, ha' thee twirl a chain

With the best lord's vermin, of 'em all.

330 *Fac.*   Away, sir.

  Mam. A Count, nay, a Count Palatine——

  Fac.   Good sir, go.

  Mam. Shall not advance thee better: no, nor faster. [*Exit*]

---

320 *Bantam*: in Java, fabled for its riches   325 *jack*: device for turning spit
326 *bite thine ear*: expression of endearment 328 *weasel*: belonging to the species
mustela erminea, whose winter fur is ermine (l. 330), worn by judges 329 *chain*:
worn by the steward in a great house 330 *vermin*: quibble on 'vermin' as a collec-
tive term including the weasel, and the 'ermine' of the judge's robe 331 *Count
Palatine*: with jurisdiction within his own territory such as belongs to the king

ACT II, Scene iv

Enter Subtle, Dol

Sub. Has he bit? Has he bit?

Fac.   And swallowed too, my Subtle.
I ha' given him line, and now he plays, i'faith.

Sub. And shall we twitch him?

Fac.   Thorough both the gills.
A wench is a rare bait, with which a man
No sooner's taken, but he straight firks mad.   5

Sub. Dol, my lord Whats'hum's sister, you must now
Bear yourself *statelich*.

Dol.   Oh, let me alone.
I'll not forget my race, I warrant you.
I'll keep my distance, laugh, and talk aloud;
Have all the tricks of a proud scurvy lady,   10
And be as rude as her woman.

Fac.   Well said, Sanguine.

Sub. But will he send his andirons?

Fac.   His jack too;
And's iron shoeing-horn: I ha' spoke to him. Well,
I must not loose my wary gamester, yonder.

Sub. Oh Monsieur Caution, that will not be gulled?   15

Fac. Aye, if I can strike a fine hook into him, now,
The Temple church, there I have cast mine angle.
Well, pray for me. I'll about it.   (*One knocks*)

Sub.   What, more gudgeons!
Dol, scout, scout [Dol *goes to window*]; stay Face, you must go to the
    door:
'Pray God, it be my Anabaptist. Who is't, Dol?   20

Dol. I know him not. He looks like a gold-end-man.

Sub. Gods so! 'Tis he, he said he would send. What call you him?
The sanctified Elder, that should deal

---

5 *firks*: threshes about   7 *statelich*: in a stately manner   8 *race*:
stock, breeding   11 *Sanguine*: the 'humour' appropriate to an amorous disposi-
tion   18 *gudgeons*: gulls   20 *Anabaptist*: of a sect emerging in Germany in
1521, advocating adult baptism, community of goods, and theocracy ('Ananias' is used
as a Puritan name)   21 *gold-end-man*: dealer in oddments of gold and other metals

For Mammon's jack and andirons! Let him in.
25 Stay, help me off, first, with my gown. [*Exit* Face *with gown*] Away
Madam, to your withdrawing chamber. [*Exit* Dol] Now,
In a new tune, new gesture, but old language.
This fellow is sent, from one negotiates with me
About the stone, too; for the holy Brethren
30 Of Amsterdam, the exiled Saints: that hope
To raise their discipline by it. I must use him
In some strange fashion now, to make him admire me.

ACT II, Scene v

Enter Ananias

  Sub. Where is my drudge?

  [*Enter* Face]

  Fac.   Sir.
  Sub.   Take away the recipient,
And rectify your menstrue, from the phlegma.
Then pour it, o' the *Sol*, in the cucurbit,
And let 'em macerate together.
  Fac.   Yes, sir.
And save the ground?
5 *Sub.*   No. *Terra damnata*
Must not have entrance in the work. Who are you?
  Ana. A faithful Brother, if it please you.
  Sub.   What's that?
A Lullianist? A Ripley? *Filius artis?*
Can you sublime, and dulcify? Calcine?

---

30 *Amsterdam*: one of the Dutch towns where the ambitions of the Anabaptists had
met resistance   (*II. v*) 1 *recipient*: vessel for receiving and condensing the product
of distillation   2 *phlegma*: tasteless and odourless substance obtained by distilla-
tion   4 *macerate*: soften by steeping   5 *Terra damnata*: sediment   7 *faithful
Brother*: taken by Subtle to refer to the Arabian alchemists so named   8 *Lullianist*:
follower of Raymond Lully (1235–1315), whose alchemical works were popularized by
Sir George Ripley (? d. 1490) *Filius artis*: cf. *Mercury Vindicated*, 26   9 *dulcify*:
wash out the soluble salts to neutralize acidity

Know you the *sapor pontic*? *Sapor stiptic*?   10
Or what is homogene, or heterogene?
   Ana. I understand no heathen language, truly.
   Sub. Heathen, you Knipper-Doling? Is *Ars sacra*,
Or *Chrysopoeia*, or *Spagyrica*,
Or the pamphysic, or panarchic knowledge,   15
A heathen language?
   Ana.   Heathen Greek, I take it.
   Sub. How? Heathen Greek?
   Ana.   All's heathen, but the Hebrew.
   Sub. Sirrah, my varlet, stand you forth, and speak to him,
Like a philosopher: answer, i'the language.
Name the vexations, and the martyrizations   20
Of metals in the work.
   Fac.   Sir, putrefaction,
Solution, ablution, sublimation,
Cohobation, calcination, ceration, and
Fixation.
   Sub.   This is heathen Greek, to you, now?
And when comes vivification?
   Fac.   After mortification.   25
   Sub. What's cohobation?
   Fac.   'Tis the pouring on
Your *Aqua Regis*, and then drawing him off,
To the trine circle of the seven spheres.
   Sub. What's the proper passion of metals?
   Fac.   Malleation.

10 in the order of 'savours', *pontick* was 'less sour' and *stiptick* 'yet less sour'
13 *Knipper-Doling*: Bernt Knipperdollinck, a leader of the Anabaptist uprising in
Munster in 1534–6, when 'the Kingdom of God' was established under John of Leyden
14 *Chrysopoeia*: making of gold   *Spagyrica*: 'separating and bringing together' (a term
associated with the methods of Paracelsus)   15 *pamphysic . . . knowledge*: knowledge
of all nature   *panarchic*: all ruling   17 *the Hebrew*: glancing at the 'Old Testa-
ment' religion of the Puritans, and at their adoption of the belief that Adam spoke
Hebrew   21 *putrefaction*: decomposition   22 *ablution*: washing away of
impurities   23 *cohobation*: redistillation   25 *mortification*: destroying the
active qualities of a substance (restored again in *vivification*)   27 *Aqua Regis*:
mixture of nitric and hydrochloric acid   28 *trine*: the process is to be repeated
three times (*H&S* x. 88)   *seven spheres*: below the alchemical 'firmament' (II.
iii. 190)   29 *passion*: attribute, property   *Malleation*: yielding to being beaten
by a hammer

Sub. What's your *ultimum supplicium auri*?

30 *Fac.*   Antimonium.

Sub. This's heathen Greek, to you? And, what's your Mercury?

Fac. A very fugitive, he will be gone, sir.

Sub. How know you him?

Fac.   By his viscosity,
His oleosity, and his suscitability.

Sub. How do you sublime him?

35 *Fac.*   With the calce of eggshells,
White marble, talc.

Sub.   Your magisterium, now?
What's that?

Fac.   Shifting, sir, your elements,
Dry into cold, cold into moist, moist in-
to hot, hot into dry.

Sub.   This's heathen Greek to you, still?
Your *lapis philosophicus*?

40 *Fac.*   'Tis a stone, and not
A stone; a spirit, a soul, and a body:
Which, if you do dissolve, it is dissolved,
If you coagulate, it is coagulated,
If you make it to fly, it flieth.

Sub.   Enough.   [*Exit* Face]

45 This's heathen Greek, to you? What are you, sir?

Ana. Please you, a servant of the exiled Brethren,
That deal with widows', and with orphans' goods;
And make a just account unto the Saints:
A deacon.

Sub.   Oh, you are sent from Master Wholesome,
Your teacher?

50 *Ana.*   From Tribulation Wholesome,
Our very zealous Pastor.

Sub.   Good. I have
Some orphans' goods to come here.

Ana.   Of what kind, sir?

---

30 *ultimum supplicium*: 'utmost punishment' (as antimony made gold less malleable)
32 *fugitive*: cf. *Mercury Vindicated*, 23   34 *suscitability*: excitability   35 *calce*:
calx   36 *talc*: III. ii. 36

Sub. Pewter, and brass, andirons, and kitchenware,
Metals, that we must use our medicine on:
Wherein the Brethren may have a penn'orth,   55
For ready money.
    Ana.   Were the orphans' parents
Sincere professors?
    Sub.   Why do you ask?
    Ana.   Because
We then are to deal justly, and give (in truth)
Their utmost value.
    Sub.   'Slid, you'd cozen, else,
And if their parents were not of the faithful?   60
I will not trust you, now I think on't,
Till I ha' talked with your Pastor. Ha' you brought money
To buy more coals?
    Ana.   No, surely.
    Sub.   No? How so?
    Ana. The Brethren bid me say unto you, sir.
Surely they will not venture any more,   65
Till they may see projection.
    Sub.   How!
    Ana.   You've had,
For the instruments, as bricks, and loam, and glasses,
Already thirty pound; and, for materials,
They say, some ninety more: and they have heard, since,
That one, at Heidelberg, made it, of an egg,   70
And a small paper of pin-dust.
    Sub.   What's your name?
    Ana. My name is Ananias.
    Sub.   Out, the varlet
That cozened the Apostles! Hence, away,
Flee Mischief; had your holy Consistory
No name to send me, of another sound,   75
Than wicked Ananias? Send your Elders
Hither to make atonement for you quickly.
And gi' me satisfaction; or out goes
The fire: and down the alembics and the furnace,

---

57 *professors*: i.e. of Anabaptism   73 *cozened the Apostles*: Acts 5: 1–10

80 *Piger Henricus*, or what not. Thou wretch,
   Both Sericon, and Bufo, shall be lost,
   Tell 'em. All hope of rooting out the Bishops,
   Or the Antichristian Hierarchy shall perish,
   If they stay threescore minutes. The Aqueity,
85 Terreity, and Sulphureity
   Shall run together again, and all be annulled,
   Thou wicked Ananias. [*Exit* Ananias] This will fetch 'em,
   And make 'em haste towards their gulling more.
   A man must deal like a rough nurse, and fright
90 Those that are froward, to an appetite.

ACT II, Scene vi

Enter Face, Drugger

   Fac. He's busy with his spirits, but we'll upon him.
   Sub. How now! What mates? What Bayards ha' we here?
   Fac. I told you he would be furious. Sir, here's Nab,
   Has brought you another piece of gold to look on:
5 (We must appease him. Give it me) and prays you,
   You would devise (what is it Nab?)
       Dru.   A sign, sir.
   Fac. Aye, a good lucky one, a thriving sign, Doctor.
   Sub. I was devising now.
   Fac.   ('Slight, do not say so,
   He will repent he ga' you any more.)
10 What say you to his constellation, Doctor?
   The Balance?
       Sub.   No, that way is stale, and common.
   A townsman, born in Taurus, gives the bull;
   Or the bull's-head: in Aries, the ram.

---

80 *Piger Henricus*: 'lazy Henry', a multiple furnace heated by a single fire   81 *Sericon*: the red tincture   *Bufo*: 'toad' (II. iii. 189) the black tincture   84 *Aqueity*:
. . . *Sulphureity*: i.e. the clarified mercury will be spoilt   90 *froward*: fractious
(*II. vi*) 2 *Bayards*: 'bold as blind Bayard' (from the magic horse given by Charlemagne
to Rinaldo) was proverbial for precipitate, blundering behaviour   10 *constellation*:
sign of the zodiac under which he was born   11 *Balance*: Libra (I. iii. 56–7)

A poor device. No, I will have his name
Formed in some mystic character; whose *radii*,   15
Striking the senses of the passers-by,
Shall, by a virtual influence, breed affections,
That may result upon the party owns it:
As thus——
   Fac.   Nab!
   Sub.   He first shall have a bell, that's Abel;
And, by it, standing one, whose name is Dee,   20
In a rug gown; there's D and Rug, that's Drug:
And, right anenst him, a Dog snarling Er;
There's Drugger, Abel Drugger. That's his sign.
And here's now mystery, and hieroglyphic!
   Fac. Abel, thou art made.
   Dru.   Sir, I do thank his worship.   25
   Fac. Six o' thy legs more will not do it, Nab.
He has brought you a pipe of tobacco, Doctor.
   Dru.   Yes, sir:
I have another thing I would impart——
   Fac. Out with it, Nab.
   Dru.   Sir, there is lodged, hard by me,
A rich young widow——
   Fac.   Good! A *bona roba*?   30
   Dru. But nineteen, at the most.
   Fac.   Very good, Abel.
   Dru. Marry, she's not in fashion, yet; she wears
A hood: but 't stands a cop.
   Fac.   No matter, Abel.
   Dru. And I do, now and then, give her a fucus——
   Fac. What! Dost thou deal, Nab?
   Sub.   I did tell you, Captain.   35
   Dru. And physic too sometime, sir: for which she trusts me

---

17 *virtual*: powerful   20 *Dee*: John Dee (1527–1608), mathematician and
astrologer   21 *rug gown*: of coarse material, worn by astrologers and mathematicians
22 *anenst*: opposite, facing   26 *legs*: bows   30 *bona roba*: well-dressed
woman; prostitute   33 *hood*: French hood (contrasted to the hat of fashion)
a cop: 'on high' (the top of the head, instead of the back)   35 *deal*: with quibble
on 'deal' in the sense of 'copulate'. For the innuendo conveyed phonetically in 'fucus'
cf. 'firks' (II. iv. 5, III. iii. 69)

With all her mind. She's come up here, of purpose
To learn the fashion.
    Fac.   Good (his match too!) on, Nab.
    Dru. And she does strangely long to know her fortune.
40   *Fac.* God's lid, Nab, send her to the Doctor, hither.
    Dru. Yes, I have spoke to her of his worship, already:
But she's afraid it will be blown abroad,
And hurt her marriage.
    Fac.   Hurt it? 'Tis the way
To heal it, if 'twere hurt; to make it more
45 Followed, and sought: Nab, thou shalt tell her this.
She'll be more known, more talked of, and your widows
Are ne'er of any price till they be famous;
Their honour is their multitude of suitors:
Send her, it may be thy good fortune. What?
Thou dost not know.
50   *Dru.*   No, sir, she'll never marry
Under a knight. Her brother has made a vow.
    Fac. What, and dost thou despair, my little Nab,
Knowing what the Doctor has set down for thee,
And seeing so many o'the city dubbed?
55 One glass o' thy water, with a Madam I know,
Will have it done, Nab. What's her brother? A knight?
    Dru. No, sir, a gentleman, newly warm in his land, sir,
Scarce cold in his one-and-twenty; that does govern
His sister, here: and is a man himself
60 Of some three thousand a year, and is come up
To learn to quarrel, and to live by his wits,
And will go down again, and die i'the country.
    Fac. How! To quarrel?
    Dru.   Yes, sir, to carry quarrels,
As gallants do, and manage 'em, by line.
65   *Fac.* 'Slid, Nab! The Doctor is the only man
In Christendom for him. He has made a table,
With mathematical demonstrations,
Touching the art of quarrels. He will give him

   54 *dubbed*: (1) as knights, (2) as cuckolds   55 *water*: a love-philtre (cf. 34–8)
   64 *by line*: with methodical accuracy

An instrument to quarrel by. Go, bring 'em, both:
Him, and his sister. And, for thee, with her   70
The Doctor happ'ly may persuade. Go to.
'Shalt give his worship a new damask suit
Upon the premises.

    Sub.   Oh, good Captain.

    Fac.   He shall,
He is the honestest fellow, Doctor. Stay not,
No offers, bring the damask, and the parties.   75

    Dru. I'll try my power, sir.

    Fac.   And thy will too, Nab.

    Sub. 'Tis good tobacco this! What is't an ounce?

    Fac. He'll send you a pound, Doctor.

    Sub.   Oh, no.

    Fac.   He will do't.
It is the goodest soul. Abel, about it.
(Thou shalt know more anon. Away, be gone.)   [*Exit* Drugger] 80
A miserable rogue, and lives with cheese,
And has the worms. That was the cause indeed
Why he came now. He dealt with me, in private,
To get a medicine for 'em.

    Sub.   And shall, sir. This works.

    Fac. A wife, a wife, for one on us, my dear Subtle: 85
We'll e'en draw lots, and he that fails shall have
The more in goods, the other has in tail.

    Sub. Rather the less. For she may be so light
She may want grains.

    Fac.   Aye, or be such a burden,
A man would scarce endure her, for the whole.   90

    Sub. Faith, best let's see her first, and then determine.

    Fac. Content. But Dol must ha' no breath on't.

    Sub.   Mum.
Away, you to your Surly yonder, catch him.

    Fac. 'Pray God, I ha' not stayed too long.

    Sub.   I fear it.   [*Exeunt*]

---

71 *happ'ly* perchance; by good fortune   87 *in tail*: quibble on the legal term
'entail' and tail = pudendum   89 *grains*: i.e. of weight, to compensate for her
'lightness'

ACT III, Scene i

Enter Tribulation Wholesome, Ananias

Tri. THESE chastisements are common to the Saints,
And such rebukes we of the Separation
Must bear, with willing shoulders, as the trials
Sent forth, to tempt our frailties.

   Ana.   In pure zeal,
5 I do not like the man: he is a heathen.
And speaks the language of Canaan, truly.

   Tri. I think him a profane person, indeed.

   Ana.   He bears
The visible mark of the Beast in his forehead.
And for his stone, it is a work of darkness,
10 And with philosophy blinds the eyes of man.

   Tri. Good Brother, we must bend unto all means,
That may give furtherance to the holy cause.

   Ana. Which his cannot: the sanctified cause
Should have a sanctified course.

   Tri.   Not always necessary.
15 The children of perdition are, oft-times,
Made instruments even of the greatest works.
Beside, we should give somewhat to man's nature,
The place he lives in, still about the fire,
And fume of metals, that intoxicate
20 The brain of man, and make him prone to passion.
Where have you greater atheists, than your cooks?
Or more profane, or choleric than your glassmen?
More Antichristian than your bell-founders?
What makes the devil so devilish, I would ask you,
25 Satan, our common enemy, but his being
Perpetually about the fire, and boiling
Brimstone and arsenic? We must give, I say,
Unto the motives, and the stirrers up

---

1 *Saints*: cf. the 'exiled Saints' of II. iv. 30   2 *Separation*: (1) by exile,
(2) by doctrinal differences   6 *the language of Canaan*: i.e. of the infidel   8 *mark
of the Beast*: i. e. of the damned (Rev. 26: 2, 19: 20)   17 *give*: concede

Of humours in the blood. It may be so,
When as the work is done, the stone is made,   30
This heat of his may turn into a zeal,
And stand up for the beauteous discipline
Against the menstruous cloth and rag of Rome.
We must await his calling, and the coming
Of the good spirit. You did fault, to upbraid him   35
With the Brethren's blessing of Heidelberg, weighing
What need we have to hasten on the work,
For the restoring of the silenced Saints,
Which ne'er will be, but by the philosophers' stone.
And so a learned Elder, one of Scotland,   40
Assured me; *aurum potabile* being
The only medicine, for the civil magistrate,
To incline him to a feeling of the cause:
And must be daily used, in the disease.
　Ana. I have not edified more, truly, by man;   45
Not since the beautiful light first shone on me:
And I am sad my zeal hath so offended.
　Tri. Let us call on him, then.
　Ana.   The motion's good,
And of the spirit; I will knock first. Peace be within.

ACT III, Scene ii

Enter Subtle

　Sub. Oh, are you come? 'Twas time. Your threescore minutes
Were at the last thread, you see; and down had gone
Furnus acediae, turris circulatorius:
Limbeck, bolt's-head, retort, and pelican

---

32 *beauteous discipline*: cant phrase for Puritanism   33 *menstruous cloth*: Rome
as 'the Scarlet Woman'   36 *Heidelberg*: II. v. 70   38 *silenced Saints*:
excommunicated by the Hampton Court Conference of 1604 for refusing the King's
supremacy, the Prayer Book, and the Thirty-Nine Articles   41 *aurum potabile*:
cordial prepared from gold (here taken as a bribe)   45 *edified*: been strengthened
by instruction   (*III. ii*) 3 *Furnus acediae*: the 'furnace of sloth' of II. v. 80
turris circulatorius: circulation tower

5   Had all been cinders. Wicked Ananias!
    Art thou returned? Nay then, it goes down yet.
      Tri. Sir, be appeased, he is come to humble
    Himself in spirit, and to ask your patience,
    If too much zeal hath carried him aside
    From the due path.
10   *Sub.*   Why, this doth qualify!
      Tri. The Brethren had no purpose, verily,
    To give you the least grievance: but are ready
    To lend their willing hands to any project
    The spirit and you direct.
      Sub.   This qualifies more!
15   *Tri.* And for the orphans' goods, let them be valued,
    Or what is needful, else, to the holy work,
    It shall be numbered: here, by me, the Saints
    Throw down their purse before you.
      Sub.   This qualifies, most!
    Why, thus it should be, now you understand.
20   Have I discoursed so unto you, of our stone?
    And of the good that it shall bring your cause?
    Showed you (beside the main of hiring forces
    Abroad, drawing the Hollanders, your friends,
    From the Indies, to serve you, with all their fleet)
25   That even the medicinal use shall make you a faction,
    And party in the realm? As, put the case,
    That some great man in state, he have the gout,
    Why, you but send three drops of your elixir,
    You help him straight: there you have made a friend.
30   Another has the palsy, or the dropsy,
    He takes of your incombustible stuff,
    He's young again: there you have made a friend.
    A lady, that is past the feat of body,
    Though not of mind, and hath her face decayed
35   Beyond all cure of paintings, you restore
    With the oil of talc; there you have made a friend:

---

10 *qualify*: moderate (the offence)   31 *incombustible stuff*: e.g. the 'oyle incombustable' that was part of the alchemist's repertoire   36 *oil of talc*: a facewash, but here probably the white elixir (II. iii. 99)

And all her friends. A lord, that is a leper,
A knight, that has the bone-ache, or a squire
That hath both these, you make 'em smooth and sound,
With a bare fricace of your medicine: still,   40
You increase your friends.
   Tri.   Aye, 'tis very pregnant.
   Sub. And, then, the turning of this lawyer's pewter
To plate, at Christmas——
   Ana.   Christ-tide, I pray you.
   Sub. Yet, Ananias?
   Ana.   I have done.
   Sub.   Or changing
His parcel gilt to massy gold. You cannot   45
But raise you friends. Withal, to be of power
To pay an army, in the field, to buy
The king of France out of his realms; or Spain,
Out of his Indies: what can you not do,
Against lords spiritual, or temporal,   50
That shall oppone you?
   Tri.   Verily, 'tis true.
We may be temporal lords ourselves, I take it.
   Sub. You may be anything, and leave off to make
Long-winded exercises: or suck up,
Your 'ha' and 'hum' in a tune. I not deny,   55
But such as are not graced in a state,
May, for their ends, be adverse in religion,
And get a tune, to call the flock together:
For (to say sooth) a tune does much with women,
And other phlegmatic people; it is your bell.   60
   Ana. Bells are profane: a tune may be religious.
   Sub. No warning with you? Then farewell my patience.
'Slight, it shall down: I will not be thus tortured.
   Tri. I pray you, sir.
   Sub.   All shall perish. I have spoke it.

---

38 *bone-ache*: venereal disease   40 *fricace*: rubbing, massage   43 *Christ-tide*:
avoiding the Popish 'mass'   45 *parcel gilt*: silverware partly gilded   51 *oppone*:
oppose   55 *'ha' and 'hum'*: Puritan mannerisms   61 *Bells are profane*:
because of their Popish associations

65   *Tri.* Let me find grace, sir, in your eyes; the man
      He stands corrected: neither did his zeal
      (But as yourself) allow a tune, somewhere.
      Which, now, being toward the stone, we shall not need.
         Sub. No, nor your holy vizard, to win widows
70 To give you legacies; or make zealous wives
      To rob their husbands, for the common cause:
      Nor take the start of bonds, broke but one day,
      And say they were forfeited, by providence.
      Nor shall you need, o'er night to eat huge meals,
75 To celebrate your next day's fast the better:
      The whilst the Brethren, and the Sisters, humbled,
      Abate the stiffness of the flesh. Nor cast
      Before your hungry hearers scrupulous bones,
      As whether a Christian may hawk or hunt;
80 Or whether Matrons of the holy assembly
      May lay their hair out, or wear doublets,
      Or have that idol starch about their linen.
         Ana. It is, indeed, an idol.
         Tri.   Mind him not, sir.
      I do command thee, spirit (of zeal, but trouble)
85 To peace within him. Pray you, sir, go on.
         Sub. Nor shall you need to libel 'gainst the prelates,
      And shorten so your ears, against the hearing
      Of the next wire-drawn grace. Nor of necessity
      Rail against plays, to please the alderman,
90 Whose daily custard you devour. Nor lie
      With zealous rage, till you are hoarse. Not one
      Of these so singular arts. Nor call yourselves,
      By names of Tribulation, Persecution,
      Restraint, Long-Patience, and such like, affected
95 By the whole family, or wood of you,
      Only for glory, and to catch the ear

---

72 *take the start of*: repudiate   *broke*: negotiated   81 *lay their hair out*: i.e.
with the wires and wreaths of fashion   *doublets*: properly worn by men, so an offence
against Deut. 22: 5   82 *starch*: condemned by the Puritans (*BF* I. iii. 118)
87 *ears*: cropped as a punishment accompanying the pillory   89 *alderman*: of
Puritan leanings   90 *custard*: *Volp.* Prol., 21 n.   95 *wood*: collection, as in
The Underwood

Of the disciple.
 Tri.   Truly, sir, they are
Ways that the godly Brethren have invented
For propagation of the glorious cause,
As very notable means, and whereby also   100
Themselves grow soon, and profitably famous.
 Sub. Oh, but the stone, all's idle to it! Nothing!
The art of angels, Nature's miracle,
The divine secret, that doth fly in clouds,
From east to west: and whose tradition   105
Is not from men, but spirits.
 Ana.   I hate traditions:
I do not trust them——
 Tri.   Peace.
 Ana.   They are Popish, all.
I will not peace. I will not——
 Tri.   Ananias.
 Ana. Please the profane, to grieve the godly: I may not.
 Sub. Well, Ananias, thou shalt overcome.   110
 Tri. It is an ignorant zeal that haunts him, sir.
But truly, else, a very faithful Brother,
A botcher: and a man, by revelation,
That hath a competent knowledge of the truth.
 Sub. Has he a competent sum, there, i' the bag, 115
To buy the goods within? I am made guardian,
And must, for charity and conscience sake,
Now see the most be made for my poor orphan:
Though I desire the Brethren, too, good gainers.
There they are, within. When you have viewed, and bought 'em, 120
And ta'en the inventory of what they are,
They're ready for projection; there's no more
To do: cast on the medicine so much silver
As there is tin there, so much gold as brass,
I'll gi' it you in, by weight.   125
 Tri.   But how long time,
Sir, must the Saints expect, yet?
 Sub.   Let me see,

 113 *botcher*: tailor who did repairs 126 *expect*: wait

How's the moon now? Eight, nine, ten days hence
He will be silver potate; then three days
Before he citronise: some fifteen days,
130 The magisterium will be perfected.
  Ana. About the second day, of the third week,
In the ninth month?
  Sub.   Yes, my good Ananias.
  Tri. What will the orphans' goods arise to, think you?
  Sub. Some hundred marks; as much as filled three cars,
135 Unladed now: you'll make six millions of 'em.
But I must ha' more coals laid in.
  Tri.   How!
  Sub.   Another load,
And then we ha' finished. We must now increase
Our fire to *ignis ardens*, we are past
Fimus equinus, *balnei*, *cineris*,
140 And all those lenter heats. If the holy purse
Should, with this draught, fall low, and that the Saints
Do need a present sum, I have a trick
To melt the pewter, you shall buy now, instantly,
And with a tincture, make you as good Dutch dollars,
As any are in Holland.
145   *Tri.*   Can you so?
  Sub. Aye, and shall bide the third examination.
  Ana. It will be joyful tidings to the Brethren.
  Sub. But you must carry it, secret.
  Tri.   Aye, but stay,
This act of coining, is it lawful?
  Ana.   Lawful?
150 We know no magistrate. Or, if we did,
This's foreign coin.
  Sub.   It is no coining, sir.
It is but casting.
  Tri.   Ha? You distinguish well.

---

128 *silver potate*: liquefied silver   129 *citronise*: achieve the colour indicating
'complete digestion'   138 *ignis ardens*: the greatest heat, exceeding the 'lenter'
stages of *fimus equinus* (I. i. 84) and *balnei* and *cineris* (II. iii. 41, 85)   150 *no
magistrate*: i.e. his authority in matters of religion was not accepted by Anabaptists or
Puritans   151-2 *coining . . . casting*: aimed at Puritan casuistry

Casting of money may be lawful.

Ana.   'Tis, sir.

Tri. Truly, I take it so.

Sub.   There is no scruple,

Sir, to be made of it; believe Ananias: 155

This case of conscience he is studied in.

Tri. I'll make a question of it to the Brethren.

Ana. The Brethren shall approve it lawful, doubt not.

Where shall't be done?   (*Knock without*)

Sub.   For that we'll talk anon.

There's some to speak with me. Go in, I pray you,   160

And view the parcels. That's the inventory.

I'll come to you straight.   [*Exeunt* Tribulation, Ananias]

Who is it? Face! Appear.

ACT III, Scene iii

Enter Face

Sub. How now? Good prize?

Fac.   Good pox! Yond' costive cheater

Never came on.

Sub.   How then?

Fac.   I ha' walked the round,

Till now, and no such thing.

Sub.   And ha' you quit him?

Fac. Quit him? And hell would quit him too, he were happy.

'Slight would you have me stalk like a mill-jade,   5

All day, for one, that will not yield us grains?

I know him of old.

Sub.   Oh, but to ha' gulled him,

Had been a maistry.

Fac.   Let him go, black boy,

And turn thee, that some fresh news may possess thee.

A noble Count, a Don of Spain (my dear   10

---

2 *walked the round*: kept a look-out, with a quibble on the 'round' of the Temple
Church (II. iii. 289)   8 *maistry*: master-stroke

Delicious compeer, and my party-bawd)
Who is come hither, private, for his conscience,
And brought munition with him, six great slops,
Bigger than three Dutch hoys, beside round trunks,
15 Furnished with pistolets, and pieces of eight,
Will straight be here, my rogue, to have thy bath
(That is the colour,) and to make his battery
Upon our Dol, our castle, our *cinque* Port,
Our Dover pier, our what thou wilt. Where is she?
20 She must prepare perfumes, delicate linen,
The bath in chief, a banquet, and her wit,
For she must milk his epididymis.
Where is the doxy?
    Sub.   I'll send her to thee:
And but dispatch my brace of little John Leydens,
And come again myself.
25   *Fac.*   Are they within then?
    Sub. Numbering the sum.
    Fac.   How much?
    Sub.   A hundred marks, boy.
                    [*Exit*]

    Fac. Why, this's a lucky day! Ten pounds of Mammon!
Three o' my clerk! A portague o' my grocer!
This o' the Brethren! Beside reversions,
30 And states, to come i' the widow, and my Count!
My share today will not be bought for forty——

              [*Enter* Dol]
    Dol.   What?
    Fac. Pounds, dainty Dorothy, art thou so near?
    Dol. Yes, say lord General, how fares our camp?
    Fac. As with the few, that had entrenched themselves

---

11 *compeer*: comrade   13 *slops*: wide puffed breeches   14 *hoys*: *Volp.* IV.
i. 60 n.   *trunks*: trunk-hose, breeches extending to the knee and stuffed to an
enormous size   15 *pistolets*: Spanish gold coins worth from 16*s*. 8*d*. to 18*s*.
pieces of eight: the Spanish *peso* worth eight reales   17 *colour*: pretext   18 *cinque*
Port: one of the five defensive ports (including Dover) on the SE coast   22 *epi-
didymis*: duct leading from the back of the testicles   24 *John Leydens*: Anabaptists
(II. v. 13 n.)   33 from the opening of Kyd's *Spanish Tragedy*

Safe, by their discipline, against a world, Dol: 35
And laughed, within those trenches, and grew fat
With thinking on the booties, Dol, brought in
Daily, by their small parties. This dear hour,
A doughty Don is taken, with my Dol;
And thou mayst make his ransom what thou wilt,   40
My Dousabel: he shall be brought here, fettered
With thy fair looks, before he sees thee; and thrown
In a down-bed, as dark as any dungeon;
Where thou shalt keep him waking, with thy drum;
Thy drum, my Dol; thy drum; till he be tame   45
As the poor blackbirds were i' the great frost,
Or bees are with a basin: and so hive him
I'the swan-skin coverlid, and cambric sheets,
Till he work honey and wax, my little God's-gift.
   Dol. What is he, General?
   Fac.   An Adelantado,   50
A Grandee, girl. Was not my Dapper here yet?
   Dol. No.
   Fac.   Nor my Drugger?
   Dol.   Neither.
   Fac.   A pox on 'em,
They are so long a-furnishing! Such stinkards
Would not be seen, upon these festival days.
               [Enter Subtle]
How now! Ha' you done?
   Sub.   Done. They are gone. The sum   55
Is here in bank, my Face. I would we knew
Another chapman, now, would buy 'em outright.
   Fac. 'Slid, Nab shall do't, against he ha' the widow,
To furnish household.
   Sub.   Excellent, well thought on,
Pray God he come.
   Fac.   I pray he keep away   60

41 *Dousabel*: lady-love, sweetheart   44 *drum*: continuing the military metaphor,
and punning on drum = belly   46 *great frost*: from December 1607 to February
1608, when the Thames was frozen over   47 *bees*: induced to hive by beating
a dish   49 *God's-gift*: Dorothea (Gr.)   50 *Adelantado*: grandee, governor
57 *chapman*: dealer

Till our new business be o'er-past.
    Sub.   But, Face,
How cam'st thou by this secret Don?
    Fac.   A spirit
Brought me the intelligence, in a paper, here,
As I was conjuring, yonder, in my circle
65 For Surly: I ha' my flies abroad. Your bath
Is famous, Subtle, by my means. Sweet Dol,
You must go tune your virginal, no losing
O' the least time. And do you hear? Good action.
Firk like a flounder; kiss like a scallop, close:
70 And tickle him with thy mother-tongue. His great
Verdugo-ship has not a jot of language:
So much the easier to be cozened, my Dolly.
He will come here, in a hired coach, obscure,
And our own coachman, whom I have sent, as guide,
No creature else. (*One knocks*) Who's that?
75   *Sub.*   It i' not he?
    Fac. Oh no, not yet this hour.
    Sub.   Who is't?
    Dol. [*At window*]   Dapper,
Your clerk.
    Fac.   God's will, then, Queen of Faery,
On with your tire; and, Doctor, with your robes.
Let's dispatch him, for God's sake.   [*Exit* Dol]
    Sub.   'Twill be long.
80   *Fac.* I warrant you, take but the cues I give you,
It shall be brief enough. 'Slight, here are more!
Abel, and I think, the angry boy, the heir,
That fain would quarrel.
    Sub.   And the widow?
    Fac.   No,
Not that I see. Away.   [*Exit* Subtle]
        Oh, sir, you are welcome.

64 *circle*: the 'round' of l. 2 taken as the magician's circle   65 *flies*: familiars
(I. ii. 43)   67 *virginal*: keyboard stringed instrument (with innuendo)   69 *Firk*:
II. iv. 5   *scallop*: cf. 'kisses close as a cockle' (*CR* V. iv. 481)   71 *Verdugo-ship*:
mock title from verdugo = hangman   82 *angry boy*: term for a quarrelsome
roisterer, like Cutting in *BF*

ACT III, Scene iv

Enter Dapper

Fac. The Doctor is within, a-moving for you;
(I have had the most ado to win him to it)
He swears, you'll be the darling o' the dice:
He never heard her Highness dote, till now (he says).
Your aunt has given you the most gracious words   5
That can be thought on.
   Dap.   Shall I see her Grace?
   Fac. See her, and kiss her, too.

           [*Enter* Drugger, Kastril]
                  What? Honest Nab!
Hast brought the damask?
   Nab.   No, sir, here's tobacco.
   Fac. 'Tis well done, Nab: thou'lt bring the damask too?
   Dru. Yes, here's the gentleman, Captain, Master Kastril,   10
I have brought to see the Doctor.
   Fac.   Where's the widow?
   Dru. Sir, as he likes, his sister (he says) shall come.
   Fac. Oh, is it so? 'Good time. Is your name Kastril, sir?
   Kas. Aye, and the best o'the Kastrils, I'd be sorry else,
By fifteen hundred, a year. Where is this Doctor?   15
My mad tobacco boy, here, tells me of one
That can do things. Has he any skill?
   Fac.   Wherein, sir?
   Kas. To carry a business, manage a quarrel, fairly,
Upon fit terms.
   Fac.   It seems sir, you're but young
About the town, that can make that a question!   20
   Kas. Sir, not so young, but I have heard some speech
Of the angry boys, and seen 'em take tobacco;
And in his shop: and I can take it too.
And I would fain be one of 'em, and go down
And practise i'the country.

13 *Kastril*: named after the wild hawk   18 *carry a business*: officiate
in a duel   in a duel

25   *Fac.*   Sir, for the *Duello*,
The Doctor, I assure you, shall inform you,
To the least shadow of a hair: and show you,
An instrument he has, of his own making,
Wherewith, no sooner shall you make report
30 Of any quarrel, but he will take the height on't,
Most instantly; and tell in what degree,
Of safety it lies in, or mortality.
And how it may be borne, whether in a right line,
Or a half-circle; or may, else, be cast
35 Into an angle blunt, if not acute:
All this he will demonstrate. And then, rules,
To give and take the lie by.
    Kas.   How? To take it?
    Fac. Yes, in oblique, he'll show you; or in circle:
But never in diameter. The whole town
40 Study his theorems, and dispute them, ordinarily,
At the eating academies.
    Kas.   But does he teach
Living by the wits too?
    Fac.   Anything, whatever.
You cannot think that subtlety, but he reads it.
He made me a Captain. I was a stark pimp,
45 Just o' your standing, 'fore I met with him:
It i' not two months since. I'll tell you his method.
First, he will enter you, at some ordinary.
    Kas. No, I'll not come there. You shall pardon me.
    Fac.   For why, sir?
    Kas. There's gaming there, and tricks.
    Fac.   Why, would you be
A gallant, and not game?
50   *Kas.*   Aye, 'twill spend a man.
    Fac. Spend you? It will repair you, when you are spent.
How do they live by their wits, there, that have vented

---

25 *Duello*: conducted by elaborate rules, expounded here (ll. 33–41) in terms of
geometry, and at IV. ii. 21–8 in terms of grammar and logic   39 *in diameter*: i.e.
directly (*EMI* IV. vii. 25)   41 *eating academies*: the ordinaries   50 *spend a
man*: i.e. waste his substance   52 *vented*: spent

Six times your fortunes?

 Kas.   What, three thousand a year!

 Fac. Aye, forty thousand.

 Kas.   Are there such?

 Fac.   Aye, sir.

And gallants, yet. Here's a young gentleman,   55
Is born to nothing, forty marks a year,
Which I count nothing. He's to be initiated,
And have a fly o'the Doctor. He will win you
By unresistable luck, within this fortnight,
Enough to buy a barony. They will set him   60
Upmost, at the groom-porter's, all the Christmas!
And for the whole year through, at every place,
Where there is play, present him with the chair;
The best attendance, the best drink, sometimes
Two glasses of canary, and pay nothing;   65
The purest linen, and the sharpest knife,
The partridge next his trencher: and, somewhere
The dainty bed, in private, with the dainty.
You shall ha' your ordinaries bid for him,
As play-houses for a poet; and the master   70
Pray him aloud to name what dish he affects,
Which must be buttered shrimps: and those that drink
To no mouth else, will drink to his, as being
The goodly, president mouth of all the board.

 Kas. Do you not gull one?

 Fac.   'Od's my life! Do you think it?   75
You shall have a cast commander (can but get
In credit with a glover, or a spurrier,
For some two pair, of either's ware, aforehand)
Will, by most swift posts, dealing with him,
Arrive at competent means, to keep himself,   80
His punk, and naked boy, in excellent fashion.
And be admired for't.

 Kas.   Will the Doctor teach this?

---

61 *groom-porter's*: officer of the Lord Chamberlain who superintended play at cards, dice, and bowls   65 *canary*: light sweet wine from Canary Is.   76 *cast*: cashiered   79 *by most swift posts*: with the speed of a post-horse

    Fac. He will do more, sir, when your land is gone,
    (As men of spirit hate to keep earth long)
85 In a vacation, when small money is stirring,
    And ordinaries suspended till the term,
    He'll show a perspective, where on one side
    You shall behold the faces, and the persons
    Of all sufficient young heirs, in town,
90 Whose bonds are current for commodity;
    On the other side, the merchants' forms, and others,
    That, without help of any second broker,
    (Who would expect a share) will trust such parcels:
    In the third square, the very street, and sign
95 Where the commodity dwells, and does but wait
    To be delivered, be it pepper, soap,
    Hops, or tobacco, oatmeal, woad, or cheeses.
    All which you may so handle, to enjoy,
    To your own use, and never stand obliged.
100   *Kas.* I'faith! Is he such a fellow?
    Fac.   Why, Nab here knows him.
    And then for making matches, for rich widows,
    Young gentlewomen, heirs, the fortunat'st man!
    He's sent to, far and near, all over England,
    To have his counsel, and to know their fortunes.
105   *Kas.* God's will, my suster shall see him.
    Fac.   I'll tell you, sir,
    What he did tell me of Nab. It's a strange thing!
    (By the way you must eat no cheese, Nab, it breeds melancholy:
    And that some melancholy breeds worms) but pass it,
    He told me, honest Nab, here, was ne'er at tavern,
110 But once in's life.
    Dru.   Truth, and no more I was not.
    Fac. And then he was so sick——
    Dru.   Could he tell you that, too?
    Fac. How should I know it?
    Dru.   In troth we had been a-shooting,

---

   84 *earth*: the basest of the elements   87 *perspective*: picture so constructed as to assume different aspects from different points of view (or possibly a magic glass) 90 *commodity*: II. i. 11 n.   97 *woad*: blue dye

And had a piece of fat ram-mutton, to supper,
That lay so heavy o' my stomach——
    Fac.   And he has no head
To bear any wine; for what with the noise o'the fiddlers,   115
And care of his shop, for he dares keep no servants——
    Dru. My head did so ache——
    Fac.   As he was fain to be brought home,
The Doctor told me. And then, a good old woman——
    Dru. (Yes, faith, she dwells in Seacoal Lane) did cure me,
With sodden ale, and pellitory o'the wall: 120
Cost me but twopence. I had another sickness,
Was worse than that.
    Fac.   Aye, that was with the grief
Thou took'st for being 'sessed at eighteen pence,
For the waterwork.
    Dru.   In truth, and it was like
To have cost me almost my life.   125
    Fac.   Thy hair went off?
    Dru. Yes, sir, 'twas done for spite.
    Fac.   Nay, so says the Doctor.
    Kas. Pray thee, tobacco boy, go fetch my suster,
I'll see this learned boy, before I go:
And so shall she.
    Fac.   Sir, he is busy now:
But, if you have a sister to fetch hither,   130
Perhaps your own pains may command her sooner;
And he, by that time, will be free.
    Kas.   I go.   *[Exit]*
    Fac. Drugger, she's thine: the damask. *[Exit* Drugger] (Subtle
    and I
Must wrestle for her.) Come on, Master Dapper.
You see, how I turn clients, here, away,   135
To give your cause dispatch. Ha' you performed
The ceremonies were enjoined you?
    Dap.   Yes, o'the vinegar,

---

119 *Seacoal Lane*: off Snow Hill in the ward of Faringdon Without   120 *sodden*:
boiled   *pellitory o' the wall*: low bushy plant used medicinally   124 *waterwork*:
II. i. 76 ('sessed = assessed)

And the clean shirt.

  Fac.   'Tis well: that shirt may do you
More worship than you think. Your aunt's afire,
140 But that she will not show it, to have a sight on you.
Ha' you provided for her Grace's servants?

  Dap. Yes, here are six score Edward shillings.

  Fac.   Good.

  Dap. And an old Harry's sovereign.

  Fac.   Very good.

  Dap. And three James shillings, and an Elizabeth groat,
Just twenty nobles.

145   *Fac.*   Oh, you are too just.
I would you had had the other noble in Maries.

  Dap. I have some Philip and Maries.

  Fac.   Aye, those same
Are best of all. Where are they? Hark, the Doctor.

ACT III, Scene v

Enter Subtle *disguised like a Priest of Faery*

  Sub. Is yet her Grace's cousin come?

  Fac.   He is come.

  Sub. And is he fasting?

  Fac.   Yes.

  Sub.   And hath cried 'hum'?

  Fac. Thrice, you must answer.

  Dap.   Thrice.

  Sub.   And as oft 'buzz'?

  Fac. If you have, say.

  Dap.   I have.

  Sub.   Then, to her coz,
5 Hoping, that he hath vinegared his senses,
As he was bid, the Faery Queen dispenses,

---

143 *old Harry's sovereign*: worth 10s.   144 *groat*: worth 4d.   145 *nobles*:
worth 6s. 8d. *just*: exact 148 *best of all*: unexplained

By me, this robe, the petticoat of Fortune;
Which that he straight put on, she doth importune.
And though to Fortune near be her petticoat,
Yet nearer is her smock, the Queen doth note: 10
And therefore, even of that a piece she hath sent,
Which, being a child, to wrap him in, was rent;
And prays him, for a scarf, he now will wear it
(With as much love, as then her Grace did tear it)
About his eyes, to show, he is fortunate.   15

                               (They blind him with a rag)

And trusting unto her to make his state,
He'll throw away all wordly pelf about him;
Which that he will perform, she doth not doubt him.
  Fac. She need not doubt him, sir. Alas, he has nothing,   20
But what he will part withal, as willingly,
Upon her Grace's word (throw away your purse)
As she would ask it: (handkerchiefs, and all)
She cannot bid that thing, but he'll obey.

                           (He throws away, as they bid him)

(If you have a ring about you, cast it off,
Or a silver seal, at your wrist, her Grace will send   25
Her faeries here to search you, therefore deal
Directly with her Highness. If they find
That you conceal a mite, you are undone.)
  Dap. Truly, there's all.
  Fac.   All what?
  Dap.   My money, truly.
  Fac. Keep nothing that is transitory about you.   30
(Bid Dol play music.) (Dol *enters with a cithern*) Look, the elves are
    come
To pinch you, if you tell not truth. Advise you.   *(They pinch him)*
  Dap. Oh, I have a paper with a spur-rial in't.
  Fac.   *Ti, ti,*
They knew't, they say.
  Sub.   *Ti, ti, ti, ti,* he has more yet.

9–10 'Ny is my kyrtell, but nere is my smocke' (Heywood's *Proverbs*)   31 *cithern*:
guitar-like instrument   33 *spur-rial*: a rial struck by Edward IV with a blazing
sun resembling the rowel of a spur on the reverse, worth 15*s*.

Fac. Ti, *ti-ti-ti.* I'the tother pocket?

35 *Sub.*   *Titi, titi, titi, titi.*
They must pinch him, or he will never confess, they say.

Dap. Oh, oh.

Fac.   Nay, 'pray you hold. He is her Grace's nephew.
Ti, ti, ti? What care you? Good faith, you shall care.
Deal plainly, sir, and shame the faeries. Show
You are an innocent.

40 *Dap.*   By this good light, I ha' nothing.

Sub. Ti ti, ti ti to ta. He does equivocate, she says:
Ti, ti do ti, ti ti do, ti da. And swears by the light, when he is blinded.

Dap. By this good dark, I ha' nothing but a half-crown
Of gold, about my wrist, that my love gave me;

45 And a leaden heart I wore, sin' she forsook me.   [*Exit* Dol]

Fac. I thought 'twas something. And would you incur
Your aunt's displeasure for these trifles? Come,
I had rather you had thrown away twenty half-crowns.
You may wear your leaden heart still.

[*Enter* Dol]

                                    How now?

Sub. What news, Dol?

50 *Dol.*   Yonder's your knight, Sir Mammon.

Fac. God's lid, we never thought of him, till now.
Where is he?

Dol.   Here, hard by. He's at the door.

Sub. [*To* Face] And you are not ready, now? Dol, get his suit.
                                        [*Exit* Dol]

He must not be sent back.

Fac.   Oh, by no means.

55 What shall we do with this same puffin, here,
Now he's o'the spit?

Sub.   Why, lay him back a while,
With some device.

[*Enter* Dol *with* Face's *suit*]

43-4 *half-crown Of gold*: first coined by Henry VIII   55 *puffin*: (1) puffed-up
person, (2) the sea bird   56 *lay him back*: i.e. from roasting

    Ti, ti ti, ti ti ti. Would her Grace speak with me?
I come. Help, Dol.
 Fac. (*He speaks through the keyhole, the other knocking*) Who's
  there? Sir Epicure;
My master's i'the way. Please you to walk   60
Three or four turns, but till his back be turned,
And I am for you. Quickly, Dol.
 Sub.   Her Grace
Commends her kindly to you, Master Dapper.
 Dap. I long to see her Grace.
 Sub.   She now is set
At dinner in her bed; and she has sent you,
From her own private trencher, a dead mouse,   65
And a piece of gingerbread, to be merry withal,
And stay your stomach, lest you faint with fasting:
Yet, if you could hold out till she saw you (she says)
It would be better for you.
 Fac.   Sir, he shall
Hold out, and 'twere this two hours, for her Highness; 70
I can assure you that. We will not lose
All we ha' done——
 Sub.   He must nor see nor speak
To anybody till then.
 Fac.   For that, we'll put, sir,
A stay in's mouth.
 Sub.   Of what?
 Fac.   Of gingerbread.
Make you it fit. He that hath pleased her Grace,   75
Thus far, shall not now crinkle, for a little.
Gape sir, and let him fit you. [*Thrusting gingerbread into his mouth*]
 Sub.   Where shall we now
Bestow him?
 Dol.   I' the privy.
 Sub.   Come along, sir,
I now must show you Fortune's privy lodgings.
 Fac. Are they perfumed? And his bath ready?
 Sub.   All.

76 *crinkle*: shrink, recoil

Only the fumigation's somewhat strong.

                      [*Exeunt* Subtle, Dol, Dapper]

  Fac. Sir Epicure, I am yours, sir, by and by.

ACT IV, Scene i

Enter Sir Epicure Mammon

  Fac. OH, sir, you're come i'the only, finest time——

  Mam. Where's master?

  Fac.   Now preparing for projection, sir.

Your stuff will be all changed shortly.

  Mam.   Into gold?

  Fac. To gold and silver, sir.

  Mam.   Silver I care not for.

  Fac. Yes, sir, a little to give beggars.

5 *Mam.*   Where's the lady?

  Fac. At hand, here. I ha' told her such brave things o' you,

Touching your bounty and your noble spirit——

  Mam.   Hast thou?

  Fac. As she is almost in her fit to see you.

But, good sir, no divinity i' your conference,

For fear of putting her in rage——

10 *Mam.*   I warrant thee.

  Fac. Six men will not hold her down. And then,

If the old man should hear, or see you——

  Mam.   Fear not.

  Fac. The very house, sir, would run mad. You know it

How scrupulous he is, and violent,

15 'Gainst the least act of sin. Physic, or mathematics,

Poetry, state, or bawdry (as I told you)

She will endure, and never startle: but

No word of controversy.

  Mam.   I am schooled, good Ulen.

  Fac. And you must praise her house, remember that,

And her nobility.

20 *Mam.*   Let me alone:

No herald, no nor antiquary, Lungs,
Shall do it better. Go.
    Fac. [*Aside*]   Why, this is yet
A kind of modern happiness, to have
Dol Common for a great lady.   [*Exit*]
    Mam.   Now, Epicure,
Heighten thyself, talk to her, all in gold;   25
Rain her as many showers, as Jove did drops
Unto his Danae: show the god a miser,
Compared with Mammon. What? The stone will do't.
She shall feel gold, taste gold, hear gold, sleep gold:
Nay, we will *concumbere* gold. I will be puissant,   30
And mighty in my talk to her! Here she comes.

[*Enter* Dol, Face]

    Fac. To him, Dol, suckle him. This is the noble knight
I told your ladyship——
    Mam.   Madam, with your pardon,
I kiss your vesture.
    Dol.   Sir, I were uncivil
If I would suffer that, my lip to you, sir.   35
    Mam. I hope, my lord your brother be in health, lady?
    Dol. My lord, my brother is, though I no lady, sir.
    Fac. (Well said my Guinea bird.)
    Mam.   Right noble madam——
    Fac. (Oh, we shall have most fierce idolatry!)
    Mam. 'Tis your prerogative.
    Dol.   Rather your courtesy.   40
    Mam. Were there naught else to enlarge your virtues to me,
These answers speak your breeding and your blood.
    Dol. Blood we boast none, sir, a poor Baron's daughter.
    Mam. Poor! And gat you? Profane not. Had your father
Slept all the happy remnant of his life   45
After the act, lain but there still, and panted,
He'd done enough to make himself, his issue,
And his posterity noble.

---

23 *modern*: ordinary, commonplace   25 *Heighten*: i.e. in the alchemical
sense   30 *concumbere gold*: breed gold (Juvenal, *Sat.* vi. 91)   38 *Guinea bird*:
prostitute

Dol.   Sir, although
We may be said to want the gilt and trappings,
50 The dress of honour; yet we strive to keep
The seeds, and the materials.
   Mam.   I do see
The old ingredient, virtue, was not lost,
Nor the drug, money, used to make your compound.
There is a strange nobility i' your eye,
55 This lip, that chin! Methinks you do resemble
One o' the Austriac princes.
   Fac. [*Aside*]   Very like,
Her father was an Irish costermonger.
   Mam. The house of Valois just had such a nose.
And such a forehead, yet the Medici
Of Florence boast.
60   *Dol.*   Troth, and I have been likened
To all these Princes.
   Fac. [*Aside*]   I'll be sworn, I heard it.
   Mam. I know not how! It is not any one,
But e'en the very choice of all their features.
   Fac. [*Aside*] I'll in, and laugh.   [*Exit*]
   Mam.   A certain touch, or air,
65 That sparkles a divinity, beyond
An earthly beauty!
   Dol.   Oh, you play the courtier.
   Mam. Good lady, gi' me leave——
   Dol.   In faith, I may not,
To mock me, sir.
   Mam.   To burn i' this sweet flame:
The phoenix never knew a nobler death.
70   *Dol.* Nay, now you court the courtier: and destroy
What you would build. This art, sir, i' your words,
Calls your whole faith in question.
   Mam.   By my soul——
   Dol. Nay, oaths are made o' the same air, sir.
   Mam.   Nature

56 *Austriac*: the Hapsburgs were noted for the fullness of the nether lip   57 *coster-*
monger: seller of apples (costards) and pears

Never bestowed upon mortality,
A more unblamed, a more harmonious feature: 75
She played the stepdame in all faces, else.
Sweet madam, let me be particular——
    Dol. Particular, sir? I pray you, know your distance.
    Mam. In no ill sense, sweet lady, but to ask
How your fair graces pass the hours? I see   80
You're lodged here, i'the house of a rare man,
An excellent artist: but what's that to you?
    Dol. Yes, sir. I study here the mathematics,
And distillation.
    Mam.   Oh, I cry your pardon.
He's a divine instructor! Can extract   85
The souls of all things, by his art; call all
The virtues, and the miracles of the sun,
Into a temperate furnace: teach dull nature
What her own forces are. A man, the emperor
Has courted, above Kelly: sent his medals,   90
And chains to invite him.
    Dol.   Aye, and for his physic, sir——
    Mam. Above the art of Aesculapius,
That drew the envy of the Thunderer!
I know all this, and more.
    Dol.   Troth, I am taken, sir,
Whole, with these studies, that contemplate nature: 95
    Mam. It is a noble humour. But, this form
Was not intended to so dark a use!
Had you been crooked, foul, of some coarse mould,
A cloister had done well: but such a feature
That might stand up the glory of a kingdom,   100
To live recluse! Is a mere solecism,
Though in a nunnery. It must not be.
I muse, my lord your brother will permit it!
You should spend half my land first, were I he.

---

75 *feature*: physical presence   77 *particular*: private, intimate (I. i. 179)
83 *mathematics*: astrology   84 *distillation*: chemistry   90 *Kelly*: Edward
Kelly (1555–95) who won the favour of Rudolph II by claiming to have the stone
92 *Aesculapius*: who restored the dead to life, and was killed by Zeus in a flash of
lightning   101 *mere solecism*: absolute impropriety

105 Does not this diamond better on my finger
    Than i' the quarry?
         Dol.   Yes.
         Mam.   Why, you are like it.
    You were created, lady, for the light!
    Hear, you shall wear it; take it, the first pledge
    Of what I speak: to bind you to believe me.
         Dol. In chains of adamant?
110   *Mam.*   Yes, the strongest bands.
    And take a secret, too. Here, by your side,
    Doth stand, this hour, the happiest man in Europe.
         Dol. You are contented, sir?
         Mam.   Nay, in true being:
    The envy of princes, and the fear of states.
         Dol. Say you so, Sir Epicure!
115   *Mam.*   Yes, and thou shalt prove it,
    Daughter of honour. I have cast mine eye
    Upon thy form, and I will rear this beauty,
    Above all styles.
         Dol.   You mean no treason, sir!
         Mam. No, I will take away that jealousy.
120 I am the lord of the philosophers' stone,
    And thou the lady.
         Dol.   How sir! Ha' you that?
         Mam. I am the master of the maistry.
    This day, the good old wretch, here, o' the house
    Has made it for us. Now, he's at projection.
125 Think therefore, thy first wish, now; let me hear it:
    And it shall rain into thy lap, no shower,
    But floods of gold, whole cataracts, a deluge,
    To get a nation on thee!
         Dol.   You are pleased, sir,
    To work on the ambition of our sex.
130   *Mam.* I'm pleased, the glory of her sex should know,
    This nook, here, of the Friars, is no climate
    For her, to live obscurely in, to learn

119 *jealousy*: suspicion   122 *maistry*: the magisterium (I. iv. 14)   126 *shower*:
cf. ll. 26-7   131 *Friars*: I. i. 17

Physic and surgery, for the constable's wife
Of some odd Hundred in Essex; but come forth,
And taste the air of palaces; eat, drink   135
The toils of emp'rics, and their boasted practice;
Tincture of pearl, and coral, gold, and amber;
Be seen at feasts, and triumphs; have it asked,
What miracle she is? Set all the eyes
Of court afire, like a burning glass,   140
And work 'em into cinders; when the jewels
Of twenty states adorn thee; and the light
Strikes out the stars; that, when thy name is mentioned,
Queens may look pale: and we but showing our love,
Nero's Poppaea may be lost in story!   145
Thus will we have it.
   Dol.   I could well consent, sir.
But, in a monarchy, how will this be?
The prince will soon take notice; and both seize
You and your stone: it being a wealth unfit
For any private subject.
   Mam.   If he knew it.   150
   Dol. Yourself do boast it, sir.
   Mam.   To thee, my life.
   Dol. Oh, but beware, sir! You may come to end
The remnant of your days, in a loathed prison,
By speaking of it.
   Mam.   'Tis no idle fear!
We'll therefore go with all, my girl, and live   155
In a free state; where we will eat our mullets,
Soused in high-country wines, sup pheasants' eggs,
And have our cockles boiled in silver shells,
Our shrimps to swim again, as when they lived,
In a rare butter, made of dolphins' milk,   160
Whose cream does look like opals: and with these
Delicate meats, set ourselves high for pleasure,

---

134 *Hundred*: subdivision of county or shire   136 *emp'rics*: quacks, charlatans
145 *Poppaea*: celebrated beauty who bathed in asses' milk   156 *mullets*: a luxury
in ancient Rome   157 *high-country wines*: wines of *le haut pays*, the mountainous
region

And take us down again, and then renew
Our youth, and strength, with drinking the elixir,
165 And so enjoy a perpetuity
Of life and lust. And thou shalt ha' thy wardrobe,
Richer than Nature's, still, to change thyself,
And vary oftener, for thy pride, than she:
Or Art, her wise, and almost-equal servant.

[*Enter* Face]

170 *Fac.* Sir, you are too loud. I hear you, every word,
Into the laboratory. Some fitter place.
The garden, or great chamber above. How like you her?
    Mam. Excellent! Lungs. There's for thee.   [*Gives money*]
    Fac.   But, do you hear?
Good sir, beware, no mention of the Rabbins.
    Mam. We think not on 'em.
175   *Fac.*   Oh, it is well, sir.

[*Exeunt* Dol, Mammon]
Subtle!

ACT IV, Scene ii

Enter Subtle

    Fac. Dost thou not laugh?
    Sub.   Yes. Are they gone?
    Fac.   All's clear.
    Sub. The widow is come.
    Fac.   And your quarrelling disciple?
    Sub. Aye.
    Fac.   I must to my captainship again then.
    Sub. Stay, bring 'em in first.
    Fac.   So I meant. What is she?
A bonnibel?
    Sub.   I know not.
5   *Fac.*   We'll draw lots,
You'll stand to that?

174 *Rabbins*: cf. II. iii. 239-40   (*IV. ii*) 5 *bonnibel*: bonny lass

Sub.   What else?

Fac.   Oh for a suit,

To fall now, like a curtain: flap.

Sub.   To the door, man.

Fac. You'll ha' the first kiss, 'cause I am not ready.

Sub. [*Aside*] Yes, and perhaps hit you through both the nostrils.

[*Enter* Kastril, Dame Pliant]

Fac. Who would you speak with?

Kas.   Where's the Captain?

Fac.   Gone, sir,   10

About some business.

Kas.   Gone?

Fac.   He'll return straight.

But Master Doctor, his lieutenant, is here.   [*Exit*]

Sub. Come near, my worshipful boy, my *terrae Fili*,

That is, my boy of land; make thy approaches:

Welcome, I know thy lusts, and thy desires,

And I will serve, and satisfy 'em. Begin,   15

Charge me from thence, or thence, or in this line;

Here is my centre: ground thy quarrel.

Kas.   You lie.

Sub. How, child of wrath, and anger! The loud lie?

For what, my sudden boy?

Kas.   Nay, that look you to,

I am aforehand.   20

Sub.   Oh, this's no true grammar,

And as ill logic! You must render causes, child,

Your first and second intentions, know your canons,

And your divisions, modes, degrees, and differences,

Your predicaments, substance, and accident,

Series extern, and intern, with their causes   25

Efficient, material, formal, final,

And ha' your elements perfect——

Kas.   What is this

6 *suit*: his Captain's uniform (l. 3)   9 *hit . . . nostrils*: make a booby of you
13 *terrae Fili*: in alchemy, a spirit (lit. one of low birth, with quibble on *terrae* and
'land')   21 *grammar . . . logic*: III. iv. 25 n.   22 *render causes*: or else forfeit
the choice of weapons

The angry tongue he talks in?
   Sub.   That false precept,
30 Of being aforehand, has deceived a number;
And made 'em enter quarrels, oftentimes,
Before they were aware: and afterward,
Against their wills.
   Kas.   How must I do then, sir?
   Sub. I cry this lady mercy. She should, first,
35 Have been saluted. I do call you lady,
Because you are to be one, ere't be long,
My soft and buxom widow.   (*He kisses her*)
   Kas.   Is she, i'faith?
   Sub. Yes, or my art is an egregious liar.
   Kas. How know you?
   Sub.   By inspection, on her forehead,
40 And subtlety of her lip, which must be tasted
Often, to make a judgement. (*He kisses her again*) 'Slight, she melts
Like a myrobalane! Here is yet a line
In *rivo frontis* tells me he is no knight.
   Pli. What is he then, sir?
   Sub.   Let me see your hand.
45 Oh, your *linea Fortunae* makes it plain;
And *stella*, here, in *monte Veneris*:
But, most of all, *junctura annularis*.
He is a soldier, or a man of art, lady:
But shall have some great honour, shortly.
   Pli.   Brother,
He's a rare man, believe me!
50   *Kas.*   Hold your peace.
Here comes the tother rare man.

              [*Enter* Face *in uniform*]
                    'Save you Captain.
   Fac. Good Master Kastril. Is this your sister?
   Kas.   Aye, sir.

---

   40 *subtlety*: a sugar delicacy   42 *myrobalane*: a plum-like fruit   43 *rivo frontis*: the frontal vein   45 *linea Fortunae*: line of fortune (on the palm)   46 *stella . . . Veneris*: a star on the hill of Venus (at the base of the thumb)   47 *junctura annularis*: joint of the ring-finger

Please you to kuss her, and be proud to know her?

 Fac. I shall be proud to know you, lady.

 Pli.   Brother,

He calls me lady, too.

 Kas.   Aye, peace. I heard it.   55

 Fac. [*To* Subtle] The Count is come.

 Sub.   Where is he?

 Fac.   At the door.

 Sub. Why, you must entertain him.

 Fac.   What'll you do

With these the while?

 Sub.   Why, have 'em up, and show 'em

Some fustian book, or the dark glass.

 Fac.   'Fore God,

She is a delicate dabchick! I must have her.   [*Exit*] 60

 Sub. Must you? Aye, if your fortune will, you must.

Come sir, the Captain will come to us presently.

I'll ha' you to my chamber of demonstrations,

Where I'll show you both the grammar, and logic,

And rhetoric of quarrelling; my whole method,   65

Drawn out in tables: and my instrument,

That hath the several scale upon't, shall make you

Able to quarrel, at a straw's breadth, by moon-light.

And, lady, I'll have you look in a glass,

Some half an hour, but to clear your eyesight,   70

Against you see your fortune: which is greater,

Than I may judge upon the sudden, trust me.   [*Exeunt*]

ACT IV, Scene iii

Enter Face

 Fac. Where are you, Doctor?

 Sub. [*Within*]   I'll come to you presently.

 Fac. I will ha' this same widow, now I ha' seen her,

On any composition.

---

 59 *fustian*: bombastic, worthless *dark glass*: magic crystal 67 *several*: i.e. for
each individual case   (*IV. iii*) 3 *composition*: arrangement (usually to settle con-
flicting claims, cf. ll. 12, 71–2)

[*Enter* Subtle]

Sub.   What do you say?

Fac. Ha' you disposed of them?

Sub.   I ha' sent 'em up.

5 *Fac.* Subtle, in troth, I needs must have this widow.

Sub. Is that the matter?

Fac.   Nay, but hear me.

Sub.   Go to,

If you rebel once, Dol shall know it all.

Therefore be quiet, and obey your chance.

Fac. Nay, thou art so violent now—— Do but conceive:

Thou art old, and canst not serve——

10 *Sub.*   Who, cannot I?

'Slight, I will serve her with thee, for a——

Fac.   Nay,

But understand: I'll gi' you composition.

Sub. I will not treat with thee: what, sell my fortune?

'Tis better than my birthright. Do not murmur.

15 Win her, and carry her. If you grumble, Dol

Knows it directly.

Fac.   Well sir, I am silent.

Will you go help to fetch in Don, in state?

Sub. I follow you, sir: [*Exit* Face] we must keep Face in awe,

Or he will overlook us like a tyrant.

20 Brain of a tailor! Who comes here? Don John!

(Surly *like a Spaniard* [*with* Face])

Sur. Señores, beso las manos, à vuestras mercedes.

Sub. Would you had stooped a little, and kissed our *anos.*

Fac. Peace Subtle.

Sub.   Stab me; I shall never hold, man.

He looks in that deep ruff, like a head in a platter,

25 Served in by a short cloak upon two trestles!

Fac. Or, what do you say to a collar of brawn, cut down

Beneath the souse, and wriggled with a knife?

---

10 *serve*: as of stallions, bulls   20 *Don John*: stock name for a Spaniard (like
Diego, l. 37)   21 'Gentlemen, I kiss your honours' hands'   25 *trestles*: i.e.
his legs   27 *souse*: ear   *wriggled*: carved with a wriggly pattern

Sub. 'Slud, he does look too fat to be a Spaniard.

Fac. Perhaps some Fleming, or some Hollander got him
In D'Alva's time: Count Egmont's bastard.

Sub.   Don,   30
Your scurvy, yellow, Madrid face is welcome.

Sur. Gratia.

Sub.   He speaks, out of a fortification.
'Pray God, he ha' no squibs in those deep sets.

Sur. Por dios, señores, muy linda casa!

Sub. What says he?

Fac.   Praises the house, I think,   35
I know no more but's action.

Sub.   Yes, the *casa*,
My precious Diego, will prove fair enough,
To cozen you in. Do you mark? You shall
Be cozened, Diego.

Fac.   Cozened, do you see?
My worthy Donzel, cozened.

Sur.   *Entiendo.*   40

Sub. Do you intend it? So do we, dear Don.
Have you brought pistolets? Or portagues?
My solemn Don? Dost thou feel any?

Fac. (He feels his pockets)   Full.

Sub. You shall be emptied, Don; pumped and drawn,
Dry, as they say.

Fac.   Milked, in troth, sweet Don.   45

Sub. See all the monsters; the great lion of all, Don.

Sur. Con licencia, se puede ver à esta señora?

Sub. What talks he now?

Fac.   O'the *señora*.

Sub.   Oh, Don,
That is the lioness, which you shall see
Also, my Don.

Fac.   'Slid, Subtle, how shall we do?   50

---

30 *D'Alva*: Fernando Alvarez, Duke of Alva, Governor of the Netherlands 1567–73
Egmont: Flemish patriot put to death by Alva in 1568   33 *sets*: folds in the ruff
34 'Gad, gentlemen, a very pretty house'   40 *Donzel*: squire (? or 'little Don')
Entiendo: 'I understand'   47 'If you please, may I see this lady?'

Sub. For what?

Fac.   Why, Dol's employed, you know.

Sub.   That's true!
'Fore heaven I know not: he must stay, that's all.

Fac. Stay? That he must not by no means.

Sub.   No, why?

Fac. Unless you'll mar all. 'Slight, he'll suspect it.
55 And then he will not pay, not half so well.
This is a travelled punk-master, and does know
All the delays: a notable hot rascal,
And looks, already, rampant.

Sub.   'Sdeath, and Mammon
Must not be troubled.

Fac.   Mammon, in no case!

Sub. What shall we do then?
60 *Fac.*   Think: you must be sudden.

Sur. Entiendo, que la señora es tan hermosa, que codicio tan
à verla, como la bien aventuránça de mi vida.

Fac. Mi vida? 'Slid, Subtle, he puts me in mind o'the widow.
What dost thou say to draw her to it? Ha?
65 And tell her, it is her fortune. All our venture
Now lies upon't. It is but one man more,
Which on's chance to have her: and, beside,
There is no maidenhead to be feared or lost.
What dost thou think on't, Subtle?

Sub.   Who, I? Why——
70 *Fac.* The credit of our house too is engaged.

Sub. You made me an offer for my share erewhile.
What wilt thou gi' me, i'faith?

Fac.   Oh, by that light,
I'll not buy now. You know your doom to me.
E'en take your lot, obey your chance, sir; win her,
And wear her, out for me.
75 *Sub.*   'Slight. I'll not work her then.

61-2 'I understand the lady is so beautiful that I am anxious to see her as the chief
fortune of my life'   73 *doom*: decision (ll. 13-14)   74-5 *win. . . And
wear*: phrase used of winning a wife   75 *work*: i.e. persuade the widow to take
the Spaniard

Fac. It is the common cause, therefore bethink you.
Dol else must know it, as you said.
    Sub.   I care not.
    Sur. Señores, por que se tarda tanta?
    Sub. Faith, I am not fit, I am old.
    Fac.   That's now no reason, sir.
    Sur. Puede ser, de hazer burla de mi amor.   80
    Fac. You hear the Don, too? By this air, I call,
And loose the hinges. Dol!
    Sub.   A plague of hell——
    Fac. Will you then do?
    Sub.   You're a terrible rogue,
I'll think of this: will you, sir, call the widow?
    Fac. Yes, and I'll take her too, with all her faults,   85
Now I do think on't better.
    Sub.   With all my heart, sir,
Am I discharged o'the lot?
    Fac.   As you please.
    Sub.   Hands.
                          [*They shake hands*]
    Fac. Remember now, that, upon any change,
You never claim her.
    Sub.   Much good joy, and health to you, sir.
Marry a whore? Fate, let me wed a witch first.   90
    Sur. Por estas honrada's barbas——
    Sub.   He swears by his beard.
Dispatch, and call the brother too.   [*Exit* Face]
    Sur.   *Tiengo duda, señores,*
Que on me hágan alguna traycion.
    Sub. How, issue on? Yes, *praesto señor.* Please you
Enthratha the *chaṃbratha*, worthy Don;   95
Where if it please the Fates, in your *bathada*,
You shall be soaked, and stroked, and tubbed, and rubbed:
And scrubbed, and fubbed, dear Don, before you go.

---

78 'Gentlemen, why this great delay?'   80 'Possibly you are making mock of
my love'   82 *hinges*: i.e. of their partnership   84 *think of*: remember
91 'By this honoured beard—'   92–3 'I fear, gentlemen, that you are practising
some treachery on me'   98 *fubbed*: cheated

You shall, in faith, my scurvy babioun Don:
100 Be curried, clawed, and flawed, and tawed, indeed.
I will the heartilier go about it now,
And make the widow a punk, so much the sooner,
To be revenged on this impetuous Face:
The quickly doing of it is the grace.   [*Exeunt*]

ACT IV, Scene iv

Enter Face, Dame Pliant, Kastril

Fac. Come lady: I knew the Doctor would not leave,
Till he had found the very nick of her fortune.
   Kas. To be a countess, say you?
   Fac.   A Spanish countess, sir.
   Pli. Why? Is that better than an English countess?
5 *Fac.* Better? 'Slight, make you that a question, lady?
   Kas. Nay, she is a fool, Captain, you must pardon her.
   Fac. Ask from your courtier, to your inns of court man,
To your mere milliner: they will tell you all,
Your Spanish jennet is the best horse. Your Spanish
10 Stoup is the best garb. Your Spanish beard
Is the best cut. Your Spanish ruffs are the best
Wear. Your Spanish pavan the best dance.
Your Spanish titillation in a glove
The best perfume. And, for your Spanish pike,
15 And Spanish blade, let your poor Captain speak.
Here comes the Doctor.
                    [*Enter* Subtle]

   Sub.   My most honoured lady,
(For so I am now to style you, having found
By this my scheme, you are to undergo
An honourable fortune, very shortly.)
What will you say now, if some——

---

100 *curried*: process of dressing leather by soaking, beating, and scraping   *flawed*:
flayed   *tawed*: softened with alum   (*IV. iv*) 2 *very nick*: critical moment,
turning-point   10 *Stoup*: bow   *garb*: fashion   12 *pavan*: a stately dance
13 *titillation*: scent   14 *Spanish pike*: the Toledo

 Fac.   I ha' told her all, sir,   20
And her right worshipful brother, here, that she shall be
A countess: do not delay 'em, sir. A Spanish countess.
 Sub. Still, my scarce worshipful Captain, you can keep
No secret. Well, since he has told you, madam,
Do you forgive him, and I do.
 Kas.   She shall do that, sir.   25
I'll look to't, 'tis my charge.
 Sub.   Well then. Naught rests
But that she fit her love, now, to her fortune.
 Pli. Truly, I shall never brook a Spaniard.
 Sub.   No?
 Pli. Never, sin' eighty-eight could I abide 'em,
And that was some three year afore I was born, in truth.   30
 Sub. Come, you must love him, or be miserable:
Choose, which you will.
 Fac.   By this good rush, persuade her,
She will cry strawberries else, within this twelve-month.
 Sub. Nay, shads, and mackerel, which is worse.
 Fac.   Indeed, sir?
 Kas. God's lid, you shall love him, or I'll kick you.
 Pli.   Why?   35
I'll do as you will ha' me, brother.
 Kas.   Do,
Or by this hand, I'll maul you.
 Fac.   Nay, good sir,
Be not so fierce.
 Sub.   No, my enraged child,
She will be ruled. What, when she comes to taste
The pleasures of a countess! To be courted——   40
 Fac. And kissed, and ruffled!
 Sub.   Aye, behind the hangings.
 Fac. And then come forth in pomp!
 Sub.   And know her state!
 Fac. Of keeping all the idolaters o'the chamber

29 *eighty-eight*: 1588, Armada year   32 *rush*: picked up by Face from the floor
33 *cry strawberries*: become a market-girl or (l. 34) a fishwife (shads = herrings)
41 *ruffled*: handled with familiarity

Barer to her, than at their prayers!
   Sub.   Is served
Upon the knee!
45   *Fac.*   And has her pages, ushers,
Footmen, and coaches——
   Sub.   Her six mares——
   Fac.   Nay, eight!
   Sub. To hurry her through London, to the Exchange,
Bedlam, the China-houses——
   Fac.   Yes, and have
The citizens gape at her, and praise her tires!
50 And my lord's goose-turd bands, that rides with her!
   Kas. Most brave! By this hand, you are not my suster,
If you refuse.
   Pli.   I will not refuse, brother.

            [*Enter* Surly]

   Sur. Que es esto, señores, que non se venga?
Esta tardanza me mata!
   Fac.   It is the Count come!
55 The Doctor knew he would be here, by his art.
   Sub. En gallanta Madama, Don! Gallantissima!
   Sur. Por tódos los dioses, la mas acabada
Hermosura, que he visto en mi vida!
   Fac. Is't not a gallant language, that they speak?
60   *Kas.* An admirable language! Is't not French?
   Fac. No, Spanish, sir.
   Kas.   It goes like law-French,
And that, they say, is the courtliest language.
   Fac.   List, sir.
   Sur. El Sol ha perdido su lumbre, con el
Resplandor, que tràe esta dama. Valgame dios!
   Fac. He admires your sister.

47 *the Exchange, Bedlam, the China-houses*: places of fashionable resort, as in *SW* I.
iii. 33, IV. iii. 22–3   50 *goose-turd*: yellowish green, a fashionable colour   *bands*:
collars   53–4 'How is it, gentlemen, that she does not come? This delay is killing
me'   57–8 'By all the gods, the most perfect beauty I have ever seen'   61 *law-*
French: a jargon not yet ousted by English in the law of the time   63–4 'The sun
has lost his light with the splendour that this lady brings, God bless me!'

Kas.   Must not she make curtsey?   65
Sub. 'Ods will, she must go to him, man; and kiss him!
It is the Spanish fashion, for the women
To make first court.
    Fac.   'Tis true he tells you, sir:
His art knows all.
    Aur.   *Per que no se acude?*
    Kas. He speaks to her, I think?
    Fac.   That he does sir.   70
Sur. Por el amor de dios, que es esto, que se tàrda?
    Kas. Nay, see: she will not understand him! Gull.
Noddy.
    Pli. What say you brother?
    Kas.   Ass, my suster,
Go kuss him, as the cunning man would ha' you,
I'll thrust a pin i' your buttocks else.
    Fac.   Oh, no sir.   75
*Sur. Señora mia, mi persona muy indigna esta
Allegar à tànta Hermosura.*
    Fac. Does he not use her bravely?
    Kas.   Bravely, i'faith!
    Fac. Nay, he will use her better.
    Kas.   Do you think so?
Sur. Señora, si sera seruida, entremos.   [*Exit with* Dame Pliant] 80
    Kas. Where does he carry her?
    Fac.   Into the garden, sir;
Take you no thought: I must interpret for her.
    Sub. Give Dol the word. [*Exit* Face] Come, my fierce child, advance,
We'll to our quarrelling lesson again.
    Kas.   Agreed.
I love a Spanish boy, with all my heart.   85
    Sub. Nay, and by this means, sir, you shall be brother
To a great Count.
    Kas.   Aye, I knew that, at first.

69 'Why does she not come?'   71 'For the love of God, why is it she delays?'
76-7 'My lady, my person is quite unworthy to approach such beauty'   80 'Lady,
if it is convenient to you, let us go in'   83 *the word*: the cue to go mad

This match will advance the house of the Kastrils.

Sub. 'Pray God, your sister prove but pliant.

Kas.   Why,

Her name is so: by her other husband.

90   *Sub.*   How!

Kas. The widow Pliant. Knew you not that?

Sub.   No faith, sir.

Yet, by erection of her figure, I guessed it.

Come, let's go practise.

Kas.   Yes, but do you think, Doctor.

I e'er shall quarrel well?

Sub.   I warrant you.   [*Exeunt*]

ACT IV, Scene v

Enter Dol (*in her fit of talking*), Sir Epicure Mammon

Dol. For, after Alexander's death——

Mam.   Good lady——

Dol. That Perdiccas, and Antigonus were slain,

The two that stood, Seleuc', and Ptolemy——

Mam. Madam.

Dol.   Made up the two legs, and the fourth Beast.

5 That was Gog-north, and Egypt-south: which after

Was called Gog Iron-leg, and South Iron-leg——

Mam.   Lady——

Dol. And then Gog-horned. So was Egypt, too.

Then Egypt clay-leg, and Gog clay-leg——

Mam.   Sweet madam.

Dol. And last Gog-dust, and Egypt-dust, which fall

10 In the last link of the fourth chain. And these

Be stars in story, which none see, or look at——

Mam. What shall I do?

Dol.   For, as he says, except

---

92 *erection of her figure*: casting her horoscope   (*IV. v*) 1–32 garbled quotations
from Hugh Broughton's *A Concent of Scripture* (1590), a study of biblical chronology
(see *H&S* x. 104–6)

We call the Rabbins, and the heathen Greeks——
  Mam. Dear lady.
  Dol.   To come from Salem, and from Athens,
And teach the people of great Britain——

[Enter Face]

  Fac.   What's the matter, sir? 15
  Dol. To speak the tongue of Eber, and Javan——
  Mam.   Oh,
She's in her fit.
  Dol.   We shall know nothing——
  Fac.   Death, sir,
We are undone.
  Dol.   Where, then, a learned Linguist
Shall see the ancient used communion
Of vowels, and consonants——
  Fac.   My master will hear!   20
  Dol. A wisdom, which Pythagoras held most high——
  Mam. Sweet honourable lady.
  Dol.   To comprise
All sounds of voices, in few marks of letters——
  Fac. Nay, you must never hope to lay her now.
(They speak together)

  Dol. And so we may arrive by Talmud skill,   25
And profane Greek, to raise the building up
Of Helen's house, against the Ismaelite,
King of Thogarma, and his Habergions
Brimstony, blue, and fiery; and the force
Of King Abaddon, and the Beast of Cittim;   30
Which Rabbi David Kimchi, Onkelos,
And Aben-Ezra do interpret Rome.
  Fac. How did you put her into't?
  Mam.   Alas I talked
Of a fifth monarchy I would erect,
With the philosophers' stone (by chance) and she   35
Falls on the other four, straight.

  24/5 s.d. The exchange between Face and Mammon (ll. 33–40) goes on while Dol
is uttering ll. 25–32.

    Fac.   Out of Broughton!
I told you so. 'Slid stop her mouth.
    Mam.   Is't best?
    Fac. She'll never leave else. If the old man hear her,
We are but faeces, ashes.
    Sub.   What's to do there?
40   *Fac.* Oh, we are lost. Now she hears him, she is quiet.
                    (*Upon* Subtle's *entry they disperse*)
    Mam. Where shall I hide me?
    Sub.   How! What sight is here!
Close deeds of darkness, and that shun the light!
Bring him again. Who is he? What, my son!
Oh, I have lived too long.
    Mam.   Nay good, dear father,
There was no unchaste purpose.
45   *Sub.*   Not? And flee me,
When I come in?
    Mam.   That was my error.
    Sub.   Error?
Guilt, guilt, my son, Give it the right name. No marvel,
If I found check in our great work within,
When such affairs as these were managing!
    Mam. Why, have you so?
50   *Sub.*   It has stood still this half hour:
And all the rest of our less works gone back.
Where is the instrument of wickedness,
My lewd false drudge?
    Mam.   Nay, good sir, blame not him.
Believe me, 'twas against his will, or knowledge.
I saw her by chance.
55   *Sub.*   Will you commit more sin,
To excuse a varlet?
    Mam.   By my hope, 'tis true, sir.
    Sub. Nay, then I wonder less, if you, for whom
The blessing was prepared, would so tempt heaven:
And lose your fortunes.
    Mam.   Why, sir?
    Sub.   This'll retard

The work, a month at least.

 Mam.   Why, if it do,   60
What remedy? But think it not, good father:
Our purposes were honest.

 Sub.   As they were,
So the reward will prove. (*A great crack and noise within*) How now!
 Ay me.
God, and all saints be good to us.

[*Enter* Face]

         What's that?

 Fac. Oh sir, we are defeated! All the works   65
Are flown *in fumo*: every glass is burst.
Furnace, and all rent down! As if a bolt
Of thunder had been driven through the house.
Retorts, receivers, pelicans, bolt-heads,
All struck in shivers! (Subtle *falls down as in a swoon*) Help, good
 sir! Alas,   70
Coldness, and death invades him. Nay, Sir Mammon,
Do the fair offices of a man! You stand
As you were readier to depart than he.   (*One knocks*)
Who's there? My lord her brother is come.

 Mam.   Ha, Lungs?

 Fac. His coach is at the door. Avoid his sight,   75
For he's as furious as his sister is mad.

 Mam. Alas!

 Fac.   My brain is quite undone with the fume, sir,
I ne'er must hope to be mine own man again.

 Mam. Is all lost, Lungs? Will nothing be preserved,
Of all our cost?

 Fac.   Faith, very little, sir.   80
A peck of coals, or so, which is cold comfort, sir.

 Mam. Oh, my voluptuous mind! I am justly punished.

 Fac. And so am I, sir.

 Mam.   Cast from all my hopes——

 Fac. Nay, certainties, sir.

 Mam.   By mine own base affections.

         (*Subtle seems to come to himself*)

Sub. Oh, the cursed fruits of vice and lust!

85 *Mam.*   Good father,
It was my sin. Forgive it.

    Sub.   Hangs my roof
Over us still, and will not fall, oh justice,
Upon us, for this wicked man!

    Fac.   Nay, look, sir,
You grieve him, now, with staying in his sight:
90 Good sir, the nobleman will come too, and take you,
And that may breed a tragedy.

    Mam.   I'll go.

    Fac. Aye, and repent at home, sir. It may be,
For some good penance, you may ha' it, yet,
A hundred pound to the box at Bedlam——

    Mam.   Yes.

    Fac. For the restoring such as ha' their wits.

95 *Mam.*   I'll do't.

    Fac. I'll send one to you to receive it.

    Mam.   Do.
Is no projection left?

    Fac.   All flown, or stinks, sir.

    Mam. Will naught be saved, that's good for medicine, thinkst
    thou?

    Fac. I cannot tell, sir. There will be, perhaps,
100 Something, about the scraping of the shards,
Will cure the itch: [*Aside*] though not your itch of mind, sir.
It shall be saved for you, and sent home. Good sir,
This way: for fear the lord should meet you.   [*Exit* Mammon]

    Sub.   Face.

    Fac. Aye.

    Sub.   Is he gone?

    Fac.   Yes, and as heavily
105 As all the gold he hoped for were in his blood.
Let us be light, though.

    Sub. [*Leaping up*]   Aye, as balls, and bound
And hit our heads against the roof for joy:
There's so much of our care now cast away.

    Fac. Now to our Don.

Sub.   Yes, your young widow, by this time
Is made a countess, Face: she's been in travail   110
Of a young heir for you.
    Fac.   Good, sir.
    Sub.   Off with your case,
And greet her kindly, as a bridegroom should,
After these common hazards.
    Fac.   Very well, sir.
Will you go fetch Don Diego off the while?
    Sub. And fetch him over too, if you'll be pleased, sir: 115
Would Dol were in her place, to pick his pockets now.
    Fac. Why, you can do it as well, if you would set to't.
I pray you prove your virtue.
    Sub.   For your sake, sir.   [*Exeunt*]

ACT IV, Scene vi

Enter Surly, Dame Pliant

    Sur. Lady, you see into what hands you are fallen;
'Mongst what a nest of villains! And how near
Your honour was to have catched a certain clap
(Through your credulity) had I but been
So punctually forward, as place, time,   5
And other circumstance would ha' made a man:
For you're a handsome woman: would yo' were wise, too.
I am a gentleman, come here disguised,
Only to find the knaveries of this citadel,
And where I might have wronged your honour, and have not,   10
I claim some interest in your love. You are,
They say, a widow, rich: and I am a bachelor,
Worth naught: your fortunes may make me a man,
As mine ha' preserved you a woman. Think upon it,
And whether I have deserved you, or no.
    Pli.   I will, sir.   15

---

111 *case*: his alchemist's dress   115 *fetch him over*: get the better of him (with
quibble on the alchemical term)   (*IV. vi*) 3 *clap*: venereal disease

Sur. And for these household-rogues, let me alone,
To treat with them.

[*Enter* Subtle]

Sub. How doth my noble Diego?
And my dear madam, Countess? Hath the Count
Been courteous, lady? Liberal? And open?
20 Donzel, methinks you look melancholic,
After your *coitum*, and scurvy! Truly,
I do not like the dullness of your eye:
It hath a heavy cast, 'tis upsee Dutch,
And says you are a lumpish whore-master.
25 Be lighter, I will make your pockets so. (*He falls to picking of them*)
    Sur. [*Revealing himself*] Will you, Don bawd, and pick-purse?
      How now? Reel you?
Stand up sir, you shall find since I am so heavy,
I'll gi' you equal weight.
    Sub. Help, murder!
    Sur. No, sir.
There's no such thing intended. A good cart,
30 And a clean whip shall ease you of that fear.
I am the Spanish Don, that should be cozened,
Do you see? Cozened? Where's your Captain Face?
That parcel-broker, and whole-bawd, all rascal.

[*Enter* Face]

Fac. How, Surly!
    Sur. Oh, make your approach, good Captain.
35 I've found from whence your copper rings and spoons
Come, now, wherewith you cheat abroad in taverns.
'Twas here, you learned to anoint your boot with brimstone,
Then rub men's gold on't, for a kind of touch,
And say 'twas naught, when you had changed the colour,
40 That you might ha't for nothing? And this Doctor,
Your sooty, smoky-bearded compeer, he
Will close you so much gold, in a bolt's-head,
And, on a turn, convey (i'the stead) another

---

23 *upsee Dutch*: Dutch (i.e. phlegmatic) fashion (cf. *CA* IV. v. 25)   29 *cart*:
for the public exposure of criminals   33 *parcel-broker*: III. ii. 45

With sublimed Mercury, that shall burst i'the heat,
And fly out all *in fumo*? [*Exit* Face]Then weeps Mammon: 45
Then swoons his worship. Or he is the Faustus,
That casteth figures, and can conjure, cures
Plague, piles, and pox, by the ephemerides,
And holds intelligence with all the bawds,
And midwives of three shires? While you send in——   50
Captain (what is he gone?) damsels with child,
Wives, that are barren, or, the waiting-maid
With the green-sickness? Nay, sir, you must tarry

                                        [*Seizing* Subtle]

Though he be scaped; and answer, by the ears, sir.

ACT IV, Scene vii

Enter Face, Kastril

  Fac. Why, now's the time, if ever you will quarrel
Well (as they say) and be a true-born child.
The Doctor, and your sister both are abused.
  Kas. Where is he? Which is he? He is a slave
What e'er he is, and the son of a whore. Are you   5
The man, sir, I would know.
  Sur.   I should be loth, sir,
To confess so much.
  Kas.   Then you lie, i'your throat.
  Sur.   How?
  Fac. A very arrant rogue, sir, and a cheater,
Employed here, by another conjurer,
That does not love the Doctor, and would cross him   10
If he knew how——
  Sur.   Sir, you are abused.
  Kas.   You lie:
And 'tis no matter.

----

  46 *Faustus*: alluding to Marlowe's play   48 *ephemerides*: astronomical almanacs
53 *green-sickness*: chlorosis: anaemic disease of girls at puberty   54 *answer, by the
ears*: be cropped in the pillory

Fac.   Well said, sir. He is
The impudentest rascal——
   Sur.   You are indeed. Will you hear me, sir?
   Fac. By no means: bid him be gone.
   Kas.   Be gone, sir, quickly.
15   *Sur.* This's strange! Lady, do you inform your brother.
                        [She tries to speak to him]
   Fac. There is not such a foist, in all the town,
The Doctor had him, presently: and finds, yet,
The Spanish count will come, here. Bear up, Subtle.
   Sub. Yes, sir, he must appear, within this hour.
20   *Fac.* And yet this rogue, would come, in a disguise,
By the temptation of another spirit,
To trouble our art, though he could not hurt it.
   Kas.   Aye,
I know——*[To* Dame Pliant] Away, you talk like a foolish mauther.
                          [Exit Dame]
   Sur. Sir, all is truth, she says.
   Fac.   Do not believe him, sir:
25 He is the lyingest swabber! Come your ways, sir.
   Sur. You are valiant, out of company.
   Kas.   Yes, how then, sir?

[Enter Drugger]

   Fac. Nay, here's an honest fellow too, that knows him,
And all his tricks. (Make good what I say, Abel,
This cheater would ha' cozened thee o'the widow.)
30 He owes this honest Drugger, here, seven pound,
He has had on him, in two-penny'orths of tobacco.
   Dru. Yes sir. And he's damned himself, three terms, to pay me.
   Fac. And what does he owe for *lotium*?
   Dru.   Thirty shillings, sir:
And for six syringes.
   Sur.   Hydra of villainy!
   Fac. Nay, sir, you must quarrel him out o'the house.

---

16 *foist*: rogue   23 *mauther*: young woman   25 *swabber*: low rank of
sailor, hence term of contempt   33 *lotium*: stale urine used by barbers as lye
34 *Hydra*: the monster which grew two heads for every one cut off

Kas.   I will.   35

Sir, if you get not out o' doors, you lie:

And you are a pimp.

    Sur.   Why, this is madness, sir,

Not valour in you: I must laugh at this.

    Kas. It is my humour: you are a pimp, and a trig,

And an Amadis de Gaul, or a Don Quixote.   40

    Dru. Or a Knight o'the curious coxcomb. Do you see?

                  [*Enter* Ananias]

    Ana. Peace to the household.

    Kas.   I'll keep peace, for no man.

    Ana. Casting of dollars is concluded lawful.

    Kas. Is he the Constable?

    Sub.   Peace, Ananias.

    Fac.   No, sir.

    Kas. Then you are an otter, and a shad, a whit,   45

A very tim.

    Sur.   You'll hear me, sir?

    Kas.   I will not.

    Ana. What is the motive?

    Sub.   Zeal, in the young gentleman,

Against his Spanish slops——

    Ana.   They are profane,

Lewd, superstitious, and idolatrous breeches.

    Sur. New rascals!

    Kas.   Will you be gone, sir?

    Ana.   Avoid Satan,   50

Thou art not of the light. That ruff of pride

About thy neck betrays thee: and is the same

With that, which the unclean birds, in seventy-seven,

Were seen to prank it with, on divers coasts.

Thou look'st like Antichrist, in that lewd hat.   55

---

    39 *trig*: dandy, coxcomb   40 *Amadis de Gaul . . . Don Quixote*: romances which
Jonson despised   41 *curious coxcomb*: the 'lewd hat' of l. 55, with a glance at
Beaumont and Fletcher's *The Coxcomb*   45 *otter*: neither fish nor flesh (*1 Henry
IV*, III. iii. 127; cf. Captain Otter in *SW*)   *shad*: fish (herring)   *whit*: ? bird (as in
'godwit'); also a trifle, a particle (cf. Captain Whit in *BF*)   46 *very tim*: ? tiny
particle (cf. Tim Item in *ML*)   48 *slops*: III. iii. 13   53 *unclean birds*: Rev.
18: 2   *seventy-seven*: misdating Alva's invasion of the Netherlands (in 1567)

    Sur. I must give way.
    Kas.   Be gone, sir.
    Sur.   But I'll take
A course with you——
    (*Ana.*   Depart, proud Spanish fiend)
    Sur. Captain, and Doctor——
    Ana.   Child of perdition.
    Kas.   Hence, sir.
                             [*Exit* Surly]
Did I not quarrel bravely?
    Fac.   Yes, indeed, sir.
60   *Kas.* Nay, and I give my mind to't, I shall do't.
    Fac. Oh, you must follow, sir, and threaten him tame.
He'll turn again else.
    Kas.   I'll return him, then.   [*Exit*]
    Fac. Drugger, this rogue prevented us, for thee:
We had determined, that thou shouldst ha' come,
65 In a Spanish suit, and ha' carried her so; and he,
A brokerly slave, goes, puts it on himself.
Hast brought the damask?
    Dru.   Yes sir.
    Fac.   Thou must borrow
A Spanish suit. Hast thou no credit with the players?
    Dru. Yes, sir, did you never see me play the fool?
70   *Fac.* I know not, Nab: thou shalt, if I can help it.
Hieronimo's old cloak, ruff, and hat will serve,
I'll tell thee more, when thou bringst 'em.   [*Exit* Drugger]
    Ana. (Subtle *hath whispered with him this while*)
                            Sir, I know
The Spaniard hates the Brethren, and hath spies
Upon their actions: and that this was one
75 I make no scruple. But the holy Synod
Have been in prayer and meditation for it.
And 'tis revealed no less, to them, than me,
That casting of money is most lawful.
    Sub.   True.

---

63 *prevented*: anticipated   66 *brokerly*: pettifogging   71 *Hieronimo*: in
Kyd's *The Spanish Tragedy*

But here, I cannot do it; if the house
Should chance to be suspected, all would out,   80
And we be locked up, in the tower, for ever,
To make gold there (for the state) never come out:
And, then, are you defeated.
    Ana.   I will tell
This to the Elders, and the weaker Brethren,
That the whole company of the Separation   85
May join in humble prayer again.
    (*Sub.*   And fasting.)
    Ana. Yea, for some fitter place. The peace of mind
Rest with these walls.
    Sub.   Thanks, courteous Ananias. [*Exit* Ananias]
    Fac. What did he come for?
    Sub.   About casting dollars,
Presently, out of hand. And so, I told him,   90
A Spanish minister came here to spy,
Against the faithful——
    Fac.   I conceive. Come Subtle,
Thou art so down upon the least disaster!
How wouldst thou ha' done, if I had not helped thee out?
    Sub. I thank thee Face, for the angry boy, i'faith.   95
    Fac. Who would ha' looked it should ha' been that rascal?
Surly? He had dyed his beard, and all. Well, sir,
Here's damask come, to make you a suit.
    Sub.   Where's Drugger?
    Fac. He is gone to borrow me a Spanish habit,
I'll be the Count, now.
    Sub.   But where's the widow?   100
    Fac. Within, with my lord's sister: Madam Dol
Is entertaining her.
    Sub,   By your favour, Face,
Now she is honest, I will stand again.
    Fac. You will not offer it?
    Sub.   Why?
    Fac.   Stand to your word,

---

  81 *locked up, in the tower*: as Raymond Lully was said to have been   92 *con-*
ceive: understand

Or——here comes Dol. She knows——

105   *Sub.*   You're tyrannous still.

   Fac. Strict for my right. How now, Dol? Hast told her,
The Spanish Count will come?

   Dol.   Yes, but another is come,
You little looked for!

   Fac.   Who's that?

   Dol.   Your master:
The master of the house.

   Sub.   How, Dol!

   Fac.   She lies.

110 This is some trick. Come, leave your quiblins, Dorothy.

   Dol. Look out, and see.

   Sub.   Art thou in earnest?

   Dol.   'Slight,
Forty o'the neighbours are about him, talking.

   Fac. [*At window*] 'Tis he, by this good day.

   Dol.   'Twill prove ill day,
For some on us.

   Fac.   We are undone, and taken.

   Dol. Lost, I'm afraid.

115   *Sub.*   You said he would not come,
While there died one a week, within the liberties.

   Fac. No: 'twas within the walls.

   Sub.   Was't so? Cry you mercy:
I thought the liberties. What shall we do now, Face?

   Fac. Be silent: not a word, if he call, or knock.

120 I'll into mine old shape again, and meet him,
Of Jeremy, the butler. I' the meantime,
Do you two pack up all the goods, and purchase,
That we can carry i' the two trunks. I'll keep him
Off for today, if I cannot longer: and then

125 At night, I'll ship you both away to Ratcliffe,
Where we'll meet tomorrow, and there we'll share.
Let Mammon's brass and pewter keep the cellar:

---

110 *quiblins*: tricks   116 *liberties*: district beyond the city bounds, but subject
to municipal authority   122 *purchase*: booty, gains   125 *Rátcliffe*: in
Stepney, reached by the river

We'll have another time for that. But, Dol,
'Pray thee, go heat a little water, quickly,
Subtle must shave me. [*Exit* Dol] All my Captain's beard
Must off, to make me appear smooth Jeremy.   130
You'll do't?

    Sub.   Yes, I'll shave you, as well as I can.
    Fac. And not cut my throat, but trim me?
    Sub.   You shall see, sir.

                                [*Exeunt*]

ACT V, Scene i

Enter Lovewit, Neighbours

    Lov. Has there been such resort, say you?
    1st Nei.   Daily, sir.
    2nd Nei. And nightly, too.
    3rd Nei.   Aye, some as brave as lords.
    4th Nei. Ladies and gentlewomen.
    5th Nei.   Citizens' wives.
    1st Nei. And knights.
    6th Nei.   In coaches.
    2nd Nei.   Yes, and oyster-women.
    1st Nei. Beside other gallants.
    3rd Nei.   Sailors' wives.
    4th Nei.   Tobacco-men.   5
    5th Nei. Another Pimlico!
    Lov.   What should my knave advance,
To draw this company? He hung out no banners
Of a strange calf, with five legs, to be seen?
Or a huge lobster, with six claws?
    6th Nei.   No, sir.
    3rd Nei. We had gone in then, sir.
    Lov.   He has no gift   10
Of teaching i' the nose, that e'er I knew of!

131-2 *shave . . . trim*: quibble on the sense 'cheat'   (*V. i*) 2 *brave*: finely dressed
6 *Pimlico*: a noted house for cakes and 'Pimlico' ale at Hoxton   11 *teaching i' the
nose*: ? like the Puritans (*CA* I. ix. 34)

You saw no bills set up, that promised cure
Of agues, or the toothache?
   2nd Nei.   No such thing, sir.
   Lov. Nor heard a drum struck, for babions, or puppets?
   5th Nei. Neither sir.
15   *Lov.*   What device should he bring forth now!
I love a teeming wit, as I love my nourishment.
'Pray God he ha' not kept such open house,
That he hath sold my hangings and my bedding:
I left him nothing else. If he have eat 'em,
20 A plague o'the moth, say I. Sure he has got
Some bawdy pictures, to call all this ging;
The friar and the nun; or the new motion
Of the knight's courser, covering the parson's mare;
The boy of six year old, with the great thing:
25 Or 't may be, he has the fleas that run at tilt,
Upon a table, or some dog to dance?
When saw you him?
   1st Nei.   Who sir, Jeremy?
   2nd Nei.   Jeremy butler?
We saw him not this month.
   Lov.   How!
   4th Nei.   Not these five weeks, sir.
   1st Nei. These six weeks, at the least.
   Lov.   You amaze me, neighbours!
30   *5th Nei.* Sure, if your worship know not where he is,
He's slipped away.
   6th Nei.   Pray God, he be not made away!
   Lov. Ha? It's no time to question, then.   (*He knocks*)
   6th Nei.   About
Some three weeks' since, I heard a doleful cry,
As I sat up, a-mending my wife's stockings.
35   *Lov.* This's strange! That none will answer! Didst thou hear
A cry, sayst thou?
   6th Nei.   Yes, sir, like unto a man

---

21 *ging*: company   22 *The friar and the nun*: 'the Fryer whipping the Nuns
arse' (*H&S* x. 109)   *motion*: puppet show   24 *The boy*: cf. Beaumont and
Fletcher, *The Knight of the Burning Pestle* (ed. Moorman), III. ii. 151–5

That had been strangled an hour, and could not speak.

    2nd Nei. I heard it too, just this day three weeks, at two o'clock
Next morning.

    Lov.   These be miracles, or you make 'em so!
A man an hour strangled, and could not speak,   40
And both you heard him cry?

    3rd Nei.   Yes, downward, sir.

    Lov. Thou art a wise fellow: give me thy hand, I pray thee.
What trade art thou on?

    3rd Nei.   A smith, and't please your worship.

    Lov. A smith? Then, lend me thy help, to get this door open.

    3rd Nei. That I will presently, sir, but fetch my tools—— [*Exit*]   45

    1st Nei. Sir, best to knock again, afore you break it.

ACT V, Scene ii

    Lov. I will.   [*Knocks*]
                        [*Enter* Face]

    Fac.   What mean you, sir?

    1st, 2nd, 4th Nei.   Oh, here's Jeremy!

    Fac. Good sir, come from the door.

    Lov.   Why! What's the matter?

    Fac. Yet farther, you are too near, yet.

    Lov.   I'the name of wonder!
What means the fellow?

    Fac.   The house, sir, has been visited.

    Lov. What? With the plague? Stand thou then farther.

    Fac.   No, sir,   5
I had it not.

    Lov.   Who had it then? I left
None else but thee i'the house!

    Fac.   Yes, sir. My fellow,
The cat, that kept the buttery, had it on her
A week before I spied it: but I got her
Conveyed away, i'the night. And so I shut   10
The house up for a month——

    Lov.   How!

Fac.   Purposing then, sir,
To have burnt rose-vinegar, treacle, and tar,
And ha' made it sweet, that you should ne'er ha' known it:
Because I knew the news would but afflict you, sir.

15   *Lov.* Breathless, and farther off. Why, this is stranger!
The neighbours tell me all, here, that the doors
Have still been open——
     Fac.   How, sir!
     Lov.   Gallants, men, and women,
And of all sorts, tag-rag, been seen to flock here
In threaves, these ten weeks, as to a second Hoxton,
In days of Pimlico, and Eye-bright!

20   *Fac.*   Sir,
Their wisdoms will not say so!
     Lov.   Today, they speak
Of coaches and gallants; one in a French hood,
Went in, they tell me: and another was seen
In a velvet gown, at the window? Divers more
Pass in and out!

25   *Fac.*   They did pass through the doors then,
Or walls, I assure their eyesights, and their spectacles;
For here, sir, are the keys: and here have been,
In this my pocket, now, above twenty days!
And for before, I kept the fort alone, there.

30 But, that 'tis yet not deep i'the afternoon,
I should believe my neighbours had seen double
Through the black-pot, and made these apparitions!
For on my faith, to your worship, for these three weeks
And upwards, the door has not been opened.
     Lov.   Strange!
     1st Nei. Good faith, I think I saw a coach!

35   *2nd Nei.*   And I too,
I'd ha' been sworn!
     Lov.   Do you but think it now?
And but one coach?
     4th Nei.   We cannot tell, sir: Jeremy

---

19 *threaves*: droves   *Hoxton*: a favourite resort   20 *Eye-bright*: also famous
for its beer   32 *black-pot*: beer mug

Is a very honest fellow.

    Fac.   Did you see me at all?

    1st Nei. No. That we are sure on.

    2nd Nei.   I'll be sworn o' that.

    Lov. Fine rogues, to have your testimonies built on!   40

[Enter 3rd Neighbour with tools]

    3rd Nei. Is Jeremy come?

    1st Nei.   Oh, yes, you may leave your tools,

We were deceived, he says.

    2nd Nei.   He's had the keys:

And the door has been shut these three weeks.

    3rd Nei.   Like enough.

    Lov. Peace, and get hence, you changelings.

    Fac. [Seeing Surly *and* Mammon]   Surly come!

And Mammon made acquainted? They'll tell all.   45

(How shall I beat them off? What shall I do?)

Nothing's more wretched, than a guilty conscience.

ACT V, Scene iii

Enter Surly, Sir Epicure Mammon

    Sur. No, sir, he was a great physician. This,

It was no bawdy-house: but mere chancel.

You knew the lord, and his sister.

    Mam.   Nay, good Surly——

    Sur. The happy word, 'be rich'——

    Mam.   Play not the tyrant——

    Sur. Should be today pronounced to all your friends.   5

And where be your andirons now? And your brass pots?

That should ha' been golden flagons, and great wedges?

    Mam. Let me but breathe. What! They ha' shut their doors,

Methinks!

---

    44 *changelings*: quibble on (1) changing of opinions, (2) idiots   (*V. iii*) 2 *mere*: absolute

  Sur. Aye, now, 'tis holy-day with them.

  Mam.   Rogues,

Cozeners, impostors, bawds.   (*Mammon and* Surly *knock*)

10 *Fac.*   What mean you, sir?

  Mam. To enter if we can.

  Fac.   Another man's house?

Here is the owner, sir. Turn you to him,

And speak your business.

  Mam.   Are you, sir, the owner?

  Lov. Yes, sir.

  Mam.   And are those knaves, within, your cheaters?

  Lov. What knaves? What cheaters?

15 *Mam.*   Subtle, and his Lungs.

  Fac. The gentleman is distracted, sir! No lungs,

Nor lights ha' been seen here these three weeks, sir,

Within these doors, upon my word!

  Sur.   Your word,

Groom arrogant?

  Fac.   Yes, sir, I am the housekeeper,

20 And know the keys ha' not been out o' my hands.

  Sur. This's a new Face?

  Fac.   You do mistake the house, sir!

What sign was't at?

  Sur.   You rascal! This is one

O' the confederacy. Come, let's get officers,

And force the door.

  Lov.   'Pray you stay, gentlemen.

  Sur. No, sir, we'll come with warrant.

25 *Mam.*   Aye, and then,

We shall ha' your doors open.   [*Exit with* Surly]

  Lov.   What means this?

  Fac. I cannot tell, sir!

  1st Nei.   These are two o'the gallants,

That we do think we saw.

  Fac.   Two o' the fools?

You talk as idly as they. Good faith, sir,

I think the moon has crazed 'em all!

---

 17 *lights*: lungs of beasts used as food for cats and dogs

[*Enter* Kastril]

                                (Oh me,   30
The angry boy come too? He'll make a noise,
And ne'er away till he have betrayed us all.)
  Kas. (*Knocks*) What rogues, bawds, slaves, you'll open the door
    anon.
Punk, cockatrice, my suster. By this light
I'll fetch the marshal to you. You are a whore,   35
To keep your castle——
  Fac.   Who would you speak with, sir?
  Kas. The bawdy Doctor, and the cozening Captain,
And Pus my suster.
  Lov.   This is something, sure!
  Fac. Upon my trust, the doors were never open, sir.
  Kas. I have heard all their tricks, told me twice over,   40
By the fat knight, and the lean gentleman.
  Lov. Here comes another.

              [*Enter* Ananias, Tribulation]

  Fac. [*Aside*]   Ananias too?
And his Pastor?
  Tri.   The doors are shut against us.
                              (*They beat too, at the door*)
  Ana. Come forth, you seed of sulphur, sons of fire,
Your stench, it is broke forth: abomination   45
Is in the house.
  Kas.   Aye, my suster's there.
  Ana.   The place,
It is become a cage of unclean birds.
  Kas. Yes, I will fetch the scavenger, and the constable.
  Tri. You shall do well.
  Ana.   We'll join, to weed them out.
  Kas. You will not come then? Punk, device, my suster!   50
  Ana. Call her not sister. She is a harlot, verily.
  Kas. I'll raise the street.

34 *cockatrice*: whore   48 *scavenger*: officer charged with keeping the streets clean
50 *punk, device*: arrant whore (*point-device*)

Lov.   Good gentlemen, a word.

Ana. Satan, avoid, and hinder not our zeal.

> [*Exit with* Tribulation, Kastril]

Lov. The world's turned Bedlam.

Fac.   These are all broke loose,

55 Out of St Katherine's, where they use to keep,
The better sort of mad-folks.

1st Nei.   All these persons

We saw go in, and out, here.

2nd Nei.   Yes, indeed, sir.

3rd Nei. These were the parties.

Fac.   Peace, you drunkards. Sir,

I wonder at it! Please you, to give me leave

60 To touch the door, I'll try, an' the lock be changed.

Lov. It mazes me!

Fac.   Good faith, sir, I believe,

There's no such thing. 'Tis all *deceptio visus*.

[*Aside*] Would I could get him away.

Dap. (Dapper *cries out within*)   Master Captain, Master Doctor.

Lov. Who's that?

Fac.   (Our clerk within, that I forgot!) I know not, sir,

Dap. [*Within*] For God's sake, when will her Grace be at leisure?

65 *Fac.*   Ha!

Illusions, some spirit o'the air: (his gag is melted,
And now he sets out the throat.)

Dap. [*Within*]   I am almost stifled——

(*Fac.* Would you were altogether.)

Lov.   'Tis i'the house.

Ha! List.

Fac.   Believe it, sir, i'the air!

Lov.   Peace, you——

Dap. [*Within*] Mine aunt's Grace does not use me well.

70 *Sub.* [*Within*]   You fool,

Peace, you'll mar all.

Fac. [*To* Subtle *within*] Or you will else, you rogue.

Lov. Oh, is it so? Then you converse with spirits!

---

55 *St Katherine's*: old hospital displaced by St. Katherine's Docks   62 *deceptio visus*: an optical illusion   67 *sets out the throat*: raises his voice

Come sir. No more o' your tricks, good Jeremy,
The truth, the shortest way.
    Fac.   Dismiss this rabble, sir.
[*Aside*] What shall I do? I am catched.
    Lov.   Good neighbours,   75
I thank you all. You may depart. [*Exeunt* Neighbours] Come sir,
You know that I am an indulgent master:
And therefore, conceal nothing. What's your medicine,
To draw so many several sorts of wildfowl?
    Fac. Sir, you were wont to affect mirth, and wit: 80
(But here's no place to talk on't i' the street.)
Give me but leave, to make the best of my fortune,
And only pardon me the abuse of your house:
It's all I beg. I'll help you to a widow,
In recompense, that you shall gi' me thanks for,   85
Will make you seven years younger, and a rich one.
'Tis but your putting on a Spanish cloak,
I have her within. You need not fear the house,
It was not visited.
    Lov.   But by me, who came
Sooner than you expected.
    Fac.   It is true, sir.   90
'Pray you forgive me.
    Lov.   Well: let's see your widow.   [*Exeunt*]

ACT V, Scene iv

Enter Subtle, Dapper

    Sub. How! Ha' you eaten your gag?
    Dap.   Yes faith, it crumbled
Away i' my mouth.
    Sub.   You ha' spoiled all then.
    Dap.   No,
I hope my aunt of Faery will forgive me.

---

89 *visited*: i.e. by the plague

Sub. Your aunt's a gracious lady: but in troth
You were to blame.
5   *Dap.*   The fume did overcome me,
And I did do't to stay my stomach. 'Pray you
So satisfy her Grace. Here comes the Captain.

[*Enter* Face]

Fac. How now! Is his mouth down?
Sub.   Aye! He has spoken!
Fac. (A pox, I heard him, and you too.) He's undone, then.
10   (I have been fain to say the house is haunted
With spirits, to keep churl back.
Sub.   And hast thou done it?
Fac. Sure, for this night.
Sub.   Why, then triumph, and sing
Of Face so famous, the precious king
Of present wits.
Fac.   Did you not hear the coil,
About the door?
15   *Sub.*   Yes, and I dwindled with it.)
Fac. Show him his aunt, and let him be dispatched:
I'll send her to you.   [*Exit*]
Sub.   Well sir, your aunt her Grace,
Will give you audience presently, on my suit,
And the Captain's word, that you did not eat your gag,
In any contempt of her Highness.
20   *Dap.*   Not I, in troth, sir.
Sub. Here she is come. (Dol *like the Queen of Faery*) Down o' your
      knees, and wriggle:
She has a stately presence. Good. Yet nearer,
And bid, God save you.
Dap.   Madam.
Sub.   And your aunt.
Dap. And my most gracious aunt, God save your Grace.
25   *Dol.* Nephew, we thought to have been angry with you:
But that sweet face of yours, hath turned the tide,

11 *churl*: countryman, because of his hop-yards (I. i. 184)   14 *coil*: disturbance

And made it flow with joy, that ebbed of love.
Arise, and touch our velvet gown.
    Sub.   The skirts,
And kiss 'em. So.
    Dol.   Let me now stroke that head,
Much, nephew, shalt thou win; much shalt thou spend;   30
Much shalt thou give away: much shalt thou lend.
    Sub. (Aye, much, indeed.) Why do you not thank her Grace?
    Dap. I cannot speak for joy.
    Sub.   See, the kind wretch!
Your Grace's kinsman right.
    Dol.   Give me the bird.
Here is your fly in a purse, about your neck, cousin,   35
Wear it, and feed it, about this day sen'night,
On your right wrist——
    Sub.   Open a vein, with a pin,
And let it suck but once a week: till then,
You must not look on't.
    Dol.   No. And, kinsman,
Bear yourself worthy of the blood you come on.   40
    Sub. Her Grace would ha' you eat no more Woolsack pies,
Nor Dagger frumenty.
    Dol.   Nor break his fast,
In heaven and hell.
    Sub.   She's with you everywhere!
Nor play with costermongers at mum-chance, tray-trip,
God make you rich (when as your aunt has done it:) but keep   45
The gallant'st company, and the best games——
    Dap.   Yes, sir.
    Sub. Gleek and primero: and what you get, be true to us.
    Dap. By this hand, I will.
    Sub.   You may bring's a thousand pound,
Before tomorrow night, (if but three thousand,
Be stirring) an' you will.

---

33 *kind*: showing natural feeling   41 *Woolsack*: tavern in Ivy Lane   42 *frumenty*:
dish made of wheat boiled in milk and seasoned (*Dagger*, I. i. 191)   43 *heaven,
and hell*: taverns on the site of the present House of Commons   44 *mum-chance,
tray-trip*: dice games popular with costermongers   45 *God make you rich*: variety
of backgammon   47 *Gleek and primero*: II. iii. 284n.

50   *Dap.*   I swear, I will then.
     Sub. Your fly will learn you all games.
     Fac. [*Within*]   Ha' you done there?
     Sub. Your Grace will command him no more duties?
     Dol.   No:
     But come and see me often. I may chance
     To leave him three or four hundred chests of treasure,
55   And some twelve thousand acres of Faeryland:
     If he game well and comely, with good gamesters.
     Sub. There's a kind aunt! Kiss her departing part,
     But you must sell your forty mark a year, now:
     Dap. Aye, sir, I mean.
     Sub.   Or, gi't away: pox on't.
60   *Dap.* I'll gi't mine aunt. I'll go and fetch the writings.
     Sub. 'Tis well, away.   [*Exit* Dapper]

                         [*Enter* Face]

     Fac.   Where's Subtle?
     Sub.   Here. What news?
     Fac. Drugger is at the door, go take his suit,
     And bid him fetch a parson presently:
     Say, he shall marry the widow. Thou shalt spend
     A hundred pound by the service!   [*Exit* Subtle]
65   Now, queen Dol,
     Ha' you packed up all?
     Dol.   Yes.
     Fac.   And how do you like
     The lady Pliant?
     Dol.   A good dull innocent.

                         [*Enter* Subtle]

     Sub. Here's your Hieronimo's cloak and hat.
     Fac.   Give me 'em.
     Sub. And the ruff too?
     Fac.   Yes, I'll come to you presently.   [*Exit*]
70   *Sub.* Now he is gone about his project, Dol,
     I told you of, for the widow.

          64 *spend*: i.e. have for spending

Dol.   'Tis direct
Against our articles.
   Sub.   Well, we'll fit him, wench.
Hast thou gulled her of her jewels, or her bracelets?
   Dol. No, but I will do't.
   Sub.   Soon at night, my Dolly,
When we are shipped, and all our goods aboard,   75
Eastward for Ratcliffe; we will turn our course
To Brainford, westward, if thou sayst the word:
And take our leaves of this o'er-weening rascal,
This peremptory Face.
   Dol.   Content, I'm weary of him.
   Sub. Thou'st cause, when the slave will run a-wiving, Dol,   80
Against the instrument, that was drawn between us.
   Dol. I'll pluck his bird as bare as I can.
   Sub.   Yes, tell her,
She must by any means, address some present
To the cunning man; make him amends, for wronging
His art with her suspicion; send a ring;   85
Or chain of pearl; she will be tortured else
Extremely in her sleep, say: and ha' strange things
Come to her. Wilt thou?
   Dol.   Yes.
   Sub.   My fine flitter-mouse,
My bird o'the night; we'll tickle it at the Pigeons,
When we have all, and may unlock the trunks,   90
And say, this's mine, and thine, and thine, and mine——

                                          (They kiss)

                    [Enter Face]

   Fac. What now, a-billing?
   Sub.   Yes, a little exalted
In the good passage of our stock-affairs.
   Fac. Drugger has brought his parson, take him in, Subtle,
And send Nab back again, to wash his face.   95

   72 *fit him: The Spanish Tragedy* (ed. Edwards), IV. i. 70   77 *Brainford:*
Brentford   88 *flitter-mouse:* bat   89 *Pigeons:* 'The Three Pigeons' in
Brentford market-place

    Sub. I will: and shave himself?

    Fac.   If you can get him.

                                        [*Exit* Subtle]

    Dol. You are hot upon it, Face, what e'er it is!

    Fac. A trick, that Dol shall spend ten pound a month by.

[*Enter* Subtle]

Is he gone?

    Sub.   The chaplain waits you i'the hall, sir.

    Fac. I'll go bestow him.   [*Exit*]

100   *Dol.*   He'll now marry her, instantly.

    Sub. He cannot yet, he is not ready. Dear Dol,

Cozen her of all thou canst. To deceive him

Is no deceit, but justice, that would break

Such an inextricable tie as ours was.

    Dol. Let me alone to fit him.

[*Enter* Face]

105   *Fac.*   Come, my venturers,

You ha' packed up all? Where be the trunks? Bring forth.

    Sub. Here.

    Fac.   Let's see 'em. Where's the money?

    Sub.   Here,

In this.

    Fac. Mammon's ten pound: eight score before.

The Brethren's money, this. Drugger's, and Dapper's.

What paper's that?

110   *Dol.*   The jewel of the waiting maid's,

That stole it from her lady, to know certain——

    Fac. If she should have precedence of her mistress?

    Dol.   Yes.

    Fac. What box is that?

    Sub.   The fishwife's rings, I think:

And the alewife's single money. Is't not Dol?

115   *Dol.* Yes: and the whistle, that the sailor's wife

Brought you, to know and her husband were with Ward.

114 *single money*: small coins not requiring change   116 *Ward*: a noted pirate
(and = if)

Fac. We'll wet it tomorrow: and our silver beakers,
And tavern cups. Where be the French petticoats,
And girdles, and hangers?
   Sub.   Here, i'the trunk,
And the bolts of lawn.
   Fac.   Is Drugger's damask there?   120
And the tobacco?
   Sub.   Yes.
   Fac.   Give me the keys.
   Dol. Why you the keys!
   Sub.   No matter, Dol: because
We shall not open 'em before he comes.
   Fac. 'Tis true, you shall not open them, indeed:
Nor have 'em forth. Do you see? Not forth, Dol.
   Dol.   No!   125
   Fac. No, my smock-rampant. The right is, my master
Knows all, has pardoned me, and he will keep 'em.
Doctor, 'tis true (you look) for all your figures:
I sent for him, indeed. Wherefore, good partners,
Both he, and she, be satisfied: for, here   130
Determines the indenture tripartite,
Twixt Subtle, Dol, and Face. All I can do
Is to help you over the wall, o' the back-side;
Or lend you a sheet, to save your velvet gown, Dol.
Here will be officers, presently; bethink you,   135
Of some course suddenly to scape the dock:
For thither you'll come else. (*Some knock*) Hark you, thunder.
   Sub. You are a precious fiend!
   Off. [*Without*]   Open the door.
   Fac. Dol, I am sorry for thee i'faith. But hear'st thou?
It shall go hard, but I will place thee somewhere: 140
Thou shalt ha' my letter to Mistress Amo.
   Dol.   Hang you——
   Fac. Or Madam Caesarean.
   Dol.   Pox upon you, rogue,
Would I had but time to beat thee.

119 *hangers*: *EMI* I. v. 71 n.   128 *figures*: horoscopes   141 *Amo* . . .
Caesarean: brothel-keepers

 Fac.   Subtle,
Let's know where you set up next; I'll send you
145 A customer, now and then, for old acquaintance:
What new course ha' you?
 Sub.   Rogue, I'll hang myself:
That I may walk a greater devil than thou,
And haunt thee i'the flock-bed, and the buttery.   [*Exeunt*]

ACT V, Scene v

Enter Lovewit [*in Spanish dress with the* Parson]

 Lov. What do you mean, my masters?
 Mam. [*Without*]   Open your door,
Cheaters, bawds, conjurers.
 Off. [*Without*]   Or we'll break it open.
 Lov. What warrant have you?
 Off. [*Without*]   Warrant enough, sir, doubt not
If you'll not open it.
 Lov.   Is there an officer there?
 Off. [*Without*] Yes, two or three for failing.
5 *Lov.*   Have but patience
And I will open it straight.

[*Enter* Face]

 Fac.   Sir, ha' you done?
Is it a marriage? Perfect?
 Lov.   Yes, my brain.
 Fac. Off with you ruff, and cloak then, be yourself, sir.
 Sur. [*Without*] Down with the door.
 Kas. [*Without*]   'Slight, ding it open.
 Lov. [*Opening door, they try to rush in*]   Hold.
10 Hold gentlemen, what means this violence?
 Mam. Where is this collier?
 Sur.   And my Captain Face?

 5 *for failing*: as a precaution against failing 9 *ding it open*: break it down
11 *collier*: I. i. 90

Mam. These day-owls.

Sur.   That are birding in men's purses.

Mam. Madam Suppository.

Kas.   Doxy, my suster.

Ana.   Locusts

Of the foul pit.

    Tri.   Profane as Bel, and the Dragon.

    Ana. Worse than the grasshoppers, or the lice of Egypt.   15

    Lov. Good gentlemen, hear me. Are you officers,

And cannot stay this violence?

    Off.   Keep the peace.

    Lov. Gentlemen, what is the matter? Whom do you seek?

    Mam. The chemical cozener.

    Sur.   And the Captain Pandar.

    Kas. The nun my suster.

    Mam.   Madam Rabbi.

    Ana.   Scorpions,   20

And caterpillars.

    Lov.   Fewer at once, I pray you.

    Off. One after another, gentlemen, I charge you,

By virtue of my staff——

    Ana.   They are the vessels

Of pride, lust, and the cart.

    Lov.   Good zeal, lie still,

A little while.

    Tri.   Peace, Deacon Ananias.   25

    Lov. The house is mine here, and the doors are open:

If there be any such persons, as you seek for,

Use your authority, search on o' God's name.

I am but newly come to town, and finding

This tumult 'bout my door (to tell you true)   30

It somewhat 'mazed me; till my man here (fearing

My more displeasure) told me he had done

Somewhat an insolent part, let out my house

(Belike, presuming on my known aversion

---

13 *Suppository*: cf. *SN*, Intermean II. 47, with quibble on 'impostor' (supposititious)   14 *Bel, and the Dragon*: in the addition to the Book of Daniel in the Apocrypha   20 *nun*: facetiously applied to prostitutes

35 From any air o'the town, while there was sickness)
   To a Doctor and a Captain: who, what they are,
   Or where they be, he knows not.
  Mam.   Are they gone?
  Lov. You may go in, and search, sir. (*They enter*) Here, I find
   The empty walls, worse than I left 'em, smoked,
40 A few cracked pots, and glasses, and a furnace,
   The ceiling filled with posies of the candle:
   And Madam, with a dildo, writ o' the walls.
   Only, one gentlewoman, I met here,
   That is within, that said she was a widow——
45 *Kas.* Aye, that's my suster. I'll go thump her. Where is she?
                  [*Exit*]

  Lov. And should ha' married a Spanish Count, but he,
   When he came to't, neglected her so grossly,
   That I, a widower, am gone through with her.
  Sur. How! Have I lost her then?
  Lov.   Were you the Don, sir?
50 Good faith, now, she does blame you extremely, and says
   You swore, and told her, you had ta'en the pains,
   To dye your beard, and umber o'er your face,
   Borrowed a suit and ruff, all for her love;
   And then did nothing. What an oversight,
55 And want of putting forward, sir, was this!
   Well fare an old harquebusier, yet,
   Could prime his powder, and give fire, and hit,
   All in a twinkling.   (Mammon *comes forth*)
  Mam.   The whole nest are fled!
  Lov. What sort of birds were they?
  Mam.   A kind of choughs,
60 Or thievish daws, sir, that have picked my purse
   Of eight-score, and ten pounds, within these five weeks,
   Beside my first materials; and my goods,
   That lie i'the cellar: which I am glad they ha' left,
   I may have home yet.

---

 41 *posies of the candle*: i.e. written with candle-smoke   42 *dildo*: phallus
56 *harquebusier*: musketeer (armed with the harquebus) 59–60 *choughs . . . daws*:
of the crow family

Lov.   Think you so, sir?

Mam.   Aye.

Lov. By order of law, sir, but not otherwise.   65

Mam. Not mine own stuff?

Lov.   Sir, I can take no knowledge,
That they are yours, but by public means.
If you can bring certificate, that you were gulled of 'em,
Or any formal writ, out of a court,
That you did cozen yourself: I will not hold them.   70

Mam. I'll rather lose 'em.

Lov.   That you shall not, sir,
By me, in troth. Upon these terms they're yours.
What should they ha' been, sir, turned into gold all?

Mam.   No.
I cannot tell. It may be they should. What then?

Lov. What a great loss in hope have you sustained?   75

Mam. Not I, the commonwealth has.

Fac.   Aye, he would ha' built
The city new; and made a ditch about it
Of silver, should have run with cream from Hoxton:
That, every Sunday in Moorfields, the younkers,
And tits, and tomboys should have fed on, *gratis*.   80

Mam. I will go mount a turnip-cart, and preach
The end o'the world, within these two months. Surly,
What! In a dream?

Sur.   Must I needs cheat myself,
With that same foolish vice of honesty!
Come let us go, and hearken out the rogues.   85
That Face I'll mark for mine, if e'er I meet him.

Fac. If I can hear of him, sir, I'll bring you word
Unto your lodging: for in troth, they were strangers
To me, I thought 'em honest, as myself, sir.

          [*Exeunt* Surly, Mammon] (Tribulation *and* Ananias *come forth*)

Tri. 'Tis well, the Saints shall not lose all yet. Go,   90
And get some carts——

Lov.   For what, my zealous friends?

Ana. To bear away the portion of the righteous,

80 *tits, and tomboys*: young girls   85 *hearken out*: find out

Out of this den of thieves.

  Lov.   What is that portion?

  Ana. The goods, sometimes the orphans', that the Brethren
Bought with their silver pence.

95 *Lov.*   What, those i'the cellar,
The knight Sir Mammon claims?

  Ana.   I do defy
The wicked Mammon, so do all the Brethren,
Thou profane man. I ask thee, with what conscience
Thou canst advance that idol against us,

100 That have the seal? Were not the shillings numbered,
That made the pounds? Were not the pounds told out,
Upon the second day of the fourth week,
In the eight month, upon the table dormant,
The year, of the last patience of the Saints,
Six hundred and ten?

  Lov.   Mine earnest vehement botcher,

105 And deacon also, I cannot dispute with you,
But, if you get you not away the sooner,
I shall confute you with a cudgel.

  Ana.   Sir.

  Tri. Be patient Ananias.

  Ana.   I am strong,

110 And will stand up, well girt, against an host,
That threaten Gad in exile.

  Lov.   I shall send you
To Amsterdam, to your cellar.

  Ana.   I will pray there,
Against thy house: may dogs defile thy walls,
And wasps, and hornets breed beneath thy roof,

115 This seat of falsehood, and this cave of cozenage.

           [*Exit with* Tribulation]

  Lov. Another too?

       Enter Drugger

  Dru.   Not I sir, I am no Brother.

---

 100 *the seal*: Rev. 9: 4 103 *table dormant*: permanent side-table (distinct from
a removable 'board') 111 Gen. 49: 19

    Lov. Away you Harry Nicholas, do you talk?

                                  (*He beats him away*)

    Fac. No, this was Abel Drugger. (*To the Parson*) Good sir, go,
And satisfy him; tell him, all is done:
He stayed too long a-washing of his face.   120
The Doctor, he shall hear of him at Westchester;
And of the Captain, tell him at Yarmouth: or
Some good port-town else, lying for a wind.   [*Exit* Parson]

                   [*Enter* Kastril]

If you get off the angry child, now, sir——

    Kas. (*To his sister*) Come on, you ewe, you have matched most
      sweetly, ha' you not?   125
Did not I say, I would never ha' you tupped
But by a dubbed boy, to make you a lady-tom?
'Slight, you are a mammet! Oh, I could touse you now.
Death, mun' you marry with a pox?

    Lov.   You lie, boy;
As sound as you: and I am aforehand with you.

    Kas.   Anon?   130

    Lov. Come, will you quarrel? I will feize you, sirrah.
Why do you not buckle to your tools?

    Kas.   God's light!
This is a fine old boy, as e'er I saw!

    Lov. What, do you change your copy, now? Proceed,
Here stands my dove: stoop at her, if you dare.   135

    Kas. 'Slight I must love him! I cannot choose, i'faith!
And I should be hanged for't. Suster, I protest,
I honour thee, for this match.

    Lov.   Oh, do you so, sir?

    Kas. Yes, and thou canst take tobacco, and drink, old boy,
I'll give her five hundred pound more, to her marriage,   140
Than her own state.

    Lov.   Fill a pipe-full, Jeremy.

---

117 *Harry Nicholas*: Henrick Niclaes, Anabaptist leader of the sect of 'the Family of
Love', suppressed by Elizabeth in 1580   121 *Westchester*: Chester   128 *mammet*:
puppet   *touse*: beat   131 *feize you*: settle your business   134 *copy*: style,
demeanour   135 *stoop at*: swoop on (falconry)

    Fac. Yes, but go in, and take it, sir.
    Lov.   We will.
I will be ruled by thee in anything, Jeremy.
    Kas. 'Slight, thou art not hidebound! Thou art a Jovy' boy!
145 Come let's in, I pray thee, and take our whiffs.
    Lov. Whiff in with your sister, brother boy. [*Exeunt* Kastril, Dame]
          That master
That had received such happiness by a servant,
In such a widow, and with so much wealth,
Were very ungrateful, if he would not be
150 A little indulgent to that servant's wit,
And help his fortune, though with some small strain
Of his own candour. Therefore, gentlemen,
And kind spectators, if I have outstripped
An old man's gravity, or strict canon, think
155 What a young wife, and a good brain may do:
Stretch age's truth sometimes, and crack it too.
Speak for thyself, knave.
    Fac.   So I will, sir. Gentlemen,
My part a little fell in this last scene,
Yet 'twas decorum. And though I am clean
160 Got off, from Subtle, Surly, Mammon, Dol,
Hot Ananias, Dapper, Drugger, all
With whom I traded; yet I put myself
On you, that are my country: and this pelf,
Which I have got, if you do quit me, rests
165 To feast you often, and invite new guests.   [*Exeunt*]

THE END

144 *Jovy'*: jovial (born under Jupiter)   152 *candour*: honour, fair repute
159 *decorum*: appropriate to his role   163 *country*: the accused pleading not
guilty was tried 'by God and the country' (i.e. jury)

BARTHOLOMEW FAIR

BARTHOLMEW FAYRE:

A COMEDIE,

ACTED IN THE
YEARE, 1614.

By the Lady *ELIZABETHS*
SERVANTS.

And then dedicated to King I AMES, of
most Blessed Memorie;

By the Author, BENIAMIN IOHNSON.

Si foret in terris, rideret Democritus : *nam*
Spectaret populum ludis attentius ipsis,
Vt sibi præbentem, mimo spectacula plura.
Scriptores autem narrare putaret asello
Fabellam surdo.   Hor.lib.2. Epist. 1.

LONDON,
Printed by *I. B.* for ROBERT ALLOT, and are
to be sold at the signe of the *Beare,* in *Pauls*
Church yard. 1631.

The title-page of the Folio, 1631, with Beale's device.

THE
PROLOGUE
TO
THE KING'S
MAJESTY.

Your Majesty is welcome to a Fair;
Such place, such men, such language and such ware,
You must expect: with these, the zealous noise
Of your land's faction, scandalized at toys,
As babies, hobby-horses, puppet-plays,   5
And suchlike rage, whereof the petulant ways
Yourself have known, and have been vexed with long.
These for your sport, without particular wrong,
Or just complaint of any private man,
(Who of himself, or shall think well or can)   10
The maker doth present: and hopes tonight
To give you for a fairing, true delight.

4 *faction*: the Puritans   5 *babies*: dolls, puppets   12 *fairing*:
present from a fair

The Persons of the Play

John Littlewit, *a proctor*
Solomon, *his man*
Win Littlewit, *his wife*
Dame Purecraft, *her mother, and a widow*
Zeal-of-the-Land Busy, *her suitor, a Banbury man*
Winwife, *his rival, a gentleman*
Quarlous, *his companion, a gamester*
Bartholomew Cokes, *an esquire of Harrow*
Humphrey Wasp, *his man*
Adam Overdo, *a justice of peace*
Dame Overdo, *his wife*
Grace Wellborn, *his ward*
Lantern Leatherhead, *a hobby-horse seller*
Joan Trash, *a gingerbread woman*
Ezekiel Edgeworth, *a cutpurse*
Nightingale, *a ballad-singer*

Ursula, *a pig-woman*
Mooncalf, *her tapster*
Jordan Knockem, *a horse-courser, and ranger of Turnbull*
Val. Cutting, *a roarer*
Captain Whit, *a bawd*
Punk Alice, *mistress of the game*
Trouble-all, *a madman*
3 watchmen [Haggis, Bristle, *and* Pocher, *a beadle*]
Costardmonger
Corncutter
Mousetrap man [also called a Tinder-box man]
Clothier [Northern]
Wrestler [Puppy]
Porters
Doorkeepers [Filcher, Sharkwell]
Puppets

THE INDUCTION
ON THE *STAGE*.

Enter Stage-keeper

Sta. GENTLEMEN, have a little patience, they are e'en upon
coming, instantly. He that should begin the play, Master Littlewit,
the proctor, has a stitch new fallen in his black silk stocking; 'twill
be drawn up ere you can tell twenty. He plays one o' the Arches,
that dwells about the Hospital, and he has a very pretty part. But 5
for the whole play, will you ha' the truth on't? (I am looking, lest
the poet hear me, or his man, Master Brome, behind the arras) it is
like to be a very conceited scurvy one, in plain English. When 't
comes to the Fair, once: you were e'en as good go to Virginia, for
anything there is of Smithfield. He has not hit the humours, he 10
does not know 'em; he has not conversed with the Bartholomew-
birds, as they say; he has ne'er a sword and buckler man in his
Fair, nor a little Davy, to take toll o' the bawds there, as in my time,
nor a Kindheart, if anybody's teeth should chance to ache in his
play. Nor a juggler with a well-educated ape to come over the chain, 15
for the King of England, and back again for the Prince, and sit still
on his arse for the Pope, and the King of Spain! None o' these fine
sights! Nor has he the canvas-cut i' the night, for a hobby-horseman
to creep in to his she-neighbour, and take his leap there! Nothing!
No, and some writer (that I know) had had but the penning o' this 20
matter, he would ha' made you such a jig-a-jog i' the booths, you
should ha' thought an earthquake had been i' the Fair! But these
Master-Poets, they will ha' their own absurd courses; they will be
informed of nothing! He has (sir-reverence) kicked me three or
four times about the tiring-house, I thank him, for but offering to 25

4 *one o' the Arches*: a proctor of the Court of Arches held in Bow Church
5 *Hospital*: St. Bartholomew in Smithfield (site of the fair)   7 *Brome*: Richard
Brome, servant and then disciple of Jonson   8 *conceited*: witty, ingenious
11-12 *Bartholomew-birds*: II. ii. 34-5   12 *sword and buckler man*: who took part
in the swordplay at West Smithfield (l. 103)   13 *little Davy*: apparently a 'bully
on the town' (l. 104)   14 *Kindheart*: itinerant tooth-drawer   24 *sir-reverence*:
saving your reverence   25 *tiring-house*: dressing-room

put in, with my experience. I'll be judged by you, gentlemen, now,
but for one conceit of mine! Would not a fine pump upon the stage
ha' done well, for a property now? And a punk set under upon her
head, with her stern upward, and ha' been soused by my witty
30 young masters o' the Inns o' Court? What think you o' this for a
show, now? He will not hear o' this! I am an ass! I! And yet I
kept the stage in Master Tarlton's time, I thank my stars. Ho!
and that man had lived to have played in *Bartholomew Fair*, you
should ha' seen him ha' come in, and ha' been cozened i' the Cloth-
35 quarter so finely! And Adams, the rogue, ha' leaped and capered
upon him, and ha' dealt his vermin about, as though they had cost
him nothing. And then a substantial watch to ha' stolen in upon
'em, and taken 'em away, with mistaking words, as the fashion is,
in the stage-practice,

Enter Book-holder, Scrivener

40 *Boo.* How now? What rare discourse are you fallen upon? Ha?
Ha' you found any familiars here, that you are so free? What's the
business?

Sta. Nothing, but the understanding gentlemen o' the ground
here asked my judgement.

45 *Boo.* Your judgement, rascal? For what? Sweeping the stage?
Or gathering up the broken apples for the bears within? Away
rogue, it's come to a fine degree in these spectacles when such a
youth as you pretend to a judgement.   [*Exit* Stage-keeper]
And yet he may, i' the most o' this matter i'faith: for the author
50 hath writ it just to his meridian, and the scale of the grounded
judgements here, his play-fellows in wit. Gentlemen; not for want
of a Prologue, but by way of a new one, I am sent out to you here,
with a scrivener, and certain articles drawn out in haste between our
author and you; which if you please to hear, and as they appear

---

28 *punk*: whore   32 *Tarlton*: principal comedian of the Queen's Men, 1583–8
34–5 *Cloth-quarter*: line of booths along the church wall: one of *Tarltons Jests* describes
his being duped out of his clothes there   35 *Adams*: fellow member of the Queen's
Men   37–8 *watch . . . mistaking words*: as in *Much Ado*, III. iii   39/40 s.d.
Book-holder: prompter   43 *understanding gentlemen o' the ground*: those in the pit
46 *bears*: the Hope Theatre was also used for bear-baiting   50 *meridian*: i.e.
capacity, level.

reasonable, to approve of; the play will follow presently. Read, 55
scribe, gi' me the counterpane.

Scr. Articles of Agreement, indented, between the Spectators or
Hearers, at the Hope on the Bankside, in the County of Surrey on
the one party; and the Author of *Bartholomew Fair* in the said place,
and County on the other party: the one and thirtieth day of October 60
1614, and in the twelfth year of the Reign of our Sovereign Lord,
James by the grace of God King of England, France, and Ireland;
Defender of the Faith. And of Scotland the seven and fortieth.

Imprimis. It is covenanted and agreed, by and between the parties
abovesaid, and the said Spectators and Hearers, as well the curious 65
and envious, as the favouring and judicious, as also the grounded
judgements and understandings, do for themselves severally cove-
nant, and agree to remain in the places, their money or friends have
put them in, with patience, for the space of two hours and an half,
and somewhat more. In which time the Author promiseth to present 70
them by us, with a new sufficient play called *Bartholomew Fair*,
merry, and as full of noise, as sport: made to delight all, and to
offend none. Provided they have either the wit or the honesty to
think well of themselves.

It is further agreed that every person here, have his or their free- 75
will of censure, to like or dislike at their own charge, the Author
having now departed with his right: it shall be lawful for any man
to judge his six pennorth, his twelve pennorth, so to his eighteen
pence, two shillings, half a crown, to the value of his place: Provided
always his place get not above his wit. And if he pay for half a 80
dozen, he may censure for all them too, so that he will undertake
that they shall be silent. He shall put in for censures here, as they
do for lots at the lottery: marry, if he drop but sixpence at the door,
and will censure a crown's worth, it is thought there is no con-
science, or justice in that.

It is also agreed that every man here exercise his own judgemen
and not censure by contagion, or upon trust, from another's voice
face, that sits by him, be he never so first in the Commission of

---

56 *counterpane*: counterpart of an indenture   76 *censure*: judgement
parted: parted   83 *lottery*: a lottery under royal patronage for fu
plantation of Virginia   88 *Commission of Wit*: as though a commiss
set up to assess the play (cf. 'Bench', l. 92)

As also, that he be fixed and settled in his censure, that what he
90 approves, or not approves today, he will do the same tomorrow,
and if tomorrow, the next day, and so the next week (if need be):
and not to be brought about by any that sits on the Bench with him,
though they indict and arraign plays daily. He that will swear,
Jeronimo, or *Andronicus* are the best plays, yet shall pass unex-
95 cepted at, here, as a man whose judgement shows it is constant, and
hath stood still, these five and twenty, or thirty years. Though it be
an ignorance, it is a virtuous and stayed ignorance; and next to truth,
a confirmed error does well; such a one, the Author knows where
to find him.

100   It is further covenanted, concluded and agreed, that how great
soever the expectation be, no person here is to expect more than he
knows, or better ware than a Fair will afford: neither to look back
to the sword and bucklerage of Smithfield, but content himself with
the present. Instead of a little Davy, to take toll o' the bawds, the
105 Author doth promise a strutting horse-courser, with a leer drunk-
ard, two or three to attend him, in as good equipage as you would
wish. And then for Kindheart, the tooth-drawer, a fine oily pig-
woman with her tapster, to bid you welcome, and a consort of
roarers for music. A wise Justice of Peace meditant, instead of a
110 juggler, with an ape. A civil cutpurse searchant. A sweet singer of
new ballads allurant: and as fresh an hypocrite, as ever was broached,
rampant. If there be never a servant-monster i'the Fair; who can
help it? he says; nor a nest of antics? He is loth to make Nature
afraid in his plays, like those that beget Tales, Tempests, and such
115 like drolleries, to mix his head with other men's heels, let the con-
cupiscence of jigs and dances reign as strong as it will amongst
you: yet if the puppets will please anybody, they shall be entreated
to come in.

        In consideration of which, it is finally agreed, by the foresaid
120 Hearers and Spectators, that they neither in themselves conceal,
nor suffer by them to be concealed, any state-decipherer, or

94 *Jeronimo* . . . *Andronicus*: Kyd's *Spanish Tragedy* and Shakespeare's *Titus An-
dronicus* (as old-fashioned plays)   105 *horse-courser*: one who buys and sells horses
(but does not breed or train them)   *leer*: sly   109–12 a mock coat of arms
12 *servant-monster*: like Caliban (cf. 'Tempests', l. 114)   113 *antics*: clowns,
grotesques; referring to the dance of Satyrs in *The Winter's Tale*, IV. iv. 334 (cf.
'Tales', l. 114)

politic picklock of the scene, so solemnly ridiculous, as to search out, who was meant by the gingerbread-woman, who by the hobby-horse-man, who by the costardmonger, nay, who by their wares. Or that will pretend to affirm (on his own inspired ignorance) what Mirror 125 of Magistrates is meant by the Justice, what great lady by the pig-woman, what concealed statesman, by the seller of mousetraps, and so of the rest. But that such person, or persons so found, be left discovered to the mercy of the Author, as a forfeiture to the stage, and your laughter, aforesaid. As also, such as shall so desperately, 130 or ambitiously, play the fool by his place aforesaid, to challenge the Author of scurrility, because the language somewhere savours of Smithfield, the booth, and the pig-broth, or of profaneness, because a madman cries, *God quit you*, or *bless you*. In witness whereof, as you have preposterously put to your seals already (which is your 135 money) you will now add the other part of suffrage, your hands. The play shall presently begin. And though the Fair be not kept in the same region that some here, perhaps, would have it, yet think, that therein the Author hath observed a special decorum, the place being as dirty as Smithfield, and as stinking every whit. 140

Howsoever, he prays you to believe, his ware is still the same, else you will make him justly suspect that he that is so loth to look on a baby, or an hobby-horse, here, would be glad to take up a commodity of them, at any laughter, or loss, in another place.

[*Exeunt*]

122 *politic picklock*: one intent on identifying the play's characters with actual people   124 *costardmonger*: apple-and-pear man   125-6 *Mirror of Magistrates*: probably 'pattern or example for magistrates' (V. vi. 30), but see further *H&S* x. 177   134 *God quit you*: God reward you   135 *preposterously*: in reverse order   144 *commodity*: *Alch.* II. i. 11 n. and *H&S* ix. 658

BARTHOLOMEW FAIR

ACT I, Scene i

[Littlewit's house]

Enter Littlewit [*reading a licence*]

Lit. A PRETTY conceit, and worth the finding! I ha' such luck to spin out these fine things still, and like a silk-worm, out of myself. Here's Master Bartholomew Cokes, of Harrow o'the hill, i'the county of Middlesex, Esquire, takes forth his licence, to marry Mistress Grace Wellborn of the said place and county: and when 5 does he take it forth? Today! the four and twentieth of August! Bartholomew day! Bartholomew upon Bartholomew! There's the device! Who would have marked such a leapfrog chance now? A very . . . less than ames-ace, on two dice! Well, go thy ways, John Littlewit, proctor John Littlewit: one o' the pretty wits o' Pauls, the 10 Littlewit of London (so thou art called) and something beside. When a quirk, or a quiblin does scape thee, and thou dost not watch, and apprehend it, and bring it afore the constable of conceit: (there now, I speak quib too) let 'em carry thee out o' the archdeacon's court, into his kitchen, and make a Jack of thee instead of a John. (There 15 I am again la!)

[*Enter* Win Littlewit]

Win, good morrow, Win. Aye, marry, Win! Now you look finely indeed, Win! This cap does convince! You'd not ha' worn it, Win, nor ha' had it velvet, but a rough country beaver, with a copper-

---

3 *Cokes*: an ass, dolt   8 *device*: emblematic figure (cf. 'leap-frog') with accompanying motto   9 *ames-ace*: double ace, the lowest possible throw   12 *quiblin*: conceit   15 *Jack*: knave   18 *convince*: overpower (Lat. *convinco*)

20 band, like the coney-skin woman of Budge Row? Sweet Win, let me
kiss it! And her fine high shoes, like the Spanish lady! Good Win,
go a little, I would fain see thee pace, pretty Win! By this fine cap,
I could never leave kissing on't.

Win. Come, indeed la, you are such a fool, still!

25 *Lit.* No, but half a one, Win, you are the tother half: man and
wife make one fool, Win. (Good!) Is there the proctor, or doctor
indeed, i' the diocese, that ever had the fortune to win him such a
Win! (There I am again!) I do feel conceits coming upon me, more
than I am able to turn tongue to. A pox o' these pretenders to wit!

30 Your Three Cranes, Mitre, and Mermaid men! Not a corn of true
salt, nor a grain of right mustard amongst them all. They may stand
for places or so, again the next wit fall, and pay twopence in a quart
more for their canary than other men. But gi' me the man can start
up a justice of wit out of six-shillings beer, and give the law to all

35 the poets and poet-suckers i' town, because they are the players'
gossips? 'Slid, other men have wives as fine as the players, and as
well dressed. Come hither, Win.   [*Kisses her*]

ACT I, Scene ii

Enter Winwife

Winw. Why, how now Master Littlewit! Measuring of lips? Or
moulding of kisses? Which is it?

Lit. Troth I am a little taken with my Win's dressing here!
Does't not fine, Master Winwife? How do you apprehend, sir? She
5 would not ha' worn this habit. I challenge all Cheapside to show
such another: Moorfields, Pimlico path, or the Exchange, in a
summer evening, with a lace to boot as this has. Dear Win, let Master

---

20 *coney-skin*: rabbit-skin   *Budge Row* street of the skin and fur merchants
22 *go*: walk   30 *Three Cranes, Mitre . . . Mermaid*: London taverns   *corn*:
grain   31 *salt*: wit   32 *wit fall*: harvest of wit   33 *canary*: a light
sweet wine from the Canary Is.   34 *six-shillings beer*: small beer at 6s. a barrel
35 *poet-suckers*: sucking poets (as in 'rabbit-sucker', a young rabbit)   36 *gossips*:
familiar acquaintances   (*I. ii*) 5 *Cheapside*: noted for its mercers' shops
6 *Moorfields*: a park outside the city   *Pimlico*: *Alch.* V. i. 6 n.   *Exchange*: The New
Exchange in the Strand, with milliners' and sempstresses' shops

Winwife kiss you. He comes a-wooing to our mother, Win, and may
be our father perhaps, Win. There's no harm in him, Win.

Winw. None i' the earth, Master Littlewit.   [*Kisses her*] 10

Lit. I envy no man my delicates, sir.

Winw. Alas, you ha' the garden where they grow still! A wife here
with a strawberry-breath, cherry-lips, apricot cheeks, and a soft
velvet head, like a melicotton.

Lit. Good i'faith! Now dullness upon me, that I had not that 15
before him, that I should not light on't, as well as he! Velvet head!

Winw. But my taste, Master Littlewit, tends to fruit of a later
kind: the sober matron, your wife's mother.

Lit. Aye! We know you are a suitor, sir. Win, and I both, wish
you well: by this licence here, would you had her, that your two 20
names were as fast in it, as here are a couple. Win would fain have
a fine young father i' law, with a feather: that her mother might hood
it and chain it, with Mistress Overdo. But, you do not take the right
course, Master Winwife.

Winw. No? Master Littlewit, why?   25

Lit. You are not mad enough.

Winw. How? Is madness a right course?

Lit. I say nothing, but I wink upon Win. You have a friend, one
(Master Quarlous) comes here sometimes?

Winw. Why? He makes no love to her, does he?   30

Lit. Not a tokenworth that ever I saw, I assure you. But—

Winw. What?

Lit. He is the more madcap o' the two. You do not apprehend me.

Win. You have a hot coal i' your mouth, now, you cannot hold.

Lit. Let me out with it, dear Win.   35

Win. I'll tell him myself.

Lit. Do, and take all the thanks, and much good do thy pretty
heart, Win.

Win. Sir, my mother has had her nativity-water cast lately by the
cunning men in Cow Lane, and they ha' told her her fortune, and 40
do ensure her, she shall never have happy hour, unless she marry

---

14 *melicotton*: peach grafted on a quince   22–3 *hood . . . chain*: the marks of
office   31 *tokenworth*: farthing's worth   39 *water cast*: usually for diagnosis
of disease from the urine; here for a horoscope (nativity)   40 *cunning*: *Alch.* I.
ii. 8 n.

within this sennight, and when it is, it must be a madman, they
say.

    Lit. Aye, but it must be a gentleman madman.

45   *Win.* Yes, so the tother man of Moorfields says.

    Winw. But does she believe 'em?

    Lit. Yes, and has been at Bedlam twice since, every day, to
enquire if any gentleman be there, or to come there, mad!

    Winw. Why, this is a confederacy, a mere piece of practice upon
50 her, by these impostors?

    Lit. I tell her so; or else say I, that they mean some young-
madcap-gentleman (for the devil can equivocate as well as a shop-
keeper) and therefore would I advise you to be a little madder than
Master Quarlous hereafter.

55   *Win.* Where is she? Stirring yet?

    Lit. Stirring! Yes, and studying an old elder, come from Banbury,
a suitor that puts in here at meal-tide, to praise the painful brethren,
or pray that the sweet singers may be restored; says a grace as long
as his breath lasts him! Sometime the spirit is so strong with him,
60 it gets quite out of him, and then my mother, or Win, are fain to
fetch it again with malmsey, or *Aqua coelestis*.

    Win. Yes indeed, we have such a tedious life with him for his
diet, and his clothes too, he breaks his buttons, and cracks seams
at every saying he sobs out.

65   *Lit.* He cannot abide my vocation, he says.

    Win. No, he told my mother, a proctor was a claw of the Beast,
and that she had little less than committed abomination in marrying
me so as she has done.

    Lit. Every line (he says) that a proctor writes, when it comes to
70 be read in the Bishops' Court, is a long black hair, kembed out of
the tail of Antichrist.

    Winw. When came this proselyte?

    Lit. Some three days since.

  42 *sennight*: week   47 *Bedlam*: *Alch*. IV. iv. 47 n.   49 *practice*: craft,
deceit   56 *Banbury*: noted as a haunt of Puritans   57–8 *painful brethren* . . .
sweet singers: the Puritans   61 *malmsey*: a strong sweet wine *Aqua coelestis*: a
cordial distilled from wine

ACT I, Scene iii

Enter Quarlous

Qua. Oh sir, ha' you ta'en soil, here? It's well a man may reach you, after three hours' running yet! What an unmerciful companion art thou, to quit thy lodging at such ungentlemanly hours? None but a scattered covey of fiddlers, or one of these rag-rakers in dung-hills, or some marrowbone man at most, would have been up, when 5 thou wert gone abroad, by all description. I pray thee what ailest thou, thou canst not sleep? Hast thou thorns i' thy eyelids, or thistles i' thy bed?

Winw. I cannot tell. It seems you had neither i' your feet; that took this pain to find me. 10

Qua. No, and I had, all the limehounds o' the city should have drawn after you, by the scent rather. Master John Littlewit! God save you, sir. 'Twas a hot night with some of us, last night, John: shall we pluck a hair o' the same wolf today, proctor John?

Lit. Do you remember, Master Quarlous, what we discoursed on 15 last night?

Qua. Not I, John: nothing that I either discourse or do, at those times I forfeit all to forgetfulness.

Lit. No? Not concerning Win? Look you: there she is, and dressed as I told you she should be: hark you sir, had you forgot? 20

Qua. By this head, I'll beware how I keep you company, John, when I am drunk, and you have this dangerous memory! That's certain.

Lit. Why sir?

Qua. Why? We were all a little stained last night, sprinkled with 25 a cup or two, and I agreed with proctor John here to come and do somewhat with Win (I know not what 'twas) today; and he puts me in mind on't now; he says he was coming to fetch me: before truth, if you have that fearful quality, John, to remember, when you are sober, John, what you promise drunk, John; I shall take heed of you, 30

---

1 *ta'en soil*: hunting term for a stag taking to water when hard pressed   4 *covey*: brood, clutch   11 *limehounds*: bloodhounds (held by a leash called a 'liam') 24 this interjection must belong to Winwife (cf. l. 26)

John. For this once, I am content to wink at you, where's your wife?
Come hither, Win.   (*He kisseth her*)

35   *Win.* Why, John! Do you see this, John? Look you! Help
me, John.

    Lit. Oh Win, fie, what do you mean, Win! Be womanly, Win;
make an outcry to your mother, Win? Master Quarlous is an honest
gentleman, and our worshipful good friend, Win: and he is Master
Winwife's friend, too: and Master Winwife comes a suitor to your
mother, Win; as I told you before, Win, and may perhaps, be our
40 father, Win: they'll do you no harm, Win, they are both our
worshipful good friends. Master Quarlous! You must know Master
Quarlous, Win; you must not quarrel with Master Quarlous, Win.

    Qua. No, we'll kiss again and fall in.

    Lit. Yes, do, good Win.

45   *Win.* I'faith you are a fool, John.

    Lit. A fool-John she calls me, do you mark that, gentlemen?
Pretty littlewit of velvet! A fool-John!

    Qua. [*Aside*] She may call you an apple-John, if you use this.
                               [*Kisses her again*]

    Winw. Pray thee forbear, for my respect somewhat.

50   *Qua.* Hoy-day! How respective you are become o' the sudden!
I fear this family will turn you reformed too, pray you come about
again. Because she is in possibility to be your daughter-in-law, and
may ask you blessing hereafter, when she courts it to Tottenham to
eat cream. Well, I will forbear, sir, but i'faith, would thou wouldst
55 leave thy exercise of widow-hunting once! This drawing after an old
reverend smock by the splay foot. There cannot be an ancient tripe
or trillibub i' the town, but thou art straight nosing it, and 'tis a
fine occupation thou'lt confine thyself to, when thou hast got one;
scrubbing a piece of buff, as if thou hadst the perpetuity of Pannier
60 Alley to stink in; or perhaps, worse, currying a carcass, that thou
hast bound thyself to alive. I'll be sworn, some of them (that thou
art, or hast been a suitor to) are so old, as no chaste or married

---

43 *fall in*: be reconciled   48 *apple-John*: pun on 'apple-squire', a pandar
50 *respective*: respectful   53 *Tottenham*: Tottenham Court, known for cakes and
cream   55 *drawing after*: tracking—a hunting term—after old women with splay
feet   56–7 *tripe or trillibub*: the entrails; used scornfully of a fat person
59 *buff*: ox-hide; also the bare skin   59–60 *Pannier Alley*: associated with the
leather trade   60 *currying*: of dressing a horse with a comb

pleasure can ever become 'em: the honest instrument of pro-
creation has (forty years since) left to belong to 'em, thou must visit
'em, as thou wouldst do a tomb, with a torch, or three handfuls of 65
link, flaming hot, and so thou mayst hap to make 'em feel thee, and
after, come to inherit according to thy inches. A sweet course for a
man to waste the brand of life for, to be still raking himself a
fortune in an old woman's embers; we shall ha' thee, after thou hast
been but a month married to one of 'em, look like the quartan ague, 70
and the black jaundice met in a face, and walk as if thou hadst
borrowed legs of a spinner, and voice of a cricket. I would endure
to hear fifteen sermons a week for her, and such coarse and loud
ones, as some of 'em must be; I would e'en desire of Fate, I might
dwell in a drum, and take in my sustenance with an old broken 75
tobacco pipe and a straw. Dost thou ever think to bring thine ears
or stomach to the patience of a dry grace, as long as thy tablecloth?
And droned out by thy son, here (that might be thy father) till all
the meat o' thy board has forgot, it was that day i' the kitchen?
Or to brook the noise made, in a question of predestination, by the 80
good labourers and painful eaters, assembled together, put to 'em
by the matron, your spouse; who moderates with a cup of wine,
ever and anon, and a sentence out of Knox between? Or the perpetual
spitting, before and after a sober drawn exhortation of six hours,
whose better part was the *hum-ha-hum*? Or to hear prayers groaned 85
out, over thy iron-chests, as if they were charms to break 'em? And
all this for the hope of two Apostle-spoons, to suffer! And a cup to
eat a caudle in! For that will be thy legacy. She'll ha' conveyed her
state safe enough from thee, an' she be a right widow.

Winw. Alas, I am quite off that scent now.

Qua. How so? 90

Winw. Put off by a Brother of Banbury, one that they say is come
here, and governs all, already.

Qua. What do you call him? I knew divers of those Banburians
when I was in Oxford. 95

66 *link*: mixture of tow and pitch   70 *quartan ague*: with the paroxysm occur-
ring every fourth day (the third in modern reckoning)   72 *spinner*: spider
82 *moderates*: arbitrates   87 *Apostle-spoons*: made of silver (like the caudle cup),
with the figure of an apostle on the handle, and a common present at christenings
88 *caudle*: warm spiced gruel, for invalids   88–9 *conveyed her state*: made her
estate over to another

Winw. Master Littlewit can tell us.

Lit. Sir! Good Win, go in, and if Master Bartholomew Cokes his man come for the licence, (the little old fellow), let him speak with me; what say you, gentlemen?   [*Exit* Win]

100 *Winw.* What call you the reverend elder, you told me of? Your Banbury man?

Lit. Rabbi Busy, sir, he is more than an elder, he is a prophet, sir.

Qua. Oh, I know him! A baker, is he not?

105 *Lit.* He was a baker, sir, but he does dream now, and see visions, he has given over his trade.

Qua. I remember that too: out of a scruple he took, that (in spiced conscience) those cakes he made were served to bridals, Maypoles, Morrises, and such profane feasts and meetings; his
110 Christian-name is Zeal-of-the-land.

Lit. Yes, sir, Zeal-of-the-land Busy.

Winw. How, what a name's there!

Lit. Oh, they have all such names, sir; he was witness for Win, here (they will not be called Godfathers) and named her Win-the-
115 fight, you thought her name had been Winifred, did you not?

Winw. I did indeed.

Lit. He would ha' thought himself a stark reprobate, if it had.

Qua. Aye, for there was a blue-starch-woman o' the name, at the same time. A notable hypocritical vermin it is; I know him. One that
120 stands upon his face more than his faith, at all times; ever in seditious motion, and reproving for vain-glory: of a most lunatic conscience and spleen, and affects the violence of singularity in all he does. (He has undone a grocer here, in Newgate market, that broke with him, trusted him with currants, as arrant a zeal as he, that's by the way.) By his
125 profession, he will ever be i' the state of innocence, though, and child-hood; derides all antiquity; defies any other learning than inspiration; and what discretion soever years should afford him, it is all prevented in his original ignorance; ha' not to do with him: for he is a fellow of a most arrogant and invincible dullness, I assure you. Who is this?

---

108 *spiced*: dainty, over-particular   109 *Morrises*: morris-dances   118 *blue-starch-woman*: selling the starch for ruffs, of which the Puritans disapproved (*Alch.* III. ii. 82)   121 *in seditious motion*: stirring up trouble   123 *broke*: dealt
125 *profession*: i.e. declaration of faith   127 *prevented*: forestalled

ACT I, Scene iv

Enter Wasp [*with* Win]

Was. By your leave, gentlemen, with all my heart to you: and God you good morrow; Master Littlewit, my business is to you. Is this licence ready?

Lit. Here, I ha' it for you in my hand, Master Humphrey.

Was. That's well, nay, never open or read it to me, it's labour in 5 vain, you know. I am no clerk, I scorn to be saved by my book, i'faith I'll hang first; fold it up o' your word and gi' it me; what must you ha' for't?

Lit. We'll talk of that anon, Master Humphrey.

Was. Now, or not at all, good Master Proctor, I am for no anons, 10 I assure you.

Lit. Sweet Win, bid Solomon send me the little black box within, in my study.

Was. Aye, quickly, good Mistress, I pray you: for I have both eggs o' the spit, and iron i' the fire, say, what you must have, good 15 Master Littlewit.   [*Exit* Win]

Lit. Why, you know the price, Master Numps.

Was. I know? I know nothing, I, what tell you me of knowing? (Now I am in haste) sir, I do not know, and I will not know, and I scorn to know, and yet (now I think on't) I will, and do know, as 20 well as another; you must have a mark for your thing here, and eightpence for the box; I could ha' saved two pence i' that, an' I had brought it myself, but here's fourteen shillings for you. Good Lord! How long your little wife stays! Pray God, Solomon, your clerk, be not looking i' the wrong box, Master Proctor.   25

Lit. Good i'faith! No, I warrant you, Solomon is wiser than so, sir.

Was. Fie, fie, fie, by your leave Master Littlewit, this is scurvy, idle, foolish and abominable; with all my heart, I do not like it.

[*Walks aside*]

---

6 *saved by my book*: escape hanging by claiming benefit of clergy (*CR*, Ind. 36)
14–15 *both eggs o' the spit*: *EMI* III. vi. 44   17 *Numps*: diminutive of Humphrey
21 *a mark*: 13*s*. 4*d*.   25 *box*: quibble on box = pudendum

30   *Winw.* Do you hear? Jack Littlewit, what business does thy pretty head think this fellow may have, that he keeps such a coil with?

  Qua. More than buying of gingerbread i' the cloister, here (for that we allow him) or a gilt pouch i' the Fair?

35   *Lit.* Master Quarlous, do not mistake him: he is his master's both-hands, I assure you.

  Qua. What? To pull on his boots, a-mornings, or his stockings, does he?

  Lit. Sir, if you have a mind to mock him, mock him softly, and look t'other way: for if he apprehend you flout him, once, he will
40 fly at you presently. A terrible testy old fellow, and his name is Wasp too.

  Qua. Pretty insect! Make much on him.

  Was. A plague o'this box, and the pox too, and on him that made it, and her that went for't, and all that should ha' sought it, sent it,
45 or brought it! Do you see, sir?

  Lit. Nay, good Master Wasp.

  Was. Good Master Hornet, turd 'i your teeth, hold you your tongue; do not I know you? Your father was a 'pothecary, and sold clysters, more than he gave, I wusse: and turd i' your little wife's
50 teeth too (here she comes) 'twill make her spit, as fine as she is, for all her velvet-custard on her head, sir.

[*Enter* Win]

  Lit. Oh! Be civil, Master Numps.

  Was. Why, say I have a humour not to be civil; how then? Who shall compel me? You?

55   *Lit.* Here is the box now.

  Was. Why a pox o' your box, once again: let your little wife stale in it, and she will. Sir, I would have you to understand, and these gentlemen too, if they please——

  Winw. With all our hearts. Sir.

60   *Was.* That I have a charge. Gentlemen.

  Lit. They do apprehend, sir.

  Was. Pardon me, sir, neither they nor you, can apprehend me,

---

31 *keeps . . . a coil*: makes a disturbance   32 *cloister*: used as a mart during the Fair   49 *I wusse*: certainly   51 *velvet-custard*: velvet hat shaped like a pie
56 *stale*: urinate

yet (you are an ass). I have a young master, he is now upon his
making and marring; the whole care of his well doing is now mine.
His foolish schoolmasters have done nothing, but run up and down 65
the country with him, to beg puddings and cake-bread of his
tenants, and almost spoiled him, he has learned nothing, but to
sing catches, and repeat *rattle bladder rattle*, and *Oh, Madge*. I dare
not let him walk alone, for fear of learning of vile tunes, which he
will sing at supper, and in the sermon-times! If he meet but a 70
carman i' the street, and I find him not talk to keep him off on him,
he will whistle him, and all his tunes over, at night in his sleep! He
has a head full of bees! I am fain now (for this little time I am absent)
to leave him in charge with a gentlewoman; 'tis true, she is a
Justice of Peace his wife, and a gentlewoman o' the hood, and his 75
natural sister: but what may happen under a woman's government,
there's the doubt. Gentlemen, you do not know him: he is another
manner of piece than you think for! But nineteen year old, and yet
he is taller than either of you, by the head, God bless him.

Qua. Well, methinks, this is a fine fellow!   80

Winw. He has made his master a finer by this description, I
should think.

Qua. 'Faith, much about one, it's cross and pile, whether for a
new farthing.

Was. I'll tell you, gentlemen——

Lit. Will't please you drink, Master Wasp?   85

Was. Why, I ha' not talked so long to be dry, sir, you see no dust
or cobwebs come out o' my mouth: do you? You'd ha' me gone,
would you?

Lit. No, but you were in haste e'en now, Master Numps.   90

Was. What an' I were? So I am still, and yet I will stay too,
meddle you with your match, your Win, there, she has as little wit
as her husband, it seems: I have others to talk to.

Lit. She's my match indeed, and as little wit as I, good!

Was. We ha' been but a day and a half in town, gentlemen, 'tis 95
true; and yesterday i' the afternoon, we walked London, to show
the city to the gentlewoman he shall marry, Mistress Grace; but,

---

68 *rattle bladder rattle, and Oh, Madge*: examples of current trivia (*H&S* x. 182)
75 *hood*: mark of her husband's office   78 *piece*: person   83 *it's cross and
pile*: it's a toss-up   92 *meddle . . . with your match*: proverbial

afore I will endure such another half-day with him, I'll be drawn
with a good gibcat through the great pond at home, as his uncle
100 Hodge was! Why, we could not meet that heathen thing, all day,
but stayed him: he would name you all the signs over, as he went,
aloud: and where he spied a parrot, or a monkey, there he was
pitched, with all the little long-coats about him, male and female;
no getting him away! I thought he would ha' run mad o'the black
105 boy in Bucklersbury, that takes the scurvy, roguey tobacco, there.

  Lit. You say true, Master Numps: there's such a one indeed.

  Was. It's no matter, whether there be or no, what's that to you?

  Qua. He will not allow of John's reading at any hand.

ACT I, Scene v

Enter Cokes, Mistress Overdo, Grace

  Cok. Oh Numps! Are you here, Numps? Look where I am,
Numps! And Mistress Grace, too! Nay, do not look angerly,
Numps: my sister is here, and all, I do not come without her.

  Was. What, the mischief, do you come with her? Or she with you?

5 *Cok.* We came all to seek you, Numps.

  Was. To seek me? Why, did you all think I was lost? Or run
away with your fourteen shillings' worth of small ware, here? Or
that I had changed it i' the Fair, for hobby-horses? 'Sprecious—to
seek me!

10 *Mrs Ove.* Nay, good Master Numps, do you show discretion, though
he be exorbitant (as Master Overdo says) and't be but for conser-
vation of the peace.

  Was. Mary gip, goody she-justice, Mistress French-hood! Turd i'
your teeth; and turd i' your French-hood's teeth, too, to do you
15 service, do you see? Must you quote your Adam to me! You think

---

  99 *gibcat*: tomcat. To wager that a cat could pull a man through a pond was a
practical joke played on an ignorant rustic   103 *little long-coats*: children
105 *Bucklersbury*: a street of apothecaries, who sold tobacco   108 *reading*: inter-
pretation   (I. v) 13 *Mary gip*: 'By St. Mary of Egypt', conflated with the excla-
mation 'gip' ('gee-up', 'get out')   *French-hood* mark of a fashionable city dame

you are Madam Regent still, Mistress Overdo; when I am in place?
No such matter, I assure you, your reign is out when I am in,
Dame.

Mrs Ove. I am content to be in abeyance, sir, and be governed
by you; so should he too, if he did well; but 'twill be expected you 20
should also govern your passions.

Was. Will't so forsooth? Good Lord! How sharp you are! With
being at Bedlam yesterday? Whetston has set an edge upon you,
has he?

Mrs Ove. Nay, if you know not what belongs to your dignity: 25
I do, yet, to mine.

Was. Very well then.

Cok. Is this the licence, Numps? For Love's sake, let me see't.
I never saw a licence.

Was. Did you not so? Why, you shall not see't then.   30

Cok. An' you love me, good Numps.

Was. Sir, I love you, and yet I do not love you, i' these fooleries,
set your heart at rest; there's nothing in't, but hard words: and
what would you see't for?

Cok. I would see the length and the breadth on't, that's all; and 35
I will see't now, so I will.

Was. You sha' not see it here.

Cok. Then I'll see't at home, and I'll look upo' the case here.

Was. Why, do so, a man must give way to him a little in trifles:
gentlemen, these are errors, diseases of youth: which he will mend 40
when he comes to judgement and knowledge of matters. I pray you
conceive so, and I thank you. And I pray you pardon him, and I
thank you again.

Qua. Well, this dry-nurse, I say still, is a delicate man.

Winw. And I am for the cosset, his charge! Did you ever see a 45
fellow's face more accuse him for an ass?

Qua. Accuse him? It confesses him one without accusing. What
pity 'tis yonder wench should marry such a Cokes?

Winw. 'Tis true.

Qua. She seems to be discreet, and as sober as she is handsome. 50

23 *Whetston*: probably the name of a keeper at Bethlehem Hospital (with a quibble
on the whetstone used for sharpening)   45 *cosset*: lit. a lamb brought up by hand;
a spoilt child

Winw. Aye, and if you mark her, what a restrained scorn she casts upon all his behaviour and speeches?

Cok. Well, Numps, I am now for another piece of business more, the Fair, Numps, and then—

55 *Was.* Bless me! Deliver me, help, hold me! The Fair!

Cok. Nay, never fidge up and down, Numps, and vex itself. I am resolute Bartholomew, in this; I'll make no suit on't to you; 'twas all the end of my journey, indeed, to show Mistress Grace my Fair: I call't my Fair, because of Bartholomew: you know my name is
60 Bartholomew, and Bartholomew Fair.

Lit. That was mine afore, gentlemen: this morning, I had that i'faith, upon his licence, believe me, there he comes, after me.

Qua. Come, John, this ambitious wit of yours (I am afraid) will do you no good i' the end.

65 *Lit.* No? Why sir?

Qua. You grow so insolent with it, and overdoing, John: that if you look not to it, and tie it up, it will bring you to some obscure place in time, and there 'twill leave you.

Winw. Do not trust it too much, John, be more sparing, and use
70 it but now and then; a wit is a dangerous thing in this age; do not over-buy it.

Lit. Think you so, gentlemen? I'll take heed on't hereafter.

Win. Yes, do John.

Cok. A pretty little soul, this same Mistress Littlewit! Would I
75 might marry her.

Gra. [*Aside*] So would I, or anybody else, so I might scape you.

Cok. Numps, I will see it, Numps, 'tis decreed: never be melancholy for the matter.

80 *Was.* Why, see it, sir, see it, do see it! Who hinders you? Why do you not go see it? 'Slid see it.

Cok. The Fair, Numps, the Fair.

Was. Would the Fair and all the drums, and rattles in't, were i' your belly for me: they are already i' your brain: he that had the
85 means to travel your head, now, should meet finer sights than any are i' the Fair; and make a finer voyage on't; to see it all hung with cockleshells, pebbles, fine wheat-straws, and here and there a chicken's feather, and a cobweb.

Qua. Goodfaith, he looks, methinks an' you mark him, like one that were made to catch flies, with his Sir Cranion-legs.

Winw. And his Numps, to flap 'em away. 90

Was. God be w'you, sir, there's your bee in a box, and much good do't you.

Cok. Why, your friend, and Bartholomew; an' you be so contumacious.

Qua. What mean you, Numps? 95

Was. I'll not be guilty, I, gentlemen.

Mrs Ove. You will not let him go, brother, and lose him?

Cok. Who can hold that will away? I had rather lose him than the Fair, I wusse.

Was. You do not know the inconvenience, gentlemen, you 100 persuade to: nor what trouble I have with him in these humours. If he go to the Fair, he will buy of everything, to a baby there; and household-stuff for that too. If a leg or an arm on him did not grow on, he would lose it i' the press. Pray heaven I bring him off with one stone! And then he is such a ravener after fruit! You will 105 not believe what a coil I had, t'other day, to compound a business between a Catherine-pear-woman, and him, about snatching! 'Tis intolerable, gentlemen.

Winw. Oh but you must not leave him now to these hazards, Numps. 110

Was. Nay, he knows too well, I will not leave him, and that makes him presume: well, sir, will you go now? If you have such an itch i' your feet, to foot it to the Fair, why do you stop, am I your tarriers? Go, will you go? Sir, why do you not go?

Cok. Oh Numps! Have I brought you about? Come Mistress 115 Grace, and sister, I am resolute Bat, i'faith, still.

Gra. Truly, I have no such fancy to the Fair; nor ambition to see it; there's none goes thither of any quality or fashion.

Cok. Oh Lord, sir! You shall pardon me, Mistress Grace, we are enough of ourselves to make it a fashion: and for qualities, let 120 Numps alone, he'll find qualities.

[*Exeunt* Cokes, Wasp, Mistress Overdo, Grace]

89 *Sir Cranion*: the crane-fly (daddy-long-legs)
104 *press*: crowd   105 *stone*: i.e. testicle
and early variety   114 *tarriers*: hinderers
102 *baby*: doll, puppet
107 *Catherine-pear*: a small

Qua. What a rogue in apprehension is this! To understand her language no better.

Winw. Aye, and offer to marry to her? Well, I will leave the chase of my widow for today, and directly to the Fair. These flies cannot this hot season but engender us excellent creeping sport.

Qua. A man that has but a spoonful of brain would think so. Farewell, John.   [*Exit with* Winwife]

Lit. Win, you see, 'tis in fashion to go to the Fair, Win: we must to the Fair too, you and I, Win. I have an affair i' the Fair, Win, a puppet-play of mine own making, say nothing, that I writ for the motion man, which you must see, Win.

Win. I would I might, John, but my mother will never consent to such a profane motion: she will call it.

Lit. Tut, we'll have a device, a dainty one (Now, Wit, help at a pinch, good Wit come, come, good Wit, and't be thy will.) I have it, Win, I have it i'faith, and 'tis a fine one. Win, long to eat of a pig, sweet Win, i' the Fair; do you see? I' the heart o'the Fair; not at Pie Corner. Your mother will do anything, Win, to satisfy your longing, you know, pray thee long, presently, and be sick o' the sudden, good Win. I'll go in and tell her, cut thy lace i' the mean time and play the hypocrite, sweet Win.

Win. No, I'll not make me unready for it. I can be hypocrite enough, though I were never so straight laced.

Lit. You say true, you have been bred i' the family, and brought up to 't. Our mother is a most elect hypocrite, and has maintained us all this seven year with it, like gentlefolks.

Win. Aye, let her alone, John, she is not a wise wilful widow for nothing, nor a sanctified sister for a song. And let me alone too, I ha' somewhat o' the mother in me, you shall see, fetch her, fetch her, ah, ah.   [*Seems to swoon. Exit* Littlewit]

---

132 *motion man*: puppet-master   135 *device*: stratagem   139 *Pie Corner*: *Alch.* I. i. 25 n.   143 *make me unready*: undress   150 *mother*: quibble on (1) taking after one's mother, (2) the cravings of pregnancy (II. ii. 99–100), and (3) 'mother' as 'hysteria'

ACT I, Scene vi

Enter Dame Purecraft *with* Littlewit

Pur. Now, the blaze of the beauteous discipline, fright away this evil from our house! How now Win-the-fight, child: how do you? Sweet child, speak to me.

Win. Yes, forsooth.

Pur. Look up, sweet Win-the-fight, and suffer not the enemy to 5 enter you at this door, remember that your education has been with the purest, what polluted one was it, that named first the unclean beast, pig, to you, child?

Win. (Uh, uh.)

Lit. Not I, o' my sincerity, mother: she longed above three hours, 10 ere she would let me know it; who was it, Win?

Win. A profane black thing with a beard, John.

Pur. Oh! Resist it, Win-the-fight, it is the Tempter, the wicked Tempter, you may know it by the fleshly motion of pig, be strong against it, and its foul temptations in these assaults, whereby it 15 broacheth flesh and blood, as it were, on the weaker side, and pray against its carnal provocations, good child, sweet child, pray.

Lit. Good mother, I pray you, that she may eat some pig, and her belly full, too; and do not you cast away your own child, and perhaps one of mine, with your tale of the Tempter: how do you, Win? 20 Are you not sick?

Win. Yes, a great deal, John (uh, uh).

Pur. What shall we do? Call our zealous brother Busy hither, for his faithful fortification in this charge of the adversary; child, my dear child, you shall eat pig, be comforted, my sweet child. 25

[*Exit* Littlewit]

Win. Aye, but i' the Fair, mother.

Pur. I mean i' the Fair, if it can be any way made, or found lawful.

[*Enter* Littlewit]

Where is our brother Busy? Will he not come? Look up, child.

Lit. Presently, mother, as soon as he has cleansed his beard. I 30

---

1 *beauteous discipline*: cant phrase for Puritanism

found him, fast by the teeth, i' the cold turkey pie, i' the cupboard,
with a great white loaf on his left hand, and a glass of malmsey on
his right.

Pur. Slander not the Brethren, wicked one.

35   *Lit.* Here he is now, purified, Mother.

[*Enter* Zeal-of-the-land Busy]

Pur. Oh brother Busy! Your help here to edify, and raise us up
in a scruple; my daughter Win-the-fight is visited with a natural
disease of women; called, a longing to eat pig.

Lit. Aye sir, a Bartholomew pig: and in the Fair.

40   *Pur.* And I would be satisfied from you, religiously-wise, whether
a widow of the sanctified assembly, or a widow's daughter, may
commit the act, without offence to the weaker sisters.

Bus. Verily, for the disease of longing, it is a disease, a carnal
disease, or appetite, incident to women: and as it is carnal, and
45 incident, it is natural, very natural. Now pig, it is a meat, and a
meat that is nourishing, and may be longed for, and so conse-
quently eaten; it may be eaten; very exceeding well-eaten: but in
the Fair, and as a Bartholomew pig, it cannot be eaten, for the very
calling it a Bartholomew pig, and to eat it so, is a spice of idolatry,
50 and you make the Fair no better than one of the high places. This
I take it, is the state of the question. A high place.

Lit. Aye, but in state of necessity: place should give place, Master
Busy (I have a conceit left, yet).

Pur. Good Brother Zeal-of-the-land, think to make it as lawful
55 as you can.

Lit. Yes sir, and as soon as you can: for it must be, sir; you see
the danger my little wife is in, sir.

Pur. Truly, I do love my child dearly, and I would not have her
miscarry, or hazard her first fruits, if it might be otherwise.

60   *Bus.* Surely, it may be otherwise, but it is subject to construction,
subject, and hath a face of offence, with the weak, a great face, a
foul face, but that face may have a veil put over it, and be shadowed,
as it were, it may be eaten, and in the Fair, I take it, in a booth,
the tents of the wicked: the place is not much, not very much, we
65 may be religious in midst of the profane, so it be eaten with a re-

50 *high places*: associated with idolatry (Lev. 26: 30)

formed mouth, with sobriety, and humbleness; not gorged in with gluttony or greediness; there's the fear: for, should she go there, as taking pride in the place, or delight in the unclean dressing, to feed the vanity of the eye, or the lust of the palate, it were not well, it were not fit, it were abominable, and not good.   70

Lit. Nay, I knew that afore, and told her on't, but courage, Win, we'll be humble enough; we'll seek out the homeliest booth i' the Fair, that's certain, rather than fail, we'll eat it o' the ground.

Pur. Aye, and I'll go with you myself, Win-the-fight, and my brother, Zeal-of-the-land, shall go with us too, for our better   75 consolation.

Win. Uh, uh.

Lit. Aye, and Solomon too, Win (the more the merrier) Win, we'll leave Rabbi Busy in a booth. Solomon, my cloak.

[*Enter* Solomon]

Sol. Here, sir.   80

Bus. In the way of comfort to the weak, I will go and eat. I will eat exceedingly, and prophesy; there may be a good use made of it, too, now I think on't: by the public eating of swine's flesh, to profess our hate and loathing of Judaism, whereof the brethren stand taxed. I will therefore eat, yea, I will eat exceedingly.   85

Lit. Good, i'faith, I will eat heartily too, because I will be no Jew, I could never away with that stiff-necked generation: and truly, I hope my little one will be like me, that cries for pig so, i' the mother's belly.

Bus. Very likely, exceeding likely, very exceeding likely. [*Exeunt*]   90

ACT II, Scene i

[The Fair]

Enter Justice Overdo [*disguised*]

Jus. WELL, in justice' name, and the King's; and for the commonwealth! Defy all the world, Adam Overdo, for a disguise and

---

84 *Judaism, whereof the brethren stand taxed*: because of their cult of the Old Testament   87 *away with*: agree with

all story; for thou hast fitted thyself, I swear; fain would I meet the
Lynceus now, that eagle's eye, that piercing Epidaurian serpent (as
5 my Quint. Horace calls him) that could discover a Justice of Peace
(and lately of the Quorum) under this covering. They may have
seen many a fool in the habit of a Justice; but never till now, a
Justice in the habit of a fool. Thus must we do, though, that wake
for the public good: and thus hath the wise magistrate done in all
10 ages. There is a doing of right out of wrong, if the way be found.
Never shall I enough commend a worthy worshipful man, some-
time a capital member of this city, for his high wisdom, in this
point, who would take you, now the habit of a porter; now of a
carman; now of the dog-killer, in this month of August; and in the
15 winter, of a seller of tinder-boxes; and what would he do in all these
shapes? Marry, go you into every alehouse, and down into every
cellar; measure the length of puddings, take the gauge of black
pots, and cans, aye, and custards with a stick; and their circum-
ference, with a thread; weigh the loaves of bread on his middle-
20 finger; then would he send for 'em, home; give the puddings to the
poor, the bread to the hungry, the custards to his children; break
the pots, and burn the cans himself; he would not trust his corrupt
officers; he would do't himself. Would all men in authority would
follow this worthy precedent! For (alas) as we are public persons,
25 what do we know? Nay, what can we know? We hear with other
men's ears; we see with other men's eyes; a foolish constable, or a
sleepy watchman, is all our information, he slanders a gentleman,
by the virtue of his place (as he calls it) and we by the vice of ours,
must believe him. As a while agone, they made me, yea me, to
30 mistake an honest zealous pursuivant, for a seminary: and a proper
young Bachelor of Music, for a bawd. This we are subject to, that
live in high place, all our intelligence is idle, and most of our intelli-
gencers, knaves: and by your leave, ourselves, thought little better,
if not arrant fools, for believing 'em. I Adam Overdo, am resolved
35 therefore, to spare spy-money hereafter, and make mine own dis-

---

4 *Lynceus*: the Argonaut, noted for his keen sight   *Epidaurian serpent*:
Horace, *Sat*. I. iii. 26–7 (serpents, reputed to have keen sight, were sacred to Aesculapius,
who was worshipped in serpent form at Epidaurus)   12 *capital member*: probably
Sir Thomas Hayes, Lord Mayor in 1614, who adopted such disguises   30 *pur-
suivant*: state messenger with power to execute warrants of arrest   *seminary*: a recusant
trained in one of the seminaries on the Continent   32 *intelligence*: information

coveries. Many are the yearly enormities of this Fair, in whose
courts of Piepowders I have had the honour during the three days
sometimes to sit as judge. But this is the special day for detection of
those foresaid enormities. Here is my black book for the purpose;
this the cloud that hides me: under this covert I shall see, and not   40
be seen. On, Junius Brutus. And as I began, so I'll end: in justice'
name, and the King's; and for the commonwealth.

ACT II, Scene ii

Enter Leatherhead, Trash [*from their booths*], Passengers

Lea. The Fair's pestilence dead, methinks; people come not
abroad today, whatever the matter is. Do you hear, sister Trash,
lady o' the basket? Sit farther with your gingerbread-progeny there,
and hinder not the prospect of my shop, or I'll ha' it proclaimed i'
the Fair what stuff they are made on.   5

Tra. Why, what stuff are they made on, brother Leatherhead?
Nothing but what's wholesome, I assure you.

Lea. Yes, stale bread, rotten eggs, musty ginger, and dead honey,
you know.

Jus. [*Aside*] Aye! Have I met with enormity, so soon?   10

Lea. I shall mar your market, old Joan.

Tra. Mar my market, thou too-proud pedlar? Do thy worst; I
defy thee, aye, and thy stable of hobby-horses. I pay for my ground,
as well as thou dost, and thou wrong'st me, for all thou art parcel-
poet, and an enginer. I'll find a friend shall right me, and make a   15
ballad of thee, and thy cattel all over. Are you puffed up with the
pride of your wares? Your arsedine?

Lea. Go to, old Joan, I'll talk with you anon; and take you down
too, afore Justice Overdo, he is the man must charm you, I'll ha'
you i' the Piepowders.   20

Tra. Charm me? I'll meet thee face to face, afore his worship,

37 *courts of Piepowders*: summary courts held at fairs to administer justice among
itinerants (Fr. 'dusty-footed')   41 *Junius Brutus*: who also adopted a disguise, and
proved an inflexible judge   (*II. ii*) 1 *pestilence dead*: plaguy dead   8 *dead*:
stale, flat   14-15 *parcel-poet*: part poet   15 *enginer*: contriver, inventor
16 *cattel*: stock ('chattels')   17 *arsedine*: alloy of copper and zinc used as gold-leaf
(cf. 'gilt gingerbread', l. 31)   19 *charm*: silence, subdue (as if by magic)

when thou dar'st: and though I be a little crooked o' my body, I'll
be found as upright in my dealing as any woman in Smithfield, I,
charm me?

25   *Jus.* [*Aside*] I am glad to hear my name is their terror yet, this is
doing of justice.

   Lea. What do you lack? What is't you buy? What do you lack?
Rattles, drums, halberts, horses, babies o' the best? Fiddles o'the
finest?

Enter Costardmonger, [Nightingale]

30   *Cos.* Buy any pears, pears, fine, very fine pears!

   Tra. Buy any gingerbread, gilt gingerbread!

   Nig. Hey, now the Fair's a-filling!
      Oh, for a tune to startle
      The birds o' the booths here billing
35   Yearly with old Saint Bartle!
      The drunkards they are wading,
      The punks and chapmen trading;
      Who'd see the Fair without his lading?
Buy any ballads; new ballads?

[*Enter* Ursula *from her booth*]

40   *Urs.* Fie upon't: who would wear out their youth and prime thus,
in roasting of pigs, that had any cooler vocation? Hell's a kind of
cold cellar to't, a very fine vault, o' my conscience! What, Mooncalf?

   Moo. [*Within*] Here, mistress.

   Nig. How now Ursula? In a heat, in a heat?

45   *Urs.* My chair, you false faucet you; and my morning's draught,
quickly, a bottle of ale, to quench me, rascal. I am all fire and fat,
Nightingale, I shall e'en melt away to the first woman, a rib again,
I am afraid. I do water the ground in knots, as I go, like a great
garden-pot, you may follow me by the S's I make.

50   *Nig.* Alas, good Urs; was Zekiel here this morning?

   Urs. Zekiel? What Zekiel?

   Nig. Zekiel Edgeworth, the civil cutpurse, you know him well
enough; he that talks bawdy to you still: I call him my secretary.

---

   28 *halberts*: toy halberts (combined spear and axe)   36 *wading*: staggering
   37 *chapmen*: pedlars   45 *faucet*: i.e. tapster   53 *secretary*: confidant

Urs. He promised to be here this morning, I remember.

Nig. When he comes, bid him stay: I'll be back again presently. 55

Urs. Best take your morning's dew in your belly, Nightingale.
(Mooncalf *brings in the chair*) Come, sir, set it here, did not I bid
you should get this chair let out o' the sides for me, that my hips
might play? You'll never think of anything, till your dame be
rumpgalled; 'tis well, changeling: because it can take in your 60
grasshoppers thighs, you care for no more. Now, you look as you
had been i' the corner o' the booth, fleaing your breech with a
candle's end, and set fire o' the Fair. Fill, stoat: fill.

Jus. [*Aside*] This pig-woman do I know, and I will put her in,
for my second enormity, she hath been before me, punk, pinnace 65
and bawd, any time these two and twenty years, upon record i' the
Piepowders.

Urs. Fill again, you unlucky vermin.

Moo. 'Pray you be not angry, mistress, I'll ha' it widened anon.

Urs. No, no, I shall e'en dwindle away to't, ere the Fair be done, 70
you think, now you ha' heated me? A poor vexed thing I am, I feel
myself dropping already, as fast as I can: two stone a suet a day is
my proportion: I can but hold life and soul together, with this
(here's to you, Nightingale) and a whiff of tobacco, at most. Where's
my pipe now? Not filled? Thou errant incubee.   75

Nig. Nay, Ursula, thou'lt gall between the tongue and the teeth
with fretting, now.

Urs. How can I hope, that ever he'll discharge his place of trust,
tapster, a man of reckoning under me, that remembers nothing I
say to him? [*Exit* Nightingale] But look to't, sirrah, you were best, 80
threepence a pipeful, I will ha' made, of all my whole half pound of
tobacco, and a quarter of a pound of coltsfoot, mixed with it too,
to itch it out. I that have dealt so long in the fire, will not be to seek
in smoke now. Then six and twenty shillings a barrel I will advance o'
my beer; and fifty shillings a hundred o' my bottle-ale, I ha' told 85
you the ways how to raise it. Froth your cans well i' the filling, at
length, rogue, and jog your bottles o' the buttock, sirrah, then

---

60 *galled*: blistered, chafed   *changeling*: idiot (left by fairies in exchange for a
stolen child)   63 *stoat*: weasel (because of his leanness); hence 'vermin' (l. 68)
64 *put her in*: i.e. his black book   65 *pinnace*: go-between   75 *incubee*:
progeny of a demon   82 *coltsfoot*: large-leafed herb smoked as a cure for asthma
83 *itch*: eke   84 *advance*: raise

skink out the first glass, ever, and drink with all companies, though
you be sure to be drunk; you'll misreckon the better, and be less
90 ashamed on't. But your true trick, rascal, must be, to be ever busy,
and mis-take away the bottles and cans, in haste, before they be
half drunk off, and never hear anybody call (if they should chance
to mark you) till you ha' brought fresh, and be able to forswear
'em. Give me a drink of ale.

95 *Jus.* [*Aside*] This is the very womb and bed of enormity!
Gross, as herself! This must all down for enormity, all, every
whit on't.   (*One knocks*)

Urs. Look, who's there, sirrah? Five shillings a pig is my price,
at least; if it be a sow-pig, sixpence more: if she be a great-bellied
100 wife, and long for't, sixpence more for that.

Jus. [*Aside*] *O tempora! O mores!* I would not ha' lost my
discovery of this one grievance, for my place, and worship o' the
Bench, how is the poor subject abused here! Well, I will fall in
with her, and with her Mooncalf, and win out wonders of enormity.
105 [*To* Ursula] By thy leave, goodly woman, and the fatness of the
Fair: oily as the King's constable's lamp, and shining as his shoeing-
horn! Hath thy ale virtue, or thy beer strength? That the tongue
of man may be tickled? And his palate pleased in the morning? Let
thy pretty nephew here go search and see.

110 *Urs.* What new roarer is this?

Moo. Oh Lord! Do you not know him, mistress, 'tis mad Arthur
of Bradley, that makes the orations. Brave Master, old Arthur of
Bradley, how do you? Welcome to the Fair, when shall we hear
you again, to handle your matters? With your back again a booth,
115 ha? I ha' been one o' your little disciples i' my days!

Jus. Let me drink, boy, with my love, thy aunt here; that I may
be eloquent: but of thy best, lest it be bitter in my mouth, and my
words fall foul on the Fair.

Urs. Why dost thou not fetch him drink? And offer him
120 to sit?

Moo. Is't ale or beer? Master Arthur?

Jus. Thy best, pretty stripling, thy best; the same thy dove
drinketh, and thou drawest on holy days.

---

88 *skink*: draw (liquor)   111-12 *Arthur of Bradley*: hero of 'The Ballad on the
Wedding of Arthur of Bradley'   116 *aunt*: crony   122 *dove*: darling

Urs. Bring him a sixpenny bottle of ale; they say, a fool's handsel is lucky.   125

Jus. Bring both, child. Ale for Arthur, and beer for Bradley. Ale for thine aunt, boy. [*Exit* Mooncalf] [*Aside*] My disguise takes to the very wish and reach of it. I shall by the benefit of this, discover enough and more: and yet get off with the reputation of what I would be. A certain middling thing, between a fool and a madman.

ACT II, Scene iii

Enter Knockem

Kno. What! My little lean Ursula! My she-bear! Art thou alive yet? With thy litter of pigs, to grunt out another Bartholomew Fair? Ha!

Urs. Yes, and to amble afoot, when the Fair is done, to hear you groan out of a cart, up the heavy hill.   5

Kno. Of Holborn, Ursula, mean'st thou so? For what? For what, pretty Urs?

Urs. For cutting halfpenny purses: or stealing little penny dogs, out o' the Fair.

Kno. Oh! Good words, good words Urs.   10

Jus. [*Aside*] Another special enormity. A cutpurse of the sword! The boot, and the feather! Those are his marks.

[*Enter* Mooncalf *with ale*]

Urs. You are one of those horseleeches, that gave out I was dead in Turnbull Street, of a surfeit of bottle ale and tripes?

Kno. No, 'twas better meat, Urs: cows' udders, cows' udders!   15

Urs. Well, I shall be meet with your mumbling mouth one day.

Kno. What? Thou'lt poison me with a newt in a bottle of ale, wilt thou? Or a spider in a tobacco pipe, Urs? Come, there's no malice

---

124 *handsel*: first money received from any enterprise   (*II. iii*) 1 *she-bear*: quibble on Lat. *ursa*   5 *up the heavy hill*: i.e. to Tyburn   13 *horseleeches*: farriers; here with the sense of rapacity   14 *Turnbull Street*: Turnmill St. in Clerkenwell, a prostitutes' haunt   16 *meet with*: even with

20 in these fat folks, I never fear thee, and I can scape thy lean Mooncalf
here. Let's drink it out, good Urs, and no vapours!   [*Exit* Ursula]

   Jus. Dost thou hear, boy? (There's for thy ale, and the remnant for
thee.) Speak in thy faith of a faucet, now; is this goodly person before
us here, this vapours, a knight of the knife?

25   *Moo.* What mean you by that, Master Arthur?

   Jus. I mean a child of the horn-thumb, a babe of booty, boy; a
cutpurse.

   Moo. Oh Lord, sir! Far from it. This is Master Dan. Knockem:
Jordan, the ranger of Turnbull. He is a horse-courser, sir.

30   *Jus.* Thy dainty dame, though, called him cutpurse.

   Moo. Like enough, sir, she'll do forty such things in an hour (an
you listen to her) for her recreation, if the toy take her i' the greasy
kerchief: it makes her fat, you see. She battens with it.

   Jus. [*Aside*] Here might I ha' been deceived now: and ha' put
35 a fool's blot upon myself, if I had not played an after game o'
discretion.

             Ursula *comes in again dropping*

   Kno. Alas poor Urs, this's an ill season for thee.

   Urs. Hang yourself, hackney-man.

   Kno. How? How? Urs, vapours! Motion breed vapours?

40   *Urs.* Vapours? Never tusk, nor twirl your dibble, good Jordan, I
know what you'll take to a very drop. Though you be captain o'the
roarers, and fight well at the case of pisspots, you shall not fright me
with your lion-chap, sir, nor your tusks; you angry? You are hungry:
come, a pig's head will stop your mouth, and stay your stomach, at
45 all times.

   Kno. Thou art such another mad merry Urs still! Troth I do
make conscience of vexing thee, now i' the dog-days, this hot weather,
for fear of foundering thee i' the body; and melting down a pillar of

---

21 *vapours*: Knockem displays the 'humours' of the roarer   26 *horn-thumb*:
thimble protecting the cutpurse's thumb from the knife   29 *Jordan*: a chamber-
pot   *ranger*: as though Turnmill St. (l. 14) were a royal park   32 *toy*: whim,
fancy   33 *battens*: thrives   35 *after game*: second game allowing the oppor-
tunity to reverse the result of the first   40 *tusk*: ? pull at a moustache   *dibble*:
the spade-beard affected by the roarer (gardening implement)   43 *lion-chap*: lion
jaw   47 *dog-days*: variously calculated (in July–August) from the rising of the
Dog-star   48 *foundering*: play on 'foundering i' the body' (of a horse with a
surfeit) and 'foundring' (of melting down metal)

the Fair. Pray thee take thy chair again, and keep state; and let's have
a fresh bottle of ale, and a pipe of tobacco; and no vapours. I'll ha' 50
this belly o' thine taken up, and thy grass scoured, wench; look!
Here's Ezekiel Edgeworth; a fine boy of his inches, as any is i' the
Fair! Has still money in his purse, and will pay all, with a kind heart;
and good vapours.

ACT II, Scene iv

Enter Edgeworth, Nightingale, Corncutter, Tinder-box Man,
Passengers

Edg. That I will, indeed, willingly, Master Knockem, fetch some
ale and tobacco.   [*Exit* Mooncalf]

Lea. What do you lack, gentlemen? Maid: see a fine hobby-horse
for your young master: cost you but a token a week his provender.

Cor. Ha' you any corns i' your feet and toes?   5

Tin. Buy a mousetrap, a mousetrap, or a tormentor for a flea.

Tra. Buy some gingerbread.

Nig. Ballads, ballads! Fine new ballads:

  Hear for your love, and buy for your money.

  A delicate ballad o' the ferret and the coney.   10

  A preservative again' the punk's evil.

  Another of goose-green-starch, and the Devil.

  A dozen of divine points, and the godly garters.

  The fairing of good counsel, of an ell and three quarters.

    What is't you buy?   15

  The windmill blown down by the witch's fart!

  Or Saint George, that Oh! did break the dragon's heart!

Edg. Master Nightingale, come hither, leave your mart a little.

Nig. Oh my secretary! What says my secretary?

---

51 phrases used of the care of horses   (*II. iv*) 4 *token*: I. ii. 31 n.   10 *ferret
... coney*: cant terms for trickster and dupe   12 *goose-green-starch, and the Devil*:
'a goodly Ballad against Pride' (*H&S* x. 190–1)   13 *A dozen ... points*: twelve
moral maxims (printed in H. E. Rollins, *Old English Ballads 1553–1625*, pp. 315–17)
godly garters: 'A pair of garters for young men to wear yet serve the Lord God and
live in his fear' (registered 20 October 1578)   14 *an ell*: 45 inches (? referring to
the length of the broadside)

[Enter Mooncalf with ale and tobacco]

20   *Jus.* Child o' the bottles, what's he? What's he?

Moo. A civil young gentleman, Master Arthur, that keeps company with the roarers, and disburses all still. He has ever money in his purse; he pays for them; and they roar for him: one does good offices for another. They call him the secretary, but he serves nobody.
25 A great friend of the ballad-man's, they are never asunder.

Jus. What pity 'tis so civil a young man should haunt this debauched company? Here's the bane of the youth of our time apparent. A proper penman, I see't in his countenance, he has a good clerk's look with him, and I warrant him a quick hand.

30   *Moo.* A very quick hand, sir.   *[Exit]*

Edg. All the purses and purchase I give you today by conveyance, bring hither to Ursula's presently. Here we will meet at night in her lodge, and share. Look you choose good places for your standing i' the Fair, when you sing, Nightingale.

               (This they whisper, that Overdo *hears it not)*
35   *Urs.* Aye, near the fullest passages; and shift 'em often.

Edg. And i' your singing, you must use your hawk's eye nimbly, and fly the purse to a mark, still, where 'tis worn, and o' which side; that you may gi' me the sign with your beak, or hang your head that way i' the tune.

40   *Urs.* Enough, talk no more on't: your friendship (masters) is not now to begin. Drink your draught of indenture, your sup of covenant, and away, the Fair fills apace, company begins to come in, and I ha' ne'er a pig ready yet.

Kno. Well said! Fill the cups, and light the tobacco: let's give fire
45 i'the works, and noble vapours.

Edg. And shall we ha' smocks Ursula, and good whimsies, ha?

Urs. Come, you are i' your bawdy vein! The best the Fair will afford, Zekiel, if bawd Whit keep his word;

[Enter Mooncalf]

how do the pigs, Mooncalf?

---

31 *purchase*: booty   *conveyance*: III. v. 159   37 *fly . . . to a mark*: of a hawk marking the place where its prey disappeared   40–1 *your friendship . . . begin*: *Canterbury Tales*, Prol. l. 428   41 *draught of indenture*: the drinking that went with the drawing up of agreements   46 *smocks . . . whimsies*: wenches

Moo. Very passionate, mistress, one on 'em has wept out an eye. 50
Master Arthur o' Bradley is melancholy here, nobody talks to him.
Will you any tobacco, Master Arthur?

Jus. No, boy, let my meditations alone.

Moo. He's studying for an oration now.

Jus. [*Aside*] If I can, with this day's travel, and all my policy, but 55
rescue this youth here, out of the hands of the lewd man and the
strange woman, I will sit down at night, and say with my friend
Ovid, *Iamqe opus exegi, quod nec Jovis ira, nec ignis, &c.*

Kno. Here Zekiel; here's a health to Ursula, and a kind vapour,
thou hast money i' thy purse still; and store! How dost thou come 60
by it? Pray thee vapour thy friends some in a courteous vapour.

Edg. Half I have, Master Dan Knockem, is always at your service.

Jus. [*Aside*] Ha, sweet nature! What goshawk would prey upon
such a lamb?

Kno. Let's see what 'tis, Zekiel! Count it, come, fill him to 65
pledge me.

ACT II, Scene v

Enter Winwife, Quarlous

Winw. We are here before 'em, methinks.

Qua. All the better, we shall see 'em come in now.

Lea. What do you lack, gentlemen, what is't you lack? A fine
horse? A lion? A bull? A bear? A dog, or a cat? An excellent fine
Bartholomew bird? Or an instrument? What is't you lack? 5

Qua. Slid! Here's Orpheus among the beasts, with his fiddle
and all!

Tra. Will you buy any comfortable bread, gentlemen?

Qua. And Ceres selling her daughter's picture, in gingerwork!

Winw. That these people should be so ignorant to think us 10
chapmen for 'em! Do we look as if we would buy gingerbread?
Or hobby-horses?

---

50 *passionate*: emotional   *wept out an eye*: sign that it is well roasted (II. v. 64)
55 *travel*: peregrinations, travail   57 *strange woman*: harlot (1 Kgs. 12: 1)
58 *Ovid*: *Metamorphoses*, xv. 871 ('And now my work is done, which neither the wrath
of Jove, nor fire, nor sword, nor the gnawing tooth of time shall ever be able to undo')
60 *store*: abundance   (*II. v*) 8 *comfortable bread*: gingerbread   11 *chapmen*:
customers

Qua. Why, they know no better ware than they have, nor better customers than come. And our very being here makes us fit to be
15 demanded as well as others. Would Cokes would come! There were a true customer for 'em.

Kno. [*To* Edgeworth] How much is't? Thirty shillings? Who's yonder! Ned Winwife? and Tom Quarlous, I think! Yes (gi' me it all) (gi' me it all) Master Winwife! Master Quarlous! Will you take
20 a pipe of tobacco with us? Do not discredit me now, Zekiel.

Winw. Do not see him! He is the roaring horse-courser, pray thee let's avoid him: turn down this way.

Qua. Slud, I'll see him, and roar with him too, and he roared as loud as Neptune, pray thee go with me.

25 *Winw.* You may draw me to as likely an inconvenience, when you please, as this.

Qua. Go to then, come along, we ha' nothing to do, man, but to see sights now.

Kno. Welcome Master Quarlous, and Master Winwife! Will you
30 take any froth, and smoke with us?

Qua. Yes, sir, but you'll pardon us, if we knew not of so much familiarity between us afore.

Kno. As what, sir?

Qua. To be so lightly invited to smoke and froth.

35 *Kno.* A good vapour! Will you sit down, sir? This is old Ursula's mansion, how like you her bower? Here you may ha' your punk and your pig in state, sir, both piping hot.

Qua. I had rather ha' my punk cold, sir.

Jus. There's for me, punk! And pig!

40 *Urs.* (*She calls within*) What Mooncalf? You rogue.

Moo. By and by, the bottle is almost off, mistress, here Master Arthur.

Urs. I'll part you and your playfellow there, i' the guarded coat, an' you sunder not the sooner.

45 *Kno.* Master Winwife, you are proud (methinks) you do not talk, nor drink, are you proud?

Winw. Not of the company I am in, sir, nor the place, I assure you.

36 *bower*: decked with boughs (III. ii. 50)—also ironical   38 *cold*:? free of infection   43 *guarded*: with trimming

Kno. You do not except at the company! Do you? Are you in vapours, sir? 50

Moo. Nay, good Master Dan Knockem, respect my mistress' bower, as you call it; for the honour of our booth, none o' your vapours here.   (Ursula *comes out with a firebrand*)

Urs. Why, you thin lean polecat you, and they have a mind to be i' their vapours, must you hinder 'em? What did you know, vermin, 55 if they would ha' lost a cloak, or such a trifle? Must you be drawing the air of pacification here? While I am tormented, within, i' the fire, you weasel?

Moo. Good mistress, 'twas in the behalf of your booth's credit, that I spoke. 60

Urs. Why? Would my booth ha' broke, if they had fallen out in't? Sir? Or would their heat ha' fired it? In, you rogue, and wipe the pigs, and mend the fire, that they fall not, or I'll both baste and roast you, till your eyes drop out, like 'em. (Leave the bottle behind you, and be cursed a while.)   [*Exit* Mooncalf] 65

Qua. Body o' the Fair! What's this? Mother o' the bawds?

Kno. No, she's mother o' the pigs, sir, mother o' the pigs!

Winw. Mother o' the Furies, I think, by her firebrand.

Qua. Nay, she is too fat to be a Fury, sure, some walking sow of tallow! 70

Winw. An inspired vessel of kitchen-stuff!

Qua. She'll make excellent gear for the coach-makers, here in Smithfield, to anoint wheels and axle-trees with.

(*She drinks this while*)

Urs. Aye, aye, gamesters, mock a plain plump soft wench o' the suburbs, do, because she's juicy and wholesome: you must ha' your 75 thin pinched ware, pent up i' the compass of a dog-collar (or 'twill not do) that looks like a long laced conger, set upright, and a green feather, like fennel, i' the jowl on't.

Kno. Well said Urs, my good Urs; to 'em Urs.

Qua. Is she your quagmire, Dan Knockem? Is this your bog? 80

Nig. We shall have a quarrel presently.

Kno. How? Bog? Quagmire? Foul vapours! Hum'h!

---

50 *vapours*: the game described in IV. iv. 22 ff. (s.d.)   61 *broke*: gone bankrupt   77 *conger*: eel   80 *quagmire . . . bog*: in which unsound horses were stood

Qua. Yes, he that would venture for't, I assure him, might sink
into her and be drowned a week, ere any friend he had could find
85 where he were.

Winw. And then he would be a fortnight weighing up again.

Qua. 'Twere like falling into a whole shire of butter: they had need
be a team of Dutchmen should draw him out.

Kno. Answer 'em, Urs, where's thy Bartholomew wit, now?
90 Urs, thy Bartholomew wit?

Urs. Hang 'em, rotten, roguey cheaters, I hope to see 'em plagued
one day (poxed they are already, I am sure) with lean playhouse
poultry, that has the bony rump, sticking out like the ace of spades,
or the point of a partisan, that every rib of 'em is like the tooth of a
95 saw: and will so grate 'em with their hips and shoulders, as (take
'em altogether) they were as good lie with a hurdle.

Qua. Out upon her, how she drips! She's able to give a man the
sweating sickness with looking on her.

Urs. Marry look off, with a patch o' your face; and a dozen i' your
100 breech, though they be o' scarlet, sir. I ha' seen as fine outsides as
either o' yours bring lousy linings to the brokers ere now, twice
a week.

Qua. Do you think there may be a fine new cuckingstool i' the
Fair to be purchased? One large enough, I mean. I know there is a
105 pond of capacity for her.

Urs. For your mother, you rascal, out you rogue, you hedge bird,
you pimp, you pannier-man's bastard, you.

Qua. Ha, ha, ha.

Urs. Do you sneer, you dog's-head, you trendle tail! You look as
110 you were begotten atop of a cart in harvest-time, when the whelp
was hot and eager. Go, snuff after your brother's bitch, Mistress
Commodity, that's the livery you wear, 'twill be out at the elbows
shortly. It's time you went to't, for the t'other remnant.

Kno. Peace, Urs, peace, Urs, they'll kill the poor whale, and
115 make oil of her. Pray thee go in.

---

86 *weighing up*: being raised   88 *Dutchmen*: noted for their consumption of
butter   94 *partisan*: long-handled spear with an axe head   99–100 *patch*
... *breech*: cf. l. 91 ('poxed ... already')   103 *cuckingstool*: for ducking scolds
('pond' = the Horsepool at West Smithfield)   106 *hedge bird*: footpad
107 *pannier-man*: hawker   109 *trendle tail*: low-bred dog   112 *Com-
modity* Ind. 144

Urs. I'll see 'em poxed first, and piled, and double piled.

Winw. Let's away, her language grows greasier than her pigs.

Urs. Dost so, snotty nose? Good Lord! Are you snivelling? You were engendered on a she-beggar, in a barn, when the bald thrasher, your sire, was scarce warm.   120

Winw. Pray thee, let's go.

Qua. No, faith: I'll stay the end of her now. I know she cannot last long; I find by her similes, she wanes apace.

Urs. Does she so? I'll set you gone. Gi' me my pigpan hither a little. I'll scald you hence, and you will not go.   [*Exit*] 125

Kno. Gentlemen, these are very strange vapours! And very idle vapours! I assure you.

Qua. You are a very serious ass, we assure you.

Kno. Humh! Ass? And serious? Nay, then pardon me my vapour. I have a foolish vapour, gentlemen: any man that does vapour me, 130 the ass, Master Quarlous——

Qua. What then, Master Jordan?

Kno. I do vapour him the lie.

Qua. Faith, and to any man that vapours me the lie, I do vapour that.   135

Kno. Nay, then, vapours upon vapours.

Edg., Nig. 'Ware the pan, the pan, the pan, she comes with the pan, gentlemen. God bless the woman.

> (Ursula *comes in, with the scalding-pan. They fight.*
> *She falls with it*)

Urs. Oh.   [*Exeunt* Quarlous, Winwife]

Tra. What's the matter?   140

Jus. Goodly woman!

Moo. Mistress!

Urs. Curse of hell, that ever I saw these fiends, oh! I ha' scalded my leg, my leg, my leg, my leg. I ha' lost a limb in the service! Run for some cream and salad oil, quickly. Are you under-peering, you 145 baboon? Rip off my hose, an' you be men, men, men.

Moo. Run you for some cream, good mother Joan. I'll look to your basket.

---

116 *double piled*: quibble on cloth with a pile of double closeness, on the baldness caused by the pox (pilled = stripped of hair), and on being afflicted with piles
133 *lie*: with quibble on 'lye' as 'urine'

Lea. Best sit up i' your chair, Ursula. Help, gentlemen.

150 *Kno.* Be of good cheer, Urs, thou hast hindered me the curry-
ing of a couple of stallions here, that abused the good race-bawd
o' Smithfield; 'twas time for 'em to go.

Nig. I' faith, when the pan came, they had made you run else.
(This had been a fine time for purchase, if you had ventured.)

155 *Edg.* Not a whit, these fellows were too fine to carry money.

Kno. Nightingale, get some help to carry her leg out o' the air; take
off her shoes; body o' me, she has the mallanders, the scratches, the
crown scab, and the quitter bone i' the tother leg.

Urs. Oh! The pox, why do you put me in mind o' my leg, thus,
160 to make it prick and shoot? Would you ha' me i' the Hospital afore
my time?

Kno. Patience, Urs, take a good heart, 'tis but a blister, as big as
a windgall; I'll take it away with the white of an egg, a little honey,
and hog's grease, ha' thy pasterns well rolled, and thou shalt pace
165 again by tomorrow. I'll tend thy booth, and look to thy affairs the
while: thou shalt sit i' thy chair, and give directions, and shine *Ursa
major.*   [*Exeunt* Ursula, Knockem, Mooncalf]

ACT II, Scene vi

Jus. These are the fruits of bottle-ale and tobacco! The foam of the
one, and the fumes of the other! Stay, young man, and despise not
the wisdom of these few hairs, that are grown grey in care of thee.

Edg. Nightingale, stay a little. Indeed I'll hear some o' this!

[*Enter* Cokes, Wasp, Mistress Overdo, Grace]

5 *Cok.* Come, Numps, come, where are you? Welcome into the
Fair, Mistress Grace.

Edg. 'Slight, he will call company, you shall see, and put us into
doings presently.

Jus. Thirst not after that frothy liquor, ale: for who knows when
10 he openeth the stopple what may be in the bottle? Hath not a snail,

---

150-1 *currying*: drubbing   154 *purchase*: acquisition   157-8 *mallanders* . . .
quitter bone: diseases of the leg and hoof in horses   160 *Hospital*: Ind. 5
163 *windgall*: small tumour above the pastern

a spider, yea, a newt been found there? Thirst not after it, youth: thirst not after it.

Cok. This is a brave fellow, Numps, let's hear him.

Was. 'Sblood, how brave is he? In a guarded coat? You were best truck with him, e'en strip, and truck presently, it will become you, 15 why will you hear him? Because he is an ass, and may be a kin to the Cokeses?

Cok. Oh, good Numps!

Jus. Neither do thou lust after that tawny weed, tobacco.

Cok. Brave words! 20

Jus. Whose complexion is like the Indian's that vents it!

Cok. Are they not brave words, sister?

Jus. And who can tell, if, before the gathering and making up thereof, the alligator hath not pissed thereon?

Was. 'Heart, let 'em be brave words, as brave as they will! And 25 they were all the brave words in a country, how then? Will you away yet? Ha' you enough on him? Mistress Grace, come you away, I pray you, be not you accessory. If you do lose your licence, or some-what else, sir, with listening to his fables: say, Numps is a witch, with all my heart, do, say so. 30

Cok. Avoid i' your satin doublet, Numps.

Jus. The creeping venom of which subtle serpent, as some late writers affirm; neither the cutting of the perilous plant, nor the drying of it, nor the lighting, or burning, can any way persway, or assuage. 35

Cok. Good, i'faith! Is't not sister?

Jus. Hence it is, that the lungs of the tobacconist are rotted, the liver spotted, the brain smoked like the backside of the pig-woman's booth here, and the whole body within, black as her pan you saw e'en now, without. 40

Cok. A fine similitude, that, sir! Did you see the pan?

Edg. Yes, sir.

Jus. Nay, the hole in the nose here, of some tobacco-takers, or the third nostril (if I may so call it) which makes, that they can vent the tobacco out, like the ace of clubs, or rather the flower-de-lys, is caused 45 from the tobacco, the mere tobacco! When the poor innocent pox,

---

14 *brave*: finely dressed   15 *truck*: barter   34 *persway*: diminish
46 *pox*: which attacked the nose

having nothing to do there, is miserably, and most unconscionably slandered.

 Cok. Who would ha' missed this, sister?

50 *Mrs Ove.* Not anybody, but Numps.

 Cok. He does not understand.

 Edg. [*Aside*] Nor you feel.   (*He picketh his purse*)

 Cok. What would you have, sister, of a fellow that knows nothing but a basket-hilt, and an old fox in't? The best music i' the Fair will
55 not move a log.

 Edg. In, to Ursula, Nightingale, and carry her comfort: see it told. This fellow was sent to us by fortune, for our first fairing.

         [*Exit* Nightingale *with purse*]

 Jus. But what speak I of the diseases of the body, children of the Fair?

60 *Cok.* That's to us, sister. Brave i'faith!

 Jus. Hark, O, you sons and daughters of Smithfield! And hear what malady it doth the mind. It causeth swearing, it causeth swaggering, it causeth snuffling and snarling, and now and then a hurt.

65 *Mrs Ove.* He hath something of Master Overdo, methinks, brother.

 Cok. So methought, sister, very much of my brother Overdo. And 'tis, when he speaks.

 Jus. Look into any angle o' the town (the Streights, or the
70 Bermudas) where the quarrelling lesson is read, and how do they entertain the time, but with bottle-ale and tobacco? The lecturer is o' one side, and his pupils o' the other; but the seconds are still bottle-ale and tobacco, for which the lecturer reads, and the novices pay. Thirty pound a week in bottle-ale! Forty in tobacco! And ten
75 more in ale again. Then for a suit to drink in, so much, and (that being slavered) so much for another suit, and then a third suit, and a fourth suit! And still the bottle-ale slavereth, and the tobacco stinketh!

 Was. Heart of a madman! Are you rooted here? Will you never
80 away? What can any man find out in this bawling fellow, to grow

  54 *basket-hilt*: sword hilt carved in the shape of a basket *fox*: sword (? from figure on blade) 69–70 *Streights . . . Bermudas*: alleys frequented by thieves and prostitutes 72 *seconds*: supports

here for? He is a full handful higher, sin' he heard him. Will you fix here? And set up a booth? Sir?

Jus. I will conclude briefly——

Was. Hold your peace, you roaring rascal, I'll run my head i' your chaps else. You were best build a booth, and entertain him, make 85 your will, and you say the word, and him your heir! Heart, I never knew one taken with a mouth of a peck afore. By this light, I'll carry you away o' my back, and you will not come.

(*He gets him up on pick-pack*)

Cok. Stay Numps, stay, set me down: I ha' lost my purse, Numps, oh, my purse! One o' my fine purses is gone.   90

Mrs Ove. Is't indeed, brother?

Cok. Aye, as I am an honest man, would I were an arrant rogue else! A plague of all roguey, damned cutpurses for me.

Was. Bless 'em with all my heart, with all my heart, do you see! Now, as I am no infidel, that I know of, I am glad on't. Aye, I am 95 (here's my witness!) do you see, sir? I did not tell you of his fables, I? No, no, I am a dull malt-horse, I, I know nothing. Are you not justly served i' your conscience now? Speak i' your conscience. Much good do you with all my heart, and his good heart that has it, with all my heart again.   100

Edg. This fellow is very charitable, would he had a purse too! But I must not be too bold, all at a time.

Cok. Nay, Numps, it is not my best purse.

Was. Not your best! Death! Why should it be your worst? Why should it be any, indeed, at all? Answer me to that, gi' me a reason 105 from you, why it should be any?

Cok. Nor my gold, Numps; I ha' that yet, look here else, sister.

Was. Why so, there's all the feeling he has!

Mrs Ove. I pray you, have a better care of that, brother.

Cok. Nay, so I will, I warrant you; let him catch this, that catch 110 can. I would fain see him get this, look you here.

Was. So, so, so, so, so, so, so, so! Very good.

Cok. I would ha' him come again, now, and but offer at it. Sister, will you take notice of a good jest? I will put it just where the other was, and if we ha' good luck, you shall see a delicate fine trap to 115 catch the cutpurse nibbling.

87 *peck*: i.e. of the capacity of a peck   97 *malt-horse*: *EMI* I. v. 78 n.

Edg. Faith, and he'll try ere you be out o' the Fair.

Cok. Come, Mistress Grace, prithee be not melancholy for my mischance; sorrow wi' not keep it, sweetheart.

120   *Gra.* I do not think on't, sir.

Cok. 'Twas but a little scurvy white money, hang it: it may hang the cutpurse one day. I ha' gold left to gi' thee a fairing, yet, as hard as the world goes: nothing angers me, but that nobody here looked like a cutpurse, unless 'twere Numps.

125   *Was.* How? I? I look like a cutpurse? Death! Your sister's a cutpurse! And your mother and father, and all your kin were cutpurses! And here is a rogue is the bawd o' the cutpurses, whom I will beat to begin with.   (*They speak all together: and* Wasp *beats the* Justice)

Jus. Hold thy hand, child of wrath, and heir of anger, make it not 130 Childermass day in thy fury, or the feast of the French Bartholomew, parent of the Massacre.

Cok. Numps, Numps.

Mrs. Ove. Good Master Humphrey.

Was. You are the Patrico! Are you? The patriarch of the cut-135 purses? You share, sir, they say, let them share this with you. Are you i' your hot fit of preaching again? I'll cool you.

Jus. Murder, murder, murder.   [*Exeunt*]

ACT III, Scene i

[The Fair]

Enter Whit, Haggis, Bristle, Leatherhead, Trash

Whi. NAY, tish all gone, now! Dish tish, phen tou vilt not be phitin call, Mashter Offisher, phat ish a man te better to lishen out noishes for tee, and tou art in an oder 'orld, being very shuffishient noishes and gallantsh too, one o' their brabblesh would have fed ush 5 all dish fortnight, but tou art so bushy about beggersh stil, tou hast no leshure to intend shentlemen, and't be.

Hag. Why, I told you, Davy Bristle.

---

121 *white money*: silver   130 *Childermass day*: the Festival of the Innocents, 28 December   131 *Massacre*: 24 August 1572   134 *Patrico*: the hedge-priest of the gipsies   (*III. i*) 1–6 the jargon of Elizabethan stage-Irish

Bri. Come, come, you told me a pudding, Toby Haggis; a matter of nothing; I am sure it came to nothing! You said, let's go to Ursula's, indeed; but then you met the man with the monsters, and 10 I could not get you from him. An old fool, not leave seeing yet?

Hag. Why, who would ha' thought anybody would ha' quarrelled so early? Or that the ale o' the Fair would ha' been up so soon?

Whi. Phy? Phat a clock toest tou tink it ish, man?

Hag. I cannot tell.   15

Whi. Tou art a vishe vatchman, i' te meanteem.

Hag. Why? Should the watch go by the clock, or the clock by the watch, I pray?

Bri. One should go by another, if they did well.

Whi. Tou art right now! Phen didst tou ever know, or hear of a 20 shuffishient vatchman, but he did tell the clock, phat bushiness soever he had?

Bri. Nay, that's most true, a sufficient watchman knows what a clock it is.

Whi. Shleeping, or vaking! Ash well as te clock himshelf, or te 25 jack dat shtrikes him!

Bri. Let's enquire of Master Leatherhead, or Joan Trash here. Master Leatherhead, do you hear, Master Leatherhead?

Whi. If it be a Ledderhead, tish a very tick Ledderhead, tat sho mush noish vill not peirsh him.   30

Lea. I have a little business now, good friends do not trouble me.

Whi. Phat? Because o' ty wrought neet cap, and ty phelvet sherkin, man? Phy? I have sheen tee in ty ledder sherkin, ere now, mashter o' de hobby-horses, as bushy and as stately as tou sheem'st to be.   35

Tra. Why, what an' you have, Captain Whit? He has his choice of jerkins, you may see by that, and his caps too, I assure you, when he pleases to be either sick, or employed.

Lea. God a mercy Joan, answer for me.

Whi. Away, be not sheen i' my company, here be shentlemen, and 40 men of vorship.   [*Exeunt* Haggis, Bristle]

26 *jack*: the figure on old public clocks which told the time by striking a bell on the outside

ACT III, Scene ii

Enter Quarlous, Winwife

Qua. We had wonderful ill luck, to miss this prologue o' the purse, but the best is, we shall have five acts of him ere night: he'll be spectacle enough! I'll answer for't.

Whi. Oh Creesh! Duke Quarlous, how dosht tou? Tou dosht not
5 know me, I fear? I am te vishesht man, but Justish Overdo, in all Bartholomew Fair, now. Gi' me twelvepence from tee, I vill help tee to a vife vorth forty marks for't, and't be.

Qua. Away, rogue, pimp, away.

Whi. And she shall show tee as fine cut 'ork for't in her shmock
10 too, as tou cansht vishe i'faith; vilt tou have her, vorshipful Vinvife? I vill help tee to her, here, be an't be, in te pig-quarter, gi' me ty twelpence from tee.

Winw. Why, there's twelpence, pray thee wilt thou be gone?

Whi. Tou art a vorthy man, and a vorshipful man still.

15 *Qua.* Get you gone, rascal.

Whi. I do mean it, man. Prinsh Quarlous, if tou hasht need on me, tou shalt find me here, at ·Ursula's, I vill see phat ale, and punk ish i' te pigshty, for tee, bless ty good vorship.   [*Exit*]

Qua. Look! Who comes here! John Littlewit!

20 *Winw.* And his wife, and my widow, her mother: the whole family.

Qua. 'Slight, you must gi' em all fairings, now!

Winw. Not I, I'll not see 'em.

Qua. They are going a-feasting. What school-master's that is with 'em?

25 *Winw.* That's my rival, I believe, the baker!

[*Enter* Busy, Purecraft, Littlewit, Win]

Bus. So, walk on in the middle way, fore-right, turn neither to the right hand, nor to the left: let not your eyes be drawn aside with vanity, nor your ear with noises.

---

9 *cut 'ork*: lace embroidery worn by superior prostitutes   26 *fore-right*: straight ahead

Qua. Oh, I know him by that start!

Lea. What do you lack? What do you buy, pretty mistress! A fine 30
hobby-horse, to make your son a tilter? A drum to make him a sol-
dier? A fiddle, to make him a reveller? What is't you lack? Little
dogs for your daughters? Or babies, male, or female?

Bus. Look not toward them, hearken not: the place is Smithfield,
or the field of Smiths, the grove of hobby-horses and trinkets, the 35
wares are the wares of devils. And the whole Fair is the shop of
Satan! They are hooks and baits, very baits, that are hung out on
every side to catch you, and to hold you as it were, by the gills; and
by the nostrils, as the fisher doth: therefore you must not look, nor
turn toward them——the heathen man could stop his ears with wax, 40
against the harlot o' the sea: do you the like, with your fingers,
against the bells of the Beast.

Winw. What flashes comes from him!

Qua. Oh, he has those of his oven! A notable hot baker 'twas, when
he plied the peel: he is leading his flock into the Fair now.   45

Winw. Rather driving 'em to the pens: for he will let 'em look
upon nothing.

[*Enter* Knockem, Whit]

Kno. Gentlewomen, the weather's hot! Whither walk you? Have
a care o' your fine velvet caps, the Fair is dusty. Take a sweet delicate
booth, with boughs, here i' the way, and cool yourselves i' the shade: 50
you and your friends. The best pig and bottle-ale i' the Fair, sir.
(Littlewit *is gazing at the sign; which is the pig's head with a large
writing under it*) Old Ursula is cook, there you may read: the pig's
head speaks it. Poor soul, she has had a stringhalt, the maryhinchco:
but she's prettily amended.   55

Whi. A delicate show-pig, little mistress, with shweet sauce and
crackling, like de bay-leaf i' de fire, la! Tou shalt ha' de clean side
o' de table-clot and di glass vash'd with phatersh of Dame Annessh
Cleare.

Lit. This's fine, verily, here be the best pigs: and she does roast 60
'em as well as ever she did; the pig's head says.

40-1 *heathen man . . . harlot*: Ulysses and the Sirens   45 *peel*: long-handled
shovel for reaching into the oven   54 *stringhalt, the maryhinchco*: twitching up
of a horse's hind legs   58-9 *Dame Annessh Cleare*: a well in Hoxton

Kno. Excellent, excellent, mistress, with fire o' juniper and rosemary branches! The oracle of the pig's head, that, sir.

Pur. Son, were you not warned of the vanity of the eye? Have you forgot the wholesome admonition, so soon?

Lit. Good mother, how shall we find a pig, if we do not look about for't? Will it run off o' the spit, into our mouths, think you? As in Lubberland? And cry, *we, we*?

Bus. No, but your mother, religiously wise, conceiveth it may offer itself, by other means, to the sense, as by way of steam, which I think it doth, here in this place (Huh, huh) yes, it doth. (*Busy scents after it like a hound*) And it were a sin of obstinacy, great obstinacy, high and horrible obstinacy, to decline, or resist the good titillation of the famelic sense, which is the smell. Therefore be bold (huh, huh, huh) follow the scent. Enter the tents of the unclean for once, and satisfy your wife's frailty. Let your frail wife be satisfied: your zealous mother, and my suffering self, will also be satisfied.

Lit. Come, Win, as good winny here as go farther, and see nothing.

Bus. We scape so much of the other vanities, by our early entering.

Pur. It is an edifying consideration.

Win. This is scurvy, that we must come into the Fair, and not look on't.

Lit. Win, have patience, Win, I'll tell you more anon.

                    [*Exeunt into the booth* Busy, Purecraft, Littlewit, Win]

Kno. Mooncalf, entertain within there, the best pig i' the booth; a porklike pig. These are Banbury-bloods, o' the sincere stud, come a pig-hunting. Whit, wait Whit, look to your charge.   [*Exit* Whit]

Bus. [*Within*] A pig prepare, presently, let a pig be prepared to us.

[*Enter* Mooncalf, Ursula]

Moo. 'Slight, who be these?

Urs. Is this the good service, Jordan, you'd do me?

Kno. Why, Urs? Why, Urs? Thou'lt ha' vapours i' thy leg again presently, pray thee go in, 't may turn to the scratches else.

---

62 *juniper*: fragrant and long-burning   63 *rosemary*: sweet-smelling
68 *Lubberland*: where pigs run about roasted, and asking to be eaten (proverbial)
74 *famelic*: hungry   78 *winny*: stay

Urs. Hang your vapours, they are stale, and stink like you, are these the guests o' the game, you promised to fill my pit withal today? 95

Kno. Aye, what ail they Urs?

Urs. Ail they? They are all sippers, sippers o' the city, they look as they would not drink off two pennorth of bottle-ale amongst 'em.

Moo. A body may read that i' their small printed ruffs.

Kno. Away, thou art a fool, Urs, and thy Mooncalf too, i' your 100 ignorant vapours, now? Hence! Good guests, I say right hypocrites, good gluttons. In, and set a couple o' pigs o' the board, and half a dozen of the biggest bottles afore 'em, and call Whit, I do not love to hear innocents abused: fine ambling hypocrites! And a stone-puritan, with a sorrel head, and beard, good-mouthed gluttons: two 105 to a pig, away.   [*Exit Mooncalf*]

Urs. Are you sure they are such?

Kno. O' the right breed, thou shalt try 'em by the teeth, Urs. Where's this Whit?

[*Enter* Whit]

Whi. Behold, man, and see, what a worthy man am ee! 110
    With the fury of my sword, and the shaking of my beard,
    I will make ten thousand men afeared.

Kno. Well said, brave Whit, in, and fear the ale out o' the bottles, into the bellies of the brethren, and the sisters, drink to the cause, and pure vapours.   [*Exeunt Knockem, Whit, Ursula*] 115

Qua. My roarer is turned tapster, methinks. Now were a fine time for thee, Winwife, to lay aboard thy widow, thou'lt never be master of a better season, or place; she that will venture herself into the Fair, and a pig-box, will admit any assault, be assured of that.

Winw. I love not enterprises of that suddenness, though. 120

Qua. I'll warrant thee, then, no wife out o' the widows' hundred: if I had but as much title to her, as to have breathed once on that straight stomacher of hers, I would now assure myself to carry her, yet, ere she went out of Smithfield. Or she should carry me, which were the fitter sight, I confess. But you are a modest undertaker, by 125 circumstances, and degrees; come, 'tis disease in thee, not judge-

---

95 *guests o' the game*: prostitutes   99 *small-printed*: small and exactly folded
104-5 *stone-puritan*: as in 'stone-horse', a stallion   105 *sorrel*: chestnut
117 *lay aboard*: of a ship coming alongside another   121 *hundred*: *Alch.* IV. i.
134 n.

ment, I should offer at all together. Look, here's the poor fool again, that was stung by the wasp erewhile.

ACT III, Scene iii

Enter Justice Overdo

Jus. I will make no more orations, shall draw on these tragical conclusions. And I begin now to think, that by a spice of collateral justice, Adam Overdo deserved this beating; for I the said Adam, was one cause (a by-cause) why the purse was lost: and my wife's
5 brother's purse too, which they know not of yet. But I shall make very good mirth with it, at supper (that will be the sport) and put my little friend, Master Humphrey Wasp's choler quite out of countenance. When, sitting at the upper end o' my table, as I use, and drinking to my brother Cokes, and Mistress Alice Overdo, as I will, my wife, for
10 their good affection to old Bradley, I deliver to 'em, it was I, that was cudgelled, and show 'em the marks. To see what bad events may peep out o' the tail of good purposes! The care I had of that civil young man I took fancy to this morning (and have not left it yet) drew me to that exhortation, which drew the company, indeed,
15 which drew the cutpurse; which drew the money; which drew my brother Cokes his loss; which drew on Wasp's anger; which drew on my beating: a pretty gradation! And they shall ha' it i' their dish, i' faith, at night for fruit: I love to be merry at my table. I had thought once, at one special blow he ga' me, to have revealed myself;
20 but then (I thank thee, fortitude) I remembered that a wise man (and who is ever so great a part o' the commonwealth in himself) for no particular disaster ought to abandon a public good design. The husbandman ought not for one unthankful year, to forsake the plough; the shepherd ought not, for one scabbed sheep, to throw by
25 his tar-box; the pilot ought not for one leak i' the poop, to quit the helm; nor the alderman ought not for one custard more, at a meal, to give up his cloak; the constable ought not to break his staff, and forswear the watch, for one roaring night; nor the piper o' the parish

---

11 *events*: consequences   25 *tar-box*: for anointing sores   26 *custard*:
Volp, Prol. 21 n.

(*Ut parvis componere magna solebam*) to put up his pipes, for one
rainy Sunday. These are certain knocking conclusions; out of which, 30
I am resolved, come what come can, come beating, come imprison-
ment, come infamy, come banishment, nay, come the rack, come the
hurdle (welcome all) I will not discover who I am, till my due time;
and yet still, all shall be, as I said ever, in justice' name, and the
King's, and for the commonwealth.   [*Exit*] 35

Winw. What does he talk to himself, and act so seriously?
Poor fool!

Qua. No matter what. Here's fresher argument, intend that.

ACT III, Scene iv

Enter Cokes, Mistress Overdo, Grace, *with* Wasp [*carrying goods*]

Cok. Come, Mistress Grace, come sister, here's more fine sights,
yet, i' faith. God's lid, where's Numps?

Lea. What do you lack, gentlemen? What is't you buy? Fine
rattles? Drums? Babies? Little dogs? And birds for ladies? What
do you lack?   5

Cok. Good honest Numps, keep afore, I am so afraid thou'lt lose
somewhat: my heart was at my mouth, when I missed thee.

Was. You were best buy a whip i' your hand to drive me.

Cok. Nay, do not mistake, Numps, thou art so apt to mistake: I
would but watch the goods. Look you now, the treble fiddle, was 10
e'en almost like to be lost.

Was. Pray you take heed you lose not yourself: your best way,
were e'en get up, and ride for more surety. Buy a token's worth of
great pins, to fasten yourself to my shoulder.

Lea. What do you lack, gentlemen? Fine purses, pouches, pin- 15
cases, pipes? What is't you lack? A pair o' smiths to wake you i' the
morning? Or a fine whistling bird?

Cok. Numps, here be finer things than any we ha' bought by odds!
And more delicate horses, a great deal! Good Numps, stay, and
come hither.   20

---

29 *Ut parvis* . . .: Virgil, *Ecl.* i. 23 ('Thus I used to compare great things with small')
32–3 *rack* . . . *hurdle*: instruments of punishment   38 *intend*: pay attention to
(*III iv.*) 16 *pair o' smiths*: ? device serving as an alarm clock

Was. Will you scourse with him? You are in Smithfield, you may
fit yourself with a fine easy-going street-nag, for your saddle again'
Michaelmas-term, do, has he ne'er a little odd cart for you, to make
a caroche on, i' the country, with four pied hobby-horses? Why the
25 measles should you stand here, with your train, cheaping of dogs,
birds, and babies? You ha' no children to bestow 'em on? Ha' you?

Cok. No, but again' I ha' children, Numps, that's all one.

Was. Do, do, do, do; how many shall you have, think you? An'
I were as you, I'd buy for all my tenants, too, they are a kind o' civil
30 savages, that will part with their children for rattles, pipes, and
knives. You were best buy a hatchet or two, and truck with 'em.

Cok. Good Numps, hold that little tongue o' thine, and save it a
labour. I am resolute Bat, thou know'st.

Was. A resolute fool, you are, I know, and a very sufficient cox-
35 comb; with all my heart; nay, you have it, sir, and you be angry, turd
i'your teeth, twice (if I said it not once afore) and much good do you.

Winw. Was there ever such a self-affliction? And so impertinent?

Qua. Alas! His care will go near to crack him, let's in, and
comfort him.

40 *Was.* Would I had been set i' the ground, all but the head on me,
and had my brains bowled at, or threshed out, when first I under-
went this plague of a charge!

Qua. How now, Numps! Almost tired i' your protectorship?
Overparted? Overparted?

45 *Was.* Why, I cannot tell, sir, it may be I am, dost grieve you?

Qua. No, I swear dost not, Numps: to satisfy you.

Was. Numps? 'Sblood, you are fine and familiar! How long ha'
we been acquainted, I pray you?

Qua. I think it may be remembered, Numps, that? 'Twas since
50 morning sure.

Was. Why, I hope I know 't well enough, sir, I did not ask to
be told.

Qua. No? Why then?

Was. It's no matter why, you see with your eyes, now, what I said
55 to you today? You'll believe me another time?

21 *scourse*: deal   22 *again'*: in anticipation of   24 *caroche*: large and
stately carriage   25 *cheaping*: asking the price   38 *crack*: craze
44 *Overparted*: given too heavy a part

Qua. Are you removing the Fair, Numps?

Was. A pretty question! And a very civil one! Yes faith, I ha' my lading, you see; or shall have anon, you may know whose beast I am, by my burthen. If the pannier-man's jack were ever better known by his loins of mutton, I'll be flayed, and feed dogs for him, when his time comes.

Winw. How melancholy Mistress Grace is yonder! Pray thee let's go enter ourselves in Grace, with her.

Cok. Those six horses, friend, I'll have——

Was. How!

Cok. And the three Jew's trumps; and half a dozen o' birds, and that drum (I have one drum already) and your smiths; I like that device o' your smiths, very pretty well, and four halberts——and (le'me see) that fine painted great lady, and her three women for state, I'll have.

Was. No, the shop; buy the whole shop, it will be best, the shop, the shop!

Lea. If his worship please.

Was. Yes, and keep it during the Fair, bobchin.

Cok. Peace, Numps. Friend, do not meddle with him, an' you be wise, and would show your head above board: he will sting thorough your wrought night-cap, believe me. A set of these violins, I would buy too, for a delicate young noise I have i' the country, that are every one a size less than another, just like your fiddles. I would fain have a fine young masque at my marriage, now I think on't: but I do want such a number o' things. And Numps will not help me now, and I dare not speak to him.

Tra. Will your worship buy any gingerbread, very good bread, comfortable bread?

Cok. Gingerbread! Yes, let's see.   (*He runs to her shop*)

Was. There's the tother springe?

Lea. Is this well, goody Joan? To interrupt my market? In the midst? And call away my customers? Can you answer this, at the Piepowders?

Tra. Why? If his mastership have a mind to buy, I hope my

---

59 *pannier-man's jack*: minor official who waited on tables in the Inns of Court
66 *trumps*: harps   74 *bobchin*: imbecile (whose chin jerks up and down)
78 *noise*: band of musicians   86 *springe*: snare

ware lies as open as another's; I may show my ware as well as
you yours.

    Cok. Hold your peace; I'll content you both: I'll buy up his shop,
and thy basket.

95   *Was* Will you i'faith?

    Lea. Why should you put him from it, friend?

    Was. Cry you mercy! You'd be sold too, would you? What's the
price on you? Jerkin, and all as you stand? Ha' you any qualities?

    Tra. Yes, goodman angry-man, you shall find he has qualities, if
100 you cheapen him.

    Was. Gods so, you ha' the selling of him! What are they? Will
they be bought for love or money?

    Tra. No indeed, sir.

    Was. For what then? Victuals?

105   *Tra.* He scorns victuals, sir, he has bread and butter at home,
thanks be to God! And yet he will do more for a good meal, if the
toy take him i' the belly, marry then they must not set him at lower
end; if they do, he'll go away, though he fast. But put him a top o'
the table, where his place is, and he'll do you forty fine things. He
110 has not been sent for, and sought out for nothing, at your great city-
suppers, to put down Coryat, and Cokeley, and been laughed at for
his labour: he'll play you all the puppets i' the town over, and the
players, every company, and his own company too; he spares
nobody!

115   *Cok.* I'faith?

    Tra. He was the first, sir, that ever baited the fellow i' the bear's
skin, an't like your worship: no dog ever came near him since. And
for fine motions!

    Cok. Is he good at those too? Can he set out a masque, trow?

120   *Tra.* Oh Lord, master! Sought to far and near, for his inventions:
and he engrosses all, he makes all the puppets i' the Fair.

    Cok. Dost thou (in troth) old velvet jerkin? Give me thy hand.

    Tra. Nay sir, you shall see him in his velvet jerkin, and a scarf,
too, at night, when you hear him interpret Master Littlewit's motion.

    108–9 *top o' the table*: the jester's place   111 *Coryat*: Thomas Coryat, traveller
and jester, to whose *Crudities* (1611) Jonson contributed mock-commendatory verses
Cokeley: a jester who improvised at entertainments   116–17 *fellow i' the bear's
skin*: commemorated in a ballad (*H&S* x. 198)   119 *trow?*: do you suppose?
124 *interpret*: speak the words at the puppet-show

Cok. Speak no more, but shut up shop presently, friend. I'll buy 125
both it, and thee too, to carry down with me, and her hamper,
beside. Thy shop shall furnish out the masque, and hers the banquet:
I cannot go less, to set out anything with credit. What's the price, at
a word, o' thy whole shop, case, and all as it stands?

Lea. Sir, it stands me in six and twenty shillings seven pence, 130
halfpenny, besides three shillings for my ground.

Cok. Well, thirty shillings will do all, then! And what comes
yours to?

Tra. Four shillings and eleven pence, sir, ground, and all, an't like
your worship.   135

Cok. Yes, it does like my worship very well, poor woman, that's
five shillings more. What a masque shall I furnish out, for forty
shillings? (twenty pounds Scotch) and a banquet of gingerbread?
There's a stately thing! Numps? Sister? And my wedding gloves
too? (That I never thought on afore). All my wedding gloves, 140
gingerbread? Oh me! What a device will there be? To make 'em
eat their fingers' ends! And delicate brooches for the bride-men!
And all! And then I'll ha' this poesy put to 'em: *For the best grace*,
meaning Mistress Grace, my wedding poesy.

Gra. I am beholden to you, sir, and to your Bartholomew-wit.   145

Was. You do not mean this, do you? Is this your first purchase?

Cok. Yes faith, and I do not think, Numps, but thou'lt say, it was
the wisest act, that ever I did in my wardship.

Was. Like enough! I shall say anything, I!

ACT III, Scene v

Enter Justice Overdo, Edgeworth, Nightingale

Jus. I cannot beget a project, with all my political brain, yet; my
project is how to fetch off this proper young man, from his debauched
company: I have followed him all the Fair over, and still I find him
with this songster: and I begin shrewdly to suspect their familiarity;
and the young man of a terrible taint, Poetry! With which idle 5

127 *banquet*: dessert   138 *pound Scotch*: equal to one-twelfth of a pound ster-
ling   139 *wedding gloves*: presented to the company at a wedding   144 *poesy*:
motto (inscribed in the ring)

disease, if he be infected, there's no hope of him, in a state-course. *Actum est*, of him for a commonwealth's-man: if he go to't in rhyme once.

    Edg. Yonder he is buying o' gingerbread: set in quickly, before he
10 part with too much on his money.

    Nig. My masters and friends, and good people, draw near, &c.

    Cok. Ballads! Hark, hark! Pray thee, fellow, stay a little, good Numps, look to the goods. What ballads hast thou? Let me see, let me see myself.   (*He runs to the ballad man*)

15   *Was.* Why so! He's flown to another lime-bush, there he will flutter as long more; till he ha' ne'er a feather left. Is there a vexation like this, gentlemen? Will you believe me now, hereafter shall I have credit with you?

    Qua. Yes faith, shalt thou, Numps, and thou art worthy on't, for
20 thou sweatest for't. I never saw a young pimp errant, and his squire better matched.

    Winw. Faith, the sister comes after 'em, well, too.

    Gra. Nay, if you saw the Justice her husband, my guardian, you were fitted for the mess, he is such a wise one his way——

25   *Winw.* I wonder, we see him not here.

    Gra. Oh! He is too serious for this place, and yet better sport than the other three, I assure you, gentlemen: where'er he is, though 't be o' the Bench.

    Cok. How dost thou call it! A caveat against cutpurses! A good
30 jest, i'faith, I would fain see that demon, your cutpurse, you talk of, that delicate-handed devil; they say he walks hereabout; I would see him walk, now. (*He shows his purse boastingly*) Look you sister, here, here, let him come, sister, and welcome. Ballad-man, does any cut-purses haunt hereabout? Pray thee raise me one or two: begin and
35 show me one.

    Nig. Sir, this is a spell against 'em, spick and span new; and 'tis made as 'twere in mine own person, and I sing it in mine own defence. But 'twill cost a penny alone, if you buy it.

    Cok. No matter for the price, thou dost not know me, I see, I am
40 an odd Bartholomew.

    Mrs Ove. Has't a fine picture, brother?

---

7 *Actum . . . him*: It's all over with him   15 *lime-bush*: bush dressed with
birdlime   24 *mess*: set of four

Cok. Oh sister, do you remember the ballads over the nursery-chimney at home o' my own pasting up, there be brave pictures. Other manner of pictures than these, friend.

Was. Yet these will serve to pick the pictures out o' your pockets, 45 you shall see.

Cok. So, I heard 'em say. Pray thee mind him not, fellow: he'll have an oar in everything.

Nig. It was intended sir, as if a purse should chance to be cut in my presence, now, I may be blameless, though: as by the sequel, will 50 more plainly appear.

Cok. We shall find that i' the matter. Pray thee begin.

Nig. To the tune of 'Paggington's Pound', sir,

Cok. Fa, la la la, la la la, fa la la la. Nay, I'll put thee in tune, and all! Mine own country dance! Pray thee begin.   55

Nig. It is a gentle admonition, you must know, sir, both to the purse-cutter, and the purse-bearer.

Cok. Not a word more, out o' the tune, an' thou lov'st me: Fa, la la la, la la la, fa la la la. Come, when?

Nig. My masters and friends, and good people draw near,   60
      And look to your purses, for that I do say;

Cok. Ha, ha, this chimes! Good counsel at first dash.

Nig. And though little money, in them you do bear,
      It cost more to get, than to lose in a day.

Cok.   Good!

Nig. You oft have been told,   65
      Both the young and the old;
      And bidden beware of the cutpurse so bold:

Cok. Well said! He were to blame that would not i'faith.

Nig. Then if you take heed not, free me from the curse,
      Who both give you warning for and the cutpurse.   70
      Youth, youth, thou hadst better been starved by thy nurse,
      Than live to be hanged for cutting a purse.

Cok. Good i'faith, how say you, Numps? Is there any harm i' this?

Nig. It hath been upbraided to men of my trade,
      That oftentimes we are the cause of this crime.   75

Cok. The more coxcombs they that did it, I wusse.

53 '*Paggington's Pound*': old dance-tune given in Chappell, i. 259 (for the stories alluded to in the ballad itself see *H&S* x. 199–200)   70 *for and*: and moreover

 Nig. Alack and for pity, why should it be said?
  As if they regarded or places, or time.
   Examples have been
80   Of some that were seen,
  In Westminster Hall, yea the pleaders between,
  Then why should the judges be free from this curse,
  More than my poor self, for cutting the purse?
 Cok. God a mercy for that! Why should they be more free indeed?
         (*He sings the burden with him*)
85 *Nig.* Youth, youth, thou hadst better been starved by thy nurse,
  Than live to be hanged for cutting a purse.
 Cok. That again, good ballad-man, that again. Oh rare! I
would fain rub mine elbow now, but I dare not pull out my
hand. On, I pray thee, he that made this ballad, shall be poet to
90 my masque.
 Nig. At Worc'ter 'tis known well, and even i' the jail,
  A knight of good worship did there show his face,
  Against the foul sinners, in zeal for to rail,
  And lost (*ipso facto*) his purse in the place.
95 *Cok.* Is it possible?
 Nig.   Nay, once from the seat
   Of judgement so great,
  A judge there did lose a fair pouch of velvet.
 Cok. I' faith?
100 *Nig.* Oh Lord for thy mercy, how wicked or worse,
   Are those that so venture their necks for a purse! Youth,
    youth, etc.
 Cok. 'Youth, youth, etc.'? Pray thee stay a little, friend, yet, o' thy
conscience, Numps, speak, is there any harm i' this?
 Was. To tell you true, 'tis too good for you, 'less you had grace to
105 follow it.
 Jus. It doth discover enormity, I'll mark it more: I ha' not liked a
paltry piece of poetry, so well, a good while.
 Cok. 'Youth, youth, etc'! Where's this youth, now? A man must
call upon him, for his own good, and yet he will not appear: look
110 here, here's for him (*He shows his purse*); handy-dandy, which hand

---

 88 *rub . . . elbow*: show enjoyment   110 *handy-dandy*: children's game of
guessing which hand conceals an object

will he have? On, I pray thee, with the rest, I do hear of him, but I
cannot see him, this Master Youth, the cutpurse.

Nig. At plays and at sermons, and at the sessions,
    'Tis daily their practice such booty to make:
    Yea, under the gallows, at executions,   115
    They stick not the stare-abouts' purses to take.
        Nay one without grace,
          At a far better place,
    At court, and in Christmas, before the King's face.

Cok. That was a fine fellow! I would have him, now.   120

Nig. Alack then for pity, must I bear the curse,
    That only belongs to the cunning cutpurse?

Cok. But where's their cunning, now, when they should use it?
They are all chained now, I warrant you. 'Youth, youth, thou hadst
better, etc.' The rat-catchers' charm, are all fools and asses to this! 125
A pox on 'em, that they will not come! That a man should have such
a desire to a thing, and want it.

Qua. 'Fore God, I'd give half the Fair, and 'twere mine, for a cut-
purse for him, to save his longing.

Cok. (*He shows his purse again*) Look you sister, here, here, where 130
is't now? Which pocket is't in? For a wager?

Was. I beseech you leave your wagers, and let him end his matter,
an't may be.

Cok. Oh, are you edified, Numps?

Jus. Indeed he does interrupt him, too much: there Numps spoke 135
to purpose.

Cok. Sister, I am an ass, I cannot keep my purse: ([*shows it*] *again*)
on, on; I pray thee, friend.

Nig. But O, you vile nation of cutpurses all,
    Relent and repent, and amend and be sound,   140
    And know that you ought not, by honest men's fall,
    Advance your own fortunes, to die above ground,
        And though you go gay,
          In silks as you may,
    It is not the high way to heaven (as they say)   145

Winw. Will you see sport? Look, there's a fellow gathers up to
him, mark.

  125 *charm*: rats were believed susceptible to music (*SN* Intermean IV. 46–7)

(Edgeworth *gets up to him, and tickles him in the ear
with a straw twice to draw his hand out of his pocket*)

Qua. Good, i'faith! Oh, he has lighted on the wrong pocket.

Winw. He has it, 'fore God he is a brave fellow; pity he should be
150 detected.

Nig. Repent then, repent you, for better, for worse:
     And kiss not the gallows for cutting a purse.
     Youth, youth, thou hadst better been starved by thy nurse,
     Than live to be hanged for cutting a purse.

155 *All.* An excellent ballad! An excellent ballad!

Edg. Friend, let me ha' the first, let me ha' the first, I pray you.

Cok. Pardon me, sir. First come, first served; and I'll buy the
whole bundle too.

Win. That conveyance was better than all, did you see 't? He has
160 given the purse to the ballad-singer.

Qua. Has he?

Edg. Sir, I cry you mercy; I'll not hinder the poor man's profit:
pray you mistake me not.

Cok. Sir, I take you for an honest gentleman, if that be mistaking;
165 I met you today afore: ha! Humh! Oh God! My purse is gone, my
purse, my purse, &c.

Was. Come, do not make a stir, and cry yourself an ass thorough
the Fair afore your time.

Cok. Why, hast thou it, Numps? Good Numps, how came you
170 by it? I mar'l!

Was. I pray you seek some other gamester to play the fool with:
you may lose it time enough, for all your Fair-wit.

Cok. By this good hand, glove and all, I ha' lost it already, if thou
hast it not: feel else, and Mistress Grace's handkercher, too, out o'
175 the tother pocket.

Was. Why, 'tis well; very well, exceeding pretty, and well.

Edg. Are you sure you ha' lost it, sir?

Cok. Oh God! Yes; as I am an honest man, I had it but e'en
now, at 'youth, youth'.

180 *Nig.* I hope you suspect not me, sir.

Edg. Thee? That were a jest indeed! Dost thou think the
gentleman is foolish? Where hadst thou hands, I pray thee? Away
ass, away.   [*Exit* Nightingale]

Jus. [*Aside*] I shall be beaten again, if I be spied.

Edg. Sir, I suspect an odd fellow, yonder, is stealing away.   185

Mrs Ove. Brother, it is the preaching fellow! You shall suspect him. He was at your tother purse, you know! Nay, stay, sir, and view the work you ha' done, an' you be beneficed at the gallows, and preach there, thank your own handiwork.

Cok. Sir, you shall take no pride in your preferment: you shall be   190
silenced quickly.

Jus. What do you mean? Sweet buds of gentility.

Cok. To ha' my pennyworths out on you: bud! No less than two purses a day, serve you? I thought you a simple fellow, when my man Numps beat you, i' the morning, and pitied you——   195

Mrs Ove. So did I, I'll be sworn, brother; but now I see he is a lewd and pernicious enormity (as Master Overdo calls him.)

Jus. [*Aside*] Mine own words turned upon me, like swords.

Cok. Cannot a man's purse be at quiet for you, i' the master's pocket, but you must entice it forth, and debauch it?   200

                              [Justice Overdo *is carried off*]

Was. Sir, sir, keep your debauch, and your fine Bartholomew-terms to yourself; and make as much on 'em as you please. But gi' me this from you, i' the meantime: I beseech you, see if I can look to this.   (Wasp *takes the licence from him*)

Cok. Why, Numps?   205

Was. Why? Because you are an ass, sir, there's a reason the shortest way, and you will needs ha' it; now you ha' got the trick of losing, you'd lose your breech, an't 'twere loose. I know you, sir, come, deliver, you'll go and crack the vermin, you breed now, will you? 'Tis very fine, will you ha' the truth on't? They are such retchless   210
flies as you are, that blow cutpurses abroad in every corner; your foolish having of money, makes 'em. An' there were no wiser than I, sir, the trade should lie open for you, sir, it should i'faith, sir. I would teach your wit to come to your head, sir, as well as your land to come into your hand, I assure you, sir.   215

Winw. Alack, good Numps.

Was. Nay, gentlemen, never pity me, I am not worth it: Lord send me at home once, to Harrow o' the Hill again, if I travel any more, call me Coryat; with all my heart. [*Exeunt* Wasp, Cokes, Mistress Overdo]

210 *retchless*: heedless   219 *Coryat*: III. iv. 111 n.

220   *Qua.* Stay, sir, I must have a word with you in private. Do you hear?

  Edg. With me, sir? What's your pleasure? Good sir.

  Qua. Do not deny it. You are a cutpurse, sir, this gentleman here, and I, saw you, nor do we mean to detect you (although we can suffi-
225 ciently inform ourselves, toward the danger of concealing you) but, you must do us a piece of service.

  Edg. Good gentlemen, do not undo me; I am a civil young man, and but a beginner, indeed.

  Qua. Sir, your beginning shall bring on your ending, for us. We
230 are no catchpoles nor constables. That you are to undertake, is this; you saw the old fellow, with the black box, here?

  Edg. The little old governor, sir?

  Qua. That same: I see, you have flown him to a mark already. I would ha' you get away that box from him, and bring it us.

235   *Edg.* Would you ha' the box and all, sir? Or only that, that is in't? I'll get you that, and leave him the box, to play with still (which will be the harder o'the two) because I would gain your worship's good opinion of me.

  Winw. He says well, 'tis the greater mastery, and 'twill make the
240 more sport when 'tis missed.

  Edg. Aye, and 'twill be the longer a-missing, to draw on the sport.

  Qua. But look you do it now, sirrah, and keep your word: or——

  Edg. Sir, if ever I break my word, with a gentleman, may I never read word at my need. Where shall I find you?

245   *Qua.* Somewhere i' the Fair, hereabouts. Dispatch it quickly. [*Exit* Edgeworth] I would fain see the careful fool deluded! Of all beasts, I love the serious ass. He that takes pains to be one, and plays the fool, with the greatest diligence that can be.

  Gra. Then you would not choose, sir, but love my guardian,
250 Justice Overdo, who is answerable to that description, in every hair of him.

  Qua. So I have heard. But how came you, Mistress Wellborn, to be his ward? Or have relation to him, at first?

  Gra. Faith, through a common calamity, he bought me, sir; and

---

230 *catchpoles*: Sheriff's officers (contemptuous)   232 *governor*: tutor   254 *bought*: the Court of Wards and Liveries permitted the sale of guardianships

now he will marry me to his wife's brother, this wise gentleman, that 255
you see, or else I must pay value o' my land.

Qua. 'Slid, is there no device of disparagement? Or so? Talk with
some crafty fellow, some picklock o' the law! Would I had studied
a year longer i'the Inns of Court, and't had been but i' your case.

Winw. [*Aside*] Aye, Master Quarlous, are you proffering? 260

Gra. You'd bring but little aid, sir.

Winw. (I'll look to you i' faith, gamester.) An unfortunate foolish
tribe you are fallen into, lady, I wonder you can endure 'em.

Gra. Sir, they that cannot work their fetters off; must wear 'em.

Winw. You see what care they have on you, to leave you thus. 265

Gra. Faith, the same they have of themselves, sir. I cannot greatly
complain, if this were all the plea I had against 'em.

Winw. 'Tis true! But will you please to withdraw with us a little,
and make them think they have lost you. I hope our manners ha'
been such hitherto, and our language, as will give you no cause to 270
doubt yourself in our company.

Gra. Sir, I will give myself no cause; I am so secure of mine own
manners, as I suspect not yours.

Qua. Look where John Littlewit comes.

Winw. Away, I'll not be seen by him. 275

Qua. No, you were not best, he'd tell his mother, the widow.

Winw. Heart, what do you mean?

Qua. Cry you mercy, is the wind there? Must not the widow be
named?   [*Exeunt* Quarlous, Winwife, Grace]

ACT III, Scene vi

Enter Littlewit, Win

Lit. Do you hear, Win, Win?

Win. What say you, John?

Lit. While they are paying the reckoning, Win, I'll tell you a
thing, Win, we shall never see any sights i' the Fair, Win, except you
long still, Win, good Win, sweet Win, long to see some hobby- 5
horses, and some drums, and rattles, and dogs, and fine devices,

---

257 *disparagement*: marriage of an heir to someone of lower degree   278 *is the*
wind there: is that how things stand

Win. The bull with the five legs, Win; and the great hog: now you ha'
begun with pig, you may long for anything, Win, and so for my
motion, Win.

10   *Win.* But we sha' not eat o' the bull, and the hog, John, how shall
I long then?

     Lit. Oh yes! Win: you may long to see, as well as to taste, Win:
how did the pothecary's wife, Win, that longed to see the anatomy,
Win? Or the lady, Win, that desired to spit i' the great lawyer's
15 mouth, after an eloquent pleading? I assure you they longed, Win,
good Win, go in, and long.   [*Exeunt*]

     Tra. I think we are rid of our new customer, brother Leatherhead,
we shall hear no more of him.   (*They plot to be gone*)

     Lea. All the better, let's pack up all, and be gone, before he find us.
20   *Tra.* Stay a little, yonder comes a company: it may be we may
take some more money.

[*Enter* Knockem, Busy]

     Kno. Sir, I will take your counsel, and cut my hair, and leave
vapours: I see, that tobacco, and bottle-ale, and pig, and Whit, and
very Ursula, herself, is all vanity.

25   *Bus.* Only pig was not comprehended in my admonition, the rest
were. For long hair, it is an ensign of pride, a banner, and the world
is full of those banners, very full of banners. And, bottle-ale is a
drink of Satan's, a diet-drink of Satan's, devised to puff us up, and
make us swell in this latter age of vanity, as the smoke of tobacco, to
30 keep us in mist and error. But the fleshly woman (which you call
Ursula) is above all to be avoided, having the marks upon her of the
three enemies of man, the world, as being in the Fair; the devil, as
being in the fire; and the flesh, as being herself.

[*Enter* Dame Purecraft]

     Pur. Brother Zeal-of-the-land! What shall we do? My daughter
35 Win-the-fight is fallen into her fit of longing again.

     Bus. For more pig? There is no more, is there?

     Pur. To see some sights, i' the Fair.

     Bus. Sister, let her fly the impurity of the place, swiftly, lest

---

13 *anatomy*: skeleton   22 *cut my hair*: a sign of reformation (*EMO*, Ind. 42–3,
Ep. xxi)   28 *diet-drink*: prescribed drink

she partake of the pitch thereof. Thou art the seat of the Beast, O Smithfield, and I will leave thee. Idolatry peepeth out on every side 40 of thee.

Kno. [*Aside*] An excellent right hypocrite! Now his belly is full, he falls a-railing and kicking, the jade. A very good vapour! I'll in, and joy Ursula, with telling, how her pig works, two and a half he eat to his share. And he has drunk a pailful. He eats with his eyes, as 45 well as his teeth.   [*Exit*]

Lea. What do you lack, gentlemen? What is't you buy? Rattles, drums, babies——

Bus. Peace, with thy apocryphal wares, thou profane publican: thy bells, thy dragons, and thy Toby's dogs. Thy hobby-horse is an 50 idol, a very idol, a fierce and rank idol: and thou, the Nebuchadnezzar, the proud Nebuchadnezzar of the Fair, that set'st it up, for children to fall down to and worship.

Lea. Cry you mercy, sir, will you buy a fiddle to fill up your noise?

[*Enter* Littlewit, Win]

Lit. Look Win, do, look a God's name, and save your longing. 55 Here be fine sights.

Pur. Aye child, so you hate 'em, as our brother Zeal does, you may look on 'em.

Lea. Or what do you say, to a drum, sir?

Bus. It is the broken belly of the Beast, and thy bellows there are 60 his lungs, and these pipes are his throat, those feathers are of his tail, and thy rattles, the gnashing of his teeth.

Tra. And what's my gingerbread? I pray you.

Bus. The provender that pricks him up. Hence with thy basket of Popery, thy nest of images: and whole legend of gingerwork.   65

Lea. Sir, if you be not quiet, the quicklier, I'll ha' you clapped fairly by the heels, for disturbing the Fair.

Bus. The sin of the Fair provokes me, I cannot be silent.

Pur. Good brother Zeal!

Lea. Sir, I'll make you silent, believe it.   70

Lit. I'd give a shilling, you could i'faith, friend.

---

50 *bells . . . dragons . . . Toby's dogs*: glancing at the books of Bel and the Dragon and Tobit in the Apocrypha (which the Puritans rejected)   65 *images*: gingerbread moulded into figures of St. Bartholomew

Lea. Sir, give me your shilling, I'll give you my shop, if I do not,
and I'll leave it in pawn with you, i' the meantime.

Lit. A match i' faith, but do it quickly, then. [*Exit* Leatherhead]

75 *Bus*. Hinder me not, woman. (*He speaks to the widow*) I was moved
in spirit, to be here, this day, in this Fair, this wicked, and foul Fair;
and fitter may it be called a foul, than a Fair. To protest against the
abuses of it, the foul abuses of it, in regard of the afflicted saints, that
are troubled, very much troubled, exceedingly troubled, with the
80 opening of the merchandise of Babylon again, and the peeping of
Popery upon the stalls, here, here, in the high places. See you not
Goldilocks, the purple strumpet, there? In her yellow gown, and
green sleeves? The profane pipes, the tinkling timbrels? A shop of
relics!

85 *Lit*. Pray you forbear, I am put in trust with 'em.

Bus. And this idolatrous grove of images, this flasket of idols!
Which I will pull down——   (*Overthrows the gingerbread*)
          (*Tra*. Oh my ware, my ware, God bless it.)

Bus. In my zeal, and glory to be thus exercised.

                         (Leatherhead *enters with officers*)

90 *Lea*. Here he is, pray you lay hold on his zeal, we cannot sell a
whistle, for him, in tune. Stop his noise, first!

Bus. Thou canst not: 'tis a sanctified noise. I will make a loud and
most strong noise, till I háve daunted the profane enemy. And for
this cause——

95 *Lea*. Sir, here's no man afraid of you, or your cause. You shall
swear it, i' the stocks, sir.

Bus. I will thrust myself into the stocks, upon the pikes of the land.

Lea. Carry him away.

Pur. What do you mean, wicked men?

100 *Bus*. Let them alone; I fear them not. [*Exit with officers*, Purecraft]

Lit. Was not this shilling well ventured, Win? For our liberty?
Now we may go play, and see over the Fair, where we list ourselves;
my mother is gone after him, and let her e'en go, and loose us.

Win. Yes John, but I know not what to do.

105 *Lit*. For what, Win?

Win. For a thing, I am ashamed to tell you, i'faith, and 'tis too far
to go home.

86 *flasket*: shallow basket

Lit. I pray thee be not ashamed, Win. Come, i'faith thou shalt not be ashamed, is it anything about the hobby-horse-man? An't be, speak freely.   110

Win. Hang him, base bobchin, I scorn him; no, I have very great, what sha'call'um, John.   [*Whispers him*]

Lit. Oh! Is that all, Win? We'll go back to Captain Jordan; to the pig-woman's, Win, he'll help us, or she with a dripping pan, or an old kettle, or something. The poor greasy soul loves you, Win, and 115 after we'll visit the Fair all over, Win, and see my puppet play, Win, you know it's a fine matter, Win.   [*Exit with* Win]

Lea. Let's away, I counselled you to pack up afore, Joan.

Tra. A pox of his Bedlam purity. He has spoiled half my ware: but the best is, we lose nothing, if we miss our first merchant.   120

Lea. It shall be hard for him to find, or know us, when we are translated, Joan.   [*Exeunt*]

ACT IV, Scene i

[The Fair]

Enter Trouble-all, Bristle, Haggis, Cokes, Justice Overdo

Tro. MY masters, I do make no doubt, but you are officers.

Bri. What then, sir?

Tro. And the King's loving, and obedient subjects.

Bri. Obedient, friend? Take heed what you speak, I advise you: Oliver Bristle advises you. His loving subjects, we grant you: but not 5 his obedient, at this time, by your leave, we know ourselves, a little better than so, we are to command, sir, and such as you are to be obedient. Here's one of his obedient subjects, going to the stocks, and we'll make you such another, if you talk.

Tro. You are all wise enough i' your places, I know.   10

Bri. If you know it, sir, why do you bring it in question?

Tro. I question nothing, pardon me. I do only hope you have warrant for what you do, and so, quit you, and so, multiply you.

                                                  (*He goes away again*)

13 *quit you*: Ind. 134 n.

Hag. What's he? Bring him up to the stocks there. Why bring you
15 him not up?

Tro. (*Comes again*) If you have Justice Overdo's warrant, 'tis well:
you are safe; that is the warrant of warrants. I'll not give this button
for any man's warrant else.

Bri. Like enough, sir, but let me tell you, an' you play away your
20 buttons, thus, you will want 'em ere night, for any store I see about
you: you might keep 'em, and save pins, I wusse.

([*Trouble-all*] *goes away*)

Jus. [*Aside*] What should he be, that doth so esteem, and advance
my warrant? He seems a sober and discreet person! It is a comfort
to a good conscience, to be followed with a good fame, in his suffer-
25 ings. The world will have a pretty taste by this, how I can bear
adversity: and it will beget a kind of reverence toward me hereafter,
even from mine enemies, when they shall see I carry my calamity
nobly, and that it doth neither break me, nor bend me.

Hag. Come, sir, here's a place for you to preach in. Will you put in
30 your leg?   (*They put him in the stocks*)

Jus. That I will, cheerfully.

Bri. O' my conscience, a seminary! He kisses the stocks.

Cok. Well my masters, I'll leave him with you; now I see him
bestowed, I'll go look for my goods, and Numps.   [*Exit*]
35 *Hag.* You may, sir, I warrant you; where's the tother bawler?
Fetch him too, you shall find 'em both fast enough.

Jus. [*Aside*] In the midst of this tumult, I will yet be the author of
mine own rest, and not minding their fury, sit in the stocks, in that
calm, as shall be able to trouble a triumph.

40 *Tro.* (*Comes again*) Do you assure me upon your words? May I
undertake for you, if I be asked the question; that you have this
warrant?

Hag. What's this fellow, for God's sake?

Tro. Do but show me Adam Overdo, and I am satisfied.

(*Goes out*)

45 *Bri.* He is a fellow that is distracted, they say; one Trouble-all: he
was an officer in the Court of Piepowders, here last year, and put out
on his place by Justice Overdo.

Jus. [*Aside*] Ha!

20 *store*: abundance   32 *seminary*: II. i. 30 n.

Bri. Upon which, he took an idle conceit, and's run mad upon't. So that ever since, he will do nothing, but by Justice Overdo's 50 warrant, he will not eat a crust, nor drink a little, nor make him in his apparel, ready. His wife, sir-reverence, cannot get him make his water, or shift his shirt, without his warrant.

Jus. [*Aside*] If this be true, this is my greatest disaster! How am I bound to satisfy this poor man, that is of so good a nature to me, out 55 of his wits! Where there is no room left for dissembling.

Tro. (*Comes in*) If you cannot show me Adam Overdo, I am in doubt of you: I am afraid you cannot answer it.   (*Goes again*)

Hag. Before me, neighbour Bristle (and now I think on't better) Justice Overdo is a very parantory person. 60

Bri. Oh! Are you advised of that? And a severe justicer, by your leave.

Jus. [*Aside*] Do I hear ill o' that side, too?

Bri. He will sit as upright o' the bench, an' you mark him, as a candle i' the socket, and give light to the whole court in every 65 business.

Hag. But he will burn blue, and swell like a bile (God bless us) an' he be angry.

Bri. Aye, and he will be angry too, when him list, that's more: and when he is angry, be it right or wrong; he has the law on's side, ever. 70 I mark that too.

Jus. [*Aside*] I will be more tender hereafter. I see compassion may become a Justice, though it be a weakness, I confess; and nearer a vice than a virtue.

Hag. Well, take him out o' the stock again, we'll go a sure way to 75 work, we'll ha' the ace of hearts of our side, if we can.

                (*They take the* Justice *out*)

[*Enter* Pocher, Busy, Purecraft]

Poc. Come, bring him away to his fellow, there. Master Busy, we shall rule your legs, I hope, though we cannot rule your tongue.

Bus. No, minister of darkness, no, thou canst not rule my tongue, my tongue it is mine own, and with it I will both knock, and mock 80

---

52 *sir-reverence*: Ind. 24   60 *parantory*: peremptory   63 *hear ill*: have
an evil reputation   67 *bile*: boil

down your Bartholomew abominations, till you be made a hissing
to the neighbour parishes, round about.

    Hag. Let him alone, we have devised better upon't.

    Pur. And shall he not into the stocks then?

85   *Bri.* No, mistress, we'll have 'em both to Justice Overdo, and let
him do over 'em as is fitting. Then I, and my gossip Haggis, and my
beadle Pocher are discharged.

    Pur. Oh, I thank you, blessed, honest men!

    Bri. Nay, never thank us, but thank this madman that comes here,
90 he put it in our heads.   ([*Trouble-all*] *comes again*)

    Pur. Is he mad? Now heaven increase his madness, and bless it,
and thank it, sir, your poor handmaid thanks you.

    Tro. Have you a warrant? An' you have a warrant, show it.

    Pur. Yes, I have a warrant out of the word, to give thanks for
95 removing any scorn intended to the brethren.

                           [*Exeunt all but* Trouble-all]

    Tro. It is Justice Overdo's warrant that I look for, if you have not
that, keep your word, I'll keep mine. Quit ye, and multiply ye.

ACT IV, Scene ii

Enter Edgeworth, Nightingale

    Edg. Come away Nightingale, I pray thee.

    Tro. Whither go you? Where's your warrant?

    Edg. Warrant, for what, sir?

    Tro. For what you go about, you know how fit it is, an' you have
5 no warrant, bless you, I'll pray for you, that's all I can do.

                               (*Goes out*)

    Edg. What means he?

    Nig. A madman that haunts the Fair, do you not know him? It's
marvel he has not more followers, after his ragged heels.

    Edg. Beshrew him, he startled me: I thought he had known of our
10 plot. Guilt's a terrible thing! Ha' you prepared the costardmonger?

    Nig. Yes, and agreed for his basket of pears; he is at the corner
here, ready. And your prize, he comes down, sailing that way, all
alone; without his protector: he is rid of him, it seems.

   94 *the word*: Puritan term for the Bible

Edg. Aye, I know; I should ha' followed his protectorship for a feat I am to do upon him: but this offered itself, so i' the way, I 15 could not let it scape. Here he comes, whistle, be this sport called dorring the dotterel.

[*Enter* Cokes]

Nig. (Nightingale *whistles*) Wh, wh, wh, wh, etc.

Cok. By this light, I cannot find my gingerbread-wife, nor my hobby-horse-man in all the Fair, now; to ha' my money again. And 20 I do not know the way out on't, to go home for more, do you hear, friend, you that whistle; what tune is that, you whistle?

Nig. A new tune, I am practising, sir.

Cok. Dost thou know where I dwell, I pray thee? Nay, on with thy tune, I ha' no such haste, for an answer: I'll practise with thee. 25

[*Enter* Costardmonger]

Cos. Buy any pears, very fine pears, pears fine.

(Nightingale *sets his foot afore him, and he falls with his basket*)

Cok. Gods so! A muss, a muss, a muss, a muss.

Cos. Good gentleman, my ware, my ware, I am a poor man. Good sir, my ware.

Nig. Let me hold your sword, sir, it troubles you. 30

Cok. Do, and my cloak, an' thou wilt; and my hat, too.

(Cokes *falls a scrambling whilst they run away with his things*)

Edg. A delicate great boy! Methinks, he out-scrambles 'em all. I cannot persuade myself, but he goes to grammar-school yet; and plays the truant, today.

Nig. Would he had another purse to cut, Zekiel.

Edg. Purse? A man might cut out his kidneys, I think; and he 35 never feel 'em, he is so earnest at the sport.

Nig. His soul is halfway out on's body, at the game.

Edg. Away, Nightingale: that way. [*Exit* Nightingale]

Cok. I think I am furnished for Catherine pears, for one 40 undermeal: gi' me my cloak.

17 *dorring the dotterel*: hoaxing the simpleton; the stupidity of the dotterel (plover) was proverbial   27 *muss*: scramble   41 *under-meal*: afternoon meal

Cos. Good gentleman, give me my ware.

Cok. Where's the fellow, I ga' my cloak to? My cloak? And my
hat? Ha! God's lid, is he gone? Thieves, thieves, help me to cry,
45 gentlemen.   (*He runs out*)

Edg. Away, costermonger, come to us to Ursula's. [*Exit* Costard-
monger] Talk of him to have a soul? 'Heart, if he have any more than
a thing given him instead of salt, only to keep him from stinking, I'll
be hanged afore my time, presently: where should it be trow? In his
50 blood? He has not so much to'ard it in his whole body, as will main-
tain a good flea; and if he take this course, he will not ha' so much
land left, as to rear a calf within this twelvemonth. Was there ever
green plover so pulled! That his little overseer had been here now,
and been but tall enough to see him steal pears, in exchange for his
55 beaver-hat and his cloak thus? I must go find him out, next, for his
black box, and his patent (it seems) he has of his place; which I think
the gentleman would have a reversion of; that spoke to me for it so
earnestly.   [*Exit*]

[*Cokes*] *comes again*

Cok. Would I might lose my doublet, and hose, too; as I am an
60 honest man, and never stir, if I think there be anything but thieving,
and cozening, i' this whole Fair. Bartholomew Fair, quoth he; an'
ever any Bartholomew had that luck in't, that I have had, I'll be
martyred for him, and in Smithfield, too. I ha' paid for my pears,
a rot on 'em, I'll keep 'em no longer; you were choke-pears to me;
65 (*Throws away his pears*) I had been better ha' gone to mumchance for
you, I wusse. Methinks the Fair should not have used me thus, and
'twere but for my name's sake, I would not ha' used a dog o' the
name so. Oh, Numps will triumph now! (*Trouble-all comes again*)
Friend, do you know who I am? Or where I lie? I do not myself,
70 I'll be sworn. Do but carry me home, and I'll please thee, I ha'
money enough there, I ha' lost myself, and my cloak and my hat;
and my fine sword, and my sister, and Numps, and Mistress Grace
(a gentlewoman that I should ha' married) and a cutwork handker-
cher she ga' me, and two purses today. And my bargain o' hobby-
75 horses and gingerbread, which grieves me worst of all.

56 *patent*: licence conferring an office or privilege   61 *cozening*: swindling
64 *choke-pears*: a coarse variety   65 *mumchance*: *Alch.* V. iv. 44 n.

Tro. By whose warrant, sir, have you done all this?

Cok. Warrant? Thou art a wise fellow, indeed, as if a man need a warrant to lose anything with.

Tro. Yes, Justice Overdo's warrant, a man may get, and lose with, I'll stand to't.

Cok. Justice Overdo? Dost thou know him? I lie there, he is my brother-in-law, he married my sister: pray thee show me the way, dost thou know the house?

Tro. Sir, show me your warrant, I know nothing without a warrant, pardon me.

Cok. Why, I warrant thee, come along: thou shalt see, I have wrought pillows there, and cambric sheets, and sweet bags, too. Pray thee guide me to the house.

Tro. Sir, I'll tell you; go you thither yourself, first, alone; tell your worshipful brother your mind: and but bring me three lines of his hand, or his clerk's, with 'Adam Overdo' underneath; here I'll stay you, I'll obey you, and I'll guide you presently.

Cok. 'Slid, this is an ass, I ha' found him, pox upon me, what do I talking to such a dull fool; farewell, you are a very coxcomb, do you hear?

Tro. I think I am, if Justice Overdo sign to it, I am, and so we are all, he'll quit us all, multiply us all.   [*Exeunt*]

ACT IV, Scene iii

Enter Grace, Quarlous, Winwife (*They enter with their swords drawn*)

Gra. Gentlemen, this is no way that you take: you do but breed one another trouble and offence, and give me no contentment at all. I am no she that affects to be quarrelled for, or have my name or fortune made the question of men's swords.

Qua. 'Sblood, we love you.

Gra. If you both love me, as you pretend, your own reason will tell you, but one can enjoy me; and to that point, there leads a directer line, than by my infamy, which must follow, if you fight. 'Tis true, I have professed it to you ingenuously, that rather than to

80

85

90

95

5

87 *wrought*: embroidered   *sweet bags*: to lie among the linen

10 be yoked with this bridegroom is appointed me, I would take up any
husband, almost upon any trust. Though subtlety would say to me,
(I know) he is a fool, and has an estate, and I might govern him, and
enjoy a friend, beside. But these are not my aims, I must have a
husband I must love, or I cannot live with him. I shall ill make one
15 of these politic wives!

   Winw. Why, if you can like either of us, lady, say, which is he,
and the other shall swear instantly to desist.

   Qua. Content, I accord to that willingly.

   Gra. Sure you think me a woman of an extreme levity, gentlemen,
20 or a strange fancy, that (meeting you by chance in such a place, as
this, both at one instant, and not yet of two hours' acquaintance,
neither of you deserving afore the other, of me) I should so forsake
my modesty (though I might affect one more particularly) as to say,
This is he, and name him.

25 *Qua.* Why, wherefore should you not? What should hinder you?

   Gra. If you would not give it to my modesty, allow it yet to my
wit; give me so much of woman, and cunning, as not to betray myself
impertinently. How can I judge of you, so far as to a choice, without
knowing you more? You are both equal, and alike to me, yet: and so
30 indifferently affected by me, as each of you might be the man, if the
other were away. For you are reasonable creatures, you have under-
standing, and discourse. And if fate send me an understanding hus-
band, I have no fear at all, but mine own manners shall make him a
good one.

35 *Qua.* Would I were put forth to making for you, then.

   Gra. It may be you are, you know not what's toward you: will you
consent to a motion of mine, gentlemen?

   Winw. Whatever it be, we'll presume reasonableness, coming
from you.

40 *Qua.* And fitness, too.

   Gra. I saw one of you buy a pair of tables, e'en now.

   Winw. Yes, here they be, and maiden ones too, unwritten in.

   Gra. The fitter for what they may be employed in. You shall write
either of you, here, a word, or a name, what you like best; but of two,

---

   15 *politic*: crafty   28 *impertinently*: inappropriately   32 *discourse*:
reasoning   35 *to making*: for training   36 *toward you*: in prospect for you
41 *tables*: writing tablets

or three syllables at most: and the next person that comes this way 45
(because Destiny has a high hand in business of this nature) I'll
demand which of the two words, he, or she doth approve; and
according to that sentence, fix my resolution, and affection, without
change.

Qua. Agreed, my word is conceived already.   50

Winw. And mine shall not be long creating after.

Gra. But you shall promise, gentlemen, not to be curious to
know, which of you it is, is taken; but give me leave to conceal that
till you have brought me, either home, or where I may safely tender
myself.   55

Winw. Why that's but equal.

Qua. We are pleased.

Gra. Because I will bind both your endeavours to work together,
friendly, and jointly, each to the other's fortune, and have myself
fitted with some means, to make him that is forsaken, a part of 60
amends.

Qua. These conditions are very courteous. Well, my word is out
of the *Arcadia*, then: Argalus.

Winw. And mine out of the play, Palemon.

(Trouble-all *comes again*)

Tro. Have you any warrant for this, gentlemen?   65

Qua., Winw. Ha!

Tro. There must be a warrant had, believe it.

Winw. For what?

Tro. For whatsoever it is, anything indeed, no matter what.

Qua. 'Slight, here's a fine ragged prophet, dropped down 70
i' the nick!

Tro. Heaven quit you, gentlemen.

Qua. Nay, stay a little, good lady, put him to the question.

Gra. You are content, then?

Winw., Qua. Yes, yes.   75

Gra, Sir, here are two names written——

Tro. Is Justice Overdo one?

---

56 *equal*: fair   63 *Argalus*: lover of Parthenia in the *Arcadia*   64 *Pale-
mon*: in *The Two Noble Kinsmen* (or possibly in Daniel's *The Queen's Arcadia*)
71 *i' the nick*: at the critical moment

Gra. How, sir? I pray you read 'em to yourself, it is for a wager
between these gentlemen, and with a stroke or any difference, mark
80 which you approve best.

Tro. They may be both worshipful names for aught I know,
mistress, but Adam Overdo had been worth three o' 'em, I assure
you, in this place, that's in plain English.

Gra. This man amazes me! I pray you, like one of 'em, sir.

85 *Tro.* I do like him there, that has the best warrant. Mistress, to
save your longing (and multiply him) it may be this. But I am still
for Justice Overdo, that's my conscience. And quit you.   [*Exit*]

Winw. Is't done, lady?

Gra. Aye, and strangely, as ever I saw! What fellow is this, trow?

90 *Qua.* No matter what, a fortune-teller we ha' made him. Which is't,
which is't?

Gra. Nay, did you not promise, not to enquire?

Qua. 'Slid, I forgot that, pray you pardon me. Look, here's our
Mercury come: the licence arrives i' the finest time, too! 'Tis but
95 scraping out Cokes his name, and 'tis done.

[*Enter* Edgeworth]

Winw. How now lime-twig? Hast thou touched?

Edg. Not yet, sir, except you would go with me, and see't, it's not
worth speaking on. The act is nothing, without a witness. Yonder he
is, your man with the box fallen into the finest company, and so
100 transported with vapours, they ha' got in a northern clothier, and
one Puppy, a western man, that's come to wrestle before my Lord
Major, anon, and Captain Whit, and one Val Cutting, that helps
Captain Jordan to roar, a circling boy: with whom your Numps is so
taken, that you may strip him of his clothes, if you will. I'll under-
105 take to geld him for you; if you had but a surgeon, ready, to sear
him. And Mistress Justice there, is the goodest woman! She does so
love 'em all over, in terms of justice, and the style of authority, with
her hood upright——that I beseech you come away, gentlemen,
and see't.

110 *Qua.* 'Slight, I would not lose it for the Fair, what'll you do, Ned?

---

94 *Mercury*: messenger of the gods   96 *lime-twig*: thief   101 *western*:
from Cornwall, noted for its wrestlers   103 *a circling boy*: ? explained by IV. iv.
117-24

Winw. Why, stay here about for you, Mistress Wellborn must not
be seen.

Qua. Do so, and find out a priest i' the meantime, I'll bring the
licence. Lead, which way is't?

Edg. Here, sir, you are o' the backside o' the booth already, you   115
may hear the noise.   [*Exeunt*]

ACT IV, Scene iv

Enter Knockem, Northern, Puppy, Cutting, Whit, Wasp,
Mistress Overdo

Kno. Whit, bid Val Cutting continue the vapours for a lift, Whit,
for a lift.

Nor. I'll ne mare, I'll ne mare, the eale's too meeghty.

Kno. How now! My Galloway nag, the staggers? Ha! Whit, gi'
him a slit i' the forehead. Cheer up, man, a needle and thread to   5
stitch his ears. I'd cure him now an' I had it, with a little butter, and
garlic, long-pepper, and grains. Where's my horn? I'll gi' him a
mash, presently, shall take away this dizziness.

Pup. Why, where are you, zurs? Do you vlinch, and leave us
i' the zuds, now?   10

Nor. I'll ne mare, I'is e'en as vull as a piper's bag, by my troth, I.

Pup. Do my northern cloth zhrink i' the wetting? Ha?

Kno. Why, well said, old flea-bitten, thou'lt never tire, I see.

Cut. No, sir, but he may tire, if it please him.

Whi. Who told dee sho? That he vuld never teer, man?   15

                    (*They fall to their vapours, again*)

Cut. No matter who told him so, so long as he knows.

Kno. Nay, I know nothing, sir, pardon me there.

[*Enter* Edgeworth *and* Quarlous]

Edg. They are at it still, sir, this they call vapours.

---

1 *lift*: theft, trick   4 *Galloway nag*: small and hardy Scottish breed
5–6 *slit . . . ears*: treatment for the staggers   7 *long-pepper*: much stronger than
the ordinary variety   *horn*: used for dosing horses   10 *i' the zuds*: in difficulties
12 *zhrink i' the wetting*: make off without paying the score   13 'A flea-bitten
horse [i.e. with bay or sorrel spots] never tires' (proverb)

    Whi. He shall not pardon dee, Captain, dou shalt not be pardoned.
20 Pre'de shweetheart, do not pardon him.

    Cut. 'Slight, I'll pardon him, an' I list, whosoever says nay to't.

    Qua. Where's Numps? I miss him.

                  (*Here they continue their game of vapours, which is*
                      nonsense. Every man to oppose the last man that
                          spoke: whether it concerned him, or no)

    Was. Why, I say nay to't.

    Qua. Oh there he is!

25   *Kno.* To what do you say nay, sir?

    Was. To anything, whatsoever it is, so long as I do not like it.

    Whi. Pardon me, little man, dou musht like it a little.

    Cut. No, he must not like it at all, sir, there you are i' the wrong.

    Whi. I tink I be, he musht not like it, indeed.

30   *Cut.* Nay, then he both must, and will like it, sir, for all you.

    Kno. If he have reason, he may like it, sir.

    Whi. By no meansh, Captain, upon reason, he may like nothing
upon reason.

    Was. I have no reason, nor I will hear of no reason, nor I will look
35 for no reason, and he is an ass, that either knows any, or looks for't
from me.

    Cut. Yes, in some sense you may have reason, sir.

    Was. Aye, in some sense, I care not if I grant you.

    Whi. Pardon me, thou ougsht to grant him nothing, in no shensh,
40 if dou doe love dyshelf, angry man.

    Was. Why then, I do grant him nothing; and I have no sense.

    Cut. 'Tis true, thou hast no sense indeed.

    Was. 'Slid, but I have sense, now I think on't better, and I will
grant him anything, do you see?

45   *Kno.* He is i' the right, and does utter a sufficient vapour.

    Cut. Nay, it is no sufficient vapour, neither, I deny that.

    Kno. Then it is a sweet vapour.

    Cut. It may be a sweet vapour.

    Was. Nay, it is no sweet vapour, neither, sir, it stinks, and I'll
50 stand to't.

    Whi. Yes, I tink it dosh shtink, Captain. All vapour dosh shtink.

    Was. Nay, then it does not stink, sir, and it shall not stink.

    Cut. By your leave, it may, sir.

Was. Aye, by my leave, it may stink, I know that.

Whi. Pardon me, thou knowesht nothing, it cannot by thy leave, 55
angry man.

Was. How can it not?

Kno. Nay, never question him, for he is i' the right.

Whi. Yesh, I am i' de right, I confesh it, so ish de little man too.

Was. I'll have nothing confessed, that concerns me. I am not in the 60
right, nor never was i' the right, nor never will be i' the right, while
I am in my right mind.

Cut. Mind? Why, here's no man minds you, sir, nor any-
thing else.   (*They drink again*)

Pup. Vreind, will you mind this that we do? 65

Qua. Call you this vapours? This is such belching of quarrel, as
I never heard. Will you mind your business, sir?

Edg. You shall see, sir.

Nor. I'll ne maire, my waimb warkes too mickle with this aureadly.

Edg. Will you take that, Master Wasp, that nobody should 70
mind you?

Was. Why? What ha' you to do? Is't any matter to you?

Edg. No, but methinks you should not be unminded, though.

Was. Nor, I wu'not be, now I think on't, do you hear, new
acquaintance, does no man mind me, say you? 75

Cut. Yes, sir, every man here minds you, but how?

Was. Nay, I care as little how, as you do, that was not my
question.

Whi. No, noting was ty question, tou art a learned man, and I am
a valiant man, i'faith la, tou shalt speak for me, and I vill fight 80
for tee.

Kno. Fight for him, Whit? A gross vapour, he can fight for
himself.

Was. It may be I can, but it may be, I wu'not, how then?

Cut. Why, then you may choose. 85

Was. Why, and I'll choose whether I'll choose or no.

Kno. I think you may, and 'tis true; and I allow it for a resolute
vapour.

Was. Nay, then, I do think you do not think, and it is no resolute
vapour. 90

67 *your business*: i.e. getting the licence from Wasp

Cut. Yes, in some sort he may allow you.

Kno. In no sort, sir, pardon me, I can allow him nothing. You mistake the vapour.

Was. He mistakes nothing, sir, in no sort.

95 *Whi.* Yes, I pre dee now, let him mistake.

Was. A turd i' your teeth, neuer pre dee mee, for I will haue nothing mistaken.

Kno. Turd, ha turd? A noisome vapour, strike Whit.

(*They fall by the ears*) [*Exit* Edgeworth *with licence from box*]

Mrs Ove. Why, gentlemen, why gentlemen, I charge you upon
100 my authority, conserve the peace. In the King's name, and my husband's, put up your weapons. I shall be driven to commit you myself, else.

Qua. Ha, ha, ha.

Was. Why do you laugh, sir?

105 *Qua.* Sir, you'll allow me my Christian liberty. I may laugh, I hope.

Cut. In some sort you may, and in some sort you may not, sir.

Kno. Nay, in some sort, sir, he may neither laugh, nor hope, in this company.

Was. Yes, then he may both laugh, and hope in any sort, an't
110 please him.

Qua. Faith, and I will then, for it doth please me exceedingly.

Was. No exceeding neither, sir.

Kno. No, that vapour is too lofty.

Qua. Gentlemen, I do not play well at your game of vapours, I
115 am not very good at it, but——

Cut. Do you hear, sir? I would speak with you in circle?

(*He draws a circle on the ground*)

Qua. In circle, sir? What would you with me in circle?

Cut. Can you lend me a piece, a Jacobus? In circle?

Qua. 'Slid, your circle will prove more costly than your vapours,
120 then. Sir, no, I lend you none.

Cut. Your beard's not well turned up, sir.

Qua. How, rascal? Are you playing with my beard? I'll break circle with you.   (*They draw all, and fight*)

Pup., Nor. Gentlemen, gentlemen!

---

106 *sort*: quibble on 'sort' meaning 'company'   118 *Jacobus*: gold coin of James I, a 'sovereign'

Kno. Gather up, Whit, gather up, Whit, good vapours. [*Exit*] 125
[Whit *gathers up the swords and cloaks*]

Mrs Ove. What mean you? Are you rebels? Gentlemen? Shall I
send out a serjeant at arms, or a writ o' rebellion, against you?
I'll commit you upon my womanhood, for a riot, upon my justice-
hood, if you persist.   [*Exeunt* Quarlous, Cutting]

Was. Upon your justice-hood? Marry shit o' your hood, you'll 130
commit? Spoke like a true Justice of Peace's wife, indeed, and a
fine female lawyer! Turd i' your teeth for a fee, now.

Mrs Ove. Why, Numps, in Master Overdo's name, I charge you.

Was. Good Mistress Underdo, hold your tongue.

Mrs. Ove. Alas! Poor Numps.   135

Was. Alas! And why alas from you, I beseech you? Or why poor
Numps, goody Rich? Am I come to be pitied by your tuftaffeta
now? Why mistress, I knew Adam, the clerk, your husband, when
he was Adam scrivener, and writ for twopence a sheet, as high as
he bears his head now, or you your hood, dame. (*The watch comes in*) 140
What are you, sir?

Bri. We be men, and no infidels; what is the matter, here, and
the noises? Can you tell?

Was. Heart, what ha' you to do? Cannot a man quarrel in
quietness? But he must be put out on't by you? What are you? 145

Bri. Why, we be His Majesty's watch, sir.

Was. Watch? 'Sblood, you are a sweet watch, indeed. A body
would think, and you watched well a nights, you should be con-
tented to sleep at this time a day. Get you to your fleas, and your
flock-beds, you rogues, your kennels, and lie down close. 150

Bri. Down? Yes, we will down, I warrant you, down with him
in His Majesty's name, down, down with him, and carry him away,
to the pigeon-holes.   [Wasp *is carried off*]

Mrs Ove. I thank you, honest friends, in the behalf o' the Crown,
and the peace, and in Master Overdo's name, for suppressing 155
enormities.

Whi. Stay, Bristle, here ish anoder brash o' drunkards [*Pointing
to* Northern *and* Puppy] but very quiet, special drunkards, will pay

---

137 *goody Rich*: the Rich family received tolls and dues from the Fair   *tuftaffeta*:
taffata with the nap woven in tufts, and affected by the fashionable   153 *pigeon-*
holes: stocks

dee, five shillings very well. Take 'em to dee, in de graish o' God:
160 one of 'em does change cloth, for ale in the Fair, here, te toder ish
a strong man, a mighty man, my Lord Mayor's man, and a wrastler.
He has wrashled so long with the bottle, here, that the man with the
beard hash almosht streek up hish heelsh.

    Bri. 'Slid, the clerk o' the market has been to cry him all the
165 Fair over, here, for my lord's service.

    Whi. Tere he ish, pre de taik him hensh, and make ty best on
him. [*Exeunt* Watch *etc.*] How now woman o' shilk, vat ailsh ty
shweet faish? Art tou melancholy?

    Mrs Ove. A little distempered with these enormities; shall I
170 entreat a courtesy of you, Captain?

    Whi. Entreat a hundred, velvet voman, I vill do it, shpeak out.

    Mrs Ove. I cannot with modesty speak it out, but——
                                                  [*Whispers him*]

    Whi. I vill do it, and more, and more, for dee. What Ursula,
and't be bitch, and't be bawd, and't be!

[*Enter* Ursula]

175   *Urs.* How now rascal? What roar you for? Old pimp.

    Whi. Here, put up de cloaks Ursh; de purchase; pre dee now,
shweet Ursh, help dis good brave voman to a jordan, and't be.

    Urs. 'Slid call your Captain Jordan to her, can you not?

    Whi. Nay, pre dee leave dy consheits, and bring the velvet woman
180 to de——

    Urs. I bring her, hang her: heart must I find a common pot for
every punk i' your purlieus?

    Whi. Oh good voordsh, Ursh, it ish a guest o' velvet, i'fait la.

    Urs. Let her sell her hood, and buy a sponge, with a pox to her,
185 my vessel is employed sir. I have but one, and 'tis the bottom of an
old bottle. An honest proctor and his wife are at it within, if she'll
stay her time, so.

    Whi. As soon ash tou cansht, shwet Ursh. Of a valiant man I
tink I am the patientsh man i' the world, or in all Smithfield.

                                            [*Exit* Ursula]

162-3 *man with the beard*: drinking jug ornamented with a bearded face
174 *and't be*: if that's what you are   182 *purlieus*: suburbs (noted for vice)

[*Enter* Knockem]

Kno. How now Whit? Close vapours, stealing your leaps? 190
Covering in corners, ha?

Whi. No fait, Captain, dough tou beesht a vishe man, dy vit is a
mile hence, now. I vas procuring a shmall courtesy for a woman of
fashion here.

Mrs Ove. Yes, Captain, though I am Justice of Peace's wife, I do 195
love men of war, and the sons of the sword, when they come before
my husband.

Kno. Say'st thou so, filly? Thou shalt have a leap presently, I'll
horse thee myself else.

[*Enter* Ursula]

Urs. Come, will you bring her in now? And let her take her turn? 200
Whi. Gramercy good Ursh, I tank dee.
Mrs Ove. Master Overdo shall thank her.   [*Exit*]

ACT IV, Scene v

Enter Littlewit, Win

Lit. Good Gammer Urs; Win and I are exceedingly beholden
to you, and to Captain Jordan, and Captain Whit. Win, I'll be bold
to leave you i' this good company, Win: for half an hour or so, Win,
while I go, and see how my matter goes forward, and if the puppets
be perfect: and then I'll come and fetch you, Win.   5

Win. Will you leave me alone with two men, John?

Lit. Aye, they are honest gentlemen, Win, Captain Jordan and
Captain Whit, they'll use you very civilly, Win, God b'w'you, Win.

[*Exit*]

Urs. What's her husband gone?
Kno. On his false gallop, Urs, away.   10
Urs. An' you be right Bartholomew-birds, now show yourselves
so: we are undone for want of fowl i' the Fair, here. Here will be
Zekiel Edgeworth, and three or four gallants, with him at night,
and I ha' neither plover nor quail for 'em: persuade this between

---

191 *Covering*: copulating (of horses)   (*IV. v*) 14 *plover . . . quail*: loose women

15 you two, to become a bird o' the game, while I work the velvet
woman within (as you call her).

    Kno. I conceive thee, Urs! Go thy ways. [*Exit* Ursula] Dost
thou hear, Whit? Is't not pity, my delicate dark chestnut here, with
the fine lean head, large forehead, round eyes, even mouth, sharp
20 ears, long neck, thin crest, close withers, plain back, deep sides, short
fillets, and full flanks: with a round belly, a plump buttock, large
thighs, knit knees, straight legs, short pasterns, smooth hoofs, and
short heels; should lead a dull honest woman's life, that might live
the life of a lady?

25   *Whi.* Yes, by my fait, and trot, it is, Captain: de honesht woman's
life is a scurvy dull life, indeed, la.

    Win. How, sir? Is an honest woman's life a scurvy life?

    Whi. Yes fait, shweetheart, believe him, de leefe of a bond-
woman! But if dou vilt hearken to me, I vill make tee a free-woman,
30 and a lady: dou shalt live like a lady, as te Captain saish.

    Kno. Aye, and be honest too sometimes: have her wires, and
her tires, her green gowns, and velvet petticoats.

    Whi. Aye, and ride to Ware and Romford i' dy coash, shee de
players, be in love vit 'em; sup vit gallantsh, be drunk, and cost de
35 noting.

    Kno. Brave vapours!

    Whi. And lie by twenty on 'em, if dou pleash, shweetheart.

    Win. What, and be honest still, that were fine sport.

    Whi. Tish common, shweetheart, tou mayst do it, by my hand:
40 it shall be justified to ty husband's faish, now: tou shalt be as
honesht as the skin between his hornsh, la!

    Kno. Yes, and wear a dressing, top, and top-gallant, to compare
with e'er a husband on 'em all, for a fore-top: it is the vapour of
spirit in the wife, to cuckold, nowadays; as it is the vapour of
45 fashion, in the husband, not to suspect. Your prying cat-eyed-
citizen is an abominable vapour.

    Win. Lord, what a fool have I been!

    Whi. Mend then, and do everyting like a lady, hereafter, never
know ty husband from another man.

---

31 *wires*: for supporting the ruff   32 *tires*: dresses   *green gowns*: colour
affected by prostitutes (l. 85)   33 *Ware and Romford*: noted for assignations
42 *top, and top-gallant*: with all sails set, in full array

Kno. Nor any one man from another, but i' the dark.   50
Whi. Aye, and then it ish no dishgrash to know any man.
Urs. [*Within*] Help, help here.
Kno. How now? What vapour's there?

[*Enter* Ursula]

Urs. Oh, you are a sweet ranger! And look well to your walks.
Yonder is your punk of Turnbull, ramping Alice, has fallen upon   55
the poor gentlewoman within, and pulled her hood over her ears,
and her hair through it.

Alice *enters, beating the* Justice's *wife*

Mrs Ove. Help, help, i' the King's name.
Ali. A mischief on you, they are such as you are, that undo us,
and take our trade from us, with your tuftaffeta haunches.   60
Kno. How now, Alice!
Ali. The poor common whores can ha' no traffic, for the privy
rich ones; your caps and hoods of velvet, call away our customers,
and lick the fat from us.
Urs. Peace you foul ramping jade, you——   65
Ali. Od's foot, you bawd in grease, are you talking?
Kno. Why, Alice, I say.
Ali. Thou sow of Smithfield, thou.
Urs. Thou tripe of Turnbull.
Kno. Cat-a-mountain-vapours! Ha!   70
Urs. You know where you were tawed lately, both lashed, and
slashed you were in Bridewell.
Ali. Aye, by the same token, you rid that week, and broke out
the bottom o'the cart, night-tub.
Kno. Why, lion face! Ha! Do you know who I am? Shall I tear   75
ruff, slit waistcoat, make rags of petticoat? Ha! Go to, vanish, for
fear of vapours. Whit, a kick, Whit, in the parting vapour. [*Exit*
Alice] Come brave woman, take a good heart, thou shalt be
a lady, too.

---

60 *haunches*: artificial shape-improvers   66 *in grease*: in prime condition
69 *tripe*: I. iii. 56–7 n.   70 *Cat-a-mountain*: leopard or panther   71 *tawed*:
softened with alum (as leather is)   74 *the cart*: for whores (*SW* III. v. 75 n.)

80   *Whi*. Yes fait, dey shal all both be ladies, and write Madam. I vill
do't myself for dem. *Do*, is the vord, and D is the middle letter of
Madam, DD, put 'em together and make deeds, without which, all
words are alike, la.

Kno. 'Tis true, Ursula, take 'em in, open thy wardrobe, and fit
85 'em to their calling. Green gowns, crimson petticoats, green women!
My Lord Mayor's green women! Guests o' the game, true bred.
I'll provide you a coach, to take the air, in.

Win. But do you think you can get one?

Kno. Oh, they are as common as wheelbarrows, where there are
90 great dunghills. Every pettifogger's wife has 'em, for first he buys a
coach, that he may marry, and then he marries that he may be made
cuckold in't: for if their wives ride not to their cuckolding, they do
'em no credit. Hide, and be hidden; ride, and be ridden, says the
vapour of experience.   [*Exeunt* Ursula, Win, Mistress Overdo]

ACT IV, Scene vi

Enter Trouble-all

Tro. By what warrant does it say so?

Kno. Ha! mad child o' the Piepowders, art thou there? Fill us a
fresh can, Urs, we may drink together.

Tro. I may not drink without a warrant, Captain.

5   *Kno*. 'Sblood, thou'll not stale without a warrant, shortly. Whit,
give me pen, ink and paper. I'll draw him a warrant presently.

Tro. It must be Justice Overdo's.

Kno. I know, man. Fetch the drink, Whit.

Whi. I pre dee now, be very brief, Captain; for de new ladies stay
10 for dee.

Kno. Oh, as brief as can be, here 'tis already. 'Adam Overdo.'

Tro. Why, now, I'll pledge you, Captain.

Kno. Drink it off. I'll come to thee, anon, again.   [*Exeunt*]

[*Enter* Quarlous, Edgeworth]

80 *write*: i.e. style themselves   (*IV. vi*) 5 *stale*: urinate   6 *presently*: at
once

Qua. Well, sir. You are now discharged: beware of being spied
hereafter.   (Quarlous *to the cutpurse*) 15

Edg. Sir, will it please you, enter in here, at Ursula's; and take
part of a silken gown, a velvet petticoat, or a wrought smock; I am
promised such: and I can spare any gentleman a moiety.

Qua. Keep it for your companions in beastliness, I am none of
'em, sir. If I had not already forgiven you a greater trespass, or 20
thought you yet worth my beating, I would instruct your manners,
to whom you made your offers. But go your ways, talk not to me,
the hangman is only fit to discourse with you; the hand of beadle
is too merciful a punishment for your trade of life. [*Exit* Edgeworth]
I am sorry I employed this fellow; for he thinks me such: *Facinus* 25
quos inquinat, aequat. But it was for sport. And would I make it
serious, the getting of this licence is nothing to me, without other
circumstances concur. I do think how impertinently I labour, if the
word be not mine, that the ragged fellow marked: and what advan-
tage I have given Ned Winwife in this time now, of working her, 30
though it be mine. He'll go near to form to her what a debauched
rascal I am, and fright her out of all good conceit of me: I should
do so by him, I am sure, if I had the opportunity. But my hope is
in her temper, yet; and it must needs be next to despair, that is
grounded on any part of a woman's discretion. I would give by my 35
troth, now, all I could spare (to my clothes, and my sword) to meet
my tattered soothsayer again, who was my judge i' the question, to
know certainly whose word he has damned or saved. For, till then,
I live but under a reprieve. I must seek him. Who be these?

Enter Wasp *with the officers*

Was. Sir, you are a Welsh cuckold, and a prating runt, and no 40
constable.

Bri. You say very well. Come put in his leg in the middle roundel,
and let him hole there.

Was. You stink of leeks, metheglin, and cheese. You rogue.

---

17 *velvet petticoat, or a wrought smock*: worn by superior prostitutes   23 *beadle*:
parish officer who punished minor offences   25 *Facinus* . . .: Lucan, *Pharsalia*,
v. 290 ('Crime levels those whom it pollutes')   28 *impertinently*: irrelevantly
31 *form*: depict   40 *runt*: uncouth, ignorant person   44 *metheglin*: Welsh
meddyglyn (made from herbs boiled with honey)

45   *Bri*. Why, what is that to you, if you sit sweetly in the stocks in
the meantime? If you have a mind to stink too, your breeches sit
close enough to your bum. Sit you merry, sir.

[They put him in the stocks]

    Qua. How now, Numps?

    Was. It is no matter, how; pray you look off.

50   *Qua*. Nay I'll not offend you, Numps. I thought you had sat
there to be seen.

    Was. And to be sold, did you not? Pray you mind your business,
an' you have any.

    Qua. Cry you mercy, Numps. Does your leg lie high enough?

[*Enter* Haggis]

55   *Bri*. How now, neighbour Haggis, what says Justice Overdo's
worship, to the other offenders?

    Hag. Why, he says just nothing, what should he say?
Or where should he say? He is not to be found, man. He ha' not
been seen i' the Fair, here, all this livelong day, never since seven
60 o'clock i' the morning. His clerks know not what to think on't.
There is no court of Piepowders yet. Here they be returned.

[*Enter officers with* Busy, Justice]

  Bri. What shall be done with 'em, then? In your discretion?

    Hag. I think we were best put 'em in the stocks, in discretion
(there they will be safe in discretion) for the valour of an hour, or
65 such a thing, till his worship come.

    Bri. It is but a hole matter, if we do, neighbour Haggis; come,
sir, here is company for you, heave up the stocks.

    Was. [*Aside*] I shall put a trick upon your Welsh diligence,
perhaps.   (*As they open the stocks*, Wasp *puts his shoe on his hand,
and slips it in for his leg*)

70   *Bri*. Put in your leg, sir.   (*They bring* Busy, *and put him in*)

    Qua. What, Rabbi Busy! Is he come?

    Bus. I do obey thee, the lion may roar, but he cannot bite. I am
glad to be thus separated from the heathen of the land, and put
apart in the stocks, for the holy cause.

75   *Was*. What are you, sir?

64 *valour*: amount (here 'duration')

Bus. One that rejoiceth in his affliction, and sitteth here to prophesy the destruction of Fairs and May-games, wakes and Whitsun ales, and doth sigh and groan for the reformation of these abuses.   [*They put the* Justice *in*]

Was. And do you sigh and groan too, or rejoice in your affliction? 80

Jus. I do not feel it, I do not think of it, it is a thing without me. Adam, thou art above these batteries, these contumelies. *In te manca ruit fortuna*, as thy friend Horace says; thou art one, *Quem neque pauperies, neque mors, neque vincula terrent*. And therefore as another friend of thine says (I think it be thy friend Persius) *Non te* 85 *quaesiveris extra*.

Qua. What's here? A Stoic i' the stocks? The fool is turned philosopher.

Bus. Friend, I will leave to communicate my spirit with you, if I hear any more of those superstitious relics, those lists of Latin, the 90 very rags of Rome, and patches of Popery.

Was. Nay, an' you begin to quarrel, gentlemen, I'll leave you. I ha' paid for quarrelling too lately: look you, a device, but shifting in a hand for a foot. God b'w'you.   (*He gets out*)

Bus. Wilt thou then leave thy brethren in tribulation?   95

Was. For this once, sir.   [*Exit*]

Bus. Thou art a halting neutral: stay him there, stop him: that will not endure the heat of persecution.

Bri. How now, what's the matter?

Bus. He is fled, he is fled, and dares not sit it out.   100

Bri. What, has he made an escape, which way? Follow, neighbour Haggis.   [*Exit* Haggis]

[*Enter* Dame Purecraft]

Pur. Oh me! In the stocks! Have the wicked prevailed?

Bus. Peace, religious sister, it is my calling, comfort yourself, an extraordinary calling, and done for my better standing, my surer 105 standing, hereafter.

The madman enters

---

78 *Whitsun ales*: festivals at Whitsuntide   83 *Horace*: *Sat.* II. vii. 88 ('In her assaults on you Fortune maims herself')   83–4 *Sat.* II. vii. 84 ('whom neither poverty, nor death, nor chains affright')   85 *Persius*: *Sat.* i. 7 ('Look to no one outside yourself')   90 *lists*: fag-ends (to the Puritans, Latin was 'the Popish tongue')   97 *halting*: (1) limping, (2) weak, defective

Tro. By whose warrant, by whose warrant, this?

Qua. Oh, here's my man, dropped in, I looked for.

Jus. Ha!

110 *Pur.* Oh good sir, they have set the faithful, here to be wondered at; and provided holes for the holy of the land.

Tro. Had they warrant for it? Showed they Justice Overdo's hand? If they had no warrant, they shall answer it.

[*Enter* Haggis]

Bri. Sure you did not lock the stocks sufficiently, neighbour Toby!

115 *Hag.* No! See if you can lock 'em better.

Bri. They are very sufficiently locked, and truly, yet something is in the matter.

Tro. True, your warrant is the matter that is in question, by what warrant?

120 *Bri.* Madman, hold your peace, I will put you in his room else, in the very same hole, do you see?

Qua. How! Is he a madman!

Tro. Show me Justice Overdo's warrant, I obey you.

Hag. You are a mad fool, hold your tongue. [*Exit with* Bristle]

125 *Tro.* In Justice Overdo's name, I drink to you, and here's my warrant.   (*Shows his can*)

Jus. [*Aside*] Alas poor wretch! How it earns my heart for him!

Qua. If he be mad, it is in vain to question him. I'll try though. Friend, there was a gentlewoman, showed you two names, some 130 hour since, Argalus and Palemon, to mark in a book, which of 'em was it you marked?

Tro. I mark no name, but Adam Overdo, that is the name of names, he only is the sufficient magistrate; and that name I reverence, show it me.

135 *Qua.* This fellow's mad indeed: I am further off, now, than afore.

Jus. [*Aside*] I shall not breathe in peace, till I have made him some amends.

Qua. Well, I will make another use of him, is come in my head: I have a nest of beards in my trunk, one something like his.

The watchmen come back again

127 *earns*: grieves   139 *trunk*: trunk-hose, stuffed breeches reaching to the knee

Bri. This mad fool has made me that I know not whether I have 140
locked the stocks or no, I think I locked 'em.

Tro. Take Adam Overdo in your mind, and fear nothing.

Bri. 'Slid, madness itself, hold thy peace, and take that.

Tro. Strikest thou without a warrant? Take thou that.

        (*The madman fights with 'em, and they leave open the stocks*)

Bus. We are delivered by miracle; fellow in fetters, let us not 145
refuse the means, this madness was of the spirit. The malice of the
enemy hath mocked itself.   [*Exit with* Justice]

Pur. Mad do they call him! The world is mad in error, but he is
mad in truth: I love him o' the sudden (the cunning man said all
true) and shall love him more and more. How well it becomes 150
a man to be mad in truth! Oh that I might be his yoke-fellow, and
be mad with him, what a many should we draw to madness in truth
with us!   [*Exit*]

            (*The watch missing them are affrighted*)

Bri. How now! All scaped? Where's the woman? It is witchcraft!
Her velvet hat is a witch, o' my conscience, or my key! t'one! The 155
madman was a devil, and I am an ass; so bless me, my place, and
mine office.   [*Exeunt*]

ACT V, Scene i

[The Fair]

Enter Leatherhead [*as a puppet-show man*], Filcher, Sharkwell

Lea. WELL, luck and Saint Bartholomew; out with the sign of
our invention, in the name of wit, and do you beat the drum the
while. All the fowl i' the Fair, I mean, all the dirt in Smithfield,
(that's one of Master Littlewit's carwhitchets now) will be thrown
at our banner today, if the matter does not please the people. Oh 5
the motions that I Lanthorn Leatherhead have given light to, i' my
time, since my Master Pod died! Jerusalem was a stately thing; and

------

155 *t'one*: the one or the other   (*V. i*) 1 *sign*: the banner of l. 5   4 *car-
whitchets*: quibbles   7 *Master Pod*: Pod was a master of motions before him
(Jonson's note)

so was Nineveh, and the city of Norwich, and Sodom and Gomor-
rah; with the rising o' the prentices; and pulling down the bawdy
10 houses there, upon Shrove Tuesday; but the Gunpowder plot,
there was a get-penny! I have presented that to an eighteen-, or
twenty-pence audience, nine times in an afternoon. Your home-born
projects prove ever the best, they are so easy and familiar, they put
too much learning i' their things nowadays: and that I fear will be
15 the spoil o' this. Littlewit? I say, Micklewit! If not too mickle!
Look to your gathering there, good man Filcher.

    Fil. I warrant you, sir.

    Lea. And there come any gentlefolks, take twopence a piece,
Sharkwell.

20   *Sha.* I warrant you, sir, threepence, an' we can.   [*Exeunt*]

ACT V, Scene ii

The Justice *comes in like a porter*

    Jus. This later disguise I have borrowed of a porter shall carry
me out to all my great and good ends; which however interrupted,
were never destroyed in me: neither is the hour of my severity yet
come, to reveal myself, wherein cloud-like, I will break out in rain
5 and hail, lightning and thunder, upon the head of enormity. Two
main works I have to prosecute: first, one is to invent some satisfac-
tion for the poor, kind wretch, who is out of his wits for my sake,
and yonder I see him coming. I will walk aside, and project for it.

[*Enter* Winwife, Grace]

    Winw. I wonder where Tom Quarlous is, that he returns not; it
10 may be he is struck in here to seek us.

    Gra. See, here's our madman again.

[*Enter* Quarlous]

    Qua. [*Aside*] I have made myself as like him as his gown and cap
will give me leave.

[*Enter* Dame Purecraft]

---

10 *Shrove Tuesday*: traditional day of riot for apprentices (*SW* I. i. 140)

Pur. Sir, I love you, and would be glad to be mad with you in truth. (Quarlous *in the habit of the madman is mistaken* 15
by Mistress Purecraft)

Winw. How! My widow in love with a madman?

Pur. Verily, I can be as mad in spirit as you.

Qua. By whose warrant? Leave your canting. Gentlewoman, have I found you? (Save ye, quit ye, and multiply ye) Where's your book? 'Twas a sufficient name I marked, let me see't, be not afraid 20 to show't me. (*He desires to see the book of* Mistress Grace)

Gra. What would you with it, sir?

Qua. Mark it again, and again, at your service.

Gra. Here it is, sir, this was it you marked.

Qua. Palemon? Fare you well, fare you well. 25

Winw. How, Palemon!

Gra. Yes faith, he has discovered it to you, now, and therefore 'twere vain to disguise it longer, I am yours, sir, by the benefit of your fortune.

Winw. And you have him, mistress, believe it, that shall never give 30 you cause to repent her benefit, but make you rather to think that in this choice she had both her eyes.

Gra. I desire to put it to no danger of protestation.

[*Exit with* Winwife]

Qua. Palemon the word, and Winwife the man?

Pur. Good sir, vouchsafe a yokefellow in your madness, shun not 35 one of the sanctified sisters, that would draw with you, in truth.

Qua. Away, you are a herd of hypocritical proud ignorants, rather wild, than mad. Fitter for woods and the society of beasts than houses and the congregation of men. You are the second part of the society of canters, outlaws to order and discipline, and the only 40 privileged church-robbers of Christendom. Let me alone. Palemon the word, and Winwife the man?

Pur. [*Aside*] I must uncover myself unto him, or I shall never enjoy him, for all the cunning men's promises. Good sir, hear me, I am worth six thousand pound, my love to you is become my rack, 45 I'll tell you all, and the truth: since you hate the hypocrisy of the party-coloured brotherhood. These seven years, I have been a wilful holy widow, only to draw feasts and gifts from my entangled suitors:

18 *canting*: pious jargon   40 *canters*: vagrant beggars (*SN* II. v. 15–17)

I am also by office an assisting sister of the Deacons, and a devourer,
50 instead of a distributer of the alms. I am a special maker of marriages
for our decayed brethren with our rich widows; for a third part of
their wealth, when they are married, for the relief of the poor elect:
as also our poor handsome young virgins, with our wealthy bachelors,
or widowers; to make them steal from their husbands, when I have
55 confirmed them in the faith, and got all put into their custodies. And
if I ha' not my bargain, they may sooner turn a scolding drab, into a
silent minister, than make me leave pronouncing reprobation, and
damnation unto them. Our elder, Zeal-of-the-land, would have had
me, but I know him to be the capital knave of the land, making
60 himself rich, by being made feoffee in trust to deceased brethren,
and cozening their heirs, by swearing the absolute gift of their
inheritance. And thus having eased my conscience, and uttered my
heart, with the tongue of my love: enjoy all my deceits together, I
beseech you. I should not have revealed this to you, but that in time
65 I think you are mad, and I hope you'll think me so too, sir?

Qua. Stand aside, I'll answer you presently. (*He considers with*
himself of it) Why should not I marry this six thousand pound, now
I think on't? And a good trade too, that she has beside, ha? The
tother wench, Winwife is sure of; there's no expectation for me
70 there! Here I may make myself some saver, yet, if she continue mad,
there the question. It is money that I want, why should I not marry
the money, when 'tis offered me? I have a licence and all, it is but
razing out one name, and putting in another. There's no playing
with a man's fortune! I am resolved! I were truly mad, an' I would
75 not! Well, come your ways, follow me, an' you will be mad, I'll
show you a warrant!   (*He takes her along with him*)

Pur. Most zealously, it is that I zealously desire.

(*The* Justice *calls him*)

Jus. Sir, let me speak with you.

Qua. By whose warrant?

80 *Jus.* The warrant that you tender, and respect so; Justice Over-
do's! I am the man, friend Trouble-all, though thus disguised (as
the careful magistrate ought) for the good of the republic, in the
Fair, and the weeding out of enormity. Do you want a house or

57 *silent minister*: *Alch.* III. i. 38 n.   60 *feoffee in trust*: trustee of a household
estate in land   70 *make . . . saver*: recover part of loss

meat, or drink, or clothes? Speak whatsoever it is, it shall be supplied
you, what want you?   85

Qua. Nothing but your warrant.

Jus. My warrant? For what?

Qua. To be gone, sir.

Jus. Nay, I pray thee stay, I am serious, and have not many
words, nor much time to exchange with thee; think what may do 90
thee good.

Qua. Your hand and seal will do me a great deal of good; nothing
else in the whole Fair, that I know.

Jus. If it were to any end, thou should'st have it willingly.

Qua. Why, it will satisfy me, that's end enough, to look on; an' 95
you will not gi' it me, let me go.

Jus. Alas! Thou shalt ha' it presently: I'll but step into the
scrivener's hereby, and bring it. Do not go away.

                                         (*The* Justice *goes out*)

Qua. [*Aside*] Why, this madman's shape will prove a very fortu-
nate one, I think! Can a ragged robe produce these effects? If this 100
be the wise Justice, and he bring me his hand, I shall go near to
make some use on't. (*And returns*) He is come already!

Jus. Look thee! Here is my hand and seal, Adam Overdo, if there
be anything to be written, above in the paper, that thou want'st now,
or at any time hereafter; think on't; it is my deed, I deliver it so, 105
can your friend write?

Qua. Her hand for a witness, and all is well.

Jus. With all my heart.   (*He urgeth* Mistress Purecraft)

Qua. [*Aside*] Why should not I ha' the conscience, to make this a
bond of a thousand pound, now? Or what I would else?   110

Jus. Look you, there it is; and I deliver it as my deed again.

Qua. Let us now proceed in madness.   (*He takes her in with him*)

Jus. Well, my conscience is much eased; I ha' done my part,
though it doth him no good, yet Adam hath offered satisfaction! The
sting is removed from hence: poor man, he is much altered with his 115
affliction, it has brought him low! Now, for my other work, reducing
the young man (I have followed so long in love) from the brink of
his bane, to the centre of safety. Here, or in some such like vain place,
I shall be sure to find him. I will wait the good time.

116 *reducing*: bringing back

ACT V, Scene iii

Enter Cokes, Sharkwell, Filcher

Cok. How now? What's here to do? Friend, art thou the Master of the Monuments?

Sha. 'Tis a motion, an't please your worship.

Jus. My fantastical brother-in-law, Master Bartholomew Cokes!

5 *Cok.* A motion, what's that? (*He reads the Bill*) The ancient modern history of Hero and Leander, otherwise called *The Touchstone of true Love*, with as true a trial of friendship between Damon and Pythias, two faithful friends o' the Bankside? Pretty i' faith, what's the meaning on't? Is't an interlude? Or what is't?

10 *Fil.* Yes sir, please you come near, we'll take your money within.

Cok. Back with these children; they do so follow me up and down.

(*The boys o' the Fair follow him*)

[*Enter* Littlewit]

Lit. By your leave, friend.

Fil. You must pay, sir, an' you go in.

Lit. Who, I? I perceive thou know'st not me: call the master o'
15 the motion.

Sha. What, do you not know the author, fellow Filcher? You must take no money of him; he must come in *gratis*: Master Littlewit is a voluntary; he is the author.

Lit. Peace, speak not too loud, I would not have any notice taken
20 that I am the author, till we see how it passes.

Cok. Master Littlewit, how dost thou?

Lit. Master Cokes! You are exceeding well met: what, in your doublet and hose, without a cloak or a hat?

Cok. I would I might never stir, as I am an honest man, and by that
25 fire; I have lost all i' the Fair, and all my acquaintance too; didst thou meet anybody that I know, Master Littlewit? My man Numps, or my sister Overdo, or Mistress Grace? Pray thee Master Littlewit, lend me some money to see the interlude here. I'll pay thee again,

---

1–2 *Master of the Monuments*: official guide (like the one in Westminster Abbey)
18 *a voluntary*: i.e. one giving his services voluntarily (and without pay)

as I am a gentleman. If thou'lt but carry me home, I have money enough there.

Lit. Oh sir, you shall command it, what, will a crown serve you?

Cok. I think it will, what do we pay for coming in, fellows?

Fil. Twopence, sir.

Cok. Twopence? There's twelve pence, friend; nay, I am a gallant, as simple as I look now; if you see me with my man about me, and my artillery again.

Lit. Your man was i' the stocks, e'en now, sir.

Cok. Who, Numps?

Lit. Yes faith.

Cok. For what i'faith? I am glad o' that; remember to tell me on't anon; I have enough now! What manner of matter is this, Master Littlewit? What kind of actors ha' you? Are they good actors?

Lit. Pretty youths, sir, all children both old and young, here's the master of 'em——

[*Enter* Leatherhead]

(*Lea.* Call me not Leatherhead, but Lantern.)

(Leatherhead *whispers to* Littlewit)

Lit. Master Lantern, that gives light to the business.

Cok. In good time, sir, I would fain see 'em, I would be glad to drink with the young company; which is the tiring-house?

Lea. Troth, sir, our tiring-house is somewhat little, we are but beginners, yet, pray pardon us; you cannot go upright in't.

Cok. No? Not now my hat is off? What would you have done with me, if you had had me, feather and all, as I was once today? Ha'you none of your pretty impudent boys now; to bring stools, fill tobacco, fetch ale, and beg money, as they have at other houses? Let me see some o' your actors.

Lit. Show him 'em, show him 'em. Master Lantern, this is a gentleman, that is a favourer of the quality.

Jus. [*Aside*] Aye, the favouring of this licentious quality, is the consumption of many a young gentleman; a pernicious enormity.

Cok. What, do they live in baskets?

Lea. They do lie in a basket, sir, they are o' the small players.

(*He brings them out in a basket*)

30

35

40

45

50

55

60

47 *In good time*: formula of polite acquiescence   57 *the quality*: the profession of the actor

Cok. These be players minors, indeed. Do you call these players?

Lea. They are actors, sir, and as good as any, none dispraised, for dumb shows: indeed, I am the mouth of 'em all!

Cok. Thy mouth will hold 'em all. I think one Tailor would go near to beat all this company, with a hand bound behind him.

Lit. Aye, and eat 'em all, too, an' they were in cakebread.

Cok. I thank you for that, Master Littlewit, a good jest! Which is your Burbage now?

Lea. What mean you by that, sir?

Cok. Your best actor. Your Field?

Lit. Good i'faith! You are even with me, sir.

Lea. This is he, that acts young Leander, sir. He is extremely beloved of the womenkind, they do so affect his action, the green gamesters, that come here, and this is lovely Hero; this with the beard, Damon; and this pretty Pythias: this is the ghost of King Dionysius in the habit of a scrivener: as you shall see anon, at large.

Cok. Well, they are a civil company, I like 'em for that; they offer not to fleer, nor jeer, nor break jests, as the great players do. And then, there goes not so much charge to the feasting of 'em, or making 'em drunk, as to the other, by reason of their littleness. Do they use to play perfect? Are they never flustered?

Lea. No, sir. I thank my industry and policy for it; they are as well governed a company, though I say it—— And here is young Leander, is as proper an actor of his inches; and shakes his head like an ostler.

Cok. But do you play it according to the printed book? I have read that.

Lea. By no means, sir.

Cok. No? How then?

Lea. A better way, sir, that is too learned, and poetical for our

---

64 *mouth*: interpreter   65 *Taylor*: Joseph Taylor, one of the company acting the play (with pun on 'beating a tailor' as an easy feat, because of his proverbial timidity)   67 *eat 'em*: tailors were proverbially voracious   69–71 *Burbage . . . Field*: Richard Burbage and Nathan Field (the 'ostler' of l. 87 may be William Ostler of the King's Men)   74–5 *green gamesters*: IV. v. 85   76 *Damon; and . . . Pythias*: from Richard Edwards's comedy of this title (1571)   77 *habit of a scrivener*: V. iv. 328   80 *fleer*: mock   88 *the printed book*: Marlowe's *Hero and Leander*, quoted at ll. 92–3

audience; what do they know what Hellespont is? Guilty of true
love's blood? Or what Abydos is? Or the other Sestos hight?

Cok. Th'art i' the right, I do not know myself. 95

Lea. No, I have entreated Master Littlewit to take a little pains to
reduce it to a more familiar strain for our people.

Cok. How, I pray thee, good Master Littlewit?

Lit. It pleases him to make a matter of it, sir. But there is no such
matter, I assure you: I have only made it a little easy, and modern 100
for the times, sir, that's all: as, for the Hellespont I imagine our
Thames here; and then Leander, I make a dyer's son, about Puddle
Wharf: and Hero a wench o' the Bankside, who going over one
morning, to old Fish Street; Leander spies her land at Trig-stairs,
and falls in love with her. Now do I introduce Cupid, having meta- 105
morphosed himself into a drawer, and he strikes Hero in love with a
pint of sherry, and other pretty passages there are, o' the friendship,
that will delight you, sir, and please you of judgement.

Cok. I'll be sworn they shall; I am in love with the actors already,
and I'll be allied to them presently. (They respect gentlemen, these 110
fellows.) Hero shall be my fairing: but, which of my fairings?
(Le'me see) i'faith, my fiddle! And Leander my fiddle-stick: then
Damon, my drum; and Pythias, my pipe, and the ghost of Dionysius,
my hobby-horse. All fitted.

ACT V, Scene iv

Enter Winwife, Grace

Winw. Look yonder's your Cokes gotten in among his playfellows;
I thought we could not miss him, at such a spectacle.

Gra. Let him alone, he is so busy, he will never spy us.

Lea. Nay, good sir.   (Cokes *is handling the puppets*)

Cok. I warrant thee, I will not hurt her, fellow; what dost think 5
me uncivil? I pray thee, be not jealous: I am toward a wife.

Lit. Well, good Master Lantern, make ready to begin, that I may
fetch my wife, and look you be perfect, you undo me else, i' my
reputation.

100 *modern*: commonplace   106 *drawer*: tapster   (*V. iv*) 6 *toward*: in
prospect of

10   *Lea.* I warrant you sir, do not you breed too great an expectation
of it, among your friends: that's the only hurter of these things.

    Lit. No, no, no.   [*Exit*]

    Cok. I'll stay here, and see; pray thee let me see.

    Winw. How diligent and troublesome he is!

15   *Gra.* The place becomes him, methinks.

    Jus. [*Aside*] My ward, Mistress Grace in the company of a
stranger? I doubt I shall be compelled to discover myself before
my time!

    [*Enter* Knockem, Whit, Edgeworth, Win, Mistress Overdo]

                             (*The doorkeepers speak*)

    Fil. Twopence a piece, gentlemen, an excellent motion.

20   *Kno.* Shall we have fine fireworks, and good vapours?

    Sha. Yes Captain, and waterworks, too.

    Whi. I pree dee, take a care o' dy shmall lady, there, Edgeworth;
I will look to dish tall lady myself.

    Lea. Welcome, gentlemen, welcome gentlemen.

25   *Whi.* Predee, mashter o' de monshtersh, help a very sick lady,
here, to a chair, to shit in.

    Lea. Presently, sir.   (*They bring* Mistress Overdo *a chair*)

    Whi. Good fait now, Ursula's ale, and aqua-vitae ish to blame
for't; shit down, shweetheart, shit down, and shleep a little.

30   *Edg.* [*To* Win] Madam, you are very welcome hither.

    Kno. Yes, and you shall see very good vapours.

    Jus. (*By* Edgeworth) Here is my care come! I like to see him in so
good company; and yet I wonder that persons of such fashion should
resort hither!

35   *Edg.* This is a very private house, madam.

                       (*The cutpurse courts* Mistress Littlewit)

    Lea. Will it please your ladyship sit, madam?

    Win. Yes good-man. They do so all-to-be-madam me, I think
they think me a very lady!

    Edg. What else madam?

40   *Win.* Must I put off my mask to him?

    Edg. Oh, by no means.

---

14 *troublesome*: painstaking   32 *By*: in reference to   37 *all-to-be-madam*:
i.e. completely, thoroughly madam me (*CR* IV. iii. 13)

Win. How should my husband know me, then?

Kno. Husband? An idle vapour; he must not know you, nor you him; there's the true vapour.

Jus. [*Aside*] Yea, I will observe more of this: is this a lady, friend? 45

Whi. Aye, and dat is anoder lady, shweetheart; if dou hasht a mind to 'em, give me twelve pence from tee, and dou shalt have eder-oder on 'em!

Just. [*Aside*] I? This will prove my chiefest enormity: I will follow this.

Edg. Is not this a finer life, lady, than to be clogged with a 50 husband?

Win. Yes, a great deal. When will they begin, trow? In the name o' the motion?

Edg. By and by madam, they stay but for company.

Kno. Do you hear, puppet master, these are tedious vapours; 55 when begin you?

Lea. We stay but for Master Littlewit, the author, who is gone for his wife; and we begin presently.

Win. That's I, that's I.

Edg. That was you, lady; but now you are no such poor thing. 60

Kno. Hang the author's wife, a running vapour! Here be ladies will stay for ne'er a Delia o' 'em all.

Whi. But hear me now, here ish one o' de ladish, ashleep, stay till she but vake, man.

[*Enter* Wasp] 65

Was. How now, friends? What's here to do?

                                        (*The doorkeepers again*)

Fil. Twopence a piece, sir, the best motion in the Fair.

Was. I believe you lie; if you do, I'll have my money again, and beat you.

Winw. Numps is come!

Was. Did you see a master of mine come in here, a tall young 70 squire of Harrow o' the Hill; Master Bartholomew Cokes?

Fil. I think there be such a one within.

Was. Look he be, you were best: but it is very likely: I wonder I found him not at all the rest. I ha' been at the Eagle, and the Black 75

---

63 *Delia*: the mistress in Daniel's sonnet sequence

Wolf, and the Bull with the five legs, and two pizzles (he was a calf
at Uxbridge Fair, two years agone). And at the Dogs that dance the
Morris, and the Hare o' the Tabor; and missed him at all these! Sure
this must needs be some fine sight, that holds him so, if it have him.

80   *Cok.* Come, come, are you ready now?

    Lea. Presently, sir.

    Was. Hoyday, he's at work in his doublet and hose; do you hear,
sir? Are you employed? That you are bareheaded, and so busy?

    Cok. Hold your peace, Numps; you ha' been i' the stocks, I hear.

85   *Was.* Does he know that? Nay, then the date of my authority is
out; I must think no longer to reign, my government is at an end.
He that will correct another, must want fault in himself.

    Winw. Sententious Numps! I never heard so much from him
before.

90   *Lea.* Sure, Master Littlewit will not come; please you take your
place, sir, we'll begin.

    Cok. I pray thee do, mine ears long to be at it; and my eyes too.
Oh Numps, i' the stocks, Numps? Where's your sword, Numps?

    Was. I pray you intend your game, sir, let me alone.

95   *Cok.* Well then, we are quit for all. Come, sit down, Numps; I'll
interpret to thee: did you see Mistress Grace? It's no matter, neither,
now I think on't, tell me anon.

    Winw. A great deal of love and care, he expresses.

    Gra. Alas! Would you have him to express more than he has?
100   That were tyranny.

    Cok. Peace, ho; now, now.

    Lea. Gentles, that no longer your expectations may wander,
Behold our chief actor, amorous Leander,
With a great deal of cloth, lapped about him like a scarf,
105   *For he yet serves his father, a dyer at* Puddle Wharf,
Which place we'll make bold with, to call it our Abydos,
As the Bankside is our Sestos, *and let it not be denied us.*
Now, as he is beating, to make the dye take the fuller,
Who chances to come by, but fair Hero, *in a sculler;*
110   *And seeing* Leander's *naked leg and goodly calf,*

---

    78 *Hare o' the Tabor*: i.e. playing the drum with its feet   87 *want*: lack
94 *intend*: pay attention to   102–13 imitating the prologue to Edwards's *Damon
and Pythias*

Cast at him, from the boat, a sheep's eye and a half.
Now she is landed, and the sculler come back;
By and by, you shall see what Leander *doth lack.*

    Pup. L. Cole, Cole, old Cole.

    Lea. That is the sculler's name without control.   115

    Pup. L. Cole, Cole, I say, Cole.

    Lea. We do hear you.

    Pup. L. Old Cole.

    Lea. Old Cole? Is the dyer turned collier? How do you sell?

    Pup. L. A pox o' your manners, kiss my hole here, and smell.   120

    Lea. Kiss your hole, and smell? There's manners indeed.

    Pup. L. Why, Cole, I say, Cole.

    Lea. It's the sculler you need!

    Pup. L. Aye, and be hanged.

    Lea. Be hanged; look you yonder,   125
Old Cole, *you must go hang with Master* Leander.

    Pup. C. Where is he?

    Pup. L. Here, Cole, what fairest of fairs,
Was that fare, that thou landedst but now at Trig-stairs?

    Cok. What was that, fellow? Pray thee tell me, I scarce   130
understand 'em.

    Lea. Leander *does ask, sir, what fairest of fairs,*
Was the fare that he landed, but now, at Trig-stairs?

    Pup. C. It is lovely Hero.

    Pup. L. Nero?   135

    Pup. C. No, Hero.

    Lea. It is Hero.
Of the Bankside, he saith, to tell you truth without erring,
Is come over into Fish Street to eat some fresh herring.
Leander *says no more, but as fast as he can,*   140
Gets on all his best clothes; and will after to the Swan.

    Cok. Most admirable good, is't not?

    Lea. Stay, sculler.

    Pup. C. What say you?

    Lea. You must stay for Leander,
And carry him to the wench.   145

---

114 *Cole:* pandar; also 'old fellow' (Horace-Jonson had been called 'old Coale' in *Satiromastix*)   119 *collier:* an insult (*Alch.* I. i. 90)

Pup. C. You rogue, I am no pandar.

Cok. He says he is no pandar. 'Tis a fine language; I understand it, now.

150   *Lea. Are you no pandar, goodman* Cole? *Here's no man says you are,*
You'll grow a hot Cole, it seems, pray you stay for your fare.

Pup. C. Will he come away?

Lea. What do you say?

Pup. C. I'd ha' him come away.

155   *Lea. Would you ha'* Leander *come away? Why 'pray, sir, stay.*
You are angry, goodman Cole; *I believe the fair maid*
Came over wi' you a' trust: tell us sculler, are you paid?

Pup. C. Yes goodman Hogrubber, o' Pict-hatch.

Lea. How, Hogrubber o' Pict-hatch?

160   *Pup. C. Aye Hogrubber o' Pict-hatch. Take you that.* (The
puppet *strikes him over the pate*)

Lea. Oh, my head!

Pup. C. Harm watch, harm catch.

Cok. Harm watch, harm catch, he says: very good i' faith, the
165 sculler had like to ha' knocked you, sirrah.

Lea. Yes, but that his fare called him away.

Pup. L. Row apace, row apace, row, row, row, row, row.

Lea. You are knavishly loaden, sculler, take heed where you go.

Pup. C. Knave i' your face, goodman rogue.

170   *Pup. L. Row, row, row, row, row, row.*

Cok. He said knave i' your face, friend.

Lea. Aye, sir, I heard him. But there's no talking to these water-
men, they will ha' the last word.

Cok. God's my life! I am not allied to the sculler, yet; he shall be
175 Dauphin my boy. But my fiddle-stick does fiddle in and out too
much; I pray thee speak to him, on't: tell him, I would have him
tarry in my sight more.

Lea. I pray you be content; you'll have enough on him, sir.
Now gentles, I take it, here is none of you so stupid,
180   *but that you have heard of a little god of love, called* Cupid.
Who out of kindness to Leander, *hearing he but saw her,*
   this present day and hour, doth turn himself to a drawer.

---

158 *Hogrubber*: derisive term for a swineherd   *Pict-hatch*: a haunt of prostitutes
175 *Dauphin my boy*: ballad quoted in *King Lear*, III. iv. 99

And because he would have their first meeting to be merry,
   he strikes Hero *in love to him, with a pint of sherry.*
Which he tells her, from amorous Leander *is sent her,*   185
   who after him, into the room of Hero, *doth venture.*

[*Enter* Puppet Jonas, *the drawer*]

Pup. J. A pint of sack, score a pint of sack, i' the Coney.
                    (Pup. Leander *goes into* Mistress Hero's *room*)
Cok. Sack? You said but e'en now it should be sherry.
Pup. J. Why so it is; sherry, sherry, sherry.
Cok. Sherry, sherry, sherry. By my troth he makes me merry. I   190
must have a name for Cupid, too. Let me see, thou mightst help me
now, an' thou wouldest, Numps, at a dead lift, but thou art dreaming
o' the stocks still! Do not think on't, I have forgot it: 'tis but a nine
days' wonder, man; let it not trouble thee.

Was. I would the stocks were about your neck, sir; condition I   195
hung by the heels in them, till the wonder were off from you, with
all my heart.

Cok. Well said, resolute Numps: but hark you, friend, where is
the friendship, all this while, between my drum, Damon; and my
pipe, Pythias?   200

Lea. You shall see by and by, sir.

Cok. You think my hobby-horse is forgotten too; no, I'll see 'em
all enact before I go; I shall not know which to love best, else.

Kno. This gallant has interrupting vapours, troublesome vapours,
Whit, puff with him.   205

Whi. No, I pre dee, Captain, let him alone. He is a child i' faith, la'.

Lea. Now gentles, to the friends, who in number, are two,
   and lodged in that ale-house, in which fair Hero *does do.*
Damon (*for some kindness done him the last week*)
   is come fair Hero, *in Fish Street, this morning to seek:*   210
Pythias *does smell the knavery of the meeting,*
   and now you shall see their true friendly greeting.

Pup. P. You whore-masterly slave, you.

Cok. Whore-masterly slave, you? Very friendly, and familiar, that.

187 *Coney*: name of a room in the tavern   188 *sack . . . sherry*: the same (sack
= generic name for white wines)   192 *a dead lift*: an extremity   202 *my
hobby-horse is forgotten*: refrain of a lost popular song

215   *Pup. D. Whore-master i' thy face,*
Thou hast lain with her thyself, I'll prove't i' this place.

   Cok. Damon says Pythias has lain with her, himself, he'll prove't
in this place.

   Lea. They are whore-masters both, sir, that's a plain case.

220   *Pup. P. You lie, like a rogue.*

   Lea. Do I lie, like a rogue?

   Pup. P. A pimp and a scab.

   Lea. A pimp, and a scab?

I say between you, you have both but one drab.

225   *Pup. D. You lie again.*

   Lea. Do I lie again?

   Pup. D. Like a rogue again.

   Lea. Like a rogue again?

   Pup. P. And you are a pimp again.

230   *Cok.* And you are a pimp again, he says.

   Pup. D. And a scab again.

   Cok. And a scab again, he says.

   Lea. And I say again, you are both whore-masters again,
And you have both but one drab again.   *(They fight)*

235   *Pup. D., P. Dost thou, dost thou, dost thou?*

   Lea. What, both at once?

   Pup. P. Down with him, Damon.

   Pup. D. Pink his guts, Pythias.

   Lea. What, so malicious?

240 *Will ye murder me, masters both, i' mine own house?*

   Cok. Ho! Well acted my drum, well acted my pipe, well acted still.

   Was. Well acted, with all my heart.

   Lea. Hold, hold your hands.

   Cok. Aye, both your hands, for my sake! For you ha' both
245 done well.

   Pup. D. Gramercy, pure Pythias.

   Pup. P. Gramercy, dear Damon.

   Cok. Gramercy to you both, my pipe, and my drum.

   Pup. P., D. Come now, we'll together to breakfast to Hero.

250   *Lea. 'Tis well, you can now go to breakfast to Hero,*
You have given me my breakfast, with a hone and honero.

251 *a hone and honero*: from the lament 'The Irish Ho-hoane' (Chappell, i. 85)

Cok. How is't friend, ha' they hurt thee?

Lea. Oh no!

Between you and I sir, we do but make show.

Thus gentles you perceive, without any denial,

    'twixt Damon *and* Pythias *here, friendship's true trial.* 255

Though hourly they quarrel thus, and roar each with other,

    they fight you no more, than does brother with brother.

But friendly together, at the next man they meet,

    they let fly their anger, as here you might see't. 260

Cok. Well, we have seen't, and thou hast felt it, whatsoever thou sayest. What's next? What's next?

Lea. This while young Leander, *with fair* Hero *is drinking,*

    and Hero *grown drunk, to any man's thinking!*

Yet was it not three pints of sherry could flaw her, 265

    till Cupid *distinguished like* Jonas *the drawer,*

From under his apron, where his lechery lurks,

    put love in her sack. Now mark how it works.

Pup. H. O Leander, Leander, *my dear, my dear* Leander,

I'll for ever be thy goose, so thou'lt be my gander. 270

Cok. Excellently well said, fiddle, she'll ever be his goose, so he'll be her gander: was't not so?

Lea. Yes, sir, but mark his answer, now.

Pup. L. And sweetest of geese, before I go to bed,

I'll swim o'er the Thames, *my goose, thee to tread.* 275

Cok. Brave! He will swim o'er the Thames, and tread his goose, tonight, he says.

Lea. Aye, peace, sir, they'll be angry, if they hear you eavesdropping, now they are setting their match.

Pup. L. But lest the Thames should be dark, my goose, my dear friend, 280

let thy window be provided of a candle's end.

Pup. H. Fear not, my gander, I protest, I should handle

my matters very ill, if I had not a whole candle.

Pup. L. Well then, look to't, and kiss me to boot.

Lea. Now, here comes the friends again, Pythias *and* Damon, 285

Damon *and* Pythias *enter*

and under their cloaks, they have of bacon, a gammon.

279 *setting their match*: appointing to meet

  Pup. P. Drawer, fill some wine here.
  Lea. How, some wine there?
  there's company already, sir, pray forbear!
290 *Pup. D. 'Tis* Hero.
  Lea. Yes, but she will not be taken,
  after sack, and fresh herring, with your Dunmow-*bacon.*
  Pup. P. You lie, it's Westfabian.
  Lea. Westphalian *you should say.*
295 *Pup. D. If you hold not your peace, you are a coxcomb, I would say.*
          (Leander *and* Hero *are kissing*)
  Pup. P. What's here? What's here? Kiss, kiss, upon kiss.
  Lea. Aye, wherefore should they not? What harm is in this? 'Tis
   Mistress Hero.
  Pup. D. Mistress Hero's *a whore.*
300 *Lea. Is she a whore? Keep you quiet, or Sir Knave out of door.*
  Pup. D. Knave out of door?
  Pup. H. Yes, knave, out of door.
     (*Here the* puppets *quarrel and fall together by the ears*)
  Pup. D. Whore out of door.
  Pup. H. I say, knave, out of door.
305 *Pup. D. I say, whore, out of door.*
  Pup. P. Yea, so say I too.
  Pup H. *Kiss the whore o' the arse.*
  Lea. Now you ha' something to do:
  you must kiss her o' the arse, she says.
310 *Pup. D., P. So we will, so we will.*
  Pup. H. Oh my haunches, Oh my haunches, hold, hold.
  Lea. Stand'st thou still?
 Leander, *where art thou? Stand'st thou still like a sot,*
  and not offer'st to break both their heads with a pot?
315 *See who's at thine elbow, there! Puppet* Jonas *and* Cupid.
  Pup. J. Upon 'em Leander, *be not so stupid.*
  Pup. L. You goat-bearded slave!   (*They fight*)
  Pup. D. You whore-master knave.
  Pup. L. Thou art a whore-master.

---

292 *Dunmow-bacon*: the flitch presented to any couple at Dunmow, Essex, who could convince a jury of bachelors and maidens that they had spent the first year of their marriage without quarrels or regrets 294 *Westphalian*: an especially prized ham

Pup. J. Whore-masters all.   320
Lea. See, Cupid *with a word has ta'en up the brawl.*
Kno. These be fine vapours!
Cok. By this good day they fight bravely! Do they not, Numps?
Was. Yes, they lacked but you to be their second all this while.
Lea. This tragical encounter, falling out thus to busy us,   325
It raises up the ghost of their friend Dionysius:
Not like a monarch, but the master of a school,
In a scrivener's furred gown, which shows he is no fool.
For therein he hath wit enough to keep himself warm.
Oh Damon, *he cries, and* Pythias; *what harm,*   330
Hath poor Dionysius *done you in his grave,*
That after his death, you should fall out thus, and rave,
And call amorous Leander *whore-master knave?*
    Pup. D. I cannot, I will not, I promise you, endure it.

ACT V, Scene v

Enter Busy

Bus. Down with Dagon, down with Dagon; 'tis I, will no longer
endure your profanations.

Lea. What mean you, sir?

Bus. I will remove Dagon there, I say, that idol, that heathenish
idol, that remains (as I may say) a beam, a very beam, not a beam   5
of the sun, nor a beam of the moon, nor a beam of a balance, neither
a house-beam, nor a weaver's beam, but a beam in the eye, in the eye
of the brethren; a very great beam, an exceeding great beam; such
as are your stage-players, rhymers, and morris-dancers, who have
walked hand in hand, in contempt of the brethren, and the cause;   10
and been borne out by instruments of no mean countenance.

Lea. Sir, I present nothing but what is licensed by authority.

Bus. Thou art all license, even licentiousness itself, Shimei!

Lea. I have the Master of the Revels' hand for't, sir.

Bus. The Master of the Rebels' hand, thou hast; Satan's! Hold   15

---

327 *master of a school*: the vocation of Dionysius the younger, after his expulsion
from Syracuse   (V. v) 1 *Dagon*: god of the Philistines   11 *instruments*: agents
13 *Shimei*: who cursed David (2 Sam. 16: 5-13)

thy peace, thy scurrility, shut up thy mouth, thy profession is damnable, and in pleading for it, thou dost plead for Baal. I have long opened my mouth wide, and gaped, I have gaped as the oyster for the tide, after thy destruction: but cannot compass it by suit, or
20 dispute; so that I look for a bickering, ere long, and then a battle.

Kno. Good Banbury vapours.

Cok. Friend, you'd have an ill match on't, if you bicker with him here; though he be no man o' the fist, he has friends that will go to cuffs for him. Numps, will not you take our side?

25 *Edg.* Sir, it shall not need, in my mind, he offers him a fairer course, to end it by disputation! Hast thou nothing to say for thyself, in defence of thy quality?

Lea. Faith, sir, I am not well studied in these controversies, between the hypocrites and us. But here's one of my motion, Puppet
30 Dionysius shall undertake him, and I'll venture the cause on't.

Cok. Who? My hobby-horse? Will he dispute with him?

Lea. Yes, sir, and make a hobby-ass of him, I hope.

Cok. That's excellent! Indeed he looks like the best scholar of 'em all. Come, sir, you must be as good as your word now.

35 *Bus.* I will not fear to make my spirit and gifts known! Assist me zeal, fill me, fill me, that is, make me full.

Winw. What a desperate, profane wretch is this! Is there any ignorance, or impudence like his? To call his zeal to fill him against a puppet?

40 *Qua.* I know no fitter match, than a puppet to commit with an hypocrite!

Bus. First, I say unto thee, idol, thou hast no calling.

Pup. D. You lie, I am called Dionysius.

Lea. The motion says you lie, he is called Dionysius i' the matter,
45 and to that calling he answers.

Bus. I mean no vocation, idol, no present lawful calling.

Pup. D. Is yours a lawful calling?

Lea. The motion asketh, if yours be a lawful calling?

Bus. Yes, mine is of the spirit.

50 *Pup. D. Then idol is a lawful calling.*

Lea. He says, then idol is a lawful calling! For you called him idol, and your calling is of the spirit.

17 *Baal*: god of the Phoenicians   27 *quality*: occupation   40 *commit*: join battle

Cok. Well disputed, hobby-horse!

Bus. Take not part with the wicked, young gallant. He neigheth and hinneyeth, all is but hinnying sophistry. I call him idol again. 55
Yet, I say, his calling, his profession is profane, it is profane, idol.

Pup. D. It is not profane!

Lea. It is not profane, he says.

Bus. It is profane.

Pup. It is not profane. 60

Bus. It is profane.

Pup. It is not profane.

Lea. Well said, confute him with *not*, still. You cannot bear him down with your bass noise, sir.

Bus. Nor he me, with his treble creaking, though he creak like the 65
chariot wheels of Satan; I am zealous for the cause——

Lea. As a dog for a bone.

Bus. And I say, it is profane, as being the page of Pride, and the waiting woman of Vanity.

Pup. D. Yea? What say you to your tire-women, then? 70

Lea. Good.

Pup. Or feather-makers i' the Friars, that are o' your faction of faith? Are not they with their perukes and their puffs, their fans and their huffs, as much pages of Pride, and waiters upon Vanity? What say you? What say you? What say you? 75

Bus. I will not answer for them.

Pup. Because you cannot, because you cannot. Is a bugle-maker a lawful calling? Or the confect-makers? Such you have there: or your French fashioner? You'd have all the sin within yourselves, would you not? Would you not? 80

Bus. No, Dagon.

Pup. What then, Dagonet? Is a puppet worse than these?

Bus. Yes, and my main argument against you, is, that you are an abomination: for the male among you putteth on the apparel of the female, and the female of the male. 85

Pup. You lie, you lie, you lie abominably.

Cok. Good, by my troth, he has given him the lie thrice.

---

72 *Friars*: Blackfriars (*Alch.* I. i. 128)   77 *bugle-maker*: maker of glass beads
79 *fashioner*: tailor, dressmaker   82 *Dagonet*: King Arthur's fool   84–5 *male
. . . female*: a charge against the players based upon Deut. 22: 5

Pup. It is your old stale argument against the players, but it will not hold against the puppets; for we have neither male nor female amongst
90 us. And that thou may'st see, if thou wilt, like a malicious purblind zeal as thou art! (The puppet *takes up his garment*)

Edg. By my faith, there he has answered you, friend; by plain demonstration.

Pup. Nay, I'll prove, against e'er a Rabbin *of 'em all, that my*
95 *standing is as lawful as his; that I speak by inspiration, as well as he; that I have as little to do with learning as he; and do scorn her helps as much as he.*

Bus. I am confuted, the cause hath failed me.

Pup. Then be converted, be converted.

100 *Lea.* Be converted, I pray you, and let the play go on!

Bus. Let it go on. For I am changed, and will become a beholder with you!

Cok. That's brave i' faith, thou hast carried it away, hobby-horse, on with the play!

Jus. Stay, now do I forbid, I Adam Overdo! Sit still, I charge you.
                                        (The Justice *discovers himself*)
105 *Cok.* What, my brother-i'law!

Gra. My wise guardian!

Edg. Justice Overdo!

Jus. It is time, to take enormity by the forehead, and brand it; for I have discovered enough.

ACT V, Scene vi

Enter Quarlous (*like the madman*), Purecraft (*a while after*)

Qua. Nay, come mistress bride. You must do as I do now. You must be mad with me, in truth. I have here Justice Overdo for it.

Jus. Peace good Trouble-all; come hither, and you shall trouble none. (*To the cutpurse, and* Mistress Littlewit) I will take the charge
5 of you, and your friend too; you also, young man, shall be my care, stand there.

Edg. Now, mercy upon me.   (*The rest are stealing away*)

103 *carried it away*: brought it off

Kno. Would we were away, Whit, these are dangerous vapours, best fall off with our birds, for fear o' the cage.

Jus. Stay, is not my name your terror? 10

Whi. Yesh faith man, and it ish for tat, we would be gone, man.

[*Enter* Littlewit]

Lit. Oh gentlemen! Did you not see a wife of mine? I ha' lost my little wife, as I shall be trusted: my little pretty Win, I left her at the great woman's house in trust yonder, the pig-woman's, with Captain Jordan, and Captain Whit, very good men, and I cannot hear of her. 15 Poor fool, I fear she's stepped aside. Mother, did you not see Win?

Jus. If this grave matron be your mother, sir, stand by her, *Et digito compesce labellum*, I may perhaps spring a wife for you anon. Brother Bartholomew, I am sadly sorry, to see you so lightly given, and such a disciple of enormity: with your grave governor Humphrey: 20 but stand you both there, in the middle place; I will reprehend you in your course. Mistress Grace, let me rescue you out of the hands of the stranger.

Winw. Pardon me, sir, I am a kinsman of hers.

Jus. Are you so? Of what name, sir? 25

Winw. Winwife, sir.

Jus. Master Winwife? I hope you have won no wife of her, sir. If you have, I will examine the possibility of it, at fit leisure. Now, to my enormities: look upon me, O London! And see me, O Smithfield; the example of Justice, and Mirror of Magistrates: the 30 true top of formality, and scourge of enormity. Hearken unto my labours, and but observe my discoveries; and compare Hercules with me, if thou dar'st, of old; or Columbus; Magellan; or our countryman Drake of latter times: stand forth, you weeds of enormity, and spread. (*To* Busy) First, Rabbi Busy, thou superlunatical 35 hypocrite, (*To* Lantern) next, thou other extremity, thou profane professor of puppetry, little better than poetry: (*To the horse courser, and cutpurse*) then thou strong debaucher, and seducer of youth; witness this easy and honest young man: (*Then* Cap. Whit) now thou esquire of dames, madams, and twelvepenny ladies: (*and* Mistress 40

9 *cage*: prison   16 *stepped aside*: gone astray   17–18 *Et digito*: Juvenal, *Sat.* i. 160 ('Put your finger to your lip')   18 *spring*: raise from cover (of birds) 30 *Mirror of Magistrates*: Ind. 125–6

Littlewit) now my green madam herself, of the price. Let me unmask
your ladyship.

Lit. O my wife, my wife, my wife!

Jus. Is she your wife? *Redde te Harpocratem!*

Enter Trouble-all, [Ursula, Nightingale]

45   *Tro.* By your leave, stand by, my masters, be uncovered.

   Urs. Oh stay him, stay him, help to cry, Nightingale; my pan,
my pan.

   Jus. What's the matter?

   Nig. He has stolen Gammer Ursula's pan.

50   *Tro.* Yes, and I fear no man but Justice Overdo.

   Jus. Ursula? Where is she? Oh, the sow of enormity, this! (*To*
Ursula, *and* Nightingale) Welcome, stand you there, you, songster,
there.

   Urs. An' please your worship, I am in no fault: a gentleman
55 stripped him in my booth, and borrowed his gown and his hat; and
he ran away with my goods, here, for it.

   Jus. (*To* Quarlous) Then this is the true madman, and you are the
enormity!

   Qua. You are i' the right, I am mad, but from the gown outward.

60   *Jus.* Stand you there.

   Qua. Where you please, sir.   (Mistress Overdo *is sick*)

   Mrs Ove. Oh lend my a basin, I am sick, I am sick; where's
Master Overdo? Bridget, call hither my Adam.

   Jus. How?   (*and her husband is silenced*)

65   *Whi.* Dy very own wife, i' fait, worshipful Adam.

   Mrs Ove. Will not my Adam come at me? Shall I see him no
more then?

   Qua. Sir, why do you not go on with the enormity? Are you
oppressed with it? I'll help you: hark you, sir, i' your ear, your
70 innocent young man, you have ta'en such care of, all this day, is a
cutpurse; that hath got all your brother Cokes his things, and
helped you to your beating, and the stocks; if you have a mind to
hang him now, and show him your magistrate's wit, you may: but I
should think it were better, recovering the goods, and to save your
75 estimation in him. I thank you, sir, for the gift of your ward,

44 *Redde to Harpocratem*: 'Reduce yourself to silence' (*Sej.* V. 414 n.)

Mistress Grace: look you, here is your hand and seal, by the way. Master Winwife, give you joy, you are Palemon, you are possessed o' the gentlewoman, but she must pay me value, here's warrant for it. And honest madman, there's thy gown and cap again; I thank thee for my wife. (*To the widow*) Nay, I can be mad, sweetheart, when I please, still; never fear me: and careful Numps, where's he? I thank him for my licence. 80

    Was. How!   (Wasp *misseth the licence*)

    Qua. 'Tis true, Numps.

    Was. I'll be hanged then. 85

    Qua. Look i' your box, Numps. [*To* Justice] Nay, sir, stand not you fixed here, like a stake in Finsbury to be shot at, or the whipping post i' the Fair, but get your wife out o' the air, it will make her worse else; and remember you are but Adam, flesh and blood! You have your frailty, forget your other name of Overdo, and invite us all to supper. There you and I will compare our discoveries; and drown the memory of all enormity in your biggest bowl at home. 90

    Cok. How now, Numps, ha' you lost it? I warrant 'twas when thou wert i' the stocks: why dost not speak?

    Was. I will never speak while I live, again, for aught I know. 95

    Jus. Nay, Humphrey, if I be patient, you must be so too; this pleasant conceited gentleman hath wrought upon my judgement, and prevailed: I pray you take care of your sick friend, Mistress Alice, and my good friends all——

    Qua. And no enormities. 100

    Jus. I invite you home, with me to my house, to supper: I will have none fear to go along, for my intents are *Ad correctionem, non ad destructionem; Ad aedificandum, non ad diruendum:* so lead on.

    Cok. Yes, and bring the actors along, we'll ha' the rest o' the play at home.   [*Exeunt*] 105

(*The end*)

87 *Finsbury*: haunt of the Finsbury Archers (*TT* III. vi. 3–6 n.)   88 *air*: thought harmful to an invalid   102–3 'For correction, not for destruction; for building up, not for tearing down'

The Epilogue

Your Majesty hath seen the play, and you
    can best allow it from your ear, and view.
You know the scope of writers, and what store
    of leave is given them, if they take not more,
5   And turn it into licence: you can tell
    if we have used that leave you gave us well:
Or whether we to rage, or licence break,
    or be profane, or make profane men speak?
This is your power to judge (great Sir) and not
10   the envy of a few. Which if we have got,
We value less what their dislike can bring.
    if it so happy be, to have pleased the King.